For Reference

Not to be taken from this room

Employee Benefit Plans

D1401378

THE JOHN J. WRIGHT LIBRARY
LA ROCHE COLLEGE
9000 BABCOCK BLVD.
PITTSBURGH, PA 15237

Employee Benefit Plans

Barry Kozak

Associate Director, Employee Benefits
The John Marshall Law School

R
344.01252
K69e
2010

CAROLINA ACADEMIC PRESS
Durham, North Carolina

Copyright © 2010
Barry Kozak
All Rights Reserved

Library of Congress Cataloging-in-Publication Data

Kozak, Barry.
  Employee benefit plans / Barry Kozak.
      p. cm.
  ISBN 978-1-59460-639-7 (alk. paper)
  1. Pension trusts--Law and legislation--United States. I. Title.
  KF3512.K687 2010
  344.7301'252--dc22

                              2009044112

CAROLINA ACADEMIC PRESS
700 Kent Street
Durham, North Carolina 27701
Telephone (919) 489-7486
Fax (919) 493-5668
www.cap-press.com

Printed in the United States of America

This book is dedicated to Steve.

I am grateful to the authors of the essays in Chapter 22 who have each provided me with mentorship, inspiration and motivation throughout my career, and to Michael Fransen (a graduate of John Marshall's LLM Employee Benefits program, currently working at the US Department of Labor Employee Benefits Security Administration), Brian Benko (a graduate of John Marshall's LLM Employee Benefits program, currently working at McDermott Will & Emery, Washington DC), Jeremy Brunner (a graduate of John Marshall's LLM Employee Benefits program), David Diaz (a graduate of John Marshall's LLM Employee Benefits program), Zafar Musvi (currently a joint JD/LLM student in John Marshall's LLM Employee Benefits program), Patrick Ryan (currently a student in John Marshall's LLM Employee Benefits program and working as a manager at Deloitte Tax LLP, Chicago) and Patrick Ryll (a graduate of Northwestern Law's LLM Tax program, currently working as a Tax Fellow at the Thomas Jefferson School of Law assisting Professor William Byrnes) who have each provided extremely useful research assistance and editorial suggestions while still law students or as recent graduates in more ways than they can appreciate.

Contents

Preface   xvii

About the Author   xxi

Section I
Preliminary Concerns

Chapter 1 • Benefits That Employers Can Offer to Employees   3
Overview   3
A. Employee Benefits in General   4
   1. Offering Benefits to Employees   4
   2. General Categories of Employee Benefits   5
   3. The "Three-legged Stool" Theory of Retirement in the United States   6
B. Employees Allowed to Be Promised Benefits   7
   1. Only Employees Can Be Promised Employee Benefits   7
   2. Common-Law Employees   7

Chapter 2 • Basic Tax Concepts   9
Overview   9
A. Calculation of Income Tax Liability   10
   Gross Income for Individual Taxpayers   10
   Adjustments to Gross Income   12
   Calculated Tax for the Individual   12
   Actual Income Tax Due from the Individual Taxpayer   13
   Income Tax Policy   13
   Corporate Income Tax Calculation   14
B. Income Tax Advantages
   of Employee Benefit Plans   15
   1. Income Tax Advantages of Non-Qualified Deferred Compensation
      (Retirement) Plans   15
   2. Income Tax Advantages of Qualified Retirement Plans   17
   3. Income Tax Advantages of Health and Welfare Benefit Plans 17

Chapter 3 • The Employee Retirement Income Security Act of 1974   21
Overview   21
A. Protection of Employees Promised Benefits   24
   1. Employers Voluntarily Promise Employee Benefits   24
      11 N.E.2d 878 (Ohio App., 1937)   24

2. The Need for Congress to Act: ERISA   28
3. Other ERISA Protections   29
B. Income Tax Provisions   31
C. The Role of the Federal Government   31
   1. The Federal Agencies That Regulate Employee Benefit Plans   31
   2. Overview of the Federal Agencies   32
   3. Jurisdiction between Departments of Treasury and Labor   33
D. Amendment of ERISA and the Code   35
E. The Various Roles of the Employer and Outside Professionals   37
   1. Some of the Roles the Employer Must Take on or Contract out to a
      Third Party   37
      Plan Administrator   38
      Fiduciary over Plan Assets   38
   2. Some of the Other Professionals the Employer Might Need Advice
      and Work Product From   39
      Attorney   39
      Accountant   40
      Actuary   40
      Insurance Advisor   41
      Investment Advisor   41
      Record Keepers   42
      Third Party Administrators and ERPAs   42

Section II
Qualified Retirement Plans

Chapter 4 · Qualification Rules   47
Overview   47
A. Retirement Plans Sponsored by Type of Employer   51
   1. How Other Employers (*i.e.*, Those That Are Not-for-Profit) Deliver
      Retirement Benefits to Employees   51
      a. Governmental Employer   51
      b. Church Employer   54
      c. Public Schools   60
      d. Non-Profit Organizations and Charities   61
   2. How For-Profit Employers Promise and Deliver Retirement Benefits
      through a Qualified Retirement Plan   61
      a. A Brief Historical Perspective   61
      b. The Requirements for Qualified Retirement Plans   62
      c. Plan Disqualification   64
      d. Ways That a Plan Can Avoid Disqualification   65
   3. Qualified Plans for Multiemployers   66
   4. Qualified Plans for Multiple Employers   69
B. Income Tax Advantages of Retirement Plans   70
   1. Income Tax Advantages of Employer-Sponsored Retirement Plans for
      Employers   70
   2. Income Tax Advantages of Employer-Sponsored Retirement Plans for
      Employees   70
C. Choices of Written Plan Documents for Qualified Retirement Plans   70

1. Types of Written Plan Documents for Qualified Plans   70
   a. Master and Prototype Plan Documents   71
   b. Volume Submitter Plan Documents   72
   c. Individually Designed Plan Documents   73
2. Retroactive and Prospective Plan Amendments   76
3. Establishment of a Trust Document   77

Chapter 5 · Defined Contribution Plans and Defined Benefit Plans   79
Overview   79
A. Distinguishing between Defined Contribution and Defined Benefit Plans   84
  1. The Two Mutually Exclusive Types of Retirement Plans   84
  2. The Main Differences between Defined Contribution and Defined Benefit
    Plans   86
  3. Different Definitions for Pension Plans   87
B. Types of Defined Contribution Plans   90
  1. Money Purchase Plan   90
  2. Profit Sharing Plan   91
    a. Allocations Based on Salary   91
    b. Allocations Based on Permitted Disparity (Social Security
      Integration)   92
    c. Allocations Based on Age and Service Weighting   92
    d. Allocations Based on Cross Testing   94
  3. Stock Ownership Plans   94
    a. Stock Bonus Plans   94
    b. Employee Stock Ownership Plans (ESOP)   95
  4. Cash or Deferred Arrangement (a.k.a. §401(k) Plan)   96
    a. Traditional 401(k) Plans   96
    b. Roth 401(k) Plans   96
    c. Automatic Enrollment Features in 401(k) Plans   97
  5. SEPs, SIMPLEs, and Payroll Deduction IRAs   98
    a. Payroll Deduction IRAs   98
    b. SEPs   99
    c. SIMPLEs   100
C. Types of Defined Benefit Plans   101
  1. Flat Benefit   101
  2. Fixed Benefit   101
  3. Unit Benefit   101
  4. Defined Benefit Plans with Permitted Disparity   102
  5. Difference between Career Average and Final Average Plans   104
D. Types of Hybrid Plans   105
  1. Target Benefit Plans   105
  2. Statutory Hybrid Plans (Cash Balance Plans and Other Hybrid Plan
    Designs)   106
  3. New Combined DB/401(k) Plans Starting in 2010   107
  4. Certain Hybrid Plans   108

Chapter 6 · Funding Plans   109
Overview   109
A. Employer Contributions   111

1. Specific Rules for Defined Contribution Plans   111
2. Specific Rules for Defined Benefit Plans   112
    a. The Role of the Plan's Enrolled Actuary   113
    b. Funding Targets   114
    c. Impact on Plan When Funding Targets Are Not Met   116
    d. Compliant IRC § 412(e)(3) Plans (Formerly Identified in § 412(i)
       before PPA Amendments)   117
    e. Special Funding Rules for Multiemployer Plans   117
B. Employee Contributions   118
  1. Specific Rules for Defined Contribution Plans   118
    a. Pre-Tax Elective Salary Deferrals   119
    b. After Tax Contributions   119
    c. Limitations on Annual Employee Contributions   119
    d. Additional Catch-Up Contributions If over Age 50   120
    e. Additional Catch-Up Contributions If Due to Qualified Military
       Service   120
    f. Special Savers Tax Credit   121
  2. Specific Rules for Defined Benefit Plans   121
C. Deduction of Employer Contributions   121
  1. Specific Rules for Defined Contribution Plans   121
  2. Specific Rules for Defined Benefit Plans   123
  3. Issues for the Sponsoring Employer's Accountant   123
D. PBGC Premiums for Defined Benefit Plans   124

Chapter 7 • Vesting and Accruals   125
Overview   125
A. Vesting   128
  1. Common Rules for All Qualified Retirement Plans   128
  2. Specific Rules for Defined Contribution Plans   130
    a. Employee Contributions and Deferrals   130
    b. Employer Contributions   130
  3. Specific Rules for Defined Benefit Plans   131
B. Accruals   132
  1. Common Rules for All Qualified Retirement Plans   132
  2. Specific Rules for Defined Contribution Plans   132
    a. Definitely Determinable Benefits   132
    b. Benefit Accrual Rules   133
  3. Specific Rules for Defined Benefit Plans   134
    a. Definitely Determinable Benefits   134
    b. Normal Form of Benefit   134
    c. Benefit Accrual Rules   134
    d. Age Discrimination   135
    e. Normal Retirement Benefits   135
    f. Early Retirement Benefits   136
    g. Alternate Forms of Distribution   136
    h. Protected Benefits   137
  4. Additional Non-Retirement Type Benefits That Can Be Promised in Any
    Qualified Retirement Plan   137
    a. Life insurance   137

b. Disability Benefits   138
c. Retiree Health Benefits   139
C. Maximum Benefits That Can Be Promised in a Qualified Plan   139
1. Specific Rules for Defined Contribution Plans   139
2. Specific Rules for Defined Benefit Plans   140
D. Minimum Benefits That Must Be Promised in a Qualified Plan That Is
Top Heavy   141
1. Specific Rules for Defined Contribution Plans   141
2. Specific Rules for Defined Benefit Plans   142
E. Examples   142
1. Employee A   143
2. Employee B   145
3. Employee C   146

Chapter 8 • Annual Testing   149
Overview   149
A. Aggregation of Employers   155
1. Members of a Controlled Group of Corporations (or Other Businesses) 156
77 TC 881 (1981)   161
2. Members of an Affiliated Service Group   163
3. Separate Lines of Business   173
B. Highly Compensated Employees   173
1. Identification of Highly Compensated Employees   174
2. Annual Tests That Require Identified Highly Compensated Employees 175
C. Minimum Coverage Requirements for All Qualified Retirement Plans 176
1. Statutory Coverage   176
2. Minimum Coverage Testing — Preliminary Matters   176
3. Minimum Coverage Testing — Actual Tests   179
4. Minimum Coverage Testing — Corrections of a Failed Test   184
D. Minimum Participation Requirements for All Qualified Defined Benefit
Plans   186
E. Nondiscrimination Requirements for All Qualified Retirement Plans 186
1. The Three Components of Annual Nondiscrimination Testing   187
2. Safe Harbor Plan Designs   187
3. General Testing if Benefits Are Not Uniform   188
4. Correction if the Plan Fails   193
5. Nondiscrimination of Compensation   194
6. Nondiscrimination Testing for Rights and Features   202
7. Nondiscrimination Testing for Plan Amendments   202
8. Nondiscrimination Testing for Former Employees   203
F. Nondiscrimination Requirements for All 401(k) Plans (Cash or
Deferred Arrangements)   204
1. The Special Tests for Salary Deferrals   204
2. The Special Tests for Employer Matching Contributions   219
3. 401(k) Safe Harbor Plans   219
4. Correction If the 401(k) Plan Fails the ADP Test   226
G. Key Employees   235
H. Top Heavy Requirements for All Qualified Retirement Plans   237

Chapter 9 · Distributions   239
Overview   239
A. Optional Forms of Benefits   244
   1. Optional Forms of Benefit Distributions   244
   2. Actuarial Equivalences Equating Different Forms of Benefit Distributions
      in a Qualified Plan   247
   3. A Participant's Choice of Form of Benefit Distribution 250
   4. Special Distribution Forms for Married Participants   252
      520 U.S. 833 (1997)   254
   5. Early Retirement Benefits and Subsidies Available under a Qualified
      Defined Benefit Plan   259
   6. Elimination of Optional Forms of Benefits or Early Retirement Benefits
      from a Defined Benefit Plan   260
B. When Participants Can Receive Distributions   262
   1. Normal and Early Retirement Benefits   262
   2. In-service Distributions   262
   3. Qualified Domestic Relations Orders and Distributions to an Ex-spouse
      or Child Pursuant to Divorce   264
   4. Hardship Distributions from a 401(k) Plan   265
   5. Plan Loans   269
C. Taxation of Plan Distributions   270
   1. Taxation of Early Retirement Benefit and Normal Retirement Benefit
      Distributions   270
   2. Procedural Aspects—Tax Notices, Withholding and Reporting 272
   3. Rollovers   273
   4. Premature Distributions   274
   5. Required Minimum Distributions   275

Chapter 10 · Role of the Internal Revenue Service   279
Overview   279
A. Organization of the IRS   280
B. Employee Plans Group   281
   1. Organization of Tax-Exempt and Government Entities Operating Division 281
   2. Organization of the Employee Plans Business Division   282
   3. Determination Letters for Plan Documents   284
   4. Employee Plans Compliance Resolution System (*i.e.*, "Self-Correction"
      of Operational Defects)   286
      Correction on Audit (Audit CAP)   288
      Evolution of EPCRS   288
   5. Examinations of Plan Operations   289
   6. Professionals That Can Represent the Plan in Front of the IRS 293

Section III
Labor Rights and Protections in ERISA Plans

Chapter 11 · ERISA Plans   297
Overview   297
A. ERISA Plans   297
   1. Employee Benefit Plans Governed by ERISA   297
   2. Employee Benefit Plans Not Governed by ERISA   298

B. ERISA Retirement Plans 300
   1. Retirement Plans Governed by ERISA 300
   2. Retirement Plans Not Governed by ERISA 300
C. ERISA Health and Welfare Benefits Plans 304
   1. Health and Welfare Benefit Plans Governed by ERISA 304
   2. Health and Welfare Benefit Plans Not Governed by ERISA 304
D. Congressional Findings and Declaration of Policy 308

Chapter 12 · Written Plan Documents 313
Overview 313
A. Written Plan Document 314
   1. The Controlling Plan Document 314
   2. Ability to Amend or Terminate the Plan 328
   3. Ability to Interpret Ambiguous Plan Provisions (the "Firestone"
      Language) 328
B. Summary Plan Description 329

Chapter 13 · Fiduciary Rules and Investment of Plan Assets 345
Overview 345
A. Fiduciary over Plan Assets 349
   1. Employee Benefit Plans That Require Fiduciary Guardianship 349
   2. Individuals Who Are Plan Fiduciaries 349
   3. Duties for Each Decision 355
   4. Special Rules for Remittance of Employee Salary Deferrals 359
B. Prohibited Transactions 361
   1. Prohibited Transactions under ERISA Title I 361
   2. Prohibited Transactions under the Internal Revenue Code 362
   3. Exemptions from Prohibited Transactions 363
C. Special Rules for Self-Directed 401(k) Plans 364
   1. Allowing Participants to Make Their Own Investment Decisions 364
   2. Black Out Periods 375
D. Liability for Breach of Fiduciary Duties 376
   1. Personal Liability 376
   2. Liability for Co-Fiduciaries 377
   3. Bonding Requirements 377
E. Paying Plan Expenses from Qualified Plan Assets 378
   1. Settlor vs. Administrator Functions 378
   2. Special Tax Credits for Small Employers 388

Chapter 14 · ERISA Causes of Action 389
Overview 389
A. Federal Preemption of State Laws 391
B. Criminal Causes of Action 393
C. Civil Causes of Action 397
   Reporting and Disclosure Failure 397
   Benefits or Other Rights 397
   Breach of Fiduciary Duty 397
   Equitable Relief for Actions or Inactions (Not Alleged by the
      Department of Labor) 398

        Reporting and Disclosure Failure (for Plan Registration Statements) 398
        Equitable Relief for Actions or Inactions (Alleged by the Department
            of Labor) 398
        Enforcement of Civil Penalties Owed to the Department of Labor 398
        Enforcement of QMCSOs 399
        Certain Medicare and Medicaid Reports 399
        Purchase of an Annuity for a Participant or Beneficiary 399
        Violations of Minimum Coverage or Vesting Rules by a Qualified Plan 399
        Equitable Relief for Actions or Inactions of the Secretary of Labor 399
        Civil Penalties for Certain Prohibited Distributions 399
    D. Importance of Plan Benefit Claims Procedures 400
        First Level Review 401
        Second Level Review (Appeals) 402
    E. Other Issues in ERISA Litigation 403

Chapter 15 · Reporting and Disclosure 405
    Overview 405
    A. Reporting to the Government 406
        1. Annual Filing of Form 5500 406
        2. PBGC Reportable Events for Certain Defined Benefit Plans 408
    B. Disclosures to Participants and Beneficiaries 408
        1. Benefit Statements in a Qualified Retirement Plan 409
        2. Summary Annual Reports 409
        3. Other Communications 411
        4. Acceptable Methods of Communications 411

Chapter 16 · Plan Terminations 413
    Overview 413
    A. PBGC Rules for Plan Terminations 414
        1. Single-Employer Defined Benefit Plans 414
        2. PBGC Rules for Single-Employer Defined Contribution Plans 416
        3. PBGC Rules for Multi-Employer Defined Benefit Plans 417
        Statutory Rules at ERISA § 4201 417
    B. IRS Rules for Termination of All Qualified Plans 417
        1. Procedures to Terminate 417
        2. Frozen Plans and Partial Plan Terminations 420

Chapter 17 · Role of the Department of Labor 425
    Overview 425
    A. Organization of the DOL 426
    B. Employee Benefits Security Administration 430
        1. Organization of EBSA 430
        2. Enforcement 431
        3. Technical Guidance and Prohibited Transaction Exemptions 435
        4. Amicus Curie Briefs 436
        5. Form 5500, Annual Reporting Forms 436

Section IV
Other Employee Benefits Plans

Chapter 18 · Basics of Executive Compensation   441
Overview   441
A. Issues with Current Compensation for Executives   446
    1. Deductibility of Current Compensation   446
    2. Other Cash-Like Benefits   448
B. Retirement Plans for Executives   449
    1. Nonqualified Deferred Compensation (NQDC) Plans, Generally   449
    2. Excess Benefit Plans and Top-Hat Plans   450
    3. Income Taxation of Retirement Plans for Executives   451
    4. Funding Retirement Promises with Rabbi Trusts   452
    5. Limitations Based on Funding Targets in the Employer's Qualified
       Defined Benefit Plan   453
C. Equity Benefits   453
    1. Stocks   453
    2. Stock Options   454
    3. Other   455
D. Securities Law Issues   456
    1. SEC Disclosures   456
    2. Financial Statements   457

Chapter 19 · Health and Welfare Benefit Plans   459
Overview   459
A. Taxation of Health and Welfare Benefits   464
    1. Health Benefits   464
    2. Welfare Benefits   466
    3. Other Fringe Benefits   469
B. Paying for Health and Welfare Benefits   471
    1. Fully Insured or Self-Funded   471
    2. Cost-Sharing with Employees   472
       a. Subsidy for Employees   472
       b. Subsidy for Employees' Spouses, Children, Dependents and
          Domestic Partners   472
       c. Pre-Tax Funding Vehicles for Employees   473
       d. Wellness Programs   476
C. ERISA Rules for Health and Welfare Benefits   477
    1. COBRA   477
    2. HIPAA   478
    3. Mental Health Parity Act   481
    4. The Newborns' and Mothers' Health Protection Act   481
    5. Women's Health and Cancer Rights Act   482

Chapter 20 · Social Security Benefits and Individual Retirement Accounts   483
Overview   483
A. Individual Savings   484
    1. Traditional IRAs   484
    2. Roth IRAs   486
B. Social Security Benefits   487

Section V
Final Issues

Chapter 21 · Ethics Issues   493
   Overview   493
     1. Other Laws That Impact Employee Benefits Plans   494
     2. Whom Does the ERISA Attorney or Other Professional Represent?   494
     3. Practice in Front of the IRS (Circular 230)   495
     4. Other Ethical Concerns   501

Chapter 22 · Career Advice Essays   503
   Nevin E. Adams, JD   504
   Mark A. Davis, QPFC, AIF®   506
   Chad R. DeGroot, JD   507
   Kathryn J. Kennedy, JD, FSA   509
   Gary S. Lesser, JD   511
   Stuart M. Lewis, JD   515
   J.J. McKinney, CPC, QPA, QKA   516
   Tom Reeder, JD   519
   Tom Terry, FSA, EA   522

Chapter 23 · Public Policy of an Aging Population   525
   Overview   525
     1. Problems with ERISA in Its Current Form   526
     2. Aging Population   526
     3. Collection of Short Articles   528

Appendix A · Law 101 Concepts for Non-Law Students   541

Appendix B · Adjustments to Statutory Limitations and Thresholds
        Due to Inflation   547

Appendix C · ERISA and Code Organizational Charts   549

Appendix D · ERPA Learning Objectives and Mapping   555

Appendix E · Conversion of ERISA Section Cites and US Code Section Cites 563

Table of Statues and Regulations   571

Table of Cases   577

Index   579

Preface

Writing this text book truly was a labor of love. As an employee benefits professional, I have generally enjoyed every day at work, every client I advocated for, and every project I worked on throughout my career. As an educator, I absolutely relish teaching the laws surrounding employee benefit plans to students who have no idea what the class is all about and who only enrolled in the class because it fit their schedule, and yet, by the end of the semester, are actually excited about the topic and consider focusing their careers on helping employers provide proper employee benefit plans, helping employees receive the benefits promised, or helping the federal government regulate the process.

The exciting aspect of a career as an employee benefits professional is that the rules are always changing—whether through actual amendment by Congress, through guidance by the Department of Treasury or Department of Labor, or through court cases interpreting the former.

Right before I began writing this text book, I was asked to rewrite a BNA Tax Management Portfolio, which is now called Kozak, "Employee Benefit Plans and Issues for Small Employers" (353–4th T.M.). Unfortunately, I did not have it in me to discuss the same basic concepts and regulatory framework in this text book in a wholly different manner using different words and different orders. Therefore, out of fairness to BNA, the publisher of the Portfolio, and to Carolina Academic Press, many portions of this book have been extracted directly from the Portfolio. Then, after starting to write this book, but before completed, I was asked to become co-editor and lead contributing author for the third edition of "A CPA's Guide to Retirement Plans for Small Businesses," published by the American Institute of Certified Public Accountants (AICPA), and again, the chapters I penned for that reference book look very similar to the corresponding provisions in this textbook and in the BNA Tax Management portfolio.

Who this book was written for: As you see from my biography, I have several different professional certifications—each of which is an aspect of expertise in employee benefit plans design, operation, or education. While I am currently a member of the faculty of a law school, and primarily teach law students interested in becoming benefits attorneys, The John Marshall Law School in Chicago also offers a Master of Science degree for non-attorney professionals, and I teach them not how to practice law, but how to understand how attorneys understand, communicate and apply the law. Before becoming an academic, as an actuary and consultant, I was responsible for training newer associates, and grew to appreciate how different individuals, from various undergraduate degrees and life experiences, were still part of the larger group of benefits professionals, and all needed to learn how Congress enacted employee benefits laws, how the federal agencies regulated those employee benefits laws, and how the courts interpreted employee benefits laws where there was ambiguity. Therefore, I have tried to incorporate all of my past experiences (some good, some bad) into a text book that can be used in a law school or in a business school class, in an actuarial or human resources management curriculum, or as a desk reference for benefits professionals who are just trying to become better at their jobs.

In addition, there is a new professional designation for benefits professionals called an "Employee Retirement Plan Agent" (ERPA). I discuss the role of ERPAs in chapters 3 and 21 and in Appendix D. The examination process to earn the ERPA designation is quite new, and I purposely have included all of the materials necessary to study for and take the exams within this book, and in Appendix D, I have copied all of the learning objectives for the ERPA exams with a pinpoint cite to where in this book that topic is discussed. Please note that I am not trying to usurp any other study materials specifically prepared for ERPA examination takers, but if you are using this book anyway, then you should not need to go to any other source.

The purpose of this book: Benefits professionals generally need to understand the three main categories of employee benefits: (1) retirement benefit plans; (2) health and welfare benefit plans; and (3) executive compensation and equity programs. This book was written primarily to discuss the rules of retirement benefit plans, and only has one chapter each devoted to health and welfare benefit plans and to executive compensation. Therefore, when you have finished the book (whether as part of a class or simply for fun), you will have a very solid understanding of the regulatory framework and practical applications in regards to retirement plans, and only a broad and cursory understanding of the other aspects of employee benefit plans.

The way this book is organized: First, you will notice that it is broken down into 5 sections, with sections II and III being the main emphasis of the book.

Section I provides a nice grounding of why employers would want to provide benefits to employees in addition to cash compensation, and the types of benefits that are most common, and then a very basic summary of basic tax concepts that any benefits practitioner should understand. Since I am writing this book from the point of view of an attorney, but I want non-law school students and non-attorney professionals to feel comfortable reading it, I have included a "Law 101" discussion in Appendix A, which provides an overview of the U.S. legal system, a summary of some vocabulary and citing standards, and some websites that you can go to for further information.

Section II is all about how certain retirement plans can be considered "qualified retirement plans." In the first chapter of the section, the book distinguishes between the for-profit employers that can sponsor qualified retirement plans and the other non-profit employers (like state and local governments and churches) that can only sponsor non-qualified retirement plans. I explain how the rules for qualified plans are more complex than the rules that govern non-qualified plans (although the trend is to make those non-qualified plans as complicated to design and administer), so that if you, as a benefits practitioner, understand the qualified plan rules, then you can easily learn the rules for non-qualified plans when you have a client in need of that knowledge. The chapters then discuss the distinction between defined benefit and defined contribution type plan designs; the manner that the sponsoring employer can deposit money into the plan to fund the benefits promised; the vesting and accrual rules which determine how employees promised retirement benefits actually earn a legal right to receive those benefits; the annual tests or safe harbor plan designs required to ensure that the plans provide "enough" benefits to "enough" lower paid employees; the time, manner, and income tax implications of distributions from qualified retirement plans to the employees or their beneficiaries; and finally, a review of how the IRS functions to regulate the income tax aspects of qualified retirement plans.

Section III is a bit broader, as it discusses the rights under the Employee Retirement Income Security Act of 1974 (ERISA) that extend to employees who are promised benefits by an employer that are delivered through an employee benefits plan (which includes qualified retirement plans, some non-qualified retirement plans, and also some group health benefit plans). The starting point is a chapter that discusses which plans, programs, schemes, or payroll practices are in fact, governed by ERISA, and if governed, then the requirements for a written plan document and a Summary Plan Description. The chapters then discuss the individuals who are legally classified as fiduciaries over plan assets and how to fulfill their fiduciary duties and obligations; the civil and criminal causes of action and remedies available when things go awry; the reporting and disclosure requirements for communication to the federal government and to the plan participants; how retirement plans can be terminated; and finally, a review of how the Department of Labor functions to regulate the employee protection aspects of ERISA employee benefit plans.

Section IV is the place where other employee benefit plans are discussed — one chapter summarizes executive compensation, another summarizes health and welfare benefit plans, and a third summarizes Social Security benefits and Individual Retirement Accounts. Remember, the focus of this book is on the taxation and employee protections of retirement plans, and this section just fills in some of the gaps without any great detail.

Section V provides some final issues. Paying attention to ethical issues is crucial for any benefits professional to maintain his or her professional certification and to help prevent law suits for malpractice, and the first chapter highlights ethical issues that are applicable to all professionals, especially those who want to represent their clients and practice in front of the IRS. The following chapter is a special treat for anyone interested in a career as a benefits professional, as nine outstanding colleagues share their thoughts with career essays specifically written for this book. Finally, the book concludes with a quick summary of my perceived problems with ERISA, and includes excerpts from a report on global issues with an aging population and some articles I wrote that summarize my retirement concerns for America's aging population.

The Appendices include summaries of the law and the way lawyers think and conduct research in Appendix A; a table showing statutory limits and thresholds included in the statutes, their primary cites, and cost of living adjustments for 2008, 2009 and 2010 in Appendix B; a set of six charts showing how ERISA is organized, how to determine whether an employee benefit plan is governed by ERISA, how the relevant sections of the Internal Revenue Code are organized, and some dissection and comparison of qualified defined contribution plans and defined benefit plans in Appendix C; a list of all of the learning objectives needed to successfully complete the ERPA exams and a mapping to where that material is found in this text book in Appendix D; and a chart showing the sections of ERISA with the corresponding cites in Title 29 of the U.S. Code.

How to read this book: Each chapter starts with an overview, which includes simply bullet-points. If you are using this book for classroom instruction and your professor decides to omit any chapter from the syllabus, I still strongly encourage you to at least read through the overview of that omitted chapter. The main part of each chapter is then the regulatory framework. Where large chunks are based on statutory provisions of the Code or ERISA (or regulations), those cites are prominently shown right below the title for that chunk of information; otherwise, the cite for a passing thought is footnoted. I am expecting that in addition to reading this textbook, you will also read the statutory provisions. Within the regulatory framework, I have included sections of regulations, other guidance, or court cases where the point I am trying to make is much better communicated through that other document. I tried to limit the use of such outside documents as to not overwhelm you, but I think I included enough primary source material that by the time you are done reading this book, any phobia you might have with going directly to the Code or ERISA when confronted with a client's issue will be eliminated. Bold horizontal lines within the regulatory framework sections of the chapter signal primary source material.

There are many complicated rules, and the book is purposely layered. When you have read through the entire text, all of the minor details should start making sense. Please realize, however, that I am only providing a summary of the general rules in this book— I implore you to never think that by reading this book, without reading the actual statutory or regulatory provisions, and without discussing the issues with other benefits professioanls, that you are competent to advise or perform any work for a client.

So, I hope that the organization of this book and the care I put into making your learning experience worthwhile and somewhat enjoyable will make you a better benefits professional, if that's the career path you choose, or at least will make you a better employee or employer, in knowing what benefits can be promised and how they can be delivered through employee benefit plans.

About the Author

Barry Kozak is an Enrolled Actuary, an Attorney, and a Chartered Financial Consultant. Kozak teaches various employee benefits, income tax, elder law and compensation law classes at The John Marshall Law School and DePaul University College of Law, and is the Associate Director of the graduate Employee Benefits programs at The John Marshall Law School in Chicago. Kozak received his BS (Applied Statistics) degree from the University at Albany, his JD and LLM (Employee Benefits) degrees from The John Marshall Law School, and his MPP (Economic and Social Policy) from the University of Chicago Harris School of Public Policy Studies.

Section I

Preliminary Concerns

Before getting into the complicated rules that govern employee benefit plans, especially qualified retirement plans, this section will provide a solid grounding of how tax laws and other labor laws affect individuals and businesses.

Chapter 1 discusses the benefits that employers can offer to employees, first with a discussion of employee benefits in general (such as where employee benefits fit into the compensation package, the general categories of employee benefits, and the concept of a "three-legged stool" of retirement benefits), and second with a discussion of which members of the workforce actually can be classified as common-law employees (as opposed to independent contractors or non-working family members).

Chapter 2 discusses some basic tax concepts, first with a summary of Gross Income and how it is ultimately subject to federal income taxes, and then a summary of the income tax advantages for employee benefit plans.

Chapter 3 discusses the impact of the Employee Retirement Income Security Act of 1974 (ERISA), first with a discussion of the rights Congress provided to employees promised benefits which are delivered through a plan, then the income tax provisions for employee benefit plans, then an exploration of the federal government's role in regulating employee benefits plans (through the IRS, Department of Labor, and the Pension Benefit Guaranty Corporation), a quick listing of the most relevant laws enacted by Congress since 1974 that amend ERISA and the Internal Revenue Code, and finally a discussion of the professionals that most employers sponsoring employee benefit plans will need to employ (such as attorneys, accountants, actuaries, and other benefits professionals).

Chapter 1

Benefits That Employers Can Offer to Employees

Overview

Why would employers offer employee benefits in addition to cash wages?

- to attract, retain and reward good employees
- to distinguish the employer from its competitors
- for income tax advantages to both the employer and employee
- paternalistic feelings of the employer to protect the health, well-being and financial security of its workforce (while they are employed and after retirement)

What are the general categories of employee benefits?

- compensation
- paid time off
- health benefits (either the employer pays the premiums to an insurance company or the employer directly reimburses the employee for certain medical expenses)
- welfare benefits (either fringe benefits to make the employee's life easier so that the employee is more productive or benefits like reimbursement of their legal expenses or their children's day care expenses)
- retirement benefits (the employer voluntarily provides some replacement income during retirement after the employee stops earning a salary as an active employee)
- severance benefits (the employer continues to pay a portion of the employee's salary for a transition period after the employee is terminated for good cause but before a successor job is secured)
- death benefits (the employer pays a certain multiple of the employee's base salary to the beneficiary or estate of the employee who dies while still an active employee)
- equity ownership (the corporate employer either gives shares of stock or the option to purchase stock at a discount; the LLC entity does the same for membership units) to transfer ownership of the employer business to employees (either for a sense of profit sharing or for true equity and succession planning)

What is the "three-legged stool" theory for sources of income during retirement?

- individual savings (including equity in the home, credit worthiness, and Individual Retirement Accounts)
- governmental pensions (through Social Security)
- employer provided retirement benefits

Who can employers promise the employee benefits to?

- qualified retirement plans: only common-law employees of the employer can be participants in a qualified retirement plan (see Chapter 4)

- health and welfare benefit plans: only common-law employees of the employer can enroll in the health and welfare plans, and the employer can then allow spouses, children and dependents to also enroll (where the cost of the coverage for these family members is excluded from the employee's taxable income, as discussed in Chapter 2), and the employer can further allow other family members, such as same-sex or opposite-sex domestic partners or same-sex spouses to enroll (but the cost for these non-traditional family members will be imputed into the employee's taxable income)

- executive compensation plans: can be offered to individuals other than common-law employees, such as independent contractors, consultants and business advisors, and members of the board of directors, as long as the individual receives remuneration for services performed

What is a common-law employee?

- it is determined based on facts and circumstances, such as the level of control the employer has over the worker (such as setting hours and deadlines, providing office space and tools, paying professional dues), and who owns the worker's creative work product

- the U.S. Supreme Court adopted the general rules for purposes of employee benefit plans

- sometimes a leased employee might be considered as a common-law employee

- by default, any worker who is not a common-law employee is considered to be an independent contractor

- although limited for other purposes, self-employed individuals (such as partners of a partnership, owners of an S-Corporation, and sole proprietors) are considered common-law employees for purposes of participating in an employee benefit plan

A. Employee Benefits in General

1. Offering Benefits to Employees

There are numerous reasons as to why employers offer benefits. Broadly speaking, an employer offers employee benefits to attract good workers, to keep them happy while working (which hopefully will be reflected in the business's bottom line) and to reward these workers for their past efforts. By providing benefits to its workers, a company seeks to engender its employees' goodwill and loyalty, thus creating a symbiotic relationship between management and labor. Somewhat less paternalistically, employee benefits can also be used as a practical and effective means of providing income tax benefits to both the employer and employee and/or for transferring ownership in the company to its employees, either as a sense of "an employee-owned business" where the profits are shared, or where the business owner(s) are looking for succession planning opportunities.

Employee benefits can also be thought of as simply another form of compensation. Some of this compensation, however, is not obtained at the end of pay cycle in the form of cash. Rather, the benefits to the worker and his or her family consist of, among other things, the payment of health insurance company premiums, an assurance of income should the worker decide to take a sabbatical, or a steady stream of revenue when the individual decides to retire after years of valuable service. This latter category is, by definition, "deferred" compensation and is the main focus of this book.

At this point, it is crucial to explain to someone new to this area that employers generally do not have the flexibility to do whatever they want, make whatever promises, and then randomly decide whether to fulfill the promises or not. Before ERISA was enacted in 1974 (the Employee Retirement Income Security Act, as introduced in Chapter 3), employees that were promised benefits basically had no rights, and employers were able to do just that. Before ERISA, a disgruntled employee only had recourse against the employer to sue in state court for such torts as breach of contract, assuming an oral promise made by the employer even constituted a contract. Before ERISA, different employees working for the same employer, but in different states, might have had the different state courts deciding the same broken promises in totally different ways. ERISA was primarily enacted, therefore, to provide consistent rights to employees promised benefits, and to provide a single federal law for similarly situated employees, although working in different states, if the employer broke its written promise to provide employee benefits. ERISA also added more specific requirements and limitations on the promises that the employer can make to employees if the employer and employee want to enjoy certain federal income tax advantages.

2. General Categories of Employee Benefits

Employee benefits come in many varieties. The following list, while not exhaustive, includes the most frequently offered benefits.

Compensation. Other than federal and state minimum wage laws, the requirements for worker's compensation and unemployment insurance, a mandatory number of paid holidays, and certain federal requirements for family, medical and uniformed service leave, the employer does not need to offer any current compensation-type benefits to its employees. An example of a compensation-type benefit is a year-end holiday bonus. As discussed in Chapter 18, other special current compensation promises paid to high paid employees, such as severance pay and golden parachute payments, must comply with a more complicated and more stringent set of rules.

Paid time off. This would consist of sick days, vacation days, sabbaticals, and other approved leaves of absence. Federal laws mandate certain allowances by the employer for family medical leave, the birth or adoption of a child, bereavement of a family member, or for being called to active military service or jury duty. This text book does not detail these rules, but refers to them in Chapter 7 in their relation to the vesting and accrual of retirement benefits.

Health benefits. In most cases, either the employer pays premiums to an insurance company or the employer directly reimburses the employee for certain medical expenses. In Chapter 19, the health benefits that are subject to requirements under the Internal Revenue Code and/or ERISA are discussed in further detail.

Welfare benefits. Welfare benefits are those benefits designed to make the employee's life easier so that the employee is more productive. Reimbursement expenses for their children's day care or pre-paid legal services would fit in this category. On the other hand, casual Fridays and payment of membership dues at a yacht club, although welfare benefits, generally are not encumbered by strict income tax and labor rules. In Chapter 19, the welfare benefits that are subject to requirements under the Internal Revenue Code and/or ERISA are discussed in further detail.

Retirement benefits. Upon the employee's retirement, or sometimes upon disability, the employer voluntarily provides a portion of the employee's pre-retirement salary. If the benefits are structured properly in the form of a qualified retirement plan, then both the employer and the employee can reap substantial tax benefits. The main focus of this textbook is on retirement benefits, especially those that are provided to low paid and rank-and-file employees. In Chapter 4, the type of employer promising the benefits is distinguished into those for-profit employers that can sponsor "qualified retirement plans" and those non-profit employers, such as state and local governments, churches, public schools, and tax-exempt entities, that can sponsor other types of non-qualified retirement plans. Since the rules have historically been more complicated for qualified retirement plans than for non-qualified retirement plans, chapters 4 through 10 of this text concentrate on the rules specific to qualified retirement plans. In addition, when any type of employer promises a certain level of retirement benefits only to high paid employees, officers, directors, or other interested individuals, then those executive compensation arrangements are subject to a different set of rules, as summarized in Chapter 18.

Severance benefits. If an employee is terminated for good cause but before a successor job is obtained, an employer may offer to continue paying a portion of the employee's salary for a period of time, even though the individual is no longer employed, and arguably, no longer productive and adding utility to the employer's business operations. Alternatively, if there is a change in control in the corporate ownership of the employer, then an employer may contract in advance to pay a certain portion of pay to the ex-employee who is terminated for redundancy, or who is relegated to a lower position of prestige within the new owner's organizational chart. In Chapter 18, severance pay and golden parachutes, as they fit within the larger classification of executive compensation, are discussed.

Death benefits. These are benefits in which the employer pays a certain multiple of the employee's salary to the beneficiary or estate of the employee who dies while still an active employee. Life insurance and death benefits can play an important role in retirement plans, and their relation to qualified retirement plans is discussed in Chapter 7, and their relation to executive compensation programs is discussed in Chapter 18.

Equity ownership. The most common type of equity ownership in a corporation consists of shares of stock or the option to purchase the stock at a below-market price; a Limited Liability Company (LLC) does the same for membership units. In Chapter 5, ownership that is passed to rank-and-file employees through an Employee Stock Ownership Plan is discussed, and in Chapter 18, ownership that is passed to executives is discussed.

3. The "Three-legged Stool" Theory of Retirement in the United States

As mentioned above, a major area of employee benefits consists of retirement benefits. Before continuing, it might be useful if we take a minute to examine the retirement system in the U.S. from 20,000 feet. Most experts analogize our current system to that of a "three-legged stool". One of the legs consists of personal savings; for example, home equity or individual retirement accounts (IRA's). The second leg consists of government aid in the form of social security retirement benefits. The third leg consists of employer provided retirement benefits. It is this latter category that this book is primarily concerned with (although the former two are summarized in Chapter 20).

In theory at least, a person will have, by the time he or she retires, a substantial nest-egg of personal savings as well as the warm assurance that Uncle Sam will begin paying out social security upon an individual's reaching his or her social security retirement age. However, as can be gleaned from a simple glance at headlines warning of the impending collapse of social security, as well as the stark reality of personal savings being wiped out by financial crises and unscrupulous money managers (*i.e.* the Crash of 2008 and Bernard Madoff's Ponzi scheme), such legs can take on the consistency of spaghetti. It is for this reason that a correct understanding of the legal compliance issues surrounding employer provided employee benefits, especially retirement benefits, is crucial.

B. Employees Allowed to Be Promised Benefits

1. Only Employees Can Be Promised Employee Benefits

Before delving into the complicated requirements under ERISA or the Internal Revenue Code, an employer must first determine which of their workers are eligible for benefits. Employers can generally only promise retirement benefits to current common-law employees, not to former employees, not to a family member or a friend of an employee, and not to individuals who do not otherwise perform services for the employer.

However, specifically limited to certain health and welfare plans, certain family members of employees (such as spouses, children and dependents) can enroll in plans and receive benefits if the employer extends coverage to them. The cost of the coverage for these family members is generally excluded from the employee's taxable income. The recent trend is for many employers to let their employees determine who they consider family members, which can include, among others, domestic partners, same-sex spouses, children from prior marriages, and special need siblings. While the federal income tax benefits do not currently extend to these non-traditional family members as they do to traditional family members, many employers still extend benefits to them in the pursuance of happy employees.

The employer might also wish to promise some executive compensation-type benefits to directors and even to connected individuals, such as attorneys, accountants and other consultants.

2. Common-Law Employees

While this requirement might seem obvious at first glance, determining who exactly is an "employee" can often be daunting. According to the Supreme Court, for purposes of classifying a service provider as an "employee" for employee benefit plans, the factors to consider include "the skill required; the source of the instrumentalities and tools; the location of the work; the duration of the relationship between the parties; whether the hiring party has the right to assign additional projects to the hired party; the extent of the hired party's discretion over when and how long to work; the method of payment; the hired party's role in hiring and paying assistants; whether the work is part of the regular business of the hiring party; whether the hiring party is in business; the provision of employee benefits; and the tax treatment of the hired party."[1] If that sounds like a laundry list, consider that the earlier test previously set out by the IRS included no less than 20 factors.[2]

Other types of "common-law" employees, under current federal law for employee benefit plans, include self-employed individuals, partners in a partnership, shareholders in an LLC or LLP, and sometimes leased employees. Owner-employees are deemed to be employees for purposes of qualified retirement plans, where an owner-employee is defined as an employee who owns the entire interest in an unincorporated trade or business or a partner that owns more than 10% of either the capital interest or the profits interest in a partnership.[3] The individual who owns the entire interest in the unincorporated trade or business shall be deemed his or her own employer (*i.e.* the employee is also the employer); in a partnership, the partnership will be deemed to be the employer of each partner who is an employee (*i.e.,* an individual who does more than merely invest capital). The same applies for purposes of ERISA: an individual in business for himself or herself is self-employed. Sole proprietors and partners are self-employed. Self-employment can include part-time work.

Common-law employees can also include leased employees. A "leased employee" generally shall be treated as an employee of the person for whom such leased employee performs services (the "recipient" of the services) even though such individual is a common law employee of the leasing organization.[4] A leased employee is any person who performs services for a recipient if: such services are provided pursuant to an agreement between the recipient and any other person (the "leasing organization"), such person has performed such services on a substantially full-time basis for a period of at least one year, and such services are of a type historically performed in the business field of the recipient by employees. If, however, the leased employee is already covered by a proper employee benefits plan maintained by the leasing organization, then he or she does not need to be covered under the recipient employer's plan. As business practices are shifting to a more transient workforce, the governing laws and regulations concerning leased employees, especially those who are affiliated with a Professional Employer Organization (PEO), is evolving. Therefore, for purposes of this text book, just realize that if your client employer uses leased employees, then you will need to do some additional research to determine whether or not the leased employees will be classified as common-law employees for purposes of employee benefit plans.

To the extent a worker fails to qualify as a common-law employee, he or she is deemed to be an independent contractor. Independent contractors are not eligible to participate in most employer-sponsored employee benefit plans. The determination of who is an independent contractor is generally up to the employer, although simply referencing a worker as an independent contractor is not dispositive: the same multi-factored employer test must be applied. As a very general rule, the more control an employer has over his or her employee, the more likely he or she is to be an employee.

---

1. Nationwide Mut. Ins. Co. v. Darden, 503 U.S. 318, 323 (1992).
2. Rev. Rul. 87-41.
3. IRC § 401(c)(3).
4. IRC § 414(n).

Chapter 2

Basic Tax Concepts

Overview

What are the general income tax rules to understand?
- According to the Internal Revenue Code (and the form 1040):
  - Gross Income
  - less deductions (all above-the-line deductions, the greater of the individual's itemized deductions or Standard deduction, and all exemptions)
  - equals Taxable Income
  - multiply by tax rate (although under current law, certain long term capital gains and dividends are taxed at a different rate)
  - equals income tax
  - tax is greater of income tax or Alternative Minimum Tax (AMT)
  - less credits (most credits reduce tax to zero, but refundable credits actually allow the tax to be negative, meaning that the government owes the individual money)
  - equals income tax liability
  - less advanced payments (like withholding)
  - plus other taxes (like self-employment tax or penalty taxes for premature distributions from IRAs or retirement plans)
  - equals income taxes owed for the year (if negative, then the IRS owes the individual a refund)
- all salary and the value of the employee benefits received in exchange for services rendered as an employee are included in the individual's Gross Income in the tax year paid or accrued, unless there is a specific Code provision excluding or deferring such income
- therefore, the true tax advantages that Congress can provide to a taxpayer is to specifically allow income to be permanently excluded from Gross Income or at least deferred and included in a future year's Gross Income, or Congress can allow certain expenses actually paid by the taxpayer to be a deduction against Gross Income to lower the calculated tax, or allowing certain expenses to be a credit against the tax to lower the actual taxes owed
- a corporate taxpayer makes a similar calculation, but is allowed to deduct salary paid to employees (which, as discussed throughout this textbook, includes con-

tributions to certain employee benefit plans which are set up to comply with whatever rules Congress requires)

What are the income tax advantages of Non-Qualified Deferred Compensation?

- if structured properly, deferred compensation provided to the favored employees and executives will not be included in their individual Gross Income until the tax year in which there is no longer a "substantial risk of forfeiture"

- the employer gets a corresponding deduction in that same future tax year

- since the assets are always considered as part of the employer's general assets until paid, the employer will pay income taxes on all fund earnings along the way

What are the income tax advantages of retirement benefits from a Qualified Plan?

- if structured properly, deferred compensation provided to plan participants will not be included in their individual Gross Income until the tax year in which it is paid

- the employer gets an immediate deduction in the year that the retirement promises are deposited into a qualified retirement trust

- since the assets are invested in a tax-exempt retirement trust, no one will pay income taxes on all fund earnings along the way

What are the income tax advantages of health and welfare benefits?

- if structured properly, the value of the health and welfare benefits provided to them as employees, and also provided to their traditional family members (such as spouses, children and dependents) will never be included in their individual Gross Income

- the employer gets an immediate deduction in the year that the health and welfare promises are funded or paid to a third party insurer

- as long as the amounts to fund the health and welfare benefits are part of the employer's general assets, the employer will pay income taxes on all fund earnings along the way

A. Calculation of Income Tax Liability

We now get into understanding the Income Tax rules (the major portion of the Internal Revenue Code) in this chapter and ERISA in Chapter 3. If you are not a law student, this would be a good time for you to first read through Appendix A before continuing.

Since certain types of employee benefits qualify for income tax advantages, a quick primer on basic tax concepts is in order. As you will see, the Internal Revenue Code, in addition to ERISA, has many provisions—some quite complicated—governing the specific tax treatment of various employee benefits. What follows in this short chapter is a very over-simplified analysis of the calculation of an individual's or a corporation's income tax owed, and some of the tax advantages enjoyed by the employer and employee through properly drafted employee benefit plans.

Gross Income for Individual Taxpayers

As a very general rule, an individual's income tax liability for any year is calculated by first determining Gross Income. Gross Income is defined as "all income from whatever source derived, including ... compensation for services, including fees, commissions, fringe benefits, and similar items."[1] As we all dutifully look forward to every April 15, we report and pay our individual income tax liability for the prior calendar year on an IRS Form 1040. As part of the reporting, we include all other forms or schedules that detail income received, especially the amounts considered to be compensation or wages. For most common-law employees, the amount shown on the Form W-2 represents total taxable compensation for the year (which reflects payroll taxes paid to fund Social Security, unemployment insurance and worker's compensation, income taxes withheld by the employer and paid to the IRS on behalf of the employee, and other voluntary payroll deductions and transfers). Independent contractors generally receive a Form 1099 from the employer or individual for whom services were performed indicating remuneration paid. Partners in a partnership will generally receive a Form K-1 (IRS Form 1065) showing his or her share of the profits (or losses), which, for purposes of simplicity in this chapter, represent compensation. Sole proprietors and self-employed individuals will complete a Schedule B attachment to Form 1040 to determine his or her business income (commonly called "earned income," which will become important for purposes of employee benefit plans).

As many find out, often times as a shock, all other income is also included in Gross Income such as alimony (but not child support or division of marital property upon divorce), the taxable portion of IRA and retirement plan distributions (see Chapter 9 for a more detailed discussion), the taxable portion of social security distributions (which, ironically, depends on the individual's Gross Income for the year), and unemployment compensation. In addition, all "other income" is included in Gross Income (unless it is specifically excluded under a provision of the Code), which includes gambling winnings, income from illegal activities (usually, the smart criminal does not voluntarily report this amount, but after being convicted of a crime, might be required to amend a prior income tax return to include such amounts), jury duty pay, and cancelled debts. Unfortunately, the question as to what actually constitutes Gross Income has bedeviled courts and taxpayers for decades, and perhaps the best definition is "instances of undeniable accession to wealth, clearly realized, and over which the taxpayers have complete dominion."[2] In addition, over the years, Treasury and the courts have developed three basic tax doctrines that assist the IRS in assessing proper calculations of Gross Income:

- The economic benefit doctrine, which helps to determine what is included in Gross Income;
- The constructive receipt doctrine, which helps to determine when (*i.e.*, the proper tax year) an amount is included in Gross Income; and
- The transfer of property doctrine, which helps to determine who (*i.e.*, which taxpayer) is responsible for including the amount in Gross Income.

However, especially in a textbook devoted to employee benefits, the key to calculating Gross Income is the opening clause in IRC §61, which states "except as otherwise provided ..." Congress has actually sprinkled the Internal Revenue Code with several income tax advantages that either totally exclude certain amounts from ever being included in Gross Income, or that at least defers the inclusion of amounts into Gross Income until a future tax year after certain events have occurred. Since this chapter is a summary of general income tax concepts, suffice it to say that when the employer properly designs an employee benefits plan, then employees will enjoy an exclusion of certain amounts from Gross In-

---

1. IRC §61(a).
2. Commissioner v. Glenshaw Glass, 348 U.S. 426 (1955).

come (such as the value of health and welfare benefits), or will enjoy a deferral until amounts are received or could have been received (such as retirement or deferred compensation benefits, respectively).

Adjustments to Gross Income

Once Gross Income is determined, the taxpayer reduces this amount with all applicable tax deductions and exemptions to arrive at taxable income. For individual taxpayers under the United States income tax regime, this includes "above the line deductions" which include expenses paid such as alimony and moving costs, but which also include contributions to a health savings account and to an Individual Retirement Account. This amount is labeled "Adjusted Gross Income," which is important for many reasons (such as a deduction for all medical expenses in excess of 7.5% of Adjusted Gross Income). Then individual taxpayers can take "below the line deductions" which is simply the greater of a standard deduction or itemized deductions. The standard deduction represents normalized living expenses for the average individual (we all have certain expenses for food, clothes, transportation, housing, and other necessities that Congress has decided to lump together and provide a very simple one-size-fits-all number), whereas the itemized deductions vary from taxpayer to taxpayer, and includes expenses such as charitable deductions, certain unreimbursed medical expenses, home mortgage interest, and property or sales taxes paid to the individual's state of residence.

But wait, there's more! The taxable income is reduced further by an exemption—currently, in 2009, each taxpayer (if his or her Adjusted Gross Income is less than a certain threshold amount) reduces this adjusted income by $3,650 for each member of the family (so a married couple with two children considered dependents will reduce taxable income by $14,600). Under the current Tax Code, for 2009, the exemption from taxable income can even be greater if the taxpayer "provided housing to a Midwestern displaced individual."

Calculated Tax for the Individual

The resulting taxable income is then multiplied by the individual's tax bracket rate, which is a graduated rate, currently from 10% (actually 0% for many indigent taxpayers) to 35%, but where the threshold taxable income for each graduated rate depends on the type of taxpayer (unmarried individuals, married individuals filing joint returns or surviving spouses, married individuals filing separate returns, heads of households, or estates and trusts). In the absence of any long-term capital gains, this amount represents the income tax due. However, since long-term capital gains and certain dividends are taxed at a favorable rate (currently 15%, or 28% in some instances), which is usually lower than the individual's ordinary income tax bracket, the taxpayer (or more generally, the CPA or other tax form preparer), will complete the Schedule D attachment to Form 1040, and will complete the "Schedule D Tax Worksheet" in the instruction portion of the Schedule. Therefore, the accompanying normal income tax is the sum of regular Taxable Income at the regular income tax rate plus special long term capital gains and dividends at the special LTGC and Dividend rate. You would probably think that either way, the taxpayer owes this resulting tax due—and yet you might be wrong. The taxpayer must now calculate the alternative minimum tax, which negates some of the "below the line" itemized deductions. Now the taxpayer can determine the greater of the AMT or the normal income tax due.

Actual Income Tax Due from the Individual Taxpayer

The final income tax owed for the year is then calculated by adjusting the income tax owed by offsetting income tax credits and adding in other taxes. On a dollar-for-dollar basis, if the taxpayer is entitled to an income tax credit, then credits reduce the income tax owed, but usually not below $0 (*i.e.,* only "refundable" credits, such as the Earned Income Credit or the first-time homebuyer credit, will cause the IRS to actually owe money to a low-income taxpayer). Credits are generally phased-out as Adjusted Gross Income reaches certain threshold levels, and represent a way that Congress uses the Internal Revenue Code to provide assistance to low-income taxpayers by reducing their income taxes. The major credits currently are for child and dependent care expenses, for education expenses, and for contributions to an employer-provided retirement plan or an Individual Retirement Account. On the other hand, the income tax owed is increased by additional non-income taxes owed, such as the payroll taxes imputed to self-employed individuals, the employment taxes imputed when hiring household assistance, and the penalty tax imputed for premature distributions from an employer-provided retirement plan.

Now that the income tax liability for the year has been determined, the taxpayer owes that amount. Amounts withheld by the employer for a common-law employee are used to offset the amount owed, as are pre-paid quarterly self-employment taxes remit by self-employed individuals, and any estimated tax payments and amounts applied voluntarily by the taxpayer from the prior year's return. If more has been withheld or pre-paid than is actually owed, then the IRS will send a refund to the taxpayer, but without any interest (which basically makes any refund check an interest-free loan made by the taxpayer to the federal government). So, while a refund is usually looked at more favorably than the need to write a check to the IRS every April 15, individuals are usually advised by their CPAs and consultants to take the time to properly anticipate the Gross Income for the year, and the corresponding withholding.

Income Tax Policy

Believe me, this is a simplification of the whole income tax calculation process. Most individuals (including CPAs, tax attorneys, and apparently Treasury Secretary-designates) have trouble understanding all of the intricacies of the exceptions to the exceptions to the exceptions to the general rules, and many of us, including tax return preparers, use computer software to minimize income taxes owed.

The provisions of the Internal Revenue Code represent the law; quite often, however, certain provisions are tweaked, repealed or expanded so as to encourage or discourage certain behavior. These Code sections can be analogized to marionette strings with Congress, cloaked behind the curtain, acting the role of a (sometimes ambiguous) puppet master. How hard these strings are "yanked" depend on many factors, including, but not limited to, the philosophy of a new Presidential administration, an unforeseen financial crisis or the successful lobbying from a special interest group.

In addition to the Internal Revenue Code provisions, Congress allows the IRS, through the U.S. Department of Treasury, to promulgate regulations and other guidance on the interpretation of ambiguous provisions of the law and on logistical methods of compliance with the law. The hierarchy and legal effect of various types of guidance are explained in further detail in Appendix A.

Not really crucial to this textbook on employee benefits, but more as a good point where you can put down your pen and just think, do you agree with the following statement "The U.S. Internal Revenue Code is way too complex."

Policy wonks and economists argue that any income tax system should be efficient (an efficient tax system causes the least cost to the economy for a given amount of revenue, since cost is excess burden); equitable (an equitable tax system divides the tax burden fairly, but does any one really have a good definition of fairness?); and simple (a simple system is transparent, comprehensible, and easy to administer and enforce). Economists would use supply and demand curves, replete with elasticities and dead weight loss calculations, to demonstrate whether our current income tax system meets the criteria. All I am asking you to do, arguably without any empirical data or charts, is to think about the efficiency of our income tax system (*i.e.*, do you think that voluntarily reporting income taxes and playing IRS audit roulette is the most cost-effective way of the federal government raising the revenue it needs to operate?); the equity of our income tax system (*i.e.*, are similarly situated taxpayers treated the same under the Code, and if you think that taxpayers with higher incomes should theoretically pay a larger share of income taxes, then do you think this is actually accomplished through the graded tax rate structure?); and the simplicity of our income tax system (I don't think you need a clue from me on this one).

Corporate Income Tax Calculation

Now, stop daydreaming about how to fix the U.S. income tax system, pick up your pen, and resume taking notes about how the current statutory framework actually works. The corporate employer (and an LLC entity treated as a corporation) is a separate taxpayer all its own. It must similarly pay taxes on its Gross Income based on corporate tax rates (but files a Form 1120 instead of a Form 1040). However, reasonable business expenses (such as salary paid and the cost of providing or funding for certain employee benefits provided) are allowed to be deducted from its Gross Income (usually in the same tax year that such payment is included in the employee's individual Gross Income). The importance of these deductions cannot be overstated: if Manure Corp., a corporation, sells $1,000,000 worth of fertilizer in 2009, it shows Gross Income of $1,000,000 on its corporate income tax return. If Manure's tax rate is 35%, then the corporation owes $350,000 to the IRS as corporate income taxes. However, suppose Manure Corp. spends $600,000 to employees as compensation and contributions to various employee benefits plans (assume all compensation is reasonable and all employee benefit plans are compliant with the Code). At year's end, Manure Corp. has an Adjusted Gross Income of $400,000, which results in a corporate income tax liability of $140,000. Assume further Manure Inc. is entitled to a total of $10,000 in appropriate general business credits, such as small employer pension plan start-up costs, expenses incurred in providing child care facilities for employees, and for expenses in making its facilities accessible by disabled individuals. The total corporate taxes owed are therefore $130,000. Thus, Manure Corp. will enjoy $270,000 in after-tax profits, which can be reinvested in the company or distributed to shareholders.

Partnerships, LLC entities treated as partnerships, S-corporations, and sole-proprietorships are not separate taxpayers and all tax attributes of the business "pass through" to the managing individuals. This simply means that the entity itself does not pay the tax; rather the partners or individuals who reap the profits of the entity pay the tax themselves (or enjoy a loss to offset other personal income). However, these businesses generally file reporting forms with the IRS, and prepare tax attribute schedules for the managing individuals to use on their respective individual income tax returns. Tax-exempt organizations, government agencies, Indian tribes, and certain public entities are governed under special income tax rules.

B. Income Tax Advantages
of Employee Benefit Plans

1. Income Tax Advantages of Non-Qualified Deferred Compensation (Retirement) Plans

If structured properly, Supplemental Executive Retirement Plans (SERPs) provide a tax-deferral to the favored employees and executives until such time that benefits are no longer subject to a "substantial risk of forfeiture". There exists a substantial risk of forfeiture if a "person's rights to full enjoyment of such property are conditioned upon the future performance of substantial services by any individual".[3] Primarily based on this statutory provision, in conjunction with another provision (the taxable year of inclusion of items in Gross Income[4]), Treasury and the courts developed the economic benefit doctrine, the constructive receipt doctrine, and the transfer of property doctrine. In summary, these three doctrines, in the aggregate, suggest that the employee includes deferred compensation into Gross Income in the tax year that the benefits are no longer subject to a "substantial risk of forfeiture." This loose and vague definition arguably allows employers and favored employees to stretch the limits of what is the true risk of forfeiture. The IRS was very well aware of this potential for abuse, and was continually trying to narrow the playing field through guidance and challenges in the federal courts, but was severely restricted in 1978 when Congress imposed a moratorium on any further restrictive regulations in this area.

However, in 2004, largely in response to the collapse of Enron and other corporate implosions, Congress kept the existing income tax regime for non-qualified deferred compensation, and added a new layer of regulation through new IRC § 409A. Basically, the new provisions place tighter restrictions on the timing of when executives deferring income can choose to receive the benefits (specifically, Congress sought to prevent an insider, with non-public knowledge of the employer's immediate financial hardships, from receiving the deferred compensation promises before they actually become subject to the employer's creditors). Under the new rules, deferred compensation plans can only allow distributions pursuant to the following circumstances:

- separation from service;
- the date the participant becomes disabled;
- death;

---

3. IRC § 83.
4. IRC § 451

- a specified time (or pursuant to a fixed schedule) specified under the plan at the date of the deferral of such compensation;
- a change in the ownership or effective control of the corporation, or in the ownership of a substantial portion of the assets of the corporation; or
- the occurrence of an unforeseeable emergency.

Thus, when an individual makes an election to defer compensation not later than the close of the preceding taxable year, the written nonqualified deferred compensation plan must satisfy one of these distribution dates in order for the individual to continue deferring the inclusion of the promised benefits into Gross Income. The participant can elect to defer distributions for at least an additional 5 years, but if he or she has the ability to receive benefits earlier (regardless of whether or not he or she actually makes the elections), or if there are any other violations of the statute, then all compensation deferred under the plan for the taxable year and all preceding taxable years shall be includible in gross income in that year, and interest (based on very unfavorable rates) and an additional 20% penalty tax are assessed.

SERP's are either mirror-images of the qualified plan without the statutory limitations or are completely independent of the qualified plans. Importantly, however, the employer's deduction is similarly deferred until the tax year in which the employee includes such benefits in his Gross Income. Thus, companies using SERP's do not get the benefit of early deductions as with qualified plans. It is important to be aware of that these deferred compensation benefits are simply promises, and are paid from the employer's general assets, rather than a separate qualified trust, so that fund earnings are immediately taxable to the employer.

As discussed in further detail in Chapter 18, while still subject to the employer's general creditors, nonqualified deferred compensation promises may be funded through certain trusts, colloquially called "Rabbi trusts" (since the first employer seeking guidance from the IRS on such a practice was a congregation seeking to segregate the retirement promises made to its Rabbi from the temple's other general operating assets). IRC § 409A curbs some of the potential abuses by prohibiting employers from investing Rabbi trust assets in "offshore property," thus keeping all assets of the Rabbi trust under the jurisdiction of federal U.S. courts. Additionally, in 2008, Congress added new IRC § 457A, which imposes restrictions on foreign corporations from promising nonqualified deferred compensation to U.S. executives, and thus circumventing the rules of IRC § 409A.

As should be apparent, the income tax rules for both the executive and the employer for nonqualified deferred compensation promises were pretty simple and executive-friendly up until 2004, when Congress started reigning in all actual or potential abuses. In the near future, the operation of nonqualified deferred compensation plans might actually become as complicated, if not more complicated, than the income tax rules associated with qualified retirement plans.

Finally, if nonqualified deferred compensation benefits are included in Gross Income while the individual is still an active employee of the employer, then those benefits are subject to the payroll taxes of FICA and FUTA for contributions to social security and unemployment insurance, respectively.[5] In some appropriate situations, the employee can voluntarily include the present value of future promised benefits in Gross Income (and subject to payroll taxes) in the year services are performed which result in the deferred compensation.[6]

---

5. IRC §§ 3121 and 3301.
6. IRC §§ 83(b) and 3121(v).

2. Income Tax Advantages of Qualified Retirement Plans

As explained in Chapter 4, if an employer provides retirement benefits through a plan that complies with all of the qualification rules of IRC § 401(a), then

> Under IRC § 402, the employee does not include the retirement benefits in Gross Income until the year they are received. Note that this more simple and advantageous analysis is different than the year that the amount is no longer subject to a substantial risk of forfeiture metric for nonqualified benefits. The actual taxation of distributions from qualified plans, including penalties for premature distributions and missed required minimum distributions, is discussed in Chapter 9. Note that with the introduction of Roth IRAs in 2002 and Roth 401(k) accounts in 2006 (as discussed in Chapter 5), and with the loosening of distribution restrictions from IRAs in 2006 (as discussed in Chapter 9), the rules for determining Gross Income have become more complicated, further requiring individual employees to seek out and pay for personal income tax, financial planning, and estate planning advice.

> Under IRC § 404, the employer is entitled to an immediate deduction in the year contributions are made to the qualified plan. Note that this is more advantageous to the employer than the need to wait to get the deduction for nonqualified benefits until the year that the individual includes the amounts in his or her Gross Income. The actual limitations on employer deductions are discussed in Chapter 6.

> Under IRC § 501(a), as part of the rules for a qualified plan, the employer must establish a separate legal entity to hold plan assets, which is a tax-exempt trust. Therefore, unless there is any incidence of Unrelated Business Income Tax,[7] then all fund earnings accumulate tax-free, and thus are not taxable to the employer or employee until actually distributed from the trust. Unlike nonqualified benefit promises, which are always subject to the employer's creditors and possibly even subject to the executive's personal creditors, qualified plan assets properly held in trust are wholly restricted from the reach of creditors of either the employer or of the employee.

In addition, since an employee oftentimes is in a lower income tax bracket after retirement, the amounts included in Gross Income in future years after retirement might actually be subjected to a lower tax liability (this, of course, assumes that the current income tax regime will remain unchanged). Also, for payroll tax purposes, most qualified retirement benefit promises (other than elective deferrals in a 401(k) plan) are not subject to FICA and FUTA taxes to fund social security and unemployment, respectively.

3. Income Tax Advantages of Health and Welfare Benefit Plans

Health benefits and welfare benefits, if designed properly by the employer, have very advantageous income tax treatment to the employees, and possibly to certain family members. A more detailed discussion of the specific income tax requirement for the plan design follows in Chapter 19.

---

7. IRC § 512.

Under IRC §§ 104, 105, and 106, collectively, the employee does not include in Gross Income the amounts paid by the employer for premiums paid for, or amounts received through, accident or health insurance (or through an arrangement or plan having the effect of accident or health insurance) for personal injuries or sickness. If the employer allows the employee to add a spouse (defined under the federal Defense of Marriage Act as "only to a person of the opposite sex who is a husband or a wife"),[8] child (which generally includes adopted children and foster children under the employee's care) or dependent (which generally includes qualified relatives and non-relative individuals primarily residing with the employee and primarily dependent on the employee for living expenses)[9] to the plan, then the amounts paid by the employer for premiums paid or amounts received are similarly excluded from the employee's Gross Income and the family member's Gross Income. However, if the employer allows other non-traditional family members to be included in the plan, such as domestic partners, same-sex spouses, same-sex civil-unioned spouses, unadopted children, and siblings, and the non-employee family member does not fit the definition of dependent, then the value of the benefits received by the non-employee family member is imputed to the employee and included in the employee's Gross Income.

Under IRC § 132, Gross Income shall not include any fringe benefit which qualifies as a—

- no-additional-cost service (for example, the employer is an airline and the employee is allowed to fly for free for non-work-related activities if there is an available seat);
- qualified employee discount (for example, the employer is a clothing retail store and the employee receives a 15% discount on all personal purchases);
- working condition fringe (for example, the employer is a multinational corporation, and in response to several death threats on the life of an executive, the executive is provided an alarm system at his home, security guards while working, and a vehicle that is specially equipped with alarms, bullet proof glass, and armor plating);
- de minimis fringe (for example, the employer is an accounting firm, and an employee occasionally uses the firm's photocopying machine for personal use);
- qualified transportation fringe (which includes reimbursement of expenses incurred in commuting to or from work via a commuter highway vehicle, a transit pass, qualified parking, or qualified bicycle purchases and repairs);
- qualified moving expense reimbursement;
- qualified retirement planning services; or
- qualified military base realignment and closure reimbursement.

Under other various Code sections (see IRC §§ 101 through 140 for all items specifically excluded from Gross Income), the value of any benefit offered by an employer to an employee as an employee benefit will be excluded from the employee's Gross Income if the employer complies with all provisions of the respective statute.

On the employer side, all health, welfare and fringe benefits provided to employees, if reasonable and compliant with the respective Code sections, represent immediately deductible trade or business expenses for salary or other compensation for services actually rendered.[10] Please note that unlike contributions to qualified retirement plans, contribu-

---

8. 1 USC § 7.
9. IRC § 152.
10. IRC § 162(a)(1).

tions or provisions of health and welfare benefits may not be entitled to a business deduction if the employer is a partnership, S Corporation, LLC or LLP, or a sole proprietorship. Therefore, choice of business entity when a business is formed, and subsequently as employees and employee benefit programs are added, needs to be carefully considered by an expert.

If the employer requires the employee to pay for some of the benefits, then the employer can establish health savings accounts, cafeteria plans, and flexible spending arrangements to allow the employee share to be withheld from the pay check and excluded from Gross Income. These types of arrangements are discussed in Chapter 19.

Chapter 3

The Employee Retirement Income Security Act of 1974

Overview

Does an employer need to provide employee benefits?

- no
- but, if the employer voluntarily makes a promise to employees, then they must deliver them through a plan that might be subject to governance under the Employee Retirement Income Security Act of 1974 (ERISA)

What is ERISA and why was it enacted?

- in 1974, there were perceived and actual abuses in retirement plans, such as
  - broken promises by the employers
  - improper use of plan assets
  - inadequate advance funding
  - failure to cover a fair cross-section of lower paid employees
- Congress enacted ERISA primarily to provide rights to the employees being promised employee benefits
- ERISA governs the requirements for employer-sponsored retirement plans and health and welfare benefits plans
- almost all of the rules and penalties under ERISA are for acts or non-acts of the employer, not for the acts of the individual employees or their beneficiaries

What protections does ERISA provide to employees promised employee benefits?

- every ERISA plan imposes certain reporting requirements to the federal government and certain disclosure requirements to the plan participants and beneficiaries (Title I, Subtitle B, Part 1 of ERISA)
- certain retirement plans (discussed throughout this textbook as "qualified retirement plans") have minimum vesting and advanced funding rules (Title I, Subtitle B, Parts 2 and 3 of ERISA)
- qualified retirement plans and certain group health plans impose specific fiduciary duties on the individuals who have management control over plan assets (Title I, Subtitle B, Part 4 of ERISA)
- every ERISA plan (and individuals associated with the plan) is subject to the criminal and civil causes of action and remedies specifically stated in the statute, and

are therefore preempted from state-level causes of action (Title I, Subtitle B, Part 5 of ERISA)

- certain group health plans are subject to continuation requirements under COBRA and portability and accountability under requirements HIPAA (Title I, Subtitle B, Parts 6 and 7 of ERISA)

- certain qualified retirement plans must pay premiums to a federal agency (the Pension Benefit Guaranty Corporation), which acts as the insurer for employer sponsors that go bankrupt before fully funding the retirement promises, and other qualified retirement plans common to a group of union employees can impose a withdrawal liability on employers that wish to stop contributing to the common collectively bargained union fund (Title IV of ERISA)

What are the corresponding income tax provisions of ERISA?

- in addition to the "labor" rights and protections under Titles I and IV of ERISA, Title II of ERISA provides the corresponding provisions under the Internal Revenue Code which allows properly drafted and operated plans to provide the income tax advantages to employees and employers as described above

What are the main agencies that regulate ERISA governed employee benefit plans?

- The U.S. Department of Labor, through the Employee Benefits Security Administration (EBSA)

- The U.S. Department of Treasury, through the Employee Plans group of the Internal Revenue Service, Tax Exempt and Governmental Entities operating division (IRS EP)

- The Pension Benefit Guaranty Corporation (PBGC)

How do federal agencies generally work?

- they are staffed with experts

- they perform audits and examinations to make sure plan are compliant with the rules under ERISA and the Internal Revenue Code ("IRC")

- they attempt to educate employers that sponsor employee benefit plans and individuals promised benefits from the plans

- they provide interpretation of the Congressional statutes where needed

  - the highest form of guidance is a regulation, which, when published in final form, either has the effect of law, if Congress specifically asked them to draft regulations, or is presumed to be correct, if Congress does not specifically ask for the regulations

  - a proposed regulation has no legal effect, but signals how the agency would like to eventually interpret a statute, and allows a period of several months where the members of the public can provide comments

  - lesser guidance (such as Revenue Rulings or Notices from the IRS or Advisory Opinions from the EBSA) just sets forth the agencies position, but can be challenged by the plan if the plan sponsor has a different interpretation of the statute

  - individual correspondence and internal memos are not supposed to be guidance, but under the Freedom of Information laws, they are made public after names and other identifiable information is retracted

Which agencies have jurisdiction to regulate the different aspects of ERISA?
- the original division of jurisdiction between the Departments of Treasury and Labor were in Title III of ERISA
- after a few years of experience, President Carter reorganized the division of jurisdiction

Is ERISA actively amended?
- yes, almost every year since enactment in 1974, ERISA has been amended (sometimes in a very minor manner, and sometimes in a major manner)
- think about the public policy between changes:
  - is it an amendment to the labor provisions?
    - if yes, then were more protections provided to plan participants and beneficiaries (thus favoring the participants) or were the rules relaxed somewhat (thus favoring the employer sponsor)
  - or is it an amendment to the income tax provisions?
    - if yes, then is it expanding the income tax benefits to employer or participant (thus costing the government tax revenue in additional subsidies) or is it restricting the income tax benefits (thus increasing expected tax revenues, which is likely just the simplest mechanism available to Congress to pay for some other law they have enacted)

When an employer voluntarily chooses to sponsor an ERISA plan, then what roles and obligations must it fulfill?
- once the promises are made through a plan, then the employer must actually administer the plan so that all promises are delivered properly and timely, and so that the regulatory agencies have a contact for audits and questions
- if there are plan assets, then at least one individual must be named as the plan fiduciary, and then that individual can delegate and transfer fiduciary duties to others

If the employer does not employ internal staff with an expertise in the governance of the employee benefits plan, then who are other employee benefits professionals that it can work with?
- attorneys to draft the plan documents, provide legal advice, and represent its interests in litigation
- accountants to tie deductions and financial accounting of the employee benefits plans with other matters of the business, and to provide independent audits of plan assets
- actuaries to perform required valuations for certain qualified retirement plans and to provide other statistical and financial forecasts as needed or desired
- insurance advisors to provide proper and adequate forms of insurance to fund, or simply be part of, the plan assets
- investment advisors to help diversify plan assets in accordance with modern portfolio theory
- record keepers to assist the employer's payroll and human resources departments in keeping specific employee data organized in order to determine the level of benefits that were promised to the employees
- third party administrators to step in the shoes of the employer and run the day to day operations of the employee benefit plan

- Enrolled Retirement Plan Agents (ERPAs) to represent the employer's qualified retirement plan in front of the IRS (because the only individuals allowed to receive power of attorney from the employer sponsor and represent the plan in front of the IRS are ERPAs, attorneys, accountants, actuaries, and Enrolled Agents)

A. Protection of Employees Promised Benefits

1. Employers Voluntarily Promise Employee Benefits

An employer hires employees when needed, and will generally need to pay competitive compensation packages, if not better-than average compensation. The employee benefits offered on top of current wages are used to attract good workers, to keep them happy while working and making the business profitable, and to reward them for their past efforts. Additionally, the employer might seek income tax advantages through these employee benefit programs, and other non-monetary advantages, such as a happy workforce or good publicity.

In exchange for services rendered, an employer must comply with federal and state minimum wage laws, family medical and leave laws, and all other relevant labor laws that concern minimum compensation.[1] Anything else that an employer promises to an individual in exchange for services is generally considered an employee benefit, and is offered on a voluntary basis. The problem for employees, however, was that until the mid-1970s, no federal or state laws truly protected the promises made, and if not delivered, whether through good intentions but poor management exercised by the employer, or because of a willful desire to renege on promises, the only recourse an employee had was to sue in state court for breach of contract, or some other tort.

Since this textbook is not truly a casebook, there are only a few cases sprinkled throughout to prove a point. The following case is included in its entirety, because it is short and it is fun to read. In reading the following case, please note the term of art that employer Wurlitzer used instead of retirement, and then based solely on the facts of this case, please determine for yourself if it looks like Wurlitzer was being an honest employer but not constrained by federal laws demanding otherwise, or if it willfully tried to screw over its employee, Mr. Sigman.

Sigman v. Rudolph Wurlitzer Co.
11 N.E.2d 878 (Ohio App., 1937)

Harmon, Colston, Goldsmith & Hoadly and Henry B. Street, all of Cincinnati, for appellant.

Roy Manogue and J. Lewis Homer, both of Cincinnati, for appellee.

TATGENHORST, Presiding Judge.

This is an appeal on questions of law from the court of common pleas of Hamilton county.

---

1. The Department of Labor's Employment Standards Administration Wage and Hour Division has information and links for all minimum wage issues at http://www.dol.gov/esa/whd.

Suit was instituted by the appellee, Thurse Sigman, to recover from the appellant, the Rudolph Wurlitzer Company, the amount of a pension claimed to be due him by reason of his compliance with the terms of the pension requirements.

The appellant was engaged in the business of manufacture and sale of musical instruments. The appellee had been in the employ of the appellant for more than twenty-seven years, when he was discharged because it had no further employment to which he was suited. He had served appellant as order clerk, salesman on the road, manager of its Victrola department, wholesale and retail, and manager in charge of its wholesale radio department.

From time to time during his employment, the appellant issued booklets containing various declarations covering the institution of a pension system, applicable to its employees and including the appellee. That such program was calculated to and did induce continued service in the corporation there can be no question. It constituted a continuing offer on the part of the company, which was continuously accepted by the employees who preserved their status with the company. We quote from the booklet:

'He who serves best receives most.

'Rules for Your Success

'And the policy outlined for your welfare

'The Rudolph Wurlitzer Co.

'Chicago, Cincinnati, New York, and all principal cities

'For You

'This booklet was written for you. It was written for your interest and the attention of every employee thruout the enormous organization of The Rudolph Wurlitzer Co.**879

'There is something on every page of this booklet that should be of vital importance to you, that is, of course, if you desire to become successful with the vast amount of opportunities before you. The employees who shoulder the greatest responsibilities and have become most successful in our organization today are only those who have strictly adhered to and closely observed the simple but necessary rules and policies.

'After all, the important part of any rule is the spirit of it. This is gained by understanding the wisdom and necessity of the rule, and not by mere obedience because it is a rule. No rule seems hard when you see that it is wise—worked out from experience—made necessary by existing conditions.

'Every possible method has been outlined for your welfare and protection while in our employ. Your saving, bonus, compensation for promptness and efficiency, protection during sickness, pension and insurance has all been thoroughly explained in this booklet.

'All that we ask is that you kindly read every page and feel that you are a part of an organization which is doing everything within its power for your success and welfare.

'The Rudolph Wurlitzer Co.

'Pension System

'In order to take care of our loyal and trustworthy employees when old age over-takes them, we have put in this pension system: We will pay 2% on the entire amount you have earned each year, which will be paid to you in monthly in-stalments, and as long as you live. The largest pension we pay any one is $100.00 per month, or $1,200.00 a year. For example, we will take an employe that has earned $900.00 per year:

'Worked 10 years at $900.00 a year—$9,000.00. Pension, $15.00 per month.

'Worked 15 years at $900.00 a year—$13,500.00. Pension, $22.50 per month.

'Worked 20 years at $900.00 a year—$18,000.00. Pension, $30.00 per month.

'Worked 25 years at $900.00 a year—$22,500.00. Pension, $37.50 per month.

'Worked 30 years at $900.00 a year—$27,000.00. Pension, $45.00 per month.

'From the above table you can easily figure what your pension would amount to.

It pays to be loyal. A rolling stone gathers no moss.'

At the bottom of the pages of the booklet are interesting statements designed apparently to encourage *7 industry, faithfulness, loyalty, and continued service with the company. Among them, appears the following:

'No man in this world ever rightfully receives more than he gives.—Adams.

'A man with push can get there, but it takes a man with character to stay there.—Shepherd.

'Forget the past. Success lies in the future.

'No one can cheat you of final success but yourself.'

There is much good advice contained in the pamphlet, and the whole effect is to produce a feeling of confidence in the fairness and sincere concern of the company for the welfare of the employee.

[1] It is a little difficult for the court to reconcile the present attitude of ap-pellant with the many assurances of concern for the benefit of the employees contained in the pamphlet. As previously stated, in considering another pamphlet issued by this company (Wilson v. Rudolph Wurlitzer Co., 48 Ohio App. 450, 194 N.E. 441), fraud is never presumed, and where two constructions are pos-sible, one of which requires a finding of fraudulent intent, and the other per-mits a conclusion of good faith, courts never hesitate in giving effect to the latter interpretation.

[2] The inducement having been accepted by the appellee, the writing of ap-pellant must be construed also most strongly against it, for it could have re-stricted the existing implications by proper words of limitation. The appellee is entitled to the benefit of all reasonable inferences applicable to the words used.

[3] The appellant places great reliance, in denying to the 52 year old ap-pellee the benefits of its pension system, upon the words 'when old age over-takes you.' Now it must be observed that these words appear only in a clause addressed to a statement of the motivating impulse prompting the initiation and continuance of the pension system. It is further a matter of common knowledge that there is an industrial old age and what may be styled a social old age, an economic human obsolescence, **880 entirely distinct from the evening of life.

It is apparent also that according to the schedule there is an implication that an employee may be paid a pension after only ten years' service. The service of appellee is within two and one-half years of the maximum service stated in the illustration table. We are aware that neither of the extremes are limits of liability, but the appellee is entitled to the value of the natural import of what was presented to him.

[4] It is to be noted also that the pension is payable during life, and would, therefore, naturally be a protection against destitution in old age. We consider the words used do not require an exhibition of senile decrepitude before the pension becomes payable any more than mere incapacity caused by accident or disease, however disastrous to the employee, would invoke the operation of the pension. The age at which men and women cease to be effective employees varies materially in the various industries and professions.

From what the record shows it can be easily concluded that the particular business carried on by appellant was of such a nature that mature youth would be at a premium, and that the appellee had reached a point where a younger man would serve the appellant much more satisfactorily. When it becomes apparent that longer employment will be a detriment to efficient service and that the alternative is a pension, a discharge is a most effective severance of the Gordian knot. While effective and most serviceable to the appellant, it results in a complete abrogation of the security upon which the appellee for twenty- seven and one-half years relied and had a right to rely.

Not one word of criticism is made of such service for this long period.

The federal pension system is mentioned. If age 65 was in the mind of appellant, why was not this or some other age specified, so that the employee could have been permitted to govern himself accordingly with all the facts before him. The illustrative table again is most forceful in its implication of ages of retirement much below the federal age.

The court charged in part as follows: 'Now, this pension system, or contract, or agreement, which has been set forth in the amended petition and shown, in Exhibit No. 1 uses the expression 'When old age overtakes them,' or overtakes him, applying to the plaintiff. I say to you that this means the age at which the average man performing the same or similar duties would ordinarily find himself unable to further perform such duties, or, to find similar employment elsewhere, and therefore I say to you if you find from a preponderance of evidence that the plaintiff at the time his services with the defendant were discontinued then was at that age at which the average man performing the same or similar services would ordinarily find himself unable to further perform such services, or, to find similar employment elsewhere, then the plaintiff is entitled to a verdict, calculated according to the table prescribed in said Exhibit No. 1.'

If there is any criticism of this charge, it is that it states too severe a rule against the appellee. Nothing is said in the pension prospectus as to incapacity. This could have been made the criterion. It was not specified.

[5] The appellee had earned while in the service of the appellant more than $54,000. During these years he was led to believe that 2 per cent of his earnings would be paid him when the company considered him more favorably in the position of a pensioner than as an employee receiving a full salary or wage. The

appellant has made its election. It has concluded that he has reached the point of industrial old age. It is to its interest to discontinue the payment of the full wage. The employee must bow to the appellant's opinion and edict. He, however, cannot be in good faith and justice denied the alternative held out by the employer as an inducement, for more than a quarter of a century, to continue service with the appellant.

The judgment is affirmed.

Judgment affirmed.
ROSS and HAMILTON, JJ., concur.

So, Wurlitzer used the term "when old age overtakes you" which seems very tenuous and objective. While it didn't seem arbitrary and capricious against the employee simply from these facts, Wurlitzer interpreted the term one way and the employee interpreted it another. Based on the laws of the state of Ohio, the facts seemed to elevate the claim to breach of contract, but would the same facts yield the same result if another Wurlitzer employee who resided in a different state brought a similar cause of action? Say what you will about the complexity of ERISA, but one of its theoretical strong points is the similar legal treatment of similarly situated employees but for the state of residence and employment. The causes of action and federal preemption issues will be discussed further in Chapter 14.

2. The Need for Congress to Act: ERISA

The first major act signed by President Ford, on Labor Day no less, was the Employee Retirement Income Security Act of 1974, or ERISA, which is the fountainhead of Employee Benefits law. By 1974, Congress was aware of perceived and actual abuses in retirement plans. Such abuses included, but were not limited to, the failure of large employers (or unions) to deliver the benefits they had promised (whether due to economic reality, negligence or malfeasance), improper use of plan assets, inadequate advance funding, excessive periods of required service as an employee before even a portion of the benefits was vested (as demonstrated with the Wurlitzer case), and the failure to cover a fair cross-section of lower-paid employees. As a result of such perceived injustices, many retired workers found themselves with little or nothing to show for the decades of work they had put in. Because employer-provided benefits constitute one of the three legs of the aforementioned "three-legged stool" of retirement, this problem hurt not only the workers, but the government itself, which might find itself saddled with a glut of elderly public wards—disastrous from a public policy standpoint.

Essentially, ERISA was the government's first comprehensive attempt in providing relief and security by protecting the rights of the employees who were promised employee benefits. It is worth noting that, under the United States Constitution, there is no right to receive employee benefits, in contrast to, for example, the constitutions of several European countries, whose governments have been more influenced by theoretical socialism over the decades. Thus, ERISA was a major legislative grace for many American workers, and many argue in direct discord with the business goals of employers.

ERISA governs the retirement benefits (and the health and welfare benefits) promised to employees by the employer through a plan. In doing so, ERISA assumes that the employer, in affirmatively offering an employee benefits plan to its employees, voluntarily and knowingly subjects itself to ERISA coverage (and all of its complex rules).

As a result, almost all of the rules and penalties under ERISA apply to acts (or non-acts) of the employer, not for the acts of the individual employees or their beneficiaries. One of the major tenets of ERISA is proper communication to employees of exactly what is promised and disclosures of how the plans are funded to the federal government. Please note that the world of health benefit promises and delivery was vastly different in the 1970s, and as a last minute compromise, the bill seeking to offer security to employees in their retirement plan promises was amended to also include security in health and welfare benefit plan promises—and as the world of health care benefits has grown more expensive and complicated over the intervening decades, many argue that the single law should be bifurcated, since different protections and rights should go to an employee's retirement promises as should go to their health and welfare benefit promises.

Chapter 11 lays out exactly where ERISA is codified, how it is laid out, and which employee benefit plans are subjected to its rules, and Chapter 19 explores some of the current ERISA rules imposed on employer-provided health and welfare benefit plans.

3. Other ERISA Protections

Communication of promised benefits. Under ERISA, when an employer promises retirement benefits or health and welfare benefits, and delivers those benefits through an ERISA plan (as discussed in Chapter 11), it is automatically encumbered by certain reporting requirements to the federal government and disclosure requirements to the employees who are, or who might, be eligible to participate in the plan and enjoy the benefits therein. The disclosure rules are, collectively, supposed to provide enough information to the participants, generally written in a manner anticipated to be understood by the average participant, so that they know what benefits they are entitled to, when and how they are entitled to receive them, the procedures they need to take to avail themselves of the plan benefits, how they can appeal any adverse benefit decisions made by the plan sponsor, and how they can seek further redress from a governmental agency (like the Department of Labor) or the federal courts. The disclosure rules extend to beneficiaries named by employees who will receive plan benefits upon their death, and has also been extended to spouses of married plan participants and ex-spouses of divorced participants. In addition, the information submitted to the federal agencies through reporting and possibly plan audits should be sufficient for the federal government to find and curb negligence and abuses before the plan participants are affected. Chapter 15 highlights some of the more relevant reporting and disclosure requirements under ERISA.

Minimum Vesting. After ERISA, employers no longer have unfettered discretion in demanding that employees work for 20 or 30 years before having any right to receive retirement benefits. Under the current rules, the most that an employer can demand is somewhere between 3 and 7 years of service before full vesting. Chapter 7 explores the vesting requirements for rights to a benefit, and the correlated benefit accrual rules that determine the amount of benefit a plan participant is entitled to if he or she terminates employment before retirement.

Advanced Funding. Before ERISA, the employer would make promises to pay deferred compensation, but would not generally set appropriate levels of assets aside. This is known as a pay-as-you-go funding scheme, which can lead to insufficient assets to pay the retirement benefits for well-intentioned employers, and fertile areas for embezzlement and fraud for the ill-intentioned employers. After ERISA, the employer is required to establish a separate trust to properly fund retirement benefits, and if desired, for health and welfare benefits that are self-funded as opposed to being purchased through an insurance company. Chapter 6 will summarize the funding rules for retirement plans.

Fiduciary Duties. Now that employers that promise and deliver certain employee benefits are required to establish a separate trust to hold plan assets, ERISA imposes specific duties on how individuals deemed as plan fiduciaries can invest those assets. The rules impose a very high standard on the procedures, level of care, and loyalty, and are the metrics used during litigation to ascertain whether the plan fiduciaries properly performed their duties owed to the plan participants. As shown in Chapter 13, some officers of the employer might be functionally deemed a fiduciaries even if they did not expect to be one, and any fiduciary that breaches their duties can be held personally liable to put the plan back to where it would have been if not for the breach.

Civil Enforcement and ERISA Preemption. One of the major effects of ERISA covered employee benefit plans is the preemption of all state laws. This is a double edged sword for both employers and disgruntled plan participants. On the one hand, there should be consistency throughout the states, so that if an employer has employees in more than one state and they are covered by the same plan, then a disgruntled employee suing the plan in one state should get the same judicial result as a fellow disgruntled employee suing the same plan in a different state. However, as indicated in Chapter 14, the employees are limited to the causes of action and remedies specifically provided for under ERISA, even if the remedies available under state law appear more generous or likely to be awarded.

Continuation Coverage and Portability of Group Health Insurance Plans. This textbook primarily provides a framework for retirement benefit plans, and just a cursory overview of health and welfare benefit plans. However, certain aspects of group health plans are quite important, and have received special attention by Congress in the years following the enactment of ERISA in 1974 as they tried to keep the law as current as the evolving landscape of healthcare delivery in the United States. In 1986, to deal with the problems that employees were having when they left an employer and its health insurance plan, or where family members of an employee had a life-changing event that caused the termination of group health plan coverage, Congress enacted COBRA to provide a way for these former employees to pay the cost of coverage to remain part of the "group." In 1996, to deal with issues like pre-existing conditions, discriminatory decisions made by the employer regarding the health plan based on an individual's specific health condition, and the lack of privacy of personal health information, Congress enacted HIPAA. A summary of the regulation of health and welfare plans is provided in Chapter 19.

Termination of retirement plans. ERISA created a governmental insurer for certain employers that go into bankruptcy without having properly funded their retirement plans. This agency, called the Pension Benefit Guaranty Corporation (the PBGC), was established to pay certain pension benefits to the employees, but as indicated in Chapter 16, too many sectors of the economy, such as steel companies, airlines, and now likely the automotive industry, have drained the agency's assets more than originally anticipated, and Congress is currently looking at ways of keeping the PBGC viable without the need for a taxpayer bailout. On the other hand, union plans, where many unaffiliated employers contribute, have different issues. The plan itself will usually not terminate, but contributing employers might decide to stop contributing to the union plan and cover their own union employees under their own plan. Here, ERISA allows the union plan itself to demand a withdrawal liability from the employer who decides to leave.

B. Income Tax Provisions

There were corporate retirement plans by the late 1800s that served the business goals of the railroad and financial sectors of the increasingly-industrialized American economy, even before there was an Internal Revenue Code with provisions providing tax benefits to the employer or employee. Many credit the wage limitations during World War II and the corresponding tax benefits under the then existing Internal Revenue Code[2] as the catalyst for the real surge in private-sector employer provided retirement and health and welfare benefit plans. Those provisions, however, were minimal, simple, and not well regulated or enforced.

A major part of ERISA (Title II of the four-titled legislation) added many provisions to the Code that refined exactly what the employer needs to do in its employee benefits plan to enjoy a tax benefit (usually a deduction for the cost of providing benefits in the year contributions are made to the plan) and for the employees promised benefits to enjoy a tax benefit (as discussed in Chapter 2, retirement benefits from a qualified retirement plan are generally not included in Gross Income until the year received, retirement benefits from non-qualified retirement plans are generally not included in Gross Income until the year in which there is no longer a substantial risk of forfeiture, and the economic value of health and welfare benefits are generally excluded from Gross Income in all years). ERISA also carved out a specific niche within the IRS for regulation of these employee plans (in the IRS Restructuring and Reform Act of 1998, one of the four operating divisions created was the Tax Exempt / Government Entities Division, within which the Employee Plans group was created—and their specific role is discussed in more detail in Chapter 10).

C. The Role of the Federal Government

1. The Federal Agencies That Regulate Employee Benefit Plans

ERISA is regulated by a variety of federal agencies: The U.S. Department of Treasury (through the Internal Revenue Service), The U.S. Department of Labor (through the Employee Benefits Security Administration, formerly known as the Pension and Welfare Benefits Administration) and The Pension Benefit Guaranty Corporation (whose Board of Directors, investment strategy and other operational functions are governed by ERISA, and whose executive director is a presidential appointment, subject to the advise and con-

---

2. The 16th Amendment to the United States Constitution, ratified in 1913, states that "The Congress shall have power to lay and collect taxes on incomes, from whatever source derived, without apportionment among the several states, and without regard to any census or enumeration." This clarified the uniformity requirement for the laying of taxes included in Article I, Section 8. After income tax statutes sprinkled throughout the United States Code, Congress first organized and created the Internal Revenue Code of 1939, totally reorganized and made substantial changes with the promulgation of the Internal Revenue Code of 1954, and then made a similar wholesale revision with the current Internal Revenue Code of 1986, as amended. If Congress heeds the current cries of simplification of the income tax rules, there might be yet another current-day wholesale revision and reorganization of the IRC.

sent of the U.S. Senate). As discussed in Chapter 10, the IRS, through its Employee Plans group of its Tax Exempt / Government Entities operating division, is mainly concerned with compliant employee benefit plans, and achieves its goals through education, guidance and enforcement. As discussed in Chapter 17, the DOL, through its Employee Benefits Security Administration, is mainly concerned with protecting employee rights, and achieves its goals through education, guidance, enforcement, and assisting the courts when an employee is suing the employer-sponsored employee benefits plan. As discussed in Chapter 16, The PBGC is a federal corporation designed to protect the pensions of American workers and retirees, and acts as an insurer of certain types of qualified retirement plan promises that are jeopardized once the sponsoring employer declares bankruptcy.

In addition, other agencies have become more relevant, such as some of the governance of some aspects of health benefit plans by the U.S. Department of Health and Human Services, the special issues faced by retirement plans by the Securities Exchange Commission and how the benefit plans affect the financial statements of public companies by the Financial Accounting Standards Board, some of the labor, union, and collectively bargained agreement issues by the National Labor Relations Board, and some age discrimination issues inherent in some retirement plan designs by the Equal Employment Opportunity Commission. Unless casually mentioned where appropriate, this text book does not focus in on the operations and regulation of these other agencies, although in the actual employee benefits practice, some of these tangential agencies are the utmost concern to the employer-client.

Finally, employee benefits professionals will also need to understand how some of the various state laws and agencies affect the employee benefit plans, such as state agencies that monitor insurance companies, banks and other financial institutions, and labor and employment concerns above and beyond the minimum levels mandated under federal law.

2. Overview of the Federal Agencies

As discussed in further detail in Appendix A, interpretations of law under ERISA, which represent federal law, are similar to that of the Tax Code. If the law is clear on its face (*i.e.*, actual Code or ERISA provisions as penned by Congress), then it must be followed. As stated before, there are no provisions in the U.S. Constitution that directly relate to employee benefit plans, so Congress is free to amend the provisions at will, and generally does so under its clear authority to write laws that effect interstate commerce.

The Departments of Treasury and Labor, as executive-branch agencies, can issue regulations which, if directed to do so by Congress (*i.e.*, legislative regulations), have the same effect as the law so long as they are reasonable and have been finalized. All other regulations issued by the agencies (*i.e.*, interpretive regulations pursuant to their general authority to interpret any ambiguous laws, or any proposed or temporary regulations before becoming final) might be persuasive to certain courts, but do not have the same effect as the law.

Aside from regulations, other purposefully promulgated rules, procedures, notices or announcements represent the agency's interpretation of the law. The agencies are bound by such pronouncements for all similarly situated individuals or plans. Individuals or plans can, however, express alternate interpretations. All other guidance (such as private letter rulings and internal technical memorandum), which would remain unpublished if not for the Freedom of Information laws, can provide insight into how the agencies might interpret the laws, but the agencies are not bound by such interpretations.

In the event that the DOL or the DOT audits the plan or individual and assess penalties that are in dispute, ERISA mandates that all causes of action regarding employee benefit plans be litigated in federal district court. For tax litigation only, the taxpayer can either pay the tax assessment and ask the IRS for a refund in district court (usually with a jury trial) or refuse to pay the tax assessment and be sued by the Commissioner in the specialized federal Tax Court. An alternate choice, still at the primary district court level, is for the taxpayer to pay the tax assessment and then sue the United States government in the U.S. Court of Claims. For ERISA causes of action, all primary litigation is at the federal district court. Regardless of the venue for primary litigation, the respective federal Circuit Courts of Appeal have appellate jurisdiction, and the U.S. Supreme Court may grant certiorari to finally settle any ambiguity in the effect or interpretation of a Code or ERISA provision. Although the U.S. Supreme Court has indicated that there is a federal "common law" developed for ERISA cases, all roots stem from contract, labor and/or trust common law principles. ERISA litigation is discussed in further detail in Chapter 14.

3. Jurisdiction between Departments of Treasury and Labor

It is quite interesting to read the history of ERISA, and the jurisdictional battles between the tax and revenue committees of Congress (the House Ways and Means Committee and the Senate Finance Committee), and the labor and employment committees (the House Education and Labor Committee and the Senate Health, Education, Labor and Employment Committee) in the lead up to the enactment of ERISA. Noted ERISA historian Professor James Wooten of University of Buffalo Law School has written several articles and books on the legislative history of ERISA, and concludes that the labor committees won out, thus ERISA is considered a labor law that has some amendments to the Internal Revenue Code.

That being said, the original division of jurisdiction between the Departments of Labor and Treasury originally contained in Title III of ERISA showed areas of duplication and other areas of neglect, and in 1978, President Carter issued the following Executive Statement:

Message of the President
5 U.S.C.A. App. 1 REORG. PLAN 4 1978

To the Congress of the United States:

Today I am submitting to the Congress may fourth Reorganization Plan for 1978. This proposal is designed to simplify and improve the unnecessarily complex administrative requirements of the Employee Retirement Income Security Act of 1974 (ERISA) [see Short Title note set out under section 1001 of Title 29, Labor]. The new plan will eliminate overlap and duplication in the administration of ERISA and help us achieve our goal of well regulated private pension plans.

ERISA was an essential step in the protection of worker pension rights. Its administrative provisions, however, have resulted in bureaucratic confusion and have been justifiably criticized by employers and unions alike. The biggest problem has been overlapping jurisdictional authority. Under current ERISA provisions, the Departments of Treasury and Labor both have authority to issue regulations and decisions.

This dual jurisdiction has delayed a good many important rulings and, more importantly, produced bureaucratic runarounds and burdensome reporting requirements.

The new plan will significantly reduce these problems. In addition, both Departments are trying to cut red tape and paperwork, to eliminate unnecessary reporting requirements, and to streamline forms wherever possible.

Both Departments have already made considerable progress, and both will continue the effort to simplify their rules and their forms.

The Reorganization Plan is the most significant result of their joint effort to modify and simplify ERISA. It will eliminate most of the jurisdictional overlap between Treasury and Labor by making the following changes:

1) Treasury will have statutory authority for minimum standards. The new plan puts all responsibility for funding, participation, and vesting of benefit rights in the Department of Treasury. These standards are necessary to ensure that employee benefit plans are adequately funded and that all beneficiary rights are protected. Treasury is the most appropriate Department to administer these provisions; however, Labor will continue to have veto power over Treasury decisions that significantly affect collectively bargained plans.

2) Labor will have statutory authority for fiduciary obligations. ERISA prohibits transactions in which self-interest or conflict of interest could occur, but allows certain exemptions from these prohibitions. Labor will be responsible for overseeing fiduciary conduct under these provisions.

3) Both Departments will retain enforcement powers. The Reorganization Plan will continue Treasury's authority to audit plans and levy tax penalties for any deviation from standards. The plan will also continue Labor's authority to bring civil action against plans and fiduciaries. These provisions are retained in order to keep the special expertise of each Department available. New coordination between the Departments will eliminate duplicative investigations of alleged violations.

This reorganization will make an immediate improvement in ERISA's administration. It will eliminate almost all of the dual and overlapping authority in the two departments and dramatically cut the time required to process applications for exemptions from prohibited transactions.

This plan is an interim arrangement. After the Departments have had a chance to administer ERISA under this new plan, the Office of Management and Budget and the Departments will jointly evaluate that experience. Based on that evaluation, early in 1980, the Administration will make appropriate legislative proposals to establish a long-term administrative structure for ERISA.

Each provision in this reorganization will accomplish one or more of the purposes in Title 5 of U.S.C. 901(a). There will be no change in expenditure or personnel levels, although a small number of people will be transferred from the Department of Treasury to the Department of Labor.

We all recognize that the administration of ERISA has been unduly burdensome. I am confident that this reorganization will significantly relieve much of that burden.

This plan is the culmination of our effort to streamline ERISA. It provides an administrative arrangement that will work.

ERISA has been a symbol of unnecessarily complex government regulation. I hope this new step will become equally symbolic of my Administration's commitment to making government more effective and less intrusive in the lives of our people.

JIMMY CARTER.
THE WHITE HOUSE, August 10, 1978.

Please note that there was a flurry of regulation by each agency from the enactment of ERISA until this reorganization plan. That is why, for example, when we look at guidance for vesting, the original Labor Regulations defining things like an "hour of service" are still in tact and given deference by subsequent guidance provided by Treasury. Vesting is described in Chapter 7, but it is more of an example of several instances where original guidance by one of the agencies is used as a starting point for later guidance by the other agency.

On a personal note, although the reorganization plan called for a reassessment of jurisdiction in 1980, to the best of my knowledge, there was no report prepared or issued in 1980 or any time thereafter.

D. Amendment of ERISA and the Code

Unfortunately, for any employee benefits student or practitioner, ERISA has been amended over almost 40 times since enactment. Some amendments were quite substantial changes while others had only minimal impact. As indicated, the main three elements of ERISA were the protection of rights for employees promised benefits from their employer, the federal income tax advantages that employers and employees are entitled to with qualified retirement and health and welfare plans, and the federal guarantee of annuity benefits in a defined benefit pension plan whose employer sponsor goes into bankruptcy. So, to understand each individual legislative amendment to ERISA, and how collectively they fit into the overall law, it helps to determine: which political party was in charge in each house of Congress and in the Presidency; was the change to add or eliminate rights under the labor side, add or eliminate tax advantages (and if to eliminate certain tax advantages, was it motivated by sound benefits policy or simply as a balance to some other totally unrelated tax policy), or add to or diminish the federal role in providing insurance for poorly funded defined benefit plans; and whether the general economy was in a surplus or deficit mode. As a student, you are certainly not expected to spend your time and effort going through the exercise of piecing together the public policy and reality surrounding prior legislative changes; however, you are now hopefully prepared to better understand future acts of Congress that amend ERISA.

A reminder of Civics 101 might be appropriate here, especially for the non-lawyers reading this book. In our bicameral legislative body, bills can be introduced either in the House of Representatives or in the Senate; however, "[a]ll Bills for raising Revenue shall originate in the House of Representatives".[3] Generally, two or more legislators assign their names to a bill (and, when possible, one will be a Democrat and one will be a Republican, to show at least ostensible bipartisanship). The committee with jurisdiction over the main topic of the proposed bill will review it (in the House, the Ways and Means committee has jurisdiction over all income tax matters, as they relate directly to raising revenue, and the Education and Labor committee has jurisdiction over retirement security and other aspects of the labor rights afforded to plan participants under ERISA, and in the Senate, the committees that mirror the House for raising revenue and labor protections are, respectively, the Finance committee and the Health, Education, Labor and Pension committee). Assisting the House Ways and Means committee and the Senate Finance committee is the staff of arguably non-partisan experts at the Joint Committee on Taxation, which provides analysis of statutory provisions and economic impacts of proposed legislation. Generally, each respective committee of the House and Senate approve competing versions of a bill touching on the same subject matter, and if approved by each general house of Congress, then a conference committee is established where the differences between the House and State versions are ironed out. The "Chairman's Markup" is then voted on in both houses, and if approved by both, then is sent to the President for either approval or veto. If approved, then the legislation has become law, is assigned an official and unique Public Law number (*i.e.,* ERISA itself has been assigned PL 93-406, meaning it is the 406th public law enacted by the 93rd Session Congress). All legislation at all stages from introduction to enactment can be reviewed at the official website of the Library of Congress—http://thomas.loc.gov.

Below is a quick summary of the pieces of legislation that have amended ERISA and/or the Code (some laws have had major impacts while others were merely minor):

- Tax Reform Act of 1976 (PL 94-455)
- Revenue Act of 1978 (PL 95-600)
- Multiemployer Pension Plan Amendments Act of 1980 (PL 96-364)
- Miscellaneous Revenue Act of 1980 (PL 96-605)
- Economic Recovery Act of 1981 (PL 97-34)
- Tax Equity and Fiscal Responsibility Act of 1982 (PL 92-248)
- Deficit Reduction Act of 1984 (PL 98-369)
- Retirement Equity Act of 1984 (PL 98-397)
- Consolidated Omnibus Budget Reconciliation Act or 1985 (PL 99-272)
- Single-Employer Pension Plan Amendments Act or 1986 (PL 99-272)
- Omnibus Budget Reconciliation Act of 1986 (PL 99-509)
- Tax Reform Act of 1986 (PL 99-514)
- Pension Protection Act of 1987 (PL 100-203)
- Technical and Miscellaneous Revenue Act of 1988 (PL 100-647)
- Debt Limitation Extension Act of 1989 (PL 101-140)
- Omnibus Budget Reconciliation Act of 1989 (PL 101-239)
- Omnibus Budget Reconciliation Act of 1990 (PL 101-508)
- Unemployment Compensation Amendments of 1992 (PL 102-318)
- Family and Medical Leave Act of 1993 (PL 103-3)

---

3. Article I, Section 7, of the Constitution of the United States.

- Omnibus Budget Reconciliation Act of of 1993 (PL 103-66)
- Uniformed Services Employment and Reemployment Rights Act of 1994 (PL 103-353)
- Pension Annuitants Protection Act of 1994 (PL 103-401)
- General Agreement of Tariffs and Trade (part of the Uruguay Round Agreements Act of 1994) (PL 103-465)
- Small Business Job Protection Act of 1996 (PL 104-188)
- Health Insurance Portability and Accountability Act of 1996 (PL 104-191)
- Taxpayer Relief Act of 1997 (PL 105-34)
- IRS Restructuring and Reform Act of 1998 (PL 105-206)
- Economic Growth and Tax Relief Reconciliation Act of 2001 (PL 107-16)
- Job Creation and Worker Assistance Act of 2002 (PL 107-147)
- Public Company Accounting Reform and Investor Protection Act of 2002 (a.k.a. Sarbanes-Oxley Act of 2002) (PL 107-204)
- Jobs and Growth Tax Relief Reconciliation Act of 2003 (PL 108-27)
- Pension Funding Equity Act of 2004 (PL 108-218)
- American Jobs Creations Act of 2004 (PL 108-357)
- Gulf Opportunity Zone Act of 2005 (PL 109-135)
- U.S. Troop Readiness, Veterans' Care, Katrina Recovery, and Iraq Accountability Appropriations Act of 2007 (PL 110-28)
- Pension Protection Act of 2006 (PL 109-280)
- Heroes Earnings Assistance and Relief Tax Act of 2007 (PL 110-245)
- Worker, Retiree, and Employer Recovery Act of 2008 (PL 110-458)

E. The Various Roles of the Employer and Outside Professionals

1. Some of the Roles the Employer Must Take on or Contract out to a Third Party

In general, an employer who institutes an employee benefit plan is responsible for seeing that the plan meets all statutory and regulatory requirements. This means that the employer must ensure that all plan documentation is in order, that the plan operates according to its documentation, that the trust (if any) is maintained according to the fiduciary rules associated with trusts, that all reporting to participants and disclosure to the federal government is properly and timely submitted, that all benefits are properly determined, delivered, and if denied, a proper claims procedure is followed, and that all plan documents and employee data records are properly maintained. Should the employer fail to maintain the form, operation, or fiduciary responsibilities associated with retirement, health or welfare plans, then the employer may lose its tax deductions for contributions, employees may be forced to include the value of the benefits amounts (including contributions and earnings thereon) in Gross Income, the employer may be subject to excise taxes and penalties, and individual fiduciaries might be personally liable to the plan for losses and disgorgement of profits, and some individuals might even go to prison.

Plan Administrator

An employee benefit plan must be established and maintained by an employer. While the planning and studies are going on, the employer simply acts as an employer (or settlor). There is a fine line, but once the concept and desire to offer employee benefits legally becomes a plan, then the plan needs to be administered and operated in accordance with the plan document and all relevant controlling laws at all times. Again, there are consultants and other professionals that will take on all or some of the responsibility and act as plan administrator on behalf of the sponsoring employer. However, as with all delegations of authority, if something goes wrong with the operation of the plan and the employer pleads ignorance, the Department of Labor and the courts will look closely at the employer's procedural selection and monitoring of the delegated consultant.

A plan administrator is either the person specifically designated by the terms of the plan document to assume those duties, or, by default, the plan sponsor. All of the reporting and disclosure rules put the onus on the plan administrator to ensure compliance, and impose civil penalties for non-compliance.

While there are no administrative procedures required by government rules and regulations, the IRS may look to whatever the plan administrator labels as its plan procedures in an examination of a plan in order to determine the extent of a violation. In addition, should a plan participant challenge a contribution or benefit under the plan, the administrative procedures of the plan, in whatever shape or form they take, can support or undermine the actions of the plan administrator. An employer should therefore establish and maintain a written set of administrative procedures covering a qualified retirement plan, specifically policies regarding areas such as: determining employee eligibility, testing contributions annually, and approving distributions (including loans and hardship withdrawals). Forms for any required actions should be included in the administrative procedures. While some attorneys might give a knee-jerk reaction that nothing should ever be in writing, most competent employee benefits attorneys and professionals will advise that a good set of written procedures can avoid problems from happening in the first place, and if something goes wrong, can make the employer look better in lieu of the problem.

Fiduciary over Plan Assets

In an ERISA plan subject to the fiduciary duties, the individuals deemed to be plan fiduciaries have a high standard of prudence and due diligence that they must exercise over: investing and distributing plan assets, monitoring the actions of their fellow fiduciaries, avoiding prohibited transactions, and choosing another employee or outside consultant to delegate such authority over to. Fiduciaries can be subject to personal liability if they breach their fiduciary duties as proscribed under ERISA. There is a legal definition of who will be considered a plan fiduciary, and a court might declare an officer of the sponsoring employer as a fiduciary, regardless of whether he or she was even aware of their authority to make decisions on behalf of the plan and the participants and beneficiaries. Therefore, it is crucial for any employer sponsor of a qualified plan, especially a small employer, to seek legal advice to figure out who will be a fiduciary under the

ERISA rules, and then provide the proper training and purchase the appropriate surety bonds and errors and omissions insurance that is required or desired. In the normal course of providing advice and counsel, the outside professionals like attorneys, accountants and actuaries, are not generally deemed to be plan fiduciaries; thus, the officers of the employer who select and delegate to such professionals will likely be the true fiduciaries. The specific fiduciary duties are discussed in more detail in Chapter 13.

2. Some of the Other Professionals the Employer Might Need Advice and Work Product From

When establishing an employee benefit plan, the employer should consider that there are several types of costs involved in establishing and maintaining the plan. The initial start-up costs will depend on the complexity of the plan being established as well as the professionals hired to assist the employer. Start-up costs will include document preparation, filings with the IRS, employee communications, internal and external administrative costs.

Ongoing maintenance costs will also depend on the complexity of the plan as well as the type of plan. For instance, a defined benefit retirement plan will need the services of an actuary while a defined contribution retirement plan will not. Yearly information reporting to the IRS/DOL for all plans (except Simplified Employer Plans (SEPs)) is required. In addition, recordkeeping and administrative costs for operating the plan are yearly maintenance costs. Further, the employer contribution that is made to the plan on a regular basis (generally, at least on an annual basis) should be included in calculating the annual cost of operating the plan.

In order to establish an employee benefit plan, the employer will usually need to employ several professionals to provide necessary documentation and administrative services. Some professionals, like attorneys and accountants, might already have a relationship with the employer, while others, like an actuary or investment advisor, might be new as a direct result of the employee benefit plan. Once an employee benefit plan is established, the ongoing maintenance of the plan will include many of the professionals needed to implement the plan. On a yearly basis, the trust fund will need to be valued, contributions and distributions will need to be recorded, and nondiscrimination testing will need to be conducted. In addition, if there are changes in the governing federal law, then plan documentation will need to be updated.

Attorney

All ERISA retirement plans and welfare benefit plans must promise and deliver benefits through a written plan document. Although nothing in ERISA requires a licensed attorney to draft and execute the document, each state has its own special rules for the unauthorized practice of law. Therefore, while an accountant, actuary or other employee benefits professional most likely has the knowledge to adequately draft a legal document, if an attorney is hired for that purpose, then there should be no problems with the document having the desired legal effect. If the employer chooses a pre-approved plan document from a financial institution, the document was probably prepared by a licensed attorney, even if the delivery is through an investment consultant.

In addition to preparation of the plan documents, legal services may include preparing submissions to the IRS regarding the qualified status of a retirement plan and providing advice on an ongoing basis regarding the operation of the plan and any necessary changes that need to be made to maintain the plan in compliance with current statutory and regulatory requirements. As indicated, fiduciary duty is key to the operation of many ERISA plans, and in order to avoid personal liability, it is probably in the best interest of every sponsoring employer to get a legal opinion as to whether the delivery of employee benefits will constitute an ERISA plan, and if so, who will be considered a fiduciary over the plan assets.

Although ERISA and the Code are federal laws, and can be interpreted the same in any state, attorneys are licensed pursuant to state bar exams and rules of conduct. An employer should first verify that their attorney is licensed in the state (a good starting place is the state supreme court's website, which will most likely have a link to a verification site), and then should make sure that the attorney focuses most or all of his or her practice in employee benefits (which can usually be easily confirmed based on the attorney's website or other marketing materials, since the ethics of most states requires that the attorney does not fraudulently claim an expertise in a particular area of the law). While it is not crucial for a qualified and licensed attorney to be a member of a local, state or national bar association, those that indicate a membership, especially with a particular committee that focuses on employee benefit issues, will suggest that the attorney takes employee benefits seriously, has a network of colleagues, and goes from time to time to educational meetings.

Accountant

Large plans require an accountant to audit the plan assets on an annual basis and to determine and the cost for the employee benefits to be included in the corporate financial statements. While small plans generally do not need to perform those annual services, the accountant can be crucial in assisting in determining the timing of contributions and their associated deductions. Additionally, the compensation or earned income of the business owners in a small business are crucial components of the operation and administration of an employee benefits plan, and the personal or corporate accountant therefore plays an integral role in understanding how compensation should be used for benefit purposes.

Each respective state administers its own examinations to certify public accountants. The largest national organization of CPAs is the American Institute of CPAs, which among other things, acts as a clearing house to disseminate information among its members from all states. They have created special sections of their website, and present various meetings, where CPAs can become experts in employee benefits matters. A small employer business owner should either ask his personal accountant or business accountant if he or she is capable of providing counsel for the employee benefit plans, or if he or she could recommend a colleague.

Actuary

In the event the employer is establishing a defined benefit retirement plan, an Enrolled Actuary will need to be engaged to calculate the necessary contributions that will need to be made to the trust to insure that sufficient funds will be available to pay promised benefits. Actuaries also generally have the software and knowledge to properly perform the annual testing required for any plan (minimum coverage, nondiscrimination, and top-heaviness), the calculation of benefits and distribution amounts, and the determination of PBGC variable premiums. Additionally, they are useful in performing risk-analysis and cost-benefit studies. Although Enrolled Actuaries are required to determine the annual funding requirements and perform certain calculations in a defined benefit plan, other actuaries are useful in other aspects of qualified plan administration, nonqualified plan valuations and funding projections for health and welfare benefit plans. Additionally, some of the larger national actuarial firms generally have the most up-to-date and useful employee benefit surveys.

Enrolled Actuaries successfully complete the single set of exams administered by the federal Joint Board for the Enrollment of Actuaries. However, Enrolled Actuaries are only subject to the professional ethics of the Joint Board. Most Enrolled Actuaries also are members of a national professional association and, as members, are bound to those additional codes of ethics and professionalism. The most common associations are the American Academy of Actuaries, the American Society of Pension Professionals and Actuaries, the Casualty Actuarial Society, the Conference of Consulting Actuaries and the Society of Actuaries, and they all have joined together to establish a single code of professional conduct for their respective members that are Enrolled Actuaries.

Insurance Advisor

A retirement plan can be invested in insurance products, as long as the plan primarily provides benefits upon retirement. Additionally, a defined benefit plan can be invested wholly in proper insurance products to avoid the annual minimum funding requirements. On the health and welfare side, the insurance professional will likely be the key consultant in any plan that is insured, and even in those self-insured plans that have stop-loss insurance to limit the employer's total exposure, insurance advisors can generally assist in securing appropriate ERISA bonds and fiduciary liability insurance.

Each respective state administers its own examinations to certify insurance agents and brokers. Two major national associations are the National Association of Professional Insurance Agents and the National Association of Insurance and Financial Advisors, which among other things, act as clearing houses to disseminate information among their members from all states. It doesn't appear that either organization has created special sections of their websites or have formed committees that specifically address employee benefit plan concerns, so the small employer is cautioned to ask questions to make sure that the insurance advisor understands the complicated rules of ERISA and the Code that govern employee benefit plans. A small employer business owner should either ask his personal or business insurance agent or broker if he or she is capable of providing counsel for the employee benefit plans, or if he or she could recommend a colleague.

Investment Advisor

The employer may wish to hire an investment advisor to assist in the management of the trust funds. In some instances, hiring an investment advisor may limit the liability of the employer if the investment advisor is assuming certain fiduciary functions with respect to the plan. Many times, a small employer will use a financial institution's pre-approved prototype plan document for a retirement plan, and the only contact with a professional consultant will be an investment agent or broker at the institution delivering the plan document and advising on the investments. Some investment advisors specifically contract to become institutional trustees or custodians over employee plan assets.

Most investment advisors for employee benefit plans have passed both a state sponsored exam (such as a Series 63 or 65 exam) and an appropriate national exam administered by the Financial Industry Regulatory Authority (such as a Series 6 or 7 exam). Investment advisors are generally individuals or groups that make investment recommendations or conduct securities analysis in return for a fee, whether through direct management of client assets or via written publications. In addition to the advice, they usually have the license to trade securities and other investments on behalf of their clients. Small employers are cautioned that there are specific terms and definitions of investment advisors under ERISA that directly impact the fiduciary duties and liabilities. Therefore, a small employer should make sure that the investment advisor understands employee benefit rules and determines whether or not he or she will be considered a plan fiduciary. Among other designations, the American Society of Pension Actuaries (ASPPA) has established a professional designation for investment advisors with a special knowledge of qualified retirement plan issues, called the Qualified Plan Financial Consultant, and Fiduciary 360 (FI360) established the Accredited Investment Fiduciary and the Accredited Investment Fiduciary Analyst professional designations.

Record Keepers

Record keeping services are key to running a qualified retirement plan correctly. On a day-to-day basis, general bookkeeping will need to be done to insure proper credit of contributions, earnings, and losses to the trust, especially in defined contribution plans. In addition, certain plan administration functions may be performed by the accountant or record keeper, including preparation of participant statements, maintenance of records documenting who is in the plan and who has retired from the plan, and the payment of benefits.

There is no real licensing nor is there an apparent professional association for record keepers, however, the American Society of Pension Professionals and Actuaries (ASPPA) now has a method of certifying firms that adhere to record keeping best practices. Most record keepers do just that, maintain data records and transmit as instructed. They generally do not provide advice or make decisions over plan assets or operation. Often times, the financial institution that holds and invests the plan assets, especially in a defined contribution plan, will provide the record keeping services. Any of the other employee benefit plan professionals described herein, especially third party administrators, often bundle record keeping services with their primary role services.

ASPPA has established a Record Keeper Certification which provides a firm-level certification addressing three business models in the recordkeeping industry: firms that bundle record keeping services along with their proprietary investment products; firms that offer record keeping independent of investment products; and firms that perform third party administration and compliance services only.

Third Party Administrators and ERPAs

The final category is generally a catch all for all other professionals that are experts in employee benefits matters, but who don't have the other professional licenses. In many cases, these consultants have wide networks of professionals, and can help the small employer manage the employee benefit plans. In general, when interviewing a prospective third party administrator (TPA), employers should ask the candidate questions about its fee arrangement. Most provide a "bundled" package for the various services offered and charge an additional fee per year based on the number of participants covered. The employer must make inquiries about the services it will receive under the package. The employer must also determine if the TPA will make administrative decisions regarding the plan or if the TPA will merely act on those decisions certified or approved by the employer, internal administrator, or other plan fiduciary. For example, the employer should ask who determines whether a participant is eligible to receive a plan distribution. The current trend is that the employer must "sign off" on any distribution request before the TPA will make the requested distribution payment.

If the plan is a retirement plan providing for individual accounts, the employer should determine if the TPA will agree to be responsible for allocating funds among the participants' accounts and tracking investment returns for each account on an account-by-account basis. The employer also must determine which nondiscrimination tests the TPA will perform and which tests the employer will be responsible for performing. In all circumstances, the employer is ultimately responsible for reviewing all plan data used by the TPA in performing nondiscrimination testing to ensure that the information on which the test results are based is accurate.

Many TPAs will prepare the annual information return/report for each plan (Form 5500), but the employer must review the Form 5500 for any errors. Review is particularly needed because the TPA may not have all of the information necessary to complete the Form 5500 fully and accurately. Before contracting with a TPA, the employer should determine if the TPA will charge for any changes made to the Form 5500 return because of incorrect or missing data.

Currently, there are many professional associations that provide training and certification exams for TPAs and consultants, such as the American Society of Pension Professionals and Actuaries, the National Institute for Pension Administrators, the International Foundation of Employee Benefit Professionals, the American College, and the Human Resource Certification Institute, among others. These professionals are generally competent in employee benefit matters, and each organization has some sort of code of ethics and disciplinary procedures for its members. However, under the technical rules of the IRS, the only professionals allowed to represent clients in front of the IRS (under Circular 230) were Attorneys, Enrolled Actuaries, Enrolled Agents and Certified Public Accountants. To fill this void, Circular 230 was amended in 2007 to establish a new professional designation: Enrolled Retirement Plan Agents (ERPAs), who after passing the administered exams, will be able to represent employee benefit plan clients in front of the IRS for the following matters: the Employee Plans Determination Letter program; the Employee Plans Compliance Resolution System; the Employee Plans Master and Prototype and Volume Submitter program; and the representation of taxpayers with respect to IRS forms under the 5300 and 5500 series which are filed by retirement plans and plan sponsors, but not with respect to actuarial forms or schedules. Once all of the rules and examinations are set forth, with no disrespect to other TPAs and consultants, small employers should ensure that their selected TPAs and consultants are ERPAs (if they are not Enrolled Actuaries, Attorneys, Certified Public Accountants or Enrolled Agents) so that they can be granted a power of attorney to represent the employee benefit plans in front of the IRS. There are apparently no similar rules or required designation for a consultant to represent an employee benefit plan in front of the Department of Labor, the Pension Benefit Guaranty Corporation, or other federal agencies.

Section II

Qualified Retirement Plans

This textbook primarily deals with retirement plans, as opposed to health and welfare plans or executive compensation programs. For-profit employers can sponsor qualified retirement plans; whereas, other employers, such as state and local governments, churches, public schools, and other non-profit organizations, can sponsor other types of plans. The rules for qualified plans remain the most onerous, so this textbook focuses on those qualified rules. It is assumed that anyone who understands the more complicated regime for qualified retirement plans, can then become familiar with the rules for other types of retirement plans if they are actually consulting a government or church employer, school, or non-profit.

Chapter 4 sets out the laundry list of statutory rules to allow a retirement plan to be considered a qualified retirement plan, with an initial discussion of rules for non-qualified plans and then the actual qualification rules, then a review of the income tax advantages for both employers and employees of a qualified retirement plan, and finally a summary of the different models for an employer choosing a written plan and trust document.

Chapter 5 is a meaty chapter that compares the two types of retirement plans: defined contribution plans and defined benefit plans, first with an overview, then an analysis of defined contribution plans (such as money purchase plans, profit sharing plans, Employee Stock Ownership Plans, 401(k) plans and other plans specifically for small employers), an analysis of defined benefit plans (such as a flat benefit plan, a fixed benefit plan or a unit benefit plan), and finally a summary of hybrid plans (such as target benefit plans and cash balance plans).

Chapter 6 discusses how money gets deposited into the plan to fund the retirement benefits promised. First is a discussion of how employers determine the required amount to be deposited into a qualified plan, then is a discussion of how employees can contribute a portion of their salary (whether it is on a pre-tax or an after-tax basis), then a discussion of how the employer can take a deduction on its corporate return for plan contributions, and finally a discussion of extra PBGC insurance premiums required for defined benefit plans.

Chapter 7 basically discusses how a plan participant earns benefits through the vesting and benefit accrual rules. First, the vesting rules are discussed, then the benefit accrual rules (which are a bit more complicated for defined benefit plans), then maximum contributions or benefits regardless of the plan provisions, and finally minimum contributions or benefits for plans that are determined to be Top-Heavy. The chapter concludes with examples that hopefully tie all of the concepts together.

Chapter 8 will likely be the toughest chapter in this book, because the rules for annual testing to prevent abuses are extremely complicated, and riddled with special rules and exceptions to exceptions. The chapter starts with defining who the employer truly will be for testing purposes. Then, the chapter provides a definition of a Highly Compensated Employee, and then highlights the minimum coverage rules (to make certain that enough non-Highly Compensated Employees participate in any qualified plan) and the minimum participation rules (to make certain that enough non-Highly Compensated Employees specifically participate in a qualified defined benefit plan) and then the nondiscrimination rules for any qualified retirement plan (to make certain that HCEs are not inappropriately favored by the plan) and the special nondiscrimination rules specifically for 401(k) plans. Finally, the chapter ends with a definition of a Key Employee and then the rules for determining when a qualified plan is Top-Heavy.

Chapter 9 discusses all aspects of distributions from qualified plans—first, a discussion of the choices a participant has in the form of benefits, then a discussion of the timing considerations of when benefits can be paid to a plan participant (including distributions while the individual is still employed), and finally a summary of the income tax rules that attach to qualified plan distributions.

After all of the qualified plan rules under the Internal Revenue Code are presented, Chapter 10 explores how the IRS operates in regulating qualified plans. First is a quick discussion of how the IRS is organized, then a focus on the Employee Plans group and how they issue determination letters, allow for corrections of mistakes either before or during an audit, and finally how they audit plans.

Chapter 4

Qualification Rules

Overview

What types of employer-sponsored retirement plans are there?
- qualified retirement plans, as described in Internal Revenue Code ("IRC") §401(a), which is the major focus of Section II of this text
- qualified annuity plans, as described in IRC §403(b)
- other employer-purchased annuity plans, as described in IRC §403(a)
- eligible deferred compensation plans, as described in IRC §457(b)
- non-eligible deferred compensation plans, as described in IRC §457(f)

What type of employers cannot deliver retirement benefits through a qualified retirement plan?
- governmental employers
- church employers
- public schools
- non-profit corporations

What is a governmental employer?
- the actual federal, state or local government unit that employs individuals
- it then also includes political subdivisions which, based on facts and circumstances, are under the control of elected officials and statutes or ordinances (like local fire departments or transit agencies)

What type of retirement plans can a governmental employer sponsor for its workforce?
- eligible deferred compensation plans, as described in IRC §457(b)
- non-eligible deferred compensation plans, as described in IRC §457(f)

What is a church employer?
- a church or covenant
- a convention or association of churches
- it then also includes related trades or businesses which, based on facts and circumstances, are under the control of the church (like a church-run hospital)

What type of retirement plans can a church employer sponsor for its workforce?
- qualified annuity plans, as described in IRC §403(b)
- other employer-purchased annuity plans, as described in IRC §403(a)
- eligible deferred compensation plans, as described in IRC §457(b)

- non-eligible deferred compensation plans, as described in IRC § 457(f)
- qualified retirement plans, as described in IRC § 401(a), but only if the church makes a certain election

What is a public school?

- an educational organization which normally maintains a regular faculty and curriculum and normally has a regularly enrolled body of pupils or students in attendance at the place where its educational activities are regularly carried on

What type of retirement plans can a public school sponsor for its workforce?

- qualified annuity plans, as described in Code § 403(b)

What is a non-profit organization or charity?

- one that is approved by the IRS and exempt from income tax under IRC § 501(c)(3)

What type of retirement plans can a non-profit organization or charity sponsor for its workforce?

- qualified annuity plans, as described in Code § 403(b)
- eligible deferred compensation plans, as described in IRC § 457(b)

Are qualified retirement plans a new concept?

- retirement plans have been around in America since the late Nineteenth Century
- Code provisions providing a loose framework of income tax advantages to both the sponsoring employer and the employee participants have been around since the 1940s

What are the requirements for a retirement plan to be considered a qualified retirement plan?

- there is a list of 37 requirements at IRC § 401(a)
- the most important ones include:
  - plans must be for the exclusive purpose of providing retirement benefits to plan participants and their beneficiaries
  - the plan must benefit at least a certain number of lower-paid employees (but not necessarily all of them)
  - the benefits, rights and features of the plan cannot discriminate in favor of the higher-paid employees
  - the plan must provide minimum vesting and accruals
  - regardless of whether the individual wants it or not, the plan must generally start paying retirement benefits to individuals once they attain age 70½
  - the plan can cover self-employed individuals, but must use earned income to determine benefits rather than salary
  - the plan must not favor high-paid owners and officers
  - if the participant is married, then certain death benefits must go to the spouse unless the spouse waives the rights to those benefits
  - the retirement benefits for any individual may not be alienated from the plan to pay any of the individual's creditors or the employer's creditors
  - payments from the plan must start within 60 days of retirement or attaining age 65

- the plan must limit benefits and contributions, and must limit the compensation used to determine plan benefits

How can a retirement plan lose its qualified income tax status?

- an improper type of employer sponsors a § 401(a) qualified plan
- the written plan document does not comply with the laws
- the written plan document complies with the laws, but the plan is not operated and administered in accordance with its terms
- the plan demographics change and it violates the minimum coverage, nondiscrimination, or other annual tests

How can a plan avoid disqualification?

- The IRS allows three methods:
  - Self-Correction of insignificant operational failures, which requires no fees to the IRS and no IRS approval;
  - Voluntary-Correction of significant operational failures or other failures requiring a plan amendment, which requires fees paid to the IRS and their approval of the correction methodology; or
  - Audit-Cap, which requires higher fees and penalties since the error was discovered by the IRS on a plan audit

What is a multiemployer plan?

- unlike a single employer plan, a multiemployer plan is a single plan, which is established and operated pursuant to a collectively bargained agreement, where the participant is a member of a union, and when he or she works for an employer, that employer contributes to the common multiemployer fund
- there are special rules for multiemployer plans that do not apply to single employer plans, but the basic framework is similar

What is a multiple employer plan?

- unlike a single employer plan or a multiemployer plan, a multiple employer plan is a single plan, which is established and operated by a group or association of related employers
- there are very few rules on what constitutes a proper group or association, and there are few special rules for these plans, so they are not very numerous in practice

What are the income tax advantages of qualified retirement plans for employers?

- if all of the rules are complied with, then within certain limits, the amount deposited in any year to fund the qualified retirement plan can be deducted on the employer's corporate income tax return (or business reporting form if the business is a pass-through entity, like a partnership, S Corporation, or LLC)

What are the income tax advantages of qualified retirement plans for employees?

- if all of the rules are complied with, then the retirement benefits promised by the employer are not included in the individual's Gross Income until the year they are actually paid

What issues does an employer need to be concerned with when drafting a qualified retirement plan document?

- the law is frequently changed by Congress, as are its enforcement guidance by federal agencies and interpretations by federal courts
- therefore, plan documents need to be amended from time to time to remain in compliance
- generally, there is a remedial amendment period (RAP) which Congress allows between the time the law changes and the need for the plan document to be amended (even though the plan must operate in accordance with the new law during that RAP)

What is a Master & Prototype plan document?

- a bank or financial institution prepares a basic plan document for any employer that chooses to invest the plan assets with them
- they provide very little flexibility in plan design
- while the employer might receive expert financial and investment advise from the sales agent, the employer is generally not receiving a high level of legal advice

What is a Volume Submitter plan document?

- an employee benefits professional (such as an attorney, accountant or actuary) prepares a basic plan document and provides a similar document to each client (the key is that there cannot be any material modifications, which is lawyer-speak for I'll know it when I see it)
- they provide very little flexibility in plan design
- while the employer might receive an adequate level of legal advice, many things that the law allows cannot be incorporated into the plan because that might cause it to be materially modified

What is an individually designed plan document?

- either an attorney affirmatively drafts a document to include all of the business goals and desires for that specific employer, or a M&P or VS plan document is amended so much that it loses its umbrella protection
- the high level of attention and legal advice comes at the price of paying attorneys at their hourly billable rates

When can a plan document be amended?

- generally, any future promises that have not accrued (see Chapter 7) can be reduced or eliminated
- for minimum funding purposes (see Chapter 6), an amendment adopted within 2½ months of the plan year end can have a retroactive effect to the first day of the plan year at issue, but cannot reduce benefits already accrued

Why does a qualified retirement plan also need a separate trust document?

- one of the requirements of a qualified plan is that all plan assets are segregated into a separate tax-exempt trust that is not part of the employer's general assets
- the trust provisions can either be part of a separate legal document, or can constitute a stand-alone document

A. Retirement Plans Sponsored by Type of Employer

1. How Other Employers (*i.e.*, Those That Are Not-for-Profit) Deliver Retirement Benefits to Employees

Since the rest of this section of the text book is about "Qualified Retirement Plans," it is important to start with a discussion of what is not a qualified plan (*i.e.*, all other types of retirement plans that are not qualified). The term "qualified" is really a legal term assigned to only those retirement plans that meet all of the qualification rules under the Internal Revenue Code, specifically those set forth at IRC § 401(a). Qualified plans provide income tax advantages to both the sponsoring employer and to the individual employees promised retirement benefits. Retirement plans that do not meet the qualification rules of IRC § 401(a) can still provide income tax advantages to the individual employees if they comply with alternate sections of the Code, even though no tax advantages extend to the sponsoring employer.

There are several varieties of employer-sponsored retirement plans available that provide income tax benefits to both employer and employee, and which might or might not be governed by ERISA (see Chapter 11):

- qualified retirement plans, as described at IRC § 401(a)
- qualified annuity plans, as described in Code § 403(b)
- other employer-purchased annuity plans, as described in Code § 403(a)
- eligible deferred compensation plans, as described in Code § 457(b)
- non-eligible deferred compensation plans, as described in Code § 457(f)

The distinction between the varieties of retirement plans is dependent upon the tax-paying status of the sponsoring employer. Only for-profit businesses can sponsor a qualified retirement plan, and all other types of employers (such as government employers; church employers, public schools, and other non-profit and charitable organizations) must sponsor a different variety.

a. *Governmental Employer*
Legal Definition at IRC § 414(d)

For tax purposes, government employers can provide tax favored retirement benefits pursuant to IRC § 457(b) or 457(f). These plans are generally not governed by ERISA.

A governmental plan means "a plan established and maintained for its employees by the Government of the United States, by the government of any State or political subdivision thereof, or by any agency or instrumentality of any of the foregoing … [and also] includes a plan which is established and maintained by an Indian tribal government…, a subdivision of an Indian tribal government…, or an agency or instrumentality of either, and all of the participants of which are employees of such entity substantially all of whose services as such an employee are in the performance of essential governmental functions but not in the performance of commercial activities (whether or not an essential government function)."

Although not detailed in this text book, the analysis of what constitutes a governmental employer is not as simple as it might seem. The following Private Letter Ruling demonstrates some of the surrounding facts and circumstances that indicate whether an employer can be considered a governmental employer for purposes of the Tax Code (although this particular request relates to a welfare benefits plan rather than a retirement plan). An advanced Private Letter Ruling is advisable whenever the legal status of the employer as a governmental employer is not clear, and the ramifications should the employer unexpectedly be deemed by a court or the IRS to be a stand alone for-profit entity would be disastrous.

Note: for the student who is not a lawyer or law student, please just read this Private Letter Ruling as an indication of how the IRS logically analyzes the regulatory framework to reach its conclusion, because, as shown in Appendix A, a Private Letter Ruling (PLR) has no legal effect and cannot be relied upon, but because of the Freedom of Information laws, the advice provided to a particular taxpayer for a particular purpose is published to the general public.

Private Letter Ruling 9529038, 04/27/1995, IRC Sec(s). 414

Date: April 27, 1995

CP:E:EP:T:4
LEGEND:
City A = ***
State B = ***
Union C = ***
Memorandum D = ***
Plan X = ***
Plan Y = ***

Gentlemen:

This is in response to a letter ruling request dated October 17, 1994, submitted by your authorized representative and supplemented by additional correspondence dated January 23, 1995, concerning whether Plan X is a governmental plan within the meaning of section 414(d) of the Internal Revenue Code.

Your authorized representative submitted the following facts and representations. Plan X is a welfare benefit plan under section 419(e) of the Code that was established by City A for the benefit of its firefighter employees in order to provide a monthly stipend for retirees to apply to the costs of their health insurance. Plan X is under the control of City A by means of municipal ordinance G-1532, section 5. Memorandum D provides that Plan X shall be administered by a five member board of trustees comprised of two individuals appointed by the City Manager of City A, two individuals appointed by Union C, and one individual (who shall serve as chairman) selected by the four appointees specified above. Plan X is currently administered by four City A employees (two firefighter trustees and two non- firefighter trustees) and one trustee voted on by the first four trustees. Plan X is a part of a collectively bargained contract that must be submitted to the city council of City A for approval as expressly stated in the preamble of Memorandum D. Plan X received a favorable determination letter from the Internal Revenue Service dated June 13, 1989, concerning its exempt status as a voluntary employees' beneficiary association under section 501(c)(9) of the Code.

Based on the representations made above, you ask for a ruling that Plan X is a governmental plan within the meaning of section 414(d) of the Code.

Section 414(d) of the Code provides that a governmental plan means a plan established and maintained for its employees by the Government of the United States, by the government of any state or political subdivision thereof, or by any agency or instrumentality of any of the foregoing.

Revenue Ruling 89-49, 1989-1 C.B. 117, provides that a plan will not be considered a governmental plan merely because the sponsoring organization has a relationship with a governmental unit or some quasi-governmental power. One of the most important factors to be considered in determining whether an organization is an agency or instrumentality of the United States or any state or political subdivision thereof is the degree of control that the state or federal government has over the organization's everyday operations. Other factors include: (1) whether there is specific legislation creating the organization; (2) the source of funds for the organization; (3) the manner in which the organization's trustees or operating board are selected; and (4) whether the applicable governmental unit considers the employees of the organization to be employees of the applicable governmental unit. Although all of the above factors are considered in determining whether an organization is an agency or instrumentality of a government, the mere satisfaction of one or all of the factors is not necessarily determinative.

In this case, Plan X is part of an agreement established under a City A ordinance for the benefit of firefighter employees of City A, a political subdivision of State B. City A makes contributions to Plan X as part of the agreement between City A and Union C as expressed in Memorandum D. Pursuant to Article 11 of Memorandum D, benefit payments from Plan X will be made to those participants in Plan X who have retired and who have qualified for a pension under Plan Y. Plan X is administered by four City A employees (two firefighter trustees and two non-firefighter trustees) and one trustee who is determined by the vote of the first four trustees. The mayor and city council of City A have control over City A employees under City A's Charter and ordinances. In addition, City A has reached agreement with its firefighter employees concerning wages, hours, and working conditions as expressed in Memorandum D. The degree of control which City A exercises over Plan X is substantial, not minimal as in the case of the entities described in Rev. Rul. 89-49 that failed to satisfy the requirements of section 414(d) of the Code.

Therefore, we have determined in this case that there is a substantial degree of control by a municipal governmental entity over the functions and operations of Plan X, and, with respect to Plan X, the requirements described in Rev. Rul. 89-49 have been satisfied. Accordingly, we conclude that Plan X is a governmental plan within the meaning of section 414(d) of the Code.

In accordance with a power of attorney on file with this office, a copy of this letter is being sent to your authorized representative.

Sincerely yours,
John G. Riddle, Jr.
Chief, Employee Plans
Technical Branch 4

The basic rules for an "eligible deferred compensation plan" are at IRC § 457(b). Basically:

- Only individuals who perform service for the employer can be participants;

- There is a dollar limit on the amount of benefits that can be paid out (which have some similarities and some differences than the benefit limitations in qualified retirement plans, as discussed in Chapter 7 of this text book);

- Compensation will be deferred for any calendar month only if an agreement providing for that deferral has been entered into before the beginning of that particular month;

- Distributions from the plan can only be made after the participant is no longer employed, or if still employed, has attained age 70½ or is faced with an unforeseeable emergency;

- All plan assets shall remain the exclusive property of the employer, subject to its creditors, even though they are set aside for the exclusive benefit of the participants or their beneficiaries.

Any plan sponsored by a governmental employer that does not meet all of the requirements of § 457(b) will, by default, be deemed a non-eligible plan, and under § 457(f)— the participants in the plan will pay taxes on the compensation and retirement benefits in the year there is no longer a substantial risk of forfeiture, rather than the year the benefits are actually distributed from the plan. One exception is for an "employment retention plan" which, under § 457(f)(4), allows local educational agencies or associations to reward employees for meeting performance criteria, and if structured properly, then the rewards will not be deemed to be deferred compensation.

There are other retirement features available to governmental employers, such as:

- a qualified governmental excess benefit arrangement, as described in IRC § 415(m); and

- an applicable employment retention plan, as described in IRC § 457(f)(4).

This ends the discussion of governmental plans for purposes of this text book. There is a lot more to it, but if as a student, you become comfortable with all of the rules for a qualified retirement plan, described in Section II of this textbook, then you understand the basic vocabulary and considerations in any employer-sponsored retirement plan; therefore, learning the specific rules under the Internal Revenue Code for governmental plans should not be too difficult once you have an actual client to counsel.

Please note that the federal income tax provisions contain rules that allow employees to defer inclusion of benefits in their Gross Income, but all other mechanics are dictated by the state or local government, through statutes, ordinances, or other legislative means.

b. Church Employer
Legal Definition at IRC § 414(e)

For tax purposes, church employers can provide tax favored retirement benefits pursuant to §§ 403(b) or 457(b), and if the employer makes a special election, a qualified plan pursuant to § 401(a). The story goes that churches and religious leaders had a very important lobbying group when Congress enacted ERISA—thus the full spectrum of choices.

These plans are generally not governed by ERISA, unless the employer makes a special election—such as an election to be subjected to ERISA's protection of employee benefit rights under Title I, or an election to be subjected to the plan termination insurance for defined benefit plans under Title IV. Actual consulting techniques for church employer clients is beyond the scope of this book, but there are some situations where knowing the legal framework, even if it's a complicated framework, is better than a total lack of legal frameworks, so some church employers actually elect to voluntarily be governed under ERISA.

A church plan means "a plan established and maintained by a church or by a convention or association of churches which is exempt from tax, but does not include a plan which is established and maintained primarily for the benefit of employees (or their beneficiaries) of such church or convention or association of churches who are employed in connection with one or more unrelated trades or businesses or if less than substantially all of the individuals included in the plan are certain individuals."

Although not detailed in this text book, the analysis of what constitutes a church employer is similar to the analysis of what constitutes a governmental employer—the employees of the United Lutheran Church are clearly church employees, but what about employees of the United Lutheran Hospital, and what about employees of the special research wing in the United Lutheran Hospital, and what about the employees of the blood laboratory next door to the United Lutheran Hospital that gets about 80% of its clients directly from the hospital, and so on. The following Private Letter Ruling demonstrates how the IRS will review the surrounding facts and circumstances.

Private Letter Ruling 9528033, 04/19/1995, IRC Sec(s). 414

Date: April 19, 1995

CP:E:EP:T:3
Attention : ***
LEGEND:
Church C = ***
Order B = ***
Hospital A = ***
Hospital B = ***
Branch A = ***
Corporation C = ***
St. B = ***
Plan X = ***
Directory M = ***
Committee N = ***
State A = ***
City A = ***

Dear ***

This letter is in response to a ruling request dated November 23, 1994, as supplemented by submissions dated March 10, 1995, March 13, 1995, and a final submission received on March 24, 1995, submitted on your behalf by your authorized representative concerning whether Plan X qualifies as a church plan under section 414(e) of the Internal Revenue Code.

The following facts and representations have been submitted on your behalf:

Hospital A is a voluntary teaching hospital and medical center that offers tertiary services in specialized care on a regional basis and clinical services, and health care and health education to those in Hospital A's service area. Hospital

A is exempt from federal income tax under section 501(a) of the Code, and is an organization described in section 501(c)(3) of the Code.

Hospital A was founded in 1849 by Order B. It was incorporated on April 14, 1870, under the laws of State A. Hospital A operates under the not-for-profit corporation law of State A which authorizes the members of a not-for-profit corporation to adopt and amend the corporation's by-laws and elect its directors and to take any other corporate action. Hospital A was created for the care, aid and support of the indigent sick. In 1961, Hospital B was consolidated with and into Hospital A. The name of Hospital A was changed in 1964 to the current name. In 1969, Hospital A's purposes were expanded to include establishing comprehensive training programs for medical professionals, engaging in clinical research and "to make available optional patient care ... for the sick, poor and disabled and all others without regard to race, color, or creed ...". Hospital A represents that the power to appoint and fill vacancies of Hospital A's membership, which in turn has the power to appoint and fill vacancies of Hospital A's board of trustees, has at all times, since the establishment of Plan X, been reserved to Order B or the archdiocese of City A.

The bylaws of Hospital A in effect when Plan X was adopted established that the persons who may be elected as members of Hospital A must be members of Order B or clergy of the archdiocese of City A. The bylaws grant members the power to amend Hospital A's certificate of incorporation and bylaws and approve the change of the general character of the operation of Hospital A as a voluntary hospital under the auspices of the Church C archdiocese of City A. In addition, the members fix the number of trustees constituting the board of trustees and elect the trustees at the annual meeting of the members. Under the bylaws, at least three members of Order B must be on the board of trustees and at least one member must serve as a trustee. The members also elect the chairman, president and administrator of Branch A of Hospital A. All the other officers of Hospital A are elected by the board of trustees.

According to the bylaws of Hospital A, Hospital A is to carry out its activities in conformity with the ethical and religious directives for Church C health facilities of the United States Church C Conference, as may be revised from time to time.

Hospital A's current mission statement sets forth its activities as conducted in accord with the medical, moral and ethical teachings of Church C as promulgated by the archbishop of the archdiocese of City A. The quality of care is based on the charism of Order B which shares sponsorship of Hospital A with the archdiocese of City A and who carries forward the dedication of the Hospital's patron, St. B.

Directory M lists all agencies and instrumentalities and all educational, charitable and religious institutions operated by Church C in the United States, its territories and possessions. Hospital A, Order B and the Church C archdiocese of City A are listed in Directory M.

Hospital A adopted Plan X effective as of July 1, 1982. Plan X was drafted to conform with the requirements of section 401(a) of the Code and has received favorable determination letters. Effective April 1, 1989, Plan X was adopted by Corporation C, a State A professional corporation, for the purpose of providing pension benefits to its employees. Corporation C is not a not-for-profit corporation. Before April 1, 1989, the employees of Corporation C had been employed by Hospital A and were eligible for participation in Plan X. Corporation C operates the emergency room facilities of Hospital A. As of December 31, 1993, thirteen employees of Corporation C participated in Plan X and 1,834 employees of Hospital A participated in Plan X. In the ruling request dated November 23, 1994, Hospital A represented that in the plan years completed since April 1, 1989, less than one percent of the employees covered by Plan X were employed by Corporation C. The supplementary submission dated March 13, 1995, stated that as of December 31, 1994, the total number of active Hospital A employees actively participating in Plan X was 1,331 and the total number of Corporation C employees actively participating in Plan X was fifteen. Thus, as of December 31, 1994, less than two percent of the employees covered by Plan X were employed by Corporation C.

Article VI of the original Plan X document, which was effective as of July 1, 1982, provides that Plan X is administered by Committee N, and Hospital A represents that Plan X has been administered by Hospital A through Committee N. Committee N consists of three members who are appointed by the board of trustees of Hospital A. Members of Committee N serve until their resignation or removal by the board of trustees. Currently, the members of Committee N are Hospital A's president, vice president of finance and vice president of human resources. Committee N has been given such powers as may be necessary to discharge its duties, including but not limited to construing and applying the provisions of Plan X, determining the eligibility of participants, employing necessary advisors, maintaining adequate records and approving payment of benefits, and performing other similarly related administrative matters. The sole function of Committee N is the administration of Plan X.

Hospital A represents that an election has never been made under section 410(d) of the Code to have the participation, vesting and funding provisions of sections 410, 411 and 412 apply with respect to Plan X.

Hospital A represents that Plan X has at all times since July 1, 1982, satisfied the coverage, vesting and minimum funding requirements that were in existence on September 1, 1974, under sections 401(a)(3), 401(a)(4) and 401(a)(7) of the Code.

Based on the foregoing facts and representations, you request rulings that:

1. Plan X is maintained by an organization described in section 414(e)(3)(A) of the Code and qualifies as a church plan within the meaning of section 414(e);
2. Plan X has qualified as a church plan within the meaning of section 414(e) of the Code since July 1, 1982; and
3. Plan X is exempt from the requirements of section 410, 411 and 412 of the Code so long as it continues to meet the coverage, vesting and funding requirements as in effect on September 1, 1974.

Section 414(e)(1) of the Code defines a church plan as a plan established and maintained for its employees (or their beneficiaries) by a church or by a convention or association of churches which is exempt from taxation under section 501 of the Code.

Section 414(e)(2) of the Code provides that the term "church plan" does not include a plan (A) which is established and maintained primarily for the benefit of employees (or their beneficiaries) of a church or a convention or association of churches who are employed in connection with one or more unrelated trades or businesses (within the meaning of section 513); or (B) if less than substantially all of the individuals included in the plan are church employees (as described in section 414(e)(1) or 414(e)(3)(B)).

Section 414(e)(3)(A) of the Code provides that a plan, otherwise qualified, will qualify as a church plan if it is maintained by an organization, whether a civil law corporation or otherwise, the principal purpose or function of which is the administration or funding of a plan or program for the provision of retirement benefits or welfare benefits, or both, for the employees of a church or a convention or association of churches, if such organization is controlled by or associated with a church or a convention or association or churches.

Section 414(e)(3)(B) of the Code defines "employee" to include a duly ordained, commissioned, or licensed minister of a church in the exercise of a ministry, regardless of the source of his or her compensation, and an employee of an organization, whether a civil law corporation or otherwise, which is exempt from tax under section 501, and which is controlled by or associated with a church or a convention or association or churches.

Section 414(e)(3)(C) of the Code provides that a church or a convention or association of churches which is exempt from tax under section 501 shall be deemed the employer of any individual included as an employee under subparagraph (B).

Section 414(e)(3)(D) of the Code provides that an organization, whether a civil law corporation or otherwise, is "associated" with a church or a convention or association of churches if the organization shares common religious bonds and convictions with that church or convention or association of churches.

In order for an organization to have a qualified church plan, it must establish that its employees are employees or deemed employees of the church or convention or association of churches under section 414(e)(3)(B) of the Code by virtue of the organization's affiliation with the church or convention or association of churches and that the plan will be administered by an organization of the type described in section 414(e)(3)(A).

Hospital A is exempt from federal income tax under section 501(a) of the Code, and is an organization described in section 501(c)(3) of the Code.

Hospital A's bylaws have provided at all times relevant that only a member of Order B or the clergy of the archdiocese of City A may be elected as a member of Hospital A. Furthermore, at least one member of Hospital A must serve as a trustee of Hospital A and no less than three members of Order B must be on the board of trustees.

Pursuant to Hospital A's bylaws, the members elect the board of trustees of Hospital A. The members also elect the chairman, the president and the administrator of Branch A. The board of trustees elects all the other officers of Hospital A. The direct election of the trustees by the members provides the members with effective control of Hospital A. Hospital A's bylaws and its mission statement state that it will be operated in accordance with the teachings of Church C. Thus, Hospital A shares common religious bonds and convictions with Church C and is deemed associated with Church C as provided in section 414(e)(3)(D) of the Code. Further, Hospital A is listed in Directory M and any organization listed in Directory M is considered associated with Church C and its employees are deemed employees of Church C. Hospital A is also associated with Church C because it is controlled by its members who must be members of Order B or clergy of the archdiocese of City A. Order B and the archdiocese of City A are listed in Directory M and are therefore considered associated with Church C. Hospital A is therefore associated with Church C as indicated by its listing in Directory M and by sharing common religious bonds and convictions with Church C.

Accordingly, pursuant to sections 414(e)(3)(B) and (C) of the Code, employees of Hospital A are deemed to be employees of Church C, and Church C is deemed to be the employer of such employees, for purposes of the church plan rules.

However, an organization must also establish that its retirement plan is established and maintained by a church or a convention or association of churches, or by an organization described in section 414(e)(3)(A) of the Code. To be described in section 414(e)(3)(A) of the Code, an organization must have as its principal purpose the administration of the plan and must also be controlled by or associated with a church or a convention or association or churches.

Plan X has always been administered by Committee N. Committee N was designated the administrator of Plan X in the original Plan X document. Members of Committee N are appointed and removed by the board of trustees of Hospital A. Committee N has been given such powers as may be necessary to discharge its duties, including but not limited to construing and applying the provisions of Plan X, determining the eligibility of participants, employing necessary advisors, maintaining adequate records and approving payment of benefits, and performing other similarly related administrative matters. The sole purpose and function of Committee N is the administration of Plan X.

Hospital A is listed in Directory M and therefore Hospital A and its board of trustees are associated with Church C. Through its power to appoint and remove the members of Committee N, the board of trustees controls Committee N. Since Committee N is controlled by Hospital A through its board of trustees, and Hospital A is associated with Church C, Committee N is indirectly associated with Church C. Further, since Committee N is not only associated with Church C, but the sole purpose of Committee N is the administration of Plan X, Committee N is an organization described in section 414(e)(3)(A) of the Code.

Plan X also covers employees of Corporation C, which is not a not-for-profit corporation. As of December 31, 1994, the total number of active Hospital A employees actively participating in Plan X was 1,331 and the total number of Corporation C employees actively participating in Plan X was fifteen. The information provided by Hospital A indicates that as of December 31, 1994, the employees of Corporation C covered by Plan X had not risen to two percent of the total number of participants covered by Plan X during the period of its existence. Accordingly, in this case the employees of Corporation C constitute an insubstantial percent of the participants in Plan X.

Therefore, with respect to ruling requests one and two, we conclude that:
1. Plan A is maintained by an organization described in section 414(e)(3)(A) of the Code and qualifies as a church plan within the meaning of section 414(e); and
2. Plan A has qualified as a church plan within the meaning of Section 414(e) of the Code since July 1, 1982.

With respect to ruling request three, to qualify under section 401(a) of the Code, an employees' plan must meet the minimum participation standards of section 410 of the Code and the minimum vesting standards of section 411. Qualified pension plans also must meet the minimum funding standards of section 412. Each of these sections, however, contains an exception for a church plan as defined in section 414(e), unless an election has been made in accordance with section 410(d). See sections 410(c)(1)(B), 411(e)(1)(B) and 412(h)(4).

As previously represented, the election made available by section 410(d) of the Code to have the participation, vesting, funding and other provisions of the Employee Retirement Income security Act of 1974 apply to Plan X has never been made.

Therefore, with respect to ruling request three, we conclude that:

3. Plan X is exempt from the requirements of section 410, 411 and 412 of the Code so long as it continues to meet the coverage, vesting and funding requirements as in effect on September 1, 1974.

This letter expresses no opinion as to whether Plan X satisfies the requirements for qualification under section 401(a) of the Code. The determination as to whether a plan is qualified under section 401(a) is within the jurisdiction of the appropriate Key District Director's office of the Internal Revenue Service.

This letter has been sent to your authorized representative in accordance with the power of attorney submitted with the ruling request.

Sincerely yours,

Frances V. Sloan
Chief, Employee Plans
Technical Branch 3

---

c. Public Schools

Legal Definition at IRC § 170(b)(1)(A)(ii)

For tax purposes, public school employers can provide retirement benefits pursuant to §403(b). These plans are generally governed by ERISA as well, especially if the school makes employer contributions.

A public school plan means "an educational organization which normally maintains a regular faculty and curriculum and normally has a regularly enrolled body of pupils or students in attendance at the place where its educational activities are regularly carried on."

Although under-regulated for decades, the IRS and Treasury have spent the last few years updating the regulations and beefing up their audit presence and outreach and information efforts.

There are three categories of funding arrangements to which §403(b) applies:

1. annuity contracts (as defined in §401(g)) issued by an insurance company;

2. custodial accounts that are invested solely in mutual funds; and

3. retirement income accounts, which are only permitted for church employees and certain ministers.

The basic elements of a 403(b) annuity plan include:

- The contract must be nonforfeitable (except for the failure to pay future premiums), regardless of the type of contribution used to purchase the contract;

- A 403(b) contract purchased under a salary reduction agreement must satisfy the requirements relating to limitations on elective deferrals;

- All contributions to a 403(b) arrangement must be expressed as annual additions and must be limited;

- All 403(b) contracts purchased for an individual by an employer are treated as purchased under a single contract;

- A 403(b) contract that provides for elective deferrals must be available to all employees on a nondiscriminatory basis (the universal availability rule, which means that other public school employees, like a janitor, nurse, school bus driver or cafeteria staff must be eligible to defer a portion of his or her salary); and

- A 403(b) contract is required to satisfy the required minimum distribution requirements, the incidental benefit requirements, and the rollover distribution rules.

d. Non-Profit Organizations and Charities
Legal Definition at IRC § 501(c)(3)

For tax purposes, non-profit and charitable organization employers can provide tax favored retirement benefits pursuant to §§ 403(b) or 457(b). These plans are governed by ERISA, but there are no special rules.

2. How For-Profit Employers Promise and Deliver Retirement Benefits through a Qualified Retirement Plan

a. A Brief Historical Perspective

While some credit The American Express Company with establishing the first private pension plan in the United States in 1875,[1] others credit the Baltimore and Ohio Railroad with establishing the first plan in 1884.[2] Either way, the idea of an employer taking care of workers financially after they no longer perform services took root sometime after the Civil War, and after the Industrial Revolution changed the society from agrarian-oriented to manufacturing-and services-oriented. Retirement benefits became a way for employers to attract, retain and reward good workers, a way for families to be relieved of caring for elderly members, especially as families decentralized, and also as a way for an employer to promise to pay $1 in the future as wages, which is always mathematically cheaper than a promise to pay $1 today.

The purpose of this textbook is not to be a historical tome. However, an understanding of the history can help you to understand how and why the current rules are the way they are. This textbook is a likely good starting point, and it is up to you to read other sources that allow you to absorb some of the historical political and policy context.

---

1. Employee Benefits Research Institute, Facts: History of Pension Plans, March 1998, available at http://www.ebri.org/publications/facts/index.cfm?fa=0398afact (last visited December 26, 2008)

2. Wikipedia, "Retirement plans in the United States," available at http://en.wikipedia.org/wiki/Retirement_plans_in_the_United_States, citing Fee, Elizabeth; Shopes, Linda; and Zeidman, Linda (1991). The Baltimore Book: New Views of Local History. Philadelphia: Temple University Press. pp. 11–14 (last visited December 26, 2008)

b. The Requirements for Qualified Retirement Plans
Requirements Listed in IRC § 401(a)

Now that you have a general understanding of what makes a retirement plan a "qualified retirement plan," we can explore the specific rules. The "laundry list" of plan requirements under the current version of the Internal Revenue Code is:

1. the sponsoring employer can only make contributions to the plan if they are intended to be distributed (with fund earnings) to participants and beneficiaries;

2. all assets must remain for the exclusive benefit of participants and beneficiaries (*i.e.*, no diversion);

3. the plan must satisfy the requirements of § 410 (minimum coverage) — as discussed in Chapter 8 of this text book, the plan does not need to cover every employee who has attained age 21 and who has completed a year of service with the employer, but if the plan does exclude any eligible employees, then the plan will need to meet certain mathematical tests each year demonstrating that enough lower paid employees are covered by the plan;

4. neither contributions nor benefits can discriminate in favor of Highly Compensated Employees — as discussed in Chapter 8 of this text book, the plan does not need to offer the same benefits, rights and features to every employee covered by the plan, but if the plan does provide different levels, then the plan will need to meet certain mathematical tests each year demonstrating that enough lower paid employees enjoy the better benefits, rights and features;

5. special rules for the nondiscrimination requirements;

6. the plan can satisfy the minimum coverage requirements on one day in each quarter;

7. the plan must satisfy the requirements of § 411 (minimum vesting and accrual rules) — as discussed in Chapter 7 of this text book, the plan must be designed to provide adequate levels of benefits and rights to those benefits even for individuals employed for a short period of time;

8. a defined benefit plan may not allow forfeitures to increase benefits;

9. a person must start taking minimum distributions upon attaining age 70½ — as discussed in Chapter 9 of this text book, some wealthier individuals who do not actually need distributions from the retirement plan would prefer to allow their qualified retirement plan assets (and Individual Retirement Account assets) to remain in the plan (or IRA) to be used later in life or passed along to their estate upon death, but Congress generally requires at least a portion be distributed and subject to income tax once a person attains age 70½;

10. the plan must satisfy the requirements of § 401(d) (contribution limit on owner-employees) and must satisfy the requirements of § 416 (special rules for top heavy plans) — as discussed in Chapter 8 of this text book, when Congress allowed owner-employees to participate in qualified retirement plans, it added a complicated regime of rules that ensure that rank-and-file employees receive certain minimum accruals and vesting credits in years where the majority of plan benefits are promised to owner-employees;

11. the plan must satisfy the Qualified Joint and Survivor Annuity and Qualified Pre-retirement Survivor Annuity rules of § 417 — as discussed in Chapter 9 of

this text book, Congress added rights and protections to the spouses of plan participants upon distribution of benefits or death of the participant, even though the spouse might not ever have been employed by the employer that sponsors and maintains the qualified plan;

12. benefits may not be reduced due to plan merger, consolidation, or transfer;

13. no benefits can be assigned or alienated, other than the statutory exclusions to the general rules—as discussed in Chapter 9 of this text book, creditors of the plan participant generally cannot receive the benefits from the plan before they are distributed to the participant, other than ex-spouses through a Qualified Domestic Relations Order and the IRS through a special lien;

14. payment of benefits must start within 60 days of the later of normal retirement date, 10 years of plan participation, or termination of employment;

15. a plan cannot decrease benefits based on increases in Social Security benefits;

16. the plan must satisfy the requirements of §415 (limits on benefits and contributions)—as discussed in Chapter 7 of this text book, regardless of what the plan document promises, Congress has limited the benefits and contributions that can actually be allocated or paid from a qualified plan, which is the main reason that many employers will provide non-qualified retirement benefit promises to executives and other highly paid and key personnel above and beyond what can be offered through a qualified plan;

17. the maximum compensation taken into account by a plan is limited to $200,000, as indexed for inflation;

18. (Repealed)

19. the employer-contribution portion of a participant's benefits may not be forfeited if he or she withdraws some benefits from the participant-contribution portion of benefits (unless certain conditions are met);

20. certain plans are permitted to make several partial distributions within one taxable year;

21. (Repealed)

22. a profit sharing plan, in which more than 10% of the assets are invested in employer stock which is not readily tradable, must satisfy the requirements of §409(e) (with certain qualifications);

23. a stock bonus plan must satisfy the requirements of §409(h) and (o) (with certain qualifications);

24. certain group trusts automatically meet these requirements;

25. a defined benefit plan must state the actuarial assumptions for benefit equivalences in the plan document—as discussed in Chapter 9 of this text book, this requirement precludes any arbitrary conversions between optional forms of benefit distributions;

26. a defined benefit plan must cover at least the lesser of 50 employees or 40% of the workforce;

27. contributions to a profit sharing plan can be made regardless of the profitability of the sponsoring employer and a defined contribution plan must specify what type of plan it intends to be;

28. additional rules for the diversification of assets in an ESOP;

29. if a defined benefit plan is amended, and such amendment causes a severe underfunding, then some collateral security is necessary;

30. a plan which allows elective deferrals (*i.e.,* a 401(k) plan) must include a provision in its plan document that the single elective deferral limit under §402(g) applies to an individual for all plans he or she participates in during that year—as discussed in Chapter 5 of this text book, this single limit applies to the individual for the year, regardless of whether he or she has worked for different employers;

31. the plan must allow a participant to elect a plan-to-plan transfer of benefits upon distribution;

32. a defined benefit plan will not be disqualified if it is subject to the liquidity rule for minimum quarterly contribution rules of §412(m) and thereby does not make such required contributions;

33. a terminating defined benefit plan may not increase benefits while its sponsoring employer is in federal bankruptcy;

34. a terminating defined benefit plan should transfer assets for missing participants over to the Pension Benefit Guaranty Corporation;

35. defined contribution plans that allow participants to choose to invest part of their accounts into employer securities must allow them to diversify their portfolios and must provide notices that highlight the benefits of investment diversification;

36. distributions from a defined benefit plan or a money purchase plan can be made after a participant attains age 62 even if the participant is still employed, even on a reduced-working-hour basis; and

37. the HEART Act of 2008 requires certain benefits for employees who are called into temporary active military service.

While each and every provision above is crucially important for a retirement plan to be deemed a qualified retirement plan, those not discussed further in this text book either are too advanced for an introductory text book, or are self-explanatory on their face. Please note that Congress frequently adds new provisions to the list or amends existing provisions, and when advising a client on a qualified plan, a complete understanding of the entire battery of qualification rules is crucial, and should not be limited to only those discussed herein.

A point must be stressed right here, right now, and will be repeated throughout this textbook. While it is easy to sum up each and every qualification rule into a pithy sentence so that the laundry list is manageable to digest upon reading it for the first time, almost each and every provision is much more complicated, involves a general rule, exceptions to the general rule, and probably even exceptions to the exceptions, and is probably interpreted in some manner through IRS guidance or court decisions, or is ambiguous and in need of clarification. This textbook is only to be used to gain a basic understanding of the general rules, and primary source material must be read thoroughly before ever attempting to provide counsel to a client.

c. Plan Disqualification

There are four main ways that a qualified plan can be disqualified:

1. *Improper Form of Employer*: As indicated above, government entities, non-electing church employers, non-profit organizations and educational institutions are

generally not allowed to sponsor § 401(a) qualified plans. If they improperly do so, then when the error is discovered, the plan will need to be nullified.

2. *Improper Form of Plan Document*: A disqualifying provision is a provision (or absence of a required provision) in a new plan or an amendment to an existing plan that causes it to violate the qualification requirements of § 401(a). There-fore, at all times, the plan document must comply with the law. As discussed in Chapter 10, employers can file a determination letter request with the IRS for their review of the plan document and a letter assuring that it is in compliance. Also, as Congress changes the statutory rules, employers have at least until the end of a remedial amendment period to actually amend the document, as long as they operate the plan in good faith compliance with the newly amended statu-tory provisions.

3. *Operation of the Plan Without Adherence to the Plan Document*: Assuming that the plan document complies with federal law, it needs to be operated and ad-ministered in accordance with the document. Upon audit by the IRS, any oper-ational failures will need to be corrected, an additional penalty might be assessed, and the IRS can ultimately disqualify the plan. As discussed in Chapter 10, the IRS allows plan sponsors to self-audit their qualified plans and correct any op-erational failures at a lower cost than if they were discovered on audit.

4. *Failure to Comply With Annual Tests*: Unless the plan satisfies certain safe harbor requirements, it will need to pass the nondiscrimination, minimum coverage, minimum participation and top heavy tests each year. As the demographics of the workforce change annually, proper employee data and calculations are cru-cial. As discussed in Chapter 8, if the plan fails any of the annual tests that are in place to prevent abuses but the plan is not self-corrected, then the plan can be disqualified.

d. Ways That a Plan Can Avoid Disqualification

The Secretary of the Treasury has the authority to disqualify a retirement plan, sub-ject to certain coordination requirements with the Secretary of Labor. The Secretary of the Treasury has delegated its enforcement authority regarding plan qualification to the IRS, which may make a determination regarding a plan's qualification status either upon receipt of the employer's application for a determination letter or as a result of the ex-amination of the plan by the IRS. The IRS may retroactively disqualify a plan and assess taxes with respect to any "open" tax year (*i.e.,* tax years for which the statute of limita-tions has not run). The extent to which a plan may be retroactively disqualified for "form" violations is limited if it has been the subject of a favorable determination letter.

The IRS is generally allowed three years after the filing of the income tax return for the applicable year in which to assess taxes on an employer who sponsored or an em-ployee who participated in the disqualified plan. In limited circumstances, however, the IRS may assess taxes within six years after a taxpayer files its return.

As of the date of disqualification, a previously tax-qualified retirement plan becomes nonqualified and its previously tax-exempt trust becomes nonexempt. Accordingly, the non-exempt trust is subject to income tax on its earnings for the years in which the plan is disqualified. Any contributions made by the employer to the plan in the years in which the plan is disqualified are not deductible by the employer (to the extent the contributions are not included in the employee's gross income). The employee must include in his or her taxable income contributions made to the plan on the employee's behalf, to the extent the employee was "substantially vested" in the contributions for the years the plan was disqualified. If the sole reason for disqualification is because the plan fails its annual minimum coverage tests, then only the Highly Compensated Employees of the plan will be affected by these adverse non-qualification rules.

In order to limit plan disqualification to the most severe case, the IRS has developed a comprehensive self-correction program called the Employee Plans Correction Resolution System ("EPCRS"):

- *Self-Correction (SCP):* A Plan Sponsor that has established compliance practices and procedures may, at any time without paying any fee or sanction, correct insignificant operational failures. In addition, in the case of a Qualified Plan that has received a favorable determination letter from the Service, then the plan sponsor generally may correct even significant operational failures without payment of any fee or sanction.

- *Voluntary correction with Service approval (VCP):* A plan sponsor, at any time before audit, may pay a limited fee and receive the Service's approval for correction of a Qualified Plan. Under VCP, there are special procedures for anonymous submissions and group submissions.

- *Correction on audit (Audit CAP):* If a failure (other than a failure corrected through SCP or VCP) is identified on audit, the plan sponsor may correct the failure and pay a sanction. The sanction imposed will bear a reasonable relationship to the nature, extent, and severity of the failure, taking into account the extent to which correction occurred before audit.

Now that the IRS has developed the EPCRS, and Congress has actually encouraged them to expand it, there is an even greater chance that they will actually disqualify a plan that makes no attempt at self-audit to find and correct problems. The self-correction program is discussed in further detail in Chapter 10.

3. Qualified Plans for Multiemployers

A multiemployer qualified retirement plan is generally associated with a group of employees who are members of the same collectively bargained unit (*i.e.,* union) where they either work for unrelated employers, or where they only work for any given employer for a short period of time. A single plan is set up and all of the various employers contribute. In many of the qualification rules, there are special exemptions or different limits for multiemployer plans than there are for the single-employer plans. For the remainder of this text book, unless specifically mentioned (such as in funding of a defined benefit plan, as discussed in Chapter 6, or withdrawal liability for plan terminations, as discussed in Chapter 16), assume that we are providing the general rules for single-employer plans and purposely omitting the multiemployer rules.

Therefore, instead of detailing all of the qualification rules for multiemployer plans, below is the top ten issues identified during IRS examinations of multiemployer plans, which should at least highlight some of the more important rules that multiemployer plans should be complying with:[3]

---

3. available at http://www.irs.gov/retirement/article/0,,id=135263,00.html.

1. Internal Revenue Code Section 401(a)(9) violation (required minimum distributions): Because administrators typically rely on participants to apply for benefits before addressing such issues, the required minimum distribution requirements of Internal Revenue Code 401(a)(9) are not being met. Specifically many plans have failed to make required distributions to participants by the first of April following the later of the year they turn 70½ or the calendar year in which they retire. In addition when participants die the rules governing the timing of such distributions to their beneficiaries are not being followed. Plan administrators should be more proactive with respect to monitoring the section 401(a)(9) requirements.

2. Accruals/service credit is dependent on employer contributions being made: Plans are failing to meet the definitely determinable benefit rules of [Treas.] Reg. 1.401-1(b)(1)(i). Plans are failing this requirement in form and in operation. The situation that usually results in such a violation is when the plan requires payment from the participating employer prior to crediting a participant for covered service associated with that employer contribution. Administrators should ensure that the crediting of participant accruals and service is not dependent on the receipt of related employer contributions.

3. Plan did not make required actuarial adjustments for benefit payments beginning after Normal Retirement Date: The required actuarial adjustments or interest adjusted back payments are not being paid to participants whose retirement benefits first commence after the Normal Retirement Date as stipulated in the plan. This issue tends to be more prevalent when plans have normal retirement ages that are less than 65 because many participants are unaware of their eligibility to receive these benefits at this earlier age and thus fail to apply for their benefits. Administrators should ensure that all missed payments due to the delayed commencement of benefits are restored and that these payments are increased by the appropriate interest factor.

4. Errors made in benefit calculations, crediting service, reduction factors, general administration: Errors are made when participant benefits are calculated. The following reasons for these mistakes have been identified:

    • benefit provisions in the plan are misapplied

    • applicable law is not understood

    • faulty participant data is used and/or provided (by employer and/or union)

    • combinations of above

    Administrators should take greater care when considering the applicable plan provisions, law changes, and the accuracy of participant data when determining benefits.

5. Internal Revenue Code Section 411 violations including cash out/forfeitures from lost participants, wrong vesting schedule used, and error in vesting percentages: Every plan is required to have provisions regarding how participants are vested in their benefits. Normally, the percentage a participant is vested is dependent on their credited service. If employers and/or union do not track a participant's service correctly, the vesting percentage could be incorrect. Errors that have been sited include the following:

    • erroneous cash outs and forfeitures

    • wrong vesting schedules being used

- errors when calculating a participant's vesting percentage
- suspension of benefit issues including Heinz type violations

Greater care should be applied to the vesting provisions contained in the plan document and legal changes to Internal Revenue Code section 411.

6. Plan fails to follow or does not have a participation agreement for each participating employers: This normally involves non-collectively bargained employees working for union and/or trust fund who are participating in the plan yet did not have an agreement signed or the agreement in place is not followed. These agreements can be in the form of a side agreement, contained within the CBA or provided for within the plan itself. The failure to properly define the plan's eligibility and participation requirements may result in its failing to constitute a definite written program under the law. Administrators should ensure that prior to admitting a non-collectively bargained employee to the plan, adequate language addressing the eligibility requirements and benefit structure pertaining to such employee is formally adopted.

7. Internal Revenue Code Section 412 violation—funding deficiency: Plans subject to Internal Revenue Code Section 412 minimum funding requirements are failing to receive contributions necessary to satisfy this code section. In addition, participating employers responsible for the excise taxes that result are not filing the appropriate excise tax return (Forms 5330) and/or paying the tax. Administrators should actively pursue the collection of delinquent employer contributions and inform any employer who has failed to satisfy its section 412 obligation of the requirement to file Form 5330 with the Service and pay the appropriate excise tax.

8. Delinquent/late contributions: Plans subject to Internal Revenue Code Section 412 minimum funding requirements are failing to receive contributions by certain dates necessary to satisfy this code section. When the plan receives these contributions late, there are consequences which can include excise taxes being assessed, and/or deductions being disallowed on the employer's tax return. Administrators should advise all employers making contributions to the plan to make them timely per section 412. This may be difficult as not all the employers involved in a plan may have the same tax year nor the same method of accounting. If contributions are not timely per section 412, employers should be advised to file Form 5330 with the Service, and pay the appropriate excise tax due.

9. Conflict between Plan Document and Other Agreements (Collectively Bargained, Joinder, Participation): This involves situations where the language in the plan document does not agree with the language in Other Written Agreements. For example, the benefit formula in the plan is not the same as the one in the Collectively Bargained Agreement, or the eligibility provisions in the plan do not agree with those in a participation agreement. Administrators should make sure that the terms in the plan document agree with all other written agreements, especially when changes are made to these Other Agreements.

10. Misuse/Diversion of Pension Funds: This involves situations where the plan's assets are used for purposes other than the benefit of plan participants or the trust. Errors that have been noted include the following:

- plan trustee is using trust assets for personal use
- plan loans money to a trustee using an interest rate that is less than the Fair Market rate

- trust sells an asset to a "disqualified person" for less than Fair Market Value
- failure to properly allocate expenses between different trusts
- improper transfer of assets between related trusts
- embezzlement of trust assets

Administrators should make sure that the trust assets are used for the exclusive benefit of plan participants.

4. Qualified Plans for Multiple Employers

A multiple-employer retirement plan is a plan maintained by one or more employers that is not a multiemployer plan.[4] Since not a multi-employer retirement plan, which has its own special rules under the Code, a multiple-employer plan is by default treated as a single-employer plan. This can lead to problems since the loose group of employers, perhaps connected through an association or industry, are not contracted to each other in the same manner as employers bound to contribute to a multiemployer plan pursuant to a collective bargained agreement.

The definition of employer under ERISA includes a group or association of employers acting for an employer in such capacity.[5] Thus, ERISA recognizes that a single plan may be established by a bona fide group or association of employers, acting in the interests of its employer members to provide benefits for their employees. However, the Department of Labor has expressed its view that, when several unrelated employers merely execute identically worded trust agreements or similar documents as a means to fund or provide benefits, in the absence of any genuine organizational relationship between employers, no employer group or association exists for purposes of ERISA.[6] Similarly, the Department of Labor has noted that, when membership in a group or association is open to anyone engaged in a particular trade or profession regardless of their status as employer, and when control of the group or association is not vested solely in employer members, then the group or association is not a bona fide group or association of employers for purposes of ERISA.[7]

There is a more formal definition for the delivery of welfare benefits, and a multiple employer welfare arrangement ("MEWA") is an employee welfare benefit plan, or any other arrangement which is established or maintained for the purpose of providing, through the purchase of insurance or otherwise, medical, surgical, or hospital care or benefits, or benefits in the event of sickness, accident, disability, death or unemployment, or vacation benefits, apprenticeship or other training programs, or day care centers, scholarship funds, or prepaid legal services to employees of two or more employers (including one or more self-employed individuals), or to their beneficiaries, as long as the plan is not pursuant to any collective bargaining agreements.[8]

---

4. Instructions to 2007 IRS Form 5500, box A(3).
5. ERISA § 3(5).
6. DOL Adv. Op. 2003-17A.
7. Id.
8. ERISA § 3(40).

B. Income Tax Advantages of Retirement Plans

1. Income Tax Advantages of Employer-Sponsored Retirement Plans for Employers

Legal Rules at IRC § 404

A for-profit employer generally takes a deduction under IRC § 162 against Gross Income for expenses incurred in the normal and ordinary operation of the business, which specifically includes reasonable salary. However, if a portion of the salary is a contribution to a qualified retirement plan, then only contributions that meet specific requirements of IRC § 404 can be deducted. A not-for-profit employer (such as a church, state or local government, public school or charitable organization) does not pay corporate income taxes anyway, so no deduction is sought.

2. Income Tax Advantages of Employer-Sponsored Retirement Plans for Employees

Legal Rules at IRC § 402(a), the Flush Language after § 403(b)(1)(E), and § 457(a)

Contributions and other additions by an employer that sponsors a qualified retirement plan, a compliant § 403(b) annuity plan or a compliant § 457(b) eligible deferred compensation plan are excluded from the Gross Income of the employee for the taxable year contributed to the plan, and will only be included in the employee's or beneficiary's Gross Income in the year distributed from the plan. The income tax rules for plan distributions described in Chapter 9 of this text book generally apply to both qualified and non-qualified retirement plans.

C. Choices of Written Plan Documents for Qualified Retirement Plans

1. Types of Written Plan Documents for Qualified Plans

Legal Requirements at IRC § 401(b)

A major requirement of a qualified plan is that it is in writing, and that the document complies with all current federal laws. There are three main ways for an employer to get its retirement program memorialized in a compliant plan document: a Master and Prototype plan, a Volume Submitter plan, or an individually designed plan. Each respective type has varying levels of costs and associated degrees of furnished legal advice. Therefore, choosing the cheapest form of document is usually coupled with the lowest level of counseling (as the retirement plan is being implemented, while it is being administered, and when things go awry).

If an existing retirement plan fails to satisfy the qualification requirements because new legislation has been enacted that changes the qualification requirements, a corrective amendment to the plan may be made effective retroactively to the effective date of the statutory amendment if the corrective amendment is adopted on or before the filing date of the adopting employer's income tax return (including extensions) for the year in which the legislation was enacted or the regulation made effective. If the corrective amendment is made within this time frame, the retirement plan will be considered to remain qualified retroactively as of the effective date of the statutory amendment.

The time period within which a corrective amendment must be adopted is referred to as "the remedial amendment period." The IRS is allowed to extend the remedial amendment period and provide additional rules regarding the amendments that may be made with respect to disqualifying provisions during the remedial amendment period.

If the document is an Master & Prototype or Volume Submitter plan, as described below, then the document drafter and owner is generally required to amend the controlling plan document and then to properly and timely communicate the necessary written and operational changes to each adopting employer. If the document is an individually designed plan, then the attorney is assumed to contact clients and suggest that the plans be amended, but the actual onus for compliance remains with the employer sponsoring the plan and not with the attorney.

The IRS has established a procedure where an Employee Plans agent will review the submitted document and issue a favorable Determination Letter if it is written properly (and those employers with a favorable Determination Letter enjoy an extended Remedial Amendment Period). The Determination Letter request, as explained further in Chapter 10, is purely voluntary, but is highly recommended at the very least for all individually designed plans.

a. Master and Prototype Plan Documents

A Master and Prototype (M&P) plan document is a document that has been prepared by an institutional sponsor (*e.g.,* a financial institution, stock brokerage firm, or insurance company) for adoption by its employer clients. The Master and Prototype plan document consists of both an adoption agreement and a basic plan document. An adoption agreement is the portion of the plan that contains all of the options that may be selected by the employer. A basic plan document is the portion of the plan that contains the provisions applicable to all adopting employers. No options may be offered in the basic plan document. When an employer adopts the basic plan document, the institutional sponsor will provide the employer with a copy of the completed adoption agreement and the basic plan document. The institutional sponsor also provides the employer with copies of the summary plan description that accompanies the basic plan document. Under a master plan, there is a single funding medium for all adopting employers; whereas, under a prototype plan, there is a separate funding medium established for each adopting employer. Plans covering self-employed individuals can use M&P documents.

The institutional sponsor will generally submit a request to the IRS to review the basic plan document and adoption agreement form to determine whether the format complies with the qualification requirements. If it determines that the form of the documents complies with § 401(a), then the IRS will issue an opinion letter to the institutional sponsor. The institutional sponsor will provide a copy of the opinion letter to each employer that adopts the Master and Prototype plan. The institutional sponsor has the responsibility to amend the basic plan document and related adoption agreements as needed in order to maintain the compliance of the documents with statutory and regulatory requirements. When such amendments are made, the institutional sponsor will provide adopting employers with copies of the amended plan documents.

To assist the drafters of Master and Prototype documents, the IRS publishes (and updates) sample plan language that will comply with the current law.[9] One advantage of the List of Required Modifications (LRMs), in addition to spelling out how a compliant document can look, is that each provision has citations to the exact part of the law that has the plan document requirement. Therefore, drafters of Volume Submitter and individually designed plan documents can also benefit by reviewing the appropriate LRMs.

Amendments allowed: M&P plans must provide a procedure for sponsor amendment, so that changes in the Code, regulations, revenue rulings, other statements published by the Internal Revenue Service, or corrections of prior approved plans may be applied to all employers who have adopted the plan. Sponsors must make reasonable and diligent efforts to ensure that adopting employers of the sponsor's M&P plan have actually received and are aware of all plan amendments and that such employers complete and sign new adoption agreements when necessary. An employer that amends any provision of an approved M&P plan including its adoption agreement (other than to change the choice of options, if the plan permits or contemplates such a change) or an employer that chooses to discontinue participation in a plan as amended by its sponsor and does not substitute another approved M&P plan is considered to have adopted an individually designed plan.[10]

b. *Volume Submitter Plan Documents*

A Volume Submitter (VS) plan document is a document that has been prepared by an employee benefits consultant (*e.g.,* an attorney, actuary, or accounting firm) for adoption by its employer clients. Employers either adopt a specimen plan of the volume submitter verbatim or with minor modifications so that it is still substantially similar to the VS specimen. The consultant represents to the IRS that it has at least 30 employer-clients, each of which is reasonably expected to timely adopt a plan that is substantially similar to the VS practitioner's specimen plan. A VS practitioner may submit any number of specimen plans for advisory letters, provided the minimum employer requirement is separately satisfied with respect to each specimen plan. An "advisory letter" is a written statement issued by the IRS to a VS practitioner or VS mass submitter as to the acceptability of the form of a specimen plan and any related trust or custodial account. The IRS may request from the VS practitioner a list of the employers that have adopted or are expected to adopt the VS practitioner's specimen plans, including the employers' business addresses and employer identification numbers.

The Volume Submitter plan is drafted initially with alternative paragraphs for particular sections of the plan document. When an employer indicates an interest in adopting the VS plan, the employer, and/or its legal advisor, selects the alternative provisions that the employer wishes to include in the plan. The resulting plan document may or may not include a recitation of the alternative paragraphs that were available under the VS plan but not selected by the adopting employer. The Volume Submitter plan document adopted by the employer generally is included in one plan document. When an employer adopts the volume submitter plan document, the preparer often also provides the employer with

---

9. http://www.irs.gov/retirement/article/0,,id=97182,00.html
10. Rev. Proc. 2005-16, section 5.

a copy of the summary plan description for the VS plan adopted by the employer. As a caution, while each adopting employer is allowed to make minor changes in the VS document, changes that cross that "minor" threshold and become substantial changes will cause that VS plan document to be considered an individually designed plan.

c. Individually Designed Plan Documents

An individually designed custom plan document is a document that is prepared by legal counsel specifically for the employer that will adopt and sponsor the plan (or a VS plan that is modified too substantially from the specimen or an M&P adoption agreement that is modified from the original options). The sponsoring employer has flexibility within the parameters of the qualification rules and other applicable statutory provisions to draft the provisions of the plan document to accommodate the specific benefit goals and employee demographics of the employer. The individually designed custom plan document adopted by the employer is contained within one plan document. An individually designed custom summary plan description must also be prepared to accompany the custom plan document adopted by the employer.

The employer that has adopted the custom plan document can apply for its own individual determination letter from the IRS (as described in Chapter 10). Further, the employer that has adopted the custom plan document is responsible for amending the plan document as needed in order to maintain the compliance of the document with statutory and regulatory requirements. The custom plan document is primarily used by employers that have unique employee demographics or that wish to offer benefit or investment options or include any other provisions not normally found in most generic pre-approved plan documents.

The employer that is sponsoring and adopting the individually designed custom plan document will incur the full cost for the legal services required to prepare the individually designed custom plan document and related summary plan description.

"Current Initiatives by IRS to Assist Small Employers That Adopt Pre-Approved Qualified Retirement Plan Documents"
Prepared by Barry Kozak, BNA Tax Management "Insights and Commentary" on http://www.bnatax.com/tm/jc_insights.htm, (c)2008

All employers that sponsor a tax qualified retirement plan must execute a plan document that clearly states how an employee becomes a plan participant, vests in and accrues retirement benefits, and can ultimately receive the promised benefits. The employer can hire an attorney to draft an individually designed document, adopt a document that is materially similar to a Volume Submitter document drafted by an attorney, accountant or other qualified pension professional, or can adopt an "off-the-shelf" prototype document prepared by the bank or financial institution where the plan assets will be invested (which generally consists of a boiler-plate document and a fill-in-the-blanks adoption agreement). Since the latter two types are usually the easiest for the plan sponsor, and the cheapest, the IRS estimates that currently over 90% of all qualified retirement plans are supported by pre-approved plans.

However, employers adopting a pre-approved plan document, especially small employers that don't necessarily have any owners or employees that are experts in employee benefit issues, must realize what they are not receiving when they purchase a pre-approved plan, especially a Master & Prototype ("M&P") plan. By analogy, let's look at married couples that divorce using pre-printed no-contest divorce decrees to dissolve their marriages, business owners that use pre-printed forms to incorporate their businesses, or individuals that download pre-printed health care power of attorney proxies to allow close family members or friend to make life or death medical decisions on their behalves in times of emergency. It is easy to understand how in all three situations, the parties to the divorce, incorporation or health proxy are not receiving legal advice. As long as no unanticipated events occur, then in the end, with hindsight, we can say that these people properly saved money and time by using pre-printed legal documents and their general knowledge to circumvent the time and expense of seeking appropriate legal advice.

When an employer is selecting a pre-approved master and prototype plan from a bank or financial institution, it is basically doing the same thing. The financial institutions are looking for a cheap way to convince the employer to select its investment vehicles, and an off-the-shelf plan document accomplishes this goal for them. This fact is not meant in any way to disparage or question the level of expertise that any particular bank or financial institution maintains—incredibly competent ERISA attorneys are generally employed in their home offices and painstakingly draft these Master & Prototype plans for IRS approval. However, the employer looking to establish a 401(k) or profit sharing plan is generally at a local branch talking to an investment salesperson and not at the legal department of the corporate headquarters. While that representative is assumedly an expert in investments and is duly licensed, not all investment advisors are experts in employee benefits issues. And even those Registered Representatives that go the extra mile and voluntarily educate themselves on the rules and regulation of qualified plans are not necessarily licensed to practice law, and therefore can only provide limited advice.

Some of the legal advice that every employer sponsoring a qualified plan should receive before executing the plan document and formally making the retirement benefit promises to its employees include:

- The corporate or other business-related action (such as a board of directors resolution) needed in that particular state to execute the initial plan document, amend it from time to time, and to ultimately terminate it;
- The timing and substantive requirements to amend the plan as new legislation, regulations or judicial opinion invalidates previously sound plan language;
- The importance of properly selecting the individual that will be the named fiduciary in the plan document, and then training and bonding that individual;
- Establishing procedures for that named fiduciary to select and monitor other individuals to either have allocated or delegated fiduciary responsibilities;
- A true determination as to whether the employer is part of a controlled group of corporations or businesses, or is part of an affiliated service group;
- The establishment of internal payroll procedures to report proper compensation and business ownership percentages to any third party ad-

ministrators so that benefits and contributions are properly calculated, and so that Highly Compensated Employees and Key Employees are properly classified on an annual basis;

- While the plan is expected to adopt certain procedures that comply with the statutes and regulations (such as a claims procedure if a benefit request is denied, a funding policy and possibly an investment policy statement, and a procedure for determining if a Qualified Domestic Relations Order is effective to distribute some of the qualified plan benefits to the ex-spouse of a divorcing plan participant), the claims procedure, specifically, generates the written record if the case is ever litigated, and different attorneys might desire it to be drafted in different ways to best support the plan in litigation.

Additionally, even if the document complies with current law and is meticulously followed, at any point in time that the Internal Revenue Service or Department of Labor audit the plan, or if a disgruntled plan participant (or class of plaintiffs) disputes the actions taken by the plan administrator or fiduciary, then the employer will probably need to hire an outside attorney that is not the financial institution attorney that drafted the M&P plan; thus, the attorney will likely charge higher fees for having to read and digest the plan provisions on an expedited basis before he or she can offer any litigation advice.

This commentary is simply meant to advise employers of the pitfalls of simply using an off-the-shelf M&P plan document in the absence of any further thought or action. The plan advisors that are employed to administer the plan (such as accountants, actuaries, attorneys, investment advisors, or other professional consultants) can generally assist the employer (as plan sponsor) in understanding these legal issues and actually getting appropriate legal advice when needed. Like the no-contest divorce, the self-incorporation form and the do-it-yourself health proxy, small employers need to balance a cheap and easy way to execute a written plan document with the legal and other professional advice that is needed to properly administer the qualified retirement plan that will probably not be provided with the M&P plan.

The IRS has taken this matter very seriously, and is currently contacting many of the banks and financial institutions that sponsor M&P plans. One of the Employee Plans Compliance Unit's (EPCU) featured projects generates a compliance contact letter that asks the targeted M&P sponsors to provide information on how they are meeting their requirements and responsibilities. Specifically, the letter asks the financial institutions, among other things, for a list of employers that have adopted their M&P plan; an explanation (and documents) supporting their efforts that they make to educate and monitor their pre-approved plan clients on the importance of properly executing and following plan documents, and also for any feedback that they can offer to the IRS to ensure compliance for the institutions and their clients. While a contact letter from the EPCU does not rise to the level of audit or examination, there is no guarantee that the banks and financial institutions will timely and completely respond. According to the website, after lists of the respective adopting employers are received, the EPCU will likely start the second phase of this project, and actually send contact letters to individual employers; however, there is no indication of what the contact letters for adopting employers will look like, when those contacts would be made, and what percentage of all employers adopting pre-approved plans will actually be contacted.

The IRS's own Advisory Committee on Tax Exempt and Government Entities (ACT), looked at the issues with M&P plans as they relate to the institutional sponsors as well as the adopting employers, and summarized the history of M&P plans, crafted conclusions based on past plan audits, and made substantive recommendations in a report titled "Improving Compliance for Adopters of Pre-Approved Plans." The recommendations to determine how seriously institutions are taking their responsibilities with the M&P documents are basically encompassed within the EPCU project. However, there are very important recommendations at the end of the report for IRS outreach and education to the adopting employers:

- Use of IRS Newsletters,
- Special IRS Publication for Adopting Employers,
- Self-Audit Checklist, and
- A specialized website.

The IRS website has a general link to "Retirement Plans Community" and then a link for "Plan Sponsor/Employer." While there are currently links to very useful information (such as fix-it guides, information on different types of plans, reporting and disclosure rules, and how to prepare for an audit), the IRS has not yet incorporated the ACT report suggestions specifically regarding M&P plan issues as they affect adopting employers. Additionally, in Exhibit C of the 2007 ACT report, the IRS was encouraged to develop a "Pre-Approved Plan Acknowledgment and Information Form" that would mandatorily need to be completed, signed, and retained by both the M&P sponsor and each adopting employer. Unfortunately, however, "some of the procedural recommendations cannot be implemented at least until the next six year remedial amendment cycle which will not begin before 2011."

Pre-approved Master and Prototype plans, as well as Volume Submitter plans, are very important methods of providing technically compliant plan documents to small employers in a very inexpensive and efficient manner. However, the adopting employers must always be aware of the types of substantive advice that they are generally not receiving from the bank or financial institution that sells them the plan document along with the investment vehicles. The adopting employers, especially small employers without any particular expertise in employee benefit issues, must therefore take affirmative steps to employ other competent plan advisors. Educating these adopting employers is crucial for the proper delivery of retirement benefits through qualified plans, and employee benefit attorneys and practitioners are encouraged to make presentations and provide summaries of basic qualified plan requirements wherever they can (at local business associations, trade shows, chambers of commerce, or other resource points for small businesses, including programs sponsored by the Small Business Association).

2. Retroactive and Prospective Plan Amendments

The qualified retirement plan can always be amended to increase, decrease, freeze or terminate promised benefits in the future. However, as discussed in Chapter 7, no plan amendment can decrease or eliminate a benefit that has been vested and accrued.

For purposes of minimum funding requirements for defined benefit plans , any amendment applying to a plan year which is adopted after the close of such plan year but no later than 2½ months after the close of the plan year (or, in the case of a multiemployer plan, no later than 2 years after the close of such plan year), does not reduce the accrued benefit of any participant determined as of the beginning of the first plan year to which the amendment applies, and does not reduce the accrued benefit of any participant determined as of the time of adoption except to the extent required by the circumstances, shall, at the election of the plan administrator, be deemed to have been made on the first day of such plan year. No amendment described in this paragraph which reduces the accrued benefits of any participant shall take effect unless the plan administrator files a notice with the Secretary notifying him of such amendment and the Secretary has approved such amendment, or within 90 days after the date on which such notice was filed, failed to disapprove such amendment.[11]

3. Establishment of a Trust Document

Legal requirements at IRC §§ 401(a) and 501(a)

The plan document describes eligibility requirements, plan benefits, rights and features, default assumptions, and anything else required under the qualification rules. The separate trust document, on the other hand, describes who has control over plan assets, how they can be invested, and how and when distributions can be paid. Technically, each plan has a separate plan document and a trust document, but oftentimes both are incorporated into a single document. Since the trust is tax-exempt, it is has a legal identity separate from the sponsoring employer, and the employer needs to apply for a separate Taxpayer Identification Number. If an employer adopts a pre-approved M&P plan, the financial institution will generally not allow any amendments to its off the shelf trust document.

---

11. IRC § 412(d)(2).

Chapter 5

Defined Contribution Plans and Defined Benefit Plans

Overview

What are the legal definitions of defined contribution plans and defined benefit plans?

- a defined contribution plan has
    - individual accounts; and
    - the benefits at retirement are based solely on the accumulation of contributions and fund earning
- a defined benefit plan is any qualified retirement plan that is not a defined contribution plan
- over the years, hybrid designs have been developed, such as target benefit plans (which are defined contribution plans with some of the attributes of a defined benefit plan) and statutory hybrid plans with a cash balance design (which are defined benefit plans with some of the attributes of a defined contribution plan)

What are the main differences between defined contribution and defined benefit plans?

- a defined contribution plan is one in which the annual contribution is defined in the plan document, but where the contribution is subject to certain minimum and maximum allocations
    - the benefit that an individual will receive upon retirement consists entirely of the accumulation of contributions and fund earnings
    - the benefit is usually paid out in a single lump sum
    - each year, the participant receives a statement reconciling the preceding year's account balance with the current year's balance
- A defined benefit plan is entirely different because it is the promised benefit at retirement that is defined in the plan document, and where the benefit is subject to certain minimum and maximum accrual rules
    - the plan document defines the benefit the employee will receive at retirement, usually as an annuity starting at retirement and continuing for the life of the employee, the joint lives of an employee and his or her chosen beneficiary, a term certain, or any combination thereof
    - the employer accumulates assets in a common pool and simply pays liabilities as they come due to retired or terminated employees

- by statutory mandate, every qualified defined benefit plan must annually use an Enrolled Actuary to value the future expected liabilities, compare them to accumulated assets, make certain actuarial assumptions, and then ultimately determine the contribution needed for that year which will properly fund the plan if all assumptions and expected future contributions are met

- almost all defined benefit plans (except those that only cover owner-employees or those sponsored by a Professional Corporation (P.C.) with less than 25 employees) must pay annual premiums into the Pension Benefit Guaranty Corporation as insurance for government protection of certain benefits guaranteed to participants pursuant to ERISA

- each year, the participant receives a statement showing the deferred retirement annuity accrued to date and the deferred annuity promised by the plan if the employee were to continue working until reaching his or her normal retirement age

Who bears the investment risk in defined contribution and defined benefit plans?

- In a defined contribution plan,
  - the employer is either responsible for making a certain mandatory contribution for each employee who participates in the plan (*i.e.*, a money purchase plan), or the employer is responsible for allocating a discretionary contribution among all accounts in any year in which a contribution is actually made (*i.e.*, a profit sharing plan)
  - as long as the employer sponsoring the plan invests the plan assets prudently and in the best interest of plan participants and beneficiaries, then the employer is not liable for losses to the accounts and the investment risk is thus shifted to the employee
  - in a 401(k) plan, with some additional steps, the plan can allow the individuals to make their own investment decisions

- In a defined benefit plan,
  - the Enrolled Actuary determines the optimal funding pattern, so there should always be adequate assets in the common pool to pay the promised benefits for each individual as they come due
  - if assets earn a lower-than-expected rate of return, the Enrolled Actuary will calculate a higher-than-expected contribution which, under current law, must be contributed by the employer (his means that the employer bears the investment risk and not the individual employee)

Which plans are better for younger (or older) participants?

- because of the special plan qualification rules (including limits on contributions into defined contribution plans and limits on benefits paid from defined benefit plans):
  - younger employees will generally have larger accounts at age 65 (or any other reasonable retirement age) from a defined contribution plan than the equivalent lump sum of any benefit that can be provided under a defined benefit plan — primarily due to the impact of compound interest over long periods of time

- older employees will generally accrue larger benefits at age 65 (or any other reasonable retirement age) from a defined benefit plan than any account that can be accumulated under a defined contribution plan—due to the large funding that is allowed over short periods of time
- these general statements assume that an individual would either get the greatest allocations allowed under a defined contribution plan each and every year, or that the individual would receive the greatest benefit allowed at retirement from a defined benefit plan

What is a money purchase plan?

- the plan document defines exactly what amount will be contributed for each plan participant (such as a certain percentage of salary)
- the employer must contribute the amount promised

What is a profit sharing plan?

- the plan document defines exactly how any contribution will be divided and allocated among the participant's accounts, which can be based on:
  - salary
  - permitted disparity (those with salaries in excess of the Social Security Taxable Wage Base will be favored)
  - a combination of age, service and/or salary (those who are older or have been employed longer are favored)
  - cross testing to pass the nondiscrimination tests (as discussed in Chapter 8) (those who are Highly Compensated Employees are favored)
- the employer determines each year what contribution it would like to make to the plan (the employer does not need to actually show a profit on its corporate returns to make a contribution)
- there are rules that if an employer goes too many years without making a substantial contribution, then the IRS may deem the plan terminated based on facts and circumstances

What is a traditional 401(k) plan?

- each year, the participant determines how much salary is not needed for current living expenses, and elects the amount he or she would like to be deferred into the plan
- the employer must honor the election (as long as it doesn't exceed statutory limits) and take the elective deferral out of the employee's pay check and timely deposit it into the plan
- salary deferrals into a traditional 401(k) plan are excluded from the employee's Gross Income until a future year when distributed (but the deferral is subject to payroll taxes in the year earned)
- the employer can voluntarily match all or a portion of salary deferrals

What is a Roth 401(k) plan?

- most of the basic rules of a traditional 401(k) plan are applicable to Roth 401(k) plans (or Roth-designated accounts within a traditional 401(k) plan)

- each year, the participant determines how much salary is not needed for current living expenses, and elects the amount he or she would like to be contributed into the plan
- the employer must honor the election (as long as it doesn't exceed statutory limits) and take the designated Roth contribution out of the employee's pay check and timely deposit it into the plan
- designated Roth contributions into a 401(k) plan are included in the employee's Gross Income in the year earned (and are subject to payroll taxes in the year earned), but will not be included in the individual's Gross Income when distributed in a future year (if the account was established for at least 5 years and distributions occur after the individual has attained age 59½)
- the employer can voluntarily match all or a portion of designated Roth contributions

What is an automatic enrollment feature in a 401(k) plan?

- Congress has accepted the psychological phenomenon of inertia, and now allows employers sponsoring a 401(k) plan to automatically enroll eligible employees on the day of hire, allowing them to cease salary deferrals at any time
  - in a plan without an automatic enrollment feature, the new employee receives tons of paperwork and information on the date of hire, including election forms and information about the 401(k) plan, and then must take an affirmative step in deciding how much salary to defer, most likely decide how the deferrals will be invested, and then go to the payroll or human resources department and submit the completed forms
  - in a plan with an automatic enrollment feature, the new employee will receive notices and information about being automatically enrolled in the 401(k) plan on the date of hire, and if he or she decides that the salary deferral election should be stopped, decreased or increased, or if the investment mix should be changed from the default, then he or she must take an affirmative step and go to the payroll or human resources department and submit the completed forms
- if the employee affirmatively contacts the plan administrator of a 401(k) plan with an automatic enrollment feature within 90 days of automatic enrollment, then he or she can request an immediate distribution of all deferrals, plus interest (after 90 days, all he or she can do is stop future deferrals, but most likely cannot get an in-service distribution while still an employee)
- there are two levels of automatic enrollment features:
  - in an eligible automatic enrollment contribution arrangement (EACA), the employer simply has assurance that the feature will not violate any state law with the feature
    - the default percentage of salary must be uniform for all employees
    - the plan sponsor selects a reasonable and prudent default investment
    - sufficient notice and communications must be provided to employees when hired and each year thereafter
  - in a qualified automatic contribution arrangement (QACA), the plan will automatically pass the nondiscrimination and Top Heavy tests (as described in Chapter 8)

- meets all requirements of an EACA
- escalating deferrals (at least 3% of salary in first year of employment, at least 4% of salary in the second year, at least 5% of salary in third year, and at least 6% of salary in successive years — but never to exceed 10% of salary unless the participant affirmatively elects to defer an amount higher than 10% of salary)
- the employer agrees to either match 100% of the first 1% of salary deferred and 50% of the next 5% of salary deferred, or agrees to make a money-purchase type contribution of 3% of salary for every eligible employee (even those that elect to make no salary deferrals)
- additional information must be included in the notices
- because of the income tax implications, an automatic enrollment feature does not make sense in a Roth 401(k) plan

What are defined benefit plans?
- any plan that is not a plan with individual accounts (usually a pool of assets) and/or where the benefits are not based solely on the accumulation of contributions and fund earnings (usually some component of the benefit is guaranteed)
- they can be based on:
  - a flat benefit (a flat dollar amount multiplied by the number of years worked with the employer)
  - a fixed benefit (an income replacement percentage multiplied by the participant's average salary)
  - a unit benefit (a unit income replacement percentage multiplied by the participant's average salary and the number of years worked with the employer)

What is a statutory hybrid plan (such as a cash balance plan)?
- although a defined benefit plan, subject to minimum funding under the direction of an Enrolled Actuary and annual premiums to the PBGC , each participant's retirement benefit is calculated and communicated as a current (hypothetical) account
- unlike a defined contribution plan, which is simply invested and the accounts increase at whatever actual rate of return is realized, in a hybrid defined benefit plan, the interest credits are guaranteed, and the employer contributions will fluctuate in order to fund those guaranteed promises
- Congress had made cash balance designs going forward absolutely legal and proper, but there is still some litigation winding through the federal courts on purported age discrimination and other issues with conversions to cash balance plans before Congress added the statutory provisions

What is a combined DB/401(k) plan?
- until 2010, pre-tax elective salary deferrals could only be deposited into a 401(k) plan that is part of a defined contribution plan
- starting in 2010, certain small employers can allow pre-tax elective salary deferrals into a 401(k) plan that is part of a defined benefit plan if:
  - in the defined benefit portion of the plan, which will most likely be a cash balance type hybrid design, the pay credit must be at least

- 2% of salary for any participant who has not attained age 30
- 4% of salary for any participant who is between 31 and 40
- 6% of salary for any participant who is between 41 and 50
- 8% of salary for any participant who has attained age 51
- in the 401(k) portion of the plan
  - the automatic enrollment rules apply
  - the employer must match at least 50% of deferrals of up to 4% of salary

A. Distinguishing between Defined Contribution and Defined Benefit Plans

1. The Two Mutually Exclusive Types of Retirement Plans

Legal Definitions at IRC §§ 414(i) and 414(j) (Although No Actual Cross-reference from IRC § 401(a))

Under IRC § 414(i), "[f]or purposes of this part, the term 'defined contribution plan' means a plan which provides for an individual account for each participant and for benefits based solely on the amount contributed to the participant's account, and any income, expenses, gains and losses, and any forfeitures of accounts of other participants which may be allocated to such participant's account."

Here is your first lesson in statutory construction:

The opening statement, "for purposes of this part," means that this definition carries through for all purposes of IRC §§ 401 through 420. If we go to the table of contents of Title 26 of the United States Code (the Internal Revenue Code), we find:

- Subtitle A is Income Taxes, which includes IRC §§ 1 through 1563
- Chapter 1 is Normal Taxes and Surtaxes, which include IRC §§ 1 through 1400U-3
- Subchapter D is Deferred Compensation, etc., which includes IRC §§ 401 through 436
- Part I is Pension, Profit-Sharing, Stock Bonus Plans, etc., which includes IRC §§ 401 through 420

Therefore, while the term "defined contribution plan" might have a different legal definition elsewhere in the Internal Revenue Code, for purposes of IRC §§ 401 through 420, anytime that term is used, it has the definition found at IRC § 414(i).

From the definition, we see that a defined contribution plan has three basic features:

First, there must be a plan. There is no special definition of a "plan" elsewhere in IRC § 414, although many of the definitions of the various subsections of IRC § 414 also use the term "plan." Therefore, the legal way to interpret a "plan" under IRC § 414 is to apply its common usage. Please note that in Chapter 11, we define a "plan" for purposes of ERISA, and even though the ERISA law amended parts of the Internal Revenue Code, we have no legal basis in applying that particular definition of "plan" for purposes of ERISA to the Code.

Second, the plan assets are either actually separated into individual accounts "owned" by each plan participant, or, if they are combined and aggregately invested, then there is a clear accounting method that separates them out into individual accounts.

Third, the benefit owed to each participant is based solely on the accumulation of contributions, forfeitures (as described in Chapter 7), and fund earnings. The key legal term here is solely, which is different than other legal terms we see sprinkled throughout the Code, like primarily or substantially. Solely indicates that there can be no other component or factor that determines a participant's benefit. This point will become clearer throughout the remainder of this chapter.

Although this Section II of the textbook deals with the income tax issues of a qualified plan and Section III of this textbook deals with the labor and employment issues of ERISA, please note an identical definition of a defined contribution plan or an "individual account plan" is found at ERISA § 3(34), other than it uses the term "pension plan" instead of simply "plan."

Then, under IRC § 414(j), "[f]or purposes of this part, the term 'defined benefit plan' means any plan which is not a defined contribution plan."

From this definition, we see that there is still a requirement for a "plan," but if it fails either or both of the requirements for a defined contribution plan, such as no way to allocate the assets on an individual basis (*i.e.*, the plan assets are simply a collective pool available for all participants) or the benefit is based on more than the accumulation of contributions, forfeitures and fund earnings (*i.e.*, the benefit is based on a formula or there is some sort of guarantee made by the employer on rates of return), then it is automatically and unconditionally considered to be a defined benefit plan.

A participant's benefits under a defined benefit plan are generally determined under a formula that takes into account factors such as plan year compensation or a stated dollar amount and years of service with the employer. A participant's benefit is generally expressed as a monthly pension payable upon the participant's retirement at a special normal retirement date. The amount of the benefit payable before a participant's normal retirement date is generally reduced on an actuarial or proportionate basis.

Please note that there is basically the same definition of a defined benefit plan at ERISA § 3(35).

Since a defined benefit plan is legally any plan not considered a defined contribution plan, then we can say that there are only two types of qualified plans, and that they are mutually exclusive. This becomes important as we define hybrid plan designs that have features of both.

Although beyond the scope of this textbook, certain hybrid plans are described in IRC § 414(k), and is treated as a defined contribution plan for certain purposes and a defined benefit plan for others.

2. The Main Differences between Defined Contribution and Defined Benefit Plans

Please note that for the remainder of this chapter, new terms and vocabulary will simply be introduced without much fanfare or explanation. Each term will be defined elsewhere in this Section II of the textbook.

The defined contribution model deals exclusively with inputs: the plan document defines either mandatory or voluntary contributions by the employer and/or the employee, and the statutes set minimum and maximum levels of contributions, and associated employee tax-deferrals and employer deductions. In any defined contribution plan, the benefit that an individual will receive upon retirement consists entirely of the accumulation of contributions, forfeitures and fund earnings, and is usually paid out in a single lump sum. At least once a year, the participant receives a statement reconciling the preceding period's ending account balance with the current period's ending balance.

The defined benefit model deals exclusively with outputs: the plan document defines the benefits that must be funded for and paid out upon retirement, and the statutes set minimum and maximum levels of benefit distributions, and associated employer funding levels and deductions. In any defined benefit plan, the benefit that an individual will receive upon retirement is whatever is promised under the plan document and accrued by the participant (usually based on a combination of compensation and years of service), and is usually expressed as an annual annuity, even though the individual participant can sometimes elect a different form of distribution. At least once every three years, the participant receives a statement reconciling the accrued benefit at the end of the preceding period with the accrued benefit at the end of the current period. Almost all defined benefit plans are insured by the Pension Benefit Guaranty Corporation, and require an annual review of funding levels by an Enrolled Actuary. Because of the required actuarial valuation, the funding requirements are sometimes quite volatile from year to year, which not only impacts the actual contribution required by the employer, but also can impact the business financial statements. Current defined benefit plans generally are funded exclusively with employer contributions, and generally do not allow for employee contributions, whether voluntary or mandatory. Employers can use normal investment vehicles to fund defined benefit plans, or can choose to invest entirely in certain insurance contracts so that no actuarial valuation is required. Defined benefit plans are often touted as being harder to understand than defined contribution plans (even though federal Social Security benefits are modeled after a defined benefit plan), and often times are adopted by small employers that are partnerships where maximizing partner retirement benefits is the primary motivation for the plan.

> *Investment risk:* In all types of defined contribution plans, the risk of large investment losses (especially as the individual approaches retirement age) remains with each individual participant, since the benefit is simply the accumulation of contributions and forfeitures, and once deposited, all associated fund earnings, which can include lower-than-expected rates of return, and in poor economic conditions, even loss of principal.

In all types of defined benefit plans, on the other hand, the risk of large investment losses remains with the employer, since lower-than-expected returns or losses will simply mean that the employer will need to make larger contributions.

Age of employee: The accepted wisdom is that defined contribution plans are generally better for younger employees. However, this argument is only realized in cases where individuals: receive substantial allocations to their accounts continually throughout their careers, whether funded through employee or employer contributions; adopt sound investment strategies that account for diversification and time until retirement, whether invested by the plan fiduciary or by their own elections; properly rollover and maintain prior accounts as they move from job to job throughout their careers; and, upon retirement, frugally withdraw only the amount needed to cover necessary expenses and keep the balance invested in a way that minimizes the risk of large losses. However, even if all of these assumptions come true and the accumulated nest egg for any individual is larger in a defined contribution plan than can have been earned by participating in a defined benefit plan, the individual still has longevity risk, and at some point in time, the defined contribution retirement account balance will be depleted if the individual lives longer than expected.

On the other hand, the accepted wisdom is that defined benefit plans are generally better for older employees. However, this argument is only realized in cases where individuals spend at least a major part of their career with an employer that sponsors a defined benefit plan, and continue working until at least normal retirement age, or until early retirement age if the early retirement benefit is subsidized. If these assumptions come true, then the mathematical present value of the retirement benefits at retirement will oftentimes be greater than the accumulated account balance under a defined contribution plan. Under a traditional retirement plan, the highest benefits accrue to a participant during the final few years before retirement (usually between the ages of 55 and 65).

3. Different Definitions for Pension Plans

Since ERISA was enacted in 1974, when §§ 414(i) and (j) were added to the Code in their current form, there are two types of retirement plans: defined contribution plans and defined benefit plans. However, before ERISA, there were income tax advantages for employer-provided retirement plans, and an old set of Treasury regulations were promulgated that divided the world into pension plans, profit-sharing plans, and stock bonus plans. Those old regulations are still effective, relevant and applicable in the post-ERISA world, and need to be understood.

I am certainly not trying to confuse you at this point. However, understanding the guiding principle from pre-ERISA tax-advantaged retirement plans that were carried over to post-ERISA tax-qualified retirement plans is important. Below are excerpts from those regulations.

Treas. Regs. § 1.401-1, Qualified Pension, Profit-sharing, and Stock Bonus Plans

(a)

***

(2) A qualified pension, profit-sharing, or stock bonus plan is a definite written program and arrangement which is communicated to the employees and which is established and maintained by an employer—

(i) In the case of a pension plan, to provide for the livelihood of the employees or their beneficiaries after the retirement of such employees through the payment of benefits determined without regard to profits (see paragraph (b)(1)(i) of this section);

(ii) In the case of a profit-sharing plan, to enable employees or their beneficiaries to participate in the profits of the employer's trade or business, or in the profits of an affiliated employer who is entitled to deduct his contributions to the plan under section 404(a)(3)(B), pursuant to a definite formula for allocating the contributions and for distributing the funds accumulated under the plan (see paragraph (b)(1)(ii) of this section); and

(iii) In the case of a stock bonus plan, to provide employees or their beneficiaries benefits similar to those of profit-sharing plans, except that such benefits are distributable in stock of the employer, and that the contributions by the employer are not necessarily dependent upon profits. ***.

(3) In order for a trust forming part of a pension, profit-sharing, or stock bonus plan to constitute a qualified trust under section 401(a), the following tests must be met:

(i) It must be created or organized in the United States *** and it must be maintained at all times as a domestic trust in the United States;

(ii) It must be part of a pension, profit-sharing, or stock bonus plan established by an employer for the exclusive benefit of his employees or their beneficiaries ***;

(iii) It must be formed or availed of for the purpose of distributing to the employees or their beneficiaries the corpus and income of the fund accumulated by the trust in accordance with the plan ***;

(iv) It must be impossible under the trust instrument at any time before the satisfaction of all liabilities with respect to employees and their beneficiaries under the trust, for any part of the corpus or income to be used for, or diverted to, purposes other than for the exclusive benefit of the employees or their beneficiaries (see § 1.401-2);

(v) It must be part of a plan which benefits prescribed percentages of the employees, or which benefits such employees as qualify under a classification set up by the employer and found by the Commissioner not to be discriminatory in favor of certain specified classes of employees (see § 1.401-3 and, in addition, see § 1.401-12 for special rules as to plans covering owner-employees);

(vi) It must be part of a plan under which contributions or benefits do not discriminate in favor of certain specified classes of employees (see § 1.401-4);

(vii) It must be part of a plan which provides the nonforfeitable rights described in section 401(a)(7) (see § 1.401-6);

(viii) If the trust forms part of a pension plan, the plan must provide that forfeitures must not be applied to increase the benefits of any employee would receive under such plan (see § 1.401-7);

(ix) It must, if the plan benefits any self-employed individual who is an owner-employee, satisfy the additional requirements for qualification contained in section 401(a)(10) and (d).

***

(b)

***

(2) The term 'plan' implies a permanent as distinguished from a temporary program. Thus, although the employer may reserve the right to change or terminate the plan, and to discontinue contributions thereunder, the abandonment of the plan for any reason other than business necessity within a few years after it has taken effect will be evidence that the plan from its inception was not a bona fide program for the exclusive benefit of employees in general. *** The permanency of the plan will be indicated by all of the surrounding facts and circumstances, including the likelihood of the employer's ability to continue contributions as provided under the plan.

***

Four points from these regulations are incredibly important to understand before dissecting all of the other specific qualification rules in the current version of IRC § 401(a).

First, any qualified retirement plan must be a definite written program and arrangement. The term "arrangement" includes the plan document that details the exact retirement benefit promises made by the employer as well as the trust document that details how employer contributions are deposited, invested, and ultimately paid out as benefits to the plan participants and their named beneficiaries upon death. One of the unique features of a qualified retirement plan is the requirement of a separate trust, with a separate legal identity—thus, once an employer makes a contribution to the trust to fund the plan, the assets are immediately considered plan assets, and no longer part of the employer's general assets.

Second is the requirement that the promises made by the employer, in writing, are actually communicated to employees. As discussed in Chapter 15 of this text book, the employer will generally only provide a Summary Plan Description to the employees, which is often simply part of the general employee handbook or intranet section of the website, but the employees always have the legal right to request a copy of the actual plan document. In addition, it is clear that qualified retirement plan benefits can only be promised to employees of the employer, which generally excludes independent contractors or leased employees (and which would normally exclude sole proprietors or partners in a partnership, had Congress not specifically amended the Code to allow them to be deemed employees only for purposes of participating in a qualified plan).

Third is the use of the term "exclusive benefit." The Regulations later state that "[i]f the plan is so designed as to amount to a subterfuge for the distribution of profits to shareholders, it will not qualify as a plan for the exclusive benefit of employees even though other employees who are not shareholders are also included under the plan." Therefore, the surrounding facts and circumstances must prove the employer's intent in establishing the plan in the first place to provide retirement benefits, even though it can thereafter take full advantage of all tax benefits associated with the plan through the Internal Revenue Code. This requirement is amplified by the requirement that the provisions of the legal trust document must make it impossible that once contributed by the employer as a plan contribution, no part of the corpus or income can be used for, or diverted to, purposes other than for the exclusive benefit of the employees or their beneficiaries, at least until all plan liabilities are satisfied.

Fourth, the clear intent of the employer in establishing the plan must be for a permanent program. The employer can always amend or terminate the plan as business goals change, but the longer the plan is maintained, the less that the original intent becomes an issue under IRS scrutiny. Thus, even in a case where a sole proprietor plans on retiring in 7 years, and at that point establishes a qualified plan for her and her two employees, the actions of the sole proprietor must clearly indicate that the business and the plan are likely to continue upon her retirement.

B. Types of Defined Contribution Plans

Please note that nondiscrimination testing is extremely important in the design of defined contribution plans, and although the rules for safe harbor designs and general testing are not discussed in detail until Chapter 8, they need to be mentioned in this chapter.

1. Money Purchase Plan

A money purchase pension plan is a defined contribution plan with a benefit formula that requires a fixed annual employer contribution based on a specified percentage of participant compensation. Thus, the employer is required to deposit the contributions necessary to meet the allocation requirements of the plan document, regardless of profitability, and is subject to a penalty in years that the minimum funding requirement is not met.

There is no formal definition of a money purchase plan, but the term was used in Treasury Regulations at least as far back as 1956, when a generic pension plan was defined as a plan established primarily to provide "definitely determinable benefits to employees over a period of years" or " … in the case of money purchase pension plans, such contributions are fixed without being geared to profits."[1]

Although defined contribution plans for almost all limitations and minimums, Money Purchase plans are considered to be "pension plans" and must therefore comply with the default distribution requirements for married participants and, unlike other qualified defined contribution plans, can only allow in-service distributions of employer contributions after age 62 (both are discussed in further detail in Chapter 9). As with all qualified defined contribution plans, a participant's benefit is based solely on an individual account established on the participant's behalf, consisting of the contributions, forfeitures, income, expenses, gains, and losses allocable to the account each year. Since a money purchase plan imposes a strict liability on employers to make the pre-determined contributions, employers sometimes establish a money purchase plan with a basic promise (such as 10% of compensation), and then couple it with a profit sharing plan that allows additional discretionary contributions in years when the employer is profitable or it is otherwise desirable to make such contributions, and a 401(k) plan that also allows participants to defer some of their compensation.

For example, a 12% money purchase plan document will state "Each participant credited with a Year of Service as of December 31 will receive an allocation of 12% of annual compensation each December 31." Therefore, hypothetically, if Employee A earns $40,000 in 2010, then she will receive an allocation of $4800, and if Employee B earns $140,000 in 2010, then he will receive an allocation of $16,800. Even though Employee B is re-

---

1. Treas. Regs. § 1.401-1(b)(1)(i).

ceiving a higher dollar amount, each employee is receiving an allocation of 12% of his or her salary for that year.

2. Profit Sharing Plan

A profit-sharing plan allows employees to share in the profits, which they arguably helped generate due to being diligent and effective workers. Generally, the employer decides on an annual basis whether or not to make a contribution, and if made, how much. The plan document must provide a definite predetermined formula for allocating the contributions made to the plan among the participants. The allocation formula is generally based on the participant's compensation, which can also consider permitted disparity with social security, an allocation method that considers age and service along with compensation, or in a manner that seems random, but in the end, complies with the nondiscrimination requirements. Since the employer has full discretion to determine the amount of the profit-sharing contributions, it is important that substantial contributions be made to the profit-sharing plan in order to avoid the de facto termination of the plan. Unlike it's name suggests, however, under IRC § 401(a)(27), a contribution to a profit sharing plan no longer depends on actual profits shown on the corporate return.

In all of the various allocation methods, there is a trade off between targeting and maximizing the allocations for the favored employees with the complexity in design, annual testing, and communication with plan participants.

a. Allocations Based on Salary

This is the simplest allocation method to understand and communicate with employees. The employer's profit sharing contribution for any plan year is allocated among all current employees in that year in the same proportion that their respective salary bears to the total of all participants' salaries. Here, every participant receives an equal allocation, when shown as a percentage of salary, and thus the plan by definition does not discriminate in favor of Highly Compensated Employees. However, this might not meet the employer's business goals, as older and longer-serviced employees have less time to accumulate retirement benefits and reap no advantage in the plan for their contributions to the business.

For example, a salary-based profit sharing plan document will state "Each participant credited with a Year of Service as of December 31 will receive an allocation of the employer's discretionary contribution for the year in proportion that his compensation bears to the total compensation for all active participants." Therefore, hypothetically, if total payroll is $2,000,000 for 2010, and the employer decides to make a $100,000 profit sharing contribution, then if Employee A earns $40,000 in 2010, she will receive an allocation of $2000 [40,000 / 2,000,000 * 100,000], and if Employee B earns $140,000 in 2010, then he will receive an allocation of $7000 [140,000 / 2,000,000 * 100,000]. Even though Employee B is receiving a higher dollar amount, each employee is receiving an allocation of 5% of his or her salary for that year, since the employer chose to deposit 5% of total payroll for that year. Notice that here, Employee B (who is assumedly our favored employee) is receiving 7% of the total contribution deposited.

b. *Allocations Based on Permitted Disparity (Social Security Integration)*

Since those employee's who earn compensation in excess of the Social Security Taxable Wage Base (SSTWB) only receive federal Social Security benefits up to the SSTWB (as discussed in Chapter 20), qualified plans are allowed to provide a larger contribution or benefit to these employees. In a profit sharing plan imputed with permitted disparity, the contribution is bifurcated into two parts, the first part is allocated only to those employees earning compensation in excess of the SSTWB (in the same proportion that their respective excess salary bears to the total of all participant's excess salaries) and the second part is allocated to all participants (including these higher paid employees) in the same proportion that their respective total salary bears to the total of all participant's total salaries. Thus, the higher paid employees get two allocations while lower paid get only one. In order for the higher paid employees to get a greater allocation from the single contribution, all other participants will necessarily receive a lesser allocation than they would under a basic allocation formula based on salary. As long as the formula complies with the permitted disparity rules, then the plan by definition does not discriminate in favor of Highly Compensated Employees. While a permitted disparity formula allows higher paid employees to receive a larger allocation as a percentage of salary than lower paid employees, sometimes employers have a difficult time explaining the virtues of such a formula to the lower paid employees.

For example, a permitted-disparity-based profit sharing plan document will state "Each participant credited with a Year of Service as of December 31 will receive an allocation of the sum of (a) and (b), where (a) is 5.7% of compensation in excess of the current year's Social Security Taxable Wage Base and (b) is the balance of the employer's discretionary contribution for the year, after offsetting all contributions defined in (a), in proportion that his compensation bears to the total compensation for all active participants." Therefore, hypothetically, if total payroll is $2,000,000 for 2010, and the employer decides to make a $100,000 profit sharing contribution, and if the SSTWB for 2010 is $106,800 and if Employee B is the only participant earning a salary in excess of $106,800, then if Employee A earns $40,000 in 2010, she will receive an allocation of (a) 0 + (b) 1962 [(40,000 / 2,000,000) * (100,000 — 1892)], for a total of $1,962, and if Employee B earns $140,000 in 2010, then he will receive an allocation of (a) 1892 [.057 * (140000 — 106800)] + (b) 6868 [(140,000 / 2,000,000) * (100,000 — 1892)], for a total of $8,760. Therefore, Employee A receives an allocation of 4.9% of her salary and Employee B receives an allocation of 6.26% of his salary. So, if the employer is still contributing the same $100,000 for 2010, in a permitted disparity plan, those employees with salaries lower than the SSTWB will receive lesser allocations than under a salary-based profit sharing plan, and those employees with salaries in excess of the SSTWB will get larger allocations. Although totally legal and sanctioned, the design of the plan document and communications to plan participants just got more complicated with this type of design, so the sponsoring employer needs to determine if the advantages of a permitted disparity profit sharing plan (*i.e.,* higher allocations to favored employees) outweighs the disadvantages (*i.e.,* higher communication costs). Notice that here, Employee B (who is assumedly our favored employee) is receiving 8.76% of the total contribution deposited.

c. *Allocations Based on Age and Service Weighting*

There are two ways to approach this method: either the plan document includes a chart or method that converts compensation, age, and/or service into points, or the document establishes a way to calculate the present value of each future $1 of expected compensation until retirement.

In a points allocation approach, each employee is credited with a specific number of points for years of service, age, and compensation (or any combination). The employer contribution is allocated among all employees in the same proportion that their respective credited points bear to the total of all participants' credited points. Although a uniform points allocation formula generally is deemed a safe harbor plan design, and is not subject to the full nondiscrimination testing, there is still a small test that needs to be performed each year to prove nondiscrimination. Uniform allocation plans are somewhat complicated to administer, but the employer is truly able to determine exactly how to reward employees who are closer to retirement, have worked longer, and who earn higher salaries.

For example, a points allocation-based profit sharing plan document will state "Each participant credited with a Year of Service as of December 31 will receive an allocation of the employer's discretionary contribution for the year in proportion that his total points bears to the total points for all active participants; where each participant is credited with 1 point per $100 of salary, 2 points per year of attained age, and 10 points per year of service." Therefore, hypothetically, if total points is 17,000 for 2010, and the employer decides to make a $100,000 profit sharing contribution, then if Employee A earns $40,000 in 2009 and is 35 years old and has been employed for 5 years, she will receive an allocation of $3,059 [((40,000 / 100) + (35 * 2) + (5*10)) / 17000 * 100,000], and if Employee B earns $140,000 in 2010 and is 50 years old and has been employed for 15 years, he will receive an allocation of $9,706 [((140,000 / 100) + (50 * 2) + (15*10)) / 17000 * 100,000]. Therefore, Employee A receives an allocation of 7.65% of her salary and Employee B receives an allocation of 6.93% of his salary. So, if the employer is still contributing the same $100,000 for 2010, in an age-weighted points profit sharing plan, those employees with higher salaries, older ages, and longer service will generally receive higher allocations. As you should be noticing the pattern, the design of the plan document and communications to plan participants just got even more complicated with this type of design, so the sponsoring employer needs to determine if the advantages of a uniform points allocation profit sharing plan (*i.e.*, higher allocations to older and longer-service employees) outweighs the disadvantages (*i.e.*, higher communication and compliance costs). Notice that here, Employee B (who is assumedly our favored employee) is receiving 9.71% of the total contribution deposited.

In an age weighted approach, the employer contribution is allocated among all employees in the same proportion that their respective present value of future salaries bear to the total of all participant's present value of future salaries. Here, some older or higher paid participants might receive an allocation, when shown as a percentage of salary, greater than other participants. If the resulting allocations are uniform for each participant, then the formula is deemed to be a safe harbor plan, compliant with the nondiscrimination tests. However, if the employer truly wants to skew the allocations as much as is legally possible in favor of the older Highly Compensated Employees, then the plan will be cross-tested to pass the nondiscrimination testing. Although not required by law, an Enrolled Actuary (or other competent retirement plan professional) can determine the present value or at least help the third party administrator develop the general software. Age weighted formulas capture some of the advantages of a defined benefit plan, in that the allocations generally increase as participants age, but without the guarantees inherent in a defined benefit plan.

For example, an age-weighted-based profit sharing plan document will state "Each participant credited with a Year of Service as of December 31 will receive an allocation of the employer's discretionary contribution for the year in proportion that the present value of his future salary bears to the total present value of the future salary for all plan participants; where present values are determined using the interest rate and mortality table shown in Appendix A." Therefore, hypothetically, if the employer decides to make a $100,000 profit sharing contribution, and the total present value of future salaries for all participants in 2010 is $12,000,000, then if Employee A has a present value of future salary of $500,000 in 2010 and is 35 years old, she will receive an allocation of $4,167 [(500000 / 12000000) * 100,000], and if Employee B has a present value of future salary of $1,500,000 in 2009 and is 50 years old, he will receive an allocation of $12,500 [(1500000 / 12000000) * 100,000]. Here, assume that an actuary or computer software calculated the present values. Therefore, Employee A receives an allocation of 10.41% of her salary and Employee B receives an allocation of 8.93% of his salary. So, if the employer is still contributing the same $100,000 for 2009, in an age-weighted profit sharing plan, those employees with higher salaries and older ages will generally receive higher allocations. Notice that here, Employee B (who is assumedly our favored employee) is receiving 12.5% of the total contribution deposited.

d. Allocations Based on Cross Testing

In a cross-tested, or new comparability approach, the employer contribution is allocated among all employees based on a table in the plan document. Here, some favored participants might receive an allocation, when shown as a percentage of salary, greater than other participants. The plan must demonstrate, on an annual basis, that the allocation does not discriminate in favor of Highly Compensated Employees. In practice, the Plan Administrator usually backs into the necessary table based on what is needed to pass the test for the year. Although not required by law, an Enrolled Actuary (or other competent retirement plan professional) generally helps to back into the table; whereas the plan's attorney will amend the plan on an annual basis to insert the proper table for that year's allocations.

For example, a new comparability profit sharing plan document will state "Each participant credited with a Year of Service as of December 31 will receive an allocation based on placement in groups in Appendix A; where every participant who is in Group A shall receive an allocation of 20.44% of salary, and every participant who is in Group B shall receive an allocation of 5% of salary." Therefore, although a profit sharing plan, it starts to look like a money purchase plan, and the employer must contribute the amounts promised to be allocated—however, unlike a money purchase plan, the plan consultants back into which employees were in group A and which employees were in group B on an annual basis (based on just passing the mathematical nondiscrimination tests, as discussed in Chapter 8), and the plan attorney amends Appendix A on an annual basis. This becomes the most complicated and costly profit sharing plan design, and the most difficult to communicate to employees.

3. Stock Ownership Plans

a. Stock Bonus Plans

A stock bonus plan is a qualified plan that mirrors the rules of a qualified profit sharing plan in all aspects, except that the benefits are distributable in stock of the employer company.[2] A stock bonus plan must[3] (1) allow participants to demand that benefits are distributed in employer securities (even if not readily tradable) but the plan can pay out in cash in certain circumstances,[4] and (2) distribute benefits within 1 year of attaining the plan's normal retirement age, becoming disabled, or dying or within 5 years of any other separation from service, and, unless the participant elects otherwise, the account balance will be distributed in substantially equal periodic payments over a period of 5 years, or, if the account balance exceeds $800,000, then 5 years plus an extra fractional year for each additional $160,000.[5]

b. Employee Stock Ownership Plans (ESOP)
Special Legal Definitions Are at IRC §§ 409(h) and 4975(e)

An employee stock ownership plan (ESOP) is a qualified defined contribution plan in which the participants' account balances must be primarily invested in qualifying employer securities. An ESOP must also:

- Allow participants to demand that benefits are distributed in employer securities (even if not readily tradable), but the plan can pay out in cash in certain circumstances;
- Distribute benefits within 1 year of attaining the plan's normal retirement age, becoming disabled, or dying or within 5 years of any other separation from service, and, unless the participant elects otherwise, the account balance will be distributed in substantially equal periodic payments over a period of 5 years, or, if the account balance exceeds $800,000, then 5 years plus an extra fractional year for each additional $160,000;
- If stock is sold to an ESOP, and the taxpayer is claiming the right to not recognize and pay taxes on a portion of the gain, then there are restrictions on the accrual of ESOP assets for certain individuals;
- If an S Corporation owns the shares allocated in an ESOP, then there are restrictions on the accrual of ESOP assets for certain individuals;
- If the employer securities need to be registered with the Securities Exchange Commission (usually if a public company), then the participants must have certain voting rights.

As long as an ESOP has no features of a cash or deferred arrangement 401(k) plan (i.e., voluntary employee contributions paired with employer matching or nonelective contributions), and as long as the ESOP plan is separate and distinct from all other plans maintained by the employer, then the ESOP does not need to comply with the new diversification requirements under IRC § 401(a)(35) for defined contribution plans.

There are many income tax advantages in ESOPS for the employer and the participants, and a leveraged ESOP is a good way for a business to receive a loan. However, other considerations are that actual ownership of the business is being transferred to the employees, leveraged ESOPs have special accounting issues, and there are securities law and corporate law aspects of ESOPs. ESOPs are therefore extremely complicated, and require expert advisors and counselors.

---

2. Treas. Regs. § 1.401-1(b)(1)(iii).
3. IRC § 401(a)(23).
4. IRC § 409(h).
5. IRC § 409(o).

4. Cash or Deferred Arrangement (a.k.a. §401(k) Plan)

Special Legal Definitions at IRC §§401(k), 401(m), and 402A

A §401(k) plan is a defined contribution plan that permits participants to elect to make pre-tax salary deferrals or after-tax Roth contributions to the plan out of their pay. The original provisions of section 401(k) allowed only pre-tax employee contributions, which is why they are officially called cash or deferred arrangements. Although employers maintaining a 401(k) plan may deposit "matching contributions" on amounts deferred, the matching requirements are defined at IRC §401(m) and the IRS deems the matching portion a "separate" 401(m) plan. Employers are also allowed to make nonelective profit-sharing contributions to all eligible participants, regardless of whether they elected to defer or contribute a portion of their salary. Special nondiscrimination rules require that the employee elective deferrals or contributions, and employer matches or nonelective contributions, will be limited for the group of Highly Compensated Employees based on the averages for the non-Highly Compensated Employees, unless the plan is designed as a safe-harbor or as a compliant automatic enrollment feature plan. Additionally, because a 401(k) plan is a retirement savings vehicle and not any participant's personal piggy bank, distributions of employee contributions while a participant is still employed are generally restricted except upon hardship of the employee.

a. Traditional 401(k) Plans

A traditional 401(k) plan is one that allows for pre-tax elective salary deferrals. The plan can include employer matching contributions or qualified nonelective contributions. Distributions of the salary deferrals while the employee is actively employed are limited, and can only be distributed as hardship withdrawals. The advantage to the participant of traditional tax-free salary deferrals is that the salary deferrals are not taxed until received as a distribution, but the amount taxable each year upon retirement will consist of both a return of contributions and associated fund earnings.

For example, if a participant's annual compensation is $50,000, and she voluntarily elects to defer 5% into her employer's 401(k) plan, then at the end of the year, she will have received $47,500 take-home pay (which will be included in her Gross Income) and will have deferred $2500 into the plan (which won't be subject to income tax until some future year when she receives it, plus associated fund earnings).

b. Roth 401(k) Plans

Statutory Rules at IRC §402A

Beginning in 2006, employers were allowed to add a qualified Roth contribution program to their traditional 401(k) plans. A qualified Roth contribution program is one that allows after-tax employee designated Roth contributions. Other than the income tax attributes of the participants' separate designated Roth accounts, the plan must conform in all other aspects to a traditional 401(k) plan, and can therefore include employer matching contributions. The advantage to the participant of after-tax designated Roth contributions is that as long as they remain invested in the qualified trust for at least five years, then all distributions of the return of contributions and associated fund earnings are received tax-free if taken after age 59½. The five-year holding period represents an additional burden on the employer, since the plan administrator is responsible for keeping track of such a period of participation for each employee and the amount of investment in the contract. Please note that if an employer added a Roth contribution program on January 1, 2006, then the earliest that any participant could possibly take a qualified Roth distribution is January 1, 2011.

For example, if a participant's annual compensation is $50,000, and she voluntarily elects to contribute 5% into her employer's Roth 401(k) plan, then at the end of the year, she will have received $47,500 take-home pay but will include the full $50,000 in her Gross Income and will have deferred $2500 into the plan (which won't be subject to income tax if she receives it, plus associated fund earnings, sometime after a five year period and after she has attained age 59½).

c. Automatic Enrollment Features in 401(k) Plans
Statutory Rules at IRC §§ 401(k)(13) and 414(w)

Beginning in 2007, a § 401(k) plan may have an automatic enrollment feature through which the employer can automatically reduce employees' wages by a fixed percentage or dollar amount and contribute that amount to the plan. An employee that does not want to be subject to this feature must opt out of the contribution via automatic wage reduction or must affirmatively choose to contribute a different percentage. Congress believes that a combination of complacency and inertia will lead to more employees being covered under a 401(k) than without the automatic enrollment feature. In both traditional and Roth 401(k) plans, it is up to the employee to affirmatively make an election before the employer can appropriately withhold money from a paycheck and deposit it into a plan; however, with the automatic enrollment features, the default is participating in the plan unless the employee makes an affirmative election to stop deferring. The employer chooses between an eligible automatic contribution arrangement ("EACA") and a qualified automatic contribution arrangement ("QACA").

Eligible Automatic Contribution Arrangement:
- Cash or deferred arrangement: participants can choose between cash or salary deferrals into the plan;
- Uniformity requirement: the default elective contribution is a uniform percentage of compensation, and the participant is treated as having made the salary deferral election;
- Default investment: in the absence of any affirmative investment election, the employer selects a proper default investment for the participants;
- Notice: within a reasonable period of time before each plan year, a notice with sufficient information about the automatic enrollment feature and the participants rights, written in a manner calculated to be understood by the average plan participant, must be provided.

Qualified Automatic Contribution Arrangement:
- Meets all of the requirements for an EACA;
- Automatic deferral: each employee eligible to participate in the arrangement is treated as having elected to have the employer make elective contributions in an amount equal to at least 3% of compensation in the first year, then at least 4% in the second year, then at least 5% in the third year, and then at least 6% of compensation in years thereafter (or any greater uniform percentages of compensation up to 10%), but has the option to elect out;

- Employer contributions: the employer chooses to either provide a nonelective contribution of at least 3% of compensation for all non Highly Compensated Employees or a matching contribution of 100% of the first 1% of compensation any non HCE deferred plus 50% of the next 5% of compensation deferred by any non Highly Compensated Employee;
- Notice: within a reasonable period of time before each plan year, a notice with sufficient information about the automatic enrollment feature and the participants rights, written in a manner calculated to be understood by the average plan participant, must be provided.

If an employee elects to withdraw salary deferrals (and related earnings) made to an EACA or QACA within 90 days of the date of the first elective contribution, the following tax consequences apply:

- The amount of any such withdrawal is includible in the employee's Gross Income for the employee's taxable year in which the distribution is made;
- No additional tax on early distributions is imposed;
- The automatic enrollment arrangement is not treated as violating any restriction on distributions under the Code solely by reason of allowing the withdrawal; and
- In the case of a corrective distribution, employer matching contributions are forfeited or subject to such other treatment as the IRS may prescribe.

ERISA preempts any state law that would prohibit or restrict the inclusion in a plan of an automatic enrollment program, subject to minimum standards to be established by the DOL for such arrangements in order for preemption to apply. A §401(k) plan consisting solely of contributions made pursuant to a qualified automatic enrollment program is not subject to the nondiscrimination and Top-Heavy rules (as discussed in Chapter 8).

5. SEPs, SIMPLEs, and Payroll Deduction IRAs

Special Legal Definitions at IRC §§ 408(a), 408(k), 408(p) and 408A

Congress allows some smaller employers to adopt plans with less administrative responsibility. Of course, in exchange for simplicity, the employer gives up options of excluding certain groups of employees or from providing different benefits to certain groups of employees. While the following plans are still technically defined contribution plans (because there are individual accounts and the benefits consist solely of the accumulation of contributions, forfeitures and fund earnings), they are much simpler to administer than the other forms of qualified defined contribution plans (although they have less flexibility on the employer's part and lower limits).

a. Payroll Deduction IRAs

Individual Retirement Accounts are not employer plans, but are rather a method for an individual to save for retirement on his or her own. Basically, an individual goes to a bank or other financial institution and either contributes money into a traditional IRA (and takes a deduction on his or her personal income tax return for deposits but will include all distributions in Gross Income when received in the future) or into a Roth IRA, (and takes no deduction on his or her personal income tax return but will exclude all distributions in Gross Income when received in the future if held for 5 years and distributions occur after attainment of age 59½). The individual then chooses an investment strategy or allows the bank or financial institution custodian to set investment strategies. As long as the individual's Adjusted Gross Income is low enough (different levels for single taxpayers as opposed to married couples), then a total contribution to all IRAs and Roth IRAs for 2010 of $5,000 is allowed for individuals under age 50, and a total contribution of $6,000 is allowed for individuals who are at least 50 years old.

When completing the 2010 income tax return (think April 15 of 2011), the individual can make the 2010 contribution. The trouble is, however, most individuals, especially those with moderate to low Adjusted Gross Incomes, do not have that spare $5,000 or $6,000 laying around to contribute. Those individuals that are responsible will take a portion out of each pay check and contribute, so that the funding is spread out throughout the year. A payroll deduction IRA is a simple gesture by the employer to automatically take a portion out of the individual employee's paycheck, obviously at his or her affirmative and voluntary election, and transfer it to the individual's IRA of choice. The employer might even select a default bank or financial institution for the employees. A payroll deduction IRA is therefore not really an employer provided retirement vehicle, but is simply a method of spreading an individual's voluntary contributions to an IRA over a year so that no single contribution seems too painful to imagine, and provides the automatic transfer so that the money can't be spent on other consumption.

Please note that at the time of the publication of this textbook, a major initiative of the Obama administration is to set up mandatory automatic enrollment IRAs (similar to automatic enrollment 401(k) programs) if the employer does not otherwise sponsor a qualified retirement plan.

b. SEPs

A simplified employee pension plan (SEP) is an arrangement in which the employer selects an appropriate bank or financial institution , and then establishes and makes contributions directly to each employee's individual retirement account (IRA) or individual retirement annuity. The employer's SEP contribution must be based on a uniform percentage of compensation that is made available to all eligible employees. The employer contribution cannot discriminate in favor of Highly Compensated Employees, but it can allow for permitted disparity integration with social security. There must be a written plan document which includes an allocation formula specifying the requirements which an employee must satisfy to share in an allocation, and the manner in which the amount allocated is computed. However, the employer may decide the level of contributions that will be made to the SEP each year, and can therefore amend the document as the level of desired contribution changes. This written agreement may be satisfied by adopting an Internal Revenue Service (IRS) model SEP using Form 5305-SEP, Simplified Employee Pension—Individual Retirement Accounts Contribution Agreement, a prototype SEP that was approved by the IRS, or an individually designed SEP may be adopted. Similar to all other defined contribution plans, the employer may contribute a deductible amount up to 25% of the participant's compensation. Normally, SEP participants may not make salary reduction elections, unless they participate in a SARSEP with a salary reduction provision in effect as of December 31, 1996.

While SEPs were proposed just for small employers, the statute does not reflect this restriction, and any employer is allowed to sponsor a SEP, even sole proprietors. The SEP must include all employees: (1) who have attained 21 years of age; (2) who have been employed by the employer for at least three of the preceding five years; and (3) who have earned at least $450 in compensation from the employer for the year. All other employees can be excluded from participation. The SEP must allow for unlimited withdrawals by the plan participants. Participants must be immediately and fully vested in employer contributions made to a SEP.

Some advantages of a SEP for a small employer are: very reduced annual reporting to the government; since all eligible employees participate and receive uniform allocations, there are no annual tests required; the bank or financial institution makes all investment choices; and notices only need to be communicated to Participants eligible to elect salary deferrals to a pre-1987 SARSEP.

c. SIMPLEs

A Savings Incentive Match Plan for Employees (SIMPLE) is a defined contribution plan that is exclusively available to small employers. For this purpose, a "small employer" is an employer which had no more than 100 employees who received at least $5,000 of compensation from the employer for the preceding year. There is a two year grace period for an employer that establishes a SIMPLE while an eligible small employer, but at some point in time, has more than 100 employees. There are two types of SIMPLE plans that an employer can choose: A SIMPLE IRA and a SIMPLE 401(k).

SIMPLE IRA: As the name indicates, the employer selects an appropriate bank or financial institution , and then establishes and makes contributions directly to each employee's individual retirement account (IRA) or individual retirement annuity. The employer must provide notice to the participants that they may be transferred without cost or penalty to another individual account or annuity. All employees who have received at least $5000 in compensation in any of the 2 preceding years, or anyone likely to receive $5000 in the current year, must participate in the plan. The SIMPLE IRA must be the only plan or qualified plan maintained by the employer. The SIMPLE IRA must be in writing, and the small employer can either adopt a document offered by the financial institution, or can use one of two forms published by the IRS.

The participants in a SIMPLE IRA must make an election to either defer a portion of their salary (or earned income if self employed) into his or her SIMPLE account, or receive that amount as cash salary. The employee can make elections during the 60-day period before the beginning of any year, and at any point during the year can cancel the salary deferral for the remainder of the year. The maximum salary deferral is $10,000, and if the participant is over age 50, then additional catch-up contributions of up to $2,500. The employer must make contributions, and can either match 100% of the first 3% of compensation deferred by any Participant or can choose to provide a non-elective employer contribution of 2% of salary to every eligible employee, regardless of whether or not they elect to make salary deferrals. Employer contributions and employee deferrals must be fully vested at all times. The employer must deposit the salary deferrals within 30 days.

SIMPLE 401(k): As the name indicates, the employer establishes a 401(k) plan, as described below, where the only elective salary deferrals and the only employer contributions (either a 100% matching contribution or a 2% across the board non elective contribution) allowed are those allowed for a SIMPLE IRA. All definitions for a SIMPLE IRA apply to a SIMPLE 401(k). Although a SIMPLE 401(k) plan is a qualified defined contribution plan, subject to all of the rules for a qualified plan (including fiduciary duties, hardship withdrawals, and the normal reporting and disclosure requirements), a

SIMPLE 401(k) plan is deemed to automatically meet the ADP tests and all of the top-heavy rules. Please note that safe harbor 401(k) plans also allow plan designs that are deemed to meet the nondiscrimination and top-heavy rules. Elective salary deferrals are limited to $10,000 and catch-up contributions are limited to $2,500 in SIMPLE 401(k), but have higher limits in a safe harbor 401(k) plan.

C. Types of Defined Benefit Plans

1. Flat Benefit

In a flat benefit plan, every participant will receive an annuity, starting at normal retirement age, based on a formula which is usually a flat dollar amount multiplied by the number of years worked with the employer.

For example, a flat-benefit defined benefit plan document will define the normal retirement benefit as "a monthly annuity, starting at age 65 and continuing for the rest of the employee's life, equal to $30 for each year of credited service." Therefore, hypothetically, Employee A who has 27 years of service will receive $810 per month starting on her 65th birthday and continuing for the rest of her life; and in the following year, after she has 28 years of service, her monthly benefit will grow to $840 per month starting on her 65th birthday and continuing for the rest of her life.

2. Fixed Benefit

In a fixed benefit plan, every participant will receive an annuity, starting at normal retirement age, based on a formula which is usually an income replacement percentage multiplied by the participant's average salary. Most often, the compensation multiplied by the percentage formula represents the participant's average prior to retirement, such as the average of the three highest consecutive years of salary earned in the final five years before retirement. As such, this type of plan design is often referred to as a final average plan, as opposed to unit benefit plans, which are often referred to as career average plans.

For example, a fixed-benefit defined benefit plan document will define the normal retirement benefit as "a monthly annuity, starting at age 65 and continuing for the rest of the employee's life, equal to 70% of the participant's highest five year consecutive salary earned within the final ten years of employment." Therefore, hypothetically, if Employee B, who has a $60,000 average salary, continues working until age 65, then she will receive $3,500 per month ($42,000 per year) starting on her 65th birthday and continuing for the rest of her life; and in the following year, after her average salary increases to $62,000, then her monthly benefit will grow to $3,617 per month ($43,400 per year) starting on her 65th birthday and continuing for the rest of her life.

3. Unit Benefit

In a unit benefit plan, every participant will receive an annuity, starting at normal retirement age, based on a formula which is usually a unit income replacement percentage multiplied by the participant's average salary and the number of years worked with the employer. This type of plan design is often referred to as a career average plan.

For example, a unit-benefit defined benefit plan document will define the normal retirement benefit as "a monthly annuity, starting at age 65 and continuing for the rest of the employee's life, equal to 1% of each year's salary for the first 10 years worked with the employer, and 1.25% of each year's salary for all remaining years worked with the employer." Therefore, hypothetically, if Employee C who has a $19,000 salary for year 1 and a $20,000 salary for year 2 will receive $33 per month starting on her 65th birthday and continuing for the rest of her life [1% of $19,000/12 plus 1% of $20,000/12]; and in the following years, if Employee C's salary increases at exactly $1000 per year, then her monthly retirement benefit will grow to $50 after the third year, $68 after the fourth year,..., $196 after the tenth year, $220 after the eleventh year, $245 after the twelfth year, ...

4. Defined Benefit Plans with Permitted Disparity

Statutory Rules at IRC § 401(l)

As with defined contribution plan, employees who earn more that the annual Social Security Taxable Wage Base (as discussed in Chapter 20) only receive benefits from Social Security based on the SSTWB. Therefore, the additional compensation earned as an employee does not count towards Social Security benefits, and qualified plans are allowed to provide these high paid individuals with slightly higher benefits. A single defined benefit plan can be designed as an excess plan, or as a floor offset plan.

> "Defined benefit excess plan" means a defined benefit plan under which the rate at which employer-provided benefits are determined with respect to average annual compensation above the integration level under the plan (expressed as a percentage of such average annual compensation) is greater than the rate at which employer-provided benefits are determined with respect to average annual compensation at or below the integration level (expressed as a percentage of such average annual compensation).[6]

> "Offset plan" means a defined benefit plan that is not a defined benefit excess plan and that provides that each employee's employer-provided benefit is reduced or offset by a specified percentage of the employee's final average compensation up to the offset level under the plan.[7]

Please be aware that the permitted disparity rules are actually quite a bit more complicated than this summary indicates (such as how to calculate average salary and then final average salary, and the reductions to the .75 percent, as described in the regulations). Therefore, the employer must determine if the extra qualified plan benefit that can be promised to certain high paid individuals is worth the cost of compliance.

Treas. Regs. § 1.401(l)-3. Permitted Disparity for Defined Benefit Plans

***

---

6. Treas. Regs. § 1.401(l)-1(c)(16)(i).
7. Treas. Regs. § 1.401(l)-1(c)(25).

(b) Maximum permitted disparity.

(1) In general. In the case of a defined benefit excess plan, the disparity provided for the plan year may not exceed the maximum excess allowance as defined in paragraph (b)(2) of this section. In the case of an offset plan, the disparity provided for the plan year may not exceed the maximum offset allowance as defined in paragraph (b)(3) of this section. In addition, either type of plan must satisfy the overall permitted disparity limits of § 1.401(l)-5.

(2)Maximum excess allowance. The maximum excess allowance for a plan year is the lesser of—

(i) 0.75 percent, reduced as required under paragraphs (d) and (e) of this section, or

(ii) The base benefit percentage for the plan year.

(3) Maximum offset allowance. The maximum offset allowance for a plan year is the lesser of—

(i) 0.75 percent, reduced as required under paragraphs (d) and (e) of this section, or

(ii) One-half of the gross benefit percentage, multiplied by a fraction (not to exceed one), the numerator of which is the employee's average annual compensation, and the denominator of which is the employee's final average compensation up to the offset level.

***

(5) Examples. The following examples illustrate this paragraph (b). Unless otherwise provided, the following facts apply. The plan is noncontributory and is the only plan ever maintained by the employer. The plan uses a normal retirement age of 65 and contains no provision that would require a reduction in the 0.75-percent factor under paragraph (b)(2) or (b)(3) of this section. In the case of a defined benefit excess plan, the plan uses each employee's covered compensation as the integration level; in the case of an offset plan, the plan uses each employee's covered compensation as the offset level and provides that an employee's final average compensation is limited to the employee's average annual compensation. Each example discusses the benefit formula applicable to an employee who has a social security retirement age of 65.

Example (1). Plan N is a defined benefit excess plan that provides a normal retirement benefit of 0.5 percent of average annual compensation in excess of the integration level, for each year of service. The plan provides no benefits with respect to average annual compensation up to the integration level. The disparity provided under the plan exceeds the maximum excess allowance because the excess benefit percentage (0.5 percent) exceeds the base benefit percentage (0 percent) by more than the base benefit percentage (0 percent).

Example (2). Plan O is an offset plan that provides a normal retirement benefit equal to 2 percent of average annual compensation, minus 0.75 percent of final average compensation up to the offset level, for each year of service up to 35. The disparity provided under the plan satisfies this paragraph (b) because the offset percentage (0.75 percent) does not exceed the maximum offset allowance equal to the lesser of 0.75 percent or one-half of the gross benefit percentage (1 percent).

Example (3). Plan P is a defined benefit excess plan that provides a normal retirement benefit of 0.5 percent of average annual compensation up to the integration level, plus 1.25 percent of average annual compensation in excess of the integration level, for each year of service up to 35. The disparity provided under the plan exceeds the maximum excess allowance because the excess benefit percentage (1.25 percent) exceeds the base benefit percentage (0.5 percent) by more than the base benefit percentage (0.5 percent).

Example (4). Plan Q is an offset plan that provides a normal retirement benefit of 1 percent of average annual compensation, minus 0.75 percent of final average compensation up to the offset level, for each year of service up to 35. The disparity under the plan exceeds the maximum offset allowance because the offset percentage exceeds one-half of the gross benefit percentage (0.5 percent).

***

Example (6). Plan S is a defined benefit excess plan that provides a base benefit percentage of 1 percent of average annual compensation up to the integration level for each year of service. The plan also provides, for each of the first 10 years of service, an excess benefit percentage of 1.85 percent of average annual compensation in excess of the integration level. For each year of service after 10, the plan provides an excess benefit percentage of 1.65 percent of the employee's average annual compensation in excess of the integration level. The disparity provided under the plan exceeds the maximum excess allowance because the excess benefit percentage for each of the first ten years of service (1.85 percent) exceeds the base benefit percentage (1 percent) by more than 0.75 percent.

***

5. Difference between Career Average and Final Average Plans

This final thought about defined benefit plans is not based on a legal definition, but rather just an idea. If an employer decides to sponsor a defined benefit plan, it needs to consider whether to design it around a participant's career average of compensation or a final average of compensation.

If a career average pay plan, the lower salaries at the beginning part of the career are offset against the larger salaries generally earned towards the end of the career. Thus, each additional year's salary increase only minimally increases the accrued benefit beyond where it would have been if not for the salary increase.

In a final average pay plan, the lower salaries at the beginning of the career are pretty much ignored. Many plans contain a formula multiplied by some final average pay, such as "the highest average salary earned over 3 consecutive years," or "the highest average salary earned over 5 consecutive years," or "the highest average salary earned over 3 consecutive years within the last 10 years of employment." Thus, each additional year's salary increase directly increases the accrued benefit beyond where it would have been if not for the salary increase.

A plan that simply multiplies a factor by the final year's compensation to determine the normal retirement benefit might not match the employer and employee goals in cases where the employee is disabled in the final year and actually earns a lot less than in the previous few years, or where an employee is entitled to earn time-and-a-half and works as many overtime hours in the final year as he possibly can.

D. Types of Hybrid Plans

1. Target Benefit Plans

A target benefit plan has no statutory definition, but is considered to be a "money purchase pension plan under which contributions to an employee's account are determined by reference to the amounts necessary to fund the employee's stated benefit under the plan."[8] Therefore, for all specific qualification rules, it is a defined contribution pension plan.

A target benefit plan does not have to comply with the safe-harbor requirements under the cross-testing regulations, but any variation will need to be tested on an annual basis for compliance with the nondiscrimination requirements. In a safe-harbor target benefit plan, an annual normal cost is calculated for each participant by: (1) determining the present value of the participant's target benefit, based on the provisions in the plan document, at age 65 (or any other standard retirement age) using factors provided in the regulations; (2) offsetting the participant's theoretical reserve; and (3) determining the required contribution by multiplying the difference by the amortization factors provided in the regulations. Each year, the theoretical reserve is the accumulation of prior normal costs, increased by the assumed interest rate. Thus, the only thing that will cause a participant's normal cost to change over his or her working years until retirement will be amendments to the plan formula, changes in the plan's actuarial assumptions, or changes in the participant's compensation if the benefits are based on compensation.

The advantages of a target benefit plan are that the employer is focusing on the accumulated account at retirement (*i.e.*, the participant's nest egg), and although there are no defined benefit plan guarantees that that targeted accumulation will be achieved, the contributions and investment strategy attempt to come as close as possible. Although not required by law, an Enrolled Actuary (or other competent retirement plan professional) will be needed to determine the funding targets and normal costs.

---

8. A target benefit plan was originally described by the IRS in Revenue Ruling 76-464, but that Revenue Ruling was obsoleted by Revenue Ruling 93-87. See Treas. Regs. § 1.401(a)(4)-8(b)(3), describing a safe harbor target benefit plan for purposes of cross-testing to satisfy the nondiscrimination requirements. However, an earlier interpretation at Treas. Regs. § 1.410(a)-4(a)(1), limited to the guidance in the paragraph concerning maximum age conditions and time of participation, gave a broader definition, and labeled it as a "defined contribution plan" as opposed to "money purchase plan." While this might seem ultra-technical, an employer that sponsors a target benefit plan needs to know if it is simply a defined contribution plan, or a money purchase plan subject to the minimum funding, married participant distribution, and in-service distribution limitation rules. The conservative approach is to therefore treat a target benefit plan as a hybrid form of a money purchase plan.

2. Statutory Hybrid Plans (Cash Balance Plans and Other Hybrid Plan Designs)

Special Legal Rules at IRC § 411(a)(13) and (b)(5)

Until 2006, cash balance plans and other hybrid defined benefit plan designs had no statutory definition, and after years of relatively little controversy, they became immersed in litigation. However, the Code now sanctions hybrid plans, and a "statutory hybrid plan" is a plan that is a lump sum based plan, which means a defined benefit plan where the accumulated benefit of a participant is expressed as the balance of a hypothetical account maintained for the participant or as the current value of the accumulated percentage of the participant's final average compensation. The introduction of statutory hybrid plans, however, was prospective only, and does not in any way shed light on the outstanding litigation for older cash balance plan designs or the issues the IRS had with issuing favorable determination letters to older traditional defined benefit plans that converted into cash balance plans before the law change.

Under a cash balance plan form of statutory hybrid plan, an individual account is established for each employee. The employer credits a certain percentage of compensation to each employee's account on an annual basis and credits each account with interest earned at a stipulated rate. The benefits accrued are pursuant to the plan are based upon a formula that calculates retirement credits. The credits are applied to each participant's account on an annual basis. Generally, the credits are based on a percentage of the salary that a participant earns each year. Participants may elect to receive their benefits in a lump sum or as an annuity generally paid on a monthly basis. Because the benefits are not based solely on the actual contributions and forfeitures allocated to an employee's account and the actual investment experience and expenses of the plan are not allocated to the account, the cash balance plan is treated as a defined benefit plan, rather than a defined contribution plan.

The advantages of a hybrid defined benefit plan are that younger and transient employees enjoy the advantages of accumulating an account, but the account is credited with guaranteed fund earnings and is generally protected by the Pension Benefit Guaranty Corporation. An Enrolled Actuary will be needed to determine the annual funding targets and normal costs.

The Pension Protection Act of 2006 also changed the rules on how a traditional defined benefit plan can be converted into a statutory hybrid plan. According to the statutory provision:

IRC § 411(b)(5)(B). Applicable Defined Benefit Plans

***

(ii) Special rule for plan conversions. If, after June 29, 2005, an applicable plan amendment is adopted, the plan shall be treated as failing to meet the requirements of paragraph (1)(H) unless the requirements of clause (iii) are met with respect to each individual who was a participant in the plan immediately before the adoption of the amendment.

(iii) Rate of benefit accrual. Subject to clause (iv) , the requirements of this clause are met with respect to any participant if the accrued benefit of the participant under the terms of the plan as in effect after the amendment is not less than the sum of—

(I) the participant's accrued benefit for years of service before the effective date of the amendment, determined under the terms of the plan as in effect before the amendment, plus

(II) the participant's accrued benefit for years of service after the effective date of the amendment, determined under the terms of the plan as in effect after the amendment.

(iv) Special rules for early retirement subsidies. For purposes of clause (iii)(I) , the plan shall credit the accumulation account or similar amount with the amount of any early retirement benefit or retirement-type subsidy for the plan year in which the participant retires if, as of such time, the participant has met the age, years of service, and other requirements under the plan for entitlement to such benefit or subsidy.

(v) Applicable plan amendment. For purposes of this subparagraph—

(I) In general. The term "applicable plan amendment" means an amendment to a defined benefit plan which has the effect of converting the plan to an applicable defined benefit plan.

***

Basically, there was some major litigation before the PPA was enacted, and this statutory provision eliminated the use of a "wear-away" formula, where the old accrued benefit would be locked in until the accrued benefit in the newer hybrid formula outgrew the preserved benefit. IRC § 411(b)(5)(B)(iii)(I) requires what is commonly called the "A+B" approach, where the ole accrued benefit is frozen and every dollar accrued under the new hybrid formula is added to the preserved benefit.

3. New Combined DB/401(k) Plans Starting in 2010

Statutory Legal Rules at IRC § 414(x)

Currently, a cash or deferred arrangement, or CODA (*i.e.*, a 401(k) plan with elective salary deferrals) is only allowed to be part of a profit sharing plan. Starting in 2010, however, a CODA can be part of a defined benefit plan. This type of design is limited to employers with less than 500 employees. A good way to integrate the advantages of a defined benefit plan with the advantages of a defined contribution plan will be through a statutory hybrid defined benefit plan with accounts that can harmonize with the CODA accounts.

If an applicable defined benefit plan is paired with a CODA, then the pay credit must be at least:

- if in the form of a traditional defined benefit plan promising an annuity at normal retirement age, then the lesser of

  - 1% of final average salary multiplied by Years of Service with the employer, or

  - 20% of final average salary;

- if in the form of a statutory hybrid cash balance plan, then
  - 2% if the participant's age at the beginning of the year is 30 or less,
  - 4% if age 31 to 40,
  - 6% if age 41 to 50, and
  - 8% if older than 50.

In the CODA portion, the new automatic contribution arrangement rules must be utilized and the employer must match at least 50% of the elective deferrals up to 4% of compensation.

Employer contributions from both portions of the combined plan must be fully vested within 3 years of credited service, and all contributions and benefits, and all other rights and features, must be provided on a uniform basis to all participants. Contributions and benefits, rights and features must apply uniformly to all participants. For purposes of the Form 5500, the combined plan arrangement will constitute a single plan.

4. Certain Hybrid Plans

Statutory Legal Rules at IRC § 414(k)

As discussed, a statutory hybrid plan design where a defined benefit plan provides a benefit derived from employer contributions which is based partly on the balance of the separate account of a participant, shall be considered a defined benefit plan for certain qualification provisions and as a defined contribution plan for others. This type of plan never really gained in popularity, and is rarely used.

Chapter 6

Funding Plans

Overview

What are the required employer contributions in a qualified retirement plan?

- in a defined contribution plan:
  - money purchase plan: the employer must contribute the proper amount so that an allocation can be made to each participant's account in accordance with the amount promised under the plan document
  - profit sharing plan: the employer must contribute the amount that it wishes to deduct for the year
  - leveraged ESOPs: the employer must contribute the amount that represents the amortized repayment of principal and interest of the loan
  - 401(k) plans: the employer must contribute the amount that has promised to the participants as a match to their voluntary pre-tax elective salary deferrals or after-tax designated Roth contributions, and if the plan fails the special 401(k) nondiscrimination tests, then it must deposit the amount determined, if any, to bring the plan into compliance
- in a defined benefit plan
  - funding is a moving target, and the true funded status is only determined once all plan liabilities have been paid out
  - the Enrolled Actuary determines how well funded the defined benefit plan is by comparing the fund assets to the fund liabilities on an annual basis (through statutory controls over minimum required contributions)
    - if a plan fails to meet minimum funding requirements, then a penalty tax is imposed
    - on the other hand, if the defined benefit plan is overfunded upon termination, then the employer pays a 50% penalty on the amount that is reverted back to the employer
    - therefore, the Enrolled Actuary assists the employer in trying to properly fund the plan over its life
  - the Enrolled Actuary will make a lot of reasonable assumptions to calculate the present value of future benefit promises, and compares that value to the plan's actual current assets to determine the mathematically appropriate minimum required contribution

- Congress hopes each plan is always at least 100% funded on a current basis
- if the ratio falls below 100% in any year, then the minimum required contribution for that year is larger than expected, and more conservative actuarial assumptions might be required in the following year
- if the ratio falls below 80% in the current year, then there is a prohibition against plan amendments that in any way increase the benefit accruals, and there are benefit distribution limitations imposed on the plan in the following year
- if the ratio falls below 60% in the current year, then all future benefit accruals automatically cease, and there are severe restrictions on benefit distributions
- don't forget that an Enrolled Actuary charges a fee for his or her professional services, and when added to the PBGC premiums described below, the annual administration of a defined benefit plan is generally more expensive than the annual administration of a defined contribution plan (irrespective of the costs of contributions to the plan)

What premiums do defined benefit plans pay to the PBGC for the insurance protection it provides?

- almost all defined benefit plans pay the sum of a flat premium rate ($30 per plan participant during the plan year) and a variable rate premium of $9 for each $1,000 (or fraction thereof) of unfunded vested benefits under the plan as of the close of the preceding plan year

What are the annual limitations on employee contributions into a defined contribution plan?

- in any year, the most that an individual may elect as the total of pre-tax salary deferrals into a traditional 401(k) plan plus after-tax designated Roth contributions into a Roth 401(k) plan is
  - $15,000 (as adjusted for inflation)
  - but, starting in the year he or she attains age 50, an extra "catch-up contribution" of $5,000 (as adjusted for inflation) is allowed
- this limit applies to the individual for the year, regardless of how many jobs he or she has had where separate employers sponsored a 401(k) plan

What are the maximum deduction rules for a qualified retirement plan?

- in a defined contribution plan
  - the maximum deduction for all contributions to all defined contribution plans sponsored by the employer is basically limited to 25% of total payroll, where payroll is the total compensation to all participating employees after limiting each participant's compensation to $200,000 (as adjusted for inflation)
- in a defined benefit plan,
  - whatever amount is calculated by the Enrolled Actuary as the minimum required contribution is always required to be deposited and can always be deducted (regardless of its percentage of payroll)

- in addition, the employer is generally allowed to contribute some extra money (about 50% of the minimum required contribution) in good years to help stave off unexpectedly high contributions in future years
- there is a special deduction limit for when the employer sponsors both a defined benefit plan and a defined contribution plan that covers the same employee

A. Employer Contributions

1. Specific Rules for Defined Contribution Plans

As described in Chapter 5, the main differentiation between the various types of defined contribution plans from the employer's point of view is the flexibility and budgeting of the employer contributions.

Mandatory in a money purchase plan or similar plan: A money purchase or target benefit plan document guarantees an employer contribution for each eligible participant each year. The employer is therefore subject to the minimum funding requirements, and the 10% penalty tax for a failure to meet those requirements in any year;[1]

Discretionary in a profit sharing or similar plan: A profit sharing, stock bonus or non-leveraged ESOP plan document only provides for an allocation method if, in its discretion, the employer decides to make a contribution to the plan for the year. The amount of contribution, if any, does not need to be tied into the actual profitability of the employer;

Matching contributions in a 401(k) plan: In safeharbor 401(k) plans, as well as SIMPLEs, the document must reflect the level of employer matching contribution, so the employer is compelled to make those contributions. In other cases where there is no legal requirement that expected matches be stated clearly in the plan document, then the employer will need to make matching contributions in a manner that does not discriminate in favor of Highly Compensated Employees. If the employer communicates its intended matching contributions in a notice to employees or in the Summary Plan Description, then the employer must comply with its written promises;

Loan repayments in a leveraged ESOP: In a leveraged ESOP, a bank or other financial institution lends money to the ESOP (collateralized with the employer's assets) and the ESOP then purchases stock from the employer or shareholders. The employer will repay the loan by making the appropriate contributions into the ESOP (principal and interest) and then the ESOP pays the bank. Therefore, the loan amortization schedule becomes the mandatory contribution amount, not due to Code provisions, but to prevent the loan from going into default. If the ESOP is not leveraged, then it works in the same manner as a profit-sharing plan, with discretionary contributions of employer stock instead of cash on an annual basis.

Salary deferrals and designated Roth contributions in a 401(k) plan: As discussed in Chapter 13, it is a breach of fiduciary duty if salary deferrals and em-

---

1. under IRC § 4971.

ployee contributions are not segregated from the employer's general assets and deposited into the 401(k) plan as soon as administratively feasible.

2. Specific Rules for Defined Benefit Plans

One major disadvantage of a defined benefit plan for the employer is the inability to budget for contributions. As discussed below, Enrolled Actuaries make assumptions that attempt to generate predictable contributions, but unexpected events, such as large investment losses, will cause volatility. There are some smoothing methods allowed, but they only minimally eliminate the volatility. The plan assets can be wholly invested in certain insurance contracts in order to avoid volatility, as the annual contribution will then be the premiums charged by the insurance company. The CFO of a large company probably hates unexpected volatility more than anything else, so even if the Director of Human Resources appreciates a defined benefit plan for the employees, the CFO, especially in the current economic environment, would probably prefer a defined contribution plan—as a benefits professional, your client is the employer, and not any of the individual officers you meet with, so you need to be sensitive to the goals and fears of the other officers that you don't even meet with.

One of the confusing aspects of defined benefit plans for employers is the difference between the required contribution amounts, as determined by the Enrolled Actuary, and the pension costs required to be accounted for on the corporate financial statements, as determined by the CPA or auditor. The purpose of required financial statement disclosure of pension costs for publicly traded companies was meant to allow investors to compare apples to apples, so regardless of how the particular actuary chooses to actually fund the particular defined benefit plan, the CPA has fewer options and must calculate the financial costs pursuant to strict rules. While small employers and non-publicly traded companies are generally not required to comply with the financial accounting rules, many times they can only get a high credit rating or financing from a bank if they develop their financial statements in a manner that complies with the generally accepted accounting principles of FASB.

As described in Chapter 5, the employer can promise any level of benefits (within statutory maximum limits, as discussed in Chapter 7), but is obligated to fund the benefits promised. Unless all plan assets are invested in proper IRC § 412(e)(3) insurance policies (as described below), an Enrolled Actuary is required to value the plan's liabilities and assets each year to determine the amount needed to meet the statutory funding targets.

Before a defined benefit plan is established, there are no promised benefits and there are no plan assets to pay for any benefits that should come due. At the end of the defined benefit plan's life (*i.e,* the day that the last retired participant or beneficiary promised retirement benefits dies, or upon plan termination if earlier), there must have been enough assets to pay out every last dollar of benefits promised. If there are extra plan assets at that point in time, then the plan will be deemed to have been overfunded, and remaining plan assets can revert to the employer with a 50% penalty excise tax or can be used to establish a replacement plan or increase benefits so that the excise tax is reduced to 20%.[2] On the other hand, if there are not enough assets at that point in time, and the plan will be deemed to have been underfunded, then the employer must immediately deposit enough assets to pay current liabilities due, regardless of deductibility (as described below).

---

2. IRC § 4980.

At any point in between, the best the employer can do is look at the current funded status of the plan, which is a useful tool in anticipating the probability of successfully funding the plan. Congress requires private-sector employer plans to use an Enrolled Actuary to value the plan assets and liabilities on an annual basis and then calculate the required contribution for the sponsoring employer. Due to a perception by Congress of problematic underfunded qualified defined benefit plans, the minimum funding rules were totally revised for single employer plans effective as of 2008. If a plan fails to meet minimum funding requirements, then an initial penalty tax of 10% is imposed.[3]

The employer sponsoring the plan is generally liable for the contribution, but if the employer is part of a controlled group, then the IRS can jointly and severally demand any member of the controlled group to satisfy the plan's minimum funding requirements. In certain situations, where the employer can demonstrate a business hardship, the IRS is authorized to allow a funding waiver for all or a portion of the otherwise required amount, but that waiver must be made up in installments over the following seven years in addition to whatever minimum funding requirements are calculated by the Enrolled Actuary.

The following minimum funding rules for single employer defined benefit plans are effective in 2008 after the Pension Protection Act of 2006 took effect. There is absolutely no need in this textbook to discuss the minimum funding rules as they existed before 2008.

a. The Role of the Plan's Enrolled Actuary

Statutory Rules at IRC §§ 412, 430 (Although No Actual Cross-Reference from IRC § 401(a))

As discussed in Chapter 3, ERISA created the professional designation of Enrolled Actuary, and all defined benefit plans must either invest all plan assets in appropriate insurance contracts (as discussed below), or needs to hire an Enrolled Actuary to certify the plan's funded status and determine the required minimum contribution.

The Enrolled Actuary will make a lot of assumptions, such as:

- Mortality (*i.e.,* the expectation of the frequency of deaths; however, as a floor, starting in 2008, Enrolled Actuaries must use a current mortality table published periodically by the IRS which is based on current trends in life expectancies);
- Interest and fund earnings (*i.e.,* based on the plan's investment strategy and the general wisdom and expectations of investment advisors; however, as a floor, starting in 2008, Enrolled Actuaries must use a yield curve published monthly by the IRS which is based on high yield corporate bond rates);
- Disability (*i.e.,* how many employees are expected to go out on disability prior to reaching normal retirement age—especially if the defined benefit plan has a provision that upon disability, an employee will receive a subsidy which provides full benefits as if he worked until retirement);
- Withdrawal (*i.e.,* how many of the current employees are expected to terminate employment before reaching their normal retirement ages);
- Increases in employees (*i.e.,* how many new employees are expected to be hired and what are their expected ages and their expected salaries);

---

3. IRC § 4971.

- Age of retirement (*i.e.,* some plans allow for enhanced early retirement benefits as an incentive for older workers to voluntarily leave the workforce early and some plans allow older employees to continue accruing benefits if they work beyond normal retirement age);
- Optional form of benefit to be selected (*i.e.,* if some optional forms of benefits are actually subsidized over others, and are not simply actuarial equivalents, as discussed in Chapter 9);
- Marital status of participant and age of spouse or other beneficiary (*i.e.,* especially for a joint and survivor benefit, as discussed in Chapter 9);
- Salary Scale (*i.e.,* if benefits are based on final salaries, what will they likely be);
- Seasonal and cyclical events which effect the employer's industry (*i.e.,* new housing demands may impact covered workers and funding constraints in a defined benefit plan established to benefit construction workers);
- Disasters (*i.e.,* a collapse of a cave may impact a defined benefit plan established to benefit coalminers); and
- Value of Plan Assets (if a "smoothing" method is used, where the immediate impact of large gains or losses are diluted and spread out over a two-year period).

These assumptions, and some others, which are crucial to proper funding, are disclosed to the federal government on the annual reporting forms (the Form 5500) on the Schedule SB, and the plan's Enrolled Actuary signs the schedule, under penalty of perjury, that the determination of any present value or other computation shall be made on the basis of actuarial assumptions and methods, each of which is reasonable (taking into account the experience of the plan and reasonable expectations), and which, in combination, offer the actuary's best estimate of anticipated experience under the plan. Therefore, because of the desire of the Enrolled Actuary to meet all professional ethical obligations and keep his or her professional certification, there is arguably little incentive for a plan's Enrolled Actuary making up assumptions, without basis in reality, simply to provide the sponsoring employer with a contribution it is hoping for.

The Enrolled Actuary simply makes annual predictions and any over-estimates, under-estimates, omitted estimates, or even mistakes, will be "fixed" in the next year (assuming the Enrolled Actuary follows his or her code of professional ethics and does not commit malpractice). Therefore, an employer sponsor is not allowed to dictate its preferred assumptions for the Enrolled Actuary to use, and once benefits have accrued, they must be funded as per the Enrolled Actuary's dictates. Accrued benefits can never be eliminated by plan amendment, but future promises that have not yet accrued can be eliminated. Since a participant is entitled to a benefit accrual once credited with 1000 hours (as discussed in Chapter 7), an employer generally has about 4 months into the plan year to determine if the current year's contribution will be unaffordable (assuming full-time employees), and therefore can amend the plan to decrease future benefits promised, including the current year's accruals.

b. Funding Targets

Statutory Rules at IRC § 430 (Although No Actual Cross-Reference from IRC § 401(a))

Under the new funding rules, regardless of the suggested funding levels determined by the Enrolled Actuary in his or her expert judgment, the Code sets the absolute minimum contribution that must be deposited, in accordance with statutorily defined funding targets. Each year, the Enrolled Actuary calculates a funding target, compares it to the plan assets, and determines if there is a funding shortfall. The minimum required contribution for the year depends on whether there is a funding shortfall or not:

- If there is no funding shortfall, then the contribution is the target normal cost, reduced by the excess of the funding target over plan assets.

- If there is a funding shortfall, then the contribution is the sum of the target normal cost, a funding shortfall amortization charge, and an amortization charge for any previously granted funding waivers.

The funding target is basically the present value of benefits as of the first day of the plan year, and the target normal cost is the present value of benefits accruing during the year.

As of the last day of the prior year, the plan will or will not be determined to be "at risk" for the following plan year, depending on it's Funding Target Attainment Percentage (FTAP), which is simply the plan assets divided by the present value of plan liabilities. Although there are transitions in the first few years of the new funding rules[4], eventually a plan will be at risk in the following year if the current year's FTAP falls below 100%. For example, if the actuarial value of assets at January 1, 2010 is calculated to be $900,000 and the present value of plan liabilities (*i.e.*, the funding target) is $1,000,000, then the FTAP is 90%; whereas, if the actuarial value of assets at January 1, 2010 is calculated to be $1,250,000 and the present value of plan liabilities is $1,000,000, then the FTAP is 125%.

If a plan is "at risk" for the current year, then both the funding target and the target normal cost are calculated with much more conservative assumptions (such as assuming every participant will retire on the earliest day allowed under the plan and that every employee will choose the most valuable optional form of benefit, and adding a load factor if the plan is at-risk status for at least 2 of the 4 preceding plan years). Fortunately, small employer plans will not be considered "at risk." In addition to determining the required minimum contribution, the ratio of the funding target to adjusted plan assets determines the plan's funding target attainment percentage, which, as described below, has substantial effects on plan benefits and distributions if it falls below 80%. This is relevant for all plans, even small plans that cannot be considered "at risk."

Each year that there is a funding shortfall, it is amortized over seven years at the appropriate interest rates published for that particular year. For the current year, the total shortfall amortization charge is the sum of this year's payment plus a single year's payment for each of the prior 6 year shortfall balances (reamortized using the current year's yield curve interest rates). In any year that there is not a funding shortfall, then all prior year bases are considered to be fully amortized. For example, if the actuarial value of assets at January 1, 2010 is calculated to be $900,000 and the present value of plan liabilities (*i.e.*, the funding target) is $1,000,000, then the funding shortfall is $100,000, which will be amortized and made up in seven payments; whereas, if the actuarial value of assets at January 1, 2010 is calculated to be $1,250,000 and the present value of plan liabil-

---

4. 92% in 2008, 94% in 2009 and 96% in 2010

ities is $1,000,000, then there is no funding shortfall, and if there was a prior shortfall being amortized, the amortization bases will be deemed to be paid in full.

As discussed below, in some years the employer might choose to contribute more than the minimum required amount, so that a cushion is built up. Before the new rules became effective in 2007, this cushion was called a credit balance, but starting in 2008, it is called a prefunding balance. The main benefit of maintaining a prefunding balance is to apply all or a portion of the balance to reduce the current year's minimum required contribution. Unfortunately, the way the funding rules were written and actually work, this cushion is automatically subtracted from the assets, and can therefore cause the plan to have a lower funding target than desirable. When that happens, the employer can elect to burn off enough of the prefunding balance so that the funding target, and the resulting funding target attainment percentage, is higher. The portion burned is forever forfeited, and thus can defeat the benefit of depositing extra money in prior years when it was affordable.

All of these various funding components (the funding target, the target normal cost, the actuarial value of plan assets, the shortfall and resulting shortfall amortization charges, and the FTAP to determine whether the plan will be at risk in the following year) must be calculated at least once a year. For most single employer defined benefit plans, the valuation must be the first day of the plan year; however, small employer plans can choose any day of the plan year as the valuation date (and most small plans will select the last day of the plan year).

c. *Impact on Plan When Funding Targets Are Not Met*
Statutory Rules at IRC § 436 (Although No Actual Cross-Reference from IRC § 401(a))

As described above, the plan's funding target attainment percentage ("FTAP") is the ratio of the plan assets to its funding target. With some adjustments (not necessary to discuss here), the Adjusted Funding Target Attainment Percentage ("AFTAP") is also calculated, which is the adjusted actuarial value of plan assets divided by the adjusted funding target. The following benefit and distribution limitations automatically kick in when the AFTAP calculated in the preceding year falls below certain levels:

Between 60% and 80%: the plan cannot be amended in any manner that increases plan liabilities (such as increasing current benefits, establishing new benefits, increasing the rate of benefit accrual, or increasing the vesting schedule), and can only pay a certain portion of prohibited payments (such as lump sums); and

Below 60%: all benefit accruals in the plan are frozen, the plan cannot pay any prohibited accelerated payments and cannot pay out any shutdown benefits or other unpredictable contingent events benefits.

Most of the above restrictions do not apply in the first 5 years of a newly established defined benefit plan. The plan's actuary needs to certify the current year's FTAP based on the prior year's information by the fourth month of the current year, or else the current AFTAP is assumed to be 10% less than last year's AFTAP (which is problematic if last year's AFTAP is between 80% and 90% or between 60% and 70%). Then, if the Enrolled Actuary still has not certified the plan's current AFTAP by the tenth month of the current year, the plan's AFTAP is deemed to be less than 60% for the entire year, and cannot be reversed. The AFTAP is determined for each plan year, and the restrictions above only apply in the years that the AFTAP is below 80%.

d. Compliant IRC § 412(e)(3) Plans (Formerly Identified in § 412(i) before PPA Amendments)

Statutory Rules at IRC § 412(e)(3) (Although No Actual Cross-Reference from IRC § 401(a))

If the sponsor of a defined benefit plan does not want to pay for and transact with an Enrolled Actuary on an annual basis to determine the required minimum funding and funded status, then all plan assets can be invested with an insurance company that provides whole life contracts for each participant where the level premiums are paid fully and timely for all years the participant is employed until normal retirement age and where the death benefits equal the benefits promised under the plan. Employers are cautioned against any type of insurance product that sounds too good to be true, because non-compliant insurance contracts means that they are just normal plan assets, that they could possibly be an abusive tax avoidance transaction, that the plan is subject to the mandatory minimum funding requirements and Enrolled Actuary certifications (as described above), and that the assets are subject to the prudent fiduciary investment rules. Therefore, while a defined benefit plan invested wholly in compliant § 412(e)(3) insurance contracts might look attractive to a small employer, caution should be exercised in choosing a reputable insurance agent and company, and reputable legal counsel should be sought out to determine compliance before the insurance contracts are purchased.

e. Special Funding Rules for Multiemployer Plans

Statutory Rules at IRC §§ 431 and 432 (Although No Actual Cross-Reference from IRC § 401(a))

A multiemployer plan is a plan "to which more than one employer is required to contribute, which is maintained pursuant to one or more collective bargaining agreements between one or more employee organizations and more than one employer, and which satisfies such other requirements as the Secretary of Labor may prescribe by regulation."[5] So an employer that employs union employees can cover those union employees in its single employer sponsored plan, or can contribute to the multiemployer plan sponsored by the union itself.

Unlike simply calculating a funding target, multiemployer defined benefit plans have a totally different set of rules for determining the minimum funding requirements. With union-maintained plans for the various, unaffiliated employers that contribute, there is a T account, where credits must equal or exceed charges on an annual basis. Charges to the T account include the normal cost to fund plan liabilities, 15 year amortization payments of certain unfunded liability bases like initial unfunded liability (if prior service before the plan was established is credited for plan benefits on the first day of the plan or if the plan is amended to increase future benefits based on prior service) and plan losses (from fund earnings or from changes in actuarial assumptions), and prior waived funding deficiencies, and some other amounts. Credits to the T account include employer contributions, 15 year amortization payments of gains from plan amendments (that decreased future benefits based on prior service) and plan gains (from fund earnings or from changes in actuarial assumptions), the amount of funding waiver granted by the

---

5. IRC § 414(f).

IRS for the current year based on facts and circumstances, and some other amounts. The minimum required contribution for any year is the lesser of the amount needed so that the T account balances out, or an artificial ceiling called the "full funding limit."

For those of you who simply must know what the minimum funding rules for single-employer plans looked like before 2008—they were based on a T account with similar charges and credits, but with different amortization periods.

Similar to single-employer plans, starting in 2008, bad things happen to a multiemployer defined benefit plan that is under funded. The terms of art for multi-employer plans are "endangered status" or "critical status." If in endangered status (the funding ratio is basically less than 80%), then the plan sponsor needs to adopt and implement a funding improvement plan, and during that period of improvement, the plan is barred from accepting a collective bargaining agreement or participation agreement with respect to the multiemployer plan that provides for a reduction in the level of contributions for any participants, a suspension of contributions with respect to any period of service, or any new direct or indirect exclusion of younger or newly hired employees from plan participation, and is barred from adopting a plan amendment that increases plan benefits and resulting plan liabilities. If the plan is in critical status (the funding ratio is basically less than 65%), then the plan needs to adopt and implement a rehabilitation plan, and during the period of rehabilitation, is barred from paying out most lump sums.

B. Employee Contributions

1. Specific Rules for Defined Contribution Plans

Participants in a § 401(k) plan must fill out a salary deferral agreement before making any deferrals of salary into the plan (or before any after-tax designated Roth contribution can be made to a Roth 401(k) plan), unless they are automatically enrolled. A valid salary deferral agreement may apply to compensation earned but not yet paid to the participant at the time the agreement is signed as well as compensation earned after the effective date. The employee may execute more than one salary deferral agreement in a year, thus revoking earlier elections. The salary deferral agreement must be executed between the employee and the employer. For § 401(k) plans, the salary deferral agreement should provide that it applies only to compensation paid after the agreement is effective and that it is legally binding on the parties. The agreement may be revoked by the participant as to amounts earned while the agreement is in effect. For purposes of determining whether an election is a cash or deferred election, it is irrelevant whether the default that applies in the absence of an affirmative election is where the employee receives an amount in cash or where the employer contributes an amount to a 401(k) plan with an automatic enrollment arrangement. Participants in SIMPLE IRAs and SIMPLE 401(k) plans must also make salary deferrals pursuant to a written agreement.

Generally, a partnership or sole proprietorship is permitted to maintain a cash or deferred arrangement, and individual partners or owners are permitted to make cash or deferred elections with respect to compensation attributable to services rendered to the entity, under the same rules that apply to other cash or deferred arrangements. Matching contributions made on behalf of a self-employed individual are not treated as elective contributions. A partner's compensation is deemed currently available on the last day of the partnership taxable year and a sole proprietor's compensation is deemed currently available on the last day of the individual's taxable year. The earned income of a self-employed individual for a taxable year constitutes payment for services during that year.

401(k), 403(b), and 457(b) governmental plans may permit employees to make voluntary employee contributions to "deemed IRAs" under which the contributions are held in separate accounts or annuities and treated as contributions to an IRA. Deemed IRA contributions are subject to the exclusive benefit, fiduciary, co-fiduciary, and administration and enforcement provisions of ERISA to the extent they otherwise apply to the employer's retirement plan. However, a deemed IRA is not subject to ERISA's reporting and disclosure, participation, vesting, and funding requirements that otherwise apply to the employer's plan.

A qualified plan and a deemed IRA generally are treated as separate entities for Code purposes; therefore, each entity is subject to the rules applicable to that entity. Accordingly, a plan participant with compensation in excess of certain limits may either not be able to make a contribution to a deemed IRA, or the deductibility of such contribution by the participant may be limited.

a. Pre-Tax Elective Salary Deferrals

As discussed, employers have several choices to allow employees to voluntarily make pre-tax elective salary deferrals: deemed IRAs, payroll deduction IRAs, SARSEPs established before 1996, SIMPLE 401(k) plans of small employers, and traditional 401(k) plans (and governmental, church, non-profit and educational employers have some choices as well).

b. After Tax Contributions

Beginning in 2006, § 401(k) plans are permitted to offer a qualified Roth contribution program to which an employee may elect to make after-tax designated Roth contributions in lieu of all of or any portion of permitted elective deferrals. Designated Roth contributions will be treated as elective deferrals for plan purposes, including contribution limitations and nondiscrimination requirements. Designated Roth contributions and associated earnings must be held in a designated Roth account and accounted for separately.

c. Limitations on Annual Employee Contributions
Statutory Rules at IRC § 402(g) (Although No Actual Cross-Reference from IRC § 401(a))

The maximum amount that any individual employee can elect to defer into all 401(k) plans in any year, regardless of employer(s), is $15,000 (as adjusted for inflation). The maximum amount that any individual employee can elect to defer into all SIMPLE 401(k) plans in any year, regardless of employer(s), is $10,000 (as adjusted for inflation, see Appendix B). It is important to combine all contributions made by a participant to all elective deferral plans, such as a § 403(b) tax-deferred annuity plan, a § 457 plan, and other § 401(k) plans, to determine the limit.

Any excess deferrals will be included in the individual's Gross Income in the year returned (as opposed to the year earned) if the excess deferrals plus fund earnings are distributed by March 1 of the year after the deferral limit is exceeded, but the deferral will not be subject to any penalty tax for premature distributions (as discussed in Chapter 9).

Many employers, in appropriate situations, will simultaneously sponsor a 401(k) plan, a profit sharing plan and a money purchase plan. If employees participate in all three types of plans, then the combined documents are generally written in tandem so that annual additions are a mix of employee elective pre-tax salary deferrals or after-tax contributions, employer matching contributions, employer mandatory money purchase plan contributions, and then, if possible, discretionary employer profit sharing contributions. Unlike annual additions (as discussed in Chapter 7), however, which are limits throughout an employer, the elective deferrals are limits for the individual for the tax year, regardless of how many separate employers he or she worked for throughout the year. Under IRC § 401(a)(30), as a qualification rule, employers need to communicate this to employees, and plan documents must be drafted accordingly (although employers are generally not supposed to be detectives to affirmatively ascertain whether every employee is actually and properly limiting employee deferrals to all 401(k) plans, including those sponsored by non-affiliated employers).

d. Additional Catch-Up Contributions If over Age 50

Statutory Rules at IRC § 414(v) (Although No Actual Cross-Reference from IRC § 401(a))

Although defined contribution plans, by design, do not allow employers or employees to make current contributions to make up for lost past contributions, the one exception is for certain permitted catch-up contributions because the individual is age 50 or over. The maximum amount that any individual employee, who will attain age 50 by the end of the taxable year, can elect to defer into all 401(k) plans in any year as an eligible catch-up contribution, regardless of employer(s), is $5,000 (as adjusted for inflation). This catch-up contribution allows an individual who is over age 50 to defer up to $20,000 (as adjusted for inflation) each year, regardless of whether he or she actually deferred the maximum amount in prior years or did not.

The catch-up limit for SIMPLE IRAs and SIMPLE 401(k) plans is $2,500 (as adjusted for inflation). Catch-up contributions are not taken into account for nondiscrimination or minimum coverage testing, ADP testing, requirements for SIMPLE 401(k) plans or SEPs, or the determination of Top-Heavy status.

e. Additional Catch-Up Contributions If Due to Qualified Military Service

Statutory Definition at IRC § 414(u) (Although No Actual Cross-Reference from IRC § 401(a))

The Uniformed Services Employment and Reemployment Rights Act of 1994 allows veterans, after completing qualified military service and returning to work, to make-up missed elective deferrals (or missed after-tax contributions) in a 401(k) plan. The "missed" elective deferrals can be made up over a period which is 3 times the length of service, up to 5 years, and these catch-up deferrals are subject to appropriate employer matches. The make-up contributions are limited to the maximum the veteran would have been able to make had he or she not been absent for qualified military leave. Make-up contributions are not taken into account for nondiscrimination, minimum coverage or minimum participation testing, ADP or ACP testing, requirements for SIMPLE 401(k) plans or SEPs, or the determination of Top-Heavy status.

f. Special Savers Tax Credit
Statutory Definition at IRC § 25B

Certain low-income individuals will receive a tax credit equal to a portion of up to $2,000 (as adjusted for inflation) in contributions if they make elective deferrals into §§ 401(k), 403(b), 457(b), SIMPLE 401(k), SIMPLE IRA, or SEP plans, contributions to a traditional or Roth IRA, or voluntary after-tax employee contributions to a qualified retirement plan. The credit is phased-in depending on Adjusted Gross Income and tax-payer filing status. The nonrefundable credit is in addition to any deduction or exclusion available for the contribution and will offset both regular income tax and alternative min-imum tax.

Neither individuals younger than age 18 nor full time students are eligible for the credit. Plan distributions, except loans and excess distributions, made in the current year and preceding two years, will reduce the amount of the tax credit. The employer is not required under law to communicate this credit to employees, but doing so may encour-age some employees to make salary deferrals or employee contributions who would not have done so without the credit.

2. Specific Rules for Defined Benefit Plans

Although prior models of private-sector defined benefit plans often called for em-ployees to contribute a portion of their salary to "purchase" benefits, it is highly rare in current defined benefit plans, so there is no need to get into it here. However, some gov-ernmental plans (i.e., those plans sponsored by a state or local government) do allow this, so those rules would need to be reviewed before providing advice to a governmental plan sponsor.

C. Deduction of Employer Contributions

Statutory Rules at IRC §§ 404 and 4972 (Although No Actual Cross-Reference from IRC § 401(a))

The employer is cautioned to only contribute an amount that can be deducted on the corporate (or other business entity) tax return. Even though non-deductible amounts can be carried over and deducted in future tax years, there is generally a 10% penalty tax assessed on non-deductible amounts. The plan's fiscal year does not necessarily need to match the plan year; however, the fiscal year must either start or end in the plan year. This allows the plan sponsor to pick a fiscal year that allows maximum flexibility for de-ductions based on its internal business cycles.

1. Specific Rules for Defined Contribution Plans

The employer is entitled to take a deduction up to the following limits in the tax year the contribution is actually deposited into the plan:

- *Stock bonus plans and profit sharing plans:* up to 25% of total payroll for those plan participants;
- *Money purchase plans:* up to 25% of total payroll for those plan participants;
- *SEPs:* up to 25% of total payroll for those plan participants;
- *SIMPLE IRAs:* up to 25% of total payroll for those plan participants;
- *Leveraged ESOPs:* employers, other than S Corporations, can deduct the portion of the loan repayments representing principal up to 25% of total payroll for those plan participants, and then additionally deduct the portion of the loan repayments representing interest. C Corporations are also allowed to deduct certain dividends paid on employer securities;
- *SIMPLE 401(k) plans:* whatever amount is required to be contributed;
- *Target benefit plans:* the conservative approach is to view these plans as ordinary money purchase plans, and thus limit the deduction to 25% of total payroll. However, the deduction is arguably whatever amount is required, since the plan "provide[s] benefits upon retirement and covering a period of years, if under the plan the amounts to be contributed by the employer can be determined actuarially";[6]
- *Multiple defined contribution plans:* two or more defined contribution plans maintained by the same employer are aggregated and deemed as a single plan, with a single 25% of compensation deduction limit; and
- *Combination defined benefit and defined contribution plans:* the deduction limitation for the combination of defined benefit and defined contribution plans is limited to 25% of total combined payroll for all participants of all plans. However, after 2006, contributions to a defined contribution plan can be up to 6% of compensation otherwise paid or accrued during the taxable year to the beneficiaries under the plans if the contributions required for the defined benefit plan(s) eat up the entire 25% of payroll limits. Amounts carried over from preceding taxable years (that were contributed but not deducted) are treated as employer contributions to one or more defined contribution plans to the extent attributable to employer contributions to such plans in those preceding taxable years.

The definition of "compensation" for purposes of determining the limitation on deductible employer contributions has the same meaning as compensation for purposes of determining the maximum annual additions. Earned income for self-employed individuals is substituted for compensation. Elective deferrals are not subject to this deduction limit or considered in applying that limit to any other contributions.

If the employer contribution is actually deposited into the trust before the due date for the filing the return for such taxable year, including extensions, then it will be deemed to have made a payment on the last day of the preceding taxable year. The corporate returns are generally due on the 15th day of the third month after the tax year ends, but can apply for an extension for an additional 6 months (for example, if the employer's fiscal year ends on December 31, 2010, then its tax return is due on March 15, 2011, and if an extension is properly filed, then the return is due on September 15, 2011). Employers, and their accountants, need to be careful, and must clearly earmark the plan year for which a contribution will be credited (in the example above, a check dated July 1, 2011 and deposited into the trust can either be a contribution to be credited to the 2010 plan year, or can be an advance contribution for the 2011 plan year).

---

6. IRC § 404(a)(3)(A)(iii).

2. Specific Rules for Defined Benefit Plans

The required minimum contribution for the plan must be deposited, and can be deducted. However, if in any year the employer wishes to contribute more than the minimum required amount in order to accumulate a prefunding balance, then the employer can contribute and deduct up to the sum of: the funding target for the plan year, the target normal cost for the plan year, and a cushion amount over the plan assets. The cushion amount is basically the sum of 50% of the funding target and a hypothetical increase in the funding target assuming salary increases. Although the Enrolled Actuary is not required by law to determine the maximum contribution, and it is really an accountant's final decision, all actuarial assumption rules and definitions under § 430 need to be used to determine deduction limits.

The employer is given 8½ months after the plan year ends to actually deposit the required contribution. However, if the plan had a funding shortfall in the prior plan year, then contributions must be made in quarterly installments during the current plan year, calculated as one fourth of the lesser of 90% of the current year's true minimum required contribution or 100% of the prior year's minimum required contribution. Any late quarterly installment will be charged at the plan's effective rate of interest plus 5 percentage points.

3. Issues for the Sponsoring Employer's Accountant

Since the for-profit employer pays no federal income taxes on business expenses taken as a deduction, Congress wants to limit the amount of money which is contributed to a plan (thus ensuring that enough money goes back into the Federal Government in the form of corporate taxes). Therefore, there is a 10% penalty tax for amounts contributed to a plan which cannot be deducted.[7] While there might be actual situations where a competent accountant advises an employer to make a non-deductible contribution and pay the penalty tax, for purposes of this class, we assume a good benefits professional would not normally advise a client to do anything that subjects them to a penalty tax.

The plan's fiscal year does not necessarily need to match the plan year; however, the fiscal year must either start or end in the plan year. This allows the plan sponsor to pick a fiscal year that allows maximum flexibility for deductions based on its internal business cycles. Since the limits are adjusted annually, and since all plans are not calendar year plans, there are rules which coordinate the calendar year limits with the non-calendar fiscal years.

For a public company subject to preparing financial statements in accordance with the Financial Accounting Standards Board (FASB), the accountant must determine the pension cost for the year, which in a defined benefit plan, is usually different than the actual cash amount contributed and deducted. This irreconcilable difference between accounting costs and actual costs drives many a Chief Financial Officer crazy, and sometimes leads to friction between the human resource department that likes a defined benefit plan design and the financial department which does not.

---

7. IRC § 4972.

D. PBGC Premiums for Defined Benefit Plans

Statutory Rules at ERISA §§ 4002, 4005, 4006, and 4007

With few exceptions, every single-employer that sponsors a qualified defined benefit plan must pay premiums to the Pension Benefit Guaranty Corporation. This is an additional expense incurred by defined benefit plan sponsors.

ERISA established the Pension Benefit Guaranty Corporation to provide for the timely and uninterrupted payment of pension benefits to participants and beneficiaries under terminated defined benefit plans that cannot meet their obligations. Although the PBGC has some autonomy, it is technically created within the Department of Labor. After amendments by the PPA, the Executive Director of the PBGC is now a Presidential appointment, subject to advice and consent by the U.S. Senate.

The PBGC was granted authority to collect premiums to be deposited into one of four revolving funds that have been created on the books of the Treasury of the United States, so that they are accounted for separately from general revenues.

Generally, the premium for a year is the sum of a flat premium rate ($30 per plan participant during the plan year) and a variable rate premium of $9 for each $1,000 (or fraction thereof) of unfunded vested benefits under the plan as of the close of the preceding plan year.

Plans with 25 or fewer participants will not need to pay variable premiums that exceed, in total, $25 per participant. However, the following plans are totally exempt from PGBC coverage, and therefore do not need to submit any premiums (but as a result do not have any protection): a plan which is established and maintained exclusively for substantial owners, and a plan which is established and maintained by a professional service employer which does not at any time have more than 25 active participants in the plan.

Chapter 7

Vesting and Accruals

Overview

What is the general concept of vesting of benefits?

- vesting is a result of ERISA's classification of benefits as property rights rather than merely gifts since vesting cuts down the benefit entitlements for short service employees

- the plan document specifies each participant's vested right to benefits depending on the number of years the individual has been employed by the sponsoring employer

- if an employee terminates employment, he or she is entitled to the vested portion of his or her accrued benefits and the non-vested portion, if any, then becomes a forfeiture

- upon attaining the plan's Normal Retirement Age, the participant is 100% vested in his or her accrued benefit

How are Years of Service for Vesting determined?

- an employee must be credited with one Year of Vesting Service in any 12-month period defined in the plan document in which he or she is credited with at least 1000 Hours of Service

- generally, an Hour of Service must be credited to an employee
  - for each hour he or she is paid or entitled to payment for the performance of duties for the employer during the computation period
  - for certain periods of non-work (such as vacation, holiday, illness, incapacity, disability, layoff, jury duty, military leave, other approved leaves of absence, or back pay awards)

- to determine the number of Hours of Service during a computation period, the employer has the option of:
  - counting each hour for each employee,
  - establishing a table which credits a certain number of hours for each unit of time worked (such as 45 Hours of Service credited for each weekly paycheck, regardless of actual hours worked), or
  - using the Elapsed Time method (where the employer determines the number of Hours of Service credited between the employee's date of employment and the determination date in accordance with complicated Labor Regulations)

What is Normal Retirement Age for the plan?

- Normal Retirement Age is the earlier of the date provided for in the plan document, or the later of age 65 or the fifth anniversary of plan participation (this allows employers to hire individuals over age 60 without the plan needing to immediately vest and accrue their benefits)

How long can an employer make a plan participant wait before becoming vested in his or her employee contributions in a defined contribution plan?

- all employee contributions, such as elective salary deferrals, and after-tax Roth contributions, must always be 100% vested (*i.e.*, non-forfeitable)

How long can an employer make a plan participant wait before becoming vested in his or her employer contributions in a qualified retirement plan?

- in a defined contribution plan, all employer contributions, such as matching contributions or profit sharing and money purchase plan allocations, must always be vested at lease as quickly as the following:
  - if cliff vesting, then 100% after 3 Years of Service
  - if graded vesting, then 20% after 2 Years of Service, 40% after 3 Years, 60% after 4 Years, 80% after 5 Years, and 100% after 6 Years of Service
- slightly different minimum vesting rules apply to defined benefit plans
- there are several situations (such as plan termination) when a participant is automatically 100% vested, regardless of the schedule contained in the plan document

What is the general concept of benefit accruals?

- accrual rights are different than vesting rights—however, both accruals and vesting serve to limit the benefits to employees who do not continue working with the employer until retirement (or death or disability)
- accruals are a concept on how a plan participant is hired without any retirement benefits (*i.e.*, a -0- accrued benefit), and at retirement has something, and the accrued benefit is what he or she is entitled to if employment is severed (death, disability, quitting, being fired) or the plan is terminated along the way
- once a benefit, right or feature has accrued, it cannot be eliminated through a plan amendment
- however, a plan amendment may reduce or eliminate a benefit, right or feature for future promises that have not yet accrued
- although the plan can have a different 12-month period for a Year of Service for purposes of accruals than for vesting, the definitions and rules of 1000 Hours of Service are the same
- at any point in time
  - in a defined contribution plan, the accrued benefit is the participant's account balance (*i.e.*, the accumulation of contributions, forfeitures, and fund earnings)
  - in a defined benefit plan, the accrued benefit is whatever life annuity is payable starting upon attainment of his or her normal retirement date (or possibly upon his or her early retirement date, if the plan allows for an early retirement benefit)

How does a qualified retirement plan satisfy the definitely determinable benefits rule?
- in a defined contribution plan, the plan document will clearly indicate how allocations will be made to each participant's individual account
  - in a profit sharing plan, the formula that will divide the single discretionary contribution
  - in a money purchase plan, the exact dollar or amount or percentage of compensation
  - in a 401(k) plan, how participants can make, revise or revoke elections to make salary deferrals or designated Roth contributions, and if the employer has a mandatory or discretionary match
- in a defined benefit plan, the plan's actuary will convert one form of benefit to another based on the plan's actuarial equivalences, which must be stated in the plan document in a way that precludes any employer discretion

What are the basic forms of distribution that can be provided through a defined benefit plan?
- single life annuity: payments from the plan are paid monthly (or annually) to the plan participant starting on his or her normal retirement date and will continue for as long as he or she lives
- single life annuity with a guaranteed term: payments from the plan are paid monthly (or annually) to the plan participant starting on his or her normal retirement date and will continue for as long as she lives, but if he or she dies within the guaranteed term, then payments continue to a designated beneficiary for the remainder of the term (this protection costs a premium)
- joint life annuity: payments from the plan are paid monthly (or annually) to the plan participant starting on his or her normal retirement date and will continue for as long as he or she lives, but if he or she dies and the designated beneficiary is still alive, then payments continue to the beneficiary for the remainder of the beneficiary's life (this protection costs a premium)
- single life annuity: an amount representing the mathematical present value of future payments is paid in a single sum currently (a participant who dies earlier than expected "wins" and a participant who lives longer than expected "loses')

What are the maximum benefit accruals in any year for a qualified retirement plan?
- in a defined contribution plan,
  - the annual addition is the sum of
    - employee contributions,
    - employer contributions, and
    - the reallocation of forfeitures
  - in any year, the annual addition cannot be more than the lesser of
    - $40,000 (as adjusted for inflation), or
    - the participant's annual compensation
- in a defined benefit plan,
  - in any year, the total benefit paid from the plan cannot be more than the lesser of

- $160,000 (as adjusted for inflation, and as adjusted for other reasons), or
- the participant's average annual compensation (the average for the highest three consecutive years)

If the plan is Top-Heavy in any given year (as discussed in Chapter 8), then what are the minimum vesting and accrual rules?

- in a defined contribution plan,
  - all non-Key employees must generally receive at least 3% of his or her compensation
  - under current rules, no special vesting rules supersede in TH years
- in a defined benefit plan,
  - all non-Key employees must generally receive at least 2% of his or her average compensation (the average for the highest five consecutive years), but after the 10th year of Top-Heavy minimum accruals, the plan does not need to provide any further minimum benefit accruals
  - a slightly accelerated minimum vesting schedule supersedes in TH years

A. Vesting

1. Common Rules for All Qualified Retirement Plans

Statutory Rules at IRC § 411(a), as Cross-Referenced by IRC § 401(a)(7), and Labor Regs. § 2530.200b-1 and -2

As a qualification requirement, plans must meet the minimum vesting requirements. Vesting cuts down the benefit entitlements for short service employees, and is a result of ERISA's classification of benefits as property rights after a few years of service rather than merely nonbinding gifts. The employer can draft the plan document to provide that all accrued benefits are fully vested and non-forfeitable at all times, in which case, the vesting rules will always be in compliance. However, since Congress has allowed employers to forfeit certain accrued benefits for employees that terminate employment in just a few years, the plan documents will generally state a vesting schedule. The vesting schedule specifies each participant's vested right to benefits depending on the number of years the individual has been employed by the sponsoring employer (or sometimes by a predecessor employer or by an affiliated employer). If a plan participant terminates employment, he or she is entitled to the vested portion of his or her accrued benefits. The nonvested portion, if any, then becomes a "forfeiture." In a defined contribution plan, forfeitures will be reallocated to remaining plan participants pursuant to an allocation formula stated in the plan document, and in a defined benefit plan, forfeitures will be used to offset the current year's required contribution.

The following definitions apply to all qualified plans for vesting purposes for both defined contribution plans and defined benefit plans, (and generally also for benefit accrual purposes and plan eligibility purposes):

Years of Service: The plan document must set 12-month periods for calculating and crediting Years of Service for vesting purposes (either a calendar year, a plan year, or any other 12-month computation period stated in the plan document). An employee must be credited with one Year of Service for vesting in any year in which he or she is credited with at least 1000 Hours of Service, The plan can credit a Year of Service for vesting for any lesser number of required hours of service stated in a plan document. Special rules apply if the employer is deemed to be in a seasonal industry or maritime industry.

Hour of Service: Generally, an Hour of Service must be credited to an employee for each hour he or she is paid or entitled to payment for the performance of duties for the employer during the computation period. Additionally, an Hour of Service must be credited during certain periods of non-work (such as vacation, holiday, illness, incapacity, disability, lay-off, jury duty, military leave, other approved leaves of absence, or backpay awards). However, Hours of Service do not need to be credited for payments which reimburse an employee for medical expenses. There is a rule precluding the double counting of hours.

Counting Hours of Service: To determine the number of Hours of Service during a computation period, the employer has the option of:

- counting each hour each employee has actually worked during the year,
- establishing a table which credits a certain number of hours for each unit of time worked (such as 45 Hours of Service credited per week regardless of actual hours worked), or
- using the Elapsed Time method (where the employer determines the number of Hours of Service credited between the employee's date of employment and the determination date in accordance with complicated Labor Regulations).

Service Included: Service means all service with the employer, but certain Years of Service may be excluded, such as Years of Service before attaining age 18, years in which an eligible employee declined to contribute to a plan requiring employee contributions, years in which the employer did not maintain this plan or a predecessor plan, and periods after a Break in Service.

1-Year Break in Service: A 1-Year Break in Service is any year in which an employee is credited with less than 500 Hours of Service (certain approved leaves of absence, such as family leave, will require a "crediting" of 501 hours in a year even though an employee does not actually "work" that many hours).

Crediting service after a Participant incurs a 1-Year Break in Service: If a participant incurs a 1-Year Break in Service, then the plan can require that he or she must complete a new Year of Service before all of the pre-1-Year Break in Service years of credited service can once again be taken into account.

Disregard of certain periods of service (only for participants in a defined contribution plan or a 412(e)(3) compliant defined benefit plan): If a current employee incurs 5 consecutive 1-Year Breaks in Service, then credited years of vesting before the 5 consecutive year period shall be applied to the pre-5 year period plan accruals, and all accruals after the 5-year consecutive period will only be vested based on years of credited service after the 5-year period. Since an employee's service with the employer includes all service with the employer or predecessor employer, and since the employer, as plan administrator, is required to retain all relevant documents and personnel files for purposes of determining benefits under a qualified plans, these Break in Service rules basically allow employers to disregard and dispose of personnel files at appropriate times.

Forfeiture: the nonvested portion of a participant's accrued benefit after he or she separates from service and receives a distribution of his or her vested accrued benefit. Special rules apply if benefits in pay status are suspended if a former employee is rehired and becomes a participant of the plan once again.

Normal Retirement Age: the earlier of the date provided for in the plan document, or the later of age 65 or the fifth anniversary of plan participation.

The above definitions generally apply to Years of Service for vesting, Years of Service for benefit accruals and Years of Service for plan participation purposes, for both defined contribution plans and defined benefit plans. However, the 12-month computation period and elections, such as method for counting hours, can be different for different plans or for different purposes in the same plan. Common sense suggests that it is always simplest when a plan, and all plans maintained by the same employer, uses a uniform definition for all purposes. With different definitions, the payroll department is required to keep complicated personnel files.

2. Specific Rules for Defined Contribution Plans

a. Employee Contributions and Deferrals

Employee contributions, such as elective salary deferrals, after-tax Roth contributions, and after-tax contributions into a thrift savings plan, must always be 100% vested (*i.e.,* non-forfeitable).

b. Employer Contributions

In any qualified defined contribution plan (other than SEPs and SIMPLEs), the vesting schedule for employer contributions must be at least as advantageous to a participant as either of the following:

* Cliff vesting:
  * 100% after 3 Years of Service.

or

* Graded vesting:
  * 2 years of service — at least 20% vested;
  * 3 years of service — at least 40% vested;
  * 4 years of service — at least 60% vested;
  * 5 years of service — at least 80% vested; and
  * 6 years of service — 100% vested.

The plan can include a different cliff or graded vesting schedule, but for each Year of Service of vesting, the participant's vested percentage must be at least as favorable as the appropriate amount in the above minimum schedules.

An employee's vested percentage may never be reduced due to a plan amendment. If the plan is amended to provide a less favorable vesting schedule in the future, then every participant credited with at least 3 Years of Service for vesting must be able to choose to be personally vested under either the old vesting schedule or under the new schedule.

In all cases, the accrued benefits are automatically 100% vesting due to any of the following events:

* the participant attains the normal retirement age as defined in the plan document;
* the plan is terminated;

- the participant is part of the reduced workforce under a partial termination;
- if the employer has discretion in the level of contributions, and the IRS deems that there is a complete discontinuance of contributions (as a rule of thumb, if there are 10 years without any employer contributions).

The employer does not have to provide any death benefits through a qualified retirement plan. Therefore, a plan won't fail to be qualified if it doesn't provide full vesting upon death (although many plans do).

A vesting schedule in which there is a pattern of abuse in favor of Highly Compensated Employees (as discussed in Chapter 8) will cause the plan to fail the nondiscrimination requirements of IRC §401(a)(4) (such as firing Non Highly Compensated Employees immediately before they vest in their respective accrued benefits). The vesting rules do not apply to government plans, church plans, and certain other statutorily excluded plans. Since the above allowable vesting schedules are currently the same as those minimum required vesting schedules if the plan is deemed to be Top Heavy (as discussed in Chapter 8), it no longer matters (as far as vesting is concerned) if the defined contribution plan is Top Heavy or not.

3. Specific Rules for Defined Benefit Plans

Traditional defined benefit plans can choose cliff vesting or graded vesting, but the allowable vesting schedules under normal circumstances are not as good as the mandatory minimum vesting schedules when the plan is Top Heavy. Therefore, unless business goals demand the normal schedules, if there is even a remote chance that the plan could become Top Heavy, using the more restrictive Top Heavy vesting schedules as the actual vesting schedule for the plan makes administration so much easier.

In any qualified defined benefit plan, the vesting schedule for employer contributions must be at least as advantageous to a participant as either of the following:

- Cliff vesting:
  - 100% after 5 Years of Service
- Cliff vesting for traditional defined benefit plans that are Top Heavy:
  - 100% after 3 Years of Service

or

- Graded vesting for traditional defined benefit plans:
  - 3 years of service—at least 20% vested;
  - 4 years of service—at least 40% vested;
  - 5 years of service—at least 60% vested;
  - 6 years of service—at least 80% vested; and
  - 7 years of service—100% vested
- Graded vesting for traditional defined benefit plans that are Top Heavy:
  - 2 years of service—at least 20% vested;
  - 3 years of service—at least 40% vested;
  - 4 years of service—at least 60% vested;

- 5 years of service — at least 80% vested; and
- 6 years of service — 100% vested

If the defined benefit plan is either a statutory hybrid plan (*a.k.a.* a cash balance plan), or if the defined benefit plan has a 401(k) feature (starting in 2010), then the plan's vesting schedule must be only a cliff vesting schedule which is at least as advantageous to a participant as:

- Cliff vesting:
  - 100% after 3 Years of Service

B. Accruals

1. Common Rules for All Qualified Retirement Plans

As a qualification requirement, plans must meet the benefit accrual requirements. Accrual rights are different than vesting rights, although they work in tandem to penalize short-service employees when they leave after only a few years. The Years of Service rules for benefit accrual are similar to those for vesting, but wherever the employer has a choice, such as the 12 month determination period, the plan may have different provisions for Years of Service for benefit accruals than for vesting.

2. Specific Rules for Defined Contribution Plans

a. Definitely Determinable Benefits

Although defined contribution plans generally provide employers with more flexibility than defined benefit plans, the flexibility is not unfettered. As a qualification requirement, defined contribution plan benefits need to be considered definitely determinable.

Profit sharing and stock bonus plans: "The plan [document] must provide a definite predetermined formula for allocating the contributions made to the plan among the participants and for distributing the funds accumulated under the plan after a fixed number of years, the attainment of a stated age, or upon the prior occurrence of some event such as layoff, illness, disability, retirement, death, or severance of employment. A formula for allocating the contributions among the participants is definite if, for example, it provides for an allocation in proportion to the basic compensation of each participant."[1]

Pension plans (such as money purchase plans and target benefit plans): "The determination of the amount of retirement benefits and the contributions to provide such benefits are not dependent upon profits. Benefits are not definitely determinable if funds arising from forfeitures on termination of service, or other reason, may be used to provide increased benefits for the remaining participants."[2]

---

1. Treas. Regs. § 1.401-1(b)(1)(ii) and (iii).
2. Treas. Regs. § 1.401-1(b)(1)(i).

401(k) plans, SEPs and SIMPLEs: The Treasury regulations that pre-date ERISA do not provide precise definitions. However, plan documents are generally required to state the level of employer match, or the method of allocating non-elective employer contributions. Therefore, mere compliance with the respective Code sections arguably indicates that these plans do, in fact, provide definitely determinable benefits.

b. Benefit Accrual Rules

Statutory Rules at IRC § 411(b)(2), as Cross-Referenced by IRC § 401(a)(7)

In a defined contribution plan, the accrued benefit is simply the participant's account balance at any point in time. The account balance, once accrued, is protected and neither its value nor optional forms of distribution can be reduced or eliminated by plan amendment (other than ESOPs that modify distribution options in a nondiscriminatory manner or in certain cases, such as plan mergers, where the employer transfers assets from one plan to another and the transferee plan does not provide some or all of the forms of distribution previously available under the transferor plan).

Basically, a participant will be entitled to an allocation of the employer's nonelective profit sharing plan contributions and money purchase plan mandatory contributions once credited with a Year of Service, which is 1000 Hours of Service after becoming a participant in the plan. A defined contribution plan is allowed to require that a participant be credited with a Year of Service must also be actively employed on the last day of the plan year to be entitled to an allocation. However, if the employer wants to penalize employees who terminate service before the last day of the year, then the last day provision must be tested and cannot discriminate in favor of Highly Compensated Employees (such as a pattern of firing non-Highly Compensated Employees so they do not share in the allocations).

Allocations are defined in the plan document:

- in a cash or deferred arrangement, employee deferrals go directly into his or her account;
- in a profit-sharing plan, the plan document clearly states how a discretionary contribution, if made, will be allocated among the participant accounts; and
- in a money purchase plan, the document clearly indicates the percentage of compensation that will be allocated to each participant's respective account.

In addition to the employer contribution, if the employer is not using forfeitures to reduce contributions, then the plan document must clearly indicate how forfeitures are reallocated (the default is by the ratio that a participant's account balance bears to the total, but the plan can state that the method of allocation of forfeitures is based on the ratio of a participant's compensation as it bears to the total compensation). Because of the Break in Service rules (as discussed above), many defined contribution plans keep all forfeitures for terminated employees in a suspense account for 5 years in case the terminated employee returns to work. After 5 years, the forfeitures are released from the segregated account and are either used to reduce the employer's contribution or are allocated to active participants, depending on the terms of the plan document.

The plan must maintain a separate accounting for each employee's accrued benefit. Allocations to the employee's accounts cannot cease or be reduced because of the attainment of any age. In years that the plan is Top Heavy, each non Key Employee must generally receive an allocation of 3% of compensation (or a lesser percentage if nondiscriminatory).

3. Specific Rules for Defined Benefit Plans

Subject to the statutory limitations described below, the plan document is allowed to promise any level of benefits to participants, payable either at normal or early retirement age, in various forms. The only catch is that the total benefits promised to all participants must be adequately funded by the time they become due.

a. Definitely Determinable Benefits
Statutory Rules at IRC § 401(a)(25)

In a defined benefit plan, the plan's actuary will convert one form of benefit to another based on the plan's actuarial equivalences, which must be stated in the plan document in a way that precludes any employer discretion.

b. Normal Form of Benefit
Statutory Rules at IRC § 411(a)(7)(A)(i)

The accrued benefit in a defined benefit plan (other than a statutory hybrid cash balance plan) must be expressed as an annual benefit commencing at normal retirement age.

c. Benefit Accrual Rules
Statutory Rules at IRC § 411(b)(1), as Cross-Referenced by IRC § 401(a)(7)

All of the general rules of accrued benefits for defined contribution plans apply to defined benefit plans; but the rules for defined benefit plan accrued benefits and benefit accruals are much more complicated.

Mathematically, all defined benefit plans are, by design, "backloaded" since accruals in the final years before retirement are more valuable than accruals in a participant's younger age and earlier stages of employment. A defined benefit plan must have an accrual formula which satisfies one of the following three rules, which minimizes the mathematical backloading into an acceptable range:

3% Rule: each participant's respective accrued benefit as of the end of each plan year is at least 3 percent of the "3 percent method benefit," multiplied by the number of years (not in excess of 33⅓) of his participation in the plan including years after his normal retirement age. The "3 percent method benefit" is the participant's normal retirement benefit which he or she would be entitled to receive if he or she commenced participation at the earliest possible entry age for any individual who is or could be a participant under the plan and if he or she served continuously until the earlier of age 65 or the normal retirement age under the plan.

Fractional Rule: each participant's respective accrued benefit is at least the "fractional rule benefit" multiplied by a fraction (not exceeding 1), the numerator of which is his total number of years of participation in the plan, and the denominator of which is the total number of years he or she would have participated in the plan if he or she separated from the service at the normal retirement age under the plan. The "fractional rule benefit" is the annual benefit commencing at the normal retirement age under the plan to which a participant would be entitled if he or she continued to earn annually the same rate of compensation until normal retirement age.

133⅓ Rule: instead of looking at each participant's respective accrued benefits, as is required for the 3% and fractional rules, the 133⅓ rule is satisfied purely at the plan formula level. The accrued benefit payable at the plan's normal retirement age is equal to the normal retirement benefit, and the annual rate at which any individual who is or could be a participant can accrue the retirement benefits payable at normal retirement age under the plan for any later plan year cannot be more than 133⅓ percent of the annual rate at which he can accrue benefits for any plan year beginning on or after such particular plan year and before such later plan year. Early retirement benefits and postponed retirement benefits are ignored for purpose of compliance with this method.

Since the formula for accrued benefits is clearly stated in the plan document, compliance with one of the three allowable rules is determined during the planning stages of initial establishment of the defined benefit plan, or for any subsequent plan amendments that affect benefit accruals. Defined benefit plans can provide faster accrual schedules, so that the benefits are frontloaded, as is the case with statutory hybrid cash balance plan designs. Additionally, social security benefits can be taken into account, and the accrual formula can include some permitted disparity which allows slightly larger benefits for those higher paid employees who "lose out" on social security benefits because their salaries exceed the Social Security Taxable Wage Base. Regardless of how the plan document defines accrued benefits, minimum benefit accrual rules apply in any year in which the plan is deemed Top Heavy.

d. Age Discrimination
Statutory Rules at IRC §§ 411(b)(1)(G), 411(b)(1)(H), and 411(b)(5)

A defined benefit plan is prohibited from ceasing or reducing the accrued benefit or the rate of an employee's benefit accrual because of the attainment of any age (including normal retirement age) or because of any increase in his age or service. New rules were added in 2006 and the accrued benefit for any participant (whether expressed as an annuity payable at normal retirement age, in the case of a traditional defined benefit plan, or as the balance of a hypothetical account or as the current value of the accumulated percentage of the employee's final average compensation, as in the case of statutory hybrid plans) will satisfy the age discrimination prohibitions if it is equal to or greater than that of any similarly situated, younger individual who is or could be a participant.

e. Normal Retirement Benefits
Statutory Rules at IRC § 411(b)(8)

As indicated, in a defined benefit plan, all focus is on the benefits payable at normal retirement age, so the plan document must state a normal retirement age. The most common is the later of age 65 or 5 years of participation (so that if an individual is hired anytime after age 61, the plan still has sufficient time to fund for that individual's benefit), but can be earlier.

Unless the participant elects to postpone the starting date, benefit distributions must generally begin by the 60th day after the close of the plan year in which the participant attains the earlier of age 65 or the normal retirement age specified under the plan (the plan can allow earlier distributions for terminated employees). However, as that participant continues working beyond retirement age, and continues to postpone benefit distributions, his benefits continue to accrue and the ultimate benefit shall be the actuarial equivalent of the annual benefit at normal retirement age. In the situation where a participant terminates, starts receiving benefit distributions, and is then rehired, the employer is allowed to suspend benefit payments while paying a salary.

f. Early Retirement Benefits

One major advantage of a defined benefit plan is that it can provide early retirement subsidiaries (which allow certain older members of the work force to voluntarily leave). Such subsidies are usually provided in a short window (*i.e.,* "for the next three months, any employee who is 55 and who has worked here for 20 years will be entitled to the early retirement subsidies") or on a permanent basis (*i.e.,* "every employee who is 55 and who has worked here for 20 years will be entitled to the early retirement subsidies"). There are two main types of early retirement subsidies:

- assume (for actuarial equivalent purposes only) that the annuity payable at a younger age is the same benefit payable at retirement age (*i.e.,* if $1000 payable as a life annuity payable at 65 equals $800 payable as a life annuity payable at age 55, then the early retirement subsidy may allow that individual to receive $1000 payable as a life annuity starting at 55), or
- assume that the individual is credited for future years of service he or she would likely have worked if there was no Early Retirement subsidy (*i.e.,* if the plan formula provides a benefit of 1% of average compensation for each year of service, and a particular individual has 23 years at age 55 (AB = 23% of compensation) but would have 33 years if he stayed until age 65 (AB = 33% of compensation), then the early retirement subsidy may allow that individual at age 55 to receive a 33% of compensation benefits).

All early retirement benefits and subsidies must be tested separately and cannot discriminate in favor of the Highly Compensated Employees.

g. Alternate Forms of Distribution

As long as each benefit is actuarially equivalent to each other, using assumptions that are specified in the plan in a way which precludes employer discretion, then the plan document is allowed to provide any type of optional form of benefit. If a plan is amended to eliminate an optional form of benefit, it can only be eliminated for all future benefit accruals, but generally must be preserved for benefits accrued on the date of the plan amendment. Employers are allowed to provide optional forms that coordinate with the individual's Social Security benefits and can add cost of living adjustments. However, in all cases, an optional form of benefit is considered to be a benefit, right, or feature, and cannot be currently or effectively available in a nondiscriminatory manner to Highly Compensated Employees. Listed below are some of the more common optional forms of benefit distributions (which are discussed in more detail in Chapter 9):

Single Life Annuity: Payments from the plan are paid monthly (or annually) to the plan participant starting on her normal retirement date and will continue for as long as she lives. An unhealthy individual who does not live out her full life expectancy will lose all benefits upon death (thus the plan has incurred an actuarial gain); whereas, a super-healthy individual who outlives her life expectancy will continue getting paid for life (thus the plan has incurred an actuarial loss).

Single Life Annuity With a Guaranteed Term: This optional form of benefit would appeal to a participant who needs a stream on money coming in for a number of years, regardless of whether or not he or she lives that entire period (for example, a participant retires and starts receiving benefits from the plan, and the youngest child has 6 more years of medical school or there are 8 more years of mortgage payments until the family home is wholly paid off).

Joint Life Annuity: This optional form of benefit would appeal to a participant who needs a stream on money coming in while another individual is alive, regardless of whether or not he or she dies first (for example, a participant retires and starts receiving benefits from the plan, and the participant is responsible for support of a spouse, parent, child or special needs sibling).

Single Sum: This optional form of benefit would appeal to a participant who wants to have unfettered investment and distribution control over his or her benefits accrued under the employer-sponsored defined benefit plan. A lump sum represents a single payment today which represents the actuarial equivalent of all future expected benefit payments.

h. Protected Benefits
Statutory Rules at IRC § 411(d)(6)

With few exceptions, no plan amendment can eliminate an early retirement benefit, a retirement-type subsidy, or an optional form of benefit that has already been accrued. There is no protection, however, for future promises that have not yet been accrued. There are complicated rules for the limited circumstances within which amendments can eliminate optional forms of benefits, such as when a plan has gotten very complicated and hard to administer due to multiple mergers of plans, each with their own set of optional forms of benefits. Under ERISA § 204(h), advance notice of a reduction in the future rate of benefit accruals in a defined benefit plan must be provided in a timely manner to all plan participants.[3]

4. Additional Non-Retirement Type Benefits That Can Be Promised in Any Qualified Retirement Plan

a. Life insurance

The qualified plan, whether defined contribution or defined benefit in design, is supposed to primarily provide retirement benefits, but can be used to provide death benefits, as long as they are incidental (meaning that the plan expects to provide the majority of plan benefits to the employee while he or she is alive in retirement than is expected to be paid to his or her beneficiary upon death).[4] To be considered merely incidental, the following rules apply:

Defined contribution plans:

---

3. The parallel provisions that impose a penalty tax for failure to timely and properly communicate a plan amendment that will reduce the rate of future benefit accruals are at IRC § 4980F.

4. See, for example, IRC § 401(a)(9)(G) and T.D. 9130 (6/14/2004), Preamble to Treas. Regs. § 1.401(a)(9)-1 through -9.

- If the employer contribution portion of the account balance is used to purchase insurance contracts, then the premiums are limited to 50% if used to purchase whole life insurance and to 25% if used to purchase term life insurance;[5]
- If the voluntary employee contributions portion of the account balance is used to purchase life insurance, then the 50% / 25% limits do not apply.[6]

Defined benefit plans:

- the face amount cannot exceed 100 times the participant's projected monthly benefit.[7]

Incidental life insurance is considered a benefit, right or feature, and therefore must be available in a nondiscriminatory manner.

b. Disability Benefits

The plan document is allowed to provide payment of benefits upon disability, if earlier than retirement.[8] A qualified disability benefit is a disability benefit provided by a plan which does not exceed the benefit which would be provided for the participant if he separated from the service at normal retirement age.[9] The excess portion of a benefit payable under a defined benefit plan payable upon disability is deemed an "ancillary benefit" and is not considered a protected benefit that cannot be eliminated through a plan amendment.[10] Normally, when an individual is classified as disabled, he or she is not an active employee, so the employer cannot deduct the premiums paid into accident and health plans,[11] and he or she is not allowed to make elective salary deferrals or after tax Roth contributions into a 401(k) plan.[12] There do not seem to be any rules in the Code allowing plan assets to be used to purchase actual short-term or long-term disability insurance policies, so if the employer wishes to provide employees with disability benefits, it can either draft the plan document to allow the distribution of all or a portion of the retirement benefits upon disability, or should establish a disability insurance plan outside of the qualified retirement plan. Unless there is a compelling business reason to do otherwise, employers are encouraged to conform definitions of disability in a qualified plan to those used by Social Security so that an individual will be deemed disabled for all purposes.

---

5. Rev. Rul. 76-353 (differentiating between level premium whole life insurance and a decreasing amount whole life insurance). The initial 50% limit is set forth in Rev. Rul. 74-307.

6. Rev. Rul. 69-408. Please note that while still relevant guidance, it pre-dates the addition of §401(k) to the Code allowing for elective salary deferrals, but which are actually considered to be employer contributions.

7. Rev. Rul. 2004-21.

8. IRC §401(a)(2)(B)(i)(I).

9. IRC §411(a)(9), flush language after subparagraph B.

10. Treas. Regs. §1.411(d)-3(g)(2)(ii).

11. IRC §§106 and 162.

12. However, see PLR 200235043, which allows a specific employer to adopt a specific voluntary insurance plan which will replace the elective deferrals, matching contributions and any nonelective contributions that would have been credited to a participant's account under a 401(k) plan had the participant not become disabled, and which will be funded as an administrative charge against the participant's account.

c. Retiree Health Benefits

Statutory Rules at IRC §§ 401(h) and 420, and Treas. Regs.
§ 1.401-14

A qualified retirement plan can provide for the payment of sickness, accident, hospitalization, and medical expenses for retired employees, their spouses and their dependents; however, the retiree medical benefits are only considered to be subordinate to the retirement benefits if at all times the aggregate of contributions and any life insurance protection does not exceed 25 percent of the aggregate contributions. To be considered "retired," an employee must generally be eligible to receive retirement benefits provided under the plan, or else be retired by an employer providing such medical benefits by reason of permanent disability. Under certain circumstances, excess assets in a defined benefit plan can be transferred into a health benefits account for retirees.

C. Maximum Benefits That Can Be Promised in a Qualified Plan

As a qualification requirement, plans must meet the requirements that limit benefits and contributions. Since the emphasis of a defined contribution plan is the contribution, it is the contributions made by both employers and employees, that are limited by Congress under the Code. On the other hand, in defined benefit plans, since the benefits are defined in the plan document, then they are limited under the Code. This limitation generally affects the higher paid employees, and this is the main reason that employers will sponsor a qualified plan for a large section of the workforce, including the lower-paid workers, and then will additionally provide non-qualified deferred compensation and executive compensation to the favored employees.

1. Specific Rules for Defined Contribution Plans

Statutory Provisions at IRC § 415(c), as Cross-Referenced by IRC
§ 401(a)(16)

The proper way to describe any credits to a participant's account in a defined contribution plan is as an annual addition, which is defined as the sum of all employer contributions, employee contributions, and reallocated forfeitures for the plan year. The following additions to a participant's account are not deemed annual additions:

- rehired employees who repay their previously distributed benefits in order to buy back prior credited Years of Service;
- catch-up contributions (if over age 50 or if returning from active military service);
- restorative payments where an employer, in certain circumstances, deposits a non-deductible contribution to mitigate certain investment losses;
- any excess deferrals after they have been distributed to Highly Compensated Employees;
- amounts rolled over from another qualified plan into the defined contribution plan;

- repayments of plan loans; and
- employee contributions to a qualified cost of living arrangement.

There are special rules for annual additions to church plans, individual medical benefit accounts, post-retirement medical benefit accounts for Key Employees, and ESOPs.

The maximum annual addition on contributions to a participant's account under a defined contribution plan in any year is the lesser of:

- the statutory dollar limit of $40,000 (as adjusted for inflation);
- 100% of the participant's compensation (since the plan participant can't be worth more to the employer in retirement than he or she is worth as a active employee); or
- the annual addition that is calculated and determined to be allocated to the participant's account under the terms of the plan document.

The definition of compensation for purposes of annual additions means compensation paid as an employee from the employer for the year, where the following are added back in even though they are excluded for income tax purposes: any elective deferrals for 401(k) plans or SIMPLEs; and all other salary deferrals made to cafeteria plans, qualified transportation fringe benefit plans, or § 457 nonqualified plans. For self-employed individuals, compensation refers to the participant's earned income (except for foreign earned income and housing costs). There is a special definition of compensation for participants that are permanently and totally disabled. The term "limitation year" is used rather than plan year because in all cases where the plan year is not the calendar year, the § 415 limits are adjusted for Cost of Living Adjustments for a calendar year and such limits are effective for the limitation year that starts in such calendar year.

Remember, as discussed in Chapter 6, under IRC § 402(g), the maximum amount that can be deferred by any individual in all 401(k) plans he or she is eligible to participate in for any year is limited, even if the plans are all sponsored by different employers. However, the § 415 limits are per employer, so if an individual works 2 jobs and participates in 2 separate plans of 2 non-affiliated employers, then he or she can receive the maximum level of annual additions in each.

Many employers, in appropriate situations, will simultaneously sponsor a 401(k) plan, a profit sharing plan and a money purchase plan. If employees participate in all three types of plans, then the combined documents are generally written in tandem so that annual additions are a mix of employee elective pre-tax salary deferrals or after-tax designated Roth contributions, employer matching contributions, employer mandatory money purchase plan contributions, and then, if possible, discretionary employer profit sharing contributions.

2. Specific Rules for Defined Benefit Plans

Statutory Provisions at IRC § 415(b), as Cross-Referenced by IRC § 401(a)(16)

The maximum annual benefit that can be paid to a participant or beneficiary from a defined benefit plan in any year is the lesser of

- the statutory dollar limit of $160,000 (as adjusted for inflation), or

- 100% of the participant's average compensation for his high 3 years (since the plan participant can't be worth more to the employer in retirement than he or she is worth as a active employee), or
- the annual benefit distribution that is calculated and determined to be accrued and payable under the terms of the plan document. However, if the plan benefit is less than $10,000, he or she may receive a $10,000 annual benefit.

Under a defined benefit plan, only the annual benefit is limited, and whatever contributions are required by the employer to properly fund the benefits are generally allowed to be deducted. The definition of compensation for purposes of the compensation limit is the same definition for purposes of limitations on annual additions in defined contribution plans. For self-employed individuals, compensation refers to the participant's earned income (except for foreign earned income and housing costs). There is a special definition of compensation for participants that are permanently and totally disabled. The term "limitation year" is used rather than plan year because in all cases where the plan year is not the calendar year, the §415 limits are adjusted for Cost of Living Adjustments for a calendar year and such limits are effective for the limitation year that starts in such calendar year.

The $160,000 annual statutory dollar limit is payable at anytime between ages 62 and 65 as a life annuity. It is adjusted for ages of distribution before age 62 or after age 65, and for forms of distribution other than a straight life annuity. This dollar limit is accrued ratably over 10 years of participation (for example, if an employee first participates in a plan at age 54 and retires at age 62, the most that he or she can get from the plan upon retirement is 80% of the statutory dollar limit). There are no adjustments for age or form for the 100% of compensation limit (or minimum $10,000 de minimis benefit), but it is accrued ratably over 10 years of service with the employer (as opposed to accruing over 10 years of participation in the plan).

D. Minimum Benefits That Must Be Promised in a Qualified Plan That Is Top Heavy

As discussed in Chapter 8, each year, each qualified retirement plan needs to be tested to determine if it is Top Heavy in the current year based on the allocation of plan benefits in the prior year. In years that the plan is considered Top Heavy, certain minimum benefit accruals must be provided to "non-Key Employees" — minimum contributions in defined contribution plans and minimum accruals in defined benefit plans.

1. Specific Rules for Defined Contribution Plans

If the defined contribution plan is Top Heavy for the current year, then the employer contribution portion of the annual addition for all non-Key employees must be at least 3% of his or her compensation (or a lower uniform percentage). Therefore, if a defined contribution plan document always provides for employer contributions of at least 3% of compensation for all non Key Employees, it doesn't matter (as far as benefit accruals are concerned) if the defined contribution plan is Top Heavy or not.

2. Specific Rules for Defined Benefit Plans

The regulations require a minimum benefit under a defined benefit plan for each non-Key Employee who has at least 1,000 hours of service for an accrual computation period.

A Top Heavy defined benefit plan will meet the minimum benefit requirements for the plan year for which the plan is Top Heavy if the accrued benefits derived from the employer's contributions for each non-Key Employee participant, when expressed as an annual retirement benefit, equals or exceeds the "applicable percentage" of the non-Key Employee participant's average annual compensation during a statutory testing period. In determining whether the benefits provided by the employer meet the minimum standards, only benefits derived from employer contributions are taken into account, and accrued benefits attributable to employee contributions are ignored. Any accruals of employer-derived benefits may be used to satisfy the defined benefit minimum even though the accruals are attributable to years for which the plan was not Top Heavy. Thus, if a non-Key Employee has already accrued the maximum amount of minimum benefits required at the time the plan became Top Heavy, then no additional minimum accruals would be required. Unlike the minimum contribution rules for defined contribution plans, the minimum benefit rules do not provide that a non-Key Employee's benefit must be at least as great as that of the Key Employee with the highest accrued benefit.

The "applicable percentage" of a non-key employee's testing period compensation that must be supplied by a Top Heavy defined benefit plan is 2% multiplied by the number of the participant's years of service with the employer, but not more than 20% of average compensation in total. A non-Key Employee, therefore, may still be subject to the maximum applicable percentage after 10 years of service if his or her average compensation increases even if the applicable percentage is frozen once it hits 20%. A plan that provides a normal retirement benefit equal to the greater of the plan's projected formula or the projected minimum benefit, if benefits accrue in accordance with the "fractional rule", might not satisfy the defined benefit minimums.

Example: A non-key employee enters a Top Heavy plan at age 21 in a plan in which the projected minimum is greater for the employee than the projected benefit under the normal formula would be. Under the fractional rule, the employee's accrued benefit 10 years later at age 31 would be 5% (20% x 10/40). Under the Top Heavy rules, the employee's minimum accrued benefit after 10 years of service must be at least 20% of average compensation. Thus, because the 5% benefit is not equal to the 20% minimum required benefit, it would not satisfy the Top Heavy rules.

E. Examples

In this section , we look at a simple defined benefit plan with three hypothetical employees, to better understand how vesting, benefit accruals, § 415 maximum benefits and Top-Heavy minimum accruals all work together.

Relevant provisions of Defined Benefit Plan X (for employees A, B and C):

- Normal Retirement Benefit: 55% of the Participant's High 3 Year Average Salary, payable as a monthly life annuity starting at age 65 (or, if the Participant is married when benefits commence, the actuarial equivalent of a Qualified Joint and Survivor Annuity starting at age 65)

- Accrued Benefit: Normal Retirement Benefit multiplied by a fraction, where the numerator is the number of years of actual plan participation and the denominator is the total number of years of plan participation expected from date of hire until Normal Retirement Age

- Top Heavy Minimum Accrued Benefit: 2% of the Participant's High 5 Year Average Salary, multiplied by the number of years (to a maximum of 10 years) that the Participant is credited with service while the Plan is Top-Heavy, payable as a monthly life annuity starting at age 65

- Maximum Accrued Benefit: The lesser of the IRC § 415(b) annual statutory dollar limit or 100% of the Participant's High 3 Year Average Salary, payable as a monthly life annuity starting at age 65. Such limit shall be adjusted annually in accordance with Cost of Living Adjustments in IRC § 415(d), and shall be reduced by 1/10 for each year of service less than 10 credited to the Participant

- Vesting: 20% after 2 years of service, 40% after 3 years, 60% after 4 years, 80% after 5 years, and 100% after 6 years of service

- Participation: Immediately on date of hire (therefore the number of years of service is the same as the number of years of participation).

Please note, in all of the following examples, first we calculate the projected Normal Retirement Benefit based on the expected High 3 Year Average Salary, then we calculate the Accrued Benefit, make certain it is at least as great as the Top-Heavy minimum accrued benefit, and make certain that it does not exceed the IRC § 415(b) maximum accrued benefit, and then we multiply the accrued benefit by the vesting percentage. The vested accrued benefit is the amount of benefits owed to the participant if he or she terminated employment on that date (if the plan terminated on that date, then all accrued benefits are automatically fully vested, so the vesting part of the calculations would not be needed).

For 2010, the IRC § 415(b) annual statutory dollar limit is $195,000 (which is $16,250 per month). While adjustments will be made in future years based on actual inflation, for this example, let's assume a 2% per year increase (rounded to next lowest $5,000 increment). Therefore, in 2014, it is assumed to be $210,000 ($17,500 monthly) and in 2020, it is assumed to be $235,000 ($19,583.33 monthly).

For 2010, the IRC § 401(a)(17) annual compensation limit is $245,000 (which is $20,416.67 per month). While adjustments will be made in future years based on actual inflation, for this example, let's assume a 2% per year increase (rounded to next lowest $5,000 increment). Therefore, in 2014, it is assumed to be $265,000 ($22,083.33 monthly) and in 2020, it is assumed to be $295,000 ($24,583.33 monthly).

1. Employee A

Info for Employee A as of December 31, 2010

- Current Age: 30
- Age at Hire: 25
- Total years of service to date: 5
- Total years of service expected at age 65: 40

- Total years of service during which the Plan was Top-Heavy: 4
- Actual High 3 Year Average Salary: $22,000 ($1,833.33 monthly)
- Actual High 5 Year Average Salary: $20,400 ($1,700.00 monthly)
- Expected High 3 Year Average Salary at 65: $25,000 ($2,083.33 monthly)

What is Employee A's projected Normal Retirement Benefit?

$1,145.83 per month, starting on her 65th birthday and continuing for the rest of her life. [2,083.33 * .55]

What is Employee A's Accrued Benefit if she terminated employment on December 31, 2010?

$136.00 per month, starting on her 65th birthday and continuing for the rest of her life. This was calculated as

- the accrued benefit based on the Plan's formula of $126.04 [1,833.33 * .55 * 5/40];
- but not less than the minimum Accrued Benefit of $136.00 [1,700.00 * .02 * 4];
- but not more than the maximum accrued benefit of $916.67 {the lesser of [16,250 * 5/10] or [1,833.33 * 5/10]}

What is Employee A's Vested Accrued Benefit that would actually be paid if she terminated employment on December 31, 2010?

$108.80 per month, starting on her 65th birthday and continuing for the rest of her life. [136.00 * .8]

Info for Employee A as of December 31, 2020 (ten years later)

- Current Age: 40
- Age at Hire: 25 (no change)
- Total years of service to date: 15
- Total years of service expected at age 65: 40 (no change)
- Total years of service during which the Plan was Top-Heavy: 12
- Actual High 3 Year Average Salary: $40,000 ($3,333.33 monthly)
- Actual High 5 Year Average Salary: $38,600 ($3,216.67 monthly)
- Expected High 3 Year Average Salary at 65: $45,000 ($3,750.00 monthly)

What is Employee A's projected Normal Retirement Benefit?

$2,062.50 per month, starting on her 65th birthday and continuing for the rest of her life. [3,750.00 * .55]

What is Employee A's Accrued Benefit if she terminated employment on December 31, 2020?

$687.50 per month, starting on her 65th birthday and continuing for the rest of her life. This was calculated as

- the accrued benefit based on the Plan's formula of $687.50 [3,333.33 * .55 * 15/40];
- but not less than the minimum Accrued Benefit of $643.33 [3,216.67 * .02 * 10];
- but not more than the maximum accrued benefit of $3,333.33 {the lesser of [19,583.33 * 10/10] or [3,333.33 * 10/10]}

What is Employee A's Vested Accrued Benefit that would actually be paid if she terminated employment on December 31, 2020?

$687.50 per month, starting on her 65th birthday and continuing for the rest of her life. [687.50 * 1.0]

2. Employee B

Info for Employee B as of December 31, 2010
- Current Age: 60
- Age at Hire: 59
- Total years of service to date: 1
- Total years of service expected at age 65: 6
- Total years of service during which the Plan was Top-Heavy: 1
- Actual High 3 Year Average Salary: $70,000 ($5,833.33 monthly)
- Actual High 5 Year Average Salary: $68,000 ($5,666.67 monthly)
- Expected High 3 Year Average Salary at 65: $80,000 ($6,666.67 monthly)

What is Employee B's projected Normal Retirement Benefit?

$3,666.67 per month, starting on her 65th birthday and continuing for the rest of her life. [6,666.67 * .55]

What is Employee B's Accrued Benefit if she terminated employment on December 31, 2010?

$534.72 per month, starting on her 65th birthday and continuing for the rest of her life. This was calculated as
- the accrued benefit based on the Plan's formula of $534.72 [5,833.33 * .55 * 1/6];
- but not less than the minimum Accrued Benefit of $113.33 [5,666.67 * .02 * 1];
- but not more than the maximum accrued benefit of $583.33 {the lesser of [16,250 * 1/10] or [5,833.33 * 1/10]}

What is Employee B's Vested Accrued Benefit that would actually be paid if she terminated employment on December 31, 2010?

Nothing (because she is 0% vested in her Accrued Benefit)

Info for Employee B as of December 31, 2014 (four years later)
- Current Age: 64
- Age at Hire: 59 (no change)
- Total years of service to date: 5
- Total years of service expected at age 65: 6 (no change)
- Total years of service during which the Plan was Top-Heavy: 5
- Actual High 3 Year Average Salary: $85,000 ($7,083.33 monthly)
- Actual High 5 Year Average Salary: $82,000 ($6,833.33 monthly)
- Expected High 3 Year Average Salary at 65: $85,500 ($7,125.00 monthly)

What is Employee B's projected Normal Retirement Benefit?

$3,918.75 per month, starting on her 65th birthday and continuing for the rest of her life. [7,125.00 * .55]

What is Employee B's Accrued Benefit if she terminated employment on December 31, 2014?

$3,246.53 per month, starting on her 65th birthday and continuing for the rest of her life. This was calculated as
- the accrued benefit based on the Plan's formula of $3,246.53 [7,083.33 * .55 * 5/6];

- but not less than the minimum Accrued Benefit of $683.33 [6,833.33 * .02 * 5];
- but not more than the maximum accrued benefit of $3,541.67 {the lesser of [17,500 * 5/10] or [7,083.33 * 5/10]}

What is Employee B's Vested Accrued Benefit that would actually be paid if she terminated employment on December 31, 2014?

$2,597.22 per month, starting on her 65th birthday and continuing for the rest of her life. [3,246.53 * .8]

3. Employee C

Info for Employee C as of December 31, 2010

- Current Age: 60
- Age at Hire: 57
- Total years of service to date: 3
- Total years of service expected at age 65: 8
- Total years of service during which the Plan was Top-Heavy: -0- (since C is classified as a Key Employee)
- Actual High 3 Year Average Salary: $500,000 — limited to $245,000 ($20,416.67 monthly)
- Actual High 5 Year Average Salary: $500,000 — limited to $245,000 ($20,416.67 monthly)
- Expected High 3 Year Average Salary at 65: $500,000 — limited to $245,000 ($20,416.67 monthly)

What is Employee C's projected Normal Retirement Benefit?

$11,229.17 per month, starting on her 65th birthday and continuing for the rest of her life. [20,416.67 * .55]

What is Employee C's Accrued Benefit if she terminated employment on December 31, 2010?

$4,210.94 per month, starting on her 65th birthday and continuing for the rest of her life. This was calculated as

- accrued benefit based on the Plan's formula of $4,210.94 [20,416.67 * .55 * 3/8];
- but not less than minimum Accrued Benefit of $-0- [since she's a Key Employee];
- but not more than the maximum accrued benefit of $4,875.00 {the lesser of [16,250 * 3/10] or [20,416.67 * 3/10]}

What is Employee C's Vested Accrued Benefit that would actually be paid if she terminated employment on December 31, 2010?

$1,684.38 per month, starting on her 65th birthday and continuing for the rest of her life. [4,210.94 * .4]

Info for Employee C as of December 31, 2014 (four years later)

- Current Age: 64
- Age at Hire: 57 (no change)
- Total years of service to date: 7
- Total years of service expected at age 65: 8 (no change)

- Total years of service during which the Plan was Top-Heavy: -0- (since C is a Key Employee)
- Actual High 3 Year Average Salary: $600,000 — limited to $265,000 ($22,083.33 monthly)
- Actual High 5 Year Average Salary: $600,000 — limited to $265,000 ($22,083.33 monthly)
- Expected High 3 Year Average Salary at 65: $600,000 — limited to $265,000 ($22,083.33 monthly)

What is Employee C's projected Normal Retirement Benefit?

$12,145.83 per month, starting on her 65th birthday and continuing for the rest of her life. [22083.33 * .55]

What is Employee C's Accrued Benefit if she terminated employment on December 31, 2014?

$10,627.60 per month, starting on her 65th birthday and continuing for the rest of her life. This was calculated as

- accrued benefit based on the Plan's formula of $10,627.60 [22,083.33 * .55 * 7/8];
- but not less than minimum Accrued Benefit of $-0- [since she's a Key Employee];
- but not more than maximum accrued benefit of $12,250 {the lesser of [17,500 * 7/10] or [22,083.33 * 7/10]}

What is Employee C's Vested Accrued Benefit that would actually be paid if she terminated employment on December 31, 2014?

$10,627.60 per month, starting on her 65th birthday and continuing for the rest of her life. [10,627.60 * 1.0]

Chapter 8

Annual Testing

Overview

Why do legally separate employers need to be aggregated for purposes of annual testing in a qualified retirement plan?

- Congress put forth the minimum coverage tests to ensure enough lower-paid employees are benefitting under a qualified retirement plan, and the nondiscrimination tests to ensure that the retirement plan does not excessively discriminate in favor of the higher-paid employees
- Congress requires that employers don't "play games" with the establishment of separate business identities (although legal for tax purposes and for liability purposes) simply to avoid these rules
- for purposes of annual testing in a qualified retirement plan, all employees within a controlled group of corporations (or businesses), or all employees within an affiliated service group, are considered to be eligible to participate in every qualified plan sponsored by any member of the controlled group or affiliated service group (and whether they are benefitting or not will determine the results of the test)
- controlled groups of corporations (or other businesses)
  - whether planned (such as through a corporate merger) or unplanned (such as having ownership in a business through inheritance or marriage),
    - a "parent-subsidiary controlled group" is one or more of a chain of corporations where the parent owns at least 80% of the stock of a subsidiary, and
    - a "brother-sister controlled group" is where 5 or fewer persons (individuals, estates or trusts) have actual ownership of at least 80% and effective control of at least 50% of one or more corporations
  - for purposes of annual testing in a qualified retirement plan, all employees within the controlled group of corporations or businesses are considered to be eligible to participate in every qualified plan sponsored by any member of the controlled group (and whether they are benefitting or not will determine the results of the test)
- affiliated service groups
  - whether planned or unplanned, based on facts and circumstances, an affiliated service group, consists of a service organization and one or more of the following:
    - any service organization which is a shareholder or partner in the first organization that regularly performs services for the first organization or is

regularly associated with the first organization in performing services for third persons, and

- any other organization if a significant portion of the business of such organization is the performance of services of a type historically performed in such service field by employees, and 10 percent or more of the interests in such organization is held by persons who are highly compensated employees of the first organization

Who are the Highly Compensated Employees?

- by default, every employee who is not classified as an HCE is classified as a non Highly Compensated Employee ("NHCE")
- since salaries and ownership can change from one year to the next, the Plan Administrator must annually go through the roster of employees and classify each and every eligible employee as either an HCE or as a NHCE
- there are three ways that an employee can be classified as a Highly Compensated Employee this year:
  - an employee had at least a 5% ownership in the sponsoring employer this year or last year,
  - an employee earned compensation in excess of the annual threshold of $80,000 (as adjusted for inflation) last year, or
  - an employee was an HCE at any time after attaining age 55
- there are two employer elections available under the compensation criteria for determining HCEs
  - the top-paid group election, where more than 20% of the employees are paid in excess of $80,000 (as adjusted for inflation), such as law firms, so the employer limits the HCEs to the top 20%, and
  - the calendar year data election, where the plan year is not a calendar year plan, but the employer chooses to determine salaries based on the calendar year, since that's how payroll records are maintained

Which annual tests compare the HCEs to the NHCEs?

- the minimum coverage test determines if enough NHCEs are benefitting in the plan when compared to the percentage of HCEs benefitting in the plan
- the minimum participation test determines if enough NHCEs are benefitting in a defined benefit plan when compared to the percentage of HCEs benefitting in that defined benefit plan
- the nondiscrimination test determines if enough NHCEs are getting comparable benefits, rights and features in the plan as are the HCEs
- the nondiscrimination tests in 401(k) plans determine if enough NHCEs are deferring percentages of their salaries and receiving employer contributions (when expressed as percentages of their salaries) as are the HCEs

How can a qualified retirement plan prove it meets the minimum coverage tests each year?

- if the plan document only excludes participants who have not yet attained age 21 or who have not yet been credited with a Year of Service, then the plan passes every year

- however, if any other eligible employees are specifically excluded by plan design, then the mathematical tests will need to be performed every year
- preliminary issues
  - the following common-law employees can be eliminated from the testing group:
    - employees who are younger than age 21,
    - employees who have not yet completed a Year of Service,
    - employees who are members of a union where retirement benefits are part of the collective bargaining negotiations,
    - employees who are non-resident aliens,
    - and certain employees in the aviation and railroad industries
  - all other common-law employees are considered "eligible" employees, and are classified as either:
    - current employee or former employee,
    - HCE or NHCE, and
    - benefitting in the plan or not benefitting in the plan
- the Plan's Ratio Percentage is calculated as a top fraction divided by a bottom fraction, where
  - the top fraction is a fraction whose numerator is the number of NHCEs benefitting in the plan and the denominator is the number of NHCEs eligible to benefit in the plan
  - the bottom fraction is a fraction whose numerator is the number of HCEs benefitting in the plan and the denominator is the number of HCEs eligible to benefit in the plan
- each year, the plan only needs to pass any one of the following tests
  - the 70% Test: the plan benefits at least 70 percent of employees who are NHCEs,
  - the Ratio Percentage Test: the plan's Ratio Percentage is at least 70%, or
  - the Average Benefit Percentage Test:
    - based on all the facts and circumstances, the classification of eligible employees who are not covered by the plan is reasonable and is established under objective business criteria,
    - based on a table in the regulations, the plan's Ratio Percentage, although lower than 70%, is greater than the plan's "safe harbor percentage" for that year, or is greater than the plan's "unsafe harbor percentage" and the IRS approves an affirmative request for determination, and
    - the average benefit percentages for NHCEs divided by the average benefit percentages for HCEs, is at least 70% (for a defined contribution plan, the average benefit percentage is basically each participant's annual addition divided by his salary, and for a defined benefit plan, the average benefit percentage is calculated by the plan's Enrolled Actuary as the normal accrual rate)
- if the plan fails to meet any of the three mathematical tests in any year, then

- the plan must satisfy such minimum coverage rules on at least one day in each quarter, so the plan administrator can try to find "better" dates for testing
- if the employer maintains more than one plan, then they may be aggregated for minimum coverage testing purposes (but they will need to be aggregated for nondiscrimination testing as well)
- otherwise, the plan must be amended to allow enough excluded employees to be covered under the plan

How can a qualified retirement plan prove it meets the nondiscrimination requirements each year?

- the three components of proving nondiscrimination each year are:
  - the amount of benefits provided in a defined benefit plan or contributions in a defined contribution plan must be nondiscriminatory—either the plan is designed as a Safe Harbor or the plan must annually meet the general nondiscrimination test (which is a mathematical test),
  - the actual availability of benefits, rights and features, and the effective availability of BRFs, cannot be discriminatory—there are no plan provisions which can automatically satisfy this requirement, and facts and circumstances must be applied annually, and
  - plan amendments and termination cannot have the effect of being discriminatory—there are no plan provisions which can automatically satisfy this requirement, and facts and circumstances must be applied every time the plan is amended or upon plan termination
- former employees who are still participating in the plan need to be tested separately for all three nondiscrimination components
- as to benefits and contributions,
  - if the plan document has a uniform contribution allocation for all participants in a defined contribution plan, or a uniform benefit accrual formula in a defined benefit plan, then the plan passes every year
  - however, if there are different allocations or accruals for any participants, then the mathematical tests will need to be performed every year
  - preliminary issues
    - the same aggregation of controlled groups and affiliated service groups for minimum coverage testing apply to nondiscrimination testing
    - the same categorization of employees for minimum coverage testing apply to nondiscrimination testing
  - the general test is very complicated, and the Treasury Regulations provide many mathematical computations and many legal definitions, exceptions, and exceptions to exceptions
  - the general test for nondiscrimination testing is performed as follows:
    - first, an allocation rate is calculated for each participant benefitting under a defined contribution plan, which is his or her allocation divided by salary

- second, all participants are organized in order of descending allocation rates, where NHCEs are put above HCEs when the rates are equal

- third, a rate group is created for every HCE benefitting under the plan, which consists of that HCE and every other employee (both HCEs and NHCEs) with an accrual rate equal to or greater than his (there are some conveniences when several HCEs have the same, or similar, allocation rates)

- fourth, each rate group must satisfy a modified minimum coverage test

- If every rate group satisfies the modified minimum coverage tests, then the plan as a whole passes the nondiscrimination tests (the rationale is that although different allocations are provided to different groups of employees, each allocation goes to enough NHCEs—so instead of sponsoring a single plan with different benefit structures, the employer could have sponsored several stand-alone plans for different segments of the workforce, and each stand-alone plan would pass the minimum coverage tests)

- when testing a defined benefit plan, replace "both the normal accrual rate and most valuable accrual rate" for "allocation rate," but the rest of the general test is the same (the defined benefit plan's Enrolled actuary will calculate the accrual rates)

- if the plan fails the general test in any year, then

  - a plan can be restructured into component parts, or two or more plans sponsored by the same employer may be aggregated by the employer

  - a plan can pass the general test based on "cross testing," where a defined contribution plan will convert contributions to accrued benefits and substitute accrual rates for allocation rates in its general test, and where a defined benefit plan will convert accrued benefits to allocations and substitute allocation rates for accrual rates in its general test

  - otherwise, the plan must be amended to provide greater benefits or allocations to the NHCEs so that the plan passes the general test

- as to rights and features,

  - if the plan has uniform rights and features for all plan participants, then the plan passes this component each year

  - otherwise, under appropriate facts and circumstances, the rights and features of the plan must be currently available and effectively available to enough NHCEs

- as to plan amendments and termination,

  - under appropriate facts and circumstances, the amendments or termination of the plan must not impermissively discriminate in favor of HCEs

- in addition to the regular nondiscrimination testing required for every qualified plan, 401(k) plans have additional nondiscrimination requirements:

  - if the plan is set up to satisfy the safe harbor requirements, then the 401(k) plan meets the special nondiscrimination rules each year

- otherwise, the plan must test for salary deferrals and employee contributions and separately test for employer contributions
  - to be a safe harbor 401(k) plan, under Treasury Regulations, the plan must properly and timely provide notice to all employees, and must either:
    - provide every eligible participant with a profit sharing contribution of 3% of salary, or
    - match 100% of the first 3% of salary deferred by every participant who elects to defer plus 50% of the next 2% of salary deferred
  - additionally, a 401(k) plan offering an automatic enrollment can also be structured as a Safe Harbor plan (satisfying both the ADP and ACP tests —see Chapter 5), as long as the employer properly and timely provides notices to all eligible employees
- to test for salary deferrals and contributions in a plan that is not designed as a safe harbor
  - the Actual Deferral Percentage for each individual is basically the total of his or her elective salary deferrals and the designated Roth contributions divided by his or her compensation
  - to pass the test, the average ADP for all HCEs, when compared to the average ADP for all NHCEs, cannot be more than the greater of:
    - 125%, or
    - 200%, but only if the difference in ratios is less than 2.0 percentage points
  - to make the testing easier, the employer can choose to use prior year data to determine the average ADP for NHCEs
- to test for employer contributions in a plan that is not designed as a safe harbor
  - the Actual Contribution Percentage for each individual is basically the total of his or her employer matching or other contributions divided by his or her compensation
  - to pass the test, the average ACP for all HCEs, when compared to the average ACP for all NHCEs, cannot be more than the greater of:
    - 125%, or
    - 200%, but only if the difference in ratios is less than 2.0 percentage points
  - to make the testing easier, the employer can choose to use prior year data to determine the average ACP for NHCEs
- if the plan fails the ADP test, then
  - enough Qualified NonElective Contributions (QNECs) may be allocated to NHCEs so that the plan passes
  - enough excess contributions are distributed,
  - or enough elective deferrals may be returned to HCEs as taxable income so that the plan passes ("recharacterization")
- the plan document must provide for the exact method of correction
- similar rules apply to plans that fail the ACP tests

Who are the Key Employees?
- a different statutory provision defines a Key Employee differently than a HCE (although, oftentimes the same individual plan participant is classified as both an HCE and a Key Employee)
- by default, every employee who is not classified as a Key Employee is classified as a non-Key Employee
- a Key Employee is defined as an employee who, during the plan year, is:
  - an officer with compensation greater than $130,000 (as adjusted for inflation),
  - a 5% owner of the employer, or
  - a 1% owner of the employer with compensation greater than $150,000 (not adjusted)

Which annual tests compare the Key Employees to the non Key Employees?
- only the Top Heavy test

When is a Plan Considered to be Top Heavy?
- to determine whether a plan is Top Heavy for the current year, the determination date is the last day of the preceding year
  - a defined benefit plan is Top Heavy if at least 60% of the plan's present value of accrued benefits are attributable to Key Employees
  - similarly, a defined contribution plan is Top Heavy if at least 60% of the plan's accounts balances are allocated to Key Employees
- there is no plan design that automatically satisfies the Top Heavy test each year
- however, if a plan document always provides benefits equal to or greater than the minimum required benefits for a TH defined benefit plan or annual additions equal to or greater than the minimum required annual additions for a TH defined contribution plan (as discussed in Chapter 7), and also provides a vesting schedule which is at least as rapid as the minimum required TH vesting schedule (as discussed in Chapter 7), then it is irrelevant whether the plan is, in fact, TH for any year—although the plan still must run the tests and report the accurate results to the federal government

A. Aggregation of Employers

The very first analysis that needs to be made on an annual basis is the determination of exactly what constitutes the employer group for purposes of testing the plan for minimum coverage, minimum participation, nondiscrimination and Top-Heaviness. Basically, when several individuals have actual and common ownership of multiple businesses, then all of those businesses are aggregated into a single happy family (for testing purposes only) and every employee of the big happy family are part of the testing group. Ownership can change over time, either purposely (such as through mergers, acquisitions and spinoffs of businesses) or unexpectedly (such as the owner of one business inheriting a family business upon the death of a parent or an ex-spouse receiving ownership in a business upon divorce). It is crucial that employee benefits professionals understand how important this concept is, and that they do everything that they can to convince their clients to disclose every aspect of individual ownership each year. In addition to businesses that are actually and effectively controlled, certain service organizations and their recipient businesses will need to be aggregated (again, for testing purposes only) depending on how dependent the service organization is upon the recipient business. Here also, as facts and circumstances can change on an annual basis, employee benefit professionals need to ask the right questions and determine if the information provided by the client is sufficient to make the proper determinations.

1. Members of a Controlled Group of Corporations (or Other Businesses)

Statutory Rules at IRC §§ 414(b) and (c) (Although No Actual Cross-Reference from IRC § 401(a))

Under IRC § 414(b), all employees of all corporations which are members of a controlled group of corporations shall be treated as employed by a single employer.

Under IRC § 414(c), all employees of trades or businesses (whether or not incorporated) which are under common control shall be treated as employed by a single employer.

I have omitted some cross-references and minor points from the two statutory provisions, but aside from that, does reading these Code sections tell you anything? Not really, and that is why guidance from Treasury, especially in the form of final regulations, are crucially important.

Basically, under Treas. Regs. § 1.414(b)-1, the term "controlled group of corporations" has the same meaning as is assigned to the term in section 1563(a), except that (1) the term "controlled group of corporations" shall not include an "insurance group" described in section 1563(a)(4), and (2) section 1563(e)(3)(C) (relating to stock owned by certain employees' trusts) shall not apply. So, bear with me on this, if we flip over to IRC § 1563(a), which has absolutely nothing to do with qualified retirement plans, we find the following definitions:

- A "parent-subsidiary controlled group" is one or more of a chain of corporations connected through stock ownership with a common parent corporation if one or more of the other corporations possesses at least 80% ownership in at least one of the other corporations and if the parent corporation owns at least 80% ownership in at least one of the other corporations.

- A "brother-sister controlled group" is where 5 or fewer persons (individuals, estates or trusts) have actual control (own at least 80%) of each of the corporations and have effective control (own at least 50%) of each of the corporations.

Quite honestly, the first time I read through the statutes, while I somewhat understood what a controlled group of corporations was, I did not understand how to make a determination for qualified plan purposes. However, after reading the regulations and going through their examples, it started making sense. The moral of the story is twofold: first, the administration of qualified retirement plans is very complicated, and you can't expect to master the rules immediately, and second, one of the most useful tools for understanding the rules is actually working through examples included in Treasury guidance.

Copied below are Treasury Regulations that discuss how to determine whether two or more businesses are under common control, complete with their examples. I decided not to make any editorial cuts, so you have the experience of reading regulations in their entirety. Please note that these regulations cross-reference definitions in Reg § 1.414(c)-

3 [exclusion of certain interests or stock in determining control] and 1.414(c)-4 [rules for determining ownership], but in the interest of not overloading you at this point, they were purposely omitted. Please feel free to find those regulations and read them for yourself.

Treas. Regs § 1.414(c)-2. Two or More Trades or Businesses under Common Control

(a) **In general.** For purposes of this section, the term "two or more trades or businesses under common control" means any group of trades or businesses which is either a "parent-subsidiary group of trades or businesses under common control" as defined in paragraph (b) of this section, a "brother-sister group of trades or businesses under common control" as defined in paragraph (c) of this section, or a "combined group of trades or businesses under common control" as defined in paragraph (d) of this section. For purposes of this section and §§ 1.414(c)-3 and 1.414(c)-4, the term "organization" means a sole proprietorship, a partnership (as defined in section 7701(a)(2)), a trust, an estate, or a corporation.

(b) **Parent-subsidiary group of trades or businesses under common control.**

(1) In general. The term "parent-subsidiary group of trades or businesses under common control" means one or more chains of organizations conducting trades or businesses connected through ownership of a controlling interest with a common parent organization if—

(i) A controlling interest in each of the organizations, except the common parent organization, is owned (directly and with the application of § 1.414(c)-4(b)(1), relating to options) by one or more of the other organizations; and

(ii) The common parent organization owns (directly and with the application of § 1.414(c)-4(b)(1), relating to options) a controlling interest in at least one of the other organizations, excluding, in computing such controlling interest, any direct ownership interest by such other organizations.

(2) Controlling interest defined.

(i) Controlling interest. For purposes of paragraphs (b) and (c) of this section, the phrase "controlling interest" means:

(A) In the case of an organization which is a corporation, ownership of stock possessing at least 80 percent of total combined voting power of all classes of stock entitled to vote of such corporation or at least 80 percent of the total value of shares of all classes of stock of such corporation;

(B) In the case of an organization which is a trust or estate, ownership of an actuarial interest of at least 80 percent of such trust or estate;

(C) In the case of an organization which is a partnership, ownership of at least 80 percent of the profits interest or capital interest of such partnership; and

(D) In the case of an organization which is a sole proprietorship, ownership of such sole proprietorship.

(ii) Actuarial interest. For purposes of this section, the actuarial interest of each beneficiary of trust or estate shall be determined by assuming the maximum exercise of discretion by the fiduciary in favor of such beneficiary. The factors and methods prescribed in § 20.2031-7 or, for certain prior periods, § 20.2031-7A (Estate Tax Regulations) for use in ascertaining the value of an interest in property for estate tax purposes shall be used for purposes of this subdivision in determining a beneficiary's actuarial interest.

(c) Brother-sister group of trades or businesses under common control.

(1) In general. The term "brother-sister group of trades or businesses under common control" means two or more organizations conducting trades or businesses if (i) the same five or fewer persons who are individuals, estates, or trusts own (directly and with the application of § 1.414(c)-4) a controlling interest in each organization, and (ii) taking into account the ownership of each such person only to the extent such ownership is identical with respect to each such organization, such persons are in effective control of each organization. The five or fewer persons whose ownership is considered for purposes of the controlling interest requirement for each organization must be the same persons whose ownership is considered for purposes of the effective control requirement.

(2) Effective control defined. For purposes of this paragraph, persons are in "effective control" of an organization if—

(i) In the case of an organization which is a corporation, such persons own stock possessing more than 50 percent of the total combined voting power of all classes of stock entitled to vote or more than 50 percent of the total value of shares of all classes of stock of such corporation;

(ii) In the case of an organization which is a trust or estate, such persons own an aggregate actuarial interest of more than 50 percent of such trust or estate;

(iii) In the case of an organization which is a partnership, such persons own an aggregate of more than 50 percent of the profits interest or capital interest of such partnership; and

(iv) In the case of an organization which is a sole proprietorship, one of such persons owns such sole proprietorship.

(d) Combined group of trades or businesses under common control. The term "combined group of trades or businesses under common control" means any group of three or more organizations, if (1) each such organization is a member of either a parent-subsidiary group of trades or businesses under common control or a brother-sister group of trades or businesses under common control, and (2) at least one such organization is the common parent organization of a parent-subsidiary group of trades or businesses under common control and is also a member of a brother-sister group of trades or businesses under common control.

(e) Examples. The definitions of parent-subsidiary group of trades or businesses under common control, brother-sister group of trades or businesses under common control, and combined group of trades or businesses under common control may be illustrated by the following examples.

Example (1).

(a) The ABC partnership owns stock possessing 80 percent of the total combined voting power of all classes of stock entitled to voting of S corporation. ABC partnership is the common parent of a parent-subsidiary group of trades or businesses under common control consisting of the ABC partnership and S Corporation.

(b) Assume the same facts as in (a) and assume further that S owns 80 percent of the profits interest in the DEF Partnership. The ABC Partnership is the common parent of a parent-subsidiary group of trades or businesses under common control consisting of the ABC Partnership, S Corporation, and the DEF Partnership. The result would be the same if the ABC Partnership, rather than S, owned 80 percent of the profits interest in the DEF Partnership.

Example (2).

L Corporation owns 80 percent of the only class of stock of T Corporation, and T, in turn, owns 40 percent of the capital interest in the GHI Partnership. L also owns 80 percent of the only class of stock of N Corporation and N, in turn, owns 40 percent of the capital interest in the GHI Partnership. L is the common parent of a parent-subsidiary group of trades or businesses under common control consisting of L Corporation, T Corporation, N Corporation, and the GHI Partnership.

Example (3).

ABC Partnership owns 75 percent of the only class of stock of X and Y Corporations; X owns all the remaining stock of Y, and Y owns all the remaining stock of X. Since interorganization ownership is excluded (that is, treated as not outstanding) for purposes of determining whether ABC owns a controlling interest of at least one of the other organizations, ABC is treated as the owner of stock possessing 100 percent of the voting power and value of all classes of stock of X and of Y for purposes of paragraph (b)(1)(ii) of this section. Therefore, ABC is the common parent of a parent-subsidiary group of trades or businesses under common control consisting of the ABC Partnership, X Corporation, and Y Corporation.

Example (4).

Unrelated individuals A, B, C, D, E, and F own an interest in sole proprietorship A, a capital interest in the GHI Partnership, and stock of corporations M, W, X, Y, and Z (each of which has only one class of stock outstanding) in the following proportions:

Organizations

Individuals	A	GHI	M	W	X	Y	Z
A	100%	50%	100%	60%	40%	20%	60%
B	—	40%	—	15%	40%	50%	30%
C	—	—	—	—	10%	10%	10%
D	—	—	—	25%	—	20%	—
E	—	10%	—	—	10%	—	—
Total	100%	100%	100%	100%	100%	100%	100%

Under these facts the following four brother-sister groups of trades or businesses under common control exist: GHI, X and Z; X, Y, and Z; W and Y; A and M. In the case of GHI, X, and Z, for example, A and B together have effective control of each organization because their combined identical ownership of GHI, X and Z is greater than 50%. (A's identical ownership of GHI, X and Z is 40% because A owns at least a 40% interest in each organization. B's identical ownership of GHI, X and Z is 30% because B owns at least a 30% interest in each organization.) A and B (the persons whose ownership is considered for purposes of the effective control requirement) together own a controlling interest in each organization because they own at least 80% of the capital interest of partnership GHI and at least 80% of the total combined voting power of corporations X and Z. Therefore, GHI, X and Z comprise a brother-sister group of trades or businesses under common control. Y is not a member of this group because neither the effective control requirement nor the 80% controlling interest requirement are met. (The effective control requirement is not met because A's and B's combined identical ownership in GHI, X, Y and Z (20% for A and 30% for B) does not exceed 50%. The 80% controlling interest test is not met because A and B together only own 70% of the total combined voting power of the stock of Y.) A and M are not members of this group because B owns no interest in either organization and A's ownership of GHI, X and Z, considered alone, is less than 80%.

Example (5).

The outstanding stock of corporations U and V, which have only one class of stock outstanding, is owned by the following unrelated individuals:

Individuals	Corporation U (percent)	Corporation V (percent)
A	12	12
B	12	12
C	12	12
D	12	12
E	13	13
F	13	13
G	13	13
H	13	13
Total	**100**	**100**

Any group of five of the shareholders will own more than 50 percent of the stock in each corporation, in identical holdings. However, U and V are not members of a brother-sister group of trades or businesses under common control because at least 80 percent of the stock of each corporation is not owned by the same five or fewer persons.

Example (6).

A, an individual, owns a controlling interest in ABC Partnership and DEF Partnership. ABC, in turn, owns a controlling interest in X Corporation. Since ABC, DEF, and X are each members of either a parent-subsidiary group or a brother-sister group of trades or businesses under common control, and ABC is the common parent of a parent-subsidiary group of trades or businesses under common control consisting of ABC and X, and also a member of a brother-sister group of trades or businesses under common control consisting of ABC and

DEF, ABC Partnership, DEF Partnership, and X Corporation are members of the same combined group of trades or businesses under common control.

Now that you have had a chance to read through actual Treasury regulations (and don't worry, the rest of this chapter is replete with complete and excerpted regulations, so you will get a lot more practice), I offer some insight from a small portion of a cases appearing in front of the Tax Court to demonstrate how courts will look, after the fact, to see if indeed there was a controlled group, and if so, were all employees of the controlled group properly aggregated for purposes of some of the annual testing (which will be explained later in this chapter). As to the case, please note that where you see ***, I have purposely removed sections of the case I don't think you need to read in order for me to make the intended point.

Achiro v. Commisioner
77 TC 881 (1981)

Official Tax Court Syllabus

Achiro and Rossi each owned 50 percent of the stock of Tahoe City Disposal, and each owned 25 percent of the stock of Kings Beach Disposal. In 1974, Achiro and Rossi incorporated A & R for the purpose of rendering management services of Tahoe City Disposal and Kings Beach Disposal. Achiro and Rossi each owned 24 percent of A & R's stock, and Renato Achiro (Achiro's brother and Rossi's brother-in-law) owned the remaining 52 percent. A & R entered into management service agreements with Tahoe City Disposal and Kings Beach Disposal pursuant to which A & R provided those corporations with management services and, in exchange, received management fees. Achiro and Rossi entered into exclusive employment contracts with A & R, and, acting in their capacities as A & R's employees, rendered management services to Tahoe City Disposal and Kings Beach Disposal.

* * *

4. Section 414(b)

The final issue is whether the employees of A & R and the employees of Tahoe City Disposal should be aggregated pursuant to section 414(b). Respondent asserts that once so aggregated, A & R's pension and profit-sharing plans (which cover only petitioners) discriminate in favor of officers, shareholders, and highly compensated persons because those plans do not include Tahoe City Disposal's employees and because the North Tahoe P-S Plan's contributions and benefits are not commensurate with A & R's plans. Accordingly, respondent contends that A & R's pension and profit-sharing plans are not qualified trusts under section 401, and the contributions made to such plans should be treated as income to petitioners under the provisions of sections 402(b) and 83(a). Petitioners agree thatif the employees of A & R are aggregated with the employees of Tahoe City Disposal, then A & R's pension and profit-sharing plans are not qualified trusts, and the contributions to those plans should be income to petitioners. Petitioners contend, however, that section 414(b) does not require the aggregation of the employees of A & R with the employees of Tahoe City Disposal.

Section 414(b) requires aggregation of the employees of all corporations which are members of a controlled group of corporations as defined in section 1563(a). Section 1563(a) applies to both parent-subsidiary and brother-sister controlled [pg. 905]groups. The brother-sister controlled group determination consists of two tests. Sec. 1563(a)(2). The 80-percent test requires that five or fewer persons alone or in combination have at least an 80-percent interest in each of two or more organizations. The 50-percent test requires that the same five or fewer persons have more than a 50-percent interest in each organization, taking into account the interests of each person only to the extent that such interests are identical with regard to each organization.

Section 1.1563-1(a)(6), Income Tax Regs., defines voting powers for purposes of section 1563(a) as follows:

in determining whether the stock owned by a person (or persons) possesses a certain percentage of the total combined voting power of all classes of stock entitled to vote of a corporation, consideration will be given to all the facts and circumstances of each case. A share of stock will generally be considered as possessing the voting power accorded to such share by the corporate charter, by-laws, or share certificate. On the other hand, if there is any agreement, whether express or implied, that a shareholder will not vote his stock in a corporation, the formal voting rights possessed by his stock may be disregarded in determining the percentage of the total combined voting power possessed by the stock owned by other shareholders in the corporation, if the result is that the corporation becomes a component member of a controlled group of corporations. Moreover, if a shareholder agrees to vote his stock in a corporation in the manner specified by another shareholder in the corporation, the voting rights possessed by the stock owned by the first shareholder may be considered to be possessed by the stock owned by such other shareholder if the result is that the corporation becomes a component member of a controlled group of corporations. [Emphasis added.]

Achiro and Rossi each owned 50 percent of the voting stock of Tahoe City Disposal and each held record title to 24 percent of the stock of A & R. Renato Achiro, Achiro's brother and Rossi's brother-in-law, held record title to the remaining 52 percent of the voting stock of A & R. Considering only record title, Tahoe City Disposal and A & R were not a brother-sister controlled group under section 1563(a)(2). However, we have found that Renato implicitly agreed that he would either not vote his stock in A & R or vote his stock in the manner specified by Achiro. Under the regulations, the validity of which has not been challenged by the parties, Renato's voting rights may be disregarded or attributed to Achiro. Therefore, Achiro and Rossi are deemed each to have 50-percent interests in Tahoe City Disposal and A & R (or Achiro is deemed to have a 76-percent interest in A & R), and the corporations constitute a brother-sister controlled group.

Since the corporations form a controlled group, the employees of A & R and the employees of Tahoe City Disposal must be aggregated under section 414(b) for purposes of section 401. Such a holding complies with the intent of Congress in enacting section 414(b) as expressed in H. Rept. 93-779, at 49 (1974), 1974-3 C.B. 292:

The committee, by this provision, intends to make it clear that the coverage and antidiscrimination provisions cannot be avoided by operating through separate corporations instead of separate branches of one corporation. For example, if managerial functions were performed through one corporation employing highly compensated personnel, which has a generous pension plan, and assembly-line functions were performed through one or more other corporations employing lower-paid employees, which have less generous plans or no plans at all, this would generally constitute an impermissible discrimination.

A & R was formed for the express purpose of rendering managerial services to Tahoe City Disposal and Kings Beach Disposal. In 1975 and 1976, A & R's employees, Achiro and Rossi, were officers, shareholders, and highly compensated. Sec. 1.401-4(a)(1)(i), Income Tax Regs. The "assembly-line functions" of the day-to-day waste disposal and dump operations were carried on by the employees of Tahoe City Disposal and Kings Beach Disposal. This is the very kind of situation Congress had in mind when it enacted section 414(b).

Accordingly, for the years 1975 and 1976, A & R's pension and profit-sharing plans were not qualified because they discriminated in favor of Achiro and Rossi who were officers, shareholders, and highly compensated. Sec. 401. Contributions made to such plans must be included in the gross income of Achiro and Rossi under sections 402(b) and 83(a).

* * *

So, to conclude this portion of controlled groups, you have hopefully learned that when there is indeed a controlled group (of corporations or trades or businesses), then all employees of the controlled group are included in the annual testing (such as minimum coverage, minimum participation, nondiscrimination and Top-Heaviness, as explained throughout this chapter). The method of determining controlled groups is a quite complicated legal exercise, but an understanding of the six examples provided in the regulations should provide at least a basic understanding of parent-subsidiary and brother-sister controlled groups. Since ownership can change annually, through affirmative actions like buying or selling ownership in other businesses, or through passivity, like inheriting a business, it is crucial for the employee benefits professional to ask the right questions each year to determine if a client's controlled group situation has changed. As seen from the small excerpted portion of a Tax Court case, when not done properly, if the IRS audits the plan and winds up challenging the plan sponsor in court, and if the court agrees with the IRS, then the plan can lose its coveted tax qualification for the years where all employees were not included in the annual tests.

2. Members of an Affiliated Service Group

Statutory Rules at IRC § 414(m) (Although No Actual Cross-Reference from IRC § 401(a))

There is a second way that seemingly separate businesses must be aggregated for purposes of testing whether a retirement plan meets the qualification requirements. All employees of the members of an affiliated service group shall be treated as employed by a single employer.

An affiliated service group means a group consisting of a service organization (the "first organization") and one or more of the following:

- any service organization which is a shareholder or partner in the first organization that regularly performs services for the first organization or is regularly associated with the first organization in performing services for third persons, and

- any other organization if a significant portion of the business of such organization is the performance of services of a type historically performed in such service field by employees, and 10 percent or more of the interests in such organization is held by persons who are highly compensated employees of the first organization.

A "service organization" means an organization the principal business of which is the performance of services.

The provision was later amended to state that the term "affiliated service group" also includes a group consisting of an organization the principal business of which is performing, on a regular and continuing basis, management functions for 1 organization, and the organization (and related organizations) for which such functions are so performed by the organization.

Okay, what does this mean. Again, let's go immediately to the Regulations. But wait, in this case, we only have Proposed regulations published in 1983, but never finalized, and never updated as Congress amended IRC 414(m) in 1982 and 1986. Therefore, all that an employer, and its employee benefits counselors, can do is use the proposed regulations as a means of complying, at least in good faith, with the statutory provisions. However, if we do a bit more research, we find that a 1981 Revenue Ruling was published immediately after Congress enacted the affiliated service group provisions.

As to the proposed regulations:

Proposed Treas. Regs. § 1.414(m)-2. Definitions.

(a) **Affiliated service group.** "Affiliated service group" means a group consisting of a service organization (First Service Organization) and

 (1) One or more A Organizations described in paragraph (b), or

 (2) One or more B Organizations described in paragraph (c), or

 (3) One or more A Organizations described in paragraph (b) and one or more B Organizations described in paragraph (c).

(b) **A Organizations.**

 (1) General rule. A service organization is an A Organization if it:

 (i) Is a partner or shareholder in the First Service Organization (regardless of the percentage interest it owns in the First Service Organization but determined with regard to the constructive ownership rules of paragraph (d)); and

 (ii) Regularly performs services for the First Service Organization, or is regularly associated with the First Service Organization in performing services for third persons.

It is not necessary that any of the employees of the organization directly perform services for the First Service Organization; it is sufficient that the organization is regularly associated with the First Service Organization in performing services for third persons.

(2) Regularly performs services for. The determination of whether a service organization regularly performs services for the First Service Organization or is regularly associated with the First Service Organization in performing services for third persons shall be made on the basis of the facts and circumstances. One factor that is relevant in making this determination is the amount of the earned income that the organization derives from performing services for the First Ser-

vice Organization, or from performing services for third persons in association with the First Service Organization.

(3) Examples. The provisions of this paragraph may be illustrated by the following examples.

Example (1). A Organization.

(i) Attorney N is incorporated, and the corporation is a partner in a law firm. Attorney N and his corporation are regularly associated with the law firm in performing services for third persons.

(ii) Considering the law firm as a First Service Organization, the corporation is an A Organization because it is a partner in the law firm and it is regularly associated with the law firm in performing services for third persons. Accordingly, the corporation and the law firm constitute an affiliated service group.

Example (2). Corporation.

(i) Corporation F is a service organization that is a shareholder in Corporation G, another service organization. F regularly provides services for G. Neither corporation is a professional service corporation within the meaning of subsection (1)(c).

(ii) Neither corporation may be considered a First Service Organization for purposes of this paragraph and, thus, aggregation will not be required by operation of the A Organization test. However, G or F may be treated as a First Service Organization and the other organization may be a B Organization under the rules of subsection (2)(c).

Example (3). Regularly associated with.

(i) R, S & T is a law partnership with offices in numerous cities. The office in the city of D is incorporated, and the corporation is a partner in the law firm. All of the employees of the corporation work directly for the corporation, and none of them work directly for any of the other offices of the law firm.

(ii) Considering the law firm as a First Service Organization, the corporation is an A Organization because it is a partner in the First Service Organization and is regularly associated with the law firm in performing services for third persons. Accordingly, the corporation and the law firm constitute an affiliated service group.

(c) B Organizations.

(1) General rule. An organization is a B Organization if:

(i) A significant portion of the business of the organization is the performance of services for the First Service Organization, for one or more A Organizations determined with respect to the First Service Organization, or for both.

(ii) Those services are of a type historically performed by employees in the service field of the First Service Organization or the A Organizations, and

(iii) Ten percent or more of the interests in the organization is held, in the aggregate, by persons who are designated group members (as defined in subparagraph (4)) of the First Service Organization or of the A Organizations, determined using the constructive ownership rules of paragraph (d).

(2) Significant portion.

(i) General rule. Except as provided in paragraphs (c)(2)(ii) and (iii), the determination of whether providing services for the First Service Organization, for one or more A Organizations, or for both, is a significant portion of the business of an organization will be based on the facts and circumstances. Wherever it appears in this paragraph (c)(2), "one or more A organizations" means one or more A organizations determined with respect to the First Service Organization.

(ii) Service Receipts safe harbor. The performance of services for the First Service Organizations, for one or more A Organizations, or for both, will not be considered a significant portion of the business of an organization if the Service Receipts Percentage is less than five percent.

(iii) Total Receipts threshold test. The performance of services for the First Service Organization, for one or more A Organizations, or for both, will be considered a significant portion of the business of an organization if the Total Receipts Percentage is ten percent or more.

(iv) Service Receipts Percentage. The Service Receipts Percentage is the ratio of the gross receipts of the organization derived from performing services for the First Service Organization, for one or more A Organizations, or for both, to the total gross receipts of the organization derived from performing services. This ratio is the greater of the ratio for the year for which the determination is being made or for the three year period including that year and the two preceding years (or the period of the organization's existence, if less).

(v) Total Receipts Percentage. The Total Receipts Percentage is calculated in the same manner as the Service Receipts Percentage, except that gross receipts in the denominator are determined without regard to whether they were derived from performing services.

(3) Historically performed. Services will be considered of a type historically performed by employees in a particular service field if it was not unusual for the services to be performed by employees of organizations in that service field (in the United States) on December 13, 1980.

(4) Designated group.

(i) Definition. "Designated group" members are the officers, the highly compensated employees, and the common owners of an organization (as defined in paragraph (c)(4)(ii)). However, even though a person is not a common owner, the interests the person holds in the potential B Organization will be taken into account if the person is an officer or a highly compensated employee of the First Service Organization or of an A Organization.

(ii) Common owner. A person who is an owner of a First Service Organization or of an A Organization is a common owner if at least three percent of the interests in the organization is, in the aggregate, held by persons who are owners of the potential B organization (determined using the constructive ownership rules of paragraph (d)).

(5) Owner. The term "owner" includes organizations that have an ownership interest described in paragraph (e).

(6) Aggregation of ownership interests. It is not necessary that a single designated group member of the First Service Organization or of an A Organization own ten percent or more of the interests, determined using the constructive ownership rules of paragraph (d), in the organization for the organization to be a B Organization. It is sufficient that the sum of the interests, determined using the constructive ownership rules of paragraph (d), held by all of the designated group members of the First Service Organization, and the designated group members of the A Organizations, is ten percent or more of the interests in the organizations.

(7) Non-service organization. An organization may be a B Organization even though it does not quality as a service organization under paragraph (f).

(8) Examples. The provisions of this paragraph may be illustrated by the following examples.

Example (1). B Organization.

(i) R is a service organization that has 11 partners. Each partner of R owns one percent of the stock in Corporation D. The corporation provides services to the partnership of a type historically performed by employees in the service field of the partnership. A significant portion of the business of the corporation consists of providing services to the partnership.

(ii) Considering the partnership as a First Service Organization, the corporation is a B organization because a significant portion of the business of the corporation is the performance of services for the partnership of a type historically performed by employees in the service field of the partnership, and more than ten percent of the interests in the corporation is held, in the aggregate, by the designated group members (consisting of the 11 common owners of the partnership). Accordingly, the corporation and the partnership constitute an affiliated service group.

(iii) A similar result would be obtained if no more than 8 percent of the 11 percent ownership in Corporation D were held by highly compensated employees of R who were not owners of R (even though no one group of the three preceding groups held 10 percent or more of the stock of Corporation D).

Example (2). Other aggregation rules.

(i) C, an individual, is a 60 percent partner in D, a service organization, and regularly performs services for D. C is also an 80 percent partner in F. A significant portion of the gross receipts of F are derived from providing services to D of a type historically performed by employees in the service field of D.

(ii) Viewing D as a First Service Organization, F is a B Organization because a significant portion of gross receipts of F are derived from performing services for D of a type historically performed by employees in that service field, and more than ten percent of the interests in F is held by the designated group member C (who is a common owner of D). Accordingly, D and F constitute an affiliated service group. Additionally, the employees of D and F are aggregated under the rules of section 414(c).

Thus, any plan maintained by a member of the affiliated service group must satisfy the aggregation rules of sections 414(c) and 414(m).

Example (3). Common owner.

(i) Corporation T is a service organization. The sole function of Corporation W is to provide services to Corporation T of a type historically performed by employees in the service field of Corporation T. Individual C owns all of the stock of Corporation W and two percent of the stock of Corporation T. C is not an officer or a highly compensated employee of Corporation T.

(ii) Considering Corporation T as a First Service Organization, Corporation W is not a B Organization because it is not 10 percent owned by designated group members. Because C owns less than 3 percent of Corporation T, C is not a common owner of T.

Example (4). B Organization.

(i) Individual M owns one-third of an employee benefit consulting firm. M also owns one-third of an insurance agency. A significant portion of the business of the consulting firm consists of assisting the insurance agency in developing employee benefit packages for sale to third persons and providing services to the insurance company in connection with employee benefit programs sold to other clients of the insurance agency. Additionally, the consulting firm frequently provides services to clients who have purchased insurance arrangements from the insurance company for the employee benefit plans they maintain. The insurance company frequently refers clients to the consulting firm to assist them in the design of their employee benefit plans. The percentage of the total gross receipts of the consulting firm that represent gross receipts from the performance of these services for the insurance agency is 20 percent.

(ii) Considering the insurance agency as a First Service Organization, the consulting firm is a B Organization because a significant portion of the business of the consulting firm (as determined under the Total Receipts Percentage Test) is the performance of services for the insurance agency of a type historically performed by employees in the service field of insurance, and more than 10 percent of the interests in the consulting firm is held by owners of the insurance agency. Thus, the insurance agency and the consulting form constitute an affiliated service group.

Example (5). B Organization.

(i) Attorney T is incorporated, and the corporation is a 6% shareholder in a law firm (which is also incorporated). All of the work of Corporation T is performed for the law firm.

(ii) Under the principles of section 267(c), T is deemed to own the shares of the law firm owned by T Corporation. Thus, T is a common owner of the law firm. Considering the law firm as a First Service Organization, Corporation T is a B Organization because a significant portion of the business of Corporation T consists of performing services for the law firm of a type historically performed by employees, and 100 percent of Corporation T is owned by a common owner of the law firm.

Example (6). Significant portion.

(i) The income of Corporation X is derived from both performing services and other business activities. The amount of its receipts derived from performing services for, and its total receipts derived from, Corporation Z and the total for all other customers is set forth below:

	Origin of Income	Corporation Z	All Customers
Year 1	Services	$4	$100
	Total	—	120
Year 2	Services	9	150
	Total	—	180
Year 3	Services	42	200
	Total	—	240

(ii) In year 1 (the first year of existence of Corporation X), the Services Receipts Percentage for Corporation X (for its business with Corporation Z) is less than five percent ($4/$100, or 4%). Thus performing services for Corporation Z will not be considered a significant portion of the business of Corporation X.

(iii) In year 2, the Service Receipts Percentage is the greater of the ratio for that year ($9/$150, or 6%) or for years 1 and 2 combined ($13/$250, or 5.2%), which is six percent. The Total Receipts Percentage is the greater of the ratio for that year ($9/$180, or 5%) or for years 1 and 2 combined ($13/$300, or 4.3%), which if five percent. Because the Services Receipts Percentage is greater than five percent and the Total Receipts Percentage is less than ten percent, whether performing services for Corporation Z constitutes a significant portion of the business of Corporation X is determined by the facts and circumstances.

(iv) In year 3, the Services Receipts Percentage is the greater of the ratio for that year ($42/$200, or 21%) or for years 1, 2, and 3 combined ($55/$450, or 12.2%), which is 21 percent. The Total Receipts Percentage is the greater of the ratio for that year ($42/$240, or 17.5%) or for years 1, 2, and 3 combined ($55/$540, or 10.1%), which is 17.5 percent. Because the Total Receipts Percentage is greater than ten percent and the Services Receipts Percentage is not less than five percent, a significant portion of the business of Corporation X is considered to be the performance of services for Corporation Z.

* * *

As to the Revenue Ruling:

Revenue Ruling 81-105

* * *

Affiliated service group.

Information is provided with respect to when various businesses will be considered an affiliated service group and how this aggregation affects the retirement plans maintained by members of the group. Rev. Ruls. 68-370 and 75-35 obsoleted.

Full Text:

1. PURPOSE

This revenue ruling provides guidance with respect to the application of section 414(m) of the Internal Revenue Code, as added by the Miscellaneous Revenue Act of 1980, Pub. L. 96-605, 1980-2 C.B. 702. The guidance emphasizes the interaction of section 414(m) of the Code with the nondiscrimination requirements of section 410(b) and 401(a)(4) in response to questions that have arisen as to how those sections interact. This revenue ruling also obsoletes Rev. Rul. 68-370, 1968-2 C.B. 174, and Rev. Rul. 75-35, 1975-1 C.B. 131.

2. APPLICABLE LAW

.01. Section 414(m)(1) of the Code provides that, for purposes of certain employee benefit requirements designated in section 414(m)(4), except to the extent otherwise provided in regulations, <Page 257> all employees of the members of an affiliated service group shall be treated as employed by a single employer.

.02. Section 414(m)(2) defines an affiliated service group as a first service organization (FSO) and one or more of:

(1) any service organization (A-ORG) which is a shareholder or partner in the FSO and which regularly performs services for the FSO or is regularly associated with the FSO in performing services for third persons, and

(2) any other organization (B-ORG) if

(A) a significant portion of the business of that organization is the performance of services for the FSO or A-ORG of a type historically performed in the service field of the FSO or A-ORG by employees, and

(B) 10 percent or more of the interest of the B-ORG is held by persons who are officers, highly compensated employees, or owners of the FSO or A-ORG.

* * *

3. EXAMPLES

.01. Example 1—

(1) Facts—P, a law partnership consists of corporate partners A, B, C and 10 individual partners. Each of the partners owns less than 10% of the partnership. The partnership employs as common law employees some lawyers, paralegals, and clerical employees. The partnership has a qualified plan, Plan P, covering some but not all of the common law employees. Corporation A and B each have only one employee, the sole shareholder. Corporation A maintains a retirement plan, Plan A. Corporation B maintains no plan. Corporation C employs the sole shareholder, a lawyer employee, and three clerical employees. Corporation C maintains a retirement plan, Plan C, for all its employees. Corporations A, B, and C regularly perform services for P. No individual is a participant in more than one plan and none of the statutory exclusions of section 410(b) applies.

(2) Determination of who are employees of a single employer under section 414(m) of the Code—In order to determine whether the employees covered by Plans A and C satisfy the coverage requirements of section 410 (b), it first must be determined what employees are considered as employed by a single employer. Under section 414(m)(2), the partnership, P, may be designated as a FSO. Corporations A, B, and C are partners in the FSO, and regularly perform services for the FSO. Accordingly Corporations A, B, and C are A-ORGS. Because Corporations A, B, and C are A-ORGS for the same FSO, Corporations A, B, and C and the FSO constitute an affiliated service group. Consequently all the employees of Corporations A, B, C, the common law employees of P, and the partners of P are

considered as employed by a single employer, and must be taken into account when testing whether the coverage requirements of section 410(b) are satisfied. This group is hereafter called the total aggregated employees.

(3) Determination of whether Plan A satisfies the coverage and nondiscrimination requirements — Plan A covers only one employee, the sole shareholder of Corporation A. Because none of the statutory exclusions of section 410(b) of the Code applies, 1 participant does not satisfy the percentage tests in section 410(b)(1)(A) when compared to the total aggregated employees. Because Plan A covers only prohibited group employees and the total aggregated employees contain several rank and file employees, the non-discriminatory classification test of section 410(b)(1) (B) is not satisfied, either. When a plan does not, considered alone, satisfy the requirements of section 410(b), the employer may designate other plans of the employer to be considered as a unit with the first plan. Such plans, considered as a unit must, among other things, satisfy the coverage and nondiscrimination requirements.

Assuming Plan P were so designated, the first question to consider is whether a plan covering only Employee A and the participants of Plan P satisfies the requirements of either section 410(b)(1)(A) or (B) of the Code when compared to the total aggregated employees. (Alternatively, the employer may designate Plans A, C, and P as a unit or simply Plans A and C as a unit.) If neither coverage test is satisfied Plan A is not a qualified plan. If either coverage test is satisfied, in order for Plan A to be qualified, Plans A and P, considered as a unit must also satisfy the non-discrimination requirements of section 401(a)(4). In making this determination the rules for testing discrimination, including rules which permit imputing social security benefits, apply. In testing for discrimination, all the compensation paid by the affiliated service group to the participants of Plan P is considered, without regard to the percentage ownership of Corporation A in the partnership.

(4) Determination of whether Plan C satisfies the coverage and nondiscrimination requirements — Plan C covers one shareholder, one lawyer<Page 258> employee, and three clerical employees. Coverage of five participants is not adequate to satisfy the percentage tests of section 410(b)(1)(A) of the Code when compared to the total aggregated employees. Whether the nondiscriminatory classification test of section 410(b)(1)(B) would be satisfied by Plan C if its participants are compared to the total aggregated employees depends on additional facts and circumstances not herein provided. See section 1.410(b)-1(d)(2) of the Income Tax Regulations. If section 410(b)(1)(B) were satisfied, the nondiscrimination requirements of section 401(a)(4) would be applied considering the participants of Plan C only (without considering the participants of Plans A or P). However, if the requirements of section 410(b) (1)(B) were not satisfied by Plan C alone, then the plan could be considered in combination with other plans, as described in (3).

.02. Example 2—

(1) Facts — Corporation S provides secretarial services. Corporations A and B, both of which are professional corporations formed by doctors, each own a portion of S. A owns 11 percent of the stock of S and B owns eight percent of the stock. Approximately one-third of S's services are performed for A and one-third for B, while the other one-third are performed for other firms. A and B

each maintain a retirement plan (Plan A and Plan B) and each plan covers the corporations only employee. None of the statutory exclusions of section 410 (b) of the Code applies.

(2) Determination of who are employees of a single employer under section 414(m) of the Code—In order to determine whether the employees covered by Plans A and B satisfy the coverage requirements of section 410 (b), it first must be determined which employees are considered as employed by a single employer. Under section 414(m)(2), Corporations A and B may each be designated as separate FSOs. Corporation S is a B-ORG for A because a significant portion of S's business is the performance of services for A, the services are of a type historically performed in the FSO's service field by employees, and 11 percent of the interest in S is held by owners of the FSO. S is not a B-ORG for B because the owners of B do not hold 10 percent or more of the interest in S.

Because Corporation S is a B-ORG for Corporation A, a FSO, the two constitute an affiliated service group. Consequently, all the employees of A and S are considered as employed by a single employer and must be taken into account when testing whether the coverage requirements of section 410(b) are satisfied. Corporation B is not part of an affiliated service group with either Corporation A or S. Thus, the employee of B is not aggregated with any other employees for purposes of testing coverage.

(3) Determination of whether Plan A satisfies the coverage and nondiscrimination requirements — Plan A covers only one employee, the sole shareholder of Corporation A. Because none of the statutory exclusions of section 410(b) of the Code applies, one participant does not satisfy the percentage tests of section 410(b) (1)(A) when compared to the total employees of the A and S affiliated service group. Because Plan A covers only prohibited group employees and the total aggregated employees of the affiliated service group includes rank and file employees, the nondiscriminatory classification test of section 410 (b)(1)(B) is not satisfied, either. Accordingly, unless a sufficient number of the employees of S were covered by Plan A or by another plan so that at least one of the tests of section 410 (b) were satisfied, Plan A is not a qualified plan. If, however, section 410(b) were satisfied, the single plan or combination of plans which satisfied that section must also satisfy the nondiscrimination requirements of section 401(a)(4). As in Example 1, the normal rules apply in testing for discrimination under section 401(a)(4) and all the compensation paid to the employees of Corporation S is considered, without regard to the percentage ownership of Corporation A in Corporation S.

(4) Determination of whether Plan B satisfies the coverage and nondiscrimination requirements — Because Plan B covers the only employee of Corporation. B, and the corporation is not a part of any affiliated service group, Plan B satisfies both sections 410(b) and 401(a)(4) of the Code.

.03. Example 3 —

(1) Corporations A and B are professional corporations formed by doctors (A and B). Corporation A and Corporation B each own one-half of P, a lock repair shop. Corporations A and B utilize the services of P, however, these corporations are an insignificant portion of P's customers.

(2) Under the rules of section 414 (m)(2) of the Code there is no affiliated service group based on these facts. Considering A or B Corporations as a FSO, P is not a B-ORG for either FSO because the services performed by P are not of a

type historically performed by employees in the service field of the FSO. Furthermore, the service performed for A and B Corporations is not a significant portion of P's business.

(3) Considering P as a FSO, A and B Corporations are not A-ORGS for P because they are not regularly associated with P in performing service for third persons.

* * *

5. EFFECTIVE DATE

This revenue ruling shall apply to plan years ending after November 30, 1980. However, in the case of a plan in existence on November 30, 1980, the amendments made by this section shall apply to plan years beginning after that date.

6. EFFECT ON OTHER DOCUMENTS

Rev. Ruls. 68-370 and 75-35 are obsoleted.

So, hopefully between the Proposed Regulations and the single Revenue Ruling, the employee benefits practitioner has a basic understanding of the abuses Congress was attempting to prevent, and how to make a good faith effort to comply with the actual words and the spirit of the statutory provision.

3. Separate Lines of Business

Statutory Rules at IRC § 414(r) (Although No Actual Cross-Reference from IRC § 401(a))

On the opposite side of the spectrum, sometimes a single employer truly has distinct and separate lines of business, and with a proper application to the IRS, can disaggregate its workforce for purposes of testing separate qualified plans that benefit only employees of one line of business.

An employer shall be treated as operating separate lines of business during any year if the employer for bona fide business reasons operates separate lines of business, which has at least 50 employees who are not excluded, but only after the IRS has approved the application. There are special rules for a safe harbor determination, but at this point, there is no need to go into excruciating detail in this text book. The term "separate line of business" includes an operating unit in a separate geographic area separately operated for a bona fide business reason. There are regulations that provide further guidance, but again, for purposes of this text book, if you just understand what a separate line of business is and where to look for the specific rules, then there is no need to have you go through the exercises at this time.

B. Highly Compensated Employees

Now, after understanding how to determine the big happy family of employers, it is time to classify individual employees.

1. Identification of Highly Compensated Employees

Statutory Definition at IRC § 414(q) (Although No Actual Cross-Reference from IRC § 401(a))

An employee is generally considered a Highly Compensated Employee ("HCE") if he or she has a substantial ownership in the sponsoring employer or if he or she earns a high salary. By default, every employee who is not classified as an HCE is classified as a non Highly Compensated Employee ("NHCE"). Since salaries and ownership can change from one year to the next, the Plan Administrator must annually go through the roster of employees and classify each and every eligible employee as either an HCE or as a NHCE. As plan administration is generally performed through computers, then as long as the software is coded correctly, and the data information is input correctly, the determination of HCE status becomes somewhat routine. However, it will be someone's ultimate responsibility to ascertain that the software works properly and that the results are acceptable. Please note that in addition to testing qualified plans for minimum participation and nondiscrimination, the bifurcation of the universe of employees into HCEs and NHCEs will be needed when testing some non-retirement employee benefits for nondiscrimination, such as dependent care assistance programs and group legal services plans, because those Code sections specifically reference this definition of HCE.

There are three ways that an employee can be classified as a Highly Compensated Employee for the current plan year:

1. An employee will be deemed a HCE for this year is if he or she has at least a 5% ownership in the sponsoring employer this plan year or in the last plan year. Ownership generally means stock ownership if the employer is incorporated or capital or profits interests if the employer is a partnership or other type of business.

2. An employee will be deemed a HCE for this plan year if he or she had compensation from the employer in excess of $80,000 (as adjusted for inflation) in the last plan year. As certain employers actually pay a substantial portion of their workforce more than the compensation threshold, and as certain employers maintain payroll records on a calendar year basis but sponsor plans on a non-calendar year basis, there are two special elections that an employer can make so that the compensation criteria is adjusted somewhat to fit their business reality. Each election is independent of the other, and the rules get more complicated when the employer sponsors more than one plan.

   • *Top-paid group election:* If the employer has a lot of employees who earn over $80,000 (as adjusted), such as law firms, medical practices, and other professional service providers, then the employer can make an election to only classify the top-paid group as HCEs, and to treat the rest as NHCEs. The top-paid group consists of the top 20% of employees when ranked on the basis of compensation, but excludes part time employees, union employees, and those under age 21.

   • *Calendar Year data election:* If the plan year is not a calendar year plan, but the payroll records are based on the calendar year, then the employer can make an election to treat the calendar year beginning in the look-back year as the 'deemed" look-back year.

3. An employee who has separated from service continues to be treated as a highly compensated employee if the individual was a HCE when the employee separated from service or if the individual was a HCE at any time after attaining age 55.

I am not going to include portions of the Treasury regulations here, but here's another lesson for you. Temporary Regulations were issued in 1988, and then amended in 1991 and again in 1994. Temporary Regulations, by their very definition, only are effective for three years. These Temporary Regulations were written in the form of 15 questions and answers. Then, in 1994, Final Regulations were issued which only changed question and answer 9 (the determination of the top-paid group), but indicates that you should look to the Temporary Regulations for all other guidance. When you use a tax service to look up the regulations, the editors note that neither the Temporary nor Final regulations have been updated to reflect changes to the provisions that Congress made in 2006. What that should mean to you, as a future employee benefits professional, is that you will need to read the statute and its history, see what was changed in 2006, and knowing that Treasury has not yet provided guidance, make sure your client's plan is properly classifying employees as either a HCE or as a NHCE.

So basically, each year, all workers of the controlled group or affiliated service group must be accounted for and divided into employees and non-employees (such as independent contractors). Then, all employees must be classified as either an HCE using the definitions and employer elections above, or, by default, a NHCE.

2. Annual Tests That Require Identified Highly Compensated Employees

This classification of HCEs and NHCEs will be crucial for proper testing for compliance with the minimum coverage, minimum participation, and nondiscrimination tests as detailed later in this chapter.

Please note that the term Highly Compensated Employee, as defined in IRC §414(q) and used for testing qualified plans for minimum coverage, minimum participation, and nondiscrimination, is a different definition than a "highly compensated participant" or a "highly compensated individual" (note the lack of capital letters), which are used to determine nondiscrimination in cafeteria plans and in accident and health plans (as defined in IRC §§125(e)(1) and 105(h), respectively, and discussed in Chapter 19). Now, stick with me, this is even a different definition than a highly-compensated individual (note the lack of capital letters and the hyphen), which is used to determine which employees are subjected to the limitations on golden parachute payments (as defined in IRC §280G(c) and discussed in Chapter 18). Now those are not the only favored employees that Congress worries about and tries to prevent abuses. Later in this chapter, we will see another definition of favored employees, now called Key Employees, which will be used for testing a qualified plan for Top-Heaviness (and, because the tax writing committees of Congress, the House Ways and Means and Senate Finance committees, needed a Tax Code definition rather than a Securities law definition, an executive of a public company that meets the definition of a Key Employee will not be able to receive a distribution from a nonqualified deferred compensation plan for at least six months after termination of employment, as defined at IRC §409A(a)(2)(B)).

C. Minimum Coverage Requirements for All Qualified Retirement Plans

Every qualified retirement plan must meet the minimum coverage requirements each year. Congress decided not to require every last employee be covered under a qualified retirement plan, but if for business purposes some employees are specifically and affirmatively excluded, then mathematical tests are imposed which determine if enough NHCEs are covered. Often times, an employer might establish several different qualified plans, each for different groups of employees, so just because a particular NHCE is excluded from one qualified plan does not necessarily mean that he or she is not covered by any of the employer's other plans.

1. Statutory Coverage

Statutory Rules at IRC § 410(a), as Cross-Referenced by IRC § 401(a)(3)

Any qualified retirement plan could exclude employees who are younger than age 21 and employees who have not yet completed 1 Year of Service. Certain tax-exempt educational institutions can exclude employees who are younger than age 26. The plan cannot have a maximum age exclusion. If a plan excludes employees who have not yet completed 2 Years of Service for participation eligibility, then all benefits must be 100% vested at all times.

Unlike a Year of Service for purposes of vesting of benefit accruals, which are a consistent 12 month period which applies to everyone as defined in the plan document (see Chapter 7), for purposes of eligibility to participate in the plan, the first 12 month period for each employee starts on the day he or she is hired. Therefore, the payroll department or human resources department in the sponsoring employer will need to see whether as of each individual employee's anniversary of their respective date of hire, the employee is credited with at least 1000 Hours of Service (the same definition as in Chapter 7). However, the plan document can set a 12 month period that applies to all employees who do not complete 1000 Hours of Service in the first year since they are hired. This default 12 month period will now allow the payroll or human resources department to thereafter monitor seasonal or part time employees on a more consistent basis 12-month period.

An employee who completes all eligibility requirements must enter the plan within 6 months of satisfying the requirements. Therefore, most plans have dual entry dates during a plan year, although some plans are more liberal with either monthly or daily entry dates. Additionally, there are break in service rules for crediting hours to certain individuals (similar to those described in Chapter 7).

2. Minimum Coverage Testing — Preliminary Matters

Statutory Rules at IRC § 410(b), as Cross-Referenced by IRC § 401(a)(3)

If a qualified plan document does exclude any other employees by classification (*i.e.*, "this plan covers all eligible employees other than secretaries" or "this plan covers all eligible employees other than those employed in the Illinois facility" or "this plan covers all eligible employees paid on an hourly basis" or any other crafted exclusion), then the plan needs to be tested on an annual basis for compliance with the minimum coverage rules. This means that as demographics change for an employer, the plan might need to be amended to allow additional employees to become participants in the plan. While annual testing might become cumbersome and expensive, the business goals might be served only by excluding certain classifications, locations or divisions of employees.

All employees of corporations which are members of a controlled group of corporations, all employees of trades or business which are under common control (such as partnerships and proprietorships), and all employees of service organizations that form an affiliated service group shall be treated as employed by a single employer for purposes of minimum coverage testing. There are special rules for a "transition period" after an employer joins into or leaves a controlled group of corporations of an affiliated service group.

Once the happy family of all potential employees that can be covered under an employer's qualified plan has been determined, then, for testing purposes, all employees that meet the statutory exclusions (*i.e.,* under age 21 or less than 1 Year of Service), as well as union employees who have their own benefits pursuant to a collectively bargained agreement, nonresident aliens who receive no earned income, and certain employees of the aviation and railroad industry, can be excluded. All other employees are classified, by default, as "eligible employees."

So far, we have classified all current workers in the controlled group or affiliated service group as either employees or non-employees. Of the employees, we have classified them as either eligible or non-eligible (depending on whether they can be statutorily excluded because of service less than 1 year or attained age less than 21). Then, every employee, whether eligible or not, must be classified as either a HCE or a NHCE.

Now, we need to classify each eligible employee as either benefitting under the plan, or by default, not benefitting under the plan. With limited exceptions, an employee is treated as benefiting under a plan for a plan year if and only if for that plan year, in the case of a defined contribution plan, the employee receives an allocation, or in the case of a defined benefit plan, the employee has an increase in a benefit accrued or treated as an accrued benefit. Here is a brief excerpt from the regulations:

Treas. Regs. § 1.410(b)-3. Employees and Former Employees Who Benefit under a Plan

(a) Employees benefiting under a plan.

(1) In general. Except as provided in paragraph (a)(2) of this section, an employee is treated as benefiting under a plan for a plan year if and only if for that plan year, in the case of a defined contribution plan, the employer receives an allocation taken into account under section 1.401(a)(4)-2(c)(2)(ii), or in the case of a defined benefit plan, the employee has an increase in a benefit accrued or treated as an accrued benefit under section 411(d)(6).

(2) Exceptions to allocation or accrual requirement.

(i) Section 401(k) and 401(m) plans. Notwithstanding paragraph (a)(1) of this section, an employee is treated as benefiting under a section 401(k) plan for a plan year if and only if the employee is an eligible employee as defined in § 1.401(k)-6 under the plan. Similarly, an employee is treated as benefiting under a section 401(m) plan for a plan year if and only if the employee is an eligible employee as defined in § 1.401(m)-5 under the plan for the plan year.

* * *

(iii) Certain employees treated as benefiting.

(A) In general. An employee is treated as benefiting under a plan for a plan year if the employee satisfies all of the applicable conditions for accruing a benefit or receiving an allocation for the plan year but fails to have an increase in accrued benefit or to receive an allocation solely because of one or more of the conditions set forth in paragraphs (a)(2)(iii)(B) through (F) of this section.

* * *

(3) Examples. The following examples illustrate the determination of whether an employee is benefiting under a plan for purposes of section 410(b).

Example (1). An employer has 35 employees who are eligible under a defined benefit plan. The plan requires 1,000 hours of service to accrue a benefit. Only 30 employees satisfy the 1,000-hour requirement and accrue a benefit. The five employees who do not satisfy the 1,000-hour requirement during the plan year are taken into account in testing the plan under section 410(b) but are treated as not benefiting under the plan.

Example (2). An employer maintains a section 401(k) plan. Only employees who are at least age 21 and who complete one year of service are eligible employees under the plan within the meaning of § 1.401(k)-6. Under the rule of paragraph (a)(2)(i) of this section, only employees who have satisfied these age and service conditions are treated as benefiting under the plan.

Example (3). The facts are the same as in Example 2, except that the employer also maintains a section 401(m) plan that provides matching contributions contingent on elective contributions under the section 401(k) plan. The matching contributions are contingent on employment on the last day of the plan year. Under § 1.401(m)-5, because matching contributions are contingent on employment on the last day of the plan year, not all employees who are eligible employees under the section 401(k) plan are eligible employees under the section 401(m) plan. Thus, employees who have satisfied the age and service conditions but who do not receive a matching contribution because they are not employed on the last day of the plan year are treated as not benefiting under the section 401(m) portion of the plan.

* * *

We're almost done, but not quite. We now also need to find the group of former employees who are still benefitting under the plan (*i.e.*, their retirement benefits have not yet been fully distributed), as they generally need to be tested separately from current employees benefitting under the plan.

3. Minimum Coverage Testing — Actual Tests

Statutory Rules at IRC § 410(b), as Cross-Referenced by IRC § 401(a)(3)

These minimum coverage rules do not apply to government plans and only apply to those church plans that elect to have the participation, vesting, funding, etc., provisions apply.

Now the fun begins! The plan can calculate the percentage of HCEs benefiting under the plan compared to all nonexcludible HCEs, and can similarly calculate the percentage of NHCEs benefiting under the plan to all nonexcludible NHCEs. This is called the plan's Ratio Percentage. It is the comparison of these two percentages that forms the basis of the mathematical tests. Former employees need to be tested separately under special rules.

A plan satisfies the minimum coverage rules for the current plan year if the plan is maintained by an employer that has no NHCEs at any time during the plan year. Similarly, a plan satisfies the minimum coverage rules for the current plan year if the plan benefits no HCEs for the plan year. Therefore, a retirement program for a small employer might include several qualified plans, but if developed properly, can still avoid the annual minimum coverage testing.

If a plan excludes any employees other than those under age 21 or with less than 1 Year of Service, and doesn't cover exclusively NHCEs or HCES, then it must pass any of the following 3 mathematical tests (listed in order of ease in actual calculations):

1. *The 70% Test:* The plan benefits at least 70 percent of employees who are NHCEs. This test is purely a head count of NHCEs benefitting under the plan.

2. *The Ratio Percentage Test:* The plan benefits a percentage of employees who are NHCEs which is at least 70 percent of the percentage of HCEs benefiting under the plan. The resulting percentage is called the plan's Ratio Percentage. Therefore, although benefiting less than 70% of all NHCEs, if the plan's Ratio Percentage for the year is at least 70%, then the plan complies with the minimum coverage rules for the current year. This test is purely a headcount in terms of the percentage of NHCEs benefiting under the plan compared to the percentage of HCEs benefiting under the plan.

3. *Average Benefit Percentage Test:* A plan passes if it satisfies both prongs of this test (*i.e.*, first, the nondiscriminatory classification test, and second, the average benefits test). Unlike the first 2 tests, which are purely head counts without any regard to the actual level of benefits provided under the plan, the ABPT is more complicated and requires a comparison of the average benefits for the NHCE group to the average benefits for the HCE group.

   • Prong 1, The Nondiscriminatory Classification Test (NCT), which has two components, both of which must be satisfied before the plan can go to the second prong of this test (*i.e.*, the ABT).

     • Reasonable classification test (RCT): The plan satisfies this requirement if, and only if, based on all the facts and circumstances, the classification of eligible employees who are not covered by the plan is reasonable and is established under objective business criteria. Reasonable classifications generally include specified job categories, nature of compensation (*i.e.*, salaried or hourly), geographic location, and similar bona fide business criteria. An enumeration of employees by name or other specific criteria having substantially the same effect as an enumeration by name is not considered a reasonable classification.

- Nondiscriminatory classification (NC): A table in the regulations shows a "Safe harbor percentage" and an "Unsafe harbor percentage" based on the plan's "NHCE concentration percentage" (meaning the percentage of all the nonexcludible employees of the employer who are NHCEs). If the Plan's Ratio Percentage, as calculated under the Ratio Percentage Test, is greater than the "Safe harbor percentage," then the plan satisfies this requirement (and can therefore go to the ABT). If the plan's Ratio Percentage is less than the "Unsafe harbor percentage," then the Plan fails minimum coverage for the plan year (and, thus, the plan fails the minimum coverage tests for the plan year). If the Plan's Ratio Percentage falls in between the "Safe" and "Unsafe harbor percentages," then the plan administrator must request the IRS to approve its passing of this requirement based on facts and circumstances (before we can get to the ABT).

- Prong 2, The Average Benefits Test (ABT), which is satisfied if, and only if, (a) the average benefit percentages for NHCEs divided by (b) the average benefit percentages for HCEs, is at least 70 percent. The actual benefit percentage calculated for each individual is basically the same percentage as calculated under the nondiscrimination regulations (which, for a defined contribution plan, is basically each participant's annual addition divided by his salary, and which, for a defined benefit plan, is calculated by the plan's Enrolled Actuary as the normal accrual rate). After each individual benefit percentage is calculated, the averages are calculated for the HCE group and for the NHCE group.

Treas. Regs. § 1.410(b)-2. Minimum Coverage Requirements (after 1993)

* * *

(b) Requirements with respect to employees.

* * *

(2) Ratio percentage test.

(i) In general. A plan satisfies this paragraph (b)(2) for a plan year if and only if the plan's ratio percentage for the plan year is at least 70 percent. This test incorporates both the percentage test of section 410(b)(1)(A) and the ratio test of section 410(b)(1)(B). See § 1.410(b)-9 for the definition of ratio percentage.

(ii) Examples. The following examples illustrate the ratio percentage test of this paragraph (b)(2).

Example (1). For a plan year, Plan A benefits 70 percent of an employer's nonhighly compensated employees and 100 percent of the employer's highly compensated employees. The plan's ratio percentage for the year is 70 percent (70 percent/100 percent), and thus the plan satisfies the ratio percentage test.

Example (2). For a plan year, Plan B benefits 40 percent of the employer's nonhighly compensated employees and 60 percent of the employer's highly compensated employees. Plan B fails to satisfy the ratio percentage test because the plan's ratio percentage is only 66.67 percent (40 percent/60 percent).

* * *

Treas. Regs. § 1.410(b)-4. Nondiscriminatory Classification Test

(a) In general. A plan satisfies the nondiscriminatory classification test of this section for a plan year if and only if, for the plan year, the plan benefits the employees who qualify under a classification established by the employer in accordance with paragraph (b) of this section, and the classification of employees is nondiscriminatory under paragraph (c) of this section.

(b) Reasonable classification established by the employer. A classification is established by the employer in accordance with this paragraph (b) if and only if, based on all the facts and circumstances, the classification is reasonable and is established under objective business criteria that identify the category of employees who benefit under the plan. Reasonable classifications generally include specified job categories, nature of compensation (*i.e.,* salaried or hourly), geographic location, and similar bona fide business criteria. An enumeration of employees by name or other specific criteria having substantially the same effect as an enumeration by name is not considered a reasonable classification.

(c) Nondiscriminatory classification.

(1) General rule. A classification is nondiscriminatory under this paragraph (c) for a plan year if and only if the group of employees included in the classification benefiting under the plan satisfies the requirements of either paragraph (c)(2) or (c)(3) of this section for the plan year.

(2) Safe harbor. A plan satisfies the requirement of this paragraph (c)(2) for a plan year if and only if the plan's ratio percentage is greater than or equal to the employer's safe harbor percentage, as defined in paragraph (c)(4)(i) of this section. See § 1.410(b)-9 for the definition of a plan's ratio percentage.

* * *

(4) Definitions.

* * *

(iii) Nonhighly compensated employee concentration percentage. The nonhighly compensated employee concentration percentage of an employer is the percentage of all the employees of the employer who are nonhighly compensated employees. Employees who are excludable employees for purposes of the average benefit test are not taken into account.

(iv) Table. The following table sets forth the safe harbor and unsafe harbor percentages at each nonhighly compensated employee concentration percentage:

Nonhighly Compensated Employee Concentration Percentage	Safe Harbor Percentage	Unsafe Harbor Percentage
0-60	50.00	40.00
61	49.25	39.25
62	48.50	38.50
63	47.75	37.75
64	47.00	37.00
65	46.25	36.25
66	45.50	35.50
67	44.75	34.75
68	44.00	34.00
69	43.25	33.25
70	42.50	32.50
71	41.75	31.75
72	41.00	31.00
73	40.25	30.25
74	39.50	29.50
75	38.75	28.75
76	38.00	28.00
77	37.25	27.25
78	36.50	26.50
79	35.75	25.75
80	35.00	25.00
81	34.25	24.25
82	33.50	23.50
83	32.75	22.75
84	32.00	22.00
85	31.25	21.25
86	30.50	20.50
87	29.75	20.00
88	29.00	20.00
89	28.25	20.00
90	27.50	20.00
91	26.75	20.00
92	26.00	20.00
93	25.25	20.00
94	24.50	20.00
95	23.75	20.00
96	23.00	20.00
97	22.25	20.00
98	21.50	20.00
99	20.75	20.00

(5) Examples. The following examples illustrate the rules in this paragraph (c).

Example (1). Employer A has 200 nonexcludable employees, of whom 120 are nonhighly compensated employees and 80 are highly compensated employees. Employer A maintains a plan that benefits 60 nonhighly compensated employees and 72 highly compensated employees. Thus, the plan's ratio percentage is 55.56 percent ([60/120] / [72/80] = 50%/90% = 0.5556), which is below the percentage necessary to satisfy the ratio percentage test of § 1.410(b)-2(b)(2). The employer's nonhighly compensated employee concentration percentage is 60 percent (120/200); thus, Employer A's safe harbor percentage is 50 percent and its unsafe harbor percentage is 40 percent. Because the plan's ratio percentage is greater than the safe harbor percentage, the plan's classification satisfies the safe harbor of paragraph (c)(2) of this section.

Example (2). The facts are the same as in Example 1, except that the plan benefits only 40 nonhighly compensated employees. The plan's ratio percentage is thus 37.03 percent ([40/120] / [72/80] = 33.33%/90% = 0.3703). Under these facts, the plan's classification is below the unsafe harbor percentage and is thus considered discriminatory.

Example (3). The facts are the same as in Example 1, except that the plan benefits 45 nonhighly compensated employees. The plan's ratio percentage is thus 41.67 percent ([45/120] / [72/80] = 37.50%/90% = 0.4167), above the unsafe harbor percentage (40 percent) and below the safe harbor percentage (50 percent). The Commissioner may determine that the classification is nondiscriminatory after considering all the relevant facts and circumstances.

Example (4). Employer B has 10,000 nonexcludable employees, of whom 9,600 are nonhighly compensated employees and 400 are highly compensated employees. Employer B maintains a plan that benefits 600 nonhighly compensated employees and 100 highly compensated employees. Thus, the plan's ratio percentage is 25.00 percent ([600/9,600] / [100/400] = 6.25%/25% = 0.2500), which is below the percentage necessary to satisfy the ratio percentage test of § 1.410(b)-2(b)(2). Employer B's nonhighly compensated employee concentration percentage is 96 percent (9,600/10,000); thus, Employer B's safe harbor percentage is 23 percent, and its unsafe harbor percentage is 20 percent. Because the plan's ratio percentage (25.00 percent) is greater than the safe harbor percentage (23.00 percent), the plan's classification satisfies the safe harbor of paragraph (c)(2) of this section.

Example (5). The facts are the same as in Example 4, except that the plan benefits only 400 nonhighly compensated employees. The plan's ratio percentage is thus 16.67 percent ([400/9,600] / [100/400] = 4.17%/25% = 0.1667). The plan's ratio percentage is below the unsafe harbor percentage and thus the classification is considered discriminatory.

Example (6). The facts are the same as in Example 4, except that the plan benefits 500 nonhighly compensated employees. The plan's ratio percentage is thus 20.83 percent ([500/9,600] / [100/400] = 5.21%/25% = 0.2083), above the unsafe harbor percentage (20 percent) and below the safe harbor percentage (23 percent). The Commissioner may determine that the classification is nondiscriminatory after considering all the facts and circumstances.

∗ ∗ ∗

Treas. Regs. § 1.410(b)-5. Average Benefit Percentage Test

(a) General rule. A plan satisfies the average benefit percentage test of this section for a plan year if and only if the average benefit percentage of the plan for the plan year is at least 70 percent. A plan is deemed to satisfy this requirement if it satisfies paragraph (f) of this section for the plan year.

(b) Determination of average benefit percentage. The average benefit percentage of a plan for a plan year is the percentage determined by dividing the actual benefit

percentage of the nonhighly compensated employees in plans in the testing group for the testing period that includes the plan year by the actual benefit percentage of the highly compensated employees in plans in the testing group for that testing period. See paragraph (d)(3)(ii) of this section for the definition of testing period.

(c) Determination of actual benefit percentage. The actual benefit percentage of a group of employees for a testing period is the average of the employee benefit percentages, calculated separately with respect to each of the employees in the group for the testing period. All nonexcludable employees of the employer are taken into account for this purpose, even if they are not benefiting under any plan that is taken into account.

* * *

4. Minimum Coverage Testing — Corrections of a Failed Test

Statutory Rules at IRC § 410(b), as Cross-Referenced by IRC § 401(a)(3)

If annual testing is required, but the plan does not pass any of the three minimum coverage tests, then there are some alternate testing methods the plan can try to satisfy before the ultimate need to amend the plan document to cover more NHCEs.

First, under IRC § 401(a)(6), a plan shall be considered as meeting the requirements of the minimum coverage tests during the whole of any taxable year of the plan if on one day in each quarter it satisfied such requirements.

Treas. Regs. § 1.410(b)-8. Additional Rules

(a) **Testing methods.**

(1) In general. A plan must satisfy section 410(b) for a plan year using one of the testing options in paragraphs (a)(2) through (a)(4) of this section. Whichever testing option is used for the plan year must also be used for purposes of applying section 401(a)(4) to the plan for the plan year. The annual testing option in paragraph (a)(4) of this section must be used in applying section 410(b) to a section 401(k) plan or a section 401(m) plan, and in applying the average benefit percentage test of § 1.410(b)-5. For purposes of this paragraph (a), the plan provisions and other relevant facts as of the last day of the plan year regarding which employees benefit under the plan for the plan year are applied to the employees taken into account under the testing option used for the plan year. For this purpose, amendments retroactively correcting a plan in accordance with § 1.401(a)(4)-11(g) are taken into account as plan provisions in effect as of the last day of the plan year.

(2) Daily testing option. A plan satisfies section 410(b) for a plan year if it satisfies § 1.410(b)-2 on each day of the plan year, taking into account only those employees (or former employees) who are employees (or former employees) on that day.

(3) Quarterly testing option. A plan is deemed to satisfy section 410(b) for a plan year if the plan satisfies § 1.410(b)-2 on at least one day in each quarter of the plan year, taking into account for each of those days only those employees (or former employees) who are employees (or former employees) on that day. The preceding sentence does not apply if the plan's eligibility rules or benefit formula operate to cause the four quarterly testing days selected by the employer not to be reasonably representative of the coverage of the plan over the entire plan year.

(4) Annual testing option. A plan satisfies section 410(b) for a plan year if it satisfies § 1.410(b)-2 as of the last day of the plan year, taking into account all employees (or former employees) who were employees (or former employees) on any day during the plan year.

(5) Example. The following example illustrates this paragraph (a).

Example. Plan A is a defined contribution plan that is not a section 401(k) plan or a section 401(m) plan, and that conditions allocations on an employee's employment on the last day of the plan year. Plan A is being tested for the 1995 calendar plan year using the daily testing option in paragraph (a)(2) of this section. In testing the plan for compliance with section 410(b) on March 11, 1995, Employee X is taken into account because he was an employee on that day and was not an excludable employee with respect to Plan A on that day. Employee X was a participant in Plan A on March 11, 1995, was employed on December 31, 1995, and received an allocation under Plan A for the 1995 plan year. Under these facts, Employee X is treated as benefiting under Plan A on March 11, 1995, even though Employee X had not satisfied all of the conditions for receiving an allocation on that day, because Employee X satisfied all of those conditions as of the last day of the plan year.

* * *

Since every plan must singularly satisfy the minimum coverage rules, regulations at § 1.410(b)-7 provide a definition of a plan and rules for voluntarily aggregating multiple qualified plans sponsored by the same employer, controlled group of employers or affiliated service groups. The catch is that if voluntarily aggregating plans for purposes of minimum coverage testing, then those same plans of the employer must be aggregated for purposes of the separate nondiscrimination requirements.

If all alternatives still yield failing results, then the plan document must be amended to include enough NHCEs so that the plan passes the tests. Employers are cautioned because if the plan had been designed to exclude a category of employees (such as "all secretaries") and then needs to be amended to include a few NHCE secretaries to pass the tests, then care should be taken to include categories rather than individuals (such as amending the plan to only exclude "all secretaries that do not report to officers of the company.") If the plan is amended, two issues should be considered: first, how the plan can be amended and communicated without affecting the morale of the employees who are still excluded while some similarly situated fellow employees are now suddenly covered, and second, that while this might be a quick fix for the current year, it probably cannot be undone in the next few years unless the demographics change substantially. Under the accrual rules of IRC § 411(d)(6), since an accrued benefit can never be reduced or eliminated by plan amendment, the plan can be amended to add participants, and can only be amended to exclude future, yet unearned, accruals for employees who were already benefitting under the plan.

D. Minimum Participation Requirements for All Qualified Defined Benefit Plans

Statutory Rules at IRC § 401(a)(26)

In addition to the minimum coverage rules, every defined benefit plan must meet the minimum participation rule. This rule was established to prevent employers from allowing only favored employees to participate in a defined benefit plan and all other employees to participate in a defined contribution plan. A qualified defined benefit pension plan must benefit the lesser of: (1) 50 employees; or (2) the greater of: (i) 40% of all employees, or (ii) 2 employees. In a memorandum issued internally to IRS agents reviewing defined benefit plan documents for determination letters, in order to count a participant as benefiting under a plan, the participant must receive "meaningful benefits."

Like most aspects of the qualification rules, this seemingly simple rule is riddled with procedures on how to aggregate and disaggregate plans, how to separately test former employees and former benefit structures, and excludable employees and testing procedures. All of those procedures are published in the regulations and other guidance promulgated under § 401(a)(26), but for purposes of this introductory textbook, just knowing that the rule exists and that every defined benefit plan must comply is enough.

E. Nondiscrimination Requirements for All Qualified Retirement Plans

Every qualified retirement plan must meet the nondiscrimination requirements each year. Congress decided not to require that every participant benefit under the plan in exactly the same manner, but if for business purposes some employees receive higher benefits or enjoy certain rights or features, then mathematical tests are imposed which determine if enough NHCEs receive comparable benefits. Often times, an employer might establish several different qualified plans, or several different benefit structures within a single plan, so just because a particular NHCE receives a seemingly lesser benefit, if a certain number of HCEs receive a similarly lesser benefit, then the plan is not discriminatory in favor of HCEs.

If the plan document only provides benefits that satisfy a safe-harbor formula, then by design, the plan will automatically meet the nondiscrimination tests each year. However, if the benefits, rights and features are not uniform, then the plan must be tested annually for the nondiscrimination requirements. While annual testing might become cumbersome and expensive, the business goals might be served only by treating different groups of employees differently.

1. The Three Components of Annual Nondiscrimination Testing

Statutory Requirements at IRC § 401(a)(4) and (a)(5)

There are the three components of annual nondiscrimination testing:

1. The amount of benefits provided in a defined benefit plan or contributions in a defined contribution plan must be nondiscriminatory—either the plan is designed as a Safe Harbor or the plan must annually meet the general nondiscrimination test;

2. The actual availability of benefits, rights and features, and the effective availability of BRFs, cannot be discriminatory—there are no plan provisions which can automatically satisfy this requirement, and facts and circumstances must be applied annually; and

3. Plan amendments and plan termination cannot have the effect of being discriminatory—there are no plan provisions which can automatically satisfy this requirement, and facts and circumstances must be applied every time the plan is amended or upon plan termination.

While all three aspects are equally important, since the latter two are based on facts and circumstances, they are not discussed in great detail in this textbook. Please feel free to read regulations at § 1.401(a)(4)-4 and -5 on your own for some of the factors that the IRS will look at in determining if there is improper discrimination in favor of HCEs in either benefits, rights and features or in plan amendments or plan termination.

2. Safe Harbor Plan Designs

The following are the only available Safe Harbors for a defined contribution plan:

-   Uniform Allocation Rate: Here the allocation is divided proportionately based on compensation under a profit sharing plan or everyone is getting the same percent of their compensation under a money purchase plan or a target benefit plan.

-   Uniform Points Allocation: A profit sharing plan can credit points (on a standard basis) for years of service, age and/or compensation. If the plan document includes a table that uniformly allocates such credits to participants, and if the contribution is allocated based on each participant's proportionate share of credited points, then the plan will be deemed nondiscriminatory, but only if it passes a simple mini-nondiscrimination test. Under this mini-test, the average allocation rate for HCEs cannot exceed the average allocation rate for NHCEs, where an allocation rate for an individual participant is his annual addition divided by his salary. There are special rules for defined contribution plans which use permitted disparity, and there are rules for plans which use multiple formulas, where each formula meets the safe harbor requirements on its own.

The following are the only available Safe Harbors for a defined benefit plan:

-   Unit Credit Plan: A plan satisfies this safe harbor if it satisfies the 133 1/3 accrual rule and if each employee's accrued benefit under the plan as of any plan year is determined by applying the plan's benefit formula to the employee's years of service and (if applicable) average annual compensation, both determined as of that plan year.

- Fractional accrual plans: A plan satisfies this safe harbor if it satisfies the fractional accrual rule and if each employee's accrued benefit under the plan as of any plan year is determined by multiplying such benefit by a fraction, the numerator of which is the employee's years of service determined as of the plan year, and the denominator of which is the employee's projected years of service as of normal retirement date. A plan must also satisfy one of three additional rules to meet this Safe Harbor (which are described in the regulations).

There are special rules for defined benefit plans which use permitted disparity, and there are special rules for uniformity in normal retirement and post-normal retirement accruals and for early retirement subsidies.

The key to drafting a good safe harbor design plan is uniformity and consistency—once any individual participant or groups of participants are treated any better, with benefits or contributions, or with rights or features of the plan, then it is no longer a safe harbor plan, and it needs to be tested annually for nondiscrimination. The employer has a choice when it has a business purpose in offering different benefits to different groups of employees: set up multiple plans, each one a safe harbor design, but each plan needing to be tested separately for minimum coverage; or, set up a single plan that meets the simpler minimum coverage tests (such as the 70% test or the Ratio Percentage test), but that offers different benefits to different employees, which needs to be tested for nondiscrimination.

3. General Testing if Benefits Are Not Uniform

Guidance Primarily at Treas. Regs. § 1.401(a)(4)-1 through -13

The general test is very complicated, and the Treasury Regulations provide many mathematical computations and many legal definitions, exceptions, and exceptions to exceptions. Although similar, there are slightly different rules for qualified defined contribution plans than for qualified defined benefit plans.

First, an allocation rate is calculated for each participant benefiting under a defined contribution plan, or both a normal accrual rate and a most valuable accrual rate are calculated for each participant benefiting under a defined benefit plan. Please note, the rules of covered employees, determination of HCEs, and the controlled group and affiliated service group rules for employers for nondiscrimination purposes are generally the same as those rules for minimum coverage testing.

Second, all participants are organized in order of descending allocation or accrual rates, where NHCEs are put above HCEs when the rates are equal. There are special rules which allow a plan administrators of large plans to set bands of rates.

Third, a rate group is created for every HCE benefiting under the plan. A rate group consists of that HCE and every other employee (both HCEs and NHCEs) with an allocation rate equal to or greater than his or hers in a defined contribution plan, or with both a normal accrual rate and a most valuable accrual rate equal to or greater than his or hers in a defined benefit plan (so, on the chart where all employees are organized by descending allocation or accrual rates, starting with the highest rate at the top of the chart and all lower rates below, a line is drawn under each HCE, and a rate group is formed for every HCE, consisting of that HCE and all HCE and NHCEs listed above that HCE). There are rules where multiple HCEs with equal, or basically equal, rates can be grouped together to form a single rate group.

Fourth, each rate group must satisfy a modified minimum coverage test.

If every rate group satisfies the minimum coverage tests, as slightly modified by the regulations, then the plan as a whole passes the nondiscrimination tests. The rationale is that although different benefits or allocations are provided to different groups of employees, each benefit or allocation goes to enough NHCEs, and therefore, the employer could have accomplished its business goals through several qualified plans but decided to simplify plan administration by establishing only a single plan and trust.

Below is an excerpt from the Treasury regulations for general testing under a defined contribution plan. They are lengthy, but please go through the examples to truly learn how the tests work.

Treas. Regs. § 1.401(a)(4)-2. Nondiscrimination in Amount of Employer Contributions under a Defined Contribution Plan

* * *

(c) General test for nondiscrimination in amount of contributions.

(1) General Rule. The employer contributions allocated under a defined contribution plan are nondiscriminatory in amount for a plan year if each rate group under the plan satisfies section 410(b). For purposes of this paragraph (c), a rate group exists under a plan for each HCE and consists of the HCE and all other employees in the plan (both HCEs and NHCEs) who have an allocation rate greater than or equal to the HCE's allocation rate. Thus, an employee is in the rate group for each HCE who has an allocation rate less than or equal to the employee's allocation rate.

(2) Determination of allocation rates.

(i) General rule. The allocation rate for an employee for a plan year equals the sum of the allocations to the employee's account for the plan year, expressed either as a percentage of plan year compensation or as a dollar amount.

(ii) Allocations taken into account. The amounts taken into account in determining allocation rates for a plan year include all employer contributions and forfeitures that are allocated or treated as allocated to the account of an employee under the plan for the plan year, other than amounts described in paragraph (c)(2)(iii) of this section. For this purpose, employer contributions include annual additions described in § 1.415(c)-1(b)(4) (regarding amounts arising from certain transactions between the plan and the employer). In the case of a defined contribution plan subject to section 412, an employer contribution is taken into account in the plan year for which it is required to be contributed and allocated to employees' accounts under the plan, even if all or part of the required contribution is not actually made.

(iii) Allocations not taken into account. Allocations of income, expenses, gains, and losses attributable to the balance in an employee's account are not taken into account in determining allocation rates.

(iv) Imputation of permitted disparity. The disparity permitted under section 401(l) may be imputed in accordance with the rules of § 1.401(a)(4)-7.

(v) Grouping of allocation rates.

(A) General rule. An employer may treat all employees who have allocation rates within a specified range above and below a midpoint rate chosen by the employer as having an allocation rate equal to the midpoint rate within that range. Allocation rates within a given range may not be grouped under this paragraph (c)(2)(v) if the allocation rates of HCEs within the range generally are significantly higher than the allocation rates of NHCEs in the range. The specified ranges within which all employees are treated as having the same allocation rate may not overlap and may be no larger than provided in paragraph (c)(2)(v)(B) of this section. Allocation rates of employees that are not within any of these specified ranges are determined without regard to this paragraph (c)(2)(v).

(B) Size of specified ranges. The lowest and highest allocation rates in the range must be within five percent (not five percentage points) of the midpoint rate. If allocation rates are determined as a percentage of plan year compensation, the lowest and highest allocation rates need not be within five percent of the midpoint rate, if they are no more than one quarter of a percentage point above or below the midpoint rate.

(vi) Consistency requirement. Allocation rates must be determined in a consistent manner for all employees for the plan year.

(3) Satisfaction of section 410(b) by a rate group.

(i) General rule. For purposes of determining whether a rate group satisfies section 410(b), the rate group is treated as if it were a separate plan that benefits only the employees included in the rate group for the plan year. Thus, for example, under § 1.401(a)(4)-1(c)(4)(iv), the ratio percentage of the rate group is determined taking into account all nonexcludable employees regardless of whether they benefit under the plan. Paragraphs (c)(3)(ii) and (iii) of this section provide additional special rules for determining whether a rate group satisfies section 410(b).

(ii) Application of nondiscriminatory classification test. A rate group satisfies the nondiscriminatory classification test of § 1.410(b)-4 (including the reasonable classification requirement of § 1.410(b)-4(b)) if and only if the ratio percentage of the rate group is greater than or equal to the lesser of—

(A) The midpoint between the safe and the unsafe harbor percentages applicable to the plan; and

(B) The ratio percentage of the plan.

(iii) Application of average benefit percentage test. A rate group satisfies the average benefit percentage test of § 1.410(b)-5 if the plan of which it is a part satisfies § 1.410(b)-5 (without regard to § 1.410(b)-5(f)). In the case of a plan that relies on § 1.410(b)-5(f) to satisfy the average benefit percentage test, each rate group under the plan satisfies the average benefit percentage test (if applicable) only if the rate group separately satisfies § 1.410(b)-5(f).

(4) Examples. The following examples illustrate the general test in this paragraph (c):

Example (1). Employer X maintains two defined contribution plans, Plan A and Plan B, that are aggregated and treated as a single plan for purposes of sections 410(b) and 401(a)(4) pursuant to § 1.410(b)-7(d). For the 1994 plan year, Employee M has plan year compensation of $10,000 and receives an allocation of $200 under Plan A and an allocation of $800 under Plan B. Employee M's allocation rate under the aggregated plan for the 1994 plan year is 10 percent (*i.e.*, $1,000 divided by $10,000).

Example (2). The employees in Plan C have the following allocation rates (expressed as a percentage of plan year compensation): 2.75 percent, 2.80 percent, 2.85 percent, 3.25 percent, 6.65 percent, 7.33 percent, 7.34 percent, and 7.35 percent. Because the first four rates are within a range of no more than one quarter of a percentage point above and below 3.0 percent (a midpoint rate chosen by the employer), under paragraph (c)(2)(v) of this section the employer may treat the employees who have those rates as having an allocation rate of 3.0 percent (provided that the allocation rates of HCEs within the range generally are not significantly higher than the allocation rates of NHCEs within the range). Because the last four rates are within a range of no more than five percent above and below 7.0 percent (a midpoint rate chosen by the employer), the employer may treat the employees who have those rates as having an allocation rate of 7.0 percent (provided that the allocation rates of HCEs within the range generally are not significantly higher than the allocation rates of NHCEs within the range).

Example (3).

(a) Employer Y has only six nonexcludable employees, all of whom benefit under Plan D. The HCEs are H1 and H2, and the NHCEs are N1 through N4. For the 1994 plan year, H1 and N1 through N4 have an allocation rate of 5.0 percent of plan year compensation. For the same plan year, H2 has an allocation rate of 7.5 percent of plan year compensation.

(b) There are two rate groups under Plan D. Rate group 1 consists of H1 and all those employees who have an allocation rate greater than or equal to H1's allocation rate (5.0 percent). Thus, rate group 1 consists of H1, H2, and N1 through N4. Rate group 2 consists only of H2 because no other employee has an allocation rate greater than or equal to H2's allocation rate (7.5 percent).

(c) The ratio percentage for rate group 2 is zero percent—*i.e.*, zero percent (the percentage of all nonhighly compensated nonexcludable employees who are in the rate group) divided by 50 percent (the percentage of all highly compensated nonexcludable employees who are in the rate group). Therefore rate group 2 does not satisfy the ratio percentage test under § 1.410(b)-2(b)(2). Rate group 2 also does not satisfy the nondiscriminatory classification test of § 1.410(b)-4 (as modified by paragraph (c)(3) of this section). Rate group 2 therefore does not satisfy section 410(b) and, as a result, Plan D does not satisfy the general test in paragraph (c)(1) of this section. This is true regardless of whether rate group 1 satisfies § 1.410(b)-2(b)(2).

Example (4).

(a) The facts are the same as in Example 3, except that N4 has an allocation rate of 8.0 percent.

(b) There are two rate groups in Plan D. Rate group 1 consists of H1 and all those employees who have an allocation rate greater than or equal to H1's allocation rate (5.0 percent). Thus, rate group 1 consists of H1, H2 and N1 through N4. Rate group 2 consists of H2, and all those employees who have an allocation rate greater than or equal to H2's allocation rate (7.5 percent). Thus, rate group 2 consists of H2 and N4.

(c) Rate group 1 satisfies the ratio percentage test under § 1.410(b)-2(b)(2) because the ratio percentage of the rate group is 100 percent—*i.e.*, 100 percent (the percentage of all nonhighly compensated nonexcludable employees who are in the rate group) divided by 100 percent (the percentage of all highly compensated nonexcludable employees who are in the rate group).

(d) Rate group 2 does not satisfy the ratio percentage test of § 1.410(b)-2(b)(2) because the ratio percentage of the rate group is 50 percent—*i.e.*, 25 percent (the percentage of all nonhighly compensated nonexcludable employees who are in the rate group) divided by 50 percent (the percentage of all highly compensated nonexcludable employees who are in the rate group).

(e) However, rate group 2 does satisfy the nondiscriminatory classification test of § 1.410(b)-4 because the ratio percentage of the rate group (50 percent) is greater than the safe harbor percentage applicable to the plan under § 1.410(b)-4(c)(4) (45.5 percent).

(f) Under paragraph (c)(3)(iii) of this section, rate group 2 satisfies the average benefit percentage test, if Plan D satisfies the average benefit percentage test. (The requirement that Plan D satisfy the average benefit percentage test applies even though Plan D satisfies the ratio percentage test and would ordinarily not need to run the average benefit percentage test.) If Plan D satisfies the average benefit percentage test, then rate group 2 satisfies section 410(b) and thus, Plan D satisfies the general test in paragraph (c)(1) of this section, because each rate group under the plan satisfies section 410(b).

Example (5).

(a) Plan E satisfies section 410(b) by satisfying the nondiscriminatory classification test of § 1.410(b)-4 and the average benefit percentage test of § 1.410(b)-5 (without regard to § 1.410(b)-5(f)). See § 1.410(b)-2(b)(3). Plan E uses the facts-and-circumstances requirements of § 1.410(b)-4(c)(3) to satisfy the nondiscriminatory classification test of § 1.410(b)-4. The safe and unsafe harbor percentages applicable to the plan under § 1.410(b)-4(c)(4) are 29 and 20 percent, respectively. Plan E has a ratio percentage of 22 percent.

(b) Rate group 1 under Plan E has a ratio percentage of 23 percent. Under paragraph (c)(3)(ii) of this section, the rate group satisfies the nondiscriminatory classification requirement of § 1.410(b)-4, because the ratio percentage of the rate group (23 percent) is greater than the lesser of—

(1) The ratio percentage for the plan as a whole (22 percent); and

(2) The midpoint between the safe and unsafe harbor percentages (24.5 percent).

(c) Under paragraph (c)(3)(iii) of this section, the rate group satisfies section 410(b) because the plan satisfies the average benefit percentage test of § 1.410(b)-5.

Please note that the general test for a defined benefit plan is similar, except that instead of a single Allocation Rate for each plan participant, there is both a Normal Accrual Rate and a Most Valuable Accrual Rate for each participant. The rules, as well as examples, are at Regs. § 1.401(a)(4)-3(c).

In determining an allocation rate or an accrual rate for Step 1 of the general test, the compensation must basically be total compensation paid, even if the plan uses a different definition of compensation for purposes of allocating contributions or for the accrual of benefits. The plan document may have a different definition of compensation for purposes of determining benefits or allocations under the plan (such as compensation exclusive of bonuses, overtime, or other categories of pay). The definition of compensation for benefits purposes can be anything the sponsoring employer wants, as long as the definition of compensation does not discriminate in favor of the HCEs. Plans may have a third definition of compensation in their plan documents that is used for calculating the maximum benefits or allocations allowed. While a plan may therefore have up to three different definitions of compensation to meet its business goals and needs, it is obviously simpler for annual plan administration if all three definitions are the same.

4. Correction if the Plan Fails

If the plan fails the nondiscrimination test in any year, then the plan can be restructured into component parts, or two or more plans sponsored by the same employer may be aggregated by the employer, or, as described below, the benefits can be cross-tested. If all else fails, the plan must be amended to provide greater benefits or allocations to the NHCEs so that the plan passes the general test. The same issues with amending the plan document when the plan fails the minimum coverage tests apply here if the plan document is amended to increase the benefits or contributions to enough NHCEs so that the nondiscrimination tests are met: first, how the plan can be amended and communicated without affecting the morale of the employees who are still receiving lower benefits or contributions while some similarly situated fellow employees are now suddenly enjoying higher benefits or contributions, and second, that while this might be a quick fix for the current year, it probably cannot be undone in the next few years unless the demographics change substantially.

Although originally anticipated as a method of passing the general test if it otherwise failed, cross-testing was added to the regulations for nondiscrimination. Under the cross testing methodology, either a defined contribution plan will convert contributions to accrued benefits and substitute accrual rates for allocation rates in its general test or a defined benefit plan will convert accrued benefits to allocations and substitute allocation rates for accrual rates in its general test. Treasury added new "gateway" requirements in 2002 which generally require defined contribution plans, which are cross-tested, to provide all NHCE's with at least a 5% allocation rate before the plan can be tested under the cross-testing rules.

Some profit sharing plans, like age-weighted and new comparability plans, are specifically designed to meet the cross-testing rules rather than the general test (and, in fact, the allocation formula in a new comparability plan is usually backed into as the formula which will produce results so that the cross-testing rules are just barely satisfied). Below is a very short excerpt from the regulations, and I don't even bother including the examples in this part of the chapter, but I just want to make sure you know they are there if you really wanted to understand the cross testing rules in more detail.

Treas. Regs. § 1.401(a)(4)-8. Cross-Testing

* * *

(b) Nondiscrimination in amount of benefits provided under a defined contribution plan.

(1) General rule and gateway.

(i) General rule. Equivalent benefits under a defined contribution plan (other than an ESOP) are nondiscriminatory in amount for a plan year if—

(A) The plan would satisfy § 1.401(a)(4)-2(c)(1) for the plan year if an equivalent accrual rate, as determined under paragraph (b)(2) of this section, were substituted for each employee's allocation rate in the determination of rate groups; and

(B) For plan years beginning on or after January 1, 2002, the plan satisfies one of the following conditions—

(1) The plan has broadly available allocation rates (within the meaning of paragraph (b)(1)(iii) of this section) for the plan year;

(2) The plan has age-based allocation rates that are based on either a gradual age or service schedule (within the meaning of paragraph (b)(1)(iv) of this section) or a uniform target benefit allocation (within the meaning of paragraph (b)(1)(v) of this section) for the plan year; or

(3) The plan satisfies the minimum allocation gateway of paragraph (b)(1)(vi) of this section for the plan year.

* * *

(viii) Examples. The following examples illustrate the rules in this paragraph (b)(1):

* * *

---

5. Nondiscrimination of Compensation

I know there is a lot coming at you, but let's revisit the calculation of the allocation rates for general testing in a defined contribution plan and the calculation of normal and most valuable accrual rates for general testing in a defined benefit plan. In determining an allocation rate or an accrual rate for the general test, the compensation must basically total compensation paid,[1] even if the plan uses a different definition of compensation for purposes of allocating contributions or for the accrual of benefits. The plan document may have a different definition of compensation for purposes of de-

---

1. Treas. Regs. § 1.401(a)(5)-1(c), referencing § 414(s).

termining benefits or allocations under the plan (such as compensation exclusive of bonuses, overtime, or other categories of pay). The definition of compensation for benefits purposes can be anything the sponsoring employer wants, as long as the definition of compensation does not discriminate in favor of the HCEs. Plans may have yet a third definition of compensation in their plan documents that is used for calculating the maximum benefits or allocations allowed.[2] While a plan may have up to three different definitions of compensation to meet its business goals and needs, it is obviously simpler for annual plan administration if all three definitions are the same. Please note there are special rules for determining the compensation for testing purposes for salary earned for less than a year, and for plans that define the 12 month period for compensation differently than the 12 month period representing the plan year. Below are excerpts from the regulations defining compensation for purposes of nondiscrimination testing.

Treas. Regs. § 1.414(s)-1. Definition of Compensation

Caution: The Treasury has not yet amended Reg § 1.414(s)-1 to reflect changes made by P.L. 104-188

(a) Introduction

(1) In general. Section 414(s) and this section provide rules for defining compensation for purposes of applying any provision that specifically refers to section 414(s) or this section. For example, section 414(s) is referred to in many of the nondiscrimination provisions applicable to pension, profit-sharing, and stock bonus plans qualified under section 401(a). In accordance with section 414(s)(1), this section defines compensation as compensation within the meaning of section 415(c)(3). It also implements the election provided in section 414(s)(2) to treat certain deferrals as compensation and exercises the authority granted to the Secretary in section 414(s)(3) to prescribe alternative nondiscriminatory definitions of compensation.

(2) Limitations on scope of section 414(s). Section 414(s) and this section do not apply unless a provision specifically refers to section 414(s) or this section. For example, even though a definition of compensation permitted under section 414(s) must be used in determining whether the contributions or benefits under a pension, profit-sharing, or stock bonus plan satisfy a certain applicable provision (such as section 401(a)(4)), except as otherwise specified, the plan is not required to use a definition of compensation that satisfies section 414(s) in calculating the amount of contributions or benefits actually provided under the plan.

(3) Overview. Paragraph (b) of this section provides rules of general application that govern a definition of compensation that satisfies section 414(s). Paragraph (c) of this section contains specific definitions of compensation that satisfy section 414(s) without satisfying any additional nondiscrimination requirement under section 414(s). Paragraph (d) of this section provides rules permitting the use of alternative definitions of compensation that satisfy section 414(s) as long as the nondiscrimination requirement and other requirements described in paragraph (d) of this section are satisfied. Paragraphs (e) and (f) of this section provides special rules permitting the use of rate of compensation, or prior-employer compensation or imputed compensation, rather than actual compensation, under

---

2. IRC § 415(c); as discussed in Chapter 7.

a definition of compensation that satisfies section 414(s). Paragraph (g) of this section provides other special rules, including a special rule for determining the compensation of a self-employed individual under an alternative definition of compensation. Paragraph (h) of this section provides definitions for certain terms used in this section.

(b) Rules of general application.

(1) Use of a definition. Any definition of compensation that satisfies section 414(s) may be used when a provision explicitly refers to section 414(s) unless the reference or this section specifically indicates otherwise.

(2) Consistency Rule.

(i) General rule. A definition of compensation selected by an employer for use in satisfying an applicable provision must be used consistently to define the compensation of all employees taken into account in satisfying the requirements of the applicable provision for the determination period. For example, although any definition of compensation that satisfies section 414(s) may be used for section 401(a)(4) purposes, the same definition of compensation generally must be used consistently to define the compensation of all employees taken into account in determining whether a plan satisfies section 401(a)(4). Furthermore, a different definition of compensation that satisfies section 414(s) is permitted to be used to determine whether another plan maintained by the same employer separately satisfies the requirements of section 401(a)(4). Although a definition of compensation must be used consistently, an employer may change its definition of compensation for a subsequent determination period with respect to the applicable provision. Rules provided under any applicable provision may modify the consistency requirements of this paragraph (b)(2).

(ii) Scope of consistency rule. Compensation will not fail to be defined consistently for a group of employees merely because some employees do not receive one or more of the types of compensation included in the definition. For example, a definition of compensation that includes salary, regular or scheduled pay, overtime, and specified types of bonuses will not fail to define compensation consistently merely because only salaried employees receive salary and these specified types of bonuses and only hourly employees receive regular or scheduled pay and overtime.

(3) Self-employed individuals. Notwithstanding paragraph (b)(1) of this section, self-employed individuals' compensation can only be determined under paragraph (c)(2) of this section (with or without the modification permitted by paragraph (c)(4) of this section or a modification permitted by paragraph (c)(5) of this section) or by using an equivalent alternative compensation amount determined in accordance with paragraph (g)(1) of this section. These limitations on self-employed individuals do not affect their common-law employees. Thus, the compensation of common-law employees of a partnership or sole proprietorship may be defined using an alternative definition, provided the definition otherwise satisfies paragraph (c)(3), (d), (e), or (f) of this section. If an alternative definition of compensation under paragraph (c)(3), (d), (e), or (f) of this section is used for other employees to satisfy an applicable provision, the consistency requirement is only met if paragraph (g) of this section is used for the self-employed individuals.

(c) Specific definitions of compensation that satisfy section 414(s).

(1) General rules. The definitions of compensation provided in paragraphs (c)(2) and (c)(3) of this section satisfy section 414(s) and need not satisfy any additional requirements under section 414(s). Paragraph (c)(2) of this section describes definitions of compensation within the meaning of section 415(c)(3). Paragraph (c)(3) of this section provides a safe harbor alternative definition that excludes certain additional items of compensation. Paragraph (c)(4) of this section permits any definition provided in paragraph (c)(2) or (c)(3) of this section to include certain types of elective contributions and deferred compensation. Paragraph (c)(5) of this section permits certain modifications to a definition otherwise provided under this paragraph (c).

(2) Compensation within the meaning of section 415(c)(3). A definition of compensation that includes all compensation within the meaning of section 415(c)(3) and excludes all other compensation satisfies section 414(s). Sections 1.415(c)-2(b) and (c) provide rules for determining items of compensation included in and excluded from compensation within the meaning of section 415(c)(3). In addition, section 414(s) is satisfied by the safe harbor definitions provided in § 1.415(c)-2(d)(2), (d)(3) and (d)(4) and any additional definitions of compensation prescribed by the Commission under the authority provided in § 1.415(c)-2(d)(1) that are treated as satisfying section 415(c)(3).

(3) Safe harbor alternative definition. Under the safe harbor alternative definition in this paragraph (c)(3), compensation is compensation as defined in paragraph (c)(2) of this section, reduced by all of the following items (even if includible in gross income): reimbursements or other expense allowances, fringe benefits (cash and non-cash), moving expenses, deferred compensation, and welfare benefits.

(4) Inclusion of certain deferrals in compensation. Any definition of compensation provided in paragraph (c)(2) or (c)(3) of this section satisfies section 414(s) even though it is modified to include all of the following types of elective contributions and all of the following types of deferred compensation—

(i) Elective contributions that are made by the employer on behalf of its employees that are not includible in gross income under section 125, section 402(e)(3), section 402(h), and section 403(b);

(ii) Compensation deferred under an eligible deferred compensation plan within the meaning of section 457(b) (deferred compensation plans of state and local governments and tax-exempt organizations); and

(iii) Employee contributions (under governmental plans) described in section 414(h)(2) that are picked up by the employing unit and thus are treated as employer contributions.

(5) Exclusions applicable solely to highly compensated employees. Any definition of compensation that satisfies paragraph (c)(2) or (c)(3) of this section, with or without the modification permitted by paragraph (c)(4) of this section, may be modified to exclude any portion of the compensation of some or all of the employer's highly compensated employees (including, for example, any one or more of the types of elective contributions or deferred compensation described in paragraph (c)(4) of this section).

(d) Alternative definitions of compensation that satisfy section 414(s).

(1) General rule. In addition to the definitions provided in paragraph (c) of this section, any definition of compensation satisfies section 414(s) with respect to employees (other than self-employed individuals treated as employees under section 401(c)(1)) if the definition of compensation does not by design favor highly compensated employees, is reasonable within the meaning of paragraph (d)(2) of this section, and satisfies the nondiscrimination requirement in paragraph (d)(3) of this section.

(2) Reasonable definition of compensation.

(i) General rule. An alternative definition of compensation under this paragraph (d) is reasonable under section 414(s) if it is a definition of compensation provided in paragraph (c) of this section, modified to exclude all or any portion of one or more of the types of compensation described in paragraph (d)(2)(ii) of this section. See paragraph (e) of this section, however, for special rules that permit definitions of compensation based on employees' rates of compensation and paragraph (f) of this section for special rules that permit definitions of compensation that include prior-employer compensation or imputed compensation.

(ii) Items that may be excluded. A reasonable definition of compensation is permitted to exclude, on a consistent basis, all or any portion of irregular or additional compensation, including (but not limited to) one or more of the following: any type of additional compensation for employees working outside their regularly scheduled tour of duty (such as overtime pay, premiums for shift differential, and call-in premiums), bonuses, or any one or more of the types of compensation excluded under the safe harbor alternative definition in paragraph (c)(3) of this section. Whether a type of compensation is irregular or additional is determined based on all the relevant facts and circumstances. A reasonable definition is also permitted to include, on a consistent basis, all or any portion of the types of elective contributions or deferred compensation described in paragraph (c)(4) of this section and, thus, need not include all those types of elective contributions or deferred compensation as otherwise required under paragraph (c)(4) of this section.

(iii) Limits on the amount excluded from compensation. A definition of compensation is not reasonable if it provides that each employee's compensation is a specified portion of the employee's compensation measured for the otherwise applicable determination period under another definition. For example, a definition of compensation that specifically limits each employee's compensation for a determination period to 95 percent of the employee's compensation using a definition provided in paragraph (c) of this section is not reasonable. Similarly, a definition of compensation that limits each employee's compensation used to satisfy an applicable provision with a 12-month determination period to compensation under a definition provided in paragraph (c) of this section for one month is not a reasonable definition of compensation. However, a definition of compensation is not unreasonable merely because it excludes all compensation in excess of a specified dollar amount.

(3) Nondiscrimination requirement.

(i) In general. An alternative definition of compensation under this paragraph (d) is nondiscriminatory under section 414(s) for a determination period if the average percentage of total compensation included under the alternative definition of compensation for an employer's highly compensated employees as a group for the determination period does not exceed by more than a de minimis amount the average percentage of total compensation included under the alternative definition for the employer's nonhighly compensated employees as a group.

(ii) Total compensation.

(A) General rule. For purposes of this paragraph (d)(3), total compensation must be determined using a definition of compensation provided in paragraph (c)(2) of this section, either with or without the modification permitted by paragraph (c)(4) of this section. Thus, total compensation does not include prior-employer compensation or imputed compensation described in paragraph (f)(1) of this section (including imputed compensation for a period during which an employee performs services for another employer). Total compensation taken into account for each employee (including, if added, the elective contributions and deferred compensation described in paragraph (c)(4) of this section) may not exceed the annual compensation limit of section 401(a)(17).

(B) Alternative definitions with exclusions applicable solely to highly compensated employees. If an alternative definition of compensation contains a provision that excludes amounts from compensation and, as described in paragraph (c)(5) of this section, the provision only applies in defining the compensation of some highly compensated employees, then, for purposes of this paragraph (d)(3), the total compensation of any highly compensated employee subject to the provision must be reduced by any amount excluded from the employee's compensation as a result of the provision. However, if the provision applies consistently in defining the compensation of all highly compensated employees, this adjustment to total compensation is not required.

(iii) Employees taken into account.

(A) General rule. In applying the requirement of this paragraph (d)(3), the employees taken into account are the same employees taken into account in satisfying the requirements of the applicable provision for the determination period. For example, in determining whether a plan satisfies section 401(a)(4), an alternative definition must satisfy this paragraph (d)(3) taking into account all employees who benefit under the plan for the plan year (within the meaning of § 1.410(b)-3(a)). If an employer is using the same alternative definition of compensation to determine whether more than one separate plan satisfies section 401(a)(4), the employer is permitted to take into account all the employees who benefit under all of those plans for the plan year in determining whether the alternative definition of compensation being used satisfies this paragraph (d)(3).

(B) Exclusion of self-employed individuals. In applying the requirement of this paragraph (d)(3), self-employed individuals are disregarded.

(C) Certain employees disregarded. If an employee's total compensation for the determination period, determined under paragraph (d)(3)(ii) and (d)(3)(vi)(B) of this section, is zero, the employee is disregarded in determining whether the nondiscrimination requirement of paragraph (d)(3) of this section is satisfied for that determination period. For example, an employee who does not receive any actual compensation during a determination period because the employee is on unpaid leave of absence for the entire period, but who is credited with imputed compensation described in paragraph (f)(1) of this section, is disregarded in determining whether the nondiscrimination requirement of this paragraph (d)(3) is satisfied for that determination period.

(iv) Calculation of average percentages.

(A) General rule. To determine the average percentages described in paragraph (d)(3)(i) of this section, an individual compensation percentage must be calculated for each employee in a group, and then the average of the separately calculated compensation percentages for each employee in the group must be determined. The individual compensation percentage for an employee is calculated by dividing the amount of the employee's compensation that is included under the alternative definition by the amount of the employee's total compensation.

(B) Other reasonable methods. Notwithstanding paragraph (d)(3)(iv)(A) of this section, any other reasonable method is permitted to be used to determine the average percentages described in paragraph (d)(3)(i) of this section for either or both of the groups (*i.e.*, highly compensated employees and nonhighly compensated employees), provided that the method cannot reasonably be expected to create a significant variance from the average percentage for that group determined using the individual-percentage method provided in paragraph (d)(3)(iv)(A) of this section. The same method is not required to be used for calculating the two average percentages. For example, to determine the average percentage for nonhighly compensated employees as a group, an employer may calculate an aggregate compensation percentage by dividing the aggregate amount of compensation of nonhighly compensated employees that is included under the alternative definition by the aggregate amount of total compensation of nonhighly compensated employees, provided the resulting percentage is not reasonably expected to vary significantly from the average percentage produced using the individual-percentage method provided in paragraph (d)(3)(iv)(A) of this section because of the extra weight given employees with higher compensation.

(v) Facts and circumstances determination. The determination of whether the average percentage of total compensation included for the employer's highly compensated employees as a group for a determination period exceeds by more than a de minimis amount the average percentage of total compensation included for the employer's nonhighly compensated employees as a group is based on all the relevant facts and circumstances. The differences between the percentages for prior determination periods may be considered in determining whether the amount of the difference between the percentages is more than de minimis. In addition, an isolated instance of a more than de minimis difference between the compensation percentages that is due to an extraordinary unforeseeable event (such as overtime payments to employees of a public utility due to a major hurricane) will be disregarded if the amount of the difference in prior determination periods was de minimis.

* * *

There is yet another issue with compensation, especially for partners (if the employer is a partnership), owners (if the employer is an S Corporation), and sole proprietors (if the employer is a sole proprietorship) who don't actually earn compensation reported on a W-4. Collectively, these individuals are considered self-employed. Contributions to a qualified pension plan on behalf of someone who is self-employed[3] will be considered to satisfy the reasonable compensation rules to the extent that such contributions do not exceed the earned income of such individual derived from the trade or business with respect to which such plan is established (determined without regard to any deductions available under IRC § 404 for contributions to a qualified plan) and to the extent that such contributions are not allocable to the purchase of life, accident, health, or other insurance.[4] In other words, contributions to plans sponsored by unincorporated entities on behalf of a self-employed individual may be subject to IRS attack under reasonable compensation principles if those contributions, determined without regard to the qualified plan deduction, would cause the individual or the entity with respect to which he is a self-employed individual to incur a net operating loss for the year.

One distinction that is made between a self-employed individual and a shareholder/employee of a corporation arises when determining the amount of compensation considered for purposes of calculating the annual contribution limit.[5] The compensation for a self-employed individual is his net earned income from self-employment, taking into account all applicable deductions, including the deduction for contributions to the pension plan made by his trade or business (including the qualified plan deduction).[6] Compensation for a shareholder/employee of a corporation is the compensation received from the corporation by the shareholder/employer for the year, without any reduction for amounts deducted by the corporate employer.[7]

The actual determination of earned income is complicated (and is usually determined by the individual's personal accountant or tax advisor). There are three possible answers to what is earned income, and although it should simply be the amount of money that a self-employed individual earns for services rendered to the business, the IRS provides a worksheet to actually calculate the amount. Effective for plan years after 1997, employer matching contributions will not be counted as employee elective deferral contributions for self-employed individuals for purposes of applying the annual limitation on elective deferrals under § 402(g).

For simplicity here, just understand the following basic definition found in the IRS' List of Required Modifications for pre-approved defined contribution plans: "Earned income means the net earnings from self-employment in the trade or business with respect to

---

3. within the meaning of IRC § 401(c)(1).
4. IRC § 404(a)(8)(c).
5. under IRC § 415(c).
6. IRC § 415(c)(3)(B); see also IRC § 404(a)(8).
7. IRC § 415(c)(3)(A); Treas. Regs. § 1.415(c)-2(a)-(b).

which the plan is established, for which personal services of the individual are a material income-producing factor. Net earnings will be determined without regard to items not included in gross income and the deductions allocable to such items. Net earnings are reduced by contributions by the employer to a qualified plan to the extent deductible under § 404 of the Code. Net earnings shall be determined with regard to the deduction allowed to the taxpayer by § 164(f) of the Code for taxable years beginning after December 31, 1989."[8]

6. Nondiscrimination Testing for Rights and Features

In addition to the contributions provided through a defined contribution plan or the benefits provided through a defined benefit plan, the plan's benefits, rights and features (BRFs) must be both (1) currently available and (2) effectively available to all plan participants in a manner that does not discriminate in favor of HCEs.

In regards to the current availability, the plan passes the nondiscrimination requirements for the year if the group of employees to whom a benefit, right, or feature is currently available during the plan year satisfies section 410(b) (without regard to the average benefit percentage test of § 1.410(b)-5).[9]

In regards to the effective availability, the plan passes the nondiscrimination requirements for the year if, based on all of the relevant facts and circumstances, the group of employees to whom a benefit, right, or feature is effectively available does not substantially favor HCEs..[10]

Specifically, the method of allocation of earnings, the availability of rollovers, transfers and buybacks, and the methods of vesting and crediting service must all be nondiscriminatory.[11]

There are lots of additional rules and exceptions, and examples, in the regulations, but for purposes of this textbook, if you just know they are there, then you can read through them when your particular client's plan offers BRFs to only a portion of the plan participants.

7. Nondiscrimination Testing for Plan Amendments

Each individual plan amendment (or a series of amendments), and the plan's termination, must not discriminate in favor of HCEs. Obviously, this part of the nondiscrimination testing is not required on an annual basis, but is required only in years that the plan is amended or terminated. It is a facts and circumstance test.

Treas. Regs. § 1.401(a)(4)-5. Plan Amendments and Plan Terminations

(a) Introduction.

---

8. Defined Contribution Listing of Required Modifications and Information Package (LRM), I.7, available at http://www.irs.gov/retirement/article/0,,id=97182,00.html.
9. Treas. Regs. § 1.401(a)(4)-4(b)(1).
10. Treas. Regs. § 1.401(a)(4)-4(c)(1).
11. Treas. Regs. §§ 1.401(a)(4)-1(c) and -11.

* * *

(2) Facts-and-circumstances determination. Whether the timing of a plan amendment or series of plan amendments has the effect of discriminating significantly in favor of HCEs or former HCEs is determined at the time the plan amendment first becomes effective for purposes of section 401(a), based on all of the relevant facts and circumstances. These include, for example, the relative numbers of current and former HCEs and NHCEs affected by the plan amendment, the relative length of service of current and former HCEs and NHCEs, the length of time the plan or plan provision being amended has been in effect, and the turnover of employees prior to the plan amendment. In addition, the relevant facts and circumstances include the relative accrued benefits of current and former HCEs and NHCEs before and after the plan amendment and any additional benefits provided to current and former HCEs and NHCEs under other plans (including plans of other employers, if relevant). In the case of a plan amendment that provides additional benefits based on an employee's service prior to the amendment, the relevant facts and circumstances also include the benefits that employees and former employees who do not benefit under the amendment would have received had the plan, as amended, been in effect throughout the period on which the additional benefits are based.

* * *

(4) Examples. The following examples illustrate the rules in this paragraph (a):

Example (1). Plan A is a defined benefit plan that covered both HCEs and NHCEs for most of its existence. The employer decides to wind up its business. In the process of ceasing operations, but at a time when the plan covers only HCEs, Plan A is amended to increase benefits and thereafter is terminated. The timing of this plan amendment has the effect of discriminating significantly in favor of HCEs.

* * *

8. Nondiscrimination Testing for Former Employees

One final aspect of annual nondiscrimination testing for purposes of this text book (although there are other issues not discussed here) is the separate testing for former employees. Here is your last excerpt from regulations (at least for this part of the chapter).

Treas. Regs. § 1.401(a)(4)-10. Testing of Former Employees

(a) Introduction. This section provides rules for determining whether a plan satisfies the nondiscriminatory amount and nondiscriminatory availability requirements of § 1.401(a)(4)-1(b)(2) and (3), respectively, with respect to former employees. Generally, this section is relevant only in the case of benefits provided through an amendment to the plan effective in the current plan year. See the definitions of employee and former employee in § 1.401(a)(4)-12.

(b) Nondiscrimination in amount of contributions or benefits.

(1) General rule. A plan satisfies § 1.401(a)(4)-1(b)(2) with respect to the amount of contributions or benefits provided to former employees if, under all of the relevant facts and circumstances, the amount of contributions or benefits provided to former employees does not discriminate significantly in favor of former HCEs. For this purpose, contributions or benefits provided to former employees includes all contributions or benefits provided to former employees or, at the employer's option, only those contributions or benefits arising out of the amendment providing the contributions or benefits. A plan under which no former employee currently benefits (within the meaning of § 1.410(b)-3(b)) is deemed to satisfy this paragraph (b).

* * *

(c) **Nondiscrimination in availability of benefits, rights, or features.** A plan satisfies section 401(a)(4) with respect to the availability of benefits, rights, and features provided to former employees if any change in the availability of any benefit, right, or feature to any former employee is applied in a manner that, under all of the relevant facts and circumstances, does not discriminate significantly in favor of former HCEs. For purposes of demonstrating that a plan satisfies section 401(a)(4) with respect to the availability of loans provided to former employees, an employer may treat former employees who are parties in interest within the meaning of section 3(14) of the Employee Retirement Income Security Act of 1974 as employees.

F. Nondiscrimination Requirements for All 401(k) Plans (Cash or Deferred Arrangements)

In addition to the normal nondiscrimination rules, 401(k) plans must satisfy additional tests. There is one test for elective salary deferrals and Roth contributions and a second, but similar, test for employer matching contributions. However, if the plan is drafted as a Safe Harbor then it automatically satisfies these special tests.

Unfortunately for you, this section of the textbook goes into a lot of tedious details. Unfortunately for many 401(k) plan sponsors, not much advance thought and planning is put into the establishment of a 401(k) plan, and while they usually try to choose the provider offering the lowest document drafting and annual administration fees, they generally get what they pay for. Therefore, in this era where the free-standing 401(k) plan is the predominant form of qualified retirement plan, all employee benefits professionals need to be extra knowledgeable in the world of 401(k) plan administration.

1. The Special Tests for Salary Deferrals

Statutory Requirements at IRC § 401(k)(3)

If not designed as a safe harbor 401(k) plan (as discussed later in this chapter), then the plan must pass the Actual Deferral Percentage test, which is basically a comparison of the average deferrals made by HCEs to the average made by NHCEs. The ADP test requires that the ADP for HCEs for the current year be compared to the ADP for NHCEs for the prior year, unless the plan makes an election to use the current-year data. The method used must be stated in the plan.

There are two ways to satisfy the ADP test:

1. the ADP for the HCEs, on average, must not be more than 125% of the ADP for the NHCEs, on average, or

2. the ADP for the HCEs, on average, must simultaneously not be more than 200% of the ADP and not be more than 2% greater than the ADP for the NHCEs, on average.

This is not difficult mathematics, so please don't freak out. The first test allows the ADP for HCEs to be 125% of the ADP for NHCEs. Simply multiply the ADP for NHCEs by 1.25 to get the limit for the ADP for HCEs. For the second test, there are two components, and we are only interested in the lesser component. The first-component of the second test allows the ADP of the HCEs to be 200% of the ADP for NHCEs. Simply multiply the ADP for NHCEs by 2 to get the first-component limit for the ADP for HCEs. The second-component of the second test allows the ADP of the HCEs to be 2.0 basis points greater than the ADP for NHCEs. Simply add 2.0 to the ADP for NHCEs to get the second-component limit for the ADP for HCEs. So for the second test, we are only interested in the lesser of the first-component or the second-component. Now, the final step is to determine the lesser of the limit from the first test and the limit from the second test.

The following excerpts from the regulations demonstrate how to calculate the ADPs for each group (the HCEs and the NHCEs), and how to perform the annual ADP testing.

Treas. Reg. § 1.401(k)-2. ADP Test

(a) Actual deferral percentage (ADP) test.

* * *

(2) Determination of ADP.

(i) General rule. The ADP for a group of eligible employees (either eligible HCEs or eligible NHCEs) for a plan year or applicable year is the average of the ADRs of the eligible employees in that group for that year. The ADP for a group of eligible employees is calculated to the nearest hundredth of a percentage point.

(ii) Determination of applicable year under current year and prior year testing method. The ADP test is applied using the prior year testing method or the current year testing method. Under the prior year testing method, the applicable year for determining the ADP for the eligible NHCEs is the plan year immediately preceding the plan year for which the ADP test is being performed. Under the prior year testing method, the ADP for the eligible NHCEs is determined using the ADRs for the eligible employees who were NHCEs in that preceding plan year, regardless of whether those NHCEs are eligible employees or NHCEs in the plan year for which the ADP test is being calculated. Under the current year testing method, the applicable year for determining the ADP for the eligible NHCEs is the same plan year as the plan year for which the ADP test is being performed. Under either method, the ADP for eligible HCEs is the average of the ADRs of the eligible HCEs for the plan year for which the ADP test is being performed. See paragraph (c) of this section for additional rules for the prior year testing method.

(3) Determination of ADR.

(i) General rule. The ADR of an eligible employee for a plan year or applicable year is the sum of the employee's elective contributions taken into account with respect to such employee for the year, determined under the rules of paragraphs (a)(4) and (5) of this section, and the qualified nonelective contributions and qualified matching contributions taken into account with respect to such employee under paragraph (a)(6) of this section for the year, divided by the employee's compensation taken into account for the year. The ADR is calculated to the nearest hundredth of a percentage point. If no elective contributions, qualified nonelective contributions, or qualified matching contributions are taken into account under this section with respect to an eligible employee for the year, the ADR of the employee is zero.

(ii) ADR of HCEs eligible under more than one arrangement.

(A) General rule. Pursuant to section 401(k)(3)(A), the ADR of an HCE who is an eligible employee in more than one cash or deferred arrangement of the same employer is calculated by treating all contributions with respect to such HCE under any such arrangement as being made under the cash or deferred arrangement being tested. Thus, the ADR for such an HCE is calculated by accumulating all contributions under any cash or deferred arrangement (other than a cash or deferred arrangement described in paragraph (a)(3)(ii)(B) of this section) that would be taken into account under this section for the plan year, if the cash or deferred arrangement under which the contribution was made applied this section and had the same plan year. For example, in the case of a plan with a 12-month plan year, the ADR for the plan year of that plan for an HCE who participates in multiple cash or deferred arrangements of the same employer is the sum of all contributions during such 12-month period that would be taken into account with respect to the HCE under all such arrangements in which the HCE is an eligible employee, divided by the HCE's compensation for that 12-month period (determined using the compensation definition for the plan being tested), without regard to the plan year of the other plans and whether those plans are satisfying this section or § 1.401(k)-3.

(B) Plans not permitted to be aggregated. Cash or deferred arrangements under plans that are not permitted to be aggregated under § 1.401(k)-1(b)(4) (determined without regard to the prohibition on aggregating plans with inconsistent testing methods set forth in § 1.401(k)-1(b)(4)(iii)(B) and the prohibition on aggregating plans with different plan years set forth in § 1.410(b)-7(d)(5)) are not aggregated under this paragraph (a)(3)(ii).

(iii) Examples. The following examples illustrate the application of this paragraph (a)(3):

Example (1).

(i) Employee A, an HCE with compensation of $120,000, is eligible to make elective contributions under Plan S and Plan T, two profit-sharing plans maintained by Employer H with calendar year plan years, each of which includes a cash or deferred arrangement. During the current plan year, Employee A makes elective contributions of $6,000 to Plan S and $4,000 to Plan T.

(ii) Under each plan, the ADR for Employee A is determined by dividing Employee A's total elective contributions under both arrangements by Employee A's compensation taken into account under the plan for the year. Therefore, Employee A's ADR under each plan is 8.33% ($10,000/$120,000).

Example (2).

(i) The facts are the same as in Example 1, except that Plan T defines compensation (for deferral and testing purposes) to exclude all bonuses paid to an employee. Plan S defines compensation (for deferral and testing purposes) to include bonuses paid to an employee. During the current year, Employee A's compensation included a $10,000 bonus. Therefore, Employee A's compensation under Plan T is $110,000 and Employee A's compensation under Plan S is $120,000.

(ii) Employee A's ADR under Plan T is 9.09% ($10,000/$110,000) and under Plan S, Employee A's ADR is 8.33% ($10,000/$120,000).

Example (3).

(i) Employer J sponsors two profit-sharing plans, Plan U and Plan V, each of which includes a cash or deferred arrangement. Plan U's plan year begins on July 1 and ends on June 30. Plan V has a calendar year plan year. Compensation under both plans is limited to the participant's compensation during the period of participation. Employee B is an HCE who participates in both plans. Employee B's monthly compensation and elective contributions to each plan for the 2005 and 2006 calendar years are as follows:

Calendar Year	Monthly Compensation	Monthly Elective Contribution to Plan U	Monthly Elective Contribution to Plan V
2005	$10,000	$500	$400
2006	11,500	700	550

(ii) Under Plan U, Employee B's ADR for the plan year ended June 30, 2006, is equal to Employee B's total elective contributions under Plan U and Plan V for the plan year ending June 30, 2006, divided by Employee B's compensation for that period. Therefore, Employee B's ADR under Plan U for the plan year ending June 30, 2006, is (($900 x 6) + ($1,250 x 6)) / (($10,000 x 6) + ($11,500 x 6)), or 10%.

(iii) Under Plan V, Employee B's ADR for the plan year ended December 31, 2005, is equal to total elective contributions under Plan U and V for the plan year ending December 31, 2005, divided by Employee B's compensation for that period. Therefore, Employee B's ADR under Plan V for the plan year ending December 31, 2005, is ($10,800/$120,000), or 9%.

Example (4).

(i) The facts are the same as Example 3, except that Employee B first becomes eligible to participate in Plan U on January 1, 2006.

(ii) Under Plan U, Employee B's ADR for the plan year ended June 30, 2006, is equal to Employee B's total elective contributions under Plan U and V for the plan year ending June 30, 2006, divided by Employee B's compensation for that period. Therefore, Employee B's ADR under Plan U for the plan year ending June 30, 2006, is (($400 x 6) + ($1,250 x 6)) / (($10,000 x 6) + ($11,500 x 6)), or 7.67%.

* * *

(7) Examples. The following examples illustrate the application of this paragraph (a):

Example (1).

(i) Employer X has three employees, A, B, and C. Employer X sponsors a profit-sharing plan (Plan Z) that includes a cash or deferred arrangement. Each year, Employer X determines a bonus attributable to the prior year. Under the cash or deferred arrangement, each eligible employee may elect to receive none, all or any part of the bonus in cash. X contributes the remainder to Plan Z. The portion of the bonus paid in cash, if any, is paid 2 months after the end of the plan year and thus is included in compensation for the following plan year. Employee A is an HCE, while Employees B and C are NHCEs. The plan uses the current year testing method and defines compensation to include elective contributions and bonuses paid during each plan year. In February of 2005, Employer X determined that no bonuses will be paid for 2004. In February of 2006, Employer X provided a bonus for each employee equal to 10% of regular compensation for 2005. For the 2005 plan year, A, B, and C have the following compensation and make the following elections:

Employee	Compensation	Elective Contribution
A	$100,00	$4,340
B	60,000	2,860
C	45,000	1,250

(ii) For each employee, the ratio of elective contributions to the employee's compensation for the plan year is:

Employee	Ratio of Elective Contribution to Compensation	ADR (percent)
A	$4,340 / $100,00	4.34
B	2,860 / 60,000	4.77
C	1,250 / 45,000	2.78

(iii) The ADP for the HCEs (Employee A) is 4.34%. The ADP for the NHCEs is 3.78% ((4.77% + 2.78%)/2). Because 4.34% is less than 4.73% (3.78% multiplied by 1.25), the plan satisfies the ADP test under paragraph (a)(1)(i) of this section.

Example (2).

(i) The facts are the same as in Example 1, except that elective contributions are made pursuant to a salary reduction agreement throughout the plan year, and no bonuses are paid. As provided by section 414(s)(2), Employer X includes elective contributions in compensation. During the year, B and C defer the same amount as in Example 1, but A defers $5,770. Thus, the compensation and elective contributions for A, B, and C are:

Employee	Compensation	Elective Contribution	ADR (percent)
A	$100,00	$5,770	5.77
B	60,000	2,860	4.77
C	45,000	1,250	2.78

(ii) The ADP for the HCEs (Employee A) is 5.77%. The ADP for the NHCEs is 3.78% ((4.77% + 2.78%)/2). Because 5.77% exceeds 4.73% (3.78% x 1.25), the plan does not satisfy the ADP test under paragraph (a)(1)(i) of this section. However, because the ADP for the HCEs does not exceed the ADP for the NHCEs by more than 2 percentage points and the ADP for the HCEs does not exceed the ADP for the NHCEs multiplied by 2 (3.78% x 2 = 7.56%), the plan satisfies the ADP test under paragraph (a)(1)(ii) of this section.

Example (3).

(i) Employees D through L are eligible employees in Plan T, a profit-sharing plan that contains a cash or deferred arrangement. The plan is a calendar year plan that uses the prior year testing method. Plan T provides that elective contributions are included in compensation (as provided under section 414(s)(2)). Each eligible employee may elect to defer up to 6% of compensation under the cash or deferred arrangement. Employees D and E are HCEs. The compensation, elective contributions, and ADRs of Employees D and E for the 2006 plan year are shown below:

Employee	Compensation for 2006 Plan Year	Elective Contributions for 2006 Plan Year	ADR for 2006 Plan Year (Percent)
D	$100,000	$10,000	10
E	95,000	4,750	5

(ii) During the 2005 plan year, Employees F through L were eligible NHCEs. The compensation, elective contributions and ADRs of Employees F through L for the 2005 plan year are shown in the following table:

Employee	Compensation for 2005 Plan Year	Elective Contributions for 2005 Plan Year	ADR for 2005 Plan Year (Percent)
F	$60,000	$3,600	6
G	40,000	1,600	4
H	30,000	1,200	4
I	20,000	600	3
J	20,000	600	3
K	10,000	300	3
L	5,000	150	3

(iii) The ADP for 2006 for the HCEs is 7.5%. Because Plan T is using the prior year testing method, the applicable year for determining the NHCE ADP is the prior plan year (*i.e.*, 2005). The NHCE ADP is determined using the ADRs for NHCEs eligible during the prior plan year (without regard to whether they are eligible under the plan during the plan year). The ADP for the NHCEs is 3.71% (the sum of the individual ADRs, 26%, divided by 7 employees). Because 7.5% exceeds 4.64% (3.71% x 1.25), Plan T does not satisfy the ADP test under paragraph (a)(1)(i) of this section. In addition, because the ADP for the HCEs exceeds the ADP for the NHCEs by more than 2 percentage points, Plan T does not satisfy the ADP test under paragraph (a)(1)(ii) of this section. Therefore, the cash or deferred arrangement fails to be a qualified cash or deferred arrangement unless the ADP failure is corrected under paragraph (b) of this section.

* * *

Please note that there is more to this, and I purposely left out portions of the regulations that discuss special types of contributions that employers can make to the plan to satisfy the ADP tests (or, if not used to satisfy the ADP tests, then used to satisfy the ACP tests for employer matching contributions, as described below). The employer can make Qualified Nonelective Contributions (QNECs) and Qualified Matching Contributions (QMACs). Now read the rest of the regulations, and realize that now you are reading sections 4, 5 and 6 of Reg. § 1.401(k)-2(a), and examples 4 through 9 of section 7. I am also including an excerpt from -2(c) on prior year testing methods. Believe me, I am not trying to confuse you, but am rather trying to break up the materials into what is the ADP test, generally, and how are ADPs calculated, generally, and now will add some complexities to the ADP test and the calculation of ADPs.

Treas. Regs. § 1.401(k)-2. ADP Test

(a) **Actual deferral percentage (ADP) test.**

* * *

(4) Elective contributions taken into account under the ADP test.

(i) General rule. An elective contribution is taken into account in determining the ADR for an eligible employee for a plan year or applicable year only if each of the following requirements is satisfied—

(A) The elective contribution is allocated to the eligible employee's account under the plan as of a date within that year. For purposes of this rule, an elective contribution is considered allocated as of a date within a year only if—

(1) The allocation is not contingent on the employee's participation in the plan or performance of services on any date subsequent to that date; and

(2) The elective contribution is actually paid to the trust no later than the end of the 12-month period immediately following the year to which the contribution relates.

(B) The elective contribution relates to compensation that either—

(1) Would have been received by the employee in the year but for the employee's election to defer under the arrangement; or

(2) Is attributable to services performed by the employee in the year and, but for the employee's election to defer, would have been received by the employee within 2½ months after the close of the year, but only if the plan provides for elective contributions that relate to compensation that would have been received after the close of a year to be allocated to

such prior year rather than the year in which the compensation would have been received.

(ii) Elective contributions for partners and self-employed individuals. For
purposes of this paragraph (a)(4), a partner's distributive share of partnership income is treated as received on the last day of the partnership taxable
year and a sole proprietor's compensation is treated as received on the last
day of the individual's taxable year. Thus, an elective contribution made on
behalf of a partner or sole proprietor is treated as allocated to the partner's
account for the plan year that includes the last day of the partnership taxable
year, provided the requirements of paragraph (a)(4)(i) of this section are met.

(iii) Elective contributions for HCEs. Elective contributions of an HCE
must include any excess deferrals, as described in § 1.402(g)-1(a), even if
those excess deferrals are distributed, pursuant to § 1.402(g)-1(e).

(5) Elective contributions not taken into account under the ADP test.

(i) General rule. Elective contributions that do not satisfy the requirements of paragraph (a)(4)(i) of this section may not be taken into account
in determining the ADR of an eligible employee for the plan year or applicable year with respect to which the contributions were made, or for
any other plan year. Instead, the amount of the elective contributions must
satisfy the requirements of section 401(a)(4) (without regard to the ADP
test) for the plan year for which they are allocated under the plan as if they
were nonelective contributions and were the only nonelective contributions for that year. See §§ 1.401(a)(4)-1(b)(2)(ii)(B) and 1.410(b)-7(c)(1).

(ii) Elective contributions for NHCEs. Elective contributions of an
NHCE shall not include any excess deferrals, as described in § 1.402(g)-
1(a), to the extent the excess deferrals are prohibited under section
401(a)(30). However, to the extent that the excess deferrals are not prohibited under section 401(a)(30), they are included in elective contributions
even if distributed pursuant to § 1.402(g)-1(e).

(iii) Elective contributions treated as catch-up contributions. Elective
contributions that are treated as catch-up contributions under section
414(v) because they exceed a statutory limit or employer-provided limit
(within the meaning of § 1.414(v)-1(b)(1)) are not taken into account
under paragraph (a)(4) of this section for the plan year for which the contributions were made, or for any other plan year.

(iv) Elective contributions used to satisfy the ACP test. Except to the
extent necessary to demonstrate satisfaction of the requirement of
§ 1.401(m)-2(a)(6)(ii), elective contributions taken into account for the
ACP test under § 1.401(m)-2(a)(6) are not taken into account under paragraph (a)(4) of this section.

(v) Additional elective contributions pursuant to section 414(u). Additional elective contributions made pursuant to section 414(u) by reason
of an eligible employee's qualified military service are not taken into account
under paragraph (a)(4) of this section for the plan year for which the contributions are made, or for any other plan year.

(vi) Default elective contributions pursuant to section 414(w). Default
elective contributions made under an eligible automatic contribution arrange-

ment (within the meaning of § 1.414(w)-1(b)) that are distributed pursuant to § 1.414(w)-1(c) for plan years beginning on or after January 1, 2008, are not taken into account under paragraph (a)(4) of this section for the plan year for which the contributions are made, or for any other plan year.

(6) Qualified nonelective contributions and qualified matching contributions that may be taken into account under the ADP test. Qualified nonelective contributions and qualified matching contributions may be taken into account in determining the ADR for an eligible employee for a plan year or applicable year but only to the extent the contributions satisfy the following requirements—

(i) Timing of allocation. The qualified nonelective contribution or qualified matching contribution is allocated to the employee's account as of a date within that year within the meaning of paragraph (a)(4)(i)(A) of this section. Consequently, under the prior year testing method, in order to be taken into account in calculating the ADP for the eligible NHCEs for the applicable year, a qualified nonelective contribution or qualified matching contribution must be contributed no later than the end of the 12-month period immediately following the applicable year even though the applicable year is different than the plan year being tested.

(ii) Requirement that amount satisfy section 401(a)(4). The amount of nonelective contributions, including those qualified nonelective contributions taken into account under this paragraph (a)(6) and those qualified nonelective contributions taken into account for the ACP test of section 401(m)(2) under § 1.401(m)-2(a)(6), satisfies the requirements of section 401(a)(4). See § 1.401(a)(4)-1(b)(2). The amount of nonelective contributions, excluding those qualified nonelective contributions taken into account under this paragraph (a)(6) and those qualified nonelective contributions taken into account for the ACP test of section 401(m)(2) under § 1.401(m)-2(a)(6), satisfies the requirements of section 401(a)(4). See § 1.401(a)(4)-1(b)(2). In the case of an employer that is applying the special rule for employer-wide plans in § 1.414(r)-1(c)(2)(ii) with respect to the cash or deferred arrangement, the determination of whether the qualified nonelective contributions satisfy the requirements of this paragraph (a)(6)(ii) must be made on an employer-wide basis regardless of whether the plans to which the qualified nonelective contributions are made are satisfying the requirements of section 410(b) on an employer-wide basis. Conversely, in the case of an employer that is treated as operating qualified separate lines of business, and does not apply the special rule for employer-wide plans in § 1.414(r)-1(c)(2)(ii) with respect to the cash or deferred arrangement, then the determination of whether the qualified nonelective contributions satisfy the requirements of this paragraph (a)(6)(ii) is not permitted to be made on an employer-wide basis regardless of whether the plans to which the qualified nonelective contributions are made are satisfying the requirements of section 410(b) on that basis.

(iii) Aggregation must be permitted. The plan that contains the cash or deferred arrangement and the plan or plans to which the qualified nonelective contributions or qualified matching contributions are made, are plans that would be permitted to be aggregated under § 1.401(k)-1(b)(4). If the plan year of the plan that contains the cash or deferred arrangement is changed to satisfy the requirement under § 1.410(b)-

7(d)(5) that aggregated plans have the same plan year, qualified non-elective contributions and qualified matching contributions may be taken into account in the resulting short plan year only if such qualified non-elective contributions and qualified matching contributions could have been taken into account under an ADP test for a plan with the same short plan year.

(iv) Disproportionate contributions not taken into account.

(A) General rule. Qualified nonelective contributions cannot be taken into account for a plan year for an NHCE to the extent such contributions exceed the product of that NHCE's compensation and the greater of 5% or two times the plan's representative contribution rate. Any qualified nonelective contribution taken into account under an ACP test under § 1.401(m)-2(a)(6) (including the determination of the representative contribution rate for purposes of § 1.401(m)-2(a)(6)(v)(B)), is not permitted to be taken into account for purposes of this paragraph (a)(6) (including the determination of the representative contribution rate under paragraph (a)(6)(iv)(B) of this section).

(B) Definition of representative contribution rate. For purposes of this paragraph (a)(6)(iv), the plan's representative contribution rate is the lowest applicable contribution rate of any eligible NHCE among a group of eligible NHCEs that consists of half of all eligible NHCEs for the plan year (or, if greater, the lowest applicable contribution rate of any eligible NHCE in the group of all eligible NHCEs for the plan year and who is employed by the employer on the last day of the plan year).

(C) Definition of applicable contribution rate. For purposes of this paragraph (a)(6)(iv), the applicable contribution rate for an eligible NHCE is the sum of the qualified matching contributions taken into account under this paragraph (a)(6) for the eligible NHCE for the plan year and the qualified nonelective contributions made for the eligible NHCE for the plan year, divided by the eligible NHCE's compensation for the same period.

(D) Special rule for prevailing wage contributions. Notwithstanding paragraph (a)(6)(iv)(A) of this section, qualified nonelective contributions that are made in connection with an employer's obligation to pay prevailing wages under the Davis-Bacon Act (46 Stat. 1494), Public Law 71-798, Service Contract Act of 1965 (79 Stat. 1965), Public Law 89-286, or similar legislation can be taken into account for a plan year for an NHCE to the extent such contributions do not exceed 10 percent of that NHCE's compensation.

(v) Qualified matching contributions. Qualified matching contributions satisfy this paragraph (a)(6) only to the extent that such qualified matching contributions are matching contributions that are not precluded from being taken into account under the ACP test for the plan year under the rules of § 1.401(m)-2(a)(5)(ii).

(vi) Contributions only used once. Qualified nonelective contributions and qualified matching contributions cannot be taken into account under this paragraph (a)(6) to the extent such contributions are taken into account for purposes of satisfying any other ADP test, any ACP test, or the requirements of § 1.401(k)-3, 1.401(m)-3 or 1.401(k)-4. Thus, for example, matching contributions that are made pursuant to § 1.401(k)-3(c) cannot be taken into account under the ADP test. Similarly, if a plan switches from the current year testing method to the prior year testing method pursuant to § 1.401(k)-2(c), qualified nonelective contributions that are taken into account under the current year testing method for a year may not be taken into account under the prior year testing method for the next year.

* * *

(7) Examples. The following examples illustrate the application of this paragraph (a):

* * *

Example (4).

(i) Plan U is a calendar year profit-sharing plan that contains a cash or deferred arrangement and uses the current year testing method. Plan U provides that elective contributions are included in compensation (as provided under section 414(s)(2)). The following amounts are contributed under Plan U for the 2006 plan year: QNECs equal to 2% of each employee's compensation; Contributions equal to 6% of each employee's compensation that are not immediately vested under the terms of the plan; 3% of each employee's compensation that the employee may elect to receive as cash or to defer under the plan. Both types of nonelective contributions are made for the HCEs (employees M and N) and the NHCEs (employees O through S) for the plan year and are contributed after the end of the plan year and before the end of the following plan year. In addition, neither type of nonelective contributions is used for any other ADP or ACP test.

(ii) For the 2006 plan year, the compensation, elective contributions, and actual deferral ratios of employees M through S are shown in the following table:

Employee	Compensation	Elective contributions	Actual deferral ratio (percent)
M	$100,000	$3,000	3
N	100,000	2,000	2
O	60,000	1,800	3
P	40,000	0	0
Q	30,000	0	0
R	5,000	0	0
S	20,000	0	0

(iii) The elective contributions alone do not satisfy the ADP test of section 401(k)(3) and paragraph (a)(1) of this section because the ADP for the HCEs, consisting of employees M and N, is 2.5% and the ADP for the NHCEs is 0.6%.

(iv) The 2% QNECs satisfies the timing requirement of paragraph (a)(6)(i) of this section because it is paid within 12-month after the plan year for which allocated. All nonelective contributions also satisfy the requirements relating to section 401(a)(4) set forth in paragraph (a)(6)(ii) of this section (because all employees receive an 8% nonelective contribution and the nonelective contributions excluding the QNECs is 6% for all employees). In addition, the QNECs are not disproportionate under paragraph (a)(6)(iv) of this section because no QNEC for an NHCE exceeds the product of the plan's applicable contribution rate (2%) and that NHCE's compensation.

(v) Because the rules of paragraph (a)(6) of this section are satisfied, the 2% QNECs may be taken into account in applying the ADP test of section 401(k)(3) and paragraph (a)(1) of this section. The 6% nonelective contributions, however, may not be taken into account because they are not QNECs.

(vi) If the 2% QNECs are taken into account, the ADP for the HCEs is 4.5%, and the actual deferral percentage for the NHCEs is 2.6%. Because 4.5% is not more than two percentage points greater than 2.6 percent, and not more than two times 2.6, the cash or deferred arrangement satisfies the ADP test of section 401(k)(3) under paragraph (a)(1)(ii) of this section.

Example (5).

(i) The facts are the same as Example 4, except the plan uses the prior year testing method. In addition, the NHCE ADP for the 2005 plan year (the prior plan year) is 0.8% and no QNECs are contributed for the 2005 plan year during 2005 or 2006.

(ii) In 2007, it is determined that the elective contributions alone do not satisfy the ADP test of section 401(k)(3) and paragraph (a)(1) of this section for 2006 because the 2006 ADP for the eligible HCEs, consisting of employees M and N, is 2.5% and the 2005 ADP for the eligible NHCEs is 0.8%. An additional QNEC of 2% of compensation is made for each eligible NHCE in 2007 and allocated for 2005.

(iii) The 2% QNECs that are made in 2007 and allocated for the 2005 plan year do not satisfy the timing requirement of paragraph (a)(6)(i) of this section for the applicable year for the 2005 plan year because they were not contributed before the last day of the 2006 plan year. Accordingly, the 2% QNECs do not satisfy the rules of paragraph (a)(6) of this section and may not be taken into account in applying the ADP test of section 401(k)(3) and paragraph (a)(1) of this section for the 2006 plan year. The cash or deferred arrangement fails to be a qualified cash or deferred arrangement unless the ADP failure is corrected under paragraph (b) of this section.

Example (6).

(i) The facts are the same as Example 4, except that the ADP for the HCEs is 4.6% and there is no 6% nonelective contribution under the plan. The employer would like to take into account the 2% QNEC in determining the ADP for the NHCEs but not in determining the ADP for the HCEs.

(ii) The elective contributions alone fail the requirements of section 401(k) and paragraph (a)(1) of this section because the HCE ADP for the plan year (4.6%) exceeds 0.75% (0.6% x 1.25) and 1.2% (0.6% x 2).

(iii) The 2% QNECs may not be taken into account in determining the ADP of the NHCEs because they fail to satisfy the requirements relating to section 401(a)(4) set forth in paragraph (a)(6)(ii) of this section. This is because the amount of nonelective contributions, excluding those QNECs that would be taken into account under the ADP test, would be 2% of compensation for the HCEs and 0% for the NHCEs. Therefore, the cash or deferred arrangement fails to be a qualified cash or deferred arrangement unless the ADP failure is corrected under paragraph (b) of this section.

Example (7).

(i) The facts are the same as Example 6, except that Employee R receives a QNEC in an amount of $500 and no QNECs are made on behalf of the other employees.

(ii) If the QNEC could be taken into account under paragraph (a)(6) of this section, the ADP for the NHCEs would be 2.6% and the plan would satisfy the ADP test. The QNEC is disproportionate under paragraph (a)(6)(iv) of this section, and cannot be taken into account under paragraph (a)(6) of this section, to the extent it exceeds the greater of 5% and two times the plan's representative contribution rate (0%), multiplied by Employee R's compensation. The plan's representative contribution rate is 0% because it is the lowest applicable contribution rate among a group of NHCEs that is at least half of all NHCEs, or all the NHCEs who are employed on the last day of the plan year. Therefore, the QNEC may be taken into account under the ADP test only to the extent it does not exceed 5% times Employee R's compensation (or $250) and the cash or deferred arrangement fails to satisfy the ADP test and must correct under paragraph (b) of this section.

Example (8).

(i) The facts are the same as in Example 4 except that the plan changes from the current year testing method to the prior year testing method for the following plan year (2007 plan year). The ADP for the HCEs for the 2007 plan year is 3.5%.

(ii) The 2% QNECs may not be taken into account in determining the ADP for the NHCEs for the applicable year (2006 plan year) in satisfying the ADP test for the 2007 plan year because they were taken into account in satisfying the ADP test for the 2006 plan year. Accordingly, the NHCE ADP for the applicable year is 0.6%. The elective contributions for the plan year fail the requirements of section 401(k) and paragraph (a)(1) of this section because the HCE ADP for the plan year (3.5%) exceeds the ADP limit of 1.2% (the greater of 0.75% (0.6% x 1.25) and 1.2% (0.6% x 2)), determined using the applicable year ADP for the NHCEs. Therefore, the cash or deferred arrangement fails to be a qualified cash or deferred arrangement unless the ADP failure is corrected under paragraph (b) of this section.

Example (9).

(i)

(A) Employer N maintains Plan X, a profit sharing plan that contains a cash or deferred arrangement and that uses the current year testing method. Plan X provides for employee contributions, elective contributions, and matching contributions. Matching contributions on behalf of NHCEs are qualified matching contributions (QMACs) and are contributed during the 2005 plan year. Matching contributions on behalf of HCEs are not QMACs, because they fail to satisfy the nonforfeitability requirement of § 1.401(k)-1(c). The elective contributions and matching contributions with respect to HCEs for the 2005 plan year are shown in the following table:

	Elective Contributions	Total Matching Contributions	Matching Contributions That Are Not QMACs	QMACs
Highly Compensated Employees	15%	5%	5%	0%

(B) The elective contributions and matching contributions with respect to the NHCEs for the 2005 plan year are shown in the following table:

	Elective Contributions	Total Matching Contributions	Matching Contributions That Are Not QMACs	QMACs
Nonhighly Compensated Employees	11%	4%	0%	4%

(ii) The plan fails to satisfy the ADP test of section 401(k)(3)(A) and paragraph (a)(1) of this section because the ADP for HCEs (15%) is more than 125% of the ADP for NHCEs (11%), and more than 2 percentage points greater than 11%. However, the plan provides that QMACs may be used to meet the requirements of section 401(k)(3)(A)(ii) provided that they are not used for any other ADP or ACP test. QMACs equal to 1% of compensation are taken into account for each NHCE in applying the ADP test. After this adjustment, the applicable ADP and ACP (taking into account the provisions of § 1.401(m)-2(a)(5)(ii)) for the plan year are as follows:

	Actual Deferral Percentage	Actual Contribution Percentage
HCEs	15	5
Nonhighly compensated employees	12	3

(iii) The elective contributions and QMACs taken into account for purposes of the ADP test of section 401(k)(3) satisfy the requirements of section 401(k)(3)(A)(ii) under paragraph (a)(1)(ii) of this section because the ADP for HCEs (15%) is not more than the ADP for NHCEs multiplied by 1.25 (12% x 1.25 = 15%).

* * *

(c) **Additional rules for prior year testing method.**

(1) Rules for change in testing method.

(i) General rule. A plan is permitted to change from the prior year testing method to the current year testing method for any plan year. A plan is permitted to change from the current year testing method to the prior year testing method only in situations described in paragraph (c)(1)(ii) of this section. For purposes of this paragraph (c)(1), a plan that uses the safe harbor method described in § 1.401(k)-3 or a SIMPLE 401(k) plan is treated as using the current year testing method for that plan year.

* * *

(2) Calculation of ADP under the prior year testing method for the first plan year.

(i) Plans that are not successor plans. If, for the first plan year of any plan (other than a successor plan), the plan uses the prior year testing method, the plan is permitted to use either that first plan year as the applicable year for determining the ADP for eligible NHCEs, or use 3% as the ADP for eligible NHCEs, for applying the ADP test for that first plan year. A plan (other than a successor plan) that uses the prior year testing method but has elected for its first plan year to use that year as the applicable year is not treated as changing its testing method in the second plan year and is not subject to the limitations on double counting on QNECs under paragraph (a)(6)(vi) of this section for the second plan year.

(ii) First plan year defined. For purposes of this paragraph (c)(2), the first plan year of any plan is the first year in which the plan provides for elective contributions. Thus, the rules of this paragraph (c)(2) do not apply to a plan (within the meaning of § 1.410(b)-7(b)) for a plan year if for such plan year the plan is aggregated under § 1.401(k)-1(b)(4) with any other plan that provided for elective contributions in the prior year.

(iii) Successor plans. A plan is a successor plan if 50% or more of the eligible employees for the first plan year were eligible employees under a qualified cash or deferred arrangement maintained by the employer in the prior year. If a plan that is a successor plan uses the prior year testing method for its first plan year, the ADP for the group of NHCEs for the applicable year must be determined under paragraph (c)(4) of this section.

* * *

Okay, I know this is a lot of information to absorb at one time, especially if you have no experience with the operation of 401(k) plans. Think about how small business owners feel when they set up a 401(k) plan to provide retirement benefits to employees, only to be bogged down with the annual administrative requirements. This isn't so complicated, however, so let's just recap what we have learned at this point:

- An ADR is calculated for every eligible employee, where the total of all elective salary deferrals are divided by his or her salary for the year (and yes, someone who chooses not to make any deferrals has an ADR of 0% for the year);

- The plan document indicates whether ADRs for NHCEs only are based on current year data or prior year data;

- The ADP for all NHCEs is determined by averaging all NHCE ADRs for the year (to make life simpler for the plan sponsor, prior year data can be used if the plan sponsor makes the appropriate election in the plan document);

- Similarly, the ADP for all HCEs is determined by averaging all HCE ADRs for the year (note that for the HCE's ADP, current year actual data must be used, and the plan sponsor cannot use prior year data for HCEs);

- The average ADP for all HCEs must either (1) be no more than 125% of the ADP for all NHCEs, or if lower, (2) be no more than 200% of and no more than 2.0 percentage points above the ADP for all NHCEs; and

- If the employer has already made QNECs or QMACs, then those might be taken into account in determining the ADPs (with complicated rules governing how and when they can be counted).

2. The Special Tests for Employer Matching Contributions

Statutory Requirements at IRC § 401(m)(2)

While employer matching contributions are tested separately than elective deferrals, the ACP test under IRC § 401(m) is very similar to the ADP test under IRC § 401(k). If not designed as a safe harbor 401(k) plan, and if there are employer matching contributions, then the plan must also pass the Actual Contribution Percentage test, which is basically a comparison of the average matching contributions credited to the HCEs to the average credited to the NHCEs. The ACP test requires that the ACP for HCEs for the current year be compared to the ACP for NHCEs for the prior year, unless the plan makes an election to use the current-year data. The method used must be stated in the plan.

There are two ways to satisfy the ACP test:

1. the ACP for the HCEs, on average, must not be more than 125% of the ACP for the NHCEs, on average, or

2. the ACP for the HCEs, on average, must simultaneously not be more than 200% of the ACP and not be more than 2% greater than the ACP for the NHCEs, on average.

If the plan fails the ACP test, then either the employer makes appropriate additional contributions or excess aggregate contributions are distributed or forfeited. The plan document must provide for the exact method. While there are subtle differences in the ADP test than the ACP test, and certain employer contributions taken into account for the ADP test are not counted for purposes of passing the ACP test, for purposes of this textbook, those subtleties (which are explained in further detail in the regulations under IRC § 401(m)) are not reproduced here.

3. 401(k) Safe Harbor Plans

Statutory Requirements at IRC § 401(k)(12)

A § 401(k) safe harbor plan is one where in addition to proper notice to employees, the employer chooses to either:

- provide a nonelective contribution of at least 3% of compensation for all NHCEs, or

- provide a matching contribution of 100% of the first 3% of compensation any NHCE deferred plus 50% of the next 2% deferred (or an enhanced matching formula).

By its plan design, a § 401(k) safe harbor plan is automatically treated as satisfying the actual deferral percentage (ADP), the actual contribution percentage (ACP) nondiscrimination requirements and the Top-Heavy rules (as described below). These employer contributions, whether matching or non elective profit-sharing, must be immediately and fully vested and subject to the same in-service hardship distribution rules that limit distributions of employee elective deferrals (as discussed in Chapter 9).

Treas. Regs. § 1.401(k)-3. Safe Harbor Requirements

(a) ADP test safe harbor.

(1) Section 401(k)(12) safe harbor. A cash or deferred arrangement satisfies the ADP safe harbor provision of section 401(k)(12) for a plan year if the arrangement satisfies the safe harbor contribution requirement of paragraph (b) or (c) of this section for the plan year, the notice requirement of paragraph (d) of this section, the plan year requirements of paragraph (e) of this section, and the additional rules of paragraphs (f), (g), and (h) of this section, as applicable.

(2) Section 401(k)(13) safe harbor. For plan years beginning on or after January 1, 2008, a cash or deferred arrangement satisfies the ADP safe harbor provision of section 401(k)(13) for a plan year if the arrangement is described in paragraph (j) of this section and satisfies the safe harbor contribution requirement of paragraph (k) of this section for the plan year, the notice requirement of paragraph (d) of this section (modified to include the information set forth in paragraph (k)(4) of this section), the plan year requirements of paragraph (e) of this section, and the additional rules of paragraphs (f), (g), and (h) of this section, as applicable. A cash or deferred arrangement that satisfies the requirements of this paragraph (a)(2) is referred to as a qualified automatic contribution arrangement.

(3) Requirements applicable to safe harbor contributions. Pursuant to section 401(k)(12)(E)(ii) and section 401(k)(13)(D)(iv), the safe harbor contribution requirement of paragraph (b), (c), or (k) of this section must be satisfied without regard to section 401(l). The contributions made under paragraph (b) or (c) of this section (and the corresponding contributions under paragraph (k) of this section) are referred to as safe harbor nonelective contributions and safe harbor matching contributions.

(b) Safe harbor nonelective contribution requirement.

(1) General rule. The safe harbor nonelective contribution requirement of this paragraph is satisfied if, under the terms of the plan, the employer is required to make a qualified nonelective contribution on behalf of each eligible NHCE equal to at least 3% of the employee's safe harbor compensation.

(2) Safe harbor compensation defined. For purposes of this section, safe harbor compensation means compensation as defined in § 1.401(k)-6 (which incorporates the definition of compensation in § 1.414(s)-1); provided, however, that the rule in the last sentence of § 1.414(s)-1(d)(2)(iii) (which generally permits a definition of compensation to exclude all compensation in excess of a specified dollar amount) does not apply in determining the safe harbor compensation

of NHCEs. Thus, for example, the plan may limit the period used to determine safe harbor compensation to the eligible employee's period of participation.

(c) Safe harbor matching contribution requirement.

(1) In general. The safe harbor matching contribution requirement of this paragraph (c) is satisfied if, under the plan, qualified matching contributions are made on behalf of each eligible NHCE in an amount determined under the basic matching formula of section 401(k)(12)(B)(i)(I), as described in paragraph (c)(2) of this section, or under an enhanced matching formula of section 401(k)(12)(B)(i)(II), as described in paragraph (c)(3) of this section.

(2) Basic matching formula. Under the basic matching formula, each eligible NHCE receives qualified matching contributions in an amount equal to the sum of—

(i) 100% of the amount of the employee's elective contributions that do not exceed 3% of the employee's safe harbor compensation; and

(ii) 50% of the amount of the employee's elective contributions that exceed 3% of the employee's safe harbor compensation but that do not exceed 5% of the employee's safe harbor compensation.

(3) Enhanced matching formula. Under an enhanced matching formula, each eligible NHCE receives a matching contribution under a formula that, at any rate of elective contributions by the employee, provides an aggregate amount of qualified matching contributions at least equal to the aggregate amount of qualified matching contributions that would have been provided under the basic matching formula of paragraph (c)(2) of this section. In addition, under an enhanced matching formula, the ratio of matching contributions on behalf of an employee under the plan for a plan year to the employee's elective contributions may not increase as the amount of an employee's elective contributions increases.

(4) Limitation on HCE matching contributions. The safe harbor matching contribution requirement of this paragraph (c) is not satisfied if the ratio of matching contributions made on account of an HCE's elective contributions under the cash or deferred arrangement for a plan year to those elective contributions is greater than the ratio of matching contributions to elective contributions that would apply with respect to any eligible NHCE with elective contributions at the same percentage of safe harbor compensation.

* * *

(7) Examples. The following examples illustrate the safe harbor contribution requirement of this paragraph (c):

Example (1).

(i) Beginning January 1, 2006, Employer A maintains Plan L covering employees in Divisions D and E, each of which includes HCEs and NHCEs. Plan L contains a cash or deferred arrangement and provides qualified matching contributions equal to 100% of each eligible employee's elective contributions up to 3% of compensation and 50% of the next 2% of compensation. For purposes of the matching contribution formula, safe harbor compensation is defined as all compensation within the meaning of section 415(c)(3) (a definition that satisfies section 414(s)). Also, each employee is permitted to make elective contributions from all safe harbor compensation within the meaning of section 415(c)(3) and may change a cash or deferred election at any time. Plan L limits the amount of an employee's elective contributions for purposes of section 402(g) and section 415, and, in the case of a hardship distribution, suspends an employee's ability to make elective contributions for 6 months in accordance with § 1.401(k)-1(d)(3)(iv)(E). All contributions under Plan L are nonforfeitable and are subject to the withdrawal restrictions of section 401(k)(2)(B). Plan L provides for no other contributions and Employer A maintains no other plans. Plan L is maintained on a calendar-year basis, and all contributions for a plan year are made within 12 months after the end of the plan year.

(ii) Based on these facts, matching contributions under Plan L are safe harbor matching contributions because they are qualified matching contributions equal to the basic matching formula. Accordingly, Plan L satisfies the safe harbor contribution requirement of this paragraph (c).

Example (2).

(i) The facts are the same as in Example 1, except that instead of providing a basic matching contribution, Plan L provides a qualified matching contribution equal to 100% of each eligible employee's elective contributions up to 4% of safe harbor compensation.

(ii) Plan L's formula is an enhanced matching formula because each eligible NHCE receives safe harbor matching contributions at a rate that, at any rate of elective contributions, provides an aggregate amount of qualified matching contributions at least equal to the aggregate amount of qualified matching contributions that would have been received under the basic safe harbor matching formula, and the rate of matching contributions does not increase as the rate of an employee's elective contributions increases. Accordingly, Plan L satisfies the safe harbor contribution requirement of this paragraph (c).

Example (3).

(i) The facts are the same as in Example 2, except that instead of permitting each employee to make elective contributions from all compensation within the meaning of section 415(c)(3), each employee's elective contributions under Plan L are limited to 15% of the employee's basic compensation. Basic compensation is defined under Plan L as compensation within the meaning of section 415(c)(3), but excluding overtime pay.

(ii) The definition of basic compensation under Plan L is a reasonable definition of compensation within the meaning of § 1.414(s)-1(d)(2).

(iii) Plan L will not fail to satisfy the safe harbor contribution requirement of this paragraph (c) merely because Plan L limits the amount of elective contributions and the types of compensation that may be deferred by eligible employees, provided that each eligible NHCE may make elective contributions equal to at least 4% of the employee's safe harbor compensation.

Example (4).

(i) The facts are the same as in Example 1, except that Plan L provides that only employees employed on the last day of the plan year will receive a safe harbor matching contribution.

(ii) Even if the plan that provides for employee contributions and matching contributions satisfies the minimum coverage requirements of section 410(b)(1) taking into account this last-day requirement, Plan L would not satisfy the safe harbor contribution requirement of this paragraph (c) because safe harbor matching contributions are not made on behalf of all eligible NHCEs who make elective contributions.

(iii) The result would be the same if, instead of providing safe harbor matching contributions, Plan L provides for a 3% safe harbor nonelective contribution that is restricted to eligible employees under the cash or deferred arrangement who are employed on the last day of the plan year.

Example (5).

(i) The facts are the same as in Example 1, except that instead of providing qualified matching contributions under the basic matching formula to employees in both Divisions D and E, employees in Division E are provided qualified matching contributions under the basic matching formula, while safe harbor matching contributions continue to be provided to employees in Division D under the enhanced matching formula described in Example 2.

(ii) Even if Plan L satisfies § 1.401(a)(4)-4 with respect to each rate of matching contributions available to employees under the plan, the plan would fail to satisfy the safe harbor contribution requirement of this paragraph (c) because the rate of matching contributions with respect to HCEs in Division D at a rate of elective contributions between 3% and 5% would be greater than that with respect to NHCEs in Division E at the same rate of elective contributions. For example, an HCE in Division D who would have a 4% rate of elective contributions would have a rate of matching contributions of 100% while an NHCE in Division E who would have the same rate of elective contributions would have a lower rate of matching contributions.

(d) Notice requirement.

(1) General rule. The notice requirement of this paragraph (d) is satisfied for a plan year if each eligible employee is given notice of the employee's rights and obligations under the plan and the notice satisfies the content requirement of paragraph (d)(2) of this section and the timing requirement of paragraph (d)(3) of this section. The notice must be in writing or in such other form as may be approved by the Commissioner. See § 1.401(a)-21 of this chapter for rules permitting the use of electronic media to provide applicable notices to recipients with respect to retirement plans.

(2) Content requirement.

(i) General rule. The content requirement of this paragraph (d)(2) is satisfied if the notice is—

(A) Sufficiently accurate and comprehensive to inform the employee of the employee's rights and obligations under the plan; and

(B) Written in a manner calculated to be understood by the average employee eligible to participate in the plan.

(ii) Minimum content requirement. Subject to the requirements of paragraph (d)(2)(iii) of this section, a notice is not considered sufficiently accurate and comprehensive unless the notice accurately describes—

(A) The safe harbor matching contribution or safe harbor nonelective contribution formula used under the plan (including a description of the levels of safe harbor matching contributions, if any, available under the plan);

(B) Any other contributions under the plan or matching contributions to another plan on account of elective contributions or employee contributions under the plan (including the potential for discretionary matching contributions) and the conditions under which such contributions are made;

(C) The plan to which safe harbor contributions will be made (if different than the plan containing the cash or deferred arrangement);

(D) The type and amount of compensation that may be deferred under the plan;

(E) How to make cash or deferred elections, including any administrative requirements that apply to such elections;

(F) The periods available under the plan for making cash or deferred elections;

(G) Withdrawal and vesting provisions applicable to contributions under the plan; and

(H) Information that makes it easy to obtain additional information about the plan (including an additional copy of the summary plan description) such as telephone numbers, addresses and, if applicable, electronic addresses, of individuals or offices from whom employees can obtain such plan information.

(iii) References to SPD. A plan will not fail to satisfy the content requirements of this paragraph (d)(2) merely because, in the case of information described in paragraph (d)(2)(ii)(B) of this section (relating to any other contributions under the plan), paragraph (d)(2)(ii)(C) of this section (relating to the plan to which safe harbor contributions will be made) or paragraph (d)(2)(ii)(D) of this section (relating to the type and amount of compensation that may be deferred under the plan), the notice cross-references the relevant portions of a summary plan description that provides the same information that would be provided in accordance with such paragraphs and that has been provided (or is concurrently provided) to employees.

(3) Timing requirement.

(i) General rule. The timing requirement of this paragraph (d)(3) is satisfied if the notice is provided within a reasonable period before the beginning of the plan year (or, in the year an employee becomes eligible, within a reasonable period before the employee becomes eligible). The determination of whether a notice satisfies the timing requirement of this paragraph (d)(3) is based on all of the relevant facts and circumstances.

(ii) Deemed satisfaction of timing requirement. The timing requirement of this paragraph (d)(3) is deemed to be satisfied if at least 30 days (and no more than 90 days) before the beginning of each plan year, the notice is given to each eligible employee for the plan year. In the case of an employee who does not receive the notice within the period described in the previous sentence because the employee becomes eligible after the 90th day before the beginning of the plan year, the timing requirement is deemed to be satisfied if the notice is provided no more than 90 days before the employee becomes eligible (and no later than the date the employee becomes eligible). Thus, for example, the preceding sentence would apply in the case of any employee eligible for the first plan year under a newly established plan that provides for elective contributions, or would apply in the case of the first plan year in which an employee becomes eligible under an existing plan that provides for elective contributions. If it is not practicable for the notice to be provided on or before the date specified in the plan that an employee becomes eligible, the notice will nonetheless be treated as provided timely if it is provided as soon as practicable after that date and the employee is permitted to elect to defer from all types of compensation that may be deferred under the plan earned beginning on the date the employee becomes eligible.

(e) **Plan year requirement.**

(1) General rule. Except as provided in this paragraph (e) or in paragraph (f) of this section, a plan will fail to satisfy the requirements of sections 401(k)(12), 401(k)(13), and this section unless plan provisions that satisfy the rules of this section are adopted before the first day of the plan year and remain in effect for an entire 12-month plan year. In addition, except as provided in paragraph (g) of this section, a plan which includes provisions that satisfy the rules of this section will not satisfy the requirements of § 1.401(k)-1(b) if it is amended to change such provisions for that plan year. Moreover, if, as described under paragraph (h)(4) of this section, safe harbor matching or nonelective contributions will be made to another plan for a plan year, provisions under that other plan specifying that the safe harbor contributions will be made and providing that the contributions will be QNECs or QMACs must also be adopted before the first day of that plan year.

* * *

There are two points with the notice requirement that are crucially important. First is the requirement of a timely and sufficient notice to plan participants regarding the mandatory employer contribution (either a QNEC or a match). Therefore, even though the plan document must be drafted to demand the appropriate employer contributions, and even though at the end of the year it is determined that the plan was operated and administered in complete compliance with the statutory mandates as reflected in the plan document, unless there is a proper notice communicated to the eligible employees, the plan will not be deemed a safe harbor and must be tested for ADP, ACP and Top-Heaviness. I have omitted the sections of the regulations that describe how the plan document must be drafted and how the employer can amend the plan during the year to get out of the safe-harbor mandatory contributions (please note that if you are advising an employer that is experiencing liquidity difficulties and wants to get out of a mandatory contribution that the second they eliminate the mandatory aspect of their contribution, the fees and expenses to calculate the ACP, ADP and Top-Heaviness of the plan, and any potential fees, expenses and additional contributions that might be needed if for some reason the plan fails the testing requirements might outweigh the potential savings).

Second, please quickly reread section (d)(2)(i) and pay special attention to the phrase "[w]ritten in a manner calculated to be understood by the average employee eligible to participate in the plan." We will revisit this in Chapter 15 on other disclosures that must be communicated to plan participants, including the Summary Plan Description (SPD) as referenced in the regulations. Take a moment to think about how you, as an employee benefits professional, would draft a notice to include all of the required information, yet in what can be considered to be in plain English. Would you use the same notice for all of your clients? If say the Department of Treasury issued a model notice, would you stake your professional reputation and certifications on altering it because, in your professional opinion, it would not meet that additional requirement of being written in a manner calculated to be understood by the average participant of your particular client's 401(k) plan? I have included an article in Chapter 15 (that I authored) that explores this paradox in more detail. However, especially if you are the plan's attorney, if push comes to shove, you will need to convince the challenging party (a disgruntled participant claiming in federal court that he or she would have made other decisions had the notice been better drafted, or the Department of Treasury questioning the words included in the notice upon audit of the plan) that you took the readability requirement seriously.

4. Correction If the 401(k) Plan Fails the ADP Test

Now, let's move on. If the plan fails the ADP test, then the employer either:

- makes appropriate qualified nonelective contributions;
- distributes excess contributions appropriately; or
- recharacterizes excess contributions.

The plan document must provide for the exact method of correction. Now back to the regulations, again, taken a bit out of chronological order to make sense in this chapter.

Treas. Regs. § 1.401(k)-2. ADP Test

* * *

(b) Correction of excess contributions.

(1) Permissible correction methods.

(i) In general. A cash or deferred arrangement does not fail to satisfy the requirements of section 401(k)(3) and paragraph (a)(1) of this section if the employer, in accordance with the terms of the plan that includes the cash or deferred arrangement, uses any of the following correction methods—

(A) Qualified nonelective contributions or qualified matching contributions. The employer makes qualified nonelective contributions or qualified matching contributions that are taken into account under this section and, in combination with other amounts taken into account under paragraph (a) of this section, allow the cash or deferred arrangement to satisfy the requirements of paragraph (a)(1) of this section.

(B) Excess contributions distributed. Excess contributions are distributed in accordance with paragraph (b)(2) of this section.

(C) Excess contributions recharacterized. Excess contributions are recharacterized in accordance with paragraph (b)(3) of this section.

(ii) Combination of correction methods. A plan may provide for the use of any of the correction methods described in paragraph (b)(1)(i) of this section, may limit elective contributions in a manner designed to prevent excess contributions from being made, or may use a combination of these methods, to avoid or correct excess contributions. Similarly, a plan may permit an HCE with elective contributions for a year that includes both pre-tax elective contributions and designated Roth contributions to elect whether the excess contributions are to be attributed to pre-tax elective contributions or designated Roth contributions. A plan may permit an HCE to elect whether any excess contributions are to be recharacterized or distributed. If the plan uses a combination of correction methods, any contribution made under paragraph (b)(1)(i)(A) of this section must be taken into account before application of the correction methods in paragraph (b)(1)(i)(B) or (C) of this section.

(iii) Exclusive means of correction. A failure to satisfy the requirements of paragraph (a)(1) of this section may not be corrected using any method other than the ones described in paragraphs (b)(1)(i) and (ii) of this section. Thus, excess contributions for a plan year may not remain unallocated or be allocated to a suspense account for allocation to one or more employees in any future year. In addition, excess contributions may not be corrected using the retroactive correction rules of § 1.401(a)(4)-11(g). See § 1.401(a)(4)-11(g)(3)(vii) and (5).

(2) Corrections through distribution.

(i) General rule. This paragraph (b)(2) contains the rules for correction of excess contributions through a distribution from the plan. Correction through a distribution generally involves a 4-step process. First, the plan must determine, in accordance with paragraph (b)(2)(ii) of this section, the total amount of excess contributions that must be distributed under the plan. Second, the plan must apportion the total amount of excess contributions among HCEs in accordance with paragraph (b)(2)(iii) of this section. Third, the plan must determine the income allocable to excess contributions in accordance with paragraph (b)(2)(iv) of this section. Finally, the plan must distribute the apportioned excess contributions and allocable income in accordance with paragraph (b)(2)(v) of this section. Paragraph (b)(2)(vi) of this section provides rules relating to the tax treatment of these distributions. Paragraph (b)(2)(vii) provides other rules relating to these distributions.

(ii) Calculation of total amount to be distributed. The following procedures must be used to determine the total amount of the excess contributions to be distributed—

(A) Calculate the dollar amount of excess contributions for each HCE. The amount of excess contributions attributable to a given HCE for a plan year is the amount (if any) by which the HCE's contributions taken into account under this section must be reduced for the HCE's ADR to equal the highest permitted ADR under the plan. To calculate the highest permitted ADR under a plan, the ADR of the HCE with the highest ADR is reduced by the amount required to cause that HCE's ADR to equal the ADR of the HCE with the next highest ADR. If a lesser reduction would enable the arrangement to satisfy the requirements of paragraph (b)(2)(ii)(C) of this section, only this lesser reduction is used in determining the highest permitted ADR.

(B) Determination of the total amount of excess contributions. The process described in paragraph (b)(2)(ii)(A) of this section must be repeated until the arrangement would satisfy the requirements of paragraph (b)(2)(ii)(C) of this section. The sum of all reductions for all HCEs determined under paragraph (b)(2)(ii)(A) of this section is the total amount of excess contributions for the plan year.

(C) Satisfaction of ADP. A cash or deferred arrangement satisfies this paragraph (b)(2)(ii)(C) if the arrangement would satisfy the requirements of paragraph (a)(1)(ii) of this section if the ADR for each HCE were determined after the reductions described in paragraph (b)(2)(ii)(A) of this section.

(iii) Apportionment of total amount of excess contributions among the HCEs. The following procedures must be used in apportioning the total amount of excess contributions determined under paragraph (b)(2)(ii) of this section among the HCEs:

(A) Calculate the dollar amount of excess contributions for each HCE. The contributions of the HCE with the highest dollar amount of contributions taken into account under this section are reduced by the amount required to cause that HCE's contributions to equal the dollar amount of the contributions taken into account under this section for the HCE with the next highest dollar amount of contributions taken into account under this section. If a lesser apportionment to the HCE would enable the plan to apportion the total amount of excess contributions, only the lesser apportionment would apply.

(B) Limit on amount apportioned to any individual. For purposes of this paragraph (b)(2)(iii), the amount of contributions taken into account under this section with respect to an HCE who is an eligible employee in more than one plan of an employer is determined by taking into account all contributions otherwise taken into account with respect to such HCE under any plan of the employer during the plan year of the plan being tested as being made under the plan being tested. However, the amount of excess contributions apportioned for a plan year with respect to any HCE must not exceed the amount of contributions actually contributed to the plan for the HCE for the plan year. Thus, in the case of an HCE who is an eligible employee in more than one plan of the same employer to which elective contributions are made and whose ADR is calculated in accordance with paragraph (a)(3)(ii) of this section, the amount required to be distributed under this paragraph (b)(2)(iii) shall not exceed the contributions actually contributed to the plan and taken into account under this section for the plan year.

(C) Apportionment to additional HCEs. The procedure in paragraph (b)(2)(iii)(A) of this section must be repeated until the total amount of excess contributions determined under paragraph (b)(2)(ii) of this section has been apportioned.

(iv) Income allocable to excess contributions.

(A) General rule. For plan years beginning on or after January 1, 2008, the income allocable to excess contributions is equal to the allocable gain or loss through the end of the plan year. See paragraph (b)(2)(iv)(D) of this section for rules that apply to plan years beginning before January 1, 2008.

(B) Method of allocating income. A plan may use any reasonable method for computing the income allocable to excess contributions, provided that the method does not violate section 401(a)(4), is used consistently for all participants and for all corrective distributions under the plan for the plan year, and is used by the plan for allocating income to participant's accounts. See § 1.401(a)(4)-1(c)(8). A plan will not fail to use a reasonable method for computing the income allocable to excess contributions merely because the income allocable to excess contributions is determined on a date that is no more than 7 days before the distribution.

(C) Alternative method of allocating plan year income. A plan may allocate income to excess contributions for the plan year by multiplying the income for the plan year allocable to the elective contributions and other amounts taken into account under this section (including contributions made for the plan year), by a fraction, the numerator of which is the excess contributions for the employee for the plan year, and the denominator of which is the sum of the —

(1) Account balance attributable to elective contributions and other contributions taken into account under this section as of the beginning of the plan year, and

(2) Any additional amount of such contributions made for the plan year.

(D) Plan years before 2008. For plan years beginning before January 1, 2008, the income allocable to excess contributions is determined under § 1.401(k)-2(b)(2)(iv) (as it appeared in the April 1, 2007, edition of 26 CFR part 1).

(v) Distribution. Within 12 months after the close of the plan year in which the excess contribution arose, the plan must distribute to each HCE the excess contributions apportioned to such HCE under paragraph (b)(2)(iii) of this section and the allocable income. Except as otherwise provided in this paragraph (b)(2)(v) and paragraph (b)(4)(i) of this section, a distribution of excess contributions must be in addition to any other distributions made during the year and must be designated as a corrective distribution by the employer. In the event of a complete termination of the plan during the plan year in which an excess contribution arose, the corrective distribution must be made as soon as administratively feasible after the date of termination of the plan, but in no event later than 12 months after the date of termination. If the entire account balance of an HCE is distributed prior to when the plan makes a distribution of excess contributions in accordance with this paragraph (b)(2), the distribution is deemed to have been a corrective distribution of excess contributions (and income) to the extent that a corrective distribution would otherwise have been required.

(vi) Tax treatment of corrective distributions.

(A) Corrective distributions for plan years beginning on or after January 1, 2008. Except as provided in this paragraph (b)(2)(vi), for plan years beginning on or after January 1, 2008, a corrective distribution of excess contributions (and allocable income) is includible in the employee's gross income for the employee's taxable year in which distributed. In addition, the corrective distribution is not subject to the early distribution tax of section 72(t). See paragraph (b)(5) of this section for additional rules relating to the employer excise tax on amounts distributed more than 2½ months (6 months in the case of certain plans that include an eligible automatic contribution arrangement within the meaning of section 414(w)) after the end of the plan year. See also § 1.402(c)-2, A-4 for restrictions on rolling over distributions that are excess contributions.

(B) Corrective distributions for plan years beginning before January 1, 2008. The tax treatment of corrective distributions for plan years beginning before January 1, 2008, is determined under § 1.401(k)-2(b)(2)(vi) (as it appeared in the April 1, 2007, edition of 26 CFR Part 1). If the total amount of excess contributions, determined under this paragraph (b)(2), and excess aggregate contributions determined under § 1.401(m)-2(b)(2) distributed to a recipient under a plan for any plan year is less than $100 (excluding income), a corrective distribution of excess contributions (and income) is includible in the gross income of the recipient in the taxable year of the recipient in which the corrective distribution is made, except to the extent provided in paragraph (b)(2)(vi)(C) of this section.

(C) Corrective distributions attributable to designated Roth contributions. Notwithstanding paragraphs (b)(2)(vi)(A) and (B) of this section, a distribution of excess contributions is not includible in gross income to the extent it represents a distribution of designated Roth contributions. However, the income allocable to a corrective distribution of excess contributions that are designated Roth contributions is included in gross income in accordance with paragraph (b)(2)(vi)(A) or (B) of this section (i.e., in the same manner as income allocable to a corrective distribution of excess contributions that are pre-tax elective contributions).

(vii) Other rules.

(A) No employee or spousal consent required. A corrective distribution of excess contributions (and income) may be made under the terms of the plan without regard to any notice or consent otherwise required under sections 411(a)(11) and 417.

(B) Treatment of corrective distributions as elective contributions. Excess contributions are treated as employer contributions for purposes of sections 404 and 415 even if distributed from the plan.

(C) No reduction of required minimum distribution. A distribution of excess contributions (and income) is not treated as a distribution for purposes of determining whether the plan satisfies the minimum distribution requirements of section 401(a)(9). See § 1.401(a)(9)-5, A-9(b).

(D) Partial distributions. Any distribution of less than the entire amount of excess contributions (and allocable income) with respect to any HCE is treated as a pro rata distribution of excess contributions and allocable income.

(viii) Examples. The following examples illustrate the application of this paragraph (b)(2). For purposes of these examples, none of the plans provide for catch-up contributions under section 414(v). The examples are as follows:

Example (1).

(i) Plan P, a calendar year profit-sharing plan that includes a cash or deferred arrangement, provides for distribution of excess contributions to HCEs to the extent necessary to satisfy the ADP test. For the 2006 plan year, Employee A, an HCE, has elective contributions of $12,000 and $200,000 in compensation, for an ADR of 6%, and Employee B, a second HCE, has elective contributions of $8,960 and compensation of $128,000, for an ADR of 7%. The ADP for the NHCEs is 3% for the 2006 plan year. Under the ADP test, the ADP of the two HCEs under the plan may not exceed 5% (*i.e.,* 2 percentage points more than the ADP of the NHCEs under the plan). The ADP for the 2 HCEs under the plan is 6.5%. Therefore, there must be a correction of excess contributions for the 2006 plan year.

(ii) The total amount of excess contributions for the HCEs is determined under paragraph (b)(2)(ii) of this section as follows: the elective contributions of Employee B (the HCE with the highest ADR) are reduced by $1,280 in order to reduce his ADR to 6% ($7,680/ $128,000), which is the ADR of Employee A.

(iii) Because the ADP of the HCEs determined after the $1,280 reduction to Employee B still exceeds 5%, further reductions in elective contributions are necessary in order to reduce the ADP of the HCEs to 5%. The elective contributions of Employee A and Employee B are each reduced by 1% of compensation ($2,000 and $1,280 respectively). Because the ADP of the HCEs determined after the reductions equals 5%, the plan would satisfy the requirements of (a)(1)(ii) of this section.

(iv) The total amount of excess contributions ($4,560 = $1,280+$2,000+$1,280) is apportioned among the HCEs under paragraph (b)(2)(iii) of this section first to the HCE with the highest amount of elective contributions. Therefore, Employee A is apportioned $3,040 (the amount required to cause Employee A's elective contributions to equal the next highest dollar amount of elective contributions).

(v) Because the total amount of excess contributions has not been apportioned, further apportionment is necessary. The balance ($1,520) of the total amount of excess contributions is apportioned equally among Employee A and Employee B ($760 to each).

(vi) Therefore, the cash or deferred arrangement will satisfy the requirements of paragraph (a)(1) of this section if, by the end of the 12 month period following the end of the 2006 plan year, Employee A receives a corrective distribution of excess contributions equal to $3,800 ($3,040 + $760) and allocable income and Employee B receives a corrective distribution of $760 and allocable income.

Example (2).

(i) The facts are the same as in Example 1, except Employee A's ADR is based on $3,000 of elective contributions to this plan and $9,000 of elective contributions to another plan of the employer.

(ii) The total amount of excess contributions ($4,560 = $1,280+$2,000+$1,280) is apportioned among the HCEs under paragraph (b)(2)(iii) of this section first to the HCE with the highest amount of elective contributions. The amount of elective contributions for Employee A is $12,000. Therefore, Employee A is apportioned $3,040 (the amount required to cause Employee A's elective contributions to equal the next highest dollar amount of elective contributions). However, pursuant to paragraph (b)(2)(iii)(B) of this section, no more than the amount actually contributed to the plan may be apportioned to an HCE. Accordingly, no more than $3,000 may be apportioned to Employee A. Therefore, the remaining $1,560 must be apportioned to Employee B.

(iii) The cash or deferred arrangement will satisfy the requirements of paragraph (a)(1) of this section if, by the end of the 12 month period following the end of the 2006 plan year, Employee A receives a corrective distribution of excess contributions equal to $3,000 (total amount of elective contributions actually contributed to the plan for Employee A) and allocable income and Employee B receives a corrective distribution of $1,560 and allocable income.

(3) Recharacterization of excess contributions.

(i) General rule. Excess contributions are recharacterized in accordance with this paragraph (b)(3) only if the excess contributions that would have to be distributed under (b)(2) of this section if the plan was correcting through distribution of excess contributions are recharacterized as described in paragraph (b)(3)(ii) of this section, and all of the conditions set forth in paragraph (b)(3)(iii) of this section are satisfied.

(ii) Treatment of recharacterized excess contributions. Recharacterized excess contributions are includible in the employee's gross income as if such amounts were distributed under paragraph (b)(2) of this section. The recharacterized excess contributions are treated as employee contributions for purposes of section 72, sections 401(a)(4), 401(m), § 1.401(k)-1(d) and § 1.401(k)-2. This requirement is not treated as satisfied unless the payor or plan administrator reports the recharacterized excess contributions as employee contributions to the Internal Revenue Service and the employee by timely providing such Federal tax forms and accompanying instructions and timely taking such other action as is prescribed by the Commissioner in revenue rulings, notices and other guidance published in the Internal Revenue Bulletin (see § 601.601(d)(2) of this chapter) as well as the applicable Federal tax forms and accompanying instructions.

(iii) Additional rules.

(A) Time of recharacterization. Excess contributions may not be recharacterized under this paragraph (b)(3) after 2½ months after the close of the plan year to which the recharacterization relates. Recharacterization is deemed to have occurred on the date on which the last of those HCEs with excess contributions to be recharacterized is notified in accordance with paragraph (b)(3)(ii) of this section.

(B) Employee contributions must be permitted under plan. The amount of recharacterized excess contributions, in combination with the employee contributions actually made by the HCE, may not exceed the maximum amount of employee contributions (determined without regard to the ACP test of section 401(m)(2)) permitted under the provisions of the plan as in effect on the first day of the plan year.

(C) Treatment of recharacterized excess contributions. Recharacterized excess contributions continue to be treated as employer contributions for all purposes under the Internal Revenue Code (other than those specified in paragraph (b)(3)(ii) of this section), including section 401(a) and sections 404, 409, 411, 412, 415, 416, and 417. Thus, for example, recharacterized excess contributions remain subject to the requirements of § 1.401(k)-1(c); must be deducted under section 404; and are treated as employer contributions described in section 415(c)(2)(A).

(4) Rules applicable to all corrections.

(i) Coordination with distribution of excess deferrals.

(A) Treatment of excess deferrals that reduce excess contributions. The amount of excess contributions (and allocable income) to be distributed under paragraph (b)(2) of this section or the amount of excess contributions recharacterized under paragraph (b)(3) of this section with respect to an employee for a plan year, is reduced by any amounts previously distributed to the employee from the plan to correct excess deferrals for the employee's taxable year ending with or within the plan year in accordance with section 402(g)(2).

(B) Treatment of excess contributions that reduce excess deferrals. Under § 1.402(g)-1(e), the amount required to be distributed to correct an excess deferral to an employee for a taxable year is reduced by any excess contributions (and allocable income) previously distributed or excess contributions recharacterized with respect to the employee for the plan year beginning with or within the taxable year. The amount of excess contributions includible in the gross income of the employee, and the amount of excess contributions reported by the payer or plan administrator as includible in the gross income of the employee, does not include the amount of any reduction under § 1.402(g)-1(e)(6).

(ii) Forfeiture of match on distributed excess contributions. A matching contribution is taken into account under section 401(a)(4) even if the match is with respect to an elective contribution that is distributed or recharacterized under this paragraph (b). This requires that, after correction of excess contributions, each level of matching contributions be currently and effectively available to a group of employees that satisfies section 410(b). See § 1.401(a)(4)-4(e)(3)(iii)(G). Thus, a plan that provides the same rate of matching contributions to all employees will not meet the requirements of section 401(a)(4) if elective contributions are distributed under this paragraph (b) to HCEs to the extent needed to meet the requirements of section 401(k)(3), while matching contributions attributable to those elective contributions remain allocated to the HCEs' accounts. Under section 411(a)(3)(G) and § 1.411(a)-4(b)(7), a plan may forfeit matching contributions attributable to excess contributions, excess aggregate contributions or excess deferrals to avoid a violation of section 401(a)(4). See also § 1.401(a)(4)-11(g)(3)(vii)(B) regarding the use of additional allocations to the accounts of NHCEs for the purpose of correcting a discriminatory rate of matching contributions.

(iii) Permitted forfeiture of QMAC. Pursuant to section 401(k)(8)(E), a qualified matching contribution is not treated as forfeitable under § 1.401(k)-1(c) merely because under the plan it is forfeited in accordance with paragraph (b)(4)(ii) of this section or § 1.414(w)-1(d)(2).

(iv) No requirement for recalculation. If excess contributions are distributed or recharacterized in accordance with paragraphs (b)(2) and (3) of this section, the cash or deferred arrangement is treated as meeting the nondiscrimination test of section 401(k)(3) regardless of whether the ADP for the HCEs, if recalculated after the distributions or recharacterizations, would satisfy section 401(k)(3).

(v) Treatment of excess contributions that are catch-up contributions. A cash or deferred arrangement does not fail to meet the requirements of section 401(k)(3) and paragraph (a)(1) of this section merely because excess contributions that are catch-up contributions because they exceed the ADP limit, as described in § 1.414(v)-1(b)(1)(iii), are not corrected in accordance with this paragraph (b).

(5) Failure to timely correct.

(i) Failure to correct within 2½ months after end of plan year. If a plan does not correct excess contributions within 2½ months after the close of the plan year for which the excess contributions are made, the employer will be liable for a 10% excise tax on the amount of the excess contributions. See section 4979 and § 54.4979-1 of this chapter. Qualified nonelective contributions and qualified matching contributions properly taken into account under paragraph (a)(6) of this section for a plan year may enable a plan to avoid having excess contributions, even if the contributions are made after the close of the 2½-month period.

(ii) Failure to correct within 12 months after end of plan year. If excess contributions are not corrected within 12 months after the close of the plan year for which they were made, the cash or deferred arrangement will fail to satisfy the requirements of section 401(k)(3) for the plan year for which the excess contributions are made and all subsequent plan years during which the excess contributions remain in the trust.

(iii) Special rule for eligible automatic contribution arrangements. In the case of excess contributions under a plan that includes an eligible automatic contribution arrangement within the meaning of section 414(w), 6 months is substituted for 2½ months in paragraph (b)(5)(i) of this section. The additional time described in this paragraph (b)(5)(iii) applies to a distribution of excess contributions for a plan year beginning on or after January 1, 2010 only where all the eligible NHCEs and eligible HCEs are covered employees under the eligible automatic contribution arrangement (within the meaning of § 1.414(w)-1(e)(3)) for the entire plan year (or for the portion of the plan year that the eligible NHCEs and eligible HCEs are eligible employees).

* * *

So there you have it. A 401(k), which seems simple on its face because it's basically about getting employees to voluntarily elect to defer a portion of their salaries into the plan, is actually quite complicated. As described, if the employer wants to simplify administration by not requiring an annual calculation of ADPs, and then if it fails, either making additional contributions it did not otherwise budget, or returning or recharacterizing deferrals already made by HCEs, then it needs to comply with the safe harbor rules.

G. Key Employees

Statutory Definition at IRC § 416(i)

Before going on, please realize that we are now addressing a different classification of employees for a different qualification rule. Although different definitions, the same employee can (and often times is) classified as both a Highly Compensated Employee and as a Key Employee.

An employee is generally considered a Key Employee if he or she is an officer, if he or she owns a substantial piece of the sponsoring employer or if he or she earns a high salary. By default, every employee who is not classified as a Key Employee is classified as a non-Key Employee. Since salaries, officer responsibilities and ownership can change from one year to the next, the Plan Administrator must annually go through the roster of employees and classify each and every eligible employee as either a Key Employee or a non-Key Employee. As plan administration is generally performed through computers, then as long as the software is coded correctly, and the data information is input correctly, the determination of Key Employee status becomes somewhat routine, as long as the classification of an individual as an officer is properly made and input. However, it will be someone's ultimate responsibility to ascertain that the software works properly and that the results are acceptable.

A "key employee" is a participant who at any time during the plan year is:

- an officer of the employer whose annual compensation exceeds $130,000 (as adjusted for inflation), but no more than 50 employees (or, if lesser, the greater of 3 or 10 percent of the employees) shall be treated as officers; or
- a 5-percent owner of the employer (without regard to compensation) or
- a 1-percent owner whose compensation exceeds $150,000 (not adjusted for inflation), where actual and constructive ownership is determined pursuant to the usual rules, whether the business is a corporation or not, but the employers of controlled groups or affiliated service groups do not need to be aggregated.

The determination of Key Employees based on the above criteria is pursuant to changes in the law made in 2001. This is important since the Regulations that provide guidance on the determination were promulgated in 1984 and have not been updated for the law changes. The discussion below represents the guidance from the existing Regulations that still ostensibly applies to the current statutory provisions.

In determining whether an employee is a Key Employee under the officer test or the one percent owner test, compensation is a relevant factor. Compensation is the amount paid as an employee from the employer for the year, where the following are added back in even though they are excluded for income tax purposes: any elective deferral s for 401(k) plans or SIMPLEs; and all other salary deferrals made to cafeteria plans, qualified transportation fringe benefit plans, or §457 nonqualified plans. If an individual is self-employed, then he or she shall be treated as an employee and earned income will be considered compensation.

The statute does not define "officer." Congress, however, indicated that an employee's officer status is to be determined by the facts and circumstances of the particular employment relationship. The Conference Report states that relevant facts will be considered, including the source of the employee's authority, the term for which he was elected or appointed, and the nature and extent of the employee's duties. An employee's position must reflect a continuity of service and should not be based on a special and single transaction. The regulations equate an officer with an administrative executive. The mere lack of an executive title, however, will not prevent an employee from being classified as an officer. Further, an employee who merely has an officer's title without an officer's authority is not considered an officer. The TEFRA Bluebook emphasizes that the "relationship between the individual and the employer is determinative." The regulation provides that, in determining the officers of the employer, an employee who is an officer must be counted as an officer for key employee purposes regardless of whether the employee is a key employee under any of the other tests. However, in testing for the plan's top-heaviness, an employee's present value of accrued benefits is counted only once.

Neither the statute nor the Conference Report clarifies whether an unincorporated employer, such as a partnership, has "officers" and if so, how they are to be identified. However, sole proprietorships, partnerships, associations, trusts, and labor organizations may have officers.

In determining which employees are Key employees, Employees who have not completed six months of service, employees who normally work less than 17½ hours per week, employees who normally do not work more than six months during any year, employees who have not reached age 21, and, employees generally covered by a collective bargaining agreement shall not be considered.

In the case of corporate employers, for purposes of determining the five percent and one percent ownership tests, the general attribution rules of IRC §318 apply with the modification that a participant need own only five percent of the corporation to have a portion of the corporation's holdings of the employer's stock attributed to the participant. Thus, a person will be treated as owning stock owned by certain family members and a proportionate share of stock owned by partnerships, estates, trusts, and corporations in which the person has any interest. Further, stocks which may be acquired under an option will be attributed to the person.

On the other hand, for noncorporate employers, a five percent owner of an unincorporated employer as any person owning more than five percent of the employer's capital or profits interest. This definition automatically includes any person qualifying as an "owner-employee."

H. Top Heavy Requirements for All Qualified Retirement Plans

The determination date as to whether the plan is Top-Heavy for the current plan year is the last day of the prior plan year, or in the case of the first plan year of any plan, the last day of the first plan year. Therefore, the plan will be Top Heavy this year if, as of the last day of the prior plan year (*i.e.,* the determination date):

- for a defined contribution plan, the aggregate of the accounts of Key Employees under the plan exceeds 60 percent of the aggregate of the accounts of all employees under such plan; or

- for a defined benefit plan, the present value of the cumulative accrued benefits under the plan for Key Employees exceeds 60 percent of the present value of the cumulative accrued benefits under the plan for all employees.

A plan's precise Top Heavy ratios need not be computed every year to determine whether it is Top Heavy. If, on examination, the IRS requests a demonstration as to whether a plan is Top Heavy, the employer must demonstrate to the IRS's satisfaction that the plan is not operating in violation of the Top Heavy rules. Thus, for example, if the employer determined the present value of accrued benefits for Key Employees in a simplified manner, which had the effect of overstating their value, and determined the present value for non-Key Employees in a simplified manner, which had the effect of understating their value, and the ratio of the Key Employee present value divided by the sum of the present values was less than 60%, then the plan would not be considered Top Heavy. This would be a sufficient demonstration because the simplified fraction could be shown to be greater than the exact fraction, and thus, the exact fraction must also be less than 60% (the statutory benchmark for Top Heaviness).

The exact rules for determining a plan's Top Heavy status are complicated, and purposely only summarized for this textbook. If a plan is Top Heavy, then the vesting schedule must meet the special Top-Heavy vesting schedule rules, and minimum contributions must be provided in a defined contribution plan or, in a defined benefit plan, minimum benefit accruals must be provided to non Key Employees (all of those rules were clearly indicated in Chapter 7). There are special rules for providing Top Heavy minimums when an individual participates in multiple qualified plans sponsored by the same employer, especially if at least one is a defined contribution plan and at least one is a defined benefit plan.

Chapter 9

Distributions

Overview

What types of distributions can come from qualified plans?

- life annuity: payments from the plan are paid monthly (or annually) to the plan participant starting on his or her normal retirement date and will continue for as long as he or she lives. An unhealthy individual who does not live out his or her full life expectancy will lose all benefits upon death (thus the plan has incurred an actuarial gain); whereas, a super-healthy individual who outlives his or her life expectancy will continue getting paid for life (thus the plan has incurred an actuarial loss)
    - the law of large numbers suggest that the cumulative gains and losses will cancel each other out from the plan sponsor's point of view (even though individual participants will either suffer losses for premature deaths or enjoy gains for extended lives)
- 10 year Certain and Life thereafter annuity: payments from the plan are paid annually (or monthly) to the plan participant starting on his or her normal retirement date and will continue until the later of the date of death or after 10 annual payments have been made (or 120 monthly payments)
    - this is sort of insurance, which obviously costs a premium, and if the participant dies before the 10 year guaranteed term ends, then the premium was worthwhile
    - any term can be substituted for 10, but 10 is the most common
- 100% Joint and Survivor annuity: payments from the plan are paid annually (or monthly) to the plan participant starting on his or her normal retirement date and will continue until the later of his or her date of death or the date of death of the second life
    - again, there is a premium, and if the participant dies before the second life, then the premium was worthwhile
    - any percentage can be substituted for 100%, but 100% is the most common
- lump sum (*a.k.a.* single sum distribution): a single payment today is paid which represents all future expected benefit payments

What is one way to differentiate between annuities and lump sums?

- Annuity = mailbox
    - picture a mailbox, and with an annuity, every month that the participant is still alive after annuities begin, that retiree can walk down to his or her mailbox and find an annuity check

- if the individual is lucky, he or she lives longer than expected, and can still receive a monthly check for every month he or she is still alive, so the individual received more benefits than the plan intended
- on the other hand, if he or she is unlucky, the individual dies sometime before he or she is expected to die, and since no longer alive, the life annuity terminates, so the individual received less benefits than the plan intended
- Lump sum = piggy bank
  - picture a piggy bank, and with a lump sum, every month that the participant is still alive, the retiree takes enough out of the bank to pay for that month's living expenses
  - if the individual is lucky, he or she dies sometime before he or she is expected to die, and assuming the retiree invested the account well while alive and frugally and conservatively withdrew living expenses, there will be a balance that can be bequeathed to his or her estate
  - if the individual is unlucky, he or she lives longer than expected, or invests poorly, or withdrew too much in any given year, but in any event, has totally depleted the account, and now only has personal savings and Social Security to pay his or her expenses for the rest of his or her life

How does the Enrolled Actuary convert the normal form of benefit into an optional form of benefit in a defined benefit plan?

- as a qualification requirement, the defined benefit plan document must provide the tables or exact method of conversion
- this will indicate the premium a participant pays for the choice of an optional form (such as an approximate 10% premium for a 10 Year Certain & Life annuity and an approximate 20% premium for a 100% Joint and Survivor annuity)

When does the plan need to start making plan distributions?

- as a qualification requirement, unless the participant otherwise elects, the plan must start distributions within 60 days of the later of the participant's
  - normal retirement date
  - 10th anniversary of participation in the plan, or
  - termination of employment

What are the distribution requirements for married participants?

- the pension plan document (*i.e.*, all defined benefit plans and money purchase plans) must provide that the Qualified Joint and Survivor Annuity will be the mandatory form of distribution for a married participant unless the spouse agrees with the participant's election for an alternate form of distribution
- the spouse's signature must be notarized or witnessed by the plan administrator
- there are two types of joint and survivor annuities:
  - Qualified Pre-Retirement Survivor Annuity (QPSA)—if a married participant dies before retirement, then the surviving spouse must be able to receive at least 50% of the participant's accrued benefit at date of death
  - Qualified Joint & Survivor Annuity (QJSA)—if a participant in a plan subject to these rules has a spouse (as determined in accordance with state law) on his

or her benefit commencement date, then the normal form of benefit must be a X% Joint and Survivor Annuity where X is any percentage between 50% and 100% and where the spouse is automatically the second life (every plan must offer a married participant the option to elect a 75% joint and survivor benefit)

What early retirement benefits and subsidies are available under a qualified defined benefit plan?

- the sponsoring employer can give credit for past years of service worked before the plan was adopted, with a predecessor employer or with an affiliated employer, or can assume future, but yet unearned, years of service
- an early retirement subsidy oftentimes entices older members of the work force to voluntarily leave
- there are two main types of Early Retirement subsidies:
  - assume that the annuity payable starting at a younger age is the same benefit payable starting at retirement age
  - assume that the individual is credited for future years of service he would likely have worked if there was no Early Retirement subsidy

Under what circumstances can a plan allow in-service distributions (i.e., while the participant is still employed and still receiving a salary)?

- pension plans (*i.e.*, money purchase plans and defined benefit plans)—no distributions are allowed while the participant is still employed by the employer (other than for death or disability) before age 62
- profit sharing plans—plans may allow participants who are still employed to withdraw a portion or all of their account balances after the money has been in the plan for a specified number of years (but at least 2 years)
- 401(k) plan—for the elective salary deferrals only, only as a hardship distribution
  - distributions of an employee's elective salary deferrals can only be withdrawn while the individual is still employed if they meet the "hardship distribution" rules for an immediate and heavy financial need, which include:
    - qualified medical expenses already incurred or about to be incurred for the employee, a spouse, and dependents,
    - the expenses necessary for the employee to purchase a principal residence (or the mortgage amount necessary to prevent foreclosure, but not regular mortgage payments),
    - tuition, related educational fees, and room and board for post-secondary education for the employee, a spouse, children or dependents for the next year,
    - funds necessary to prevent the eviction of the employee from his or her principal residence,
    - burial or funeral expenses for the employee's deceased spouse, parent, child, or dependent, or
    - certain expenses to repair the participant's primary residence.
  - the employer can only pay an amount equal to the immediate and heavy need, but not greater than the sum of the employee's elective deferrals (less the amount of any previously distributed hardship withdrawal)

- although exempt from the premature penalty tax, a hardship distribution is included in Gross Income in the year distributed
- after a hardship distribution, the employee cannot elect salary deferrals for at least 6 months
- Roth 401(k) plan — any time after the money has been in the participant's account for at least 5 years, and after the participant attains age 59½
- all qualified plans must distribute appropriate benefits to an ex-spouse upon divorce from a plan participant, but only if the parties provide a valid Qualified Domestic Relations Order (QDRO)
  - A domestic relations order is merely some document that is certified in state court to divide marital property between former spouses upon divorce (a common marital property to be divided might be the benefits one of the spouses has accrued in his or her qualified retirement plan)
  - the benefits of a qualified retirement plan can only be alienated if the domestic relations order is determined, by the plan administrator, to be a Qualified Domestic Relations Order
  - the QDRO must provide clear instructions to the plan administrator (drafted specifically for that particular qualified plan) on how and when to pay the "alternate payee" former spouse
  - plans are required to have a QDRO determination procedure which clearly informs all parties what they will look for in a DRO to determine whether it is a QDRO, the time frame in which it will make such determination, and how either party can dispute the plan administrator's determination
  - if a plan administrator is on notice that a QDRO might be forthcoming, then there is a statutory 18 month period where the plan administrator must act in good faith and segregate any benefits which might become distributable to an alternate payee should a valid QDRO be communicated
- a loan is generally not considered a distribution
  - if loans are specifically allowed under the plan document, then each participant who is an employee of the sponsoring employer can take out the lesser of:
    - $50,000, as reduced by the largest outstanding loan balance in the previous 12 months or
    - 50% of the participant's accrued benefits
  - the loan must be paid back within 5 years (unless it is being used for the purchase of a first home), and must be paid at least quarterly
  - there must be a reasonable interest rate (the rule of thumb is that the IRS will not question rates which are one point above prime on that loan date)
  - if a participant defaults on the loan, then the unpaid balance is deemed a distribution and is included in Gross Income in the year of default and is subject to the premature penalty tax

How is a normal distribution from a qualified retirement plan taxed?
- if the participant has no basis in his or her plan benefits, then the total amount received in each plan year is included in Gross Income

- basis generally includes:
  - nondeductible (*i.e.*, after-tax) employee contributions,
  - P.S. 58 costs attributable to insurance included in income as an "economic benefit"
  - employer contributions which have already been taxed and
  - amounts paid by an employee as principal payments on any loans that were treated as "deemed distributions"
- if the participant has a basis in his plan benefits, then the exclusion ratio for annuities paid from qualified retirement plans will use special factors to determine the dollar amount of each distribution excluded from taxation (until the basis is fully recovered)

What are some of the procedural aspects of plan distributions?

- a statement of benefit options and procedures, including a disclosure of the relative values of optional forms of benefits
- a notice explaining all of the income tax aspects of a distribution or a rollover
- the plan sponsor must withhold 20% of any distribution and submit them to the federal government as advanced income taxes paid by the individual

What is a rollover?

- any portion of a distribution from a qualified retirement plan may be rolled over into a Traditional IRA or into another qualified retirement plan which accepts roll over contributions, unless the distribution:
  - is a minimum distribution under IRC § 401(a)(9), or
  - is a hardship distribution from a 401(k) plan
- if a participant rolls over a distribution, then the participant keeps the same tax advantages (*i.e.*, deferral of taxation of benefits and interest until distributed)
- a distribution of designated Roth contributions, and associated earnings, can be rolled over into a Roth IRA

What is a premature distribution and how is it taxed?

- a 10% penalty is assessed for premature distributions (generally made prior to age 59½)
- Congress decided that anyone who receives money before 59½ is probably not really retired and therefore such individuals are penalized for taking the money too early
- distributions which are excluded from this penalty tax are those which are:
  - paid due to death, disability, or separation of service after attainment of age 55;
  - used as qualifying medical expenses;
  - paid to an alternate payee pursuant to a QDRO;
  - used by unemployed individuals to pay health insurance premiums; or
  - paid for any reason to certain qualified reservists called into active duty before December 2008, as long as they are repaid within 2 years after the period of active duty ends
  - only if paid from a traditional IRA, are used for qualified education or qualified first time home purchase expenses.

- each individual taxpayer is required to indicate premature distributions on his individual tax return and thus pay the penalty

What are the required minimum distributions?

- this provision basically applies to wealthier individuals who have other assets available during retirement, and wish to pass the tax-qualified benefits to their beneficiaries
- a participant must start receiving annual minimum distributions in the year after he or she attains age 70½ , or, if not a 5% owner, after retirement if still working at age 70½ (the employee's required beginning date)
- if the plan is a defined contribution plan (or other individual account plan), then the minimum amount that must be distributed (and included in Gross Income) for the current year equals the account balance as of the last valuation date in the preceding year divided by a life expectancy factor
- if the plan is a defined benefit plan, then certain distribution options automatically meet the minimum distribution rules, whereas other options need to be tested against the minimum distribution incidental benefit rules (where non-spouse beneficiaries, depending on their age, cannot mathematically be expected to receive more benefits after the employee's death than the employee is expected to receive during his lifetime).
- the designated beneficiary is determined on September 30 of the calendar year following the year of the employee's death — which allows accountants and estate planners ample time to fix things for their client since there are certain income tax advantages if the spouse is the sole designated beneficiary and there are income tax disadvantages if the beneficiary is not an individual
- if the employee dies before his required beginning date, then all of the benefits must be distributed either:
  - within 5 years of his or her death;
  - over the life of the designated beneficiary, starting in the year following the year of death; or
  - over the life of the surviving spouse, starting in the year that the employee would be required to start taking distributions, if the surviving spouse is the sole designated beneficiary
- the person who fails to receive a distribution upon turning age 70½, and not the employer, will pay a 50% penalty tax for failing to take a required minimum distribution

A. Optional Forms of Benefits

1. Optional Forms of Benefit Distributions

The plan document will be drafted in a way that dictates the methods of distribution available to a participant, or upon a participant's death, to his or her beneficiary. While the most basic forms are described below, the sponsoring employer can choose to not offer some options, or can choose to offer a variety of hybrid options. Like anything else in life, while the participants might prefer a larger set of options, it will be up to the employer (or outside plan administrator) to properly explain all options to participants and to ensure that actual disbursements from the plan comply with both the terms of the plan document and with each individual's selected form of payment. Therefore, unless necessary to further the employer's business goals, a set of fewer options will be easier to administer. At this point, we are talking about distributions of retirement benefits to participants after they have retired. In part B of this chapter, we discuss other ways to pay benefits to participants who are still actively employed, such as through a plan loan or upon divorce, and there are generally much fewer options available to plan participants under those scenarios.

So, when a participant retires from the employer, he or she stops earning a salary, and, unless wealthy to start with, will need all or part of the qualified retirement benefits to live on for the rest of his or her life. The most common choices available are:

- *Life Annuity:* Payments from the plan are paid monthly (or annually) to the plan participant starting on his or her normal retirement date and will continue for as long as he or she lives. An unhealthy individual who does not live out his or her full life expectancy will lose all benefits upon death (thus the plan has incurred an actuarial gain); whereas, a super-healthy individual who outlives his or her life expectancy will continue getting paid for life (thus the plan has incurred an actuarial loss). The law of large numbers suggest that the cumulative gains and losses will cancel each other out from the plan sponsor's point of view (even though individual participants will either suffer losses for premature deaths or enjoy gains for extended lives). However, in a defined benefit plan, if the plan's actuary determines that the actuarial equivalents stated in the plan document do not accurately reflect the mortality (and other discounts) of this particular cohort of employees, then the actuary can change the equivalents (within certain statutory parameters).

Please note that when we use the term life expectancy, we mean the average future number of years an individual from this particular group of employees is expected to live—as a mathematical average, half of the individuals are expected to die before that mean age and half are expected to live beyond it. If calculated accurately (which it generally cannot be), incidences of health issues, such as vulnerability to cancer or heart disease, should be factored in.

- *10 Year Certain and Life Thereafter Annuity:* Payments from the plan are paid monthly (or annually) to the plan participant starting on his or her normal retirement date and will continue until the later of his or her her date of death or after 10 annual payments have been made (or 120 monthly payments). Therefore, if the participant dies within 10 years, the estate or beneficiary will still receive some pension payments until the 10 year period has expired. This is sort of insurance, which obviously comes with a "premium". If a 10 year C&L annuity is chosen by the participant and he or she lives beyond the 10 year period, then the "premium" was entirely wasted. However, the participant must make an election before benefits commence, so he or she must decide whether the "premium" is worth it. Any number can be substituted for 10, but 10 is the most common choice allowed in plans.

- *100% Joint and Survivor Annuity:* Payments from the plan are paid monthly (or annually) to the plan participant starting on his or her normal retirement date and will continue until the later of his or her date of death or the date of death of the second life (which he or she chooses). Even if two people are the same age, there is a positive probability that at least one of them will outlive the life expectancy. Again, there is a "premium" for this annuity which might seem "better" than a life annuity to that participant. Any number can be substituted for 100%, but 100% is the most common choice allowed in plans (although Congress currently believes that a 75% joint and survivor benefit is the most appropriate for a married couple).

- *Lump Sum (a.k.a. Single Sum Distribution):* A single payment today is paid which represents the mathematical present value of all future expected benefit payments (similar to a state lottery winner who chooses to receive a single sum this year in lieu of annual payments over the next 20 years). If the participant elects this form of distribution, then she or he is subject to longevity and investment risk. An unhealthy individual who does not live out his or her full life expectancy will likely have some balance of the lump sum distribution left over to be passed to the estate of beneficiary upon death; whereas, a super-healthy individual who outlives his or her life expectancy will most likely have spent through the entire lump sum distribution while still alive.

The way I always think about the difference between annuities (for now, let's only concentrate on life annuities) and lump sums is:

Annuity = mailbox. Picture a mailbox, and with an annuity, every month that the participant is still alive after annuities begin, that retiree can walk down to the mailbox and find his or her annuity check. For simplicity, assume that the average American alive at 65 has a life expectancy of about 81. If this particular retiree dies on his or her 81st birthday, then he or she will have received exactly what the employer wanted to provide through the retirement plan. If he or she is lucky, the retiree lives longer than his or her 81st birthday, and can still receive a monthly check for every month he or she is still alive (even at age 104), so the retiree received more benefits than the plan intended. On the other hand, if the retiree is unlucky, he or she dies sometime before his or her 81st birthday, and since he or she is no longer alive, the life annuity terminates, so the retiree received less benefits than the plan intended. The law of large numbers suggests that, from the plan's point of view, the actuarial gains from retirees dying before life expectancy will cancel out the losses from retirees living beyond life expectancy.

Lump sum = piggy bank. Picture a piggy bank, and with a lump sum, every month that the participant is still alive, the retiree takes enough out of the bank to pay for that month's living expenses. If this particular retiree dies on his or her 81st birthday, and assuming he or she properly calculated how much to withdraw each month and properly invested the balance, then on his or her 81st birthday, he or she will withdraw the last dollar, and then die. If the retiree is lucky, he or she dies before his or her 81st birthday, and whatever is left in the bank is available to the estate. On the other hand, if the retiree is unlucky, he or she lives beyond his or her 81st birthday, and has likely depleted the entire piggy bank account. From the plan's point of view, the lump sum represents the mathematical present value of benefits, so every retiree who receives a lump sum receives exactly what the plan intended.

I am being purposely dramatic with the use of the terms "lucky" and "unlucky" to emphasize the longevity, investment, and frugality risks put on individuals who choose a lump sum in lieu of a life annuity, especially if that person relies primarily on employer-provided benefits during retirement (as opposed to Social Security benefits and other accumulated personal and family wealth). Please note that Social Security as we now know it takes the form of a life annuity, and whenever a personal or private account is proposed, it would take the form of a lump sum.

2. Actuarial Equivalences Equating Different Forms of Benefit Distributions in a Qualified Plan

Statutory Rules at Various Paragraphs within IRC § 401(a)

The rules regarding qualified retirement plans were drafted based on existing practices in 1974, and back then, defined benefit pension plans were the most dominant model. Therefore, the concept of annuities, and the conversion from one form to the other, was key. As such, as a qualification rule, a "defined benefit plan shall not be treated as providing definitely determinable benefits unless, whenever the amount of any benefit is to be determined on the basis of actuarial assumptions, such assumptions are specified in the plan in a way which precludes employer discretion."[1] The IRS provided guidance in Rev. Rul. 79-90 on how a defined benefit plan document can be drafted to comply with this rule (please try to sift through and find the two acceptable fixed methods and the two acceptable variable methods, and think under what circumstances different sponsoring employers would adopt different methods for their respective defined benefit plans):

Revenue Ruling 79-90

Defined benefit plan; actuarial assumptions.

A defined benefit plan which provides optional forms of retirement benefits which are, according to the provisions of the plan, "actuarially equivalent" to the normal benefit must specify the actuarial assumptions used to compute the amounts of such optional benefits. Standards which satisfy this requirement are described.

Full Text:

Advice has been requested concerning whether a defined benefit pension plan which provides optional forms of benefit at normal retirement age which are "actuarially equivalent" to the normal benefit satisfies the "definitely determinable benefits" requirement of section 1.401-1(b)(1)(i) of the Income Tax Regulations.

The ABC Company established a defined benefit pension plan which provides a normal retirement benefit at age 65 equal to X dollars, payable as a single life annuity. A participant may alternatively select an optional form of annuity, but that annuity will equal the "actuarial equivalent" of the X dollar normal benefit. The plan does not specify what actuarial assumptions will be used to compute this "actuarial equivalent."

Section 1.401-1(b)(1)(i) of the regulations defines a pension plan, within the meaning of section 401(a), as "a plan established and maintained by an employer ... to provide ... definitely determinable benefits to his employees ... after retirement."

Rev. Rul. 74-385, 1974-2 C.B. 130 provides that, in the case of a defined benefit plan, the definitely determinable benefit requirement of section 1.401-1(b)(1)(i) of the regulations is satisfied where the benefits for each participant can be computed in accordance with an express formula contained in the plan that is not subject to the discretion of the employer.

Whenever the amount of a benefit in a defined benefit plan is to be determined by some procedure (such as "actuarial equivalent", "actuarial reserve", or

---

1. IRC § 401(a)(25).

"actuarial reduction") which requires the use of actuarial assumptions (interest, mortality, etc.) the assumptions to be used must be specified within the plan in a manner which precludes employer discretion. For purposes of this revenue ruling, employer discretion includes discretion of the employer, plan administrator, fiduciary, actuary, etc.

Two acceptable fixed standards which satisfy this requirement are:

(1) specifying the actuarial assumptions (interest, mortality, etc.) to be used, or

(2) including a table of adjustment factors to be used.

As an alternative to these fixed standards, the plan may specify a variable standard which provides for self-adjusting changes which are independent of employer discretion.

Two acceptable variable standards are:

(1) specifying that the procedure will be performed by reference to a specified insurance or annuity contract available at the time of benefit determination from a specified insurance company, or

(2) specifying that the interest rate will be a designated percentage of the prime interest rate of a specified bank or banks at the time of benefit determination (while all other assumptions are also specified).

Accordingly, since the subject plan does not sufficiently describe the procedure to be used in benefit computations, and the actuarial assumptions to be used in the computation are not definitely determinable, the plan benefits themselves are held to be not definitely determinable as required by section 1.401-1(b)(1)(i) of the regulations.

* * *

This ruling will be immediately effective for any plan not in existence on March 12, 1979.

* * *

The actuarial equivalents selected for the particular defined benefit plan are supposed to have the actuarial gains from unhealthy participants dying before the life expectancy used to offset the actuarial losses from super-healthy participants dying after the life expectancy. The plan document might need to be amended from time to time to adjust the actuarial equivalents if there are too many actuarial gains or too many actuarial losses; however, there should be a procedure in place on how and when the employer will evaluate its actuarial equivalents and update, if needed.

In a defined benefit plan, if an employee's accrued benefit is to be determined as an amount other than an annual benefit commencing at normal retirement age (*i.e.,* a life annuity), then the optional form of benefit shall be the actuarial equivalent of the life annuity benefit.[2]

We need to keep in mind that these are intended to be retirement plans, and the plan documents must clearly define the normal retirement benefit. As explained later in this chapter, if the plan document allows it, then participants might have access to plan benefits earlier than normal retirement age, such as through an in-service distribution, a plan

---

2. Treas. Reg. § 1.411(c)-1(e).

loan or hardship distribution, or through a phased retirement where current working hours are reduced. In addition, the plan can offer incidental benefits to participants, such as certain whole life or term life insurance policies, but the plan must still primarily be for the delivery of retirement benefits[3] (this becomes apparent in the discussion below of minimum required distributions at age 70½, where Congress requires that more benefits are required to be distributed and taxable to the participant while he or she is alive than is expected to be distributed to his or her beneficiaries after death).

That being said, let's get back to the discussion of the normal form of benefits payable at retirement and the other options available under the plan. The term "normal retirement benefit" means the greater of the early retirement benefit under the plan, or the benefit under the plan commencing at normal retirement age.[4] This definition basically applies to defined benefit plans, since a defined benefit plan document defines the benefit, form and age to be distributed; as opposed to a defined contribution plan, which simply pays out the account balance at the time of distribution. The accrued benefit in a defined benefit plan is "expressed in the form of an annual benefit commencing at normal retirement age."[5] Therefore, before complicating matters with the 1984 amendments to the Code that provide rights to the spouses of plan participants, let's just assume that the normal form of benefit is a life annuity. Let's see how a normal retirement benefit of $1000 per month, payable as a life annuity, can be converted to different forms of benefit.

- *Life Annuity:* A life annuity of $1000 per month commencing at age 65 has a greater actuarial present value than a life annuity of $1000 per month starting at age 70 because we expect the 65 year old to receive more actual $1000 payments until he dies than the 70 year old is expected to receive. Therefore, the Present Value of a life annuity starting at age 65 is greater than the Present Value of that same dollar amount of annuity starting at age 70. Pension plans do not take into account the health of any particular plan participant, so, for purposes of pension plans, this statement would be true even if we actually knew that a particular 65 year old has cancer and is expected to die within months and we know that a particular 70 year old runs marathons three times a year—these life expectancies are for the average 65 year old and the average 70 year old.

- *10 Year Certain and Life Thereafter Annuity:* The plan's actuarial equivalents will equate a life annuity to a 10 year C&L annuity. As a general rule of thumb, the premium is about 10%. Therefore, a life annuity of $1000 per month commencing at 65 is roughly the actuarial equivalent of a 10 year C&L annuity of $900 per month commencing at 65, continuing for 10 years, and then for life thereafter if the participant survives the 10 year term. Again, each particular plan would have its particular actuarial equivalence, so a 10 year Certain and Life conversion in one plan might actually be $902.41 per month and in another plan might be $888.67 in another—the 10% premium is a rough estimate.

- *100% Joint and Survivor Annuity:* The plan's actuarial equivalents will equate a life annuity to a 100% J&S annuity. As a general rule of thumb, the premium is about 20%. Therefore, a life annuity of $1000 per month commencing at 65, is roughly the actuarial equivalent of a 100% J&S annuity of $800 per month commencing at age 65, when both lives are 65, continuing for the life of the participant, and then continuing for the life of the beneficiary if he or she survives the participant.

---

3. Treasury Regulations under § 1.401-1(b)
4. IRC § 411(a)(9).
5. IRC § 411(a)(7).

On the other hand, a premium for a 50% J&S is closer to 16%, so a life annuity of $1000 per month commencing at 65, when both lives are 65, is roughly the actuarial equivalent of a 50% J&S annuity of $840 per month commencing at normal retirement date, continuing for the life of the participant, and then continuing for the life of the beneficiary if he or she survives the participant, but reduced to $420 per month for the beneficiary's life (*i.e.,* 50% of what the participant was getting). Please note that the actuarial equivalents will equate a J&S benefit regardless of the age of the second life, but if a 65 year old names her teenage grandchild as the second life, then the equivalent 100% J&S of a $1000 life annuity starting at age 65 might be in the range of $350 per month starting at the participant's age 65, when the second life is 17, and continuing for the participant's life, and if the second life survives the participant, then continuing for the remainder of the beneficiary's life.

- *Lump Sum Distribution:* There is a general "rule of 13" which means that under most acceptable mortality tables and interest rate assumptions, a lump sum is roughly equal to 13 times the annual life annuity commencing at age 65. Therefore, a life annuity of $1000 per month commencing at normal retirement (*i.e.,* $12,000 annually) is roughly the actuarial equivalent of a lump sum payment of $156,000. Similarly, if a 65 year old has an account balance of $156,000 in a defined contribution plan or a statutory hybrid plan, that is roughly the actuarial equivalent of a life annuity of $12,000 per year (*i.e.,* $1000 per month). However, some of the emerging financial theory opines that an individual with 25 or 30 expected years in retirement actually needs $250,000 at 65 for every $10,000 per year. There seems to be a large discrepancy between a plan issuing a check for $156,000 and the current financial theory that the participant actually needs $250,000 to fund that same benefit. Again, in my personal view, one of the reasons that annuities are superior to lump sum distributions.

In a defined benefit plan, if a participant has attained his or her normal retirement age but is still employed and if the distribution of benefits has not commenced as of the end of that year, then the plan sponsor can actually suspend benefit accruals.[6] "For example, if a plan with a normal retirement age of 65 provides a benefit of $400 a month payable at age 65, the same $400 benefit (with no upward adjustment) could be paid to an employee who retires at age 68."[7] However, for purposes of minimum required distributions (as discussed later in this chapter), the benefits not distributed while the individual is still employed beyond normal retirement age must be actuarially increased.

3. A Participant's Choice of Form of Benefit Distribution

Statutory Rules at Various Paragraphs within IRC § 401(a)

Therefore, the employer sponsoring the qualified plan will include any optional forms of benefit that it wants the plan participants to choose from (for example, if the plan does not allow for lump sum distributions, no participant can request such a form of distribution). As stated, in a defined benefit plan, the normal retirement benefit will be in the form of a life annuity, and a specific set of actuarial equivalents will be used to convert

---

6. Treas. Reg. § 1.411(c)-1(f)(1); ERISA § 206(a)(3)
7. Treas. Reg. § 1.411(c)-1(f)(2).

the life annuity into any optional forms of distribution allowed under the plan. In a defined contribution plan, however, the normal form of benefit is the account balance, and although the plan can allow optional forms of distribution, in most cases, if the participant wants some form of annuity or installment payments, then the proceeds can be used to purchase such a financial product through an insurance company, rather than the plan holding onto the account and making annual distributions of the equivalent annuity.

As a qualification rule, "unless the participant otherwise elects, the payment of benefits under the plan to the participant will begin not later than the 60th day after the latest of the close of the plan year in which—

> (A) the date on which the participant attains the earlier of age 65 or the normal retirement age specified under the plan,

> (B) occurs the 10th anniversary of the year in which the participant commenced participation in the plan, or

> (C) the participant terminates his service with the employer."[8]

Therefore, the plan document should contain default procedures for a plan participant who doesn't timely elect his or her benefit option. This requirement protects the individual, even if he or she changes jobs before retirement and even if the employer fired the individual for cause—however, it is generally the former participant's responsibility to notify the plan administrator of current contact information. As discussed in Chapter 16, if the plan terminates, then all benefits owed must be immediately distributed to current and former plan participants.

We have used the term "normal retirement age" several times in this chapter, and while the plan can generally set any reasonable age as the normal retirement age, recent regulations shed light on which ages might be subject to scrutiny:

Treas. Regs. § 1.401(a)-1
Post-ERISA Qualified Plans and Qualified Trusts in General

* * *

(b) Requirements for Pension Plans.

* * *

(2) Normal retirement age.

> (i) General rule. The normal retirement age under a plan must be an age that is not earlier than the earliest age that is reasonably representative of the typical retirement age for the industry in which the covered workforce is employed.

> (ii) Age 62 safe harbor. A normal retirement age under a plan that is age 62 or later is deemed to be not earlier than the earliest age that is reasonably representative of the typical retirement age for the industry in which the covered workforce is employed.

> (iii) Age 55 to age 62. In the case of a normal retirement age that is not earlier than age 55 and is earlier than age 62, whether the age is not earlier than the earliest age that is reasonably representative of the typical re-

---

8. IRC § 401(a)(14).

tirement age for the industry in which the covered workforce is employed is based on all of the relevant facts and circumstances.

(iv) Under age 55. A normal retirement age that is lower than age 55 is presumed to be earlier than the earliest age that is reasonably representative of the typical retirement age for the industry in which the covered workforce is employed, unless the Commissioner determines that under the facts and circumstances the normal retirement age is not earlier than the earliest age that is reasonably representative of the typical retirement age for the industry in which the covered workforce is employed.

(v) Age 50 safe harbor for qualified public safety employees. A normal retirement age under a plan that is age 50 or later is deemed to be not earlier than the earliest age that is reasonably representative of the typical retirement age for the industry in which the covered workforce is employed if substantially all of the participants in the plan are qualified public safety employees (within the meaning of section 72(t)(10)(B)).

* * *

4. Special Distribution Forms for Married Participants

Statutory Rules at IRC §§ 401(a)(11) and 417

In general, distributions from a qualified defined benefit plan or money purchase plan are subject to the joint and survivor annuity requirements. Under these requirements, vested benefits must be paid in the form of a qualified joint and survivor annuity or a qualified pre-retirement survivor annuity. A plan participant may waive this form of benefit only with the consent of his or her spouse (either witnessed by a plan representative or a notary public). If benefits are paid from a profit-sharing plan, a 401(k) plan, or any other individual account plan (other than a money purchase plan) as a single sum distribution with benefits payable in full upon the death of the participant to the participant's surviving spouse, then the defined contribution plan is not subject to the joint and survivor annuity requirements.

Please note that the reason a money purchase plan, which is a defined contribution plan, is lumped in with defined benefit plans goes back to the pre-1974 differentiation in the Internal Revenue Code between a "pension" plan, which includes a money purchase plan, and a profit sharing plan—even after the enactment of ERISA, which formally divided the world of qualified plans into defined benefit plans and defined contribution plans, the pre-ERISA concept of "pension" plan still lingers for several statutory requirements, including this requirement for distributions to married plan participants.[9]

In 1984, Congress took note than many married plan participants were selecting a lump sum distribution, when offered, and many times without their spouses even knowing that the retirement money was distributed. Therefore, to provide rights under ERISA to the spouses of the plan participants, Congress added the following qualification rules to IRC §401(a)(11), which are then explained in further detail in IRC §417:

---

9. Technically, IRC §401(a)(11)(B)(ii) indicates that these rules apply to all defined contribution plans subject to the minimum funding requirements of IRC §412, and when you look at IRC §412, you see that the contributions dictated under a money purchase plan document are mandatory, and subject to a penalty tax if not deposited properly and timely.

Qualified Pre-Retirement Survivor Annuity (QPSA): This is for a married participant who dies before retirement. If a participant in a plan subject to these rules dies leaving a surviving spouse (as determined in accordance with state law), then his surviving spouse must be able to receive at least 50% of the participant's accrued benefit at date of death. It is payable at the earliest date that the participant would have been able to receive his accrued benefit. The plan could provide more, but it has to provide at least a 50% death benefit to surviving spouses for participants who are married upon their pre-retirement death.

Qualified Joint & Survivor Annuity (QJSA): This is for a married participant who dies after reaching his normal retirement date. If a participant in a plan subject to these rules has a spouse (as determined in accordance with state law) on his benefit commencement date, then the normal form of benefit must be a X% Joint and Survivor Annuity where X is any percentage between 50% and 100% and where the spouse is automatically the second life. The rules recently became more complicated, and now, a plan must include a qualified optional survivor annuity (QOSA), which basically demands that a plan always offer a 75% Joint and Survivor Annuity where the spouse is automatically the second life, regardless of the choices of X% that otherwise satisfy the QJSA requirements.[10]

To make it easier on the plan administrator, the plan document can provide that benefits will not be payable to the surviving spouse of the participant unless the participant and such spouse had been married throughout the 1-year period ending on the earlier of the participant's annuity starting date or the date of the participant's death.[11] If the participant says he or she is single, then the plan administrator is generally not liable unless it has knowledge otherwise.

Notwithstanding the spousal consent rules of a QPSA and QJSA, if the present value of accrued benefits in a defined benefit plan, or the account balance in a money purchase plan, is less than $5,000, then in order to simplify the plan's operation for the plan administrator, the plan may simply "cash out" the participant and distribute the plan benefits in the form of a single lump sum, regardless of the participant's marital status and irrelevant of the optional form of distribution the participant would actually prefer.[12] There are complicated rules for the interest rates and mortality tables used to determine whether the present value of benefits in a defined benefit plan meets this $5,000 di minimis threshold (known as the GATT rates).

Here is a summary of some of the other rules relating to the participant's choice in timing and form of distribution:

- Often times, a defined benefit plan will offer the participants optional forms of distribution in addition to the life annuity or Qualified Joint and Survivor Annuity. The participant is expected to irrevocably choose which form of payment he or she desires before the first distribution is made. The single lump sum usually looks, to the untrained eye, as the most valuable benefit. This is not always the case, and sometimes a purposeful subsidy offered by the employer in another form is overlooked. Therefore, the participant must receive a statement that shows the normal form of benefit, and compares the relative values of each optional form when compared to the normal form. Although defined benefit plans and the available

10. The Pension Protection Act of 2006 added IRC §417(g), which contains this recent additional requirement.

11. IRC §401(a)(11)(D).

12. IRC §417(e).

optional forms of benefit can get complicated, the onus is upon the plan administrator to draft an explanation that is "written in a manner calculated to be understood by the average participant." The rules generally require that the qualified joint and survivor annuity must always be the most valuable form of benefit (*i.e.*, the plan can provide subsidies to the QJSA only, or provide the most valuable subsidy to the QJSA if it also provides subsidies to other optional forms). Again, the purpose of the disclosure of relative values is to show that while a lump sum option might look appealing, it might actually be worth say 90% of the relative value of the QJSA if the plan provides a 10% subsidy to the QJSA.

- A plan must provide written notices to participants and their spouses explaining in full detail what qualified survivor benefits are, the rights of the spouse, and how an election made by the participant and signed by the spouse for an alternate form of benefit divests the spouse of all of his or her rights. Statutorily, there is a 180 day election period (between distribution of the required notice and the commencement of benefits) to give the spouse ample time to understand the notice and to seek personal advice from a professional. However, the period may be shortened if the spouse also consents that he or she is fully aware of all rights.

- It is important for the plan to have appropriate forms and procedures to allow a participant to name a beneficiary to receive plan benefits should he or she die. The participant must also be able to subsequently rescind or revise any earlier elections. If the participant is married, then the spouse is automatically deemed to be the beneficiary, and if another individual is to be named, then the spouse must consent in writing to waive the qualified preretirement survivor annuity rights. There are differences, however, between a normal beneficiary designation form for purposes of death before starting to receive benefits and a special beneficiary designation form for minimum required distributions that must start at age 70½ (discussed in further detail below).

- There is no statutory requirement, but it is a good idea for the plan administrator to provide a beneficiary designation form to an employee upon eligibility to participate in the qualified plan. Therefore, if the individual dies while still an employee, and the plan document provides any sort of pre-retirement death benefit, the plan can comply with the participant's wishes. The brief excerpt from the following U.S. Supreme Court opinion shows that Louisiana's state law that automatically revokes any beneficiary form that names the ex-spouse was preempted by ERISA (and the qualified plan rules under the Code) — thus, holding that the participant's neglect in not affirmatively revoking his beneficiary election form upon his divorce required the plan to consider his first wife as the plan beneficiary and not his second wife who survived him upon his death. Therefore, plan administrators might want to remind participants upon notice of marriage or divorce that they can and should revoke existing beneficiary designation forms and submit a new form.

Boggs v. Boggs

520 U.S. 833 (1997)

Justice Breyer dissented and filed opinion in which Justice O'Connor joined, and in which Chief Justice Rehnquist and Justice Ginsburg joined in part.

We consider whether the Employee Retirement Income Security Act of 1974 (ERISA), 88 Stat. 832, as amended, 29 U.S.C. § 1001 et seq. , pre-empts a state law allowing a nonparticipant*836 spouse to transfer by testamentary instrument an interest in undistributed pension plan benefits. Given the pervasive significance of pension plans in the national economy, the congressional mandate for their uniform and comprehensive regulation, and the fundamental importance of community property law in defining the marital partnership in a number of States, the question is of undoubted importance. We hold that ERISA pre-empts the state law.

I

Isaac Boggs worked for South Central Bell from 1949 until his retirement in 1985. Isaac and Dorothy, his first wife, were married when he began working for the company, and they remained husband and wife until Dorothy's death in 1979. They had three sons. Within a year of Dorothy's death, Isaac married Sandra, and they remained married until his death in 1989.

Upon retirement, Isaac received various benefits from his employer's retirement plans. One was a lump-sum distribution from the Bell System Savings Plan for Salaried Employees (Savings Plan) of $151,628.94, which he rolled over into an Individual Retirement Account (IRA). He made no withdrawals and the account was worth $180,778.05 when he died. He also received 96 shares of AT & T stock from the Bell South Employee Stock Ownership Plan (ESOP). In addition, Isaac enjoyed a monthly annuity payment during his retirement of $1,777.67 from the Bell South Service Retirement Program.

[1] The instant dispute over ownership of the benefits is between Sandra (the surviving wife) and the sons of the first marriage. The sons' claim to a portion of the benefits is based on Dorothy's will. Dorothy bequeathed to Isaac one-third of her estate, and a lifetime usufruct in the remaining two-thirds. A lifetime usufruct is the rough equivalent of a common-law life estate. See La. Civ.Code Ann., Art. 535 (West 1980). She bequeathed to her sons the naked ownership*837 in the remaining two-thirds, subject to Isaac's usufruct. All agree that, absent pre-emption, Louisiana law controls and that under it Dorothy's will would dispose of her community property interest in Isaac's undistributed pension plan benefits. A Louisiana state court, in a 1980 order entitled "Judgment of Possession," ascribed to Dorothy's estate a community property interest in Isaac's Savings Plan account valued at the time at $21,194.29.

Sandra contests the validity of Dorothy's 1980 testamentary transfer, basing her claim to those benefits on her interest under Isaac's will and 29 U.S.C. § 1055. Isaac bequeathed to Sandra outright certain real property including the family home. His will also gave Sandra a lifetime usufruct in the remainder of his estate, with the naked ownership interest being held by the sons. Sandra argues that the sons' competing claim, **1759 since it is based on Dorothy's 1980 purported testamentary transfer of her community property interest in undistributed pension plan benefits, is pre-empted by ERISA. The Bell South Service Retirement Program monthly annuity is now paid to Sandra as the surviving spouse.

After Isaac's death, two of the sons filed an action in state court requesting the appointment of an expert to compute the percentage of the retirement benefits they would be entitled to as a result of Dorothy's attempted testamentary transfer. They further sought a judgment awarding them a portion of: the IRA; the ESOP shares of AT & T stock; the monthly annuity payments received by Isaac during his retirement; and Sandra's survivor annuity payments, both received and payable.

In response, Sandra Boggs filed a complaint in the United States District Court for the Eastern District of Louisiana, seeking a declaratory judgment that ERISA pre-empts the application of Louisiana's community property and succession laws to the extent they recognize the sons' claim to an interest in the disputed retirement benefits. The District *838 Court granted summary judgment against Sandra Boggs. 849 F.Supp. 462 (1994). It found that, under Louisiana community property law, Dorothy had an ownership interest in her husband's pension plan benefits built up during their marriage. The creation of this interest, the court explained, does not violate 29 U.S.C. § 1056(d)(1), which prohibits pension plan benefits from being "assigned" or "alienated," since Congress did not intend to alter traditional familial and support obligations. In the court's view, there was no assignment or alienation because Dorothy's rights in the benefits were acquired by operation of community property law and not by transfer from Isaac. Turning to Dorothy's testamentary transfer, the court found it effective because "[ERISA] does not display any particular interest in preserving maximum benefits to any particular beneficiary." 849 F.Supp., at 465.

A divided panel of the Fifth Circuit affirmed. 82 F.3d 90 (1996). The court stressed that Louisiana law affects only what a plan participant may do with his or her benefits after they are received and not the relationship between the pension plan administrator and the plan beneficiary. Id., at 96. For the reasons given by the District Court, it found ERISA's pension plan anti-alienation provision, § 1056(d)(1), inapplicable to Louisiana's creation of Dorothy Boggs' community property interest in the pension plan benefits. It concluded that the transfer of the interest from Dorothy to her sons was not a prohibited assignment or alienation, as this transfer was "two steps removed from the disbursement of benefits." Id., at 97.

* * *

[4] [5] [6] This case lies at the intersection of ERISA pension law and state community property law. None can dispute the central role community property laws play in the nine community property States. It is more than a property regime. It is a commitment to the equality of husband and wife and reflects the real partnership inherent in the marital relationship. State community property laws, many of ancient lineage, "must have continued to exist through such lengths of time because of their manifold excellences and are not lightly to be abrogated or tossed aside." 1 W. de Funiak, Principles of Community Property 11 (1943). The community property regime in Louisiana dates from 1808 when the territorial legislature of Orleans drafted a civil code which adopted Spanish principles of community property. Id., at 85–89. Louisiana's community property laws, and the community property regimes enacted in other States, implement policies and values lying within the traditional domain of the States. These considerations inform our pre-emption analysis. See Hisquierdo v. Hisquierdo, 439 U.S. 572, 581, 99 S.Ct. 802, 808, 59 L.Ed.2d 1 (1979).

The nine community property States have some 80 million residents, with perhaps $1 trillion in retirement plans. See Brief for Estate Planning, Trust and Probate Law Section of the State Bar of California as Amicus Curiae 1. This case involves a community property claim, but our ruling will affect as well the right to make claims or assert interests based on the law of any State, whether or not it recognizes community property. Our ruling must be consistent with the congressional scheme to assure the security of plan participants and their families in every State. In enacting ERISA, Congress noted the importance of pension plans in its findings and declaration of policy, explaining:

"[T]he growth in size, scope, and numbers of employee benefit plans in recent years has been rapid and substantial; … the continued well-being and security of millions of employees and their dependents are directly affected by these plans; … they are affected with a national public interest [and] they have become an important factor affecting the stability of employment and the successful development of industrial relations.…" 29 U.S.C. § 1001(a).

ERISA is an intricate, comprehensive statute. Its federal regulatory scheme governs employee benefit plans, which include both pension and welfare plans. All employee benefit plans must conform to various reporting, disclosure, and fiduciary requirements, see §§ 1021–1031, 1101–1114, while pension plans must also comply with participation, vesting, and funding requirements, see §§ 1051–1086. The surviving spouse annuity and QDRO provisions, central to the dispute here, are part of the statute's mandatory participation and vesting requirements. These provisions provide detailed protections to spouses of plan participants which, in some cases, exceed what their rights would be were community property law the sole measure.

ERISA's express pre-emption clause states that the Act "shall supersede any and all State laws insofar as they may now or hereafter relate to any employee benefit plan.…" § 1144(a). We can begin, and in this case end, the analysis by simply asking if state law conflicts with the provisions of ERISA or operates to frustrate its objects. We hold that there is a conflict, which suffices to resolve the case. We need not inquire whether the statutory phrase "relate to" provides further and additional support for the pre-emption claim. Nor need we consider the applicability of field pre-emption, see Fidelity Fed. Sav. & Loan Assn. v. De la Cuesta, 458 U.S. 141, 153, 102 S.Ct. 3014, 3022, 73 L.Ed.2d 664 (1982).

We first address the survivor's annuity and then turn to the other pension benefits.

III

[7] Sandra Boggs, as we have observed, asserts that federal law pre-empts and supersedes state law and requires the surviving spouse annuity to be paid to her as the sole beneficiary. We agree.

The annuity at issue is a qualified joint and survivor annuity mandated by ERISA. Section 1055(a) provides:

"Each pension plan to which this section applies shall provide that—

"(1) in the case of a vested participant who does not die before the annuity starting date, the accrued benefit payable to such participant shall be provided in the form of a qualified joint and survivor annuity."

ERISA requires that every qualified joint and survivor annuity include an annuity payable to a nonparticipant surviving spouse. The survivor's annuity may not be less than 50% of the amount of the annuity which is payable during the joint lives of the participant and spouse. § 1055(d)(1). Provision of the survivor's annuity may not be waived by the participant, absent certain limited circumstances, unless the spouse consents in writing to the designation of another beneficiary, which designation also cannot be changed without further spousal consent, witnessed by a plan representative or notary public. § 1055(c)(2). Sandra Boggs, as the surviving spouse, is entitled to a survivor's annuity under these provisions. She has not waived her right to the survivor's annuity, let alone consented to having the sons designated as the beneficiaries.

Respondents say their state-law claims are consistent with these provisions. Their claims, they argue, affect only the disposition of plan proceeds after they have been disbursed by the Bell South Service Retirement Program, and thus nothing is required of the plan. ERISA's concern for securing national uniformity in the administration of employee benefit plans, in their view, is not implicated. They argue Sandra's community property obligations, after she receives the survivor annuity payments, "fai[l] to implicate the regulatory concerns of ERISA." Fort Halifax Packing Co. v. Coyne, 482 U.S. 1, 15, 107 S.Ct. 2211, 2219, 96 L.Ed.2d 1 (1987).

[8] We disagree. The statutory object of the qualified joint and survivor annuity provisions, along with the rest of § 1055, is to ensure a stream of income to surviving spouses. Section 1055 mandates a survivor's annuity not only where a participant dies after the annuity starting date but also guarantees one if the participant dies before then. See §§ 1055(a)(2), (e). These provisions, enacted as part of the Retirement Equity Act of 1984 (REA), Pub. L. 98-397, 98 Stat. 1426, enlarged ERISA's protection of surviving spouses in significant respects. Before REA, ERISA only required that pension plans, if they provided for the payment of benefits in the form of an annuity, offer a qualified joint and survivor annuity as an option entirely within a participant's discretion. 29 U.S.C. §§ 1055(a), (e) (1982 ed.). REA modified ERISA to permit participants to designate a beneficiary for the survivor's annuity, other than the nonparticipant spouse, only when the spouse agrees. § 1055(c)(2). Congress' concern for surviving spouses is also evident from the expansive coverage of § 1055, as amended by REA. Section 1055's requirements, as a general matter, apply to all "individual account plans" and "defined benefit plans." § 1055(b)(1). The terms are defined, for § 1055 purposes, so that all pension plans fall within those two categories. See § 1002(35). While some individual account plans escape § 1055's surviving spouse annuity requirements under certain conditions, Congress still protects the interests of the surviving spouse by requiring those plans to pay the spouse the nonforfeitable accrued benefits, reduced by certain security interests, in a lump-sum payment. § 1055(b)(1)(C).

ERISA's solicitude for the economic security of surviving spouses would be undermined by allowing a predeceasing spouse's heirs and legatees to have a community property interest in the survivor's annuity. Even a plan participant cannot defeat a nonparticipant surviving spouse's statutory entitlement to an annuity. It would be odd, to say the least, if Congress permitted a predeceasing nonparticipant spouse *844 to do so. Nothing in the language of ERISA supports concluding that Congress made such an inexplicable decision. Testamentary transfers could reduce a surviving spouse's guaranteed annuity below the minimum set by ERISA (defined as 50% of the annuity payable during the joint lives of the participant and spouse). In this case, Sandra's annuity would be reduced by approximately 20%, according to the calculations contained in the sons' state-court filings. There is no reason why testamentary transfers could not reduce a survivor's annuity by an even greater amount. Perhaps even more troubling, the recipient of the testamentary transfer need not be a family member. For instance, a surviving spouse's § 1055 annuity might be substantially reduced so that funds could be diverted to support an unrelated stranger.

[9] [10] In the face of this direct clash between state law and the provisions and objectives of ERISA, the state law cannot stand. Conventional conflict pre-emption principles require pre-emption "where compliance with both federal and state regulations is a physical impossibility, ... or where state law stands as an obstacle to the accomplishment and execution of the full purposes and objectives of Congress." Gade v. National Solid Wastes Management Assn., 505 U.S. 88, 98, 112 S.Ct. 2374, 2383, 120 L.Ed.2d 73 (1992) (internal quotation marks and citation omitted). It would undermine the purpose of ERISA's mandated survivor's annuity to allow Dorothy, the predeceasing spouse, by her testamentary transfer to defeat in part Sandra's entitlement to the annuity § 1055 guarantees her as the surviving spouse. This cannot be. States are not free to change ERISA's structure and balance.

Louisiana law, to the extent it provides the sons with a right to a portion of Sandra Boggs' § 1055 survivor's annuity, is pre-empted.

* * *

The axis around which ERISA's protections revolve is the concepts of participant and beneficiary. When Congress has chosen to depart from this framework, it has done so in a careful and limited manner. Respondents' claims, if allowed to succeed, would depart from this framework, upsetting the deliberate balance central to ERISA. It does not matter that respondents have sought to enforce their rights only after the retirement benefits have been distributed since their asserted rights are based on the theory that they had an interest in the undistributed pension plan benefits. Their state-law claims are pre-empted. The judgment of the Fifth Circuit is

Reversed.

---

5. Early Retirement Benefits and Subsidies Available under a Qualified Defined Benefit Plan

One advantage of defined benefit plan is that the sponsoring employer can give credit for past years of service worked before the plan was adopted, with a predecessor employer or with an affiliated employer. Defined benefit plans can also allow a participant to retire before his or her normal retirement age and start receiving retirement benefits at an earlier age, thus allowing certain older members of the work force to voluntarily leave.

There are two main types of Early Retirement subsidies:

- Assume (for actuarial equivalent purposes only) that the annuity payable at a younger age is the same benefit payable at retirement age (*i.e.*, if $1000 payable as a life annuity payable at 65 is actuarially equivalent to $913 payable as a life annuity payable at age 60, then the Early Retirement subsidy may allow that individual to receive $1000 payable as a life annuity starting at 60).

- Assume that the individual is credited for future years of service he would likely have worked if there was no early retirement subsidy (*i.e.*, if the plan formula provides a benefit of 1% of average compensation for each year of service, and a particular individual has 23 years at age 55 (AB = 23% of compensation) but would have 33 years if he stayed until age 65 (AB = 33% of compensation), then the early retirement subsidy may allow the individual at age 55 to begin receiving a 33% of compensation benefit for the remainder of his life.

All early retirement benefits and subsidies must be tested under IRC § 401(a)(4) and cannot discriminate in favor of the Highly Compensated Employees.

6. Elimination of Optional Forms of Benefits or Early Retirement Benefits from a Defined Benefit Plan

As noted in Chapter 7, under IRC § 411(d)(6), a plan cannot be amended to reduce or eliminate a benefit already accrued.

As to optional forms of benefits, since defined benefit plans can get quite cumbersome with optional forms of benefits that apply to only certain groups of employees, especially after the employer has amended the plan to account for serial corporate mergers and acquisitions, recent Treasury Regulations provided guidance on what optional forms of benefits are actually protected under IRC § 411(d)(6), but which, under appropriate circumstances can actually be eliminated to make the plan document less cumbersome to administer (either several optional forms are redundant with each other and the elimination of some optional forms have only a de minimis impact on plan participants; or the plan is amended to eliminate all non-core types of optional forms of benefits; or certain optional forms have never been utilized).

As to early retirement benefits, once a participant has met the age, service, and other requirements to be eligible for early retirement, then that benefit can not be eliminated.

Here is a brief section from the regulations:

Treas. Regs. § 1.411(d)-3. Section 411(d)(6) protected benefits.

* * *

(g) Definitions and use of terms.

* * *

(6) Definitions of types of section 411(d)(6)(B) protected benefits.

(i) Early retirement benefit. The term early retirement benefit means the right, under the terms of a plan, to commence distribution of a retirement-type benefit at a particular date after severance from employment with the employer and before normal retirement age. Different early retirement benefits result from differences in terms relating to timing.

(ii)   (A) In general. The term optional form of benefit means a distribution alternative (including the normal form of benefit) that is available under the plan with respect to an accrued benefit or a distribution alternative with respect to a retirement-type benefit. Different optional forms of benefit exist if a distribution alternative is not payable on substantially the same terms as another distribution alternative. The relevant terms include all terms affecting the value of the optional form, such as the method of benefit calculation and the actuarial factors or assumptions used to determine the amount distributed. Thus, for example, different optional forms of benefit may result from differences in terms relating to the payment schedule, timing, commencement, medium of distribution (e.g., in cash or in kind), election rights, differences in eligibility requirements, or the portion of the benefit to which the distribution alternative applies. Likewise, differences in the normal retirement ages of employees or in the form in which the accrued benefit of employees is payable at normal retirement age under a plan are taken into account in determining whether a distribution alternative constitutes one or more optional forms of benefit.

(B) Death benefits. If a death benefit is payable after the annuity starting date for a specific optional form of benefit and the same death benefit would not be provided if another optional form of benefit were elected by a participant, then that death benefit is part of the specific optional form of benefit and is thus protected under section 411(d)(6). A death benefit is not treated as part of a specific optional form of benefit merely because the same benefit is not provided to a participant who has received his or her entire accrued benefit prior to death. For example, a $5,000 death benefit that is payable to all participants except any participant who has received his or her accrued benefit in a single-sum distribution is not part of a specific optional form of benefit.

(iii) Retirement-type benefit. The term retirement-type benefit means—

(A) The payment of a distribution alternative with respect to an accrued benefit; or

(B) The payment of any other benefit under a defined benefit plan (including a QSUPP as defined in § 1.401(a)(4)-12) that is permitted to be in a qualified pension plan, continues after retirement, and is not an ancillary benefit.

(iv) Retirement-type subsidy. The term retirement-type subsidy means the excess, if any, of the actuarial present value of a retirement-type benefit over the actuarial present value of the accrued benefit commencing at normal retirement age or at actual commencement date, if later, with both such actuarial present values determined as of the date the retirement-type benefit commences. Examples of retirement-type subsidies include a subsidized early retirement benefit and a subsidized qualified joint and survivor annuity.

(v) Subsidized early retirement benefit or early retirement subsidy. The terms subsidized early retirement benefit or early retirement subsidy mean the right, under the terms of a plan, to commence distribution of a retirement-type benefit at a particular date after severance from employment with the employer and before normal retirement age where the actuarial present value of the optional forms of benefit available to the participant under the plan at that annuity starting date exceeds the actuarial present value of the accrued benefit commencing at normal retirement age (with such actuarial present values determined as of the annuity starting date). Thus, an early retirement subsidy is an early retirement benefit that provides a retirement-type subsidy.

B. When Participants Can Receive Distributions

1. Normal and Early Retirement Benefits

Generally, an employee who is promised benefits through a qualified retirement plan can only receive the benefits he or she has accrued upon attaining the plan's "Normal Retirement Age" or "Early Retirement Age," and then only if he or she actually terminates employment with the employer and retires. Normal retirement age means "the earlier of the time a plan participant attains normal retirement age under the plan, or the later of the time a plan participant attains age 65 or the 5th anniversary of the time a plan participant commenced participation in the plan."[13] Therefore, the plan document can name any age as the normal retirement age, but due to concerns over age discrimination, the plan's normal retirement age cannot be mandatory at age 65, and in order to allow the hiring of individuals over age 60, must be at least 5 years after any individual's date of hire.

There is no formal definition of early retirement date, and can be whatever is defined in the plan (either on a permanent basis or through a temporary early retirement window). The only requirement is that "in the case of a plan which provides for the payment of an early retirement benefit, ... a participant who satisfied the service requirements for such early retirement benefit, but separated from the service (with any nonforfeitable right to an accrued benefit) before satisfying the age requirement for such early retirement benefit, is entitled upon satisfaction of such age requirement to receive a benefit not less than the benefit to which he would be entitled at the normal retirement age, actuarially, reduced under regulations prescribed by the Secretary."[14] Please note that early retirement windows are sometimes a good way for employers to trim the workforce of some of the older employees without actually violating any of the age discrimination laws since the employee who takes advantage of the early retirement window is doing so on a voluntary basis.

Unless the plan document allows for earlier distributions, the individual who terminates employment might need to wait until attaining the plan's normal retirement age to receive a distribution of plan benefits (a defined contribution plan generally allows a distribution of the participant's account balance at any age after termination of employment whereas a defined benefit plan that does not offer a lump sum distribution generally postpones distributions until the individual attains the normal retirement age—which is why defined contribution plans are seen as being more portable).

In addition, if the plan terminates, then all participants with vested accrued benefits must be paid out as soon as administratively feasible after the termination has been approved. Although not required, plans might also allow for distributions upon the participant's death or disability.

2. In-service Distributions

Congress is weary of "leakage," where individuals while still employed and earning a salary are receiving retirement benefits from a qualified retirement plan. However, they do allow in-service distributions under the following circumstances:

---

13. IRC §411(a)(8).
14. IRC §401(a)(14), flush language after subparagraph C.

Pension Plans (i.e., Money Purchase Plans and Defined Benefit Plans): For distributions in plan years beginning after 2006, qualified pension plans are allowed to make in-service distributions to employees who have reached age 62 and who have not separated from employment at the time of the distribution.[15] The current trend is for older workers to "partially retire" (*i.e,* working reduced hours either to enhance their retirement pensions, to supplement their current income, or simply to continue adding utility to themselves and society as they enjoy greater life expectancies). Proposals are floating around Congress which may define what "working" means, and which might allow certain distributions from pension plans while an older employee is working reduced hours. The IRS had published Proposed Regulations in 2004 that would have allowed bona fide phased retirement programs where the amount of allowable distribution would be tied to the reduction in work hours, but the Proposed Regulations have not been published in final form, and there does not seem to be too much traction with the ideas set forth in the proposed regulations.

Profit Sharing Plan: A profit sharing plan can allow distributions after a fixed period of years or other stated event. The fixed period of time must be at least 5 years, and the distribution must have been plan assets for at least 2 years.[16]

401(k) plan: The accounts in a "traditional" 401(k) plan derived from employer contributions pursuant to the participants' elective salary deferrals "(i) may not be distributable to participants or other beneficiaries earlier than (I) severance from employment, death, or disability, (II) an event described in paragraph (10), (III) in the case of a profit-sharing or stock bonus plan, the attainment of age 59½, (IV) in the case of contributions to a profit-sharing or stock bonus plan to which section 402(e)(3) applies, upon hardship of the employee, or (V) in the case of a qualified reservist distribution (as defined in section 72(t)(2)(G)(iii)), the date on which a period referred to in subclause (III) of such section begins, and (ii) will not be distributable merely by reason of the completion of a stated period of participation or the lapse of a fixed number of years."[17] Additionally, distributions may be made to HCEs to correct a failed ADP test (even though such distributions are not voluntarily requested by the participant),[18] and now that 401(k) plans can allow eligible automatic enrollment programs, participants can make an affirmative election to cease the automatic salary deferrals and receive the small amounts already deferred within 90 days.[19] Hardship distributions will be explained in detail shortly.

Roth 401(k) plan: The accounts in a Roth 401(k) plan (technically called a "Qualified Roth contribution program") derived from designated employee contributions can be distributed at any time. However, as described below, the distributions will be subject to income taxation if not a qualified distribution (*i.e.,* held in the plan for at least 5 years and after the individual has attained age 59½).[20]

---

15. IRC § 401(a)(36).
16. See Rev. Rul. 73-553.
17. IRC § 401(k)(2)(B)(i).
18. IRC § 401(k)(8).
19. IRC § 414(w)(2).
20. IRC § 402A(d)(2).

3. Qualified Domestic Relations Orders and Distributions to an Ex-spouse or Child Pursuant to Divorce

Statutory Definition at IRC § 414(p).

One of the most important advantages of a qualified retirement plan for an employee is that benefits may generally not be assigned or alienated (*i.e.*, creditors of that individual cannot seize the retirement benefits promised to the individual employee and funded and delivered through a qualified retirement plan).[21] One major exception is for a "Qualified Domestic Relations Order."

A domestic relations order is merely a valid legal document that is certified in an appropriate state court to divide marital property between former spouses upon divorce. A common marital property to be divided might be the benefits one of the spouses has accrued in his or her employer's qualified retirement plan. However, the benefits of a qualified retirement plan cannot be assigned or alienated to a former spouse (or to children) pursuant to any domestic relations order. Benefits can only be alienated if the domestic relations order meets the statutory rules and is determined, by the plan administrator, to be a Qualified Domestic Relations Order.

A QDRO must clearly specify:

- the names, addresses, and social security numbers of the parties;
- the amount and manner that benefits will be paid to the alternate payee(s);
- the number of payments or term of such distributions to alternate payee(s); and
- the exact name of the plan to which the QDRO applies (*i.e.*, it cannot be a general statement like "any plan in which the husband participated").

On the other hand, a QDRO cannot:

- require the plan to provide any type or form of benefit, or any option, not otherwise provided by the plan;
- order the plan to pay increased benefits to the alternate payee(s); or
- order the plan to pay a portion of the benefits to this alternate payee(s) which are supposed to be paid to other alternate payee(s) under a previously submitted QDRO by the participant.

An "alternate payee" is the non-participant party who, upon providing a valid QDRO to the plan administrator, is entitled to receive a portion of the participant's benefits (an alternate payee can be a spouse, a former spouse, or children of the marriage). A QDRO can allow the alternate payee to start receiving benefits at the earliest retirement age that the participant could have received retirement benefits from the plan if he or she had actually terminated employment, even though in reality the participant spouse is still employed.

Plans are required to have a QDRO determination procedure which clearly informs all parties what they will look for in a DRO to determine whether it is a QDRO, the time frame in which it will make such determination, and how either party can dispute the plan administrator's determination. Once a document purporting to be a QDRO is received by the plan administrator, the administrator shall promptly notify the participant

---

21. IRC § 401(a)(13).

and each alternate payee of the receipt of the order and the plan's procedures for determining the qualified status of domestic relations orders, and within a reasonable period after receipt, the plan administrator shall determine whether such order is a qualified domestic relations order and notify the participant and each alternate payee of its determination. Once a legal document is accepted by the Plan Administrator as a valid QDRO, then the alternate payee enjoys all of the distribution and communication rights that all other plan participants enjoy, and bears the same timing, procedure and notification requirements that all plan participants bear. Additionally, for purposes of litigation, an alternate payee generally has standing to sue (as discussed in Chapter 14).

If a plan administrator is on notice that a QDRO might be forthcoming, then there is a statutory 18 month period where the plan administrator must act in good faith and segregate any benefits which might become distributable to an alternate payee should a valid QDRO be communicated. For example, if a participant presents a DRO on April 1 of year 1, but for some reason the Plan Administrator determines that the DRO is not qualified under the statutory rules on May 1 of year 1, then for 18 months, until October 31 of year 2, the plan administrator must act in "good faith" where the errors are expected to be corrected, and where a new document which will comply with the QDRO rules is expected to be submitted by the participant. In this example, if the participant spouse is eligible for a distribution in the 18 month period, then an appropriate portion should be put in a segregated account on behalf of the potential alternate payee—if a revised QDRO is submitted within 18 months then the segregated account can be paid to the alternate payee and if no revised QDRO is submitted then the segregated account can be paid to the participant.

There are two basic theories for dividing the participant's benefits and paying them out to an alternate payee(s):

- Shared interest: the alternate payee only gets a specified portion of the participant's benefits for each and every payment he receives from the plan, and

- Separate interest: the alternate payee becomes a quasi-participant of the plan, and is entitled to choose how and when she receives her share of benefits based on the options available under the plan.

Please note that from personal experience, I find that family lawyers who are extremely competent at divorcing a married couple are often times incompetent in dividing marital property through QDROs when a qualified retirement plan is involved. I have therefore spent a considerable amount of time writing articles on QDROs and giving speeches to that targeted group of professionals. The worst thing for all is for the plan administrator to deny a QDRO as being ambiguous (under the statutory rules), and then forcing the family law attorney to get the now-divorced couple back at the bargaining table simply to divide the qualified retirement plan benefits.

4. Hardship Distributions from a 401(k) Plan

Statutory Definition at IRC § 401(k)(2)(B)

Congress does not want employer provided 401(k) retirement plans to be thought of by the participants as their high-powered personal savings account—deferring portions of salary until needed, and then withdrawing whatever they want whenever they want it. Therefore, there are only limited circumstances as to when a current employee can withdraw amounts from the 401(k) plan that were deferred from their salary.

A distribution is made on account of hardship only if the distribution both is made on account of an immediate and heavy financial need of the employee and is limited to the amount necessary to satisfy the financial need. The determination of the existence of an immediate and heavy financial need and of the amount necessary to meet the need must be made in accordance with nondiscriminatory and objective standards set forth in the plan. An immediate and heavy financial need generally may be treated as not capable of being relieved from other resources that are reasonably available to the employee if the employer relies upon the employee's representation (made in writing or such other form as may be prescribed by the Commissioner), unless the employer has actual knowledge to the contrary.

Treas. Regs. § 1.401(k)-1
Ceretain Cash or Deferred Arrangements

* * *

(d) Distribution Limitation.

* * *

(3) Rules applicable to hardship distributions.

(i) Distribution must be on account of hardship. A distribution is treated as made after an employee's hardship for purposes of paragraph (d)(1)(ii) of this section if and only if it is made on account of the hardship. For purposes of this rule, a distribution is made on account of hardship only if the distribution both is made on account of an immediate and heavy financial need of the employee and is necessary to satisfy the financial need. The determination of the existence of an immediate and heavy financial need and of the amount necessary to meet the need must be made in accordance with nondiscriminatory and objective standards set forth in the plan.

(ii) Limit on maximum distributable amount.

(A) General rule. A distribution on account of hardship must be limited to the maximum distributable amount. The maximum distributable amount is equal to the employee's total elective contributions as of the date of distribution, reduced by the amount of previous distributions of elective contributions. Thus, the maximum distributable amount does not include earnings, QNECs or QMACs, unless grandfathered under paragraph (d)(3)(ii)(B) of this section.

* * *

(iii) Immediate and heavy financial need.

(A) In general. Whether an employee has an immediate and heavy financial need is to be determined based on all the relevant facts and circumstances. Generally, for example, the need to pay the funeral expenses of a family member would constitute an immediate and heavy financial need. A distribution made to an employee for the purchase of a boat or television would generally not constitute a distribution made on account of an immediate and heavy financial need. A financial need may be immediate and heavy even if it was reasonably foreseeable or voluntarily incurred by the employee.

(B) Deemed immediate and heavy financial need. A distribution is deemed to be on account of an immediate and heavy financial need of the employee if the distribution is for—

(1) Expenses for (or necessary to obtain) medical care that would be deductible under section 213(d) (determined without regard to whether the expenses exceed 7.5% of adjusted gross income);

(2) Costs directly related to the purchase of a principal residence for the employee (excluding mortgage payments);

(3) Payment of tuition, related educational fees, and room and board expenses, for up to the next 12 months of post-secondary education for the employee, or the employee's spouse, children, or dependents (as defined in section 152, and, for taxable years beginning on or after January 1, 2005, without regard to section 152(b)(1), (b)(2) and (d)(1)(B));

(4) Payments necessary to prevent the eviction of the employee from the employee's principal residence or foreclosure on the mortgage on that residence;

(5) Payments for burial or funeral expenses for the employee's deceased parent, spouse, children or dependents (as defined in section 152, and, for taxable years beginning on or after January 1, 2005, without regard to section 152(d)(1)(B)); or

(6) Expenses for the repair of damage to the employee's principal residence that would qualify for the casualty deduction under section 165 (determined without regard to whether the loss exceeds 10% of adjusted gross income).

(iv) Distribution necessary to satisfy financial need.

(A) Distribution may not exceed amount of need. A distribution is treated as necessary to satisfy an immediate and heavy financial need of an employee only to the extent the amount of the distribution is not in excess of the amount required to satisfy the financial need. For this purpose, the amount required to satisfy the financial need may include any amounts necessary to pay any federal, state, or local income taxes or penalties reasonably anticipated to result from the distribution.

(B) No alternative means available. A distribution is not treated as necessary to satisfy an immediate and heavy financial need of an employee to the extent the need may be relieved from other resources that are reasonably available to the employee. This determination generally is to be made on the basis of all the relevant facts and circumstances. For purposes of this paragraph (d)(3)(iv), the employee's resources are deemed to include those assets of the employee's spouse and minor children that are reasonably available to the employee. Thus, for example, a vacation home owned by the employee and the employee's spouse, whether as community property, joint tenants, tenants by the entirety, or tenants in common, generally will be deemed a resource of the employee. However, property held for the employee's child under an irrevocable trust or under the Uniform Gifts to Minors Act (or comparable State law) is not treated as a resource of the employee.

(C) Employer reliance on employee representation. For purposes of paragraph (d)(3)(iv)(B) of this section, an immediate and heavy financial need generally may be treated as not capable of being relieved from other resources that are reasonably available to the employee, if the employer relies upon the employee's representation (made in writing or such other form as may be prescribed by the Commissioner), unless the employer has actual knowledge to the contrary, that the need cannot reasonably be relieved—

(1) Through reimbursement or compensation by insurance or otherwise;

(2) By liquidation of the employee's assets;

(3) By cessation of elective contributions or employee contributions under the plan;

(4) By other currently available distributions (including distribution of ESOP dividends under section 404(k)) and nontaxable (at the time of the loan) loans, under plans maintained by the employer or by any other employer; or

(5) By borrowing from commercial sources on reasonable commercial terms in an amount sufficient to satisfy the need.

(D) Employee need not take counterproductive actions. For purposes of this paragraph (d)(3)(iv), a need cannot reasonably be relieved by one of the actions described in paragraph (d)(3)(iv)(C) of this section if the effect would be to increase the amount of the need. For example, the need for funds to purchase a principal residence cannot reasonably be relieved by a plan loan if the loan would disqualify the employee from obtaining other necessary financing.

(E) Distribution deemed necessary to satisfy immediate and heavy financial need. A distribution is deemed necessary to satisfy an immediate and heavy financial need of an employee if each of the following requirements are satisfied—

(1) The employee has obtained all other currently available distributions (including distribution of ESOP dividends under section 404(k), but not hardship distributions) and nontaxable (at the time of the loan) loans, under the plan and all other plans maintained by the employer; and

(2) The employee is prohibited, under the terms of the plan or an otherwise legally enforceable agreement, from making elective contributions and employee contributions to the plan and all other plans maintained by the employer for at least 6 months after receipt of the hardship distribution.

(F) Definition of other plans. For purposes of paragraph (d)(3)(iv)(C)(4) and (E)(1) of this section, the phrase plans maintained by the employer means all qualified and nonqualified plans of deferred compensation maintained by the employer, including a cash or deferred arrangement that is part of a cafeteria plan within the meaning of section 125. However, it does not include the mandatory employee contribution portion of a defined benefit plan or a health or welfare benefit plan (including one that is part of a cafeteria plan). In addition, for purposes of paragraph (d)(3)(iv)(E)(2) of this section, the phrase plans maintained by the employer also includes a stock option, stock purchase, or similar plan maintained by the employer. See § 1.401(k)-6 for the continued treatment of suspended employees as eligible employees.

(v) Commissioner may expand standards. The Commissioner may prescribe additional guidance of general applicability, published in the Internal Revenue Bulletin (see §601.601(d)(2) of this chapter), expanding the list of deemed immediate and heavy financial needs and prescribing additional methods for distributions to be deemed necessary to satisfy an immediate and heavy financial need.

As indicated by the regulations, this becomes a very embarrassing and stressful situation for the employee. He or she must go into the employer's human resources department, present extremely personal information about the financial need and why there is no source other than the 401(k) plan that can be used to pay for it, and then hope that the human resources department approves of the distribution. Please note that under (iv)(E)(2) of the regulations above, once the employee receives a hardship distribution, he or she is barred from making further salary deferrals for at least 6 months.

In general, hardship withdrawals may only be made out of salary deferral contributions (as opposed to employer contributions). However, hardship withdrawals may not include earnings attributable to the salary deferral contributions. A determination should be made by the employer or plan administrator that the participant has met the hardship withdrawal requirements before a hardship withdrawal is distributed. In determining if the participant has met the hardship withdrawal requirements, the employer may use a discretionary facts-and-circumstances test or a safe harbor determination of hardship, pursuant to the terms of the plan. As plan fiduciary and plan administrator, the employer should monitor any hardship withdrawals and apply a uniform nondiscriminatory test to determine if the various requirements for a hardship are met.

Remember, there is a difference between pre-tax salary deferrals and after-tax Roth designated contributions. These hardship distribution requirements only apply to pretax salary deferrals in a traditional 401(k) plan. The taxation for after-tax designated Roth contributions are described below. However, if the 401(k) plan allows for both types of accounts and the participant seeking a hardship distribution needs a portion of the Roth 401(k) account to make up the entire hardship distribution, then the plan must "separately determine the amount of elective deferrals available for hardship and the amount of investment in the contract attributable to designated Roth contributions" for purposes of income taxation.[22]

5. Plan Loans

Statutory Rules at IRC §§ 72(p) and 4975(d)(1)

If the plan document permits plan loans, then in order for the loan to not be deemed a taxable distribution, the loans must generally be:

- For an amount of up to $50,000 (as reduced by the highest outstanding loan balance for that participant during the preceding 12 months), or if less, the greater of one-half of the participant's present value of vested accrued benefit in a defined benefit plan of vested account balance in a defined contribution plan. However, a deminimis loan of up to $10,000 can always be provided;

---

22. Treas. Reg. § 1.402A-1, Q&A-8.

- repayable within five years (unless used to purchase a primary residence); and
- subject to level amortization of at least quarterly repayments.[23]

In addition, the loans must generally be:

- made available on a basically equivalent and nondiscriminatory basis to all plan participants and beneficiaries;
- made in accordance with the written plan document;
- subject to a reasonable interest rate (the unofficial rule of thumb is that the IRS will not question rates which are at least one point above prime on that loan date); and
- adequately secured (which is generally satisfied by the participant's current level of vested accrued benefits).[24]

If a distribution meets these requirements, then the distribution will be treated as a proper loan, and will not be a taxable event. However, if the distribution fails to meet these requirements, then the distribution is treated as a taxable distribution to the participant, and the participant may be subject to an additional tax for taking an early distribution (as defined below). Additionally, a violation of the loan rules might cause a Prohibited Transaction penalty tax to be assessed against the plan (see Chapters 10 and 13). If the loan is made to a married participant, then the spouse must consent to the portion of the benefit being used as collateral for the loan.[25]

Although not required, payroll reduction procedures and voluntary election forms are often established so that while a participant is still receiving compensation, there is no chance of an inadvertent default. All "employees" can take participant loans, including partners in a partnership and sole proprietors.[26]

C. Taxation of Plan Distributions

1. Taxation of Early Retirement Benefit and Normal Retirement Benefit Distributions

Statutory Rules at IRC §§ 402(a) and 72(d)

Okay. Now you understand the complicated rules of the form and timing of distributions from qualified plans, so now we can discuss income taxation. As discussed in Chapter 2, for federal income tax purposes, inclusion in Gross Income is technically the trigger for potential taxation (even if an individual has enough losses, deductions and credits to reduce actual tax liability to zero—if the retirement benefits are included in Gross Income, we refer to those retirement benefits as being currently taxable).

One of the main advantages of an employer sponsored qualified retirement plan is that the employer deducts contributions as they are deposited along the way, but the employee participants do not include the amounts in Gross Income until they receive the

---

23. IRC § 72(p)(2).
24. IRC § 4975(d)(1).
25. IRC § 417(e)(4).
26. Before being amended by Taxpayer Relief Act of 1997, IRC § 4975(f)(6) had not allowed such individuals to be classified as "employees" for purposes of plan loans.

benefits. A normal distribution is simply a distribution subject to regular income taxes, and rollovers are generally available to further defer taxation. The employer will provide notices to participants about the taxation of distributions, but is cautioned to refrain from providing any personal tax advice unless qualified to do so; however, the individual participants should be advised to seek their own personal tax advisor.

All distributions made from a qualified retirement plan after a participant ceases to be an employee receiving compensation (whether for retirement, death, termination due to being fired, quitting, or becoming disabled, or termination of the plan) will be either included in Gross Income in the year distributed or excluded from Gross Income currently and deferred to a future tax year if properly rolled over. In addition to regular income tax treatment, the individual might also be subjected to a penalty tax if the distributions are premature or failed required minimum distributions.

Only the portion of benefits that has not previously been taxed is now subject to taxation, since the general principle of our federal income tax system is to only subject the same income to taxation once over the individual's life. The plan sponsor merely provides information about the portion previously taxed (*i.e.*, the participant's basis) and then it's up to each individual participant to figure out which portion of his or her distribution(s) is actually included in Gross Income.

If the participant has no basis in his plan benefits, then the total amount received in each plan year is included in his Gross Income,[27] and taxes will be paid at whatever his or her tax rate happens to be based on all taxable income for the tax year.

Basis generally includes:

- Nondeductible (*i.e.*, after-tax) employee contributions, such as Roth contributions,
- P.S. 58 costs attributable to insurance included in income as an "economic benefit,"
- Employer contributions which have already been taxed, and
- Amounts paid by an employee as principal payments on any loans after they were treated as "deemed distributions."

If the participant has a basis in his benefits, then the participant (*i.e.*, the individual, through his or her personal tax counsel, and not the Plan Administrator) must choose a recovery method to determine the portion which is included in his gross income and the portion which is not included in his gross income:

> *Regular method*: the exclusion ratio is calculated and is applied to each annuity distribution (even those distributions that do not come from qualified retirement plans). The exclusion ratio is obtained by dividing the basis in the annuity by the expected return (which is calculated based on life annuities stated in regulations). The exclusion ratio is multiplied by each distribution, and the result is the portion of the distribution which is not included in gross income (and is therefore received tax-free).[28]

> *Simplified method*: the exclusion ratio for annuities paid from qualified retirement plans can use special factors to determine the dollar amount of each distribution excluded from taxation (until the basis is fully recovered).[29]

Again, the responsibility of understanding the complicated basis recovery rules for annuity distributions and properly applying them lies with each individual plan participant

---

27. IRC § 402(a)
28. IRC § 72(c).
29. IRC § 72(d).

receiving a distribution with basis, and their personal CPAs and tax advisors, and never lies with the employer or plan administrator. Therefore, in this textbook, a thorough dissection of the complexities of the income tax rules is not necessary.

If a spouse or ex-spouse receives a distribution pursuant to a QDRO, then such alternate payee will include the distribution in his or her Gross Income; however, if a child gets a distribution pursuant to a QDRO, then the distribution amount will be taxable to the participant.

If employer securities are distributed rather than cash, then different rules apply depending on whether they are attributable to employee contributions or to employer contributions. If special conditions are met, then the unrealized appreciation of the stock may be excluded from taxable income at the time of distribution and will only be taxed upon a subsequent sale of the securities.[30]

2. Procedural Aspects — Tax Notices, Withholding and Reporting

Statutory Rules at IRC § 402(f)

Unless the benefit distribution is any distribution which is one of a series of substantially equal periodic payments made for the life, a minimum required distribution after age 70½, a hardship distribution from a 401(k) plan, or a qualified disaster-relief distribution, it is eligible to be rolled over into another retirement plan or IRA. The plan administrator must provide a written explanation within a reasonable amount of time before the distribution to the recipient that explains:

- the provisions under which the recipient may have the distribution directly transferred to an eligible retirement plan and that the automatic distribution by direct transfer applies to certain distributions,

- the provision which requires the withholding of tax on the distribution if it is not directly transferred to an eligible retirement plan,

- the provisions under which the distribution will not be subject to tax if transferred to an eligible retirement plan within 60 days after the date on which the recipient received the distribution, and

- the provisions under which distributions from the eligible retirement plan receiving the distribution may be subject to restrictions and tax consequences which are different from those applicable to distributions from the plan making such distribution.

A safe harbor § 402(f) notice was published by the IRS in 2002,[31] but was technically out of date for a period of time due to additional rollover requirements added through the Pension Protection Act of 2006. Therefore, it was up to the plan administrator to either draft a notice that complied with IRC § 402(f), or to modify the 2002 model 402(f) notice so that it to complied with current law. A new model notice was issued in 2009.[32]

If the plan participant does not elect a direct rollover of his or her retirement benefits from a trustee of one qualified plan to the trustee of another qualified plan, as explained

---

30. IRC § 402(e)(4).
31. Notice 2002-3.
32. Notice 2009-68 (modifying and superceding Notice 2002-3).

below, then an amount equal to 20% of the amount distributed must be withheld from the distribution by the plan administrator for federal income taxes.[33] Therefore, the individual will actually receive 80% of the lump sum amount, but the 20% withheld will be used as part of the calculation as to whether the individual still owes income taxes or is a due a refund from the IRS. If the individual receives a distribution, he or she has 60 days to decide to rollover the full amount (*i.e.,* he or she can find the 20% withheld amount from other personal assets and roll over the full 100% of the normal distribution). However, if the employer transfers it directly under a trustee-to-trustee transfer, then there is no withholding requirement.

The employer is required to complete a Form 1099-R for each distribution,[34] and it is up to the individual taxpayer to properly and timely include the distribution in Gross Income.

3. Rollovers

Statutory Rules at IRC §§ 402(c)(4) and 401(a)(31)

A plan participant must be given the option to elect a direct rollover of his or her retirement benefits from a qualified plan to another employer's qualified plan or into his or her individual retirement account (IRA) upon a distributable event. Distributions from a qualified plan may also be rolled over into a § 403(a) qualified annuity, § 403(b) tax-deferred annuity plan, or a § 457(b) governmental plan. Further, taxable amounts held in an IRA and distributions from a qualified plan, § 403(a) qualified annuity, § 403(b) tax-deferred annuity plan or § 457(b) governmental plan may be rolled over into a qualified plan. However, qualified plans do not have to receive rollovers, so it is up to each plan administrator to decide whether the particular plan will receive and account for rollovers.

After-tax contributions can be directly rolled over from a qualified retirement plan to a qualified defined benefit or a § 403(b) annuity as long as the receiving plan separately accounts for the after-tax contributions and associated earnings. Also, distributions from a deceased participant's account in an eligible retirement plan can be directly rolled over by a nonspouse beneficiary to a traditional IRA. Distributions from an eligible retirement plan can be directly rolled over to a Roth IRA, subject to the same restrictions that apply to rollovers from a traditional IRA to a Roth IRA. However, for tax years prior to 2010, restrictions that previously applied to rollovers from a traditional IRA to a Roth IRA apply to any direct rollover from an eligible retirement plan to a Roth IRA.

Involuntary cash-outs of more than $1,000 but less than $5,000 must be automatically rolled over to an IRA designated by the plan unless the distributee elects otherwise. A written explanation must be provided to participants advising them that this automatic direct rollover will occur unless the participant elects to have the distribution transferred to a different IRA or qualified plan or to receive it directly. If an automatic default transfer is made to a designated IRA, then the distributee will be treated as the fiduciary over the IRA assets upon the earlier of a rollover of any portion of the assets to another IRA or one year after the initial transfer to the designated IRA. There is a safe harbor under which a pension plan fiduciary is deemed to have satisfied its fiduciary responsibilities with respect to both the selection of an IRA provider and the investment of funds in con-

---

33. IRC § 3405(c).
34. Proposed Treas. Regs. § 1.402(e)-2(f).

nection with the automatic rollover of mandatory distributions of $5,000 or less. The DOL also issued a final class exemption from certain Prohibited Transaction restrictions of ERISA and related excise taxes under the Code.[35] The class exemption permits a plan fiduciary that is also the employer maintaining the plan to establish, on behalf of its separated employees, an IRA at a financial institution that is the employer or an affiliate, in connection with a mandatory distribution. A plan fiduciary may select a proprietary product as the initial investment for that IRA, and for the receipt of certain fees by the IRA provider in connection with the establishment or maintenance of the IRA and the initial investment of the mandatory distribution.

The IRS provided guidance in question-and-answer format on the automatic rollover rules.[36] The guidance clarifies that the automatic rollover provisions apply to the entire amount of a mandatory distribution, without regard to the amount of the distribution, as long as the amount exceeds $1,000, so that amounts attributable to rollover contributions that exceed $5,000 are subject to the automatic rollover provisions. Thus, the portion of the distribution attributable to a rollover contribution is subject to the automatic rollover requirements even if that amount is excludible from the determination of whether the present value of the nonforfeitable accrued benefit exceeds $5,000. Also, the guidance provides that the plan administrator must notify the distributee in writing (either separately or as part of the required tax notice) that the distribution may be paid in a direct rollover to an IRA. In addition, the guidance includes a sample plan amendment, advises that all plans must establish administrative procedures for processing automatic rollovers, and clarifies that rollover IRAs can be set up without the participant's participation.

4. Premature Distributions

Statutory Rules at IRC § 72(t)

Congress adds a non-deductible penalty tax onto the regular income tax for distributions from a qualified retirement plan that are taken earlier than expected retirement. The penalty tax is 10%, and some argue that it is too low to truly be a deterrent against leakage. This is especially true in a defined contribution plan where the total benefits at retirement consist of the account balance—the more withdrawn before retirement will result in lower nest eggs at retirement.

As discussed, distributions from a qualified plan generally may not be made before the employee attains age 59½ , separates from service, dies, becomes disabled, encounters financial hardship, or before the termination of the plan; however, certain in-service distributions are allowed. There are several specific uses of a premature distribution that will still be subject to income tax, but which will not be subject to the 10% additional penalty tax.

Distributions which are excluded from the 10% penalty tax are those paid from a qualified plan:

- which are paid due to attainment of age 59½ , death, disability, part of a series of substantially equal periodic payments, or separation of service after attainment of age 55;

---

35. PTE 2004-16, 69 Fed. Reg. 57964 (9/28/04), effective for mandatory distributions made on or after Mar. 28, 2005.
36. Notice 2005-5, effective Mar. 28, 2005, as modified by Notice 2005-95.

- which are used as qualifying medical expenses (up to the amount that could be deducted on the individual's personal federal income tax return);
- which are paid to an alternate payee pursuant to a QDRO;
- which are used by certain unemployed individuals to pay health insurance premiums; or
- which are paid for any reason to certain qualified reservists called into active duty September 11, 2001, and before December 31, 2007, as long as they are repaid within 2 years after the period of active duty ends.

In addition, distributions which are excluded from the 10% penalty tax are those paid from an individual retirement account (but not from a qualified retirement plan):

- which are used for qualified higher education expenses; or
- which are used for qualified first time home purchase expenses.

Each individual taxpayer is required to indicate premature distributions on his individual tax return and thus pay the penalty. The plan administrator will simply code the form 1099-R appropriately.

5. Required Minimum Distributions

Statutory Rules at IRC §§ 401(a)(9) and 4974(a)

Just as Congress was concerned with participants improperly taking distributions from a qualified retirement plan before retirement, it is also concerned with wealthy participants who do not actually need their qualified plan and IRA benefits in retirement and who would prefer to maintain the tax deferred status. Therefore, minimum required distributions must be taken starting at age 70½, and a 50% penalty tax will be assessed on missed required distributions. The 50% penalty tax may be waived if the payee establishes to the satisfaction of the IRS that the shortfall in the amount distributed was due to reasonable error, and reasonable steps are being taken to remedy the shortfall.[37]

Qualified retirement plans and IRAs are required to make minimum distributions; however, Roth accounts in a 401(k) plan or in Roth IRAs are not (as long as the account has been established for at least 5 years). Required minimum distributions must begin in the year after a participant attains age 70½ , or, if not a 5% owner, then upon retirement if he or she is still working at age 70½. The way this is worded, and works in practice, is that someone born between January 1 and June 30 will turn age 70 and age 70½ in the same calendar year; whereas someone born between July 1 and December 31 will turn age 70 in one year and age 70½ in the following calendar year. The required beginning date means the April 1 of the following calendar year, so if a participant's first distribution is due and calculated for 2010, then either:

- the 2010 required minimum distribution is paid by December 31, 2010, and then each successive year's distribution is paid by the successive December 31, or
- the 2010 required minimum distribution is postponed and paid by April 1, 2011, the 2011 minimum distribution is paid by December 31, 2011, and then each successive year's distribution is paid by the successive December 31 (thus, the individual chooses to include two distributions in his or her 2011 Gross Income).

---

37. Treas. Regs. § 54.4974-2, Q&A-7.

The minimum required distribution rules are somewhat complicated, and Treasury Regulations at § 1.401(a)(9)-1 through -9 provide guidance, but there were not any succinct portions that would be appropriately excepted here in this text. The distributions are generally determined as follows:

defined contribution plan (or other individual account plan): the minimum amount that must be distributed (and subject to income tax) for the current year equals the account balance as of the last valuation date in the preceding year divided by a factor. The factor is based on life expectancies and is found in one of three tables in the regulations, depending on whether (1) the employee is alive with either a spouse, who is less than 10 years younger, or any non-spouse, as the designated beneficiary; (2) the employee is alive with a spouse, who is more than 10 years younger, as the sole designated beneficiary; or (3) the employee dies and has designated an individual as a beneficiary.

defined benefit plan (or other annuity): certain distribution options automatically meet the minimum distribution rules, whereas other options need to be tested against the minimum distribution incidental benefit rules (where non-spouse beneficiaries, depending on their age, cannot be expected to receive more benefits after the employee's death than the employee is expected to receive during his lifetime).

If the employee who participates in either a defined benefit plan or a defined contribution plan dies before his or her required beginning date, then all of the benefits must be distributed either (1) within 5 years of his or her death, (2) over the life of the designated beneficiary, starting in the year following the year of the participant's death, or (3) over the life of the surviving spouse, starting in the year that the employee would be required to start taking distributions, if the surviving spouse is the sole designated beneficiary. Therefore, a married participant who names his or her spouse as the sole beneficiary will allow benefits to be tax-deferred as long as possible should the participant die before turning age 70½ and before distributions have begun.

Distributions taken before an employee's required beginning date are irrelevant. Similarly, if in any year an employee receives a distribution in excess of the minimum distribution required for that year, such excess will not count as a credit to reduce a subsequent year's minimum required distribution.

The beneficiary named for purposes of required minimum distributions can be different than the beneficiary named for normal pre-retirement death benefits. While a spouse named as a beneficiary for minimum required contributions receives tax advantages that any other individual does not receive, there is no statutory mandate that the spouse is, in fact, named. This is because required minimum distributions basically target wealthy individuals who would prefer to use the tax-deferred retirement assets to fund their estate planning bequests.

The designated beneficiary for minimum required distributions is determined on September 30 of the calendar year following the year of the employee's death — which allows accountants and estate planners ample time to "fix" things for their client since there are certain income tax advantages if the spouse is the sole designated beneficiary and there are income tax disadvantages if the beneficiary is not an individual. The regulations go into great detail explaining how beneficiaries are determined, especially if the employee names them through a marital or a QTIP trust, and whether certain named individuals are considered contingent or successor beneficiaries. An employee is considered married under a plan only if he or she is considered married under applicable state law.

For defined contribution plans and IRAs, Congress provided "relief" from the poor economic conditions, and allows an individual to not take any required minimum distribution calculated and due for the 2009 calendar year. As of the publication of this book, there is talk that Congress might extend the relief to 2010 or raise the age for required minimum distributions to 75, but until legislation is actually enacted into law, we can only understand what Congress is thinking of doing.

Chapter 10

Role of the Internal Revenue Service

Overview

Which operating division of the IRS has jurisdiction over qualified retirement plans?

- the Tax Exempt / Government Entities division, through its Employee Plans group

What does the Employee Plans group do?

- Rulings & Agreements provides guidance, both in general and to specific plans, on how they can comply with the statutory requirements (including determination letters for compliant plan documents and voluntary compliance submissions)

- Customer Education and Outreach keeps the website ripe with compliance tools, prepares newsletters, and holds live and webcasted programs to communicate the rules to plan sponsors

- Examinations agents will go out and audit the plan to ensure compliance.

What is a favorable determination letter and how is a FDL request processed?

- although voluntary, a plan should always apply for a determination letter request upon adoption, upon amendments, and upon plan termination, where the IRS indicates that the plan document complies with the laws, so that if the plan is operated and administered in accordance with the document, then the plan will be deemed to be qualified

- individually designed plans should seek a renewed favorable determination letter every 5 years, and the cycles are based on the last digit of the plan's Taxpayer Identification Number (TIN)

- Master & Prototype and Volume Submitter plans seek a renewed favorable determination letter every 6 years

Why would a plan voluntarily perform an audit to find mistakes?

- The IRS clearly signals that if they discover mistakes on audit, that the penalties and correction costs will be much more severe than if self-discovered

- The Self Correction Program (SCP) is available only for insignificant operational failures (as opposed to plan document failures)—if the plan has established compliance practices and procedures, and has received a favorable determination letter, then the plan sponsor may correct operational failures without payment of any fee or sanction, and without any contact whatsoever with the IRS

- The Voluntary Correction Program (VCP) provides general procedures for correction of all qualification failures after paying a fee and making a submission to the IRS
- Correction on Audit (CAP) allows the plan sponsor to correct qualification failures that are discovered by the IRS during an audit, but before the audit has concluded

What are some issues with the IRS auditing qualified plan administration and operation?

- The IRS is responsible for ensuring that retirement plans are qualified, and over time, has learned some effective ways to maximize their limited resources, such as:
  - focused audits that hit more plans on only the most commonly expected errors
  - team audits on large plans (with agents with different areas of specialty)
  - Abusive Tax Avoidance Transactions require certain activities, which are outside of the bounds of a reasonable interpretation of the Internal Revenue Code, to be listed, so that the IRS can control the spread of such bad activities

A. Organization of the IRS

After the IRS Restructuring and Reform Act of 1998, the IRS is divided into four operating divisions:

- Wage and Investment;
- Large and Mid-Size Business;
- Small Business/Self-Employed; and
- Tax-Exempt and Government Entities.

As described below, for purposes of qualified retirement plans, we are mostly concerned with the Tax-Exempt and Government Entities (TE/GE) division. However, the other three divisions remain incredibly important because the employer that sponsors an employee benefits plan will necessarily be a large, mid-sized, or small business or a self-employed individual. The deductions reflected on those tax returns might trigger issues with the qualified plan it sponsors. Additionally, as individuals receive retirement benefits and either include the amounts in Gross Income or determine they should be deferred, the Wage and Investment agents will be reviewing those tax returns.

Other principal offices of the IRS include:

- Office of Chief Counsel;
- Taxpayer Advocate Service;
- Office of Professional Responsibility (OPR);
- Criminal Investigation;
- Appeals;
- Communications and Liaison;
- Whistleblower Office; and
- Office of Privacy, Information Protection and Data Security.

In the administration of qualified plans, benefits professionals oftentimes need to deal with office of chief counsel and appeals when examinations of plan operations are in dispute between the IRS and the plan sponsor. Additionally, as attorneys, accountants,

Enrolled Actuaries, Enrolled Agents, and now Enrolled Retirement Plan Agents practice in front of the IRS pursuant to Circular 230 (and power of attorney pursuant to Form 2848), we need to deal with the Office of Professional Responsibility. All of the other IRS offices are important in general, but do not usually impact the operation of qualified plans.

B. Employee Plans Group

1. Organization of Tax-Exempt and Government Entities Operating Division

Now let's focus in on the TE/GE Operating division. Taken from their website:[1]

The Division is designed to serve the needs of three very distinct customer segments: Employee Plans, Exempt Organizations, and Government Entities. The customers range from small local community organizations and municipalities to major universities, huge pension funds, state governments, Indian tribal governments and participants of complex tax exempt bond transactions. These organizations represent a large economic sector with unique needs. Although generally paying no income tax, this sector does pay over $220 billion in employment taxes and income tax withholding and controls approximately $8.2 trillion in assets. Governed by complex, highly specialized provisions of the tax law, this sector is not designed to generate revenue, but rather to ensure that the entities fulfill the policy goals that their tax exemption was designed to achieve.

The TE/GE Division was created to address four basic key customer needs: education and communication, rulings and agreements, examination, and customer account services. Education and communication efforts will focus on helping customers understand their tax responsibilities with outreach programs and activities tailored to their specific needs. Rulings and agreements efforts will provide a strong emphasis on up-front compliance programs, such as the determination, voluntary compliance, and private letter ruling programs. Examination initiatives will identify and address non-compliance, through customized activities within each customer segment, and Customer Account Services will provide taxpayers with efficient tax filings as well as accurate and timely responses to questions and requests for information.

The Commissioner of the Tax Exempt and Government Entities Division is responsible for the uniform interpretation and application of the Federal tax laws on matters pertaining to the Division's customer base. In addition, the Commissioner provides advice and assistance throughout the Service, to the Department of the Treasury, other government agencies, including state governments and Congressional committees, and maintains a particularly close liaison with the Department of Labor and the Pension Guaranty Corporation.

TE/GE is Comprised of Three Distinct Business Divisions:

- Employee Plans (EP) (which we are concerned with);
- Exempt Organizations (EO) (which has jurisdiction with respect to federal income tax issues concerning charities and other non-profit organizations); and

---

1. http://www.irs.gov/irs/article/0,,id=100971,00.html.

- Government Entities (GE) (which has jurisdiction with respect to federal income tax issues concerning federal, state and local governments, Indian Tribal governments, and tax-exempt bonds).

2. Organization of the Employee Plans Business Division

We are interested in the Employee Plans Business Division. Their main website is either http://www.irs.gov/ep or http://www.irs.gov/retirement/index.html. There are three major functions within Employee Plans:

Rulings & Agreements. As Congress enacts the statutory provisions for qualified plans, the members of the R&A team provide guidance, both in general and to specific plans, on how they can comply with the statutory requirements. The main functions they have are coordinating technical guidance and quality assurance, issuing determination letters for compliant plan documents, and accepting voluntary compliance from plan administrators that discover errors in the operation of the plans. The latter two functions will be discussed in further detail below.

Customer Education and Outreach. Many employers, especially small businesses, might not know all of the specific qualification requirements for their employee benefit plans and might not hire effective plan advisors, so CE&O keeps the website ripe with compliance tools, prepares newsletters, and holds live and webcasted programs to communicate the rules to plan sponsors.

Examinations. As is generally feared in all aspects of IRS regulation, employee plan agents in the examination group will go out and audit the plan to ensure compliance.

To sum up, here is a quote from Sarah Hall Ingram, the Commissioner of TE/GE: "In EP, we take a ... holistic approach and work with the plan throughout its life cycle. The various EP programs make this easy. For example, we start with the determination/opinion/advisory letter program to ensure a plan's document is in compliance. Rulings and Agreements generates guidance to keep the plan on track; Customer Education & Outreach (CE&O) ensures the plan's administrator knows about and understands the rules; the plan can use the Employee Plans Compliance Resolution Program (EPCRS) to correct most mistakes; and Examinations may audit the plan to ensure compliance and protect the participants."[2] Asked whether, in her new role as Commissioner of TE/GE, she sees many changes in the operation of EP, Ingram indicated "I do not foresee any fundamental shift for EP but rather continuing to support the core programs we have. I especially want to continue to support and grow the EPCRS and the CE&O programs since these provide great tools and resources for the community. I would also like to expand our outreach efforts to reach not just benefits practitioners and plan administrators but also those people who may not work exclusively in the EP arena and the participants. Of course, there is always new legislation that we will need to deal with in a timely fashion rather than simply adding it to the end of the list."[3]

More specifically, Michael Julianelle, the Director of Employee Plans, indicated his priorities as: "Protecting plan participants[;] Listening to the benefits practitioner com-

---

2. IRS Employee Plan News, Summer 2009, Vol. 9, available at http://www.irs.gov/pub/irs-tege/sum09.pdf.
3. Id.

munity[;] Enhancing our relationship with the Advisory Committee on Tax Exempt and Government Entities (ACT)[;] Developing employees' skills and providing training for them to do their job in administering the law[; and] Doing the right thing—even when it's difficult[.] I care about plan participants and employers that sponsor retirement plans. EP's mission is vital to the well-being of all Americans. I value our partnership with the benefits community in promoting sound retirement plan administration. EP will face challenges as we continue to help sponsors, participants, and practitioners understand and comply with the law. Partnering with the benefits practitioner community is critical to the success of our programs. In future editions of this newsletter, I will share the challenges that we face together."[4]

From my personal experience, I can safely opine that the main concern of the EP group, at least since its reorganization in 1998, is to have compliant plans that deliver the promised benefits to the plan participants—and that working out a method of keeping the plan ongoing, and listening to the practitioner community, is generally more important than actual dollars collected as a result of imposing penalties or disqualifying a retirement plan.

As far as customer education and outreach, Julianelle, when asked what efforts are underway to improve the service that is provided to the benefits community, replied: "Let me address your question in terms of improvements to our educational/outreach services. In 2008 EP will accomplish the following:

- Expand the scope of EP events offered to the community. For example, we are developing a workshop to increase small business employers' awareness and knowledge of our retirement plan correction programs. The workshop will cover our new 'fix-it guides' outlining how to find, fix, and avoid common plan mistakes.

- Increase plain language information for the community. Our goal is to enhance Employee Plans News and Retirement News for Employers to include more relevant content for their respective audiences and provide plain language information, with a focus on guidance related to the Pension Protection Act of 2006 (PPA). All information related to PPA will be noted in the PPA of 2006 Chart (sorted by topic) and PPA of 2006 Chart (sorted by Code/ERISA section).

- Assess the effectiveness of EP outreach products. By conducting dialogues with our customers, we can validate and improve our products. The first priority will be on sponsor/employer-based products.

- Use video to educate the community. For example, we will host 30 minutes of EP produced videos on an external web site enabling customers to link from our web page. One video is promoting The Navigator.

- Enhance education to plan participants/employees. For example, we are developing a marketing campaign to promote the upcoming enhancement of the 'Plan Participant/Employee' segment (www.irs.gov/ep) and 'Timing is Everything.' This effort's signature item will include a video on 'What You Can Expect to Get Out of Your Retirement Plan' based on 'life events.'"[5]

The Employee Plans website, although collectively shown as the "Retirement Plans Community," is divided into three general areas: one for plan participants and employees, one for plan sponsors and employers, and one for benefits practitioners. A

---

4. EP Connections: Interview With Michael Julianelle, available at http://www.irs.gov/retirement/article/0,,id=176389,00.html.

5. Id. Live links appear on the actual web page.

good page to save in your favorites is http://www.irs.gov/retirement/article/0,,id=
96763,00.html, which has links to "EP Forms/Publications/Products."

3. Determination Letters for Plan Documents

A qualified plan is not required to get an advance determination from the IRS on its
qualified status, but it is highly recommended. In a determination letter request, the plan
document is reviewed by the IRS EP Rulings and Agreements agents. They will issue a
favorable determination letter stating that, in its opinion, the plan document is in compliance with all controlling laws and regulations, and that if the Plan Administrator operates the plan in accordance with its plan document, then the Plan should maintain its
tax-qualified status under IRC § 401(a).

As shown in Chapter 3, ERISA, and the corresponding Internal Revenue Code provisions, seem to be amended almost annually by Congress. Some laws make minor changes,
while others make major changes. Similarly, some laws change the requirements for compliance while others offer alternatives for the plan sponsor. Theoretically, since the plan
document must always comply with current law, then it would seem that every plan document must be amended immediately as any new statutory provision becomes effective.
Historically, however, Congress and the IRS usually group several successive laws together,
and set a deadline for the single plan amendment or total restatement to incorporate all
of those laws — however, it is fully expected that the plan will operate in accordance with
the new laws even before the plan is officially amended. This is known as the plan's remedial amendment period.[6]

However, the remedial amendment period can be extended if the plan sponsor files a
determination letter request. "If on or before the end of a remedial amendment period …
the employer or plan administrator files a request … for a determination letter with respect to the initial or continuing qualification of the plan, or a trust which is part of such
plan, such remedial amendment period shall be extended until the expiration of 91 days
after: (i) The date on which notice of the final determination with respect to such request
for a determination letter is issued by the Internal Revenue Service.…"[7]

The current iteration of the determination request program, which is based on submission cycles that are supposed to smooth out workflows for R&A personnel, is fairly
new, and therefore is still evolving and improving. The portion of the IRS website providing information to benefits professionals and plan sponsors is at http://www.irs.gov/re-
tirement/article/0,,id=128189,00.html, and there are many links on the "EP Determination
Letter Resource Guide" to more specific information, forms, and IRS Publication 794. As
different laws are enacted, the IRS publishes an annual Cumulative List of Changes in
Plan Qualification Requirements (Cumulative List) for statutory amendments required
for the current submission cycle.

The following rules summarize how the determination letter program works:

- A plan should always apply for a determination letter request upon plan termination
  (even though it is not required to under law).

---

6. IRC § 401(b).
7. Treas. Regs. § 1.401(b)-1(e)(3).

- Individually designed plans should seek a renewed favorable determination letter every 5 years, and the cycles are based on the last digit of the plan's Taxpayer Identification Number (TIN).

- Master, Prototype and Volume Submitter plans seek a renewed favorable determination letter every 6 years (all defined contribution plans are submitted and reviewed over a 2 year period, and then all employers that indicate advanced intent to adopt a Master, Prototype or Volume Submitter plan have automatic approval of the plan document, and do not need to apply for its own unique determination letter). However, often times if the sponsoring employer is engaged in a merger, acquisition, or other corporate transaction, the contract will require the application.

The application package must include Form 8717, User Fee for Employee Plan Determination, Opinion, and Advisory Letter Request and one of the following Employee Plans forms:

- Form 5300, Application for Determination for Employee Benefit Plan (or Form 6406, Short Form Application for Determination for Minor Amendment of Employee Benefit Plan) and possibly Form 5300 Schedule Q, Elective Determination Requests;

- Form 5307, Application for Determination for Adopters of Master or Prototype or Volume Submitter Plans (plus either a form 4461, Application for Approval of Master or Prototype or Volume Submitter Defined Contribution Plans or a form 4461-A, Application for Approval of Master or Prototype or Volume Submitter Defined Benefit Plan);

- Form 5309, Application for Determination of Employee Stock Ownership Plan;

- Form 5310, Application for Determination for Terminating Plan; or

- Form 5310-A, Notice of Plan Merger or Consolidation, Spin-off, or Transfer of Plan Assets or Liabilities; Notice of Qualified Separate Lines of Business.

The determination request program is quite complicated, especially when it comes to plans needing a determination letter during an off-cycle or if the sponsoring employer is part of a corporate merger or acquisition, or when a pre-approved M&P or VS plan is amended in such a major way that it becomes an individually designed plan.[8]

Individually designed plans will receive a determination letter, while M&P and VS master documents will only receive an opinion and advisory letter.

A favorable determination letter is limited in scope. A determination letter generally applies to qualification requirements regarding the form of the plan, and might also apply to certain operational (non-form) requirements. Generally, a favorable determination letter does not consider, and may not be relied on with regard to: certain requirements under IRC § 401(a)(4), including the requirement that the plan be nondiscriminatory in the amounts of contributions or benefits for Highly Compensated and non Highly Compensated employees; the coverage requirements under IRC §§ 410(b) and 401(a)(26); and the definition of compensation under IRC section 414(s). In addition, a favorable determination letter may not be relied on for any qualification change that becomes effective, any guidance published, or any statutes enacted, after the issuance of the applicable Cumulative List of Changes in Plan Qualification Requirements (Cumulative List) unless the item has been identified in that Cumulative List for the cycle under which the application was submitted.

---

8. See Rev. Proc. 2007-44.

An opinion and advisory letter suggests that the master document is compliant, but that each employer that adopts the M&P or VS plan must properly and timely adopt, or certify its intent to adopt through IRS form 8905, in order for the actual plan adopted by any particular employer to be qualified.

4. Employee Plans Compliance Resolution System (*i.e.,* "Self-Correction" of Operational Defects)

As discussed in Chapter 4, the Secretary of the Treasury (through the IRS Employee Plans Business Division of TE/GE) has the authority to disqualify a retirement plan, subject to certain coordination requirements with the Secretary of Labor. The IRS may retroactively disqualify a plan and assess taxes with respect to any "open" tax year (*i.e.,* tax years for which the statute of limitations has not run). The extent to which a plan may be retroactively disqualified for "form" violations is limited if it has been the subject of a favorable determination letter.

The IRS is generally allowed three years after the filing of the income tax return for the applicable year in which to assess taxes on an employer who sponsored or an employee who participated in the disqualified plan. The IRS may assess taxes within six years after a taxpayer files its return if the taxpayer omits from Gross Income an includible amount that exceeds 25% of the amount of Gross Income stated on its return. For plan years beginning in 2006, Schedule P is no longer required to be filed with the Form 5500, so the statute of limitations starts running with the filing of the Form 5500 itself.

As of the date of disqualification, a previously tax-qualified retirement plan becomes nonqualified and its previously tax-exempt trust becomes nonexempt. Accordingly, the non-exempt trust is subject to income tax on its earnings for the years in which the plan is disqualified. Any contributions made by the employer to the plan in the years in which the plan is disqualified are not deductible by the employer (to the extent the contributions are not included in the employee's Gross Income). The employee must include in his or her taxable income contributions made to the plan on the employee's behalf, to the extent the employee was "substantially vested" in the contributions for the years the plan was disqualified. If the sole reason for disqualification is because the plan fails its annual minimum coverage tests, then only the Highly Compensated Employees of the plan will be affected by these adverse non-qualification rules.

In order to limit plan disqualification to the most severe case, the IRS has developed a comprehensive self-correction program called the Employee Plans Correction Resolution System ("EPCRS"):

Self-Correction

The Self Correction Program (SCP) is available only for Operational Failures (as opposed to plan document failures). Qualified Plans and 403(b) Plans are eligible for SCP with respect to significant and insignificant Operational Failures. SEPs and SIMPLE IRA Plans are eligible for SCP only with respect to insignificant Operational Failures. A Plan Sponsor that has established compliance practices and procedures may, at any time without paying any fee or sanction, correct insignificant Operational Failures under a Qualified Plan or a SEP or a SIMPLE IRA Plan, provided the SEP or SIMPLE IRA Plan is established and maintained on a document approved by the Service. In addition, in the case of a Qualified Plan that is the subject of a favorable determination letter from the Service or in the case of a 403(b) Plan, the Plan Sponsor generally may correct even significant Operational Failures without payment of any fee or sanction.

The factors to be considered in determining whether or not an Operational Failure under a plan is insignificant include, but are not limited to: (1) whether other failures occurred during the period being examined (for this purpose, a failure is not considered to have occurred more than once merely because more than one participant is affected by the failure); (2) the percentage of plan assets and contributions involved in the failure; (3) the number of years the failure occurred; (4) the number of participants affected relative to the total number of participants in the plan; (5) the number of participants affected as a result of the failure relative to the number of participants who could have been affected by the failure; (6) whether correction was made within a reasonable time after discovery of the failure; and (7) the reason for the failure (for example, data errors such as errors in the transcription of data, the transposition of numbers, or minor arithmetic errors). No single factor is determinative. Additionally, factors (2), (4), and (5) should not be interpreted to exclude small businesses. In the case of a plan with more than one Operational Failure in a single year, or Operational Failures that occur in more than one year, the Operational Failures are eligible for correction under SC only if all of the Operational Failures are insignificant in the aggregate.[9]

Other Operational Failures (even if significant) can be corrected under SC if the Operational Failure is corrected and the correction is either completed or substantially completed by the last day of the correction period, which is the last day of the second plan year following the plan year for which the failure occurred. The correction period for an Operational Failure that occurs for any plan year ends, in any event, on the first date the plan or Plan Sponsor is Under Examination for that plan year.[10]

Voluntary Correction with Service Approval (VCP)

VCP provides general procedures for correction of all Qualification Failures: Operational, Plan Document, Demographic, and Employer Eligibility. A Plan Sponsor, at any time before audit, may pay a limited fee and receive the Service's approval for correction of a Qualified Plan, 403(b) Plans, SEP or SIMPLE IRA Plan. Under VCP, there are special procedures for anonymous submissions and group submissions.

VCP is not based upon an examination of the plan by the Service. Only the failures raised by the Plan Sponsor or failures identified by the Service in processing the application are addressed under VCP, and only those failures are covered by a VCP compliance statement. The Service will not make any investigation or finding under VCP concerning whether there are failures. Because VCP does not arise out of an examination, consideration under VCP does not preclude or impede a subsequent examination of the Plan Sponsor or the plan by the Service with respect to the taxable year (or years) involved with respect to matters that are outside the compliance statement. However, a Plan Sponsor's statements describing failures are made only for purposes of VCP and will not be regarded by the Service as an admission of a failure for purposes of any subsequent examination.[11]

In general, a request under VCP consists of a letter from the Plan Sponsor (which may be a letter from the Plan Sponsor's representative) or Eligible Organization (or represen-

---

9. See Rev. Proc. 2008-50, Section 8.
10. See Rev. Proc. 2008-50, Section 9.
11. See Rev. Proc. 2008-50, Section 10.

tative) to the Service that contains a description of the failures, a description of the proposed methods of correction, and other procedural items. Appendix D and Appendix F of the revenue procedure are provided to assist the applicant in satisfying these requirements. If agreement is reached, the Service will send to the Plan Sponsor a compliance statement specifying the corrective action required.[12]

In most cases, the fee is determined by the following chart:[13]

Number of Participants	Fee
20 or fewer	$ 750
21 to 50	$ 1,000
51 to 100	$ 2,500
101 to 500	$ 5,000
501 to 1,000	$ 8,000
1,001 to 5,000	$15,000
5,001 to 10,000	$20,000
Over 10,000	$25,000

Correction on Audit (Audit CAP)

If a failure (other than a failure corrected through SCP or VCP) is identified on audit, the Plan Sponsor may correct the failure and pay a sanction. The sanction imposed will bear a reasonable relationship to the nature, extent, and severity of the failure, taking into account the extent to which correction occurred before audit. The program has been designed so that the Audit CAP sanction will be much more punitive than the fees for VCP.

Evolution of EPCRS

The EPCRS program continues to evolve, and all relevant information is available through the IRS website at http://www.irs.gov/retirement/article/0,,id=96907,00.html. The "Correcting Plan Errors" page has links to reasons as to why a plan sponsor should spend money to perform self-audits to find and correct mistakes rather than waiting for the IRS to find the mistakes through a plan audit, "fix-it" guides to help plan sponsors find and correct the most common operational mistakes, and specific procedures and model cover letters for the most recent version of EPCRS, which is through Rev. Proc. 2008-50. While the EPCRS program had been improving and evolving on its own over time to allow for more mistakes to be corrected and to allow for simpler procedures for plan sponsors to follow, Congress granted the Secretary of the Treasury the full authority to establish and implement EPCRS and, among other things, instructs the Secretary to continue to update and improve EPCRS, giving special attention to the following: (1) increasing the awareness and knowledge of small employers concerning the availability and use of the program; (2) taking into account special concerns and circumstances that small employers face with respect to compliance and correction of compliance failures; (3) extending the duration of the self-correction period under SCP for significant compliance failures; (4) expanding the availability to correct insignificant compliance failures under SCP during audit; and (5) assuring that any tax, penalty, or sanction that is imposed by reason of a compliance failure is not excessive and bears a reasonable relationship to the nature, extent, and severity of the failure.[14] Therefore, it remains a

---

12. See Rev. Proc. 2008-50, Section 11.
13. See Rev. Proc. 2008-50, Section 12.
14. Pension Protection Act of 2006, section 1101.

high priority in Employee Plans to continue expanding the EPCRS program in conjunction with a greater examination presence and the imposition of much more expensive penalties if mistakes are discovered by the IRS on audit rather than by the plan administrator.

5. Examinations of Plan Operations

The Plan Administrator must operate all aspects of the plan in accordance with the plan documents. The plan document should always be in compliance with ERISA, the Code, and other federal and state laws. Therefore, the actions (or affirmative inactions) of the Plan Administrator and Trustees should always be in compliance with controlling laws and regulations.

Some of the recurring operations of the Plan Administrator can be outsourced to a third party with a particular expertise in such things as:

- Benefit determinations and calculations;
- Minimum Required Distributions;
- Record Keeping Services (especially maintenance of account balances in defined contribution plans);
- Allocation of employer contributions to a defined contribution plan;
- Annual testing (nondiscrimination, special 401(k) nondiscrimination, minimum coverage, and Top Heavy);
- Determining eligibility for plan participation;
- Satisfying all reporting and disclosure requirements;
- Monitoring beneficiary designations;
- Loan processing (if the plan document allows for plan loans); and
- Ensuring operational compliance.

However, that does not relieve the plan administrator from its duties. When audited, the plan administrator is responsible for meeting with the EP examination agent, or providing appropriate power of attorney to a benefits professional who can assist the examination agent with answering all questions and providing all requested data regarding the plan's operation.

Monika Templeman, Manager of EP Examinations, employs efficiencies with her team, which includes "focused examinations, data-driven case selection methodologies, and using Employee Plans Compliance Unit (EPCU) compliance checks to leverage resources."[15] There is plenty of public information available at the EP Examinations and Enforcement page,[16] such as links to "Technical/Procedural Guidelines for EP Examination Employees" and "EP Examination Process Guide."

Let's look at some of the current EP Examination priorities in a bit more detail, since the impact and extent of the examination program has a great affect on the level of advice and assistance plan sponsors should seek from competent benefits professionals. The IRS EP Examination group is transparent in what they look for in examinations and ways to correct any discovered problems without draconian remedies, and therefore, as bene-

---

15. IRS Employee Plan News, Summer 2008, Vol. 8, available at http://www.irs.gov/pub/irs-tege/sum08.pdf.

16. see http://www.irs.gov/retirement/article/0,,id=147731,00.html

fits professionals, the more we know about how they operate, the better we can advise our plan sponsor clients.

Focused Examinations

According to the Employee Plans FY 2009 Working Plan,[17] It will continue to optimize case selection methodology and complete audits using the focused examination approach, and will identify areas of non-compliant behavior and develop additional Risk-Based Targeted (RBT) examination projects, with a special emphasis on 401(k) plans. RBT examinations are expected to improve the use of resources by leading to more productive examinations by, focusing on less compliant market segments. This, in turn, will reduce the burden on the compliant taxpayers. Issues are pre-selected based upon the analysis of the completed baseline segments. Current examination procedures call for field agents to use Focused Examination techniques for all examinations with the exception of training cases, cases assigned to new hires and certain specified projects. Pre-determined issues are chosen using plans or industry type or other criteria based upon historical information from results of prior examinations. This concept has proven to allow agents to perform examinations more effectively and efficiently. As a result, examinations are completed in less time, allowing for increased examination coverage and reduced burden in terms of time and expense incurred by the compliant taxpayer. Focused Examination techniques are characterized by several key concepts and examination activities:

Cases are assigned with the expectation that the audit will be primarily focused on three mandatory pre-determined issues.

The agent takes the following actions:
- performs a comprehensive pre-audit analysis selecting two additional issues;
- solicits only documents required to resolve these issues;
- uses effective interview techniques;
- evaluates a taxpayer's system of internal controls;
- expands the audit scope based on facts and circumstances; and,
- closes the case as soon as the known issues are resolved.

The Learn, Educate, Self-Correct, and Enforce (LESE) concept was started in FY 2007 and uses "judgment sampling" as selection criteria. Selections are based upon personal, informed judgments that cases contain issues of interest. To identify issues of interest, all available information from agents, referrals, media, determinations, outreach, and other sources are considered. The LESE Project Selection Team, which is a cross selection of employees from all functions within EP, will be responsible for recommending and developing future projects for the program.

Large Cases and the Employee Plans Team Audit

Of the approximately 1 million qualified plans, about 4,500 (<1%) are EPTA plans (having 2,500 or more participants), yet they cover approximately 60% of plan participants and they hold approximately 70% of plan assets.[18] EPTA teams review each plan to ensure they are compliant in form and in operation, and the primary objective is protection

---

17. available at http://www.irs.gov/pub/irs-tege/epwrkpln_09.pdf.
18. Large Case Examinations: The IRS Viewpoint, presentation prepared April 2009, available at http://www.irs.gov/pub/irs-tege/epta.pdf.

of plan assets and participants. The EPTA team coordinates with other operating divisions of the IRS (mainly Large and Mid-Size Business), and coordinates with the Department of Labor and the Pension Benefit Guaranty Corporation.

Abusive Tax Avoidance Transactions

The IRS is engaged in extensive efforts to curb abusive tax shelter schemes and transactions. The Tax Exempt and Government Entities Division of the IRS, including the office of Employee Plans, participates in this IRS-wide effort by devoting substantial resources to the identification, analysis, and examination of abusive tax shelter schemes and promotions. A "listed transaction" is a transaction that is the same as, or substantially similar to, one that the IRS has determined to be a tax avoidance transaction and identified by IRS notice or other form of published guidance. The parties who participate in listed transactions may be required to disclose the transaction as required by the regulations, register the transaction with the IRS, or maintain lists of investors in the transactions and provide the list to the IRS on request.

The IRS had identified the following transactions involving employee benefit plans as listed transactions:

- Deductions for Excess Life Insurance in a Section 412(i) or Other Defined Benefit Plan (as discussed in Chapter 5, such plans are now defined at IRC § 412(e)(3);
- S Corporation ESOP Abuses: Certain Business Structures Held to Violate Code Section 409(p);
- S Corporation ESOP Abuse of Delayed Effective Date for Section 409(p);
- 401(k) Accelerated Deductions;
- Collectively Bargained Welfare Benefit Funds under Section 419A(f)(5);
- Certain Trust Arrangements Seeking to Qualify for Exemption from Section 419; and
- Abusive Roth IRA Transactions.

While not currently a listed transaction, there seem to be many problems with rollovers used as business startups, usually where a franchise is bought from the proceeds of an IRA or qualified retirement plan rollover.[19]

The bottom line is that the IRS has taken the approach that "if it sounds too good to be true" then it probably is. IRS officials have indicated that the listed transactions are only a starting point, and any employee benefit plan that is not established for the sole purpose of providing the promised benefits to employees will be suspect. Therefore, any promotional materials or discussions that a small business owner receives regarding their current or potential employee benefit plans should be discussed with their trusted employee benefits advisor before being acted upon, especially when they sound too good to be true.[20]

Employee Plans Compliance Unit

The EPCU focuses on compliance projects and performs data analysis, and was established to address pension compliance in a whole new way. Through the use of com-

---

19. See http://www.irs.gov/pub/irs-tege/rollover_guidelines.pdf.

20. The catch phrase used consistently by IRS officials to describe Abusive Tax Avoidance Transactions that affect employee benefit plans, first appeared in print in the Spring 2004 edition of their "Employee Plan News" available at http://www.irs.gov/pub/irs-tege/spr04.pdf.

pliance contacts by correspondence, telephone and other media, the EPCU will focus on project activity where there are indications of potential non-compliance. The EPCU will address compliance issues on more plans with less staffing resources than by performing traditional field examinations. The EPCU has performed over 4,700 compliance checks, contacting nearly 4,200 taxpayers since the Unit was established in 2005. The EPCU resolves issues without the necessity for a full scope examination of the books and records of the plan. This approach will not replace field audits. However, when simple verification or clarification of issues is needed, this can be accomplished with less burden to the taxpayer, saving time and money for both the taxpayer and the IRS by utilizing compliance contacts. One of the major projects currently underway is the design and implementation of a 401(k) compliance questionnaire in order to gain a better understanding of compliance behaviors of the 401(k) market segment and to recommend strategies to address the identified areas of non-compliance. Other EPCU priorities include a governmental plans questionnaire; a Master & Prototype compliance survey; a multiemployer actuarial certification review; universal availability compliance in 403(b) plans; and a review of form 5330's and determining whether plans have actually corrected the prohibited transactions that they reported.[21]

International Issues

IRS Commissioner Douglas Shulman has stated "In the U.S., international tax issues have moved to center stage. It is a major priority for President Obama, and last month he outlined a bold suite of international legislative proposals. At the same time, the IRS has been stepping up enforcement measures in this area. We are aggressively tracking down tax evaders hiding their wealth overseas and the promoters who aid and abet these schemes. We are steadily increasing the pressure on offshore financial institutions that facilitate concealment of taxable income by U.S. citizens. Indeed, I have made international issues a top priority since 'Day One' of my tenure as IRS Commissioner and it's not just because we live in a global world."[22] The EP international strategies include enhanced coordination with the Large & Mid-Size Business (LMSB) Division Territories (Hacienda Project) and targeting areas of significant risk through education and outreach and compliance/enforcement activities (EPCU Projects).[23]

Improving Communication between Plans Sponsors and EP Examination Agents before and during an Audit

The IRS has drafted an "Employee Plan Audit Efficiency Guide,"[24] which advises the plan sponsor and agent of the coming audit, and is intended to help establish a reasonable working relationship so the audit can proceed as efficiently as possible and so both parties will know what to expect during the audit. This guide outlines how the EP examination agent and the plan sponsor will work with each other during the course of the audit. It contains links information relevant in preparing for the audit.

---

21. Hot Topics: A View From the Top, presentation by Monika Templeman and Janice Gore, 2009 Hot Topics Program for EP Examination Agents of the IRS, Chicago.

22. Prepared Remarks of IRS Commissioner Doug Shulman Before the Organization For Economic Co-Operation And Development Washington, DC, June 2, 2009, available http://www.irs.gov/newsroom/article/0,,id=209342,00.html.

23. Hot Topics: A View From the Top, presentation by Monika Templeman and Janice Gore, 2009 Hot Topics Program for EP Examination Agents of the IRS, Chicago.

24. available at http://www.irs.gov/pub/irs-tege/audit_eff_guide.pdf.

Michael Julianelle, Director of Employee Plans, has indicated that the "role [of EP] is to make sure that the plan is operating in accordance with the plan terms and providing appropriate benefits to plan participants. Obviously, when our presence diminishes, the opportunity for noncompliance increases. We strive to avoid that as much as possible. Considering that there are over one million filers, we will focus our efforts on those returns that demonstrate audit potential and then spend additional time only on those returns that indicate areas of noncompliance. One way to do this is by refining our inventory selection methods using a market segment approach, and then using information derived from those examinations in order to better select returns in the future. We'll also improve our analysis of the data we have at hand to ensure we are focused on our critical priorities and we will remain nimble by shifting our resources to areas of potential abuse. Our expansion into abusive schemes is an example of this.

As stated in Revenue Procedure 64-22, an examinations program should be both reasonable and vigorous. It should be conducted with as little delay as possible and with appropriate courtesy and considerateness. It should also be vigorous in requiring compliance with the law. In applying this concept, we will look at issues from the customer's perspective to improve the process and to make it less burdensome on everyone. In summary, EP Examinations recognizes our responsibility for maintaining the private retirement system, borne through compliance enforcement with a customer focus."[25]

If the plan is audited by the IRS and the Plan Administrator is found to have violated the plan document in operation, then a "correction" must be made (generally to bring the plan assets and benefits to exactly (or approximately) where they would have been if the plan had been operated in proper compliance with the document). Additionally, statutory penalties will generally be assessed.

One of the major tools used by the IRS in pre-examination targeting, is the information disclosed on the annual Form 5500. However, since the form 5500 is now submitted to the Department of Labor, and since they have a self-correction program for late filings, the requirements for filing a form 5500 are described in Chapter 17.

6. Professionals That Can Represent the Plan in Front of the IRS

Each qualified retirement plan is provided with a unique taxpayer identification number (TIN), which is different than the sponsoring employer's TIN. When a plan is established, the plan sponsor should apply for a TIN for the plan by submitting an IRS form SS-4, and checking "Trust" or "Plan Administrator," whichever is more appropriate for the actual situation, in question 9a. Once established, then the individuals with authority through that TIN are the only people that the IRS can talk to, whether during an informal communication or through a more formal examination.

Pursuant to Circular 230, only Attorneys, Certified Public Accountants, Enrolled Actuaries, Enrolled Agents, and now Enrolled Retirement Plan Agents, can represent a plan sponsor on audit. The ethics requirements for Circular 230 are explained in more detail in Chapter 21. The IRS Form 2848, "Power of Attorney and Declaration of Representative(Rev. June 2008)" is used by the plan sponsor to delegate the extent and tax years for

---

25. EP Connections: Interview With Michael Julianelle, available at http://www.irs.gov/retirement/article/0,,id=176389,00.html.

which a benefits professional can act on its behalf (for example, if the 2009 plan year is being audited, the plan sponsor can submit a form 2848 that limits a professional's scope of authority to the audit of the form 5500 and attachments for the plan filed for its 2009 plan year). In addition to the above professionals, the form 2848 allows other officers or full-time employees of the sponsoring employer to be granted power of attorney, as well as family members, unenrolled return preparers, student attorneys and student CPAs. An IRS form 8821, Tax Information Information, is a much more restrictive form, as it allows an individual to inspect and/or receive confidential tax information about the plan, but unlike the form 2848, an individual named on a form 8821 cannot advocate a position on behalf of the plan.

Section III

Labor Rights and Protections in ERISA Plans

Now, after focusing on the income tax aspects of the Internal Revenue Code specifically for qualified retirement plans, the textbook changes focus to the rights that attach to employees promised employee benefits by their employer which are delivered through a written plan. These rules extend beyond qualified retirement plans, and go to other retirement plans and to health and welfare benefit plans.

Chapter 11 discusses the requirements for a plan, fund, program or scheme to be classified as an ERISA plans (regardless of intent). First is a discussion of the employee benefits plans subject to ERISA, in general, and then a focus on those plans that are classified as retirement plans under ERISA and then finally those plans that are classified as health and welfare benefit plans under ERISA.

Chapter 12 discusses the requirements for written plan documents (which is not necessarily always the attorney's responsibility). The chapter first provides the rules for a good written plan document, and then compares the controlling plan document with the plan's required Summary Plan Description.

One of the most important aspects of ERISA are the fiduciary requirements. Chapter 13 first discusses the legal classification of fiduciary for any individual who has any control over the investment and distribution of plan assets and their duties for each decision, then discusses the special limitations and exceptions under the prohibited transactions rules, and then a discussion of the special rules for self-directed 401(k) plans. The chapter continues with a discussion of the personal liability an individual will owe to the plan if he or she breaches a fiduciary duty, and ends with a discussion of how plan assets can be used to pay expenses.

Chapter 14 discusses the specific ERISA causes of action. The chapter starts with a discussion of how ERISA preempts all state laws that attempt to regulate employee benefits plans, and then a discussion of the specific criminal and civil causes of action, and their respective remedies, and then a discussion of the importance an the benefits claim provision in an ERISA plan, before concluding with some miscellaneous ERISA litigation issues.

Chapter 15 highlights the reporting and disclosure obligations an employer is responsible for once it decides to sponsor an ERISA plan. First, the governmental reporting issues are discussed, and then the participant disclosures are summarized.

Chapter 16 is a small chapter, but is important as retirement plan terminations are only allowed after certain events and thresh holds, and not simply the moment that the employer decides it no longer wants to sponsor an ERISA plan. First, the rules for termination of single-employer defined benefit and defined contribution plans are discussed, and then the rules for withdrawal from a multi-employer defined benefit plan are summarized. There are generally no plan termination restrictions imposed on health and welfare plans.

After all of the labor and employment rules under ERISA are presented, Chapter 17 explores how the Department of Labor's Employee Benefits Security Administration (EBSA) operates in regulating ERISA plans. First is a quick overview of the organization of the Department, and then a focus on EBSA and its various roles in enforcement, publishing technical guidance and Prohibited Transaction exemptions, drafting amicus curie briefs, and collecting annual forms 5500.

Chapter 11

ERISA Plans

Overview

What is a plan for purposes of ERISA?

- the general rule of thumb is: every time an employer promises benefits to employees, ERISA will govern unless a specific statutory or regulatory provision (or binding judicial decree) specifically excludes ERISA coverage
- generally, any scheme, program or payroll procedure which promises retirement or health and welfare benefits to employees (generally at least two) can be deemed a plan by the Department of Labor or by a court, even if the employer did not intend for the scheme to be a plan
- certain plans are statutorily excluded from ERISA coverage (*i.e.*, plans sponsored by churches and plans sponsored by state and local governments)
- certain plans are excluded from ERISA coverage by regulations (*i.e.*, sick and vacation day plans, certain severance pay plans and short-term disability plans)
- certain plans are excluded only from certain provisions of ERISA but are subject to others (*i.e.*, Top Hat non-qualified deferred compensation plans)

A. ERISA Plans

1. Employee Benefit Plans Governed by ERISA

Statutory Definition at ERISA § 3(3)

The term "employee benefit plan" or "plan" means an employee welfare benefit plan or an employee pension benefit plan or a plan which is both an employee welfare benefit plan and an employee pension benefit plan.

Certain types of plans are excepted from coverage under Title I of ERISA, including: (1) individual retirement annuities or accounts (IRAs); (2) church plans; (3) governmental plans; (4) unfunded excess benefit plans; (5) plans outside the United States for the benefit of nonresident aliens; (6) plans maintained solely for compliance with applicable workman's compensation and unemployment laws; and (7) certain tax-sheltered annuity programs with limited employer involvement.[1] Therefore, these types of plans must comply with any applicable state laws, which might be different if the employer

---

1. ERISA § 4(b).

does business in different states, and with the Code, whether or not there are certain statutory provisions.

2. Employee Benefit Plans Not Governed by ERISA

As indicated in the Labor Regulations below, plans without employees are not governed by ERISA.

Labor Regs. § 2510.3-3. Employee Benefit Plan

(a) **General.** This section clarifies the definition in section 3(3) of the term "employee benefit plan" for purposes of title I of the Act and this chapter. It states a general principle which can be applied to a large class of plans to determine whether they constitute employee benefit plans within the meaning of section 3(3) of the Act. Under section 4(a) of the Act, only employee benefit plans within the meaning of section 3(3) are subject to title I.

(b) **Plans without employees.** For purposes of title I of the Act and this chapter, the term "employee benefit plan" shall not include any plan, fund or program, other than an apprenticeship or other training program, under which no employees are participants covered under the plan, as defined in paragraph (d) of this section. For example, a so-called "Keogh" or "H.R. 10" plan under which only partners or only a sole proprietor are participants covered under the plan will not be covered under title I. However, a Keogh plan under which one or more common law employees, in addition to the self-employed individuals, are participants covered under the plan, will be covered under title I. Similarly, partnership buyout agreements described in section 736 of the Internal Revenue Code of 1954 will not be subject to title I.

(c) **Employees.** For purposes of this section:

(1) An individual and his or her spouse shall not be deemed to be employees with respect to a trade or business, whether incorporated or unincorporated, which is wholly owned by the individual or by the individual and his or her spouse, and

(2) A partner in a partnership and his or her spouse shall not be deemed to be employees with respect to the partnership.

(d) **Participant covered under the plan.**

(1) (i) An individual becomes a participant covered under an employee welfare benefit plan on the earlier of—

(A) The date designated by the plan as the date on which the individual begins participation in the plan;

(B) The date on which the individual becomes eligible under the plan for a benefit subject only to occurrence of the contingency for which the benefit is provided; or

(C) The date on which the individual makes a contribution to the plan, whether voluntary or mandatory.

(ii) An individual becomes a participant covered under an employee pension plan—

(A) In the case of a plan which provides for employee contributions or defines participation to include employees who have not yet retired, on the earlier of—

(1) The date on which the individual makes a contribution, whether voluntary or mandatory, or

(2) The date designated by the plan as the date on which the individual has satisfied the plan's age and service requirements for participation, and

(B) In the case of a plan which does not provide for employee contributions and does not define participation to include employees who have not yet retired, the date on which the individual completes the first year of employment which may be taken into account in determining—

(1) Whether the individual is entitled to benefits under the plan, or

(2) The amount of benefits to which the individual is entitled,

whichever results in earlier participation.

(2) (i) An individual is not a participant covered under an employee welfare plan on the earliest date on which the individual—

(A) Is ineligible to receive any benefit under the plan even if the contingency for which such benefit is provided should occur, and

(B) Is not designated by the plan as a participant.

(ii) An individual is not a participant covered under an employee pension plan or a beneficiary receiving benefits under an employee pension plan if—

(A) The entire benefit rights of the individual—

(1) Are fully guaranteed by an insurance company, insurance service or insurance organization licensed to do business in a State, and are legally enforceable by the sole choice of the individual against the insurance company, insurance service or insurance organization; and

(2) A contract, policy or certificate describing the benefits to which the individual is entitled under the plan has been issued to the individual; or

(B) The individual has received from the plan a lump-sum distribution or a series of distributions of cash or other property which represents the balance of his or her credit under the plan.

(3) (i) In the case of an employee pension benefit plan, an individual who, under the terms of the plan, has incurred a one-year break in service after having become a participant covered under

the plan, and who has acquired no vested right to a benefit before such break in service is not a participant covered under the plan until the individual has completed a year of service after returning to employment covered by the plan.

(ii) For purposes of paragraph (d)(3)(i) of this section, in the case of an employee pension benefit plan which is subject to section 203 of the Act the term "year of service" shall have the same meaning as in section 203(b)(2)(A) of the Act and any regulations issued under the Act and the term "one-year break in service" shall have the same meaning as in section 203(b)(3)(A) of the Act and any regulations issued under the Act.

B. ERISA Retirement Plans

1. Retirement Plans Governed by ERISA

Statutory Definition at ERISA § 3(2)

An "employee pension benefit plan" generally means any plan, fund, or program which, by its express terms or as a result of surrounding circumstances, provides retirement income to employees, or results in a deferral of income by employees for periods extending to the termination of covered employment or beyond, or until age 62, regardless of the method of calculating the contributions made to the plan, the method of calculating the benefits under the plan or the method of distributing benefits from the plan.

This means that when the surrounding facts indicate that an employer is providing retirement income, then the Department of Labor or a Court can declare that the method of delivering the benefits constitutes an employee pension benefit plan, which is subject to all of the rules in ERISA. This can be when the employer inadvertently makes certain retirement promises to more than one employee (especially through statements made by its human resources department), or when the employer purposely attempts to avoid ERISA governance.

This includes qualified retirement plans and Top-Hat non-qualified deferred compensation plans (but not excess-benefits plans), as discussed in Chapter 18. Excess benefit plans, if drafted properly, are wholly exempt from ERISA, while top-hat plans, if drafted properly, are only subject to limited ERISA governance. Because both types of plans are outside the full purview of ERISA, they are collectively known as non-qualified retirement plans for executives.

2. Retirement Plans Not Governed by ERISA

As shown in more detail in the excerpt from the Labor Regulations below, the following plans are not deemed to be employee benefit pension plans:

- Severance pay plans of up to 200% of pay paid out within 24 months;

- Bonus programs that do not systematically defer compensation for work performed until termination or retirement;
- Individual Retirement Accounts;
- Gratuitous payments to former participants that retired before ERISA was effective; and
- 403(b) Tax Sheltered Annuities that are purely voluntary and have minimal involvement by employers.

Labor Regs. § 2510.3-2. Employee Pension Benefit Plan

(a) **General.** This section clarifies the limits of the defined terms "employee pension benefit plan" and "pension plan" for purposes of title I of the Act and this chapter by identifying certain specific plans, funds and programs which do not constitute employee pension benefit plans for those purposes. To the extent that these plans, funds and programs constitute employee welfare benefit plans within the meaning of section 3(1) of the Act and § 2510.3-1 of this part, they will be covered under title I; however, they will not be subject to parts 2 and 3 of title I of the Act.

(b) **Severance pay plans.**

(1) For purposes of title I of the Act and this chapter, an arrangement shall not be deemed to constitute an employee pension benefit plan or pension plan solely by reason of the payment of severance benefits on account of the termination of an employee's service, provided that:

(i) Such payments are not contingent, directly or indirectly, upon the employee's retiring;

(ii) The total amount of such payments does not exceed the equivalent of twice the employee's annual compensation during the year immediately preceding the termination of his service; and

(iii) All such payments to any employee are completed,

(A) In the case of an employee whose service is terminated in connection with a limited program of terminations, within the later of 24 months after the termination of the employee's service, or 24 months after the employee reaches normal retirement age; and

(B) In the case of all other employees, within 24 months after the termination of the employee's service.

(2) For purposes of this paragraph (b),

(i) "Annual compensation" means the total of all compensation, including wages, salary, and any other benefit of monetary value, whether paid in the form of cash or otherwise, which was paid as consideration for the employee's service during the year, or which would have been so paid at the employee's usual rate of compensation if the employee had worked a full year.

(ii) "Limited program of terminations" means a program of terminations:

(A) Which, when begun, was scheduled to be completed upon a date certain or upon the occurrence of one or more specified events;

(B) Under which the number, percentage or class or classes of employees whose services are to be terminated is specified in advance; and

(C) Which is described in a written document which is available to the Secretary upon request, and which contains information sufficient to demonstrate that the conditions set forth in paragraphs (b)(2)(ii)(A) and (B) of this section have been met.

(c) Bonus program. For purposes of title I of the Act and this chapter, the terms "employee pension benefit plan" and "pension plan" shall not include payments made by an employer to some or all of its employees as bonuses for work performed, unless such payments are systematically deferred to the termination of covered employment or beyond, or so as to provide retirement income to employees.

(d) Individual Retirement Accounts. (1) For purposes of title I of the Act and this chapter, the terms "employee pension benefit plan" and "pension plan" shall not include an individual retirement account described in section 408(a) of the Code, an individual retirement annuity described in section 408(b) of the Internal Revenue Code of 1954 (hereinafter "the Code") and an individual retirement bond described in section 409 of the Code, provided that

* * *

(f) Tax sheltered annuities. For the purpose of title I of the Act and this chapter, a program for the purchase of an annuity contract or the establishment of a custodial account described in section 403(b) of the Internal Revenue Code of 1954 (the Code), pursuant to salary reduction agreements or agreements to forego an increase in salary, which meets the requirements of 26 CFR 1.403(b)-1(b)(3) shall not be "established or maintained by an employer" as that phrase is used in the definition of the terms "employee pension benefit plan" and "pension plan" if

(1) Participation is completely voluntary for employees;

(2) All rights under the annuity contract or custodial account are enforceable solely by the employee, by a beneficiary of such employee, or by any authorized representative of such employee or beneficiary;

(3) The sole involvement of the employer, other than pursuant to paragraph (f)(2) of this section, is limited to any of the following:

(i) Permitting annuity contractors (which term shall include any agent or broker who offers annuity contracts or who makes available custodial accounts within the meaning of section 403(b)(7) of the Code) to publicize their products to employees,

(ii) Requesting information concerning proposed funding media, products or annuity contractors;

(iii) Summarizing or otherwise compiling the information provided with respect to the proposed funding media or products which are made available, or the annuity contractors whose services are provided, in order to facilitate review and analysis by the employees;

(iv) Collecting annuity or custodial account considerations as required by salary reduction agreements or by agreements to forego salary increases, remitting such considerations to annuity contractors and maintaining records of such considerations;

(v) Holding in the employer's name one or more group annuity contracts covering its employees;

(vi) Before February 7, 1978, ***; or

(vii) After February 6, 1978, limiting the funding media or products available to employees, or the annuity contractors who may approach employees, to a number and selection which is designed to afford employees a reasonable choice in light of all relevant circumstances. Relevant circumstances may include, but would not necessarily be limited to, the following types of factors:

(A) The number of employees affected,

(B) The number of contractors who have indicated interest in approaching employees,

(C) The variety of available products,

(D) The terms of the available arrangements,

(E) The administrative burdens and costs to the employer, and

(F) The possible interference with employee performance resulting from direct solicitation by contractors; and

(4) The employer receives no direct or indirect consideration or compensation in cash or otherwise other than reasonable compensation to cover expenses properly and actually incurred by such employer in the performance of the employer's duties pursuant to the salary reduction agreements or agreements to forego salary increases described in this paragraph (f) of this section.

(g) **Supplemental payment plans**—

(1) General rule. Generally, an arrangement by which a payment is made by an employer to supplement retirement income is a pension plan. Supplemental payments made on or after September 26, 1980, shall be treated as being made under a welfare plan rather than a pension plan for purposes of title I of the Act if all of the following conditions are met:

(i) Payment is made for the purpose of supplementing the pension benefits of a participant or his or her beneficiary out of:

(A) The general assets of the employer, or

(B) A separate trust fund established and maintained solely for that purpose.

(ii) The amount payable under the supplemental payment plan to a participant or his or her beneficiary with respect to a month does not exceed the payee's supplemental payment factor ("SPF," as defined in paragraph (g)(3)(i) of this section) for that month, provided however, that unpaid monthly amounts may be cumulated and paid in subsequent months to the participant or his or her beneficiary.

(iii) The payment is not made before the last day of the month with respect to which it is computed.

(2) Safe harbor for arrangements concerning pre-1977 retirees. ***

(3) Definitions and special rules. For purposes of this paragraph (g)—

(i) The term "supplemental payment factor" (SPF) is, for any particular month, the product of:

(A) The individual's pension benefit amount (as defined in paragraph (g)(3)(ii) of this section), and

(B) The cost of living increase (as defined in paragraph (g)(3)(v) of this section) for that month.

* * *

(5) *Examples.* The following examples illustrate how this paragraph (g) works.

* * *

C. ERISA Health and Welfare Benefits Plans

1. Health and Welfare Benefit Plans Governed by ERISA

Statutory Definition at ERISA § 3(1)

The terms "employee welfare benefit plan" and "welfare plan" mean any plan, fund, or program which was heretofore or is hereafter established or maintained by an employer or by an employee organization, or by both, to the extent that such plan, fund, or program was established or is maintained for the purpose of providing for its participants or their beneficiaries, through the purchase of insurance or otherwise, (A) medical, surgical, or hospital care or benefits, or benefits in the event of sickness, accident, disability, death or unemployment, or vacation benefits, apprenticeship or other training programs, or day care centers, scholarship funds, or prepaid legal services, or (B) any benefit described in section 186(c) of this title (other than pensions on retirement or death, and insurance to provide such pensions).

2. Health and Welfare Benefit Plans Not Governed by ERISA

As shown in more detail in the excerpt from the Labor Regulations below, the following plans are not deemed to be employee welfare pension plans:

- Payroll practices that provide overtime pay, shift premiums, holiday premiums or weekend premiums;
- On-premises facilities;
- Holiday gifts;

- Sales to employees;
- Hiring halls;
- Remembrance funds;
- Strike funds;
- Industry advancement programs;
- Certain group or group-type insurance programs; and
- Unfunded scholarship programs.

Labor Regs. § 2510.3-1. Employee Welfare Benefit Plan

(a) General.

(1) The purpose of this section is to clarify the definition of the terms "employee welfare benefit plan" and "welfare plan" for purposes of Title I of the Act and this chapter by identifying certain practices which do not constitute employee welfare benefit plans for those purposes. In addition, the practices listed in this section do not constitute employee pension benefit plans within the meaning of section 3(2) of the Act, and, therefore, do not constitute employee benefit plans within the meaning of section 3(3). Since under section 4(a) of the Act, only employee benefit plans within the meaning of section 3(3) are subject to Title I of the Act, the practices listed in this section are not subject to Title I.

(2) The terms "employee welfare benefit plan" and "welfare plan" are defined in section 3(1) of the Act to include plans providing "(i) medical, surgical, or hospital care or benefits, or benefits in the event of sickness, accident, disability, death or unemployment, or vacation benefits, apprenticeship or other training programs, or day care centers, scholarship funds, or prepaid legal services, or (ii) any benefit described in section 302(c) of the Labor Management Relations Act, 1947 (other than pensions on retirement or death, and insurance to provide such pensions)." Under this definition, only plans which provide benefits described in section 3(1)(A) of the Act or in section 302(c) of the Labor-Management Relations Act, 1947 (hereinafter "the LMRA")(other than pensions on retirement or death) constitute welfare plans. For example, a system of payroll deductions by an employer for deposit in savings accounts owned by its employees is not an employee welfare benefit plan within the meaning of section 3(1) of the Act because it does not provide benefits described in section 3(1)(A) of the Act or section 302(c) of the LMRA. (In addition, if each employee has the right to withdraw the balance in his or her account at any time, such a payroll savings plan does not meet the requirements for a pension plan set forth in section 3(2) of the Act and, therefore, is not an employee benefit plan within the meaning of section 3(3) of the Act).

(3) Section 302(c) of the LMRA lists exceptions to the restrictions contained in subsections (a) and (b) of that section on payments and loans made by an employer to individuals and groups representing employees of the employer. Of these exceptions, only those contained in paragraphs (5), (6), (7) and (8) describe benefits provided through employee benefit plans. Moreover, only paragraph (6) describes benefits not described in section 3(1)(A) of the Act. The benefits described in section 302(c)(6) of

the LMRA but not in section 3(1)(A) of the Act are " * * * holiday, severance or similar benefits". Thus, the effect of section 3(1)(B) of the Act is to include within the definition of "welfare plan" those plans which provide holiday and severance benefits, and benefits which are similar (for example, benefits which are in substance severance benefits, although not so characterized).

(4) Some of the practices listed in this section as excluded from the definition of "welfare plan" or mentioned as examples of general categories of excluded practices are inserted in response to questions received by the Department of Labor and, in the Department's judgment, do not represent borderline cases under the definition in section 3(1) of the Act. Therefore, this section should not be read as implicitly indicating the Department's views on the possible scope of section 3(1).

(b) **Payroll practices.** For purposes of Title I of the Act and this chapter, the terms "employee welfare benefit plan" and "welfare plan" shall not include—

(1) Payment by an employer of compensation on account of work performed by an employee, including compensation at a rate in excess of the normal rate of compensation on account of performance of duties under other than ordinary circumstances, such as—

(i) Overtime pay,

(ii) Shift premiums,

(iii) Holiday premiums,

(iv) Weekend premiums;

(2) Payment of an employee's normal compensation, out of the employer's general assets, on account of periods of time during which the employee is physically or mentally unable to perform his or her duties, or is otherwise absent for medical reasons (such as pregnancy, a physical examination or psychiatric treatment); and

(3) Payment of compensation, out of the employer's general assets, on account of periods of time during which the employee, although physically and mentally able to perform his or her duties and not absent for medical reasons (such as pregnancy, a physical examination or psychiatric treatment) performs no duties; for example—

(i) Payment of compensation while an employee is on vacation or absent on a holiday, including payment of premiums to induce employees to take vacations at a time favorable to the employer for business reasons,

(ii) Payment of compensation to an employee who is absent while on active military duty,

(iii) Payment of compensation while an employee is absent for the purpose of serving as a juror or testifying in official proceedings,

(iv) Payment of compensation on account of periods of time during which an employee performs little or no productive work while engaged in training (whether or not subsidized in whole or in part by Federal, State or local government funds), and

(v) Payment of compensation to an employee who is relieved of duties while on sabbatical leave or while pursuing further education.

(c) On-premises facilities. For purposes of Title I of the Act and this chapter, the terms "employee welfare benefit plan" and "welfare plan" shall not include—

(1) The maintenance on the premises of an employer or of an employee organization of recreation, dining or other facilities (other than day care centers) for use by employees or members; and

(2) The maintenance on the premises of an employer of facilities for the treatment of minor injuries or illness or rendering first aid in case of accidents occurring during working hours.

(d) Holiday gifts. For purposes of Title I of the Act and this chapter the terms "employee welfare benefit plan" and "welfare plan" shall not include the distribution of gifts such as turkeys or hams by an employer to employees at Christmas and other holiday seasons.

(e) Sales to employees. For purposes of Title I of the Act and this chapter, the terms "employee welfare benefit plan" and "welfare plan" shall not include the sale by an employer to employees of an employer, whether or not at prevailing market prices, of articles or commodities of the kind which the employer offers for sale in the regular course of business.

(f) Hiring halls. For purposes of Title I of the Act and this chapter, the terms "employee welfare benefit plan" and "welfare plan" shall not include the maintenance by one or more employers, employee organizations, or both, of a hiring hall facility.

(g) Remembrance funds. For purposes of Title I of the Act and this chapter, the terms "employee welfare benefit plan" and "welfare plan" shall not include a program under which contributions are made to provide remembrances such as flowers, an obituary notice in a newspaper or a small gift on occasions such as the sickness, hospitalization, death or termination of employment of employees, or members of an employee organization, or members of their families.

(h) Strike funds. For purposes of Title I of the Act and this chapter, the terms "employee welfare benefit plan" and "welfare plan" shall not include a fund maintained by an employee organization to provide payments to its members during strikes and for related purposes.

(i) Industry advancement programs. For purposes of Title I of the Act and this chapter, the terms "employee welfare benefit plan" and "welfare plan" shall not include a program maintained by an employer or group or association of employers, which has no employee participants and does not provide benefits to employees or their dependents, regardless of whether the program serves as a conduit through which funds or other assets are channeled to employee benefit plans covered under Title I of the Act.

(j) Certain group or group-type insurance programs. For purposes of Title I of the Act and this chapter, the terms "employee welfare benefit plan" and "welfare plan" shall not include a group or group-type insurance program offered by an insurer to employees or members of an employee organization, under which

(1) No contributions are made by an employer or employee organization;

(2) Participation the program is completely voluntary for employees or members;

(3) The sole functions of the employer or employee organization with respect to the program are, without endorsing the program, to permit the insurer to publicize the program to employees or members, to collect premiums through payroll deductions or dues checkoffs and to remit them to the insurer; and

(4) The employer or employee organization receives no consideration in the form of cash or otherwise in connection with the program, other than reasonable compensation, excluding any profit, for administrative services actually rendered in connection with payroll deductions or dues checkoffs.

(k) **Unfunded scholarship programs.** For purposes of Title I of the Act and this chapter, the terms "employee welfare benefit plan" and "welfare plan" shall not include a scholarship program, including a tuition and education expense refund program, under which payments are made solely from the general assets of an employer or employee organization.

D. Congressional Findings and Declaration of Policy

Below are the provisions actually included in ERISA that show the official rationale and policy behind the law (feel free to be cynical as to the exact reasons Congress did what they did). The first was part of the original ERISA statute, and the other two were added after 1974.

29 USC § 1001; ERISA § 2, Congressional Findings and Declaration of Policy

(a) Benefit plans as affecting interstate commerce and the Federal taxing power

The Congress finds that the growth in size, scope, and numbers of employee benefit plans in recent years has been rapid and substantial; that the operational scope and economic impact of such plans is increasingly interstate; that the continued well-being and security of millions of employees and their dependents are directly affected by these plans; that they are affected with a national public interest; that they have become an important factor affecting the stability of employment and the successful development of industrial relations; that they have become an important factor in commerce because of the interstate character of their activities, and of the activities of their participants, and the employers, employee organizations, and other entities by which they are established or maintained; that a large volume of the activities of such plans are carried on by means of the mails and instrumentalities of interstate commerce; that owing to the lack of employee information and adequate safeguards concerning their operation, it is desirable in the interests of employees and their beneficiaries, and to provide for the general welfare and the free flow of commerce, that disclosure be made and safeguards be provided with respect to the establishment, operation, and administration of such plans; that they substantially affect the revenues of the United States because they are afforded preferential Federal tax treatment; that despite the enormous growth in such plans many employees with long years of employment are losing anticipated retirement benefits owing to the lack of vesting provisions in such plans; that owing to the inadequacy of current minimum standards, the soundness and stability of plans with respect to adequate funds to pay promised benefits may be endangered; that owing to the termination of plans before requisite funds have been accumulated, employees and their beneficiaries have been deprived of anticipated benefits; and that it is therefore desirable in the interests of employees and their beneficiaries, for the protection of the revenue of the United States, and to provide for the free flow of commerce, that minimum standards be provided assuring the equitable character of such plans and their financial soundness.

(b) Protection of interstate commerce and beneficiaries by requiring disclosure and reporting, setting standards of conduct, etc., for fiduciaries

It is hereby declared to be the policy of this chapter to protect interstate commerce and the interests of participants in employee benefit plans and their beneficiaries, by requiring the disclosure and reporting to participants and beneficiaries of financial and other information with respect thereto, by establishing standards of conduct, responsibility, and obligation for fiduciaries of employee benefit plans, and by providing for appropriate remedies, sanctions, and ready access to the Federal courts.

(c) Protection of interstate commerce, the Federal taxing power, and beneficiaries by vesting of accrued benefits, setting minimum standards of funding, requiring termination insurance

It is hereby further declared to be the policy of this chapter to protect interstate commerce, the Federal taxing power, and the interests of participants in private pension plans and their beneficiaries by improving the equitable character and the soundness of such plans by requiring them to vest the accrued benefits of employees with significant periods of service, to meet minimum standards of funding, and by requiring plan termination insurance.

§ 1001a. (No Corresponding Section of ERISA). Additional Congressional Findings and Declaration of Policy

(a) Effects of multiemployer pension plans — The Congress finds that —

(1) multiemployer pension plans have a substantial impact on interstate commerce and are affected with a national public interest;

(2) multiemployer pension plans have accounted for a substantial portion of the increase in private pension plan coverage over the past three decades;

(3) the continued well-being and security of millions of employees, retirees, and their dependents are directly affected by multiemployer pension plans; and

(4)

(A) withdrawals of contributing employers from a multiemployer pension plan frequently result in substantially increased funding obligations for employers who continue to contribute to the plan, adversely affecting the plan, its participants and beneficiaries, and labor-management relations, and

(B) in a declining industry, the incidence of employer withdrawals is higher and the adverse effects described in subparagraph (A) are exacerbated.

(b) Modification of multiemployer plan termination insurance provisions and replacement of program. The Congress further finds that—

(1) it is desirable to modify the current multiemployer plan termination insurance provisions in order to increase the likelihood of protecting plan participants against benefit losses; and

(2) it is desirable to replace the termination insurance program for multiemployer pension plans with an insolvency-based benefit protection program that will enhance the financial soundness of such plans, place primary emphasis on plan continuation, and contain program costs within reasonable limits.

(c) Policy—It is hereby declared to be the policy of this Act—

(1) to foster and facilitate interstate commerce,

(2) to alleviate certain problems which tend to discourage the maintenance and growth of multiemployer pension plans,

(3) to provide reasonable protection for the interests of participants and beneficiaries of financially distressed multiemployer pension plans, and

(4) to provide a financially self-sufficient program for the guarantee of employee benefits under multiemployer plans.

§ 1001b. (No Corresponding Section of ERISA). Findings and Declaration of Policy

(a) Findings—The Congress finds that—

(1) single-employer defined benefit pension plans have a substantial impact on interstate commerce and are affected with a national interest;

(2) the continued well-being and retirement income security of millions of workers, retirees, and their dependents are directly affected by such plans;

(3) the existence of a sound termination insurance system is fundamental to the retirement income security of participants and beneficiaries of such plans; and

(4) the current termination insurance system in some instances encourages employers to terminate pension plans, evade their obligations to pay benefits, and shift unfunded pension liabilities onto the termination insurance system and the other premium-payers.

(b) Additional findings—The Congress further finds that modification of the current termination insurance system and an increase in the insurance premium for single-employer defined benefit pension plans—

(1) is desirable to increase the likelihood that full benefits will be paid to participants and beneficiaries of such plans;

(2) is desirable to provide for the transfer of liabilities to the termination insurance system only in cases of severe hardship;

(3) is necessary to maintain the premium costs of such system at a reasonable level; and

(4) is necessary to finance properly current funding deficiencies and future obligations of the single-employer pension plan termination insurance system.

(c) Declaration of policy—It is hereby declared to be the policy of this title—

(1) to foster and facilitate interstate commerce;

(2) to encourage the maintenance and growth of single-employer defined benefit pension plans;

(3) to increase the likelihood that participants and beneficiaries under single-employer defined benefit pension plans will receive their full benefits;

(4) to provide for the transfer of unfunded pension liabilities onto the single-employer pension plan termination insurance system only in cases of severe hardship;

(5) to maintain the premium costs of such system at a reasonable level; and

(6) to assure the prudent financing of current funding deficiencies and future obligations of the single-employer pension plan termination insurance system by increasing termination insurance premiums.

Chapter 12

Written Plan Documents

Overview

What are the drafting requirements for ERISA plan documents?

- although ERISA requires a plan to be in the form of a written document, it does not specify its actual form

- case law has helped somewhat by suggesting the right words to use for certain provisions

- the reason for the requirement of a written plan document is to assure that every employee may, on examining the plan documents, determine exactly what his or her rights and obligations are under the plan

- the plan's written provisions control and cannot be altered by oral amendments or informal written communications (such as film strips, company newsletters, or letters to employees)—there is a trend, however, of an increasing willingness on the part of many courts to enforce oral amendments to plans under a theory of promissory estoppel

- the term "plan document" is usually comprised of four elements:

  - the plan document which describes in detail the rules under which the plan operates,

  - the trust agreement which establishes the trust under which the plan's assets are held (which may be incorporated in the same instrument or may be a separate document),

  - the summary plan description (SPD) which explains the plan's provisions in plain English for the plan participants and beneficiaries, and

  - the ancillary procedures which are adopted by the plan administrator

What is the importance of the Summary Plan Description?

- every employee must be provided with a Summary Plan Description (SPD) once they have met the eligibility requirements of the plan

- although they have the right to request a copy of the actual plan document, the SPD in reality is the only document the employees generally see regarding their benefits and other participant rights

- an SPD may be drafted in a variety of ways, as long as all of the required provisions are included and as long as it is written in a manner calculated to be understood by the average plan participant

- although the plan document is the controlling document, courts have held in some occasions that the terms of the SPD are controlling for those employees who relied on them

A. Written Plan Document

1. The Controlling Plan Document

The term "plan document" is usually comprised of four elements:

1. The plan document which describes in detail the rules under which the plan operates.

2. The trust agreement which establishes the trust under which the plan's assets are held (which may be incorporated in the same instrument or may be a separate document). Such trust must conform with the requirements of IRC § 501(a).

3. The summary plan description (SPD) which explains the plan's provisions in plain English for the plan participants and beneficiaries.

4. The ancillary procedures which are adopted by the plan administrator, such as those for:

- Establishing and implementing a funding policy and method to carry out the plan's short- and long-term objectives;

- Describing the procedure for an internal appeal of denied benefit claims;

- Describing the allocation of responsibilities for the operation and administration of the plan, including the allocation of duties among named fiduciaries and the designation of persons other than named fiduciaries to carry out fiduciary duties; providing ;

- Amending and terminating the plan;

- Specifying the basis on which contributions are made to, and payments are made from, the plan; and

- Determining whether a state court issued domestic relations order meets the requirements for a Qualified Domestic Relations Order.

ERISA does not always require a plan document. Under ERISA, only those plans subject to fiduciary duties (such as qualified retirement plans and non-insured health and welfare benefit plans) require a plan document, since one of the fiduciary duties is to follow the terms of the written document.[1] An unwritten plan, fund or program can still be determined to be an ERISA plan if it provides health or welfare benefits or the deferral of income.

The following few excerpts from court cases sum up how unwritten plans are viewed.

---

1. Under ERISA § 402(a)(1), only those plans subject to fiduciary duties "shall be established and maintained pursuant to a written instrument."

Diak v. Dwyer, Costello & Knox, P.C.

33 F.3d 809 (7th Circuit 1994)

Before CUDAHY and COFFEY, Circuit Judges, and NORGLE, District Judge.[*]

CUDAHY, Circuit Judge.

Mark Diak, an accountant, was hired by the accounting firm Dwyer, Costello & Knox, P.C. (DCK) in late 1973. After retiring in 1985, he discovered that DCK had paid pension benefits to some retired employees. Believing he had been wrongfully denied pension benefits, Diak sued DCK and officers John Dwyer and Terrance Knox for breach of fiduciary duties under the Employee Retirement Income Security Act, 29 U.S.C. § 1001 et seq. (ERISA). The district court granted summary judgment for DCK, finding that DCK had not established a pension plan. Diak appeals, arguing that there was a "plan" under which he is entitled to benefits. Diak also argues that the district court abused its discretion when it denied his motion to compel discovery. We affirm.

I.

DCK began as a partnership (DCK Partnership) with Dwyer and his son-in-law Knox as partners. DCK incorporated in 1982 and Dwyer and Knox became officers and shareholders. In January 1984, Diak also became a shareholder and officer. In 1985, at the age of 32, Diak resigned from DCK and started a competing accounting firm.

Diak was never told that DCK had a pension plan. But in 1989, Diak learned that four retirees had received pension payments. In 1973, Abraham Schaffer retired from employment with DCK after 16 years of service as an accountant. Since his retirement, DCK has paid Schaffer $75/month as well as providing medical and dental coverage. In 1974, Della Chellist retired after 36 years of service as a secretary. Chellist has received $100/month and payment of medical and dental insurance. In June 1981, Mary Wiley retired after 5 years of service; DCK continued to pay her medical and dental insurance.

John Dwyer retired in 1981 after 55 years of service. After retirement Dwyer remained active in the firm on a limited basis, but received no salary. In 1983, Dwyer began to receive $1000/month from DCK; the amount increased so that by 1989 he was receiving $30,000/year. In his deposition, Dwyer testified that he and Knox established the amount of his pension, which in 1991 amounted to $30,000. When asked about the criteria for determining a pension amount, Dwyer replied:

> The only guideline we have dealing with pensions is if somebody is with our firm, had been with our firm for twenty years and was 65, they got a pension, and a health and welfare that was established. We just established it. There was no particular plan. It was just established-if somebody had been with us all that time, they were entitled to something from us, no written plan....

Dwyer reported the payments on his income tax returns as pension payments. Dwyer also testified that he was familiar with pension plans and ERISA, having

---

* The Honorable Charles R. Norgle, Sr., of the United States District Court for the Northern District of Illinois, is sitting by designation.

advised pension funds as clients and served as the executive director of the Central States Teamsters Pension Fund in 1978/1979.

According to DCK, the pension payments were not made pursuant to a "pension plan" but were individual contracts executed upon each person's retirement. Of the approximately 25 employees who left DCK after 1970, only the above-named four employees received any post-employment benefits. Moreover, DCK maintains that these contracts were made only with individuals who reached retirement age and retired from the partnership; no benefits have ever been paid to employees of the corporation DCK.

All of the pensions were paid out of DCK's general revenues. From 1984 until 1990, Schaffer, Chellist and Dwyer received from DCK an annual Form W-P2, and its successor, Form 1099-R. DCK's corporate income tax returns included deductions for pension contributions in each year from 1983 to 1990. In 1985, Diak noticed a deduction for pensions on the 1984 DCK tax return; when he inquired, Knox told him that the deduction did not reflect a pension, but only compensation for Dwyer.

In 1990, Diak made a formal demand for benefits. DCK responded that it had no pension plan. In 1991, Diak brought suit alleging that DCK, Knox and Dwyer breached their fiduciary duties under ERISA, and seeking clarification of the terms of the plan and recovery of benefits. The district court denied Diak's motion to compel discovery of Dwyer's tax returns for 1984 to 1991. The parties filed cross-motions for summary judgment, agreeing that there were no disputed issues of fact. DCK argued that it was entitled to relief as a matter of law because DCK never had a pension plan covered by ERISA; or if it did, Diak was not a participant in the plan; and that in any event Diak's claims were time-barred. The district court granted DCK's motion for summary judgment, finding DCK had not established a pension plan. We review the district court's grant of summary judgment de novo.

II.

ERISA imposes numerous fiduciary duties on employers in connection with pension plans. Employers are required to establish plans in writing, 29 U.S.C. § 1102(1), create a fund or trust for benefit payments, 29 U.S.C. § 1103(a), and maintain various records. 29 U.S.C. § 1059. However, fiduciary duties arise only if there is a pension plan as defined by ERISA. The Act defines a pension plan as any plan, fund or program established or maintained by an employer that by its express terms or as a result of surrounding circumstances provides retirement income to employees. 29 U.S.C. § 1002(2). A plan need not be in writing to be covered by ERISA so long as the plan is a reality, meaning something more than a mere decision to extend benefits. James v. National Business Systems, Inc., 924 F.2d 718, 719 (7th Cir.1991); Ed Miniat, Inc. v. Globe Life Ins. Group, Inc., 805 F.2d 732, 739 (7th Cir.1986), cert. denied, 482 U.S. 915, 107 S.Ct. 3188, 96 L.Ed.2d 676 (1987); Donovan v. Dillingham, 688 F.2d 1367, 1372 (11th Cir.1982). Rather, we look to whether the decision "constituted an expressed intention by the employer to provide benefits on a regular and long-term basis." Wickman v. Northwestern Nat'l Life Ins. Co., 908 F.2d 1077, 1083 (1st Cir.), cert. denied, 498 U.S. 1013, 111 S.Ct. 581, 112 L.Ed.2d 586 (1990). DCK's decision to extend benefits to certain employees does not compel the conclusion that it had established a pension plan. "A mere allegation that an employer or employee organization ultimately decided to provide an employee [pension] benefits is not enough to invoke ERISA's coverage." Scott v. Gulf Oil Corp., 754 F.2d 1499, 1504 (9th Cir.1985); Pritchard v. Rainfair, Inc., 945 F.2d 185 (7th Cir.1991) (plaintiff's belief he would receive health benefits and company's extension of health benefits to two other retirees did not establish a plan); Harris v. Arkansas Book Co., 794 F.2d 358, 360 (8th Cir.1986) (worker suddenly fired after 49 years of service; company's promise of a pension and payment of benefits to other retiree did not establish a plan).

In Donovan, the Eleventh Circuit set out the prevailing test for determining whether a "plan" has been established within the meaning of ERISA: "In determining whether a plan, fund or program (pursuant to a writing or not) is a reality a court must determine whether from the surrounding circumstances a reasonable person could ascertain the intended benefits, beneficiaries, source of financing, and procedures for receiving benefits." 688 F.2d at 1373. See also Ed Miniat, 805 F.2d at 739; Deibler v. United Food and Commercial Workers' Local Union 23, 973 F.2d 206, 209 (3d Cir.1992); Elmore v. Cone Mills Corp., 6 F.3d 1028, 1035 (4th Cir.1993); Landry v. Air Line Pilots Assoc. Int'l, 901 F.2d 404, 415 (5th Cir.1990); Brown v. Ampco-Pittsburgh Corp., 876 F.2d 546, 551 (6th Cir.1989); accord Fort Halifax Packing Co. v. Coyne, 482 U.S. 1, 12, 107 S.Ct. 2211, 2217, 96 L.Ed.2d 1 (1987).

Applying the Donovan criteria, the district court found that Diak's claim foundered at the first step-ascertaining the benefits due under DCK's "plan." Dwyer testified that pension payments were determined on an ad hoc basis in consultation with Knox. Each of the individuals who received pensions received different packages, ranging from $75/month for Schaffer to $2500/month for Dwyer. Wiley received only health benefits (a welfare benefit rather than a pension). It is difficult to divine a formula at work in this distribution of payments. Diak's "expert" witness opined that DCK had a pension plan that guaranteed $2500/month to retired officers of the corporation (like Dwyer and Diak) and $100/month to other employees. But this fails to explain all of the payments-Dwyer received nothing at first, eventually received $1000/month, and did not receive $2500/month until 1989. Moreover, Schaffer and Wiley received less than $100/month, and numerous other employees who left the company received nothing.

It would also be difficult to ascertain the appropriate amount of benefits by years of service. Schaffer's 16 years of service netted him $75/month; Chellist's 36 years gave her $100/month; Wiley had worked only 5 years, and received only health benefits. Knox's affidavit indicates that at least two other employees worked for at least 10 years (Fred Siegel and Patricia Costello Thoman) but received nothing. Even if we were to accept Diak's argument that pensions were commensurate with years of service, Diak, who served 12 years at DCK, would be entitled to something less than $75/month.

* * *

The decision of the district court is AFFIRMED.

O'Leary v. Provident Life & Accident Ins. Co.,
456 F.Supp2d 285 (DC Mass, 2006)

MEMORANDUM AND ORDER

SAYLOR, District Judge.

This is an action concerning an employee disability policy. Plaintiff James R. O'Leary seeks to recover benefits under a disability policy issued by defendant Provident Life and Accident Insurance Company. O'Leary alleges that he became disabled on December 23, 1998, and has remained so since that time. Provident paid disability benefits for about a year and a half, but then determined that O'Leary was not totally disabled and discontinued paying benefits.

The complaint, which alleges only state law claims, was filed in the Worcester Superior Court. Defendant removed the action to federal court, contending that the case is governed by the Employee Retirement Income Security Act of 1974, 29 U.S.C. § 1001 et seq ("ERISA"), and that plaintiff's state law claims are accordingly preempted. Plaintiff contends, however, that Massachusetts state law governs the action in all respects. Pursuant to an order of this Court, the parties conducted limited discovery and submitted memoranda as to whether the claims are governed by federal or state law. While neither party has formally moved for summary judgment, defendant's memorandum requests that the Court dismiss plaintiff's state law claims on the ground that they are preempted by ERISA. Because both memoranda make reference to evidence outside the pleadings, the Court will treat defendant's memorandum as a motion for summary judgment, arising under Federal Rule of Civil Procedure 56.[1]

For the reasons stated below, summary judgment will be granted. Plaintiff, however, will be given thirty days to seek reconsideration or move for other relief.

I. Factual Background

The facts, which are largely undisputed, are set forth in the light most favorable to the plaintiff.

A. O'Leary's Employment

The New England Carpenters Training Fund (the "Fund") is a trust, whose Board of Trustees consists of representatives of both labor unions and employers.[2] The Fund's purpose is to train apprentice carpenters. It is a stand-alone entity with a training facility located in Millbury, Massachusetts. While the number of Fund employees has varied, it presently has an administrator, seven instructors, three secretaries, and four kitchen workers.

O'Leary was hired as the Fund's administrator in 1988. As administrator, his duties were to oversee training, develop curriculum, supervise office staff and instructors, attend various apprenticeship training committee meetings throughout the country, and administer the school. O'Leary reported directly to the Fund's Board of Trustees.

The Board of Trustees decided to hire O'Leary at a meeting held on August 25, 1988. The minutes of that meeting indicate that the Fund would provide him with health benefits, pension benefits, and a deferred compensation plan. There is no mention in the minutes of a disability policy. Subsequently, O'Leary

---

1. Specifically, both parties cite to the deposition of Thomas J. Harrington and the accompanying exhibits. Harrington is the current Executive Secretary/Treasurer for the New England Regional Council of Carpenters, which is one of many settlors of the New England Carpenters Training Fund. Harrington is also currently chairman of the Fund's Board of Trustees and has served as a trustee since 1989.

2. Prior to 1997 or 1998, the Fund was known as the Massachusetts Carpenters Training Fund.

received several documents from the fund, including: (1) a personnel policy for salaried employees; (2) a James O'Leary Employee Benefit Plan for deferred compensation; (3) a Pension Fund summary plan description; (4) an Annuity Fund summary plan description; and (5) a Health Benefits summary plan description. None of these documents make reference to a disability policy or disability insurance benefits.

B. Disability Coverage

A few weeks after O'Leary began working for the Fund, it decided to provide him with disability insurance coverage. Apparently, a number of business agents of local unions had received disability coverage, and the Board of Trustees had decided to provide the same benefit to the Fund's administrator. It is undisputed that the decision to provide disability insurance was made by the Board of Trustees. It is further undisputed that O'Leary was the only Fund employee to receive this coverage.

Following the Board's decision to provide coverage, O'Leary applied for a disability policy with Provident. On his application, O'Leary stated that his employer would "pay for all disability coverage to be carried by [me] with no portion of the premium to be included in [my] taxable income." (Harrington Dep., Ex. 9).

The disability policy took effect at some point in 1988. The policy included a "Salary Allotment Premium Payment" rider, which provides: "In consideration of the Salary Allotment Agreement between your employer and us, we agree to accept Policy Premiums as billed to your employer. The conditions of this rider are:

1. The policy will not continue in force beyond the time for which the premium is paid, subject to the grace period.

2. If your employer fails to pay premiums when due because of clerical error or negligence, your insurance under the policy will not be prejudiced.

3. This rider will be void if:

a. your employment with your employer ends;

b. the Salary Allotment Agreement is terminated; or

c. for any reason, your employer fails to pay premiums.

4. If this rider is voided, premiums will be due and payable as required in the policy.

(Harrington Dep., Ex. 9)

O'Leary issued payments for the premium amount on Massachusetts Carpenters Training Fund checks, which he was authorized to sign. There is no dispute that the Fund paid 100% of the premium amount. The policy provided annual opportunities to increase the amount of the disability benefit. In order to accept such increases, O'Leary had to obtain the Board's approval. The Board gave its approval on a number of occasions, and at least once disapproved an increase in the benefit.

Although the Board of Trustees had discretion to terminate O'Leary's disability coverage at any time, it kept the policy in place during the entirety of his employment with the Fund. O'Leary never received a summary plan description or any other such documentation in connection with the disability policy. The Fund kept a physical copy of the disability policy.

C. Denial of Disability Benefits

O'Leary contends that he became disabled under the terms of the disability policy on December 23, 1998. The nature of the disability is unclear. He subsequently applied for benefits, and on April 23, 1999, Provident began making payments to him-informing him nonetheless that the company reserved the right to make a different formal determination regarding benefits after its investigation into his alleged disability. By letter dated October 11, 2000, Provident informed him of its determination that his inability to work was not due to an injury or sickness, that he therefore did not meet the policy's definition of disabled, and that it owed him no further benefits. O'Leary thereafter appealed the decision. A letter dated May 7, 2001, indicated that his appeal had been denied.

II. Procedural History

Following Provident's denial of disability benefits, O'Leary filed suit in Worcester Superior Court. Count I of his four-count complaint, filed on October 10, 2003, alleges breach of contract. It is unclear what causes of action, if any, are stated in the remaining counts. He alleges that Provident acted "arbitrarily and capriciously" (Count II) and "unreasonably" (Count III) in failing to continue his disability benefits and asserting that his condition did not meet the terms of the policy. In Count IV, he alleges that "[t]he available evidence clearly indicates that [he] was and is disabled under the terms of the policy ... and he is entitled to recover benefits for that disability under the terms and provisions of the policy."

Provident removed the case to this Court. Following a hearing on July 30, 2004, the Court ordered limited discovery as to the issue of whether ERISA governed this case and requested briefing by the parties. The parties filed memoranda on the applicability of ERISA in March 2005.

III. Analysis

Summary judgment may be entered if the record shows that "there is no genuine issue as to any material fact and that the moving party is entitled to a judgment as a matter of law." Fed.R.Civ.P. 56(c). The evidence must be viewed in the light most favorable to the non-moving party. Mesnick v. General Elec. Co., 950 F.2d 816, 822 (1st Cir.1991).

There are two questions presented in this case: (1) whether the disability policy provided to O'Leary by the Fund qualifies as an employee welfare benefit plan for purposes of ERISA; and (2) if so, whether ERISA preempts O'Leary's state law claims.

A. ERISA Employee Welfare Benefit Plan

ERISA protects employee benefit rights in connection with any "employee benefit plan" unless the plan is specifically exempted. 29 U.S.C. § 1003(a).[3] ERISA

---

3. Earlier in this litigation, O'Leary argued that the disability policy qualified as a "top hat" plan, and was therefore exempted from ERISA's provisions. A "top hat" employee benefit plan is one that is unfunded and "maintained by an employer primarily for the purpose of providing deferred compensation for a select group of management or highly compensated employees." Cogan v. Phoenix Life Ins. Co., 310 F.3d 238, 242 (1st Cir.2002) (citing 29 U.S.C. § 1101(a)(1)). Provident argued that the policy was not a "top hat" plan, as it was not deferred. O'Leary now appears to have abandoned this argument. In any event, while a "top hat" plan is exempt from certain ERISA requirements, it is not exempt from ERISA's reporting, disclosure, administration, or enforcement provisions, and any state law concerning such plans are preempted. See, e.g., Reliable Home Health Care, Inc. v. Union

generally covers two types of employee benefit plans: employee welfare benefit plans and employee pension benefit plans (or plans that are both). 29 U.S.C. §§ 1002(1), 1002(2), and 1002(3). Provident contends that O'Leary's disability policy qualifies as an employee welfare benefit plan.

ERISA defines an "employee welfare benefit plan" as: "any plan, fund, or program which ... is ... established or maintained by an employer or by an employee organization, or by both, to the extent that such plan, fund, or program was established or is maintained for the purpose of providing for its participants or their beneficiaries, through the purchase of insurance or otherwise, (A) medical, surgical, or hospital care or benefits, or benefits in the event of sickness, accident, disability, [or] death ..." 29 U.S.C. § 1002(1). The First Circuit has adopted the so-called Donovan test for determining whether an ERISA employee welfare benefit plan exists. See Wickman v. Northwestern Nat'l Ins. Co., 908 F.2d 1077, 1082 (1st Cir.1990) (citing Donovan v. Dillingham, 688 F.2d 1367, 1370 (11th Cir.1982)). Under the Donovan test, an employee welfare benefit plan has five elements: (1) a plan, fund, or program (2) established or maintained (3) by an employer or by an employee organization, or by both, (4) for the purpose of providing ... disability ... benefits (5) to participants or their beneficiaries. Donovan, 688 F.2d at 1371. "The question of whether an ERISA plan exists is 'a question of fact, to be answered in light of all the surrounding facts and circumstances from the point of view of a reasonable person.'" Wickman, 908 F.2d at 1082 (citation omitted).

There does not appear to be any dispute that elements three, four, and five have been met: the Fund is an employer that provided disability benefits to O'Leary, who was a participant. The issues in this case are whether the policy is a "plan" that the Fund "established or maintained." The Donovan court formulated the standard for determining whether a "plan" has been "established":

In summary, a "plan, fund, or program" under ERISA is established if from the surrounding circumstances a reasonable person can ascertain the intended benefits, a class of beneficiaries, the source of financing, and procedures for receiving benefits. Donovan, 688 F.2d at 1373. In applying this standard, " '[t]he [p]lan may adopt some of its essential provisions from sources outside itself,' including 'insurance policies that provide the [p]lan's funding.'" Reber v. Provident Life & Acc. Ins. Co., 93 F.Supp.2d 995, 999 (S.D.Ind.2000) (quoting Ed Miniat, Inc. v. Globe Life Ins. Group, Inc., 805 F.2d 732, 739 (7th Cir.1986)). This standard is easily met here: a reasonable person can ascertain that disability benefits are the intended benefits; that O'Leary is the beneficiary; that the Fund is the source of the financing; and that the procedures for receiving benefits are those set forth in the disability policy. This suggests that by providing the disability coverage to O'Leary, the Fund established a "plan" for purposes of ERISA.

Plaintiff nonetheless argues that the disability policy does not qualify as an "employee welfare benefit plan" within the meaning of ERISA. In support of this argument, he asserts: (1) that the mere purchase of insurance is insufficient to establish an ERISA plan; (2) there was no ongoing administrative scheme; (3) the disability policy was not permanent and was subject to termination by

---

Cent. Ins. Co., 295 F.3d 505, 515 (5th Cir.2002); In re New Eng. Mut. Life Ins. Co. Sales Practices Litig., 324 F.Supp.2d 288, 310 (D.Mass.2004).

the Board of Trustees at any time; (4) there was no written plan; (5) the disability coverage was only provided to O'Leary and not to any other Fund employee; (6) the policy was an individual, rather than group, policy; (7) O'Leary, rather than the Fund, applied for the benefits; and (8) the disability coverage was not part of his original hiring package. The Court will consider each of these arguments in turn.

1. Whether the Purchase of Insurance Was Sufficient to Establish an ERISA Plan

Plaintiff argues that the mere purchase of insurance by an employer is insufficient to establish an ERISA plan. It is true that because "no single act in itself necessarily constitutes the establishment" of an ERISA plan, the "purchase of insurance does not conclusively establish a plan." Donovan, 688 F.2d at 1373. However, this does not mean that an employer cannot establish an ERISA plan through the purchase of insurance. Indeed, such a proposition is foreclosed by the text of ERISA itself, which expressly defines an "employee welfare benefit plan" as one that is established "through the purchase of insurance or otherwise." 29 U.S.C. § 1002(1). Moreover, "[a] number of courts have held that an employer's payment of insurance premiums, standing alone, is substantial evidence of the existence of an ERISA plan." Robinson v. Linomaz, 58 F.3d 365, 368 (8th Cir.1995); see also Madonia v. Blue Cross & Blue Shield of Va., 11 F.3d 444, 447 (4th Cir.1993); Randol v. Mid-West Nat'l Life Ins. Co. of Tenn., 987 F.2d 1547, 1551 (11th Cir.1993); Donovan, 688 F.2d at 1373; Kidder v. H & B Marine, Inc., 932 F.2d 347, 353 (5th Cir.1991) (payment of premiums on behalf of employees is substantial evidence that a plan, fund, or program was established). Thus, an ERISA plan may be established where, as here, an employer purchases a disability insurance policy for an employee.

While an ERISA plan can be established through the purchase of insurance, not every insurance purchase qualifies as a plan. The First Circuit has indicated that "[t]he crucial factor in determining if a 'plan' has been established is whether the purchase of the insurance policy constituted an expressed intention by the employer to provide benefits on a regular and long term basis." Wickman, 908 F.2d at 1083. In making that determination, a "very important consideration is whether, in light of all the surrounding facts and circumstances, a reasonable employee would perceive an ongoing commitment by the employer to provide employee benefits," and "evidence that an employer committed to provide long-term or periodic benefits to its employees will often be telling." Belanger v. Wyman-Gordon Co., 71 F.3d 451, 455 (1st Cir.1995).

Here, there is considerable evidence that the Fund intended to provide O'Leary with longterm benefits: (1) the Fund entered into a contractual agreement with Provident to pay the policy premiums; (2) the Fund in fact paid 100% of the policy premiums; (3) the Board of Trustees approved an increase in benefits on a number of occasions; and (4) the Board kept the coverage in place for the entirety of O'Leary's employment, which spanned ten years.

In arguing that the Fund's purchase of disability coverage for O'Leary did not constitute an ERISA plan, O'Leary relies on New Eng. Mut. Life Ins. Co., Inc. v. Baig, 166 F.3d 1 (1st Cir.1999). Baig, which held that no ERISA plan had been established, states:

New England Mutual argues that an employer's reimbursement of premiums paid directly by an employee should constitute substantial evidence of the existence of an ERISA plan. The policy at issue here was not initially established by a contractual arrangement between Cardiology Associates and New England Mutual; rather, Baig made the initial purchase directly. Baig paid the premiums directly to New England Mutual. The policy was an individual policy covering only Baig himself. Under these particular circumstances, the reimbursement by his employer of premiums paid directly by Baig did not create a plan under ERISA. Baig, 166 F.3d at 4. The present case, however, is clearly distinguishable. Here, the policy was initially established by a contractual agreement between the employer and Provident (*i.e.* the Salary Allotment Agreement), and the premium was directly paid by the employer out of employer funds. In fact, the Baig court explicitly distinguished between the circumstances in that case and the situation in the present litigation. See id. at 4 n. 3 (distinguishing cases where there was a "a direct contractual arrangement between the insurer and the employer establishing the policy in question" or where "direct payments of premiums [were made] by the employer to the insurer, with the payments ... made out of employer funds").

O'Leary attempts to evade this distinction by quoting the Baig court as stating that "[e]ven where an employer actually purchases an insurance policy, or makes payments directly, there may not be a 'plan' for ERISA purposes." Id. at 4-5. He fails, however, to reference the footnote attached to this statement, which sets forth specific circumstances in which direct payments would not qualify as an ERISA plan. The footnote explains that "[a] plan is not created in certain situations where an employer makes direct payments to an insurer as an intermediary, acting as a channel for premium payments from individuals." Id. at 5, n. 5. The footnote further refers to a Department of Labor regulation that states a policy will not constitute a plan "where the employer does not make contributions to the coverage, participation in the program by employees is voluntary, and the employer does no more than (1) permit the insurer to publicize the program (without endorsing it) and (2) 'collect premiums through payroll deductions or dues checkoffs and remit them to the insurer.' " Id. (citing 29 C.F.R. § 2510.3-1(j) (1998)). These conditions simply are not met here, as the Fund (1) contributed 100% of the premium amount; (2) had a prior contractual relationship with the insurer to pay this premium amount; and (3) periodically decided whether or not to increase the benefit. The Court is therefore satisfied that the Fund's purchase of disability insurance in this case established an ERISA plan.

2. Whether There Was an "Ongoing Administrative Scheme"

Plaintiff contends the disability insurance policy in this case does not constitute an ERISA plan because it does not implicate an "ongoing administrative scheme." The requirement of an "ongoing administrative scheme" comes from the Supreme Court's opinion in Fort Halifax Packing Co., Inc. v. Coyne, 482 U.S. 1, 107 S.Ct. 2211, 96 L.Ed.2d 1 (1987). In Fort Halifax, the Court "construed the word 'plan' to connote some minimal, ongoing 'administrative' scheme or practice." District of Columbia v. Greater Wash. Bd. of Trade, 506 U.S. 125, 130 n. 2, 113 S.Ct. 580, 121 L.Ed.2d 513 (1992). In describing the "administrative realities of employee benefit plans," the Court stated that "[a]n employer that makes a commitment systematically to pay certain benefits undertakes a host of obligations, such as determining the eligibility of claimants, calculating benefit levels, making disbursements, monitoring the availability of funds for benefit payments, and keeping appropriate records in order to comply with applicable reporting requirements." Fort Halifax, 482 U.S. at 9, 107 S.Ct. 2211. It then held that the severance benefit at issue in that case-"a one-time, lump-sum payment triggered by a single event"-did not qualify as an employee benefit plan. Id. at 12, 107 S.Ct. 2211.

The disability insurance policy in this case, however, did implicate an "ongoing administrative scheme." The Fund's Board of Trustees had to consider, on an annual basis, whether to approve increases in the level of benefits. It is clear from the record that the Board did improve increases on a number of occasions, and declined to approve an increase at least once. Further, the policy imposed other obligations, such as reviewing O'Leary's claim for benefits, determining whether or not he qualified as "disabled," monitoring his condition to determine whether he remained eligible for benefits, disbursing the benefits, and considering the appeal of any denial of benefits. That the Fund delegated many of these administrative obligations to the insurer does not take the policy out of ERISA coverage. See Brundage-Peterson v. Compcare Health Serv. Ins. Corp., 877 F.2d 509, 511 (7th Cir.1989) (stating that the delegation of administration of the plan to an insurance company is "in fact contemplated by the [ERISA] statute"); Robinson, 58 F.3d at 368 ("[T]here is no requirement that the employer play any role in the administration of the plan in order for it to be deemed an [employee welfare benefit plan] under ERISA.") (citation omitted); Randol, 987 F.2d at 1550-51 n. 5 ("[A] commercially purchased insurance policy under which the procedures for receiving benefits are all dictated by the insurance carrier can constitute a plan for ERISA purposes."). Because the disability coverage in this case-unlike the one-time severance payment at issue in Fort Halifax-involved a substantial "ongoing administrative scheme," it does not fall outside the requirements of an ERISA plan.

3. Whether There Was a Plan Where the Policy Was Subject to Termination at Any Time

Plaintiff further contends that his disability policy should not be governed by ERISA because his employer, the Fund, reserved the right to withdraw the insurance coverage at any time. This contention, however, is directly contrary to the applicable law. ERISA expressly exempts welfare benefit plans from a number of its requirements, including vesting requirements. 29 U.S.C. § 1051. Because welfare benefit plans are not vested, employers are "generally free under ERISA, for any reason at any time, to adopt, modify, or terminate welfare plans." Curtiss-Wright Corp. v. Schoonejongen, 514 U.S. 73, 78, 115 S.Ct. 1223, 131 L.Ed.2d 94 (1995); Cf. Campbell v. BankBoston, N.A., 327 F.3d 1, 7 (1st Cir.2003) ("A severance plan is defined as a 'welfare benefit plan'... [t]hus, employers may amend or eliminate a severance pay plan at any time."); Reichelt v. Emhart Corp., 921 F.2d 425, 430 (2nd Cir.1990) ("[U]nder ERISA, the employer has the right at any time to amend or terminate a severance pay plan."). Accordingly, the Board of Trustee's ability to terminate O'Leary's policy at any time does not remove the plan from the scope of ERISA.

4. Whether There Was a Plan in the Absence of Formal Documentation

Plaintiff next points to the absence of a formal, written summary plan description or other documentation describing the disability benefits as evidence that ERISA is inapplicable in this case. Again, however, his position lacks legal support. In Donovan, the Eleventh Circuit made clear that a written document is not a prerequisite to ERISA coverage, as "[t]here is no requirement of a formal, written plan in either ERISA's coverage section ... or its definitions section." Donovan, 688 F.2d at 1372. The court stated:

Furthermore, because the policy of ERISA is to safeguard the well-being and security of working men and women and to apprise them of their rights and obligations under any employee benefit plan … it would be incongruous for persons establishing or maintaining informal or unwritten employee benefit plans, or assuming the responsibility of safeguarding plan assets, to circumvent the Act merely because an administrator or other fiduciary failed to satisfy reporting or fiduciary standards. Id. The First Circuit has similarly indicated that a written document is not required for ERISA to apply. See Baig, 166 F.3d at 5 n. 6 ("[T]he absence of [written] documentation should not necessarily lead to a finding that there was no plan under ERISA."); see also Scott v. Gulf Oil Corp., 754 F.2d 1499, 1503 (9th Cir.1985) ("We agree with the Eleventh Circuit, however, that the existence of a written instrument is not a prerequisite to ERISA coverage."); Diak v. Dwyer, Costello & Knox, P. C., 33 F.3d 809, 811 (7th Cir.1994) ("A plan need not be in writing to be covered by ERISA so long as the plan is a reality, meaning something more than a mere decision to extend benefits."). Because a formal, written plan is not a requirement for ERISA coverage, the absence of written documentation does not alter this Court's determination that ERISA governs the present case.

5. Whether There Was a Plan Where Coverage Was Provided Only to One Employee

According to plaintiff, ERISA is inapplicable in this case because the disability insurance coverage was provided solely to him and no other Fund employees. He fails, however, to provide any statutory or case law to support this argument, and there is ample authority to the contrary. See, e.g., Cvelbar v. CBI Illinois Inc., 106 F.3d 1368, 1376 (7th Cir.1997), abrogated on other grounds, ("[The court has] no difficulty in holding that it is possible for a one-person arrangement to qualify as an ERISA plan."); Williams v. Wright, 927 F.2d 1540, 1545 (11th Cir.1991) (plan not excluded from ERISA coverage because it only applies to a single employee); Biggers v. Wittek Indus., Inc., 4 F.3d 291, 297 (4th Cir.1993) ("We are not aware of any requirement that a plan must cover more than one employee in order to be controlled by ERISA."). Furthermore, the Department of Labor has indicated that an ERISA plan can cover only a single employee. See Cvelbar, 106 F.3d at 1373.[4] Plaintiff's argument to the contrary is without merit.

6. Whether There Was a Plan Where the Policy Was for an Individual Rather than a Group

Plaintiff next argues that state law, rather than ERISA, applies because the disability coverage provided by the Fund was an individual policy. Once again, he has cited no legal authority for this contention. Provident correctly responds that the statute expressly allows an ERISA plan to be established or maintained "through the purchase of insurance," but contains no requirement that the purchased insurance be a group, rather than individual, policy. See 29 U.S.C. § 1002(1). Furthermore, courts have found ERISA applicable in cases where the benefit plan was funded by individual policies. See, e.g., Paul Revere Life Ins. Co. v. Bromberg, 382 F.3d 33, 35 (1st Cir.2004) (plan, funded by individual dis-

---

4. "The Secretary [of Labor] has been charged by Congress with responsibility for interpreting and enforcing the definitional, coverage, reporting and disclosure, and fiduciary responsibility provisions of Title I of ERISA." Cvelbar, 106 F.3d at 1373 n. 3. The interpretation by the Department of Labor of its own regulations and the statute is entitled to substantial deference. See Johnson v. Watts Regulator Co., 63 F.3d 1129, 1134-35 (1st Cir.1995).

ability insurance policies, governed by ERISA); Reber, 93 F.Supp.2d at 999 (ERISA found to govern individual disability policy issued by Provident to employee). Again, plaintiff's argument must be rejected.

7. Whether There Was a Plan Where the Participant Applied for the Policy

Plaintiff's memorandum on the inapplicability of ERISA emphasizes that O'Leary, not the Fund, was the applicant for the disability policy. His argument, however, is unclear. The Court assumes he is contending that he, rather than the Fund, "established" the plan. This argument, however, is unpersuasive.

First, the Salary Allotment Premium Payment rider contained in the policy suggests that the Fund had established a contractual relationship (the Salary Allotment Agreement) with the insurer prior to O'Leary's submission of an application. The decision in Reber, which confronted facts nearly identical to those at issue here, is instructive. See id. In Reber, the court considered whether ERISA governed a disability policy which had similarly been issued by Provident to an employee. Id. at 996-97. The policy at issue contained a Salary Allotment rider identical to the rider in O'Leary's policy, and the plaintiff employee had submitted her own application to Provident. Id. at 997. The court stated that the employer "dealt directly with Provident in establishing its plan," and that it had "established a contractual relationship with Provident (*i.e.*, the Salary Allotment Agreement) before [the employee] did." Id. at 1004-6.

Second, even if the Court assumes, for the sake of argument, that O'Leary (rather than the Fund) established the disability plan, that fact would not remove the policy from ERISA's coverage. The statute defines an "employee welfare benefit plan" as one that is "established or maintained " by an employer. 29 U.S.C. § 1002(1) (emphasis added). It is undisputed that the Fund paid 100% of the premium amount. In addition, the Board of Trustees had the authority to terminate the policy at any time, yet kept it in place for the entirety of O'Leary's employment, and even approved increases in the benefits level on a number of occasions. Thus, even if O'Leary established the policy, it still qualifies as an ERISA plan because the Fund maintained it.

8. Whether There Was a Plan Where the Disability Policy Was Not Part of the Original Hiring Package

Finally, plaintiff notes that the disability policy was not part of his compensation package at the time that he was hired. The Board of Trustees did not make the decision to provide him with disability benefits until a few weeks after he had begun working. However, the Court is not aware of-and plaintiff has not cited to-any requirement under ERISA that a plan be established at the outset of employment.[5]

* * *

---

5. While the timing of the disability coverage is not determinative of whether ERISA applies, it does have some relevance in this case. Specifically, it undermines Provident's additional argument that the disability benefits should be considered together with the other Fund benefits in determining the applicability of ERISA. There is considerable doubt as to whether the benefits provided to all salaried employees and the disability insurance provided only to O'Leary formed a single "plan, fund or program." However, the Court need not decide whether the disability benefits and other benefits constituted a single ERISA plan. Even if the other benefits provided by the Fund are disregarded, there is still substantial evidence that the employer established or maintained a disability plan. As such, the disability policy qualifies as an employee welfare benefit plan, regardless of its relationship to the other benefits.

In summary, this case involves a plan that was established or maintained by the Fund (an employer) for the purpose of providing disability benefits to O'Leary (a participant). The Court holds that it qualifies as an employee welfare benefit plan and that ERISA therefore governs.

* * *

However, even if the employer determines that ERISA will control and memorializes the promises in writing, several issues still remain, including: (i) whether the plan document has properly been executed and adopted, (ii) whether other written procedures are considered part of the plan document, and (iii) how the plan document coordinates with the Summary Plan Description. For purposes of this textbook, I am keeping the following discussion simple, and am only citing to the court cases, and not asking you to read them. The issues discussed in this part of the chapter are truly legal issues, and not necessarily tied to ERISA.

Legal effect of the plan document: For an ERISA plan document to have legal effect, in addition to meeting the requirements delineated under ERISA (and possibly the Code), it must be executed in accordance with appropriate state laws. While many professionals may have the knowledge and experience to draft a plan document, because all procedures and surrounding circumstances provide a legal foundation for the plan document, a licensed attorney should be the only professional hired to actually draft documents and plan amendments. Master & Prototype and Volume Submitter qualified retirement plans are generally drafted by attorneys at the financial institutions and service providers, even if they are not the professionals actually selling the plan. In addition, other required business procedures (such as the need for a corporate resolution or a quorum of the partners) must be properly recorded before the plan can be established, and the properly authorized officers of the employer must execute the document. One court found that a plan was effective as of 1982 due to the agreement letter between the employer and a union to establish a trust, even though the actual document was not signed until 1985.[2]

What is the actual plan document: Whether the document is comprised solely of the "four corners" of the actual pieces of paper stapled together or if other written procedures and memorializations will be deemed to be part of the larger plan document are all issues that have no clear answers. Although most ERISA plans must be established and maintained pursuant to written document, it need not be a single, formal document.[3] Another court has opined that "[t]his kind of confusion is all too common in ERISA land; often the terms of an ERISA plan must be inferred from a series of documents none clearly labeled as 'the plan.'"[4] Sometimes the employer wants several ancillary documents to be included as part of the legal document (such as a wrap welfare benefits plan that incorporates actual insurance policies), but other times, the employer believes that the final executed document is the legal document, and that other written documents should be ignored. Therefore, the plan's attorney should be consulted to determine which documents legally constitute the employee benefits plan. Understanding which documents govern the plan can protect against not only litigation regarding the plan, but also from being surprised to discover, during the course of litigation, that a document has more legal affect than previously believed.

Coordination with the summary plan description: Under a strict reading of ERISA, a Summary Plan Description is a summary, written in plain English, of the controlling

---

2. See Landry v. Airline Pilots Ass'n, 892 F.2d 1238 (5th Cir. 1990).

3. Cerasoli v Xomed, Inc., 47 F.Supp2d 401 (WD NY 1999).

4. Health Cost Controls, Inc., v. Washington, 187 F.3d 703, 712 (7th Cir. 1999) (quotations in original).

legal document. However, courts often times hold that if there is a discrepancy between the two, then the Summary Plan Description controls.[5] This has unfortunately led to the drafting of summary plan descriptions with legal disclaimers and qualifications that move them away from the plain English requirement.

2. Ability to Amend or Terminate the Plan

Every employee benefit plan shall "provide a procedure for amending such plan, and for identifying the persons who have authority to amend the plan."[6] There is no definitive procedure for amending a plan, so the sponsoring employer should choose a procedure and authorize only certain individuals to best meet its business goals - it should not be too easy nor too difficult to amend the plan. The termination of the plan is itself a plan amendment, and regardless of the business conditions, the sponsoring employer must follow the procedures to terminate a plan and cannot simply "wish" it away. However, caution is urged. One court determined that a plan amendment may take the form of corporate board resolution where the makers of resolution were also empowered to amend the plan, and thus the only difference between the plan amendment and the board resolution is purely a matter of form (namely title of document).[7] There are generally reporting and disclosure requirements that need to be communicated prior to or concurrently with a plan amendment or termination.

3. Ability to Interpret Ambiguous Plan Provisions (the "Firestone" Language)

The U.S. Supreme Court has determined that ERISA is consistent with the established principles of trust law, and held that if a plan participant brings a civil action against the plan to recover benefits due him under the terms of the plan, the denial of any benefit is to be reviewed by the courts under a de novo standard unless the benefit plan gives the administrator or fiduciary discretionary authority to determine eligibility for benefits or

---

5. See Washington v. Murphy Oil USA, Inc., 497 F.3d 453, 458, n.1 (5th Cir. 2007), "We certainly do not write on a clean slate. Indeed, there appears to be a five-way circuit split regarding whether an ERISA claimant needs to establish reliance and/or prejudice based on the conflicting terms of an SPD. The Third and Sixth Circuits do not require a showing of reliance. See Burstein v. Ret. Account Plan for Employees of Allegheny Health Edu. and Research Found., 334 F.3d 365, 380-82 (3rd Cir. 2003); Edwards v. State Farm Mut. Auto. Ins. Co., 851 F.2d 134, 137 (6th Cir. 1988). The Second Circuit also does not require a showing of reliance, but does require a showing of a likelihood of prejudice, which an employer may then rebut through evidence that the deficient SPD was in effect a harmless error. See Burke v. Kodak Ret. Income Plan, 336 F.3d 103, 111-14 (2nd Cir. 2003). The Seventh and Eleventh Circuits require a showing of reliance. See Health Cost Controls of Illinois, Inc. v. Washington, 187 F.3d 703, 711 (7th Cir. 1999); Branch v. G. Bernd Co., 955 F.2d 1574, 1579 (11th Cir. 1992). The First, Fourth, and Tenth Circuits require a showing of reliance or prejudice, though it appears that the terms "reliance" and "prejudice" are sometimes treated synonymously. See Govoni v. Bricklayers, Masons & Plasterers International Union, Local No. 5 Pension Fund, 732 F.2d 250, 252 (1st Cir. 1984); Aiken v. Policy Management Sys. Corp., 13 F.3d 138, 141 (4th Cir. 1993); Chiles v. Ceridian Corp., 95 F.3d 1505, 1519 (10th Cir. 1996). Finally, the Eighth Circuit requires a showing of reliance or prejudice, but only if the SPD is "faulty." See Palmisano v. Allina Health Sys., 190 F.3d 881, 887-88 (8th Cir.1999); Marolt v. Alliant Techsystems, 146 F.3d 617, 621-22 (8th Cir. 1998)."

6. ERISA § 402(b)(3).

7. Horn v. Berdon, Inc. Defined Benefit Pension Plan, 938 F.2d 125 (9th Cir. 1991).

to construe the terms of the plan.[8] If the court reviews the decision under the de novo standard, then it will look at all of the information the plan sponsor had, and will make a decision based on the facts. On the other hand, if the Firestone language is in the plan document, then the court will apply the arbitrary and capricious standard. In other words, the plan sponsor's denial of benefits will be assumed to be correct and reasonable, and the court will only reverse it if it is not supported by a fair or substantial cause or reason, or is inconsistent or erratic with respect to prior benefit claims for other plan participants. Therefore, it is good practice for all plan sponsors to reserve the right to interpret ambiguous provisions of the plan document so that their initial decisions regarding a benefit claim will be given the highest level of deference should it be reviewed by a court.

B. Summary Plan Description

Statutory Provisions at ERISA § 104(b)(1) and Labor Regs. § 2520.102-2 through -4

A Summary Plan Description, which is a summary of plan provisions written in a manner intended to be understood by plan participants, must be distributed to all plan participants, generally within 90 days after the employee becomes a participant. If amendments are made to the plan, a new SPD need not be drafted, as long as a summary of material modifications describing the amendments is distributed to all employees. Every five years, the plan administrator must draft and provide each participant and each beneficiary receiving benefits under the plan an updated SPD that includes all plan amendments made within the last five-year period. If no amendments have been made to the plan during the five-year period, this requirement need not be met, but an SPD must be furnished to plan participants and beneficiaries receiving benefits under the plan every 10 years regardless of whether plan amendments have been made.

SPDs must be written in a "manner calculated to be understood by the average plan participant and shall be sufficiently comprehensive to apprise the plan's participants and beneficiaries of their rights and obligations under the plan." Further, the format of an SPD "must not have the effect of misleading, misinforming or failing to inform participants and beneficiaries." If a small plan that covers fewer than 100 participants at the beginning of a plan year in which 25 percent or more of all plan participants are literate only in the same non-English language, then the plan administrator must provide these participants with an English-language SPD which prominently displays a notice, in the non-English language common to these participants, offering them assistance. Although the SPD is supposed to be the simple, easy to understand summary, since courts have been holding against the plan where the official plan document and the SPD differ, many SPDs are drafted by attorneys to lose the simple aura and more closely mirror the complicated language of the plan document.

A sponsor of an ERISA plan must distribute to participants a description of any material modification (actual term is Summary of Material Modifications) to a plan or change in information within 210 days after the close of the plan year in which the adoption or change occurs. The copy of the SPD furnished to new plan participants and beneficiaries receiving benefits must be accompanied by all summaries of material modifications or

---

8. Firestone Tire & Rubber Co. v. Bruch, 489 US 101, 115 (1989).

changes in information required to be included in the SPD which have not been incorporated. The information about material changes and amendments to the plan must be provided to participants via a summary of material modifications within 60 days after the modification or change is adopted or occurs.

Below are some excerpts from Labor regulations about style and content of SPDs, and then an article I wrote in 2007 that sums up some of my personal concerns with SPDs and other reporting and disclosure issues.

Labor Regs. § 2520.102-2
Style and Format of Summary Plan Description.

(a) **Method of presentation.** The summary plan description shall be written in a manner calculated to be understood by the average plan participant and shall be sufficiently comprehensive to apprise the plan's participants and beneficiaries of their rights and obligations under the plan. In fulfilling these requirements, the plan administrator shall exercise considered judgment and discretion by taking into account such factors as the level of comprehension and education of typical participants in the plan and the complexity of the terms of the plan. Consideration of these factors will usually require the limitation or elimination of technical jargon and of long, complex sentences, the use of clarifying examples and illustrations, the use of clear cross references and a table of contents.

(b) **General format.** The format of the summary plan description must not have the effect to misleading, misinforming or failing to inform participants and beneficiaries. Any description of exception, limitations, reductions, and other restrictions of plan benefits shall not be minimized, rendered obscure or otherwise made to appear unimportant. Such exceptions, limitations, reductions, or restrictions of plan benefits shall be described or summarized in a manner not less prominent than the style, captions, printing type, and prominence used to describe or summarize plan benefits. The advantages and disadvantages of the plan shall be presented without either exaggerating the benefits or minimizing the limitations. The description or summary of restrictive plan provisions need not be disclosed in the summary plan description in close conjunction with the description or summary of benefits, provided that adjacent to the benefit description the page on which the restrictions are described is noted.

(c) **Foreign languages.** In the case of either—

(1) A plan that covers fewer than 100 participants at the beginning of a plan year, and in which 25 percent or more of all plan participants are literate only in the same non-English language, or

(2) A plan which covers 100 or more participants at the beginning of the plan year, and in which the lesser of (i) 500 or more participants, or (ii) 10% or more of all plan participants are literate only in the same non-English language, so that a summary plan description in English would fail to inform these participants adequately of their rights and obligations under the plan, the plan administrator for such plan shall provide these participants with an English-language summary plan description which prominently displays a notice, in the non-English language common to these participants, offering them assistance. The assistance provided need not

involve written materials, but shall be given in the non-English language common to these participants and shall be calculated to provide them with a reasonable opportunity to become informed as to their rights and obligations under the plan. The notice offering assistance contained in the summary plan description shall clearly set forth in the non-English language common to such participants offering them assistance. The assistance provided need not involve written materials, but shall be given in the non-English language common to these participants and shall be calculated to provide them with a reasonable opportunity to become informed as to their rights and obligations under the plan. The notice offering assistance contained in the summary plan description shall clearly set forth in the non-English language common to such participants the procedures they must follow in order to obtain such assistance.

Example. Employer A maintains a pension plan which covers 1000 participants. At the beginning of a plan year five hundred of Employer A's covered employees are literate only in Spanish, 101 are literate only in Vietnamese, and the remaining 399 are literate in English. Each of the 1000 employees receives a summary plan description in English, containing an assistance notice in both Spanish and Vietnamese stating the following:

"This booklet contains a summary in English of your plan rights and benefits under Employer A Pension Plan. If you have difficulty understanding any part of this booklet, contact Mr. John Doe, the plan administrator, at his office in Room 123, 456 Main St., Anywhere City, State 20001. Office hours are from 8:30 A.M. to 5:00 P.M. Monday through Friday. You may also call the plan administrator's office at (202) 555-2345 for assistance."

Labor Regs. § 2520.102-3
Contents of Summary Plan Description

Section 102 of the Act specifies information that must be included in the summary plan description. The summary plan description must accurately reflect the contents of the plans as of the date not earlier than 120 days prior to the date such summary plan description is disclosed. The following information shall be included in the summary plan description of both employee welfare benefit plans and employee pension benefit plans, except as stated otherwise in paragraphs (j) through (n):

(a) The name of the plan, and, if different, the name by which the plan is commonly known by its participants and beneficiaries;

(b) The name and address of—

(1) In the case of a single employer plan, the employer whose employees are covered by the plan,

(2) In the case of a plan maintained by an employee organization for its members, the employee organization that maintains the plan,

(3) In the case of a collectively-bargained plan established or maintained by one or more employers and one or more employee organizations, the association, committee, joint board of trustees, parent

or most significantly employer of a group of employers all of which contribute to the same plan, or other similar representative of the parties who established or maintain the plan, as well as

(i) A statement that a complete list of the employers and employee organizations sponsoring the plan may be obtained by participants and beneficiaries upon written request to the plan administrator, and is available for examination by participants and beneficiaries, as required by §§ 2520.104b-1 and 2520.104b-30; or

(ii) A statement that participants and beneficiaries may receive from the plan administrator, upon written request, information as to whether a particular employer or employee organization is a sponsor of the plan and, if the employer or employee organization is a plan sponsor, the sponsor's address.

(4) In the case of a plan established or maintained by two or more employers, the association, committee, joint board of trustees, parent or most significant employer of a group of employers all of which contribute to the same plan, or other similar representative of the parties who established or maintain the plan, as well as

(i) A statement that a complete list of the employers sponsoring the plan may be obtained by participants and beneficiaries upon written request to the plan administrator, and is available for examination by participants and beneficiaries, as required by §§ 2520.104b-1 and 2520.104b-30, or,

(ii) A statement that participants and beneficiaries may receive from the plan administrator, upon written request, information as to whether a particular employer is a sponsor of the plan and, if the employer is a plan sponsor, the sponsor's address.

* * *

(g) The name of the person designated as agent for service of legal process, and the address at which process may be served on such person, and in addition, a statement that service of legal process may be made upon a plan trustee or the plan administrator;

(h) The name, title and address of the principal place of business of each trustee of the plan;

* * *

(j) The plan's requirements respecting eligibility for participation and for benefits. The summary plan description shall describe the plan's provisions relating to eligibility to participate in the plan and the information identified in paragraphs (j)(1), (2) and (3) of this section, as appropriate.

(1) For employee pension benefit plans, it shall also include a statement describing the plan's normal retirement age, as that term is defined in section 3(24) of the Act, and a statement describing any other conditions which must be met before a participant will be eligible to receive benefits. Such plan benefits shall be described or summarized. In addition, the summary plan description shall in-

clude a description of the procedures governing qualified domestic relations order (QDRO) determinations or a statement indicating that participants and beneficiaries can obtain, without charge, a copy of such procedures from the plan administrator.

(2) For employee welfare benefit plans, it shall also include a statement of the conditions pertaining to eligibility to receive benefits, and a description or summary of the benefits. In the case of a welfare plan providing extensive schedules of benefits (a group health plan, for example), only a general description of such benefits is required if reference is made to detailed schedules of benefits which are available without cost to any participant or beneficiary who so requests. In addition, the summary plan description shall include a description of the procedures governing qualified medical child support order (QMCSO) determinations or a statement indicating that participants and beneficiaries can obtain, without charge, a copy of such procedures from the plan administrator.

(3) For employee welfare benefit plans that are group health plans, as defined in section 733(a)(1) of the Act, the summary plan description shall include a description of: any cost-sharing provisions, including premiums, deductibles, coinsurance, and copayment amounts for which the participant or beneficiary will be responsible; any annual or lifetime caps or other limits on benefits under the plan; the extent to which preventive services are covered under the plan; whether, and under what circumstances, existing and new drugs are covered under the plan; whether, and under what circumstances, coverage is provided for medical tests, devices and procedures; provisions governing the use of network providers, the composition of the provider network, and whether, and under what circumstances, coverage is provided for out-of-network services; any conditions or limits on the selection of primary care providers or providers of speciality medical care; any conditions or limits applicable to obtaining emergency medical care; and any provisions requiring preauthorizations or utilization review as a condition to obtaining a benefit or service under the plan. In the case of plans with provider networks, the listing of providers may be furnished as a separate document that accompanies the plan's SPD, provided that the summary plan description contains a general description of the provider network and provided further that the SPD contains a statement that provider lists are furnished automatically, without charge, as a separate document.

* * *

(p) The sources of contributions to the plan—for example, employer, employee organization, employees—and the method by which the amount of contribution is calculated. Defined benefit pension plans may state without further explanation that the contribution is actuarially determined.

* * *

(s) The procedures governing claims for benefits (including procedures for obtaining preauthorizations, approvals, or utilization review decisions in the case of group health plan services or benefits, and procedures for filing claim forms, providing notifications of benefit determinations, and reviewing denied claims in the case of any plan), applicable time limits, and remedies available under the plan for the redress of claims which are denied in whole or in part (including procedures required under section 503 of Title I of the Act). The plan's claims procedures may be furnished as a separate document that accompanies the plan's SPD, provided that the document satisfies the style and format requirements of 29 CFR 2520.102-2 and, provided further that the SPD contains a statement that the plan's claims procedures are furnished automatically, without charge, as a separate document.

(t)(1) The statement of ERISA rights described in section 104(c) of the Act, containing the items of information applicable to the plan included in the model statement of paragraph (t)(2) of this section. Items which are not applicable to the plan are not required to be included. The statement may contain explanatory and descriptive provisions in addition to those prescribed in paragraph (t)(2) of this section. However, the style and format of the statement shall not have the effect of misleading, misinforming or failing to inform participants and beneficiaries of a plan. All such information shall be written in a manner calculated to be understood by the average plan participant, taking into account factors such as the level of comprehension and education of typical participants in the plan and the complexity of the items required under this subparagraph to be included in the statement. Inaccurate, incomprehensible or misleading explanatory material will fail to meet the requirements of this section. The statement of ERISA rights (the model statement or a statement prepared by the plan), must appear as one consolidated statement. If a plan finds it desirable to make additional mention of certain rights elsewhere in the summary plan description, it may do so. The summary plan description may state that the statement of ERISA rights is required by Federal law and regulation.

(2) A summary plan description will be deemed to comply with the requirements of paragraph (t)(1) of this section if it includes the following statement; items of information which are not applicable to a particular plan should be deleted:

As a participant in (name of plan) you are entitled to certain rights and protections under the Employee Retirement Income Security Act of 1974 (ERISA). ERISA provides that all plan participants shall be entitled to:

Receive Information About Your Plan and Benefits

Examine, without charge, at the plan administrator's office and at other specified locations, such as worksites and union halls, all documents governing the plan, including insurance contracts and collective bargaining agreements, and a copy of the latest annual report (Form 5500 Series) filed by the plan with the U.S. Department of Labor and available at the Public Disclosure Room of the Pension and Welfare Benefit Administration.

Obtain, upon written request to the plan administrator, copies of documents governing the operation of the plan, including insurance contracts and collective bargaining agreements, and copies of the latest annual report (Form 5500 Series) and updated summary plan description. The administrator may make a reasonable charge for the copies.

Receive a summary of the plan's annual financial report. The plan administrator is required by law to furnish each participant with a copy of this summary annual report.

Obtain a statement telling you whether you have a right to receive a pension at normal retirement age (age * * *) and if so, what your benefits would be at normal retirement age if you stop working under the plan now. If you do not have a right to a pension, the statement will tell you how many more years you have to work to get a right to a pension. This statement must be requested in writing and is not required to be given more than once every twelve (12) months. The plan must provide the statement free of charge.

Continue Group Health Plan Coverage

Continue health care coverage for yourself, spouse or dependents if there is a loss of coverage under the plan as a result of a qualifying event. You or your dependents may have to pay for such coverage. Review this summary plan description and the documents governing the plan on the rules governing your COBRA continuation coverage rights.

Reduction or elimination of exclusionary periods of coverage for pre-existing conditions under your group health plan, if you have creditable coverage from another plan. You should be provided a certificate of creditable coverage, free of charge, from your group health plan or health insurance issuer when you lose coverage under the plan, when you become entitled to elect COBRA continuation coverage, when your COBRA continuation coverage ceases, if you request it before losing coverage, or if you request it up to 24 months after losing coverage. Without evidence of creditable coverage, you may be subject to a preexisting condition exclusion for 12 months (18 months for late enrollees) after your enrollment date in your coverage.

Prudent Actions by Plan Fiduciaries

In addition to creating rights for plan participants ERISA imposes duties upon the people who are responsible for the operation of the employee benefit plan. The people who operate your plan, called "fiduciaries" of the plan, have a duty to do so prudently and in the interest of you and other plan participants and beneficiaries. No one, including your employer, your union, or any other person, may fire you or otherwise discriminate against you in any way to prevent you from obtaining a (pension, welfare) benefit or exercising your rights under ERISA.

Enforce Your Rights

If your claim for a (pension, welfare) benefit is denied or ignored, in whole or in part, you have a right to know why this was done, to obtain copies of documents relating to the decision without charge, and to appeal any denial, all within certain time schedules.

Under ERISA, there are steps you can take to enforce the above rights. For instance, if you request a copy of plan documents or the latest annual report from the plan and do not receive them within 30 days, you may file suit in a Federal court. In such a case, the court may require the plan administrator to provide the materials and pay you up to $110 a day until you receive the materials, unless the materials were not sent because of reasons beyond the control of the administrator. If you have a claim for benefits which is denied or ignored, in whole or in part, you may file suit in a state or Federal court. In addition, if you disagree with the plan's decision or lack thereof concerning the qualified status of a domestic relations order or a medical child support order, you may file suit in Federal court. If it should happen that plan fiduciaries misuse the plan's money, or if you are discriminated against for asserting your rights, you may seek assistance from the U.S. Department of Labor, or you may file suit in a Federal court. The court will decide who should pay court costs and legal fees. If you are successful the court may order the person you have sued to pay these costs and fees. If you lose, the court may order you to pay these costs and fees, for example, if it finds your claim is frivolous.

Assistance with Your Questions

If you have any questions about your plan, you should contact the plan administrator. If you have any questions about this statement or about your rights under ERISA, or if you need assistance in obtaining documents from the plan administrator, you should contact the nearest office of the Employee Benefits Security Administration, U.S. Department of Labor, listed in your telephone directory or the Division of Technical Assistance and Inquiries, Employee Benefits Security Administration, U.S. Department of Labor, 200 Constitution Avenue N.W., Washington, D.C. 20210. You may also obtain certain publications about your rights and responsibilities under ERISA by calling the publications hotline of the Employee Benefits Security Administration.

* * *

Please don't lose sight of two important aspects of an SPD: first, it must be written in a manner calculated to be understood by the average plan participant, and second, it shall be sufficiently comprehensive to apprise the plan's participants and beneficiaries of their rights and obligations under the plan. As discussed, there has been a lot of litigation over discrepancies between the controlling plan document (which participants usually never see until there is litigation) and the Summary Plan Description (which is either included in the employee handbook or company's intranet site available on the first day an individual is employed).

Communicating Benefits Promised: Best Practices for Meeting ERISA's Disclosure Requirements

By Barry Kozak, *CCH Pension Plan Guide, Benefit Practice Portfolios*
(July 2007)

When an employer voluntarily chooses to sponsor a retirement or health and welfare plan for its employees, it needs to communicate the terms of the plan to all participants and beneficiaries in order to achieve the results it desires through offering the plan. This would be true even in the absence of all of the complex statutory rules under ERISA. The disclosure rules under ERISA, as amplified by the Pension Protection Act of 2006 ("PPA" P.L. 109-280), require that these disclosures are accurate and truthful, yet understandable and helpful. Unfortunately, even though these employers generally want to comply with all of the disclosure requirements, they generally lack the resources to conform in all aspects, especially small- and medium-sized employers.

Adding to the problem is the fact that many ERISA advisors, such as attorneys, actuaries, accountants, and other consultants, simply don't have the inclination or billable time to learn all the specific legal requirements for each specific disclosure. However, they are hired by the plan sponsors as experts, and are usually expected to draft personalized communications in a very quick turnaround time without an accompanying large bill for services. The main impetus for this article is my recent experiences speaking about the disclosure of relative values in front of such ERISA advisor groups. Each time I gave a presentation, I was continually shocked as many audience members were not looking for me to provide guidance so that they can thereafter draft their own compliant notices, but were simply looking for my "sample" notice. My answer was always that the existing benefit disclosure notice should be used as the starting point, because it was what plan participants and administrators were already familiar with, and then the ERISA advisor should go through the requirements of the regulations and add the various required elements where appropriate. To my dismay, many ERISA advisors who seemingly appreciated my lecture, left disappointed that they were going to need to read through the regulations themselves and draft their own notices for their clients. As discussed in this article, I see the same logic and reasoning for all disclosure notices from the same plan to be of a uniform style, with each respective notice being tweaked to comply with its governing statute and regulations.

Although there are numerous disclosure requirements for both retirement and health and welfare plans under ERISA,[1] this article will focus in on notices that communicate the benefits promised, and not the financial status of the plan or that merely that describe their rights under ERISA. First the readability of a Summary Plan Description, which is required for both retirement and health plans, will be discussed. Then the information needed during the life-cycle of a retirement plan participant and a health plan participant will be discussed, respectively. Finally, this article will explore ways that plan sponsors can find a best practices solution to providing compliant communications that are (1) written in a manner anticipated to be understood by the average participant and (2) uniformly inform the participants throughout their life-cycles as plan participants.

Three major assumptions made in this article, whether justified or not, are that all employers that sponsor an employee benefits plan: (1) primarily establish plans to attract, retain or reward its valued employees, and not primarily because of income tax advantages; (2) have internal employees or outside ERISA advisors that competently understand all of the complex rules and nuances of ERISA and the Code; and (3) actually operate the plans in complete adherence to the written plan documents and the law. Providing proper notices to participants and beneficiaries becomes much more difficult when any of these assumptions is absent.

---

1. For a complete list, see "Reporting and Disclosure Guide for Employee Benefit Plans," U.S. Department of Labor Employee Benefits Security Administration (Reprinted August 2006) available at http://www.dol.gov/ebsa/pdf/rdguide.pdf.

Disclosure Required Under ERISA

Most for-profit employers that sponsor employee benefit plans must comply with the tax rules under the Internal Revenue Code and labor rules under ERISA. Part of this compliance involves reporting to the government and disclosure to the participants and beneficiaries.[2] The government controls the forms that it publishes for reporting, but disclosure notices are generally drafted by each plan sponsor, even if the regulatory agencies provide model notices or suggested language.[3]

Summary Plan Descriptions

Generally, the first plan-related communication that an employee will see is a Summary Plan Description ("SPD"), either on her date of employment, or within 90 days after she becomes a participant. Following that, a participant may anticipate receiving an updated SPD at least every five years (or a Summary of Material Modifications when the plan is materially amended in the interim).[4] While there are certain content requirements for the SPD,[5] the form and style are totally in the discretion of the plan sponsor,[6] as long as it is "written in a manner calculated to be understood by the average plan participant and shall be sufficiently comprehensive to apprise the plan's participants and beneficiaries of their rights and obligations under the plan."[7] The regulations state further that "[i]n fulfilling these requirements, the plan administrator shall exercise considered judgment and discretion by taking into account such factors as the level of comprehension and education of typical participants in the plan and the complexity of the terms of the plan. Consideration of these factors will usually require the limitation or elimination of technical jargon and of long, complex sentences, the use of clarifying examples and illustrations, the use of clear cross references and a table of contents."[8]

An SPD is generally required for all ERISA plans, and is supposed to be a nice summary, in understandable language, of the official written plan document.[9] However, over time, some courts have determined that the provisions of the SPD will control where there are inconsistencies with the actual provisions in the plan document. As courts began elevating the legal importance of these summaries to the level of actual plan documents, the attorneys representing plan sponsors

---

2. ERISA §§ 101 to 111 contain most of the statutory requirements for reporting and disclosure for plans subject to ERISA (i.e., those plans sponsored by employers, or their associated employee representative organizations, that are engaged in commerce, other than government employers or church employers electing not to be covered, and a few other types of plans not covered under ERISA § 4).

3. Under Title III of ERISA, as amplified by President Carter's Reorganization Plan No. 4 of 1978 (43 F.R. 47713, 92 Stat. 3790), the Department of Labor had jurisdiction over the content of most reporting and disclosure requirements, but over time, the Department of Treasury has been given jurisdiction and has issued guidance on the content of some disclosure as well.

4. ERISA § 104(b).

5. ERISA § 102(b), ERISA Reg. § 2520.102-3.

6. ERISA Reg. § 2520.102-2 (and ERISA Reg. § 2520.102-4 when there is a reason to draft different SPDs for the same plan).

7. Id., at -2(a).

8. Id.

9 See, e.g., Aiken v. Policy Management Systems Corp., 13 F.3d 138 (4th Cir. 1993) (CCH Pension Plan Guide ¶ 50,178) (holding that representations in the SPD control over inconsistent provisions in the official ERISA plan document). For a complete discussion, see Michael C. Joyce, "Setting a Standard to Rely On: ERISA Benefit Claims Where the Summary Plan Description and Plan Document Conflict," 90 Iowa L. Rev. 765 (January 2005, Note).

had no choice but to draft them in anticipation of litigation, which sometimes seems to supersede the actual requirement that they be drafted in a manner calculated to be understood by the average plan participant. While some have suggested that Congress should clarify that SPDs are not substitutes for the plan document unless there is fraud, Congress has not yet acted.[10]

Even if attorneys did not worry about conflicts between the SPD and the document, however, plan sponsors are still arguably not drafting the SPDs in the style and format required by the ERISA regulations. In 2006, a study looked at the readability of health care plans and found that: the average readability level for important information concerning eligibility, benefits, and participant rights and responsibilities in summary plan descriptions is written at a first year college reading level. The average level of readability for SPDs is higher than the recommended reading level for technical material. Some of the SPDs in the study sample use language written at a 9th grade reading level. Other SPDs use language written at nearly a college graduate (16th grade) reading level.[11]

The study concludes that fundamental improvements are needed in the readability of written SPDs, and that employers and plan administrators should explore the use of alternative methods of communication to plan participants beyond the written SPD."[12] While the author of this article does not disagree with the conclusions of this study, it seems that the plan sponsors should arguably first try to draft a legally compliant SPD in an understandable manner before exploring alternate methods of communication beyond the SPD.

The life-cycle of a retirement plan participant

In ERISA retirement plans, after the individual becomes a participant in the plan and has received the SPD, she will receive notices along the way informing her of the benefits that have vested and accrued under the plan. After the PPA changes become effective, she will receive such notice:

• at least quarterly if she participates in a self-directed defined contribution plan,

• at least annually if she participates in any other type of defined contribution plan, and

• at least once every three years if she participates in a defined benefit plan.[13]

Like the SPDs, these benefit statements "shall be written in a manner calculated to be understood by the average plan participant."[14] An additional requirement is that if the plan is a pension plan and it is amended to reduce the rate of future benefit accruals, then an ERISA § 204(h) notice must be distributed, and such notice must be "written in a manner calculated to be understood

---

10. For example, see Advisory Council on Employee Welfare and Pension Benefit Plans Report Of The Working Group On Communications To Retirement Plan Participants, presented to U.S. Department of Labor, November 2005 (available at http://www.dol.gov/ ebsa/publications/AC_1105b_report.html).

11. "How Readable Are Summary Plan Descriptions For Health Care Plans?" Employee Benefits Research Institute (Notes, October 2006, Vol. 27, No. 10).

12. Id.

13. ERISA § 105(a), as amended by PPA.

14. ERISA § 105(a)(2)(A)(iii).

by the average plan participant and to apprise the applicable individual of the significance of the notice."[15]

When the participant retires or is otherwise entitled to plan benefits, she will receive a notice that explains the taxation and rollover treatment allowed under Code Sec. 402(f).[16] If the plan is subject to the Qualified Joint and Survivor Annuity rules,[17] then she will also receive a disclosure of the relative values of different distribution options.[18] After the IRS provided a model notice for Code Sec. 402(f), almost all plan sponsors blindly use the model notice, sometimes not aware that the model language is outdated and that they are required to amend it to comply with current law even in the absence of further guidance from the IRS, and sometimes not aware that they are still responsible for altering the model language to comply with the actual provisions of the controlling plan document. The Treasury applied the familiar standard, requiring that the disclosure of relative values notice "must be written in a manner calculated to be understood by the average participant."[19]

The life-cycle of a group health plan participant

Participants in a health plan have the need for different information. Basically, they need to know if a certain medical procedure or treatment will be covered by the plan, as well as how their coverage will be continued or will become portable after they cease to be an employee. The SPD for the employer's group health plan has the same requirements as for a retirement plan, and must also be "written in a manner calculated to be understood by the average plan participant and shall be sufficiently comprehensive to apprise the plan's participants and beneficiaries of their rights and obligations under the plan."

Unlike a retirement plan sponsor, the plan sponsor of a group health plan is not required to provide statements along the way; therefore, the participant generally will not know with certainty that a particular medical expense will be covered. All that the participant can do is make a claim for benefits and follow the plan's claims procedures if the benefit claim is denied,[20] or bring an action against the plan to clarify her rights to future benefits under the terms of the plan.[21] Because both of these remedial procedures are burdensome, especially with many of the urgent life or death decisions that are made with respect to one's medical treatment, a clear and readable SPD is especially crucial.

As a participant in a group health plan, when employment is terminated for certain reasons, or certain qualified life events happen, the plan is required to

---

15. Treas. Regs. § 54-4980F-1, Q&A-11 (in order to add a penalty tax on untimely or ineffective notices, Congress added section 4980F to the Code to supplement existing ERISA § 204(h) and associated Labor Regulations).

16. The IRS published a model notice for compliance with the Code Sec. 402(f) requirements titled "Special Tax Notice Regarding Plan Payments" in Notice 2002-3 (CCH Pension Plan Guide ¶ 17,122Y), but which has not been updated by subsequent tax law changes (see, e.g., the letter from the ASPPA Government Affairs Committee to the IRS dated April 12, 2007, available at http://www.aspa.org/pdf_files/402(f)_Notice_coverletter.pdf).

17. IRC § 401(a)(11).

18. IRC § 417(a)(3).

19. Treas. Regs. § 1.417(a)-3(a)(4).

20. ERISA § 503.

21. ERISA § 502(a)(1)(B).

provide COBRA continuation notices in a timely manner.[22] Of course, the familiar phrase governs these notices as well, and they must be "written in a manner calculated to be understood by the average plan participant."[23]

Best practices for drafting disclosure notices

Most of the important disclosure notices that inform plan participants of their benefits under the plan, as opposed to the notices that provide general financial information about the plan or that merely convey ERISA rights, have as a basic premise that they are "written in a manner calculated to be understood by the average plan participant." Although this phrase is a statutory requirement for the SPD, and is merely a regulatory requirement for the other notices in the life-cycle of a participant, that term is not defined anywhere. Neither the Departments of Treasury nor Labor have provided guidance. A few courts have reviewed specific language of communications, but have not provided any bright-line tests.[24]

So how does a plan sponsor meet its primary threshold of drafting notices in a manner calculated to be understood by the average participant? Although not controlling, a source that might provide some level of security might be an alternate federal agency, the Department of Health and Human Services. HIPAA privacy notices are required to be drafted in "Plain Language." Because group health plans are considered covered entities under HIPAA's privacy rule, there is arguably a link between HIPAA covered entities and ERISA employee benefit plans. In its "Plain Language Principles and Thesaurus for Making HIPAA Privacy Notices More Readable,"[25] the HHS suggests:

- a layered notice, where the first layer is a short notice that summarizes individual's rights and other information, and then the second layer would be a more comprehensive notice satisfying the statutory elements of the notice;

- arranging the required information in the order that would be in the reader's best interest (including appropriate preambles and appendices);

- drafting the notice at a 9th grade reading level;

- making the notice easier to read by using a conversational style rather than a formal style, using common words, using short sentences, avoiding hyphens and compound words, providing examples to explain problem words, using lower case rather than all capital letters;

- making the notice look easier to read by allowing more white space by using wider margins, chunking long lists into smaller bites, by inserting pictures, graphs or other visuals where appropriate, using large fonts

---

22. ERISA §606.

23. Labor Regs. §§2590.606-1(c) and 2590.606-4(b)(4).

24. See, e.g., Wilson v. Southwestern Bell, 55 F.3d 399, 407 (8th Cir. 1995) (holding that it "appears to be an objective standard rather than requiring an inquiry into the subjective perception of the individual participants" and that the readability requirement does not extend to other correspondence); Hickman v. GEM Ins. Co., 299 F.3d 1208, 1212 (10th Cir. 2002) (holding that "the trial court followed the correct procedure in first resolving the question of ambiguity before proceeding to examine the question of an alleged violation of the notice requirements. This procedure is appropriate in ERISA cases, where the plan language should be construed first in order to determine whether that language was clear and unambiguous.").

25. Available at ftp://ftp.hrsa.gov/hrsa/hipaaplainlang.pdf.

and high contrasts, giving the context first before supplementing with new
information;

> • making it suitable for the culture by matching logic, language and ex-
> perience; and

> • preparing in some situations to draft all or some of the notices in an
> even simpler manner for those plan participants and beneficiaries with
> limited reading skills.

Again, there is no guarantee that following the guidance set forth by the Department of Health and Human Services for "Plain English" HIPAA privacy
notices will fulfill the ERISA notice requirements that they be drafted in a "manner calculated to be understood by the average plan participant." However,
every plan sponsor must start somewhere, and why not start with those suggestions (at least until the Departments of Treasury or Labor issue pertinent
guidance).

In most instances, the small- or midsized-employer outsources its ERISA
compliance, and its outside counsel or other advisor drafts the notices. However, this article is suggesting a brand new approach that forces the plan sponsor to take an active role in drafting these notices. The author suggests that the
plan sponsor, knowing the true reasons it established the plan in the first place
and the needs and culture of its employee population, at least draft the skeletal
outline of the SPD, benefit statements, and benefit distribution forms in the language they think will convey the relevant information. This will allow all forms
delivered throughout the participant's life-cycle to have a certain feel and style,
and provide that most of the material terms of the plan will be used consistently.
This drafting exercise should be done without any assistance from its outside
counsel or advisor. Then, after the initial outline draft by the employer, the ERISA
specialist can then insert all of the statutorily required elements. However, the
ERISA counsel would be forced to do so in a way that minimally affects the tem-
plate provided by the plan sponsor.

This should arguably be done for every notice, including those that either the
Departments of Treasury or Labor provide model language. Whether it's a notice that explains the vested and accrued benefits to date, the tax rules for a distribution, or the relative values of alternative forms of distribution, if the plan
sponsor sketches out the style of communication for its unique workforce, then
the final product after review by the ERISA counsel will likely meet the readability requirement. This article argues that it is easy for an ERISA expert to meet
the content requirements for any form, but usually misses the mark on making
that content understandable. Further, this article argues that model notices and
language provided by the regulatory agencies should be looked at as simply guidance, and not the Holy Grail. Model notices are scary in that even though the content will comply with the regulation, there is usually nothing in such model
language that expounds how such model notices will satisfy the readability and
understandability requirements. And, as discussed above, when a model notice
becomes outdated by the enactment of new law, it is wholly the responsibility of
the plan sponsor, or its ERISA counsel, to recognize the law changes and change
the model notice; once the model notice is altered in any way, however, it is no
longer a safe harbor model notice, even if the only changes are due to law changes.

Conclusion

Yes, an employer who is considering sponsorship of an employee benefits plan should acknowledge that extra thought and effort by the employer, as well as money, may be required to draft understandable language for required disclosures to participants and beneficiaries. And, yes, this also requires the competent ERISA counsel or advisor to spend time bringing each client's respective templates into compliance, rather than having a "shelved" set of SPDs and other notices that simply get attached to each plan. However, if this becomes the business model of the ERISA counsel or advisor, then as each new client meets to discuss and shape its employee benefits programs, they can be instructed as to their responsibilities. After all, if the plan sponsor takes no role at all, it is more likely that a suit by disgruntled plan participants or beneficiaries will compel the plan sponsor to appear in court where they will argue that they were not informed, inadequately informed, or misinformed and that information about their employee benefit plan that was not written in a manner calculated to be understood by them. And it is the plan sponsor that will be at the other end of that lawsuit, not its ERISA counsel or other advisor.

Chapter 13

Fiduciary Rules and Investment of Plan Assets

Overview

Who is a Plan Fiduciary?
- each plan must name at least one individual as a fiduciary, and the plan document can allow the delegation of duties and assignment of additional fiduciaries
- however, every individual is a fiduciary of the plan to the extent that he or she:
  - exercises any authority or control over the management or disposition of the plan assets,
  - renders investment advice for a fee regarding plan assets or has authority to do so, or
  - has any discretionary authority or responsibility in the administration of the plan
- the DOL takes the view that attorneys, accountants, actuaries, consultants, etc., performing their usual professional duties are not ordinarily considered fiduciaries.
- a person may not be a fiduciary of the plan if he or she has been convicted of, or imprisoned for, any of the delineated felonies (such as robbery, bribery, extortion, embezzlement, and fraud)

What are the fiduciary duties and how are they discharged?
- a fiduciary is required to discharge his or her duties:
  - solely in the interest of the plan participants and beneficiaries,
  - for the exclusive purpose of providing benefits to participants and beneficiaries and defraying reasonable plan expenses (*i.e.,* this is the only reason that the plan is set up and a fiduciary cannot have self-concerns),
  - with the skill, care, prudence and diligence under the circumstances then prevailing that a prudent person would use acting in a like capacity and with like aims (this is stricter than the common law prudent man standard is since ERISA presumes a higher degree of expertise for any individual serving as a plan fiduciary),
  - by diversifying the investments of the plan in order to minimize the risk of large losses unless under the circumstances it is clearly prudent not to do so, and

- in accordance with the documents and instruments governing the plan insofar as such documents and instruments are consistent with the provision of Titles I and IV of ERISA.
- in addition, a fiduciary is prohibited from:
  - dealing with plan assets in his or her own interest or for his or her own account,
  - involving the plan in any transaction which is adverse to the interests of the plan or to the interests of the participants and beneficiaries, or
  - receiving any consideration for his or her own personal account from any party for a transaction involving the plan assets
- this is an on-going standard, and therefore, every decision a fiduciary makes is based on this standard, even the decision to delegate certain duties to another individual and the monitoring of such individual to ensure that he or she is properly exercising their delegated fiduciary duties
- the fiduciary is required to maintain the indicia of ownership of all plan assets within the jurisdiction of the district courts of the United States
- any person who is a fiduciary of a plan and who breaches any of the responsibilities, obligations, or duties shall be personally liable to reimburse the plan for losses and to restore any lost profits (however, no fiduciary shall be liable if the breach was committed before he or she became a fiduciary or after he or she ceased to be a fiduciary)
- every fiduciary and every person who handles plan assets must generally be bonded for 10% of the value of assets he or she specifically is responsible for (up to $500,000)

How can plan assets generally be invested?

- basically, the fiduciaries and trustees can make any investment (*i.e.,* stocks, bonds, real property, futures, artwork, joint ventures, …) as long as they satisfy the delineated fiduciary duties (discussed above), don't constitute a Prohibited Transaction (discussed below), and comply with the plan document
- some of the main considerations in plan investments are:
  - whether the aggregate of plan assets are diversified, prudently invested, invested in and in accordance with the plan's investment policy and short-term liquidity needs
  - if the plan invests in real property, is it limited to the statutory amount of 10% of the aggregate of assets immediately after acquisition and does it meet the rules of Qualified Employer Real Property (QERP)
  - if the plan invests in its sponsoring employer's securities, is it limited to the statutory amount of 10% of the aggregate of assets immediately after acquisition and does it meet the rules of Qualified Employer Securities (QES)

What are the special rules for depositing elective salary deferrals or designated Roth contributions?

- salary deferral contributions must be physically deposited into the plan's trust as of the earliest date on which such contributions can reasonably be segregated from the employer's general assets, but no later than the 15th business day of the month next following the month in which the deferrals are withheld or received by the employer

What are Prohibited Transactions?

- a fiduciary shall not cause the plan to engage in a PT if he or she knows (or should know) that such transaction will directly or indirectly constitute a PT
- fiduciaries will be personally liable to make up for any plan losses due to the PT and must restore any personal profits resulting from the PT
- additionally, a court might assess other equitable relief and might remove the fiduciary
- under ERISA, some of the more common transactions prohibited between a plan and a "party in interest" are:
  - a sale, exchange or lease of any property between the plan and a party in interest,
  - the lending of money or other extension of credit between the plan and a party in interest,
  - the furnishing of goods, services, or facilities between the plan and a party in interest, or
  - the transfer of any plan assets to a party in interest, or allowing a party in interest to use or benefit from the use of any plan assets
- the term "party in interest" is defined under ERISA as basically any individual that has an interest in the plan, including employees who are plan participants
- basically the same transactions are prohibited under the Code as are prohibited under ERISA, but the term used by the Code is "disqualified person" rather than "party in interest"
- A penalty tax is imposed under the Code, whereas civil liability is imposed under ERISA

What transactions are exemptions to a Prohibited Transaction?

- The Secretary of Labor is required to establish a procedure where plans can ask the DOL in advance whether a desired business transaction will be deemed a PT or whether the DOL will issue a private PT exemption letter for the plan
- the following transactions are some of the more important statutory PT exemptions:
  - qualified loans to plan participants,
  - contracting or making reasonable arrangements with a party in interest for office space, or for legal, accounting, or other necessary services to the plan for reasonable compensation,
  - investing assets in a bank or other financial institution which is a fiduciary if certain conditions are met,
  - the purchase of life insurance, health insurance or annuities with insurers who are fiduciaries if certain conditions are met;
  - the providing of ancillary services by a bank or other financial institution which is a fiduciary if certain conditions are met;
  - distributions authorized by the fiduciary which comply with the plan provisions and Title IV of ERISA;
- although the PT rules seem to bar most transactions, nothing shall be construed to prohibit any fiduciary from:

- receiving any benefit he or she is entitled to from the plan as a participant of the plan,
- receiving reasonable compensation for actual services performed and reimbursement for reasonable expenses incurred in the performance of duties, or
- serving as a fiduciary in addition to being an officer, employee, agent, or other representative of a party in interest

Can participants in a 401(k) plan be allowed to self-direct their accounts?

- if done properly, the true fiduciaries of the plan will not be subject to a breach of fiduciary duty for losses in the participant's respective account balances due to their individual investment choices, but only if:
  - the participants have an opportunity to exercise control, which includes the communication of all information and prospectuses that are necessary for any individual to make an informed decision, and
  - the participants are given a broad range of investment alternatives (they must have at least have three alternatives which are diversified, offer materially different risk and return characteristics, aggregately enable each participant to achieve a risk and return level normally appropriate for him or her, and collectively tend to minimize through diversification the overall risk of each participant's portfolio)
- the plan fiduciary is still subject to all fiduciary duties in all actions he or she takes to choose and establish the initial investment alternatives (either through one or several investment companies), monitor their performance, and determine if new or alternative investment choices are necessary
- in choosing the array of investment choices, the plan fiduciary must take into consideration the fees charged to each individual account (currently, one of the top priorities at the DOL, and a growing concern in Congress, is looking at fees charged to plan accounts and determining whether abuses or negligence is rampant)
- there are strict parameters in which plan sponsors can provide individual investment advice to plan participants

What is a blackout period?

- a blackout period occurs when there will be at least a 3-day period where participants will not be able to transfer money in or out of an investment vehicle
- the plan sponsor must provide notices to the affected participants at least 30 days prior to the blackout period

What liabilities attach to fiduciaries?

- fiduciaries who breach their duties can be held personally liable for any losses to the plan caused by their action or inaction, and can be ordered to disgorge all personal profits

What liabilities attach to co-fiduciaries?

- one fiduciary will be liable for a breach of fiduciary duty by another plan fiduciary if:
  - he or she participates knowingly in, or knowingly undertakes to conceal, an act or omission of another fiduciary, knowing such act or omission is a breach,

- he or she has enabled the other fiduciary to commit the breach if he or she has failed to comply with the fiduciary duty specifically required for him or her, or

- he or she has knowledge of a breach by such other fiduciary, unless he or she makes reasonable efforts under the circumstances to remedy the breach

- if the assets are held by two or more trustees, then each trustee shall use reasonable care to prevent a co-trustee from committing a breach and shall jointly control and manage the plan assets and can, by agreement, allocate and limit specific trustee duties

- a trustee will not be subject to liability if he or she merely follows instructions of the plan fiduciaries or for the acts or omissions of properly named investment managers

A. Fiduciary over Plan Assets

1. Employee Benefit Plans That Require Fiduciary Guardianship

Statutory Rules at ERISA § 401

All qualified retirement plans (defined contribution, defined benefit, and hybrid plans) and all non-insured (*i.e.,* self insured) health and welfare plans are subject to the fiduciary rules.

2. Individuals Who Are Plan Fiduciaries

Statutory Definition at ERISA § 3(21)(A)

The starting point is that in order for a plan to be properly established, the plan document must specify at least one individual as the named fiduciary (which can just be a reference to an officer position at the employer that will always be filled). Then, if the named fiduciary has the right to allocate responsibilities for the operation and administration of the plan, the plan document must describe the procedures. However, any person convicted or imprisoned for certain crimes (such as robbery, bribery, extortion, embezzlement, fraud, grand larceny, burglary, arson, or other similar felonies) cannot serve as fiduciary.[1]

In addition to the named fiduciary(ies) and any other fiduciaries that are specifically allocated authority, ERISA contains a function test for the Department of Labor or a court to deem an individual a fiduciary over plan assets, whether or not the individual knows of such classification or even wants it. An individual may be considered a plan fiduciary to the extent that he or she maintains any authority or control over the management of the plan's assets or the plan in general or have any responsibility for the administration of the plan. Specifically, a fiduciary is a person who:

---

1. ERISA § 411.

1. exercises discretionary authority or control respecting the management of the plan or exercises any authority or control over the management or disposition of its assets;

2. renders investment advice for a fee or other compensation (direct or indirect) as to any assets of the plan or has any authority or responsibility to do so; or

3. has discretionary authority or discretionary responsibility in the administration of the plan.

The determination of an individual's fiduciary status is an inherently factual inquiry and will require analysis of the specific facts and circumstances of each case. However, employers will generally be fiduciaries at some level, especially in the discretionary authority exercised over the administration of the plan (*i.e.*, choosing the plan administrator or reviewing plan loans or distributions).

Custer v. Sweeney
89 F.3d 1156 (4th Cir. 1996)

NIEMEYER, Circuit Judge:

Robert D. Custer, a trustee of and participant in the Sheet Metal Workers' National Pension Fund, an employee benefit plan regulated by the Employee Retirement Income Security Act of 1974 (ERISA), 29 U.S.C. § 1001 et seq. , sued the plan's attorneys, alleging breach of ERISA fiduciary duties and legal malpractice. The district court dismissed Custer's ERISA claim on the ground that the attorney named in the ERISA count was not a plan fiduciary and declined to exercise jurisdiction over the malpractice claims, allowing Custer to prosecute those claims in state court. The court also denied a defendant's motion for attorneys fees.

Custer appeals the dismissal of his ERISA claim, and Raymond J. Sweeney, one of the defendant attorneys, cross-appeals, contending that the district court erred in failing to dismiss Custer's malpractice claims with prejudice as preempted by ERISA. Sweeney also cross-appeals the district court's refusal to award him attorneys fees. We now affirm.

I

Until his resignation in mid-1993, the late Edward J. Carlough served as chairman of the Sheet Metal Workers' National Pension Fund and president of the Sheet Metal Workers' International Association, the pension plan's affiliated union. While holding those positions, Carlough allegedly squandered millions of dollars of the pension plan's assets (1) to subsidize the lease of a private jet primarily for his personal use and (2) to purchase, improve, furnish, operate, and reside at a lavish mansion under the guise that it was needed as a second conference center. Sweeney, Carlough's nephew, served as legal counsel to the pension plan and to the two trustee committees that oversaw the airplane and conference center transactions.

In July 1994, Custer filed this action against Sweeney and the pension plan's other attorneys, alleging (1) that Sweeney breached fiduciary duties imposed by ERISA by making the arrangements for Carlough to consummate the airplane and conference center transactions and (2) that Sweeney and the other legal counsel to the pension plan committed legal malpractice in their representation of the plan. Custer predicated federal jurisdiction over the legal malpractice claims on diversity of citizenship, 28 U.S.C. § 1332, and supplemental jurisdiction, 28 U.S.C. § 1367.

The district court granted the defendants' Rule 12(b)(6) motion to dismiss Custer's suit on the ground that Custer's allegations failed to establish that Sweeney, as counsel to the pension plan, qualified as a fiduciary under ERISA. The court, however, granted Custer*1161 leave to amend his complaint to allege sufficient "indicia of fiduciary position." The court also dismissed without prejudice Custer's malpractice claims. It found an absence of complete diversity and declined to exercise its discretionary supplemental jurisdiction over the malpractice claims.

Custer filed an amended complaint, reasserting in more detail his ERISA claim against Sweeney. He alleged that Sweeney not only had exercised "de facto control over [the] arrangements for leasing the [a]irplane and the acquisition, build-out, furnishing, operation, and maintenance" of the conference center, but also had authorized expenditures and approved payments for those purposes from pension plan funds. Custer appended dozens of documents that purported to illustrate Sweeney's discretionary control over plan assets and management. In the amended complaint, Custer predicated federal subject matter jurisdiction over his malpractice claims against Sweeney and the other former counsel to the pension plan solely on the court's supplemental jurisdiction.

Again the defendants moved to dismiss the complaint. While Sweeney argued that he was not an ERISA fiduciary, all of the defendants argued that Custer's malpractice claims were preempted by ERISA and failed to establish their duty to monitor the pension plan's airplane and conference center investments for compliance with ERISA. Sweeney also requested attorneys fees under both Federal Rule of Civil Procedure 11(c) and ERISA § 502(g), 29 U.S.C. § 1132(g), on the ground that Custer lacked a good faith basis for his claims.

The district court dismissed Custer's ERISA claim against Sweeney with prejudice, concluding that Custer's second attempt to plead Sweeney's fiduciary status under ERISA was "at best hopeless or at worst contrived." It dismissed the legal malpractice claims without prejudice, declining to exercise supplemental jurisdiction over them. Finally, the court denied Sweeney's motion for attorneys fees because it did "not believe that there [was] a sufficient inference of bad faith" on Custer's part.

Custer appeals the district court's dismissal of his ERISA claim, and Sweeney cross-appeals the district court's failure to dismiss the malpractice claim with prejudice as preempted by ERISA. Sweeney also contends that the district court abused its discretion in refusing to award him attorneys fees.[*]

II

[1] We begin with Custer's contention that the district court erred in dismissing his ERISA claim against Sweeney for breach of fiduciary duty. After affording Custer the opportunity to replead that claim, the district court observed that Custer's amended complaint still alleged "that Sweeney was at most an attorney and consultant who took care of the ministerial, day-to-day payment of bills, securing of funds with which to meet Fund obligations, and monitoring the progress

---

[*] None of the fund's other counsel is a party to this appeal. But Harry Huge and his former law firm, Rogovin, Huge & Schiller, have filed an amicus brief arguing that ERISA substantively preempts Custer's malpractice claims.

of construction and operations on Fund property." Concluding that such activities "completely fail[ed] to establish the exercise of the type of discretion or control necessary to hold Sweeney liable as an ERISA fiduciary," the court dismissed Custer's ERISA claim with prejudice. Whether the district court acted properly thus depends on whether Sweeney qualifies as a "fiduciary" under ERISA.

[2] "[T]he concept of a fiduciary under ERISA is broader than the common law concept of a trustee." Custer v. Pan Am. Life Ins. Co., 12 F.3d 410, 418 n. 3 (4th Cir.1993). It includes not only those "named [as fiduciaries] in the plan instrument, or who, pursuant to a procedure specified in the plan, [are] identified as ... fiduciar[ies]," 29 U.S.C. § 1102(a)(2), but any individual who de facto performs specified discretionary functions with respect to the management, assets, or administration of a plan. According to § 3(21)(A) of ERISA:

[A] person is a fiduciary with respect to a plan to the extent (i) he exercises any *1162 discretionary authority or discretionary control respecting management of such plan or exercises any authority or control respecting management or disposition of its assets, (ii) he renders investment advice for a fee or other compensation, direct or indirect, with respect to any moneys or other property of such plan, or has any authority or responsibility to do so, or (iii) he has any discretionary authority or discretionary responsibility in the administration of such plan. 29 U.S.C. § 1002(21)(A).

[3] [4] While an attorney's duty to his client is that of a fiduciary, see F.H. Krear & Co. v. Nineteen Named Trustees, 810 F.2d 1250, 1259 (2d Cir.1987), the mere fact that an attorney represents an ERISA plan does not make the attorney an ERISA fiduciary because legal representation of ERISA plans rarely involves the discretionary authority or control required by the statute's definition of "fiduciary." According to the regulations promulgated by the Department of Labor — the agency charged with enforcing ERISA — an attorney or other professional service provider who represents an ERISA plan will not qualify as an ERISA fiduciary so long as he "performs purely ministerial functions ... within a framework of policies, interpretations, rules, practices and procedures made by other persons." 29 C.F.R. § 2509.75-8(D-2); see also 29 C.F.R. § 2509.75-5(D-1) (applying ERISA's definition of "fiduciary" to attorneys); Useden v. Acker, 947 F.2d 1563, 1577 (11th Cir.1991) (holding that law firm was not ERISA fiduciary because it did not "depart[ ] from the usual functions of a law firm or otherwise effectively or realistically control[ ] the [ERISA] Plan"), cert. denied, 508 U.S. 959, 113 S.Ct. 2927, 124 L.Ed.2d 678 (1993); Nieto v. Ecker, 845 F.2d 868, 870 (9th Cir.1988); Yeseta v. Baima, 837 F.2d 380, 385 (9th Cir.1988); F.H. Krear, 810 F.2d at 1259–60. Moreover, negligence in the provision of professional services does not create ERISA fiduciary status. See Pappas v. Buck Consultants, Inc., 923 F.2d 531, 538 (7th Cir.1991); Nieto, 845 F.2d at 870–71. ERISA's careful allocation of fiduciary liability is consonant with the statute's "clear purpose" of ensuring ERISA plans "access to ordinary legal advice." Useden, 947 F.2d at 1578.

[5] But merely because a person serves as legal counsel to a pension plan does not automatically preclude a finding that the attorney is also an ERISA fiduciary, at least as to some activities. Fiduciary status under ERISA is not "an all-or-nothing concept." Coleman v. Nationwide Life Ins. Co., 969 F.2d 54, 61 (4th Cir.1992), cert. denied, 506 U.S. 1081, 113 S.Ct. 1051, 122 L.Ed.2d 359 (1993). As we explained in Coleman, "the inclusion of the phrase 'to the extent' in [ERISA's definition of 'fiduciary'] means that a party is a fiduciary only as to the activities

which bring the person within the definition." Id.; see also F.H. Krear, 810 F.2d at 1259. Therefore, to determine whether Custer has sufficiently alleged Sweeney's status as an ERISA fiduciary, we must discern from Custer's amended complaint the functions that Sweeney allegedly performed.

Conceding that the pension plan's documents do not expressly confer ERISA fiduciary status on Sweeney, Custer argues only that his amended complaint sufficiently pled Sweeney's de facto fiduciary status by alleging that Sweeney's activities "transcended the normal legal services rendered by plan counsel." Custer contends that his amended complaint reveals that Sweeney "caused the Fund to enter into, and continue with," both the airplane and conference center transactions by (1) exercising discretionary decisionmaking authority over "all aspects" of those transactions and (2) "with [holding] vital information [from] and actively deceiv[ing]" the pension plan's trustees. Sweeney argues, on the other hand, that the district court properly dismissed Custer's ERISA claim because his amended complaint "allege [s] not one fact tending to show that Mr. Sweeney exercised control or authority specifically over the decisions to acquire and retain [the conference center] or the [a]irplane." He maintains that, to the contrary, the substance of the complaint's allegations support the conclusion that Sweeney "performed purely ministerial functions." And, according to Sweeney, Custer's assertions that Sweeney usurped the other plan fiduciaries' decisionmaking authority over the airplane and conference*1163 center transactions amount to no more than allegations of negligence in the performance of ordinary professional services.

Having carefully reviewed the amended complaint de novo, accepting all of Custer's well-pleaded allegations as true and construing them in the light most favorable to Custer, see Mylan Lab., Inc. v. Matkari, 7 F.3d 1130, 1134 (4th Cir.1993), cert. denied, 510 U.S. 1197, 114 S.Ct. 1307, 127 L.Ed.2d 658 (1994), we agree with Sweeney. While Custer's amended complaint is replete with assertions of Sweeney's "discretionary authority, control, and responsibility over the management of the Fund and certain assets of the Fund," it nevertheless lacks any specific allegations capable of demonstrating that Sweeney transcended his role as legal counsel. See 5A Charles A. Wright & Arthur R. Miller, Federal Practice and Procedure § 1357, 317–18 (2d ed.1990) (noting that court need not accept plaintiff's " 'unwarranted deductions,' 'footless conclusions of law,' or 'sweeping legal conclusions cast in the form of factual allegations' " (footnotes omitted)); see also Randall v. United States, 30 F.3d 518, 522 (4th Cir.1994), cert. denied, 514 U.S. 1107, 115 S.Ct. 1956, 131 L.Ed.2d 849 (1995). The amended complaint discloses that the trustee subcommittees that Sweeney represented made only non-binding recommendations to the pension plan's board of trustees, who ultimately decided to enter into the airplane and conference center transactions and retained authority over spending the pension plan's funds. And the documents appended to Custer's amended complaint illustrate that Sweeney performed only ministerial functions for the pension plan, such as soliciting bids for contracting work and approving the payment of bills, and that he lacked check-writing authority. See Useden, 947 F.2d at 1577 (affirming summary judgment for law firm on ground that firm was not ERISA fiduciary where plaintiff alleged that "law firm deeply penetrat[ed] the governance of the Plan" by, inter alia, "drafting ... amendments to the Plan on its own initiative" and providing "hybrid business-legal ... advice").

[6] Custer's allegations that Sweeney usurped trustee decisionmaking authority by controlling information relevant to the propriety of the airplane and

conference center transactions also fail to state an ERISA claim. If true, the assertions establish at most that Sweeney violated legal duties arising from his representation of the ERISA plan. But they do not satisfy the requirement that Sweeney caused the plan's trustees "to relinquish [their] independent discretion in investing the plan's funds and follow the course [he] prescribed." Schloegel v. Boswell, 994 F.2d 266, 271–72 (5th Cir.), cert. denied, 510 U.S. 964, 114 S.Ct. 440, 126 L.Ed.2d 374 (1993).

The amended complaint that the district court dismissed represents Custer's second attempt to plead Sweeney's ERISA fiduciary status and impose on Sweeney personal liability under ERISA for his role in advising the Sheet Metal Workers' National Pension Fund. Given the district court's explicit instructions to Custer to allege in his amended complaint all that he could properly allege about Sweeney's role and the inadequacy of Custer's latest attempt, we affirm the district court's dismissal with prejudice of Custer's ERISA claim against Sweeney.

* * *

For the foregoing reasons, we affirm the judgment of the district court.

AFFIRMED.

This case shows two points: first, the way courts will look at facts and circumstances to conclude whether an individual is a fiduciary under ERISA, and second, that sometimes even outside attorneys (or other plan advisors) can be deemed a fiduciary. Luckily, as in this case, individuals who have no power to make any decisions as to plan policy, interpretations, practices or procedures, but who perform the following administrative functions for an employee benefit plan are not considered plan fiduciaries:

- Application of rules determining eligibility for participation or benefits;
- Calculation of services and compensation credits for benefits;
- Preparation of employee communications material;
- Maintenance of participants' service and employment records;
- Preparation of reports required by government agencies;
- Calculation of benefits;
- Orientation of new participants and advising participants of their rights and options under the plan;
- Collection of contributions and application of contributions as provided in the plan;
- Preparation of reports concerning participants' benefits;
- Processing of claims; and
- Making recommendations to others for decisions with respect to plan administration.

However, although such a person may not be a plan fiduciary, he or she may be subject to the bonding requirements (as described below) if he or she handles funds or other property of the plan within the meaning of applicable regulations. A person does not automatically become a plan fiduciary by reason of holding certain positions in the administration of the plan, or by being an officer or employee, but the surrounding facts and circumstances must be examined to see if someone actually has authority to make fiduciary decisions, regardless of title or position. Similarly, a director of the sponsoring employer will only be classified as a fiduciary if he or she has actual authority over plan assets, but not solely because of his or her position as a member of the board of directors.

Fiduciary status subjects an individual to personal liability for either his or her action or inaction, or even for a co-fiduciary's action or inaction in certain situations. As described below, each action or inaction must satisfy the delineated fiduciary duties, which includes the selection and monitoring of a non-employee fiduciary that is delegated some or all of the named fiduciary's original duties.

3. Duties for Each Decision

Statutory Provisions at ERISA § 404

Once an individual is deemed to be a plan fiduciary, then every decision and action (or inaction) must be discharged within each of the following parameters:

1. *solely in the interest of plan participants and beneficiaries*—the main problems here are deciding when a decision that favors the majority of plan participants over another group of participants is proper (as long as the disfavored group are actually not harmed, but just do not benefit in the same way that the majority group is favored); or, further, where the fiduciary is also an individual who participates in the plan, and is in the favored group.

2. *for the exclusive purpose of providing benefits and defraying reasonable expenses of administering the plan*—in order to meet the exclusive benefit requirement, every investment decision should be in the context of what investment vehicle or consultant will ensure the delivery of benefits when promised. This includes understanding the amount of liabilities expected to be paid in the short-term, and making sure there are enough liquid assets to cover them, which is one of the exceptions to the diversification requirement. In order to meet the defraying reasonable expenses requirement, the fiduciary, in theory, should have a list of services that will be performed on behalf of the plan and a corresponding schedule of fees that will be charged. In the realm of actual investment fees (as opposed to an attorney's fees or an accountant's fees), there is a swelling of law suits and a very heightened interest on the part of the Department of Labor in mandating the proper disclosure.[2] In the mean time, until rules are eventually issued through law or regulations, the fiduciary should at least ask the prospective investment advisor about the various fees that will be assessed to the plan and who will receive them, and the fiduciary should at least document why or why not the disclosure seems truthful and complete. After all, if a plan fiduciary does not possess the necessary expertise to evaluate the appropriate factors to make a prudent decision, then they would need to obtain the advice of a qualified, independent expert.[3] In making an actual selection, the trustworthiness of all potential consultants should be factored in, so hopefully just an inquiry about the potential fees in the absence of further guidance from Congress or the Department of Labor will suffice. Arguably, the lack of this inquiry will not support the fiduciary's decision should the defraying of reasonable expenses requirement be challenged.

3. *with the care, skill, prudence, and diligence of a prudent man in similar circumstances*—this requirement focuses on setting out advanced procedures and fol-

---

2. See Proposed Labor Regulations, Fiduciary Requirements for Disclosure in Participant-Directed Individual Account Plans, 73 FR 43013 [7/23/2008].

3. Labor Regs. § 2509.95-1(c)(6) (although this 1995 Interpretive Bulletin was issued specifically for the selection of an annuity provider).

lowing them, as opposed to focusing on the results. Again, every decision with hindsight can be considered wrong, as long as process was followed and decisions were based on the results of an investigation, and are not arbitrary or random. A good paper trail is the best defense. Please note that the metric is whether another fiduciary of a similar ERISA plan would set similar procedures and make a similar decision after a similar investigation.

4. *diversification of investments of the plan so as to minimize the risk of large losses (unless under the circumstances it is not prudent to do so)*—in order to meet this requirement, an investment or investment course of action taken by a fiduciary is proper if he or she "(i) has given appropriate consideration to those facts and circumstances that, given the scope of such fiduciary's investment duties, the fiduciary knows or should know are relevant to the particular investment or investment course of action involved, including the role the investment or investment course of action plays in that portion of the plan's investment portfolio with respect to which the fiduciary has investment duties; and (ii) [h]as acted accordingly." Courts have recently held that in lieu of the traditional law of trusts, investment diversification should adopt modern portfolio theory.

The use of a written investment policy is recommended. "[I]nherent in the authority to appoint an investment manager, the named fiduciary ... has the authority to condition the appointment on acceptance of a statement of investment policy. Thus, such a named fiduciary may expressly require, as a condition of the investment management agreement, that an investment manager comply with the terms of a statement of investment policy which sets forth guidelines concerning investments and investment courses of action which the investment manager is authorized or is not authorized to make.... In the absence of such an express requirement to comply with an investment policy, the authority to manage the plan assets placed under the control of the investment manager would lie exclusively with the investment manager."[4]

As to the allowable investments in a plan, any legal investment is allowed (such as options, index futures, repurchase agreements, state and municipal securities, collectibles and other personal property), but such investments require annual valuations of fair market value and are generally appropriate in large plans; small plans, on the other hand, are strongly encouraged to stick with the more traditional investments (such as stocks, bonds, mutual funds, and insurance company guaranteed investment contracts), If any investment is selected by the fiduciary that does not have a readily ascertainable fair market value, then the fiduciary needs to arrange for an independent and objective assessment of fair market value. Although not actually prohibited, if more than 20% of the entire plan portfolio are invested in a single asset that is not professionally managed, the IRS or Department of Labor might be concerned and feel the need to investigate. The Department of Labor tries to assist when it can—for example, in light of the Bernie Madoff scandal, the DOL has posted "Guidance on fiduciary duties in response to recent events involving the Madoff investment firm."[5]

5. *in accordance with the terms of the plan and related documents, to the extent such documents are consistent with the provisions of ERISA*—in order to meet this requirement, the plan fiduciaries, together with the plan administrator, must be

4. Labor Regs. § 2509.94-2.
5. Available at http://www.dol.gov/ebsa/newsroom/2009/ebsa020509.html.

aware that the provisions of the executed plan document are legally binding,
Therefore, even if designating all of the fiduciary and administrative duties to various consultants and professionals, the named fiduciary must always have a copy
of the controlling plan document readily available, and he or she needs to attempt to understand it as best as he or she can, relying on legal counsel for the
minutia—just like an individual buying a house can rely on their real estate attorney to explain the minutia, but the individual still has some responsibility for
understanding at least the most material aspects of the contract.

The plan document must always comply with current law, so either the named
fiduciary needs to keep track of amendments to ERISA, or must pay a consultant to monitor legislative activity. As to the actual investments, the plan or trust
document must describe the types of investment allowed in the plan, and can be
purposely narrow and include only "stocks, bonds and other corporate deben-
tures" or can be as broad as possible and allow "any legal investment." However,
in practice, the actual plan investments must comply with those specifically allowed under the document.

6. *the indicia of ownership of all plan assets must be subject to the jurisdiction of the
   district courts of the United States at all times*—in order to meet this requirement, if the plan fiduciaries think that investing in non-U.S. companies or other
   foreign property is a prudent decision that will help diversify the assets, then it
   should only be done through a licensed U.S. agent that holds title (such as an Amer-
   ican-based mutual fund that has a portfolio of foreign investments).

In addition, as discussed later in this chapter, there are a few Prohibited Transactions
that a fiduciary has a duty to *avoid*:[6]

- dealing with plan assets in his or her own interest or for his or her own account;
- entering into a transaction that is adverse to the interests of the plan or its participants
  or beneficiaries; or
- receiving personal remuneration from any party entering into a transaction with
  the plan.

There is a lot of risk for an individual classified as a plan fiduciary packed into these
requirements. If the individual actually exercises his or her fiduciary duties, then there are
generally two ways to determine if they are proper and prudent: first, the diligent investigation of the transaction, and second, whether the decision was based on the information obtained from a diligent investigation.[7] In the end, the decisions do not need to be
looked at with hindsight as to whether it was the best decision; it simply needs to be justified by the process of investigation and decision-making. In proving this, should there
be a claim of breach of fiduciary duty, as described below, a paper trail showing the review of various alternatives and the reason one option was actually chosen over the other
will go a long way in front of the Department of Labor or a court in validating the fiduciary's decision.

Investments Allowed in a Qualified Plan

Any legal investment is allowed (such as options, index futures, repurchase agreements, state and municipal securities, collectibles and other personal property), but such

---

6. ERISA § 406(b).
7. See, e.g., Riley v. Murdock, 890 F.Supp. 444, 458 (E.D.N.C. 1995).

investments require annual valuations of fair market value and are generally appropriate in large plans.

If the plan invests in securities of the sponsoring employer, then the securities must be "qualifying employer securities"[8] and, unless part of the investment choices in a self-directed 401(k) plan as described below, cannot comprise more than 10% of the fair market value of the assets of the plan. Similarly, if the plan invests in real property, then the real property must be "qualifying employer real property"[9] and cannot comprise more than 10% of the fair market value of the plan assets. The rules for compliance with proper qualifying employer securities or qualifying employer real property are extremely complicated, and appropriate legal advice should be sought out ahead of time.

Basically, employer contributions into the plan should be made in cash, and then invested as desired by the fiduciaries. It seems clear that in-kind contributions, such as unencumbered property, are prohibited in a defined benefit plan or a money purchase plan, but can, under very specific circumstances, be allowed in a profit sharing plan or a welfare plan.[10] Additionally, the Department of Labor has opined that plan fiduciaries can invest in economically targeted investments if that investment strategy complies with their fiduciary obligations inherent in all decisions about investing plan assets.[11]

Delegation of Fiduciary Duties

The individuals actually classified as fiduciaries are allowed to, and in fact are generally encouraged to, delegate their responsibility over the management of plan assets to a third party. However, the selection and monitoring of that professional must similarly comply with the investigation and decision, and subsequent monitoring, of that consultant. "A plan fiduciary may rely on information, data, statistics or analyses furnished by persons performing ministerial functions for the plan, provided that he has exercised prudence in the selection and retention of such persons. The plan fiduciary will be deemed to have acted prudently in such selection and retention if, in the exercise of ordinary care in such situation, he has no reason to doubt the competence, integrity or responsibility of such persons."[12] Therefore, in entering into a contract with a consultant to act as fiduciary over some or all of the plan assets, the actual plan fiduciaries must: first determine the needs of the plan's participants; second, compare services and fees of at the very least two different consultants; and third, select the consultant based on the best match of their services and fees to the plan's needs and budgetary constraints.

---

8. As defined in ERISA § 407(d)(5).

9. As defined in ERISA § 407(d)(4).

10. Labor Regs. § 2509.94-3 (in response to and reflective of the decision in Commissioner of Internal Revenue Service v. Keystone Consolidated Industries, Inc., 508 US 152 (1993)).

11. Labor Regs. § 2509.94-1. According to the Joint Economic Committee of the U.S. Congress brief titled "Economically Targeted Investments (ETI's): The Issues" (May 23, 1995), available at http://www.house.gov/jec/cost-gov/regs/eti/issues.htm, "[w]hile many disagree on a precise definition [of ETIs], the essential characteristic of ETIs involves adding a second goal to the traditional pension fund investment strategy of maximizing return for the pension's beneficiaries. That second goal may be to build public housing, to provide union jobs, or even to forward the investor's political agenda."

12. Labor Regs. § 2509.75-8, FR-11.

Adoption of an Investment Policy Statement

An employer who sponsors a retirement plan should consider drafting a statement of investment policy; such a policy statement is consistent with the employer's fiduciary obligations. The investment policy statement should be distinguished from directions regarding the purchase or sale of a specific investment at a specific time. An employer may condition the appointment of an investment manager on acceptance of the statement of investment policy of the plan. In the absence of such an express requirement to comply with an investment policy, the authority to manage plan assets placed under the investment manager's control would lie exclusively with the investment manager. Although a plan is required to establish a funding policy,[13] there is no affirmative mandate to establish an investment policy. The plan document can either be very specific as to the investments allowed in the plan, or can allow any legal investment under the sun. The investment policy and actual selection must always comply with the plan document.

4. Special Rules for Remittance of Employee Salary Deferrals

Department of Labor regulations require employers to deposit the contributions made by a participant (*i.e.,* the employee elective deferrals) on the earliest date that the funds can reasonably be segregated from the employer's general assets but in no event later than the 15th business day of the month following the month in which the participant contributions are withheld or received by the employer.

Labor Regs. § 2510.3-102.
Definition of "Plan Assets" — Participant Contributions

(a) **General rule.** For purposes of subtitle A and parts 1 and 4 of subtitle B of title I of ERISA and section 4975 of the Internal Revenue Code only (but without any implication for and may not be relied upon to bar criminal prosecutions under 18 U.S.C. 664), the assets of the plan include amounts (other than union dues) that a participant or beneficiary pays to an employer, or amounts that a participant has withheld from his wages by an employer, for contribution to the plan as of the earliest date on which such contributions can reasonably be segregated from the employer's general assets.

(b) **Maximum time period for pension benefit plans.**

(1) Except as provided in paragraph (b)(2), of this section, with respect to an employee pension benefit plan as defined in section 3(2) of ERISA, in no event shall the date determined pursuant to paragraph (a) of this section occur later than the 15th business day of the month following the month in which the participant contribution amounts are received by the employer (in the case of amounts that a participant or beneficiary pays to an employer) or the 15th business day of the month following the month in which such amounts would otherwise have been payable to the participant in cash (in the case of amounts withheld by an employer from a participant's wages).

---

13. ERISA § 402(b)(1).

(2) With respect to a SIMPLE plan that involves SIMPLE IRAs (*i.e.*, Simple Retirement Accounts, as described in section 408(p) of the Internal Revenue Code), in no event shall the date determined pursuant to paragraph (a) of this section occur later than the 30th calendar day following the month in which the participant contribution amounts would otherwise have been payable to the participant in cash.

* * *

But wait. Proposed Regulations have been published, and will, if finalized, provide a safe harbor for small plans of the seventh business day following the day on which the amounts would have been payable to the participant in cash.

Proposed Labor Regs. § 2510.3-102. Amendment of Regulation Relating to Definition of "Plan Assets"—Participant Contributions
73 FR 11072 [2/29/2008]

* * *

2. Revise Sec. 2510.3-102, paragraphs (a) and (f), to read as follows:

Sec. 2510.3-102 Definition of "plan assets"—participant contributions.

(a) *(1) General rule.* For purposes of subtitle A and parts 1 and 4 of subtitle B of title 1 of ERISA and section 4975 of the Internal Revenue Code only (but without any implication for and may not be relied upon to bar criminal prosecutions under 18 U.S.C. 664), the assets of the plan include amounts (other than union dues) that a participant or beneficiary pays to an employer, or amounts that a participant has withheld from his wages by an employer, for contribution or repayment of a participant loan to the plan, as of the earliest date on which such contributions or repayments can reasonably be segregated from the employer's general assets.

(2) Safe harbor. For purposes of paragraph (a)(1) of this section, in the case of a plan with fewer than 100 participants at the beginning of the plan year, any amount deposited with such plan not later than the 7th business day following the day on which such amount is received by the employer (in the case of amounts that a participant or beneficiary pays to an employer), or the 7th business day following the day on which such amount would otherwise have been payable to the participant in cash (in the case of amounts withheld by an employer from a participant's wages), shall be deemed to be contributed or repaid to such plan on the earliest date on which such contributions or participant loan repayments can reasonably be segregated from the employer's general assets.

* * *

(f) Examples. The requirements of this section are illustrated by the following examples:

(1) Employer A sponsors a 401(k) plan. There are 30 participants in the 401(k) plan. A has one payroll period for its employees and uses an outside payroll processing service to pay employee wages and process deductions. A has established a system under which the payroll processing service provides payroll deduction information to A within 1 business day after

the issuance of paychecks. A checks this information for accuracy within 5 business days and then forwards the withheld employee contributions to the plan. The amount of the total withheld employee contributions is deposited with the trust that is maintained under the plan on the 7th business day following the date on which the employees are paid. Under the safe harbor in paragraph (a)(2) of this section, when the participant contributions are deposited with the plan on the 7th business day following a pay date, the participant contributions are deemed to be contributed to the plan on the earliest date on which such contributions can reasonably be segregated from A's general assets.

(2) Employer B is a large national corporation which sponsors a 401(k) plan with 600 participants. B has several payroll centers and uses an outside payroll processing service to pay employee wages and process deductions. Each payroll center has a different pay period. Each center maintains separate accounts on its books for purposes of accounting for that center's payroll deductions and provides the outside payroll processor the data necessary to prepare employee paychecks and process deductions. The payroll processing service issues the employees' paychecks and deducts all payroll taxes and elective employee deductions. The payroll processing service forwards the employee payroll deduction data to B on the date of issuance of paychecks. B checks this data for accuracy and transmits this data along with the employee 401(k) deferral funds to the plan's investment firm within 3 business days. The plan's investment firm deposits the employee 401(k) deferral funds into the plan on the day received from B. The assets of B's 401(k) plan would include the participant contributions no later than 3 business days after the issuance of paychecks.

* * *

B. Prohibited Transactions

1. Prohibited Transactions under ERISA Title I

Statutory Rules at ERISA § 406

ERISA contains Prohibited Transactions, which basically prohibits every conceivable transaction with the plan and a person even remotely connected to the plan, and then certain transactions are specifically and narrowly exempted. Under ERISA, "parties in interest" are the individuals prohibited from transacting with the plan, and include:[14]

- any fiduciary (including, but not limited to, any administrator, officer, trustee, or custodian), counsel, or employee of such employee benefit plan;
- a person providing services to such plan;
- an employer any of whose employees are covered by such plan;
- an employee organization any of whose members are covered by such plan;

---

14. ERISA § 3(14).

- an owner, direct or indirect, of 50 percent or more of—(i) the combined voting power of all classes of stock entitled to vote or the total value of shares of all classes of stock of a corporation, (ii) the capital interest or the profits interest of a partnership, or (iii) the beneficial interest of a trust or unincorporated enterprise, which is an employer or an employee organization;
- a relative (*i.e.,* a spouse, ancestor, lineal descendant, or spouse of a lineal descendant) of any person described above;
- a corporation, partnership, or trust or estate of which (or in which) 50 percent or more of—(i) the combined voting power of all classes of stock entitled to vote or the total value of shares of all classes of stock of such corporation, (ii) the capital interest or profits interest of such partnership, or (iii) the beneficial interest of such trust or estate, is owned directly or indirectly, or held by persons described above;
- an employee, officer, director (or an individual having powers or responsibilities similar to those of officers or directors), or a 10 percent or more shareholder directly or indirectly, of a person described above; or
- a 10 percent or more (directly or indirectly in capital or profits) partner or joint venturer of a person above.

In addition to the prohibition of general financial transactions, a plan fiduciary is further prohibited from dealing with the plan assets in his own interest or for his own account; enter into a transaction that is adverse to the interests of the plan or its participants or beneficiaries; or, receive personal remuneration from any party entering into a transaction with the plan. Therefore, in addition to complying with the duties described above, any individual that is classified as a plan fiduciary must avoid general or specific Prohibited Transactions.

2. Prohibited Transactions under the Internal Revenue Code

Statutory Rules at IRC § 4975(e)

The Code, which has a parallel set of penalty taxes imposed on Prohibited Transactions in addition to the civil penalties under ERISA, calls the group of affected individuals "disqualified persons" (instead of "party in interest") and includes basically all of the same individuals except for counsel and employees of the plan. The plan is generally subject to either a total 20% penalty upon discovery of a Prohibited Transaction (if the plan is subject to the ERISA fiduciary rules) or a total 15% penalty upon discovery (if the plan is not subject to the ERISA fiduciary rules), and then in either case a 100% penalty tax if not corrected timely after discovery.

The period during which a prohibited transaction may be corrected begins with the date the prohibited transaction occurs and ends 90 days after the date the IRS mails a notice of deficiency[15] to the taxpayer regarding the 100% excise tax. The correction of a prohibited transaction generally involves undoing the self-dealing transaction to the extent possible, while placing the plan in a financial position no worse than that it would have

---

15. IRC § 4963(e)(1); Treas. Regs. § 53.4963-1(e).

been in if the disqualified person were acting under the highest fiduciary standards. An IRS Form 5330 needs to be completed in the event that a Prohibited Transaction is discovered.

3. Exemptions from Prohibited Transactions

Statutory Rules at ERISA § 408 and IRC § 4975(f)

Luckily, there are some major exemptions which, whether by statute or regulations or granted by the Department of Labor to a plan on a facts and circumstances basis, allow some of the most basic financial transactions to go forward, but only in a reasonable and transparent manner. Some of the more important statutory Prohibited Transaction Exemptions that affect most small employers include:

- loans made by the plan (but only if such loans are available to all participants and beneficiaries on a reasonably equivalent basis, are not made available to highly compensated employees in an amount greater than the amount made available to other employees, are made in accordance with specific provisions regarding such loans set forth in the plan, bear a reasonable rate of interest, and are adequately secured);
- contracting or making reasonable arrangements with a party in interest for office space, or legal, accounting, or other services necessary for the establishment or operation of the plan, if no more than reasonable compensation is paid;
- certain loans to an employee stock ownership plan;
- the providing of any ancillary service by a bank or similar financial institution supervised by the United States or a State, under certain circumstances if the bank or other institution is a fiduciary of such plan;
- the exercise of a privilege to convert securities, but only if the plan receives no less than adequate consideration pursuant to such conversion;
- any transaction between a plan and a common or collective trust fund or pooled investment fund maintained by a party in interest which is a bank or trust company supervised by a State or Federal agency or a pooled investment fund of an insurance company qualified to do business in a State, with certain conditions;
- the making by a fiduciary of a distribution of the assets of the plan in accordance with the terms of the plan if the assets are distributed in a certain manner;
- the sale by a plan to a party in interest of certain stock;
- any transfer made before January 1, 2014, of excess pension assets from a defined benefit plan to a retiree health account in a qualified transfer;
- purchasing real estate from a disqualified person or party in interest using plan assets;
- purchasing art or other collectibles (coins, stamps, etc.) that are held by a disqualified person or party in interest with plan assets; and
- purchasing jewelry that is used by a disqualified person or party in interest with plan assets.

Recent amendments to the Prohibited Transaction Exemptions favor small employers, and now loans can be made to sole proprietors, partners and 5% shareholder/employees of S corporations. However, plan loans may not be made to IRA owners and beneficiaries.[16]

---

16. IRC § 4975(f)(6).

C. Special Rules for Self-Directed 401(k) Plans

One way to reduce fiduciary exposure is to have a defined contribution plan, such as a 401(k) plan, in which the individual participant directs the investment of his or her own individual account, (*i.e.*, "self-directed" accounts). If all of the requirements are met, then if a plan participant exercises his or her right to make investment decisions but the account loses value, the plan fiduciary should not be held personally liable for the loss. Before this protection attaches, however, the appropriate named, allocated or delegated fiduciaries must select and monitor the prudence of each investment choice available for the plan participants (which includes the current enforcement of the cost/benefit analysis of services provided against fees charged) and must follow the affirmative allocation instructions communicated by the participants.[17] Under recent legislative changes, if the plan fiduciary wants to provide individual investment advice to those participants that desire it, then the advice must be based on the risk-taking characteristics, age, and other personal attributes of each respective participant, and must be either provided by an advisor whose fees do not vary based on the choices the participant ultimately makes or is delivered through an appropriate and neutral computer model.[18]

1. Allowing Participants to Make Their Own Investment Decisions

Statutory Rules at ERISA § 404(c)

The fiduciary may select the investment options available to the participants of a 401(k) plan (or for any other individual account plan), and then may allow the participants to self-direct the asset portfolio mix of their individual accounts. Although almost all self-directed plans allow participants investment discretion over their elective salary deferrals, after-tax Roth contributions, and rollover accounts from a prior employer's plan, each fiduciary should decide whether they will also have investment discretion over their employer contribution accounts (such as matches, profit sharing amounts or forfeiture allocations). Arguably, the decision to allow self-directed accounts, and the extent to which participants have the ability, are fiduciary decisions in the first order, and a participant that ultimately loses value in his account can argue that it was a breach of fiduciary duty to allow him or her that choice in the first place.

Labor Regs. § 2550.404c-1. ERISA Section 404(c) Plans

(a) In general.

(1) Section 404(c) of the Employee Retirement Income Security Act of 1974 (ERISA or the Act) provides that if a pension plan that provides for individual accounts permits a participant or beneficiary to exercise control over assets

---

17. LaRue v. DeWolff, Boberg & Assoc., 128 S.Ct. 1020 (2008).
18. ERISA §§ 408(b)(14) and 408(g), as amplified by DOL Field Assistance Bulletin 2007-01, and IRC § 4975(d)(17). However, even though the new statutory provisions allow a fiduciary to offer individual investment advice, under Labor Regs. § 2550.404c-1(c)(4), which are still effective, "[a] fiduciary has no obligation under part 4 of title I of the Act to provide investment advice to a participant or beneficiary under an ERISA section 404(c) plan."

in his account and that participant or beneficiary in fact exercises control over assets in his account, then the participant or beneficiary shall not be deemed to be a fiduciary by reason of his exercise of control and no person who is otherwise a fiduciary shall be liable for any loss, or by reason of any breach, which results from such exercise of control. This section describes the kinds of plans that are "ERISA section 404(c) plans," the circumstances in which a participant or beneficiary is considered to have exercised independent control over the assets in his account as contemplated by section 404(c), and the consequences of a participant's or beneficiary's exercise of control.

(2) The standards set forth in this section are applicable solely for the purpose of determining whether a plan is an ERISA section 404(c) plan and whether a particular transaction engaged in by a participant or beneficiary of such plan is afforded relief by section 404(c). Such standards, therefore, are not intended to be applied in determining whether, or to what extent, a plan which does not meet the requirements for an ERISA section 404(c) plan or a fiduciary with respect to such a plan satisfies the fiduciary responsibility or other provisions of title I of the Act.

(b) ERISA section 404(c) plans—

(1) In general. An "ERISA section 404(c) Plan" is an individual account plan described in section 3(34) of the Act that:

(i) Provides an opportunity for a participant or beneficiary to exercise control over assets in his individual account (see paragraph (b)(2) of this section); and

(ii) Provides a participant or beneficiary an opportunity to choose, from a broad range of investment alternatives, the manner in which some or all of the assets in his account are invested (see paragraph (b)(3) of this section).

(2) Opportunity to exercise control.

(i) a plan provides a participant or beneficiary an opportunity to exercise control over assets in his account only if:

(A) Under the terms of the plan, the participant or beneficiary has a reasonable opportunity to give investment instructions (in writing or otherwise, with opportunity to obtain written confirmation of such instructions) to an identified plan fiduciary who is obligated to comply with such instructions except as otherwise provided in paragraph (b)(2)(ii)(B) and (d)(2)(ii) of this section; and

(B) The participant or beneficiary is provided or has the opportunity to obtain sufficient information to make informed decisions with regard to investment alternatives available under the plan, and incidents of ownership appurtenant to such investments. For purposes of this subparagraph, a participant or beneficiary will not be considered to have sufficient investment information unless—

(1) The participant or beneficiary is provided by an identified plan fiduciary (or a person or persons designated by the plan fiduciary to act on his behalf):

(i) An explanation that the plan is intended to constitute a plan described in section 404(c) of the Employee Retirement Income Security Act, and title 29 of the Code of Federal Regulations, § 2550.440c-1, and that the fiduciaries of the plan may be relieved of liability for any losses which are the direct and necessary result of investment instructions given by such participant or beneficiary;

(ii) A description of the investment alternatives available under the plan and, with respect to each designated investment alternative, a general description of the investment objectives and risk and return characteristics of each such alternative, including information relating to the type and diversification of assets comprising the portfolio of the designed investment alternative;

(iii) Identification of any designated investment managers;

(iv) An explanation of the circumstances under which participants and beneficiaries may give investment instructions and explanation of any specified limitations on such instructions under the terms of the plan, including any restrictions on transfer to or from a designated investment alternative, and any restrictions on the exercise of voting, tender and similar rights appurtenant to a participant's or beneficiary's investment in an investment alternative;

(v) A description of any transaction fees and expenses which affect the participant's or beneficiary's account balance in connection with purchases or sales of interests in investment alternatives (e.g., commissions, sales load, deferred sales charges, redemption or exchange fees);

(vi) The name, address, and phone number of the plan fiduciary (and, if applicable, the person or persons designated by the plan fiduciary to act on his behalf) responsible for providing the information described in paragraph (b)(2)(i)(B)(2) upon request of a participant or beneficiary and a description of the information described in paragraph (b)(2)(i)(B)(2) which may be obtained on request;

(vii) In the case of plans which offer an investment alternative which is designed to permit a participant or beneficiary to directly or indirectly acquire or sell any employer security (employer security alternative), a description of the procedures established to provide for the confidentiality of information relating to the purchase, holding and sale of employer securities, and the exercise of voting, tender and similar rights, by participants and beneficiaries, and the name, address and phone number of the plan fiduciary responsible for monitoring compliance with the procedures (see paragraphs (d)(2)(ii)(E)(4)(vii), (viii) and (ix) of this section); and

(viii) In the case of an investment alternative which is subject to the Securities Act of 1933, and in which the participant or beneficiary has no assets invested, immediately following the participant's or beneficiary's initial investment, a copy of the most recent prospectus provided to the plan. This condition will be deemed satisfied if the participant or beneficiary has been provided with a copy of such most recent prospectus immediately prior to the participant's or beneficiary's initial investment in such alternative;

(ix) Subsequent to an investment in a investment alternative, any materials provided to the plan relating to the exercise of voting, tender or similar rights which are incidental to the holding in the account of the participant or beneficiary of an ownership interest in such alternative to the extent that such rights are passed through to participants and beneficiaries under the terms of the plan, as well as a description of or reference to plan provisions relating to the exercise of voting, tender or similar rights.

(2) The participants or beneficiary is provided by the identified plan fiduciary (or a person or persons designated by the plan fiduciary to act on his behalf), either directly or upon request, the following information, which shall be based on the latest information available to the plan:

(i) A description of the annual operating expenses of each designated investment alternative (e.g., investment management fees, administrative fees, transaction costs) which reduce the rate of return to participants and beneficiaries, and the aggregate amount of such expenses expressed as a percentage of average net assets of the designated investment alternative;

(ii) Copies of any prospectuses, financial statements and reports, and of any other materials relating to the investment alternatives available under the plan, to the extent such information is provided to the plan;

(iii) A list of the assets comprising the portfolio of each designated investment alternative which constitute plan assets within the meaning of 29 CFR 2510.3-101, the value of each such asset (or the proportion of the investment alternative which it comprises), and, with respect to each such asset which is a fixed rate investment contract issued by a bank, savings and loan association or insurance company, the name of the issuer of the contract, the term of the contract and the rate of return on the contract;

(iv) Information concerning the value of shares or units in designated investment alternatives available to participants and beneficiaries under the plan, as well as the past and current investment performance of such alternatives, determined, net of expenses, on a reasonable and consistent basis; and

(v) Information concerning the value of shares or units in designated investment alternatives held in the account of the participant or beneficiary.

(ii) A plan does not fail to provide an opportunity for a participant or beneficiary to exercise control over his individual account merely because it—

(A) Imposes charges for reasonable expenses. A plan may charge participants' and beneficiaries' accounts for the reasonable expenses of carrying out investment instructions, provided that procedures are established under the plan to periodically inform such participants and beneficiaries of actual expenses incurred with respect to their respective individual accounts;

(B) Permits a fiduciary to decline to implement investment instructions by participants and beneficiaries. A fiduciary may decline to implement participant and beneficiary instructions which are described at paragraph (d)(2)(ii) of this section, as well as instructions specified in the plan, including instructions—

(1) Which would result in a prohibited transaction described in ERISA section 406 or section 4975 of the Internal Revenue Code, and

(2) Which would generate income that would be taxable to the plan;

(C) Imposes reasonable restrictions on frequency of investment instructions. A plan may impose reasonable restrictions on the frequency with which participants and beneficiaries may give investment instructions. In no event, however, is such a restriction reasonable unless, with respect to each investment alternative made available by the plan, it permits participants and beneficiaries to give investment instructions with a frequency which is appropriate in light of the market volatility to which the investment alternative may reasonably be expected to be subject, provided that—

(1) At least three of the investment alternatives made available pursuant to the requirements of paragraph (b)(3)(i)(B) of this section, which constitute a broad range of investment alternatives, Permit participants and beneficiaries to give investment instructions no less frequently than once within any three month period; and

(2)(i) At least one of the investment alternatives meeting the requirements of paragraph (b)(2)(ii)(C)(1) of this section permits participants and beneficiaries to give investment instructions with regard to transfers into the investment alternative as frequently as participants and beneficiaries are permitted to give investment instructions with respect to any investment alternative made available by the plan which permits participants and beneficiaries to give investment instructions more frequently than once within any three month period; or

(ii) With respect to each investment alternative which permits participants and beneficiaries to give investment instructions more frequently than once within any three month period, participants and beneficiaries are permitted to direct their investments from such alternative into an income producing, low risk, liquid fund, subfund, or account as frequently as they are permitted to give investment instructions with respect to each such alternative and, with respect to such fund, subfund or account, participants and beneficiaries are permitted to direct investments from the fund, subfund or account to an investment alternative meeting the requirements of paragraph (b)(2)(ii)(C)(1) as frequently as they are permitted to give investment instructions with respect to that investment alternative; and

(3) With respect to transfers from an investment alternative which is designed to permit a participant or beneficiary to directly or indirectly acquire or sell any employer security (employer security alternative) either:

(i) All of the investment alternatives meeting the requirements of paragraph (b)(2)(ii)(C)(1) of this section must permit participants and beneficiaries to give investment instructions with regard to transfers into each of the investment alternatives as frequently as participants and beneficiaries are permitted to give investment instructions with respect to the employer security alternative; or

(ii) Participants and beneficiaries are permitted to direct their investments from each employer security alternative into an income producing, low risk, liquid fund, subfund, or account as frequently as they are permitted to give investment instructions with respect to such employer security alternative and, with respect to such fund, subfund, or account, participants and beneficiaries are permitted to direct investments from the fund, subfund or account to each investment alternative meeting the requirements of paragraph (b)(2)(ii)(C)(1) as frequently as they are permitted to give investment instructions with respect to each such investment alternative.

(iii) Paragraph (c) of this section describes the circumstances under which a participant or beneficiary will be considered to have exercised independent control with respect to a particular transaction.

(3) Broad range of investment alternatives.

(i) A plan offers a broad range of investment alternatives only if the available investment alternatives are sufficient to provide the participant or beneficiary with a reasonable opportunity to:

(A) Materially affect the potential return on amounts in his individual account with respect to which he is permitted to exercise control and the degree of risk to which such amounts are subject;

(B) Choose from at least three investment alternatives:

(1) Each of which is diversified;

(2) Each of which has materially different risk and return characteristics;

(3) Which in the aggregate enable the participant or beneficiary by choosing among them to achieve a portfolio with aggregate risk and return characteristics at any point within the range normally appropriate for the participant or beneficiary; and

(4) Each of which when combined with investments in the other alternatives tends to minimize through diversification the overall risk of a participant's or beneficiary's portfolio;

(C) Diversify the investment of that portion of his individual account with respect to which he is permitted to exercise control so as to minimize the risk of large losses, taking into account the nature of the plan and the size of participants' or beneficiaries' accounts. In determining whether a plan provides the participant or beneficiary with a reasonable opportunity to diversify his investments, the nature of the investment alternatives offered by the plan and the size of the portion of the individual's account over which he is permitted to exercise control must be considered. Where such portion of the account of any participant or beneficiary is so limited in size that the opportunity to invest in look-through investment vehicles is the only prudent means to assure an opportunity to achieve appropriate diversification, a plan may satisfy the requirements of this paragraph only by offering look-through investment vehicles.

(ii) Diversification and look-through investment vehicles. Where look-through investment vehicles are available as investment alternatives to participants and beneficiaries, the underlying investments of the look-through investment vehicles shall be considered in determining whether the plan satisfies the requirements of subparagraphs (b)(3)(i)(B) and (b)(3)(i)(C).

(c) Exercise of control—

(1) In general.

(i) Sections 404(c)(1) and 404(c)(2) of the Act and paragraphs (a) and (d) of this section apply only with respect to a transaction where a participant or beneficiary has exercised independent control in fact with respect to the investment of assets in his individual account under an ERISA section 404(c) plan.

(ii) For purposes of sections 404(c)(1) and 4040(c)(2) of the Act and paragraphs (a) and (d) of this section, a participant or beneficiary will be deemed to have exercised control with respect to the exercise of voting, tender and similar rights appurtenant to the participant's or beneficiary's ownership interest in an investment alternative, provided that the participant's or beneficiary's investment in the investment alternative was itself the result of an exercise of control, the participant or beneficiary was provided a reasonable opportunity to give instruction with respect to such incidents of ownership, including the provision of the information described in paragraph (b)(2)(i)(B)(1)(ix) of this section, and the participant or beneficiary has not failed to exercise control by reason of the circumstances described in paragraph (c)(2) with respect to such incidents of ownership.

(2) Independent control. Whether a participant or beneficiary has exercised independent control in fact with respect to a transaction depends on the facts and circumstances of the particular case. However, a participant's or beneficiary's exercise of control is not independent in fact if:

(i) The participant or beneficiary is subjected to improper influence by a plan fiduciary or the plan sponsor with respect to the transaction;

(ii) A plan fiduciary has concealed material non-public facts regarding the investment from the participant or beneficiary, unless the disclosure of such information by the plan fiduciary to the participant or beneficiary would violate any provision of federal law or any provision of state law which is not preempted by the Act; or

(iii) The participant or beneficiary is legally incompetent and the responsible plan fiduciary accepts the instructions of the participant or beneficiary knowing him to be legally incompetent.

(3) Transactions involving a fiduciary. In the case of a sale, exchange or leasing of property (other than a transaction described in paragraph (d)(2)(ii)(E) of this section) between an ERISA section 404(c) plan and a plan fiduciary or an affiliate of such a fiduciary, or a loan to a plan fiduciary or an affiliate of such a fiduciary, the participant or beneficiary will not be deemed to have exercised independent control unless the transaction is fair and reasonable to him. For purposes of this paragraph (c)(3), a transaction will be deemed to be fair and reasonable to a participant or beneficiary if he pays no more than, or receives no less than, adequate consideration (as defined in section 3(18) of the Act) in connection with the transaction.

(4) No obligation to advise. A fiduciary has no obligation under part 4 of title I of the Act to provide investment advice to a participant or beneficiary under an ERISA section 404(c) plan.

(d) Effect of independent exercise of control—

(1) Participant or beneficiary not a fiduciary. If a participant or beneficiary of an ERISA section 404(c) plan exercises independent control over assets in his individual account in the manner described in paragraph (c), then such participant or beneficiary is not a fiduciary of the plan by reason of such exercise of control.

(2) Limitation on liability of plan fiduciaries.

(i) If a participant or beneficiary of an ERISA section 404(c) plan exercises independent control over assets in his individual account in the manner described in paragraph (c), then no other person who is a fiduciary with respect to such plan shall be liable for any loss, or with respect to any breach of part 4 of title I of the Act, that is the direct and necessary result of that participant's or beneficiary's exercise of control.

* * *

(f) Examples. The provisions of this section are illustrated by the following examples. Examples (5) through (11) assume that the participant has exercised independent control with respect to his individual account under an ERISA section

404(c) plan described in paragraph (b) and has not directed a transaction described in paragraph (d)(2)(ii).

(1) Plan A is an individual account plan described in section 3(34) of the Act. The plan states that a plan participant or beneficiary may direct the plan administrator to invest any portion of his individual account in a particular diversified equity fund managed by an entity which is not affiliated with the plan sponsor, or any other asset administratively feasible for the plan to hold. However, the plan provides that the plan administrator will not implement certain listed instructions for which plan fiduciaries would not be relieved of liability under section 404(c) (see paragraph (d)(2)(ii)). Plan participants and beneficiaries are permitted to give investment instructions during the first week of each month with respect to the equity fund and at any time with respect to other investments. The plan provides for the pass-through of voting, tender and similar rights incidental to the holding in the account of a participant or beneficiary of an ownership interest in the equity fund or any other investment alternative available under the plan. The plan administrator of plan A provides each participant and beneficiary with the information described in subparagraphs (i), (ii), (iii), (iv), (v), (vi) and (vii) of paragraph (b)(2)(i)(B)(1) upon their entry into the plan, and provides updated information in the event of any material change in the information provided. Immediately following an investment by a participant or beneficiary in the equity fund, the plan administrator provides a copy of the most recent prospectus received from the fund to the investing participant or beneficiary. Immediately following any investment by a participant or beneficiary in any other investment alternative which is subject to the Securities Act of 1933, the plan administrator provides the participant or beneficiary with the most recent prospectus received from that investment alternative (see paragraph (b)(2)(i)(B)(1)(viii)). Finally, subsequent to any investment by a participant or beneficiary, the plan administrator forwards to the investing participant or beneficiary any materials provided to the plan relating to the exercise of voting, tender or similar rights attendant to ownership of an interest in such investment (see paragraph (b)(2)(i)(B)(1)(ix)). Upon request, the plan administrator provides each participant or beneficiary with copies of any prospectuses, financial statements and reports, and any other materials relating to the investment alternatives available under the plan which are received by the plan (see paragraph (b)(2)(i)(B)(2)(ii)). Also upon request, the plan administrator provides each participant and beneficiary with the other information required by paragraph (b)(2)(i)(B)(2) with respect to the equity fund, which is a designated investment alternative, including information concerning the latest available value of the participant's or beneficiary's interest in the equity fund (see paragraph (b)(2)(i)(B)(2)(v)). Plan A meets the requirements of paragraphs (b)(2)(i)(B)(1) and (2) of this section regarding the provision of investment information.

Note: The regulation imposes no additional obligation on the administrator to furnish or make available materials relating to the companies in which the equity fund invests (e.g., prospectuses, proxies, etc.).

(2) Plan C is an individual account plan described in section 3(34) of the Act under which participants and beneficiaries may choose among three investment alternatives which otherwise meet the requirements of

paragraph (b) of this section. The plan permits investment instruction with respect to each investment alternative only on the first 10 days of each calendar quarter, *i.e.* January 1–10, April 1–10, July 1–10 and October 1–10. Plan C satisfies the condition of paragraph (b)(2)(ii)(C)(1) that instruction be permitted not less frequently than once within any three month period, since there is not any three month period during which control could not be exercised.

(3) Assume the same facts as in paragraph (f)(2), except that investment instruction may only be given on January 1, April 4, July 1 and October 1. Plan C is not an ERISA section 404(c) plan because it does not satisfy the condition of paragraph (b)(2)(ii)(C)(1) that instruction be permitted not less frequently than once within any three month period. Under these facts, there is a three month period, e.g., January 2 through April 1, during which control could not be exercised by participants and beneficiaries.

(4) Plan D is an individual account plan described in section 3(34) of the Act under which participants and beneficiaries may choose among three diversified investment alternatives which constitute a broad range of investment alternatives. The plan also permits investment instruction with respect to an employer securities alternative but provides that a participant or beneficiary can invest no more than 25% of his account balance in this alternative. This restriction does not affect the availability of relief under section 404(c) inasmuch as it does not relate to the three diversified investment alternatives and, therefore, does not cause the plan to fail to provide an opportunity to choose from a broad range of investment alternatives.

(5) A participant, P, independently exercises control over assets in his individual account plan by directing a plan fiduciary, F, to invest 100% of his account balance in a single stock. P is not a fiduciary with respect to the plan by reason of his exercise of control and F will not be liable for any losses that necessarily result form P's investment instruction.

(6) Assume the same facts as in paragraph (f)(5), except that P directs F to purchase the stock from B, who is a party in interest with respect to the plan. Neither P nor F has engaged in a transaction prohibited under section 406 of the Act: P because he is not a fiduciary with respect to the plan by reason of his exercise of control and F because he is not liable for any breach of part 4 of title I that is the direct and necessary consequence of P's exercise of control. However, a prohibited transaction under section 4975(c) of the Internal Revenue Code may have occurred, and, in the absence of an exemption, tax liability may be imposed pursuant to sections 495 (a) and (b) of the Code.

(7) Assume the same facts as in paragraph (f)(5), except that P does not specify that the stock be purchased from B, and F chooses to purchase the stock from B. In the absence of an exemption, F has engaged in a prohibited transaction described in 406(a) of ERISA because the decision to purchase the stock from B is not a direct or necessary result of P's exercise of control.

(8) Pursuant to the terms of the plan, plan fiduciary F designates three reputable investment managers whom participants may appoint to manage assets in their individual accounts. Participant P selects M, one of the designated managers, to manage the assets in his account. M prudently

manages P's account for 6 months after which he incurs losses in managing the account through his imprudence. M has engaged in a breach of fiduciary duty because M's imprudent management of P's account is not a direct or necessary result of P's exercise of control (the choice of M as manager). F has no fiduciary liability for M's imprudence because he has no affirmative duty to advise P (see paragraph (c)(4)) and because F is relieved of co-fiduciary liability by reason of section 404(c)(2) (see paragraph (d)(2)(iii)). F does have a duty to monitor M's performance to determine the suitability of continuing M as an investment manager, however, and M's imprudence would be a factor which F must consider in periodically reevaluating its decision to designate M.

* * *

Default investments selected by plan fiduciaries when participant does not make a valid investment allocation: For plan years beginning after 2006, the fiduciary of a defined contribution plan may invest amounts in a default arrangement without liability for the investment decision, and any related loss, if the participant fails to make the investment decision. Final Labor Regulations provide that the fiduciary can select a Qualified Default Investment Alternative if the participant or beneficiary is automatically enrolled through a qualified automatic contribution arrangement ("QACA") or an eligible automatic contribution arrangement ("EACA"), or under any other situation that the participant fails to make and communicate a proper affirmative allocation choice.[19] A Qualified Default Investment Alternative is generally: a "life cycle" fund (where the investment product or model portfolio is based on the participant's age, targeted retirement date, or life expectancy); a "balanced" fund (where the investment fund product or model portfolio is consistent with a target level of risk appropriate for the aggregate group of plan participants at that time); a "managed account" (where an investment management service selects a portfolio mix based on the participant's age and targeted retirement age or life expectancy); or, just for the first 120 days after an employee participates in the plan and defers a portion of his salary, a capital preservation fund (where there is a very low probability of the account losing value and provides a very high probability of yielding an appropriate rate of return and liquidity).[20] The fiduciary must provide appropriate advance notice of the participant's rights and obligations under the arrangement to obtain relief.[21]

Also, if investment options offered under a defined contribution plan change and the participant or beneficiary fails to provide affirmative investment instructions, the participant or beneficiary still may be considered to exercise control over the account assets.

2. Black Out Periods

Statutory Rules at ERISA § 101(i)

A Blackout Period is an anticipated period of at least three consecutive business days when plan participants will not be allowed to direct or diversify their assets or request a loan or distribution otherwise allowed under the plan (for example, if the named fidu-

---

19. Labor Regs. § 2550.404c-5(c).
20. Labor Regs. § 2550.404c-5(e).
21. Labor Regs. § 2550.404c-5(d). No model notice is provided under the Regulations, so the required content must be drafted into a plan's notice.

ciary decides to transfer the assets held by one financial institution into another or if the computer system needs to be shut down for a few days for maintenance or software upgrades). A blackout period does not include a period of time where federal securities laws require the suspension of activity, which is part of a regularly scheduled suspension that is clearly communicated to employees, or because it only affects a participant or alternate-payee spouse pursuant to a Qualified Domestic Relations Order as part of a divorce.

The plan fiduciaries must comply with the advance notice, and general fiduciary care in authorizing and implementing the black out period, in order to avoid any personal liability should a self-directed account lose value during the blackout period. The notice must indicate the reason for the blackout period, identify the investments and other rights affected, and indicate the expected beginning and ending date, convey that it is in the best interest of each participant or beneficiary to evaluate the appropriateness of their current investment decisions in light of the expected blackout period. With certain limited exceptions, the notice should be delivered at least 30 days in advance of the start of the expected blackout period.

D. Liability for Breach of Fiduciary Duties

1. Personal Liability

Statutory Rules at ERISA § 409

As indicated, the big deal with being classified as a plan fiduciary is that if an individual breaches his fiduciary duties or responsibilities by acting improperly or by not acting when it would have been proper to do so, then the individual shall be personally liable to put the plan back into the financial position it would have been at had the breach not occurred, and additionally shall disgorge all personal profits from the breach and restore them to the plan. There is no real guidance, but in addition, the fiduciary shall be subject to other equitable or remedial relief that a court may deem appropriate (such as the removal of the individual as a plan fiduciary). Luckily, however, no fiduciary shall be liable for a breach that occurred before he or she became a fiduciary or for a breach that occurs after he or she ceases being a fiduciary. Additionally, as indicated above, between the Internal Revenue Service and the Department of Labor, breaches of fiduciary duty that constitute a Prohibited Transaction can cause a penalty of up to 20% of the amount in violation to be assessed against the sponsoring employer, even if the transaction is reversed.

Congress has indicated that agreements and instruments that purport to relieve a fiduciary from responsibility or liability is void and against public policy. However, Congress still allows the employer, or individual plan fiduciary, to pay premiums to an insurance carrier to cover the risk of liability for a breach.[22]

The Department of Labor has authority to audit and investigate perceived breaches of fiduciary duty, and has the right to enter the sponsoring employer's premises to review plan documents and books.[23] A participant, beneficiary, other fiduciary of the same plan, or the Secretary of the Department of Labor may file a civil action for appropriate relief (*i.e.*, personal liability to restore lost profits or disgorge personal profits) against a plan

---

22. ERISA § 410.
23. ERISA § 504(a).

fiduciary for breach of fiduciary duties.[24] This relief had generally been viewed as making the plan whole, not making any individual participant whole, but a recent Supreme Court case clearly allows a single plan participant that loses value in his self-directed account to file a breach of fiduciary claim only to restore his personal loss.[25] A claim of fiduciary breach can only be filed within 6 years of the last date of an action leading to a breach, or the last date that an omitted act could have been taken to cure the breach; however, once a plaintiff has actual knowledge that a breach has occurred, then he must file the breach of fiduciary action claim within 3 years; however, if there is fraud or concealment shown on the part of the fiduciary, then the civil action can be filed within 6 years of the discovery of the breach.[26]

2. Liability for Co-Fiduciaries

Statutory Rules at ERISA § 405

In addition to a fiduciary's potential personal liability for his or her own breach, fiduciaries can also be personally liable for breaches of their co-fiduciaries. Specifically, a fiduciary shall be liable for a co-fiduciary's breach if: he or she knowingly participates or knowingly conceals a co-fiduciary's breach; breaches his or her own fiduciary duties and that breach enables a co-fiduciary to breach; or has knowledge of another fiduciary's actual breach but makes no reasonable efforts under the circumstances to remedy the breach. Even if the delegation of fiduciary duties is clearly bifurcated to two or more trustees over separate plan assets, they still need to use reasonable care to prevent a co-trustee from committing a breach; further, without proper provisions in the trust document allocating responsibilities, each trustee shall be deemed to jointly manage and control the plan assets. Trustees, however, that simply follow instructions of other plan fiduciaries pursuant to the trust document (such as being told to make a distribution of benefits or to make specific investment choices), will not be liable if the instructions themselves constitute a breach by the person giving them.

3. Bonding Requirements

Statutory Rules at ERISA § 412

As a general rule, every fiduciary of an employee benefit plan and every person who handles funds or property of the plan must be bonded. The amount of the bond is required to be $1,000 or 10% of the amount of funds handled, whichever is greater, but does not need to exceed $500,000; however, if the plan assets are invested in qualifying employer securities, then the maximum bond amount is $1 million. A bond must furnish protection to the plan against loss through fraud or dishonesty on the part of a plan official, directly or through connivance with others. Often an employer may have an insurance policy that will cover potential breaches by the plan fiduciaries; however, the Department of Labor may require a separate rider to an insurance policy to specifically meet the bonding requirements to cover violations of ERISA.

---

24. ERISA § 502(a)(2).
25. LaRue v. DeWolff, Boberg & Assoc., 128 S.Ct. 1020 (2008).
26. ERISA § 413.

Welfare benefit plans that are fully insured and/or totally self-funded and do not receive employee contributions are not required to have a fidelity bond or fiduciary insurance for the plan fiduciaries. The rationale for this exception is that such plans do not have any assets that are "handled" by the plan fiduciaries because all claims are paid directly out of the employer's general assets for self-funded plans and all premiums are paid directly from the employer's general assets to the insurance company for insured plans.

E. Paying Plan Expenses from Qualified Plan Assets

The employer wears two hats when sponsoring a qualified retirement plan: a settlor that makes decisions on behalf of the best interests of the employer; and a plan administrator that implements and operates the employee benefit plans decided by the settlor, but whose loyalty now lies with the plan and its participants and beneficiaries. When the employer is deemed a settlor, then plan expenses incurred cannot be paid directly from the qualified plan, but when the employer is deemed a plan administrator or fiduciary, then reasonable plan expenses can be paid directly from the plan. If expenses can be paid directly from a qualified plan, then there are different rules for defined benefit plans and for defined contribution plans.

1. Settlor vs. Administrator Functions

Generally, activities that benefit the employer (such as, whether to promise employee benefits in the first place, deciding how ERISA and the Code impact the delivery of those benefits, or how the employer needs to prepare to operate the plans the moment they become effective), would be classified as settlor expenses that must be paid from the general assets of the employer, rather than from plan assets. On the other hand, other expenses required to comply with the requirements of ERISA and the Code (such as, reporting and disclosure mandates, nondiscrimination and other annual testing, the distribution and delivery of benefits, the termination or amendment of the plans, and claims procedures and civil litigation) could be considered plan administration or fiduciary expenses, and under the right facts and circumstances, can be paid directly from the plan. The following are simply guidelines for types of expenses that can be paid directly from plan assets.

DOL Advisory Opinion 2001-01A

January 18, 2001

Mr. Carl J. Stoney, Jr.
Crosby, Heafey, Roach & May
Two Embarcadero Center, Suite 2000
San Francisco, California 94111-4106

 ERISA Sec. 403—404

Dear Mr. Stoney:

This is in response to your recent correspondence in which you request confirmation of the continued viability of the Department of Labor's views expressed in Advisory Opinion 97-03A (January 23, 1997), discussing the application of the Employee Retirement Income Security Act (ERISA) to the payment of certain plan termination expenses by tax-qualified plans administered by the Insurance Commissioner of the State of California in its capacity as liquidator of the companies which sponsored the plans. Further, you request any other guidance that the department may be able to provide on the issue of permissible plan expenses. In this regard, you indicate that you represent the Conservation and Liquidation Office of the State of California Department of Insurance in connection with the termination of, and attendant distribution of assets from, tax-qualified retirement plans sponsored by now-insolvent insurance companies.

Since the issuance of Advisory Opinion 97-03A, questions have been raised concerning the extent to which an employee benefit plan may pay the costs attendant to maintaining tax-qualified status, without regard to the fact that tax qualification confers a benefit on the plan sponsor. The following is intended to clarify the views of the Department of Labor on this issue.

As discussed in Advisory Opinion 97-03A, a determination as to whether to pay a particular expense out of plan assets is a fiduciary act governed by ERISA's fiduciary responsibility provisions. ERISA provides that, subject to certain exceptions, the assets of an employee benefit plan shall never inure to the benefit of any employer and shall be held for the exclusive purpose of providing benefits to participants and beneficiaries and defraying reasonable expenses of administering the plan. In discharging their duties under ERISA, fiduciaries must act prudently and solely in the interest of the plan participants and beneficiaries, and in accordance with the documents and instruments governing the plan insofar as they are consistent with the provisions of ERISA. See ERISA sections 403(c)(1), 404(a)(1)(A), (B), and (D).

With regard to sections 403 and 404 of ERISA, we noted that, as a general rule, reasonable expenses of administering a plan include direct expenses properly and actually incurred in the performance of a fiduciary's duties to the plan. We also noted, however, that the department has long taken the position that there is a class of discretionary activities which relate to the formation, rather than the management, of plans, explaining that these so-called settlor functions include decisions relating to the establishment, design and termination of plans and, except in the context of multi-employer plans, generally are not fiduciary activities governed by ERISA. Expenses incurred in connection with the performance of settlor functions would not be reasonable expenses of a plan as they would be incurred for the benefit of the employer and would involve services for which an employer could reasonably be expected to bear the cost in the normal course of its business operations. However, reasonable expenses incurred in connection with the implementation of a settlor decision would generally be payable by the plan.

In Advisory Opinion 97-03A, the department expressed the view that the tax-qualified status of a plan confers benefits upon both the plan sponsor and the plan and, therefore, in the case of a plan that is intended to be tax-qualified and that otherwise permits expenses to be paid from plan assets, a portion of the expenses attendant to tax-qualification activities may be reasonable plan expenses. This view has been construed to require an apportionment of all tax qualification-related expenses between the plan and plan sponsor. The department does not agree with this reading of the opinion. The opinion recognizes that, in the context of tax-qualification activities, fiduciaries must consider, consistent with the principles articulated in earlier letters,[1] whether the activities are settlor in nature for purposes of determining whether the expenses attendant thereto may be reasonable expenses of the plan. However, in making this determination, the department does not believe that a fiduciary must take into account the benefit a plan's tax-qualified status confers on the employer. Any such benefit, in the opinion of the department, should be viewed as an integral component of the incidental benefits that flow to plan sponsors generally by virtue of offering a plan.[2]

In the context of tax-qualification activities, it is the view of the department that the formation of a plan as a tax-qualified plan is a settlor activity for which a plan may not pay. Where a plan is intended to be a tax-qualified plan, however, implementation of this settlor decision may require plan fiduciaries to undertake activities relating to maintaining the plan's tax-qualified status for which a plan may pay reasonable expenses (*i.e.*, reasonable in light of the services rendered). Implementation activities might include drafting plan amendments required by changes in the tax law, nondiscrimination testing, and requesting IRS determination letters. If, on the other hand, maintaining the plan's tax-qualified status involves analysis of options for amending the plan from which the plan sponsor makes a choice, the expenses incurred in analyzing the options would be settlor expenses.

The foregoing views are intended to clarify, rather than supersede, the views of the department set forth in Advisory Opinion 97-03A. We hope the information provided is of assistance to you.

This letter constitutes an advisory opinion under ERISA Procedure 76-1 (41 Fed. Reg. 36281, August 27, 1976).

Sincerely,
Robert J. Doyle
Director of Regulations and Interpretations

Guidance on Settlor v. Plan Expenses (Addendum to DOL Advisory Opinion 2001-01A)

In conjunction with investigations involving reviews of plan expenses, a number of questions have been raised concerning the extent to which plans may pay certain expenses that might be viewed as conferring a benefit on the plan sponsor. In this regard, the department has issued a number of letters which have at-

---

1. See letter to John N. Ernlenborn from Dennis M. Kass (March 13, 1986); letter to Kirk F. Maldonado from Elliot I. Daniel (March 2, 1987).

2. The Supreme Court has recognized that plan sponsors receive a number of incidental benefits by virtue of offering an employee benefit plan, such as attracting and retaining employees, providing increased compensation without increasing wages, and reducing the likelihood of lawsuits by encouraging employees who would otherwise be laid off to depart voluntarily. It is the view of the department that the mere receipt of such benefits by plan sponsors does not convert a settlor activity into a fiduciary activity or convert an otherwise permissible plan expense into a settlor expense. See Lockheed Corp. v. Spink, 517 U.S. 882 (1996); Hughes Aircraft Company v. Jacobson, 525 U.S. 432 (1999).

tempted to lay out the fiduciary provisions, principles and considerations relevant to an analysis of this question.[1]

Nonetheless, it has been determined that further clarification and guidance will facilitate both compliance and enforcement efforts in this area.

In an effort to specifically address the most frequently raised questions, the Pension and Welfare Benefits Administration has developed a set of six hypothetical fact patterns in which various plan expense issues are both presented and addressed.[2]

Questions concerning this guidance may be addressed to:

U.S. Department of Labor
Pension and Welfare Benefits Administration
Office of Regulations and Interpretations
200 Constitution Avenue, NW, Suite N-5669
Washington, DC 20210
Attention: Settlor Expense Guidance
Tel 202.693.8510

Fact Pattern Number One

During 1997, ACD Inc. agreed to sell a business segment to EFG Inc., a friendly competitor. The closing date for the sale was January 1, 1998. As a result of this sale, 1,600 participants and $180 million (the amount of accrued benefits attributable to the transferring employees) were to be transferred from the ACD defined benefit plan to the EFG defined benefit plan on the sale closing date. In December 1997, the companies were forced, through no fault of the parties, to postpone the sale closing date until May 1, 1998. The following expenses were paid by the ACD plan as a result of the business segment sale:

$80,000 for a plan design study;

$30,000 to amend the ACD Plan to provide for the spin-off;

$75,000 to compute the amount necessary to implement the transfer of plan assets from the ACD Plan to the EFG Plan and an additional $75,000 to re-compute the amount of the asset transfer due to the changed closing date; and

$25,000 for negotiations with various unions related to the transfer of assets and participants

Which of the above expenses, if otherwise reasonable, may be paid by the ACD Plan?

Answer

The department has taken the position that there is a class of activities which relates to the formation, rather than the management, of plans. These activities, generally referred to as settlor functions, include decisions relating to the formation, design and termination of plans and, except in the context of multi-

---

1. See Letters to Carl J. Stoney, Jr. from Robert J. Doyle (Advisory Opinion 01-01A, January 18, 2001); Samuel Israel from Robert J. Doyle (Advisory Opinion 97-03A, January 23, 1997); Kirk Maldonado from Elliot I. Daniel (March 2, 1987); John Erlenborn from Dennis M. Kass (March 13, 1986).

2. The expense information set forth in the following hypotheticals are for illustrative purposes only and are not intended to reflect a determination by the department on the reasonableness of an expense.

employer plans, generally are not activities subject to Title I of ERISA. Expenses incurred in connection with settlor functions would not be reasonable expenses of a plan. The department also has taken the position that, while expenses attendant to settlor activities do not constitute reasonable plan expenses, expenses incurred in connection with the implementation of settlor decisions may constitute reasonable expenses of the plan. See Letters to Carl J. Stoney, Jr. (2001, Advisory Opinion 01-01A); Samuel Israel (1997, Advisory Opinion 97-03A); Kirk Maldonado (1987); and John Erlenborn (1986).

Applying the foregoing principles, the $80,000 for a plan design study clearly constitutes an expense for a settlor activity and, therefore, cannot be paid by the ACD Plan. The $30,000 to amend the ACD Plan to provide for the spin off should, in the view of the department, be treated as a settlor/plan design expense inasmuch as the plan fiduciary would have no implementation responsibilities under the plan until such time as the plan is actually amended.

The $75,000 expense incurred to determine the amount of plan assets to be transferred to the EFG Plan would be a permissible plan expense if the expense is attendant to implementing ACD's decision to spin off certain participants, rather than for assisting ACD in formulating the spin-off. The second $75,000 expense incurred to re-compute the amount of the asset transfer due to the changed closing date also may be a reasonable plan expense, where, for example, the delay in the closing date was through no fault of the sponsor and the plan was duly amended to accomplish the merger at the new closing date.

The $25,000 expense related to negotiations with various unions would be a settlor expense. The described union negotiations typically take place in advance of plan changes. Activities (such as union negotiations, benefit studies, actuarial analyses) that take place in advance of, or in preparation for, a plan change will almost always constitute settlor activities, the expenses for which would not constitute reasonable plan expenses.

Fact Pattern Number Two

MNOP Corp., a Georgia gold mining company with pharmaceutical operations in the Miami area, decided to reduce its staff after several years of poor mining results, falling gold prices, and failed marketing projects in the Miami area. After exploring several other staff reduction options, MNOP decided to initiate an early retirement window (window) in their defined benefit plan (plan) to induce older workers to retire. The plan paid the following expenses related to the window:

$150,000 for a plan design study to determine the components of the window;

$80,000 for cost projections and to determine the impact of the window on MNOP's financial statements in accordance with FASB Statement No. 87 (Employer's Accounting for Pension);

Following adoption of the early retirement window, $90,000 to compute potential benefits for those participants that would be eligible for the window;

$30,000 to communicate selected components of the window and the plan benefits under the window to encourage eligible participants to take advantage of the early retirement benefit offer;

$50,000 for benefit calculations for those opting to retire under the window;

$20,000 to communicate plan benefits to the participants that opted to retire under the window; and

$10,000 for FASB Statement No. 88 (Employer's Accounting for Settlements and Curtailments of Defined Benefit Pension plans and for Termination of Benefits') calculations, as the window resulted in a plan curtailment

Which of the above expenses, if otherwise reasonable, may be paid by the plan?

Answer

The expenses incurred in hypothetical question 2 fall into three basic categories—plan design, benefit computation and communication expenses.

Plan design expenses clearly constitute settlor expenses and, therefore, are not payable by the plan. Typically, plan design expenses are incurred in advance of the adoption of the plan or a plan amendment. In the case at hand, the $150,000 for plan design study and the $80,000 for cost projections to determine financial impact of the plan change on the sponsor are settlor expenses and may not be paid by the plan. Similarly, the $10,000 for FASB Statement No. 88 expense relate to the plan sponsor's financial statements and are not payable by the plan.

Calculating the actual benefits to which a participant is entitled under the plan is an administrative function of the plan and, accordingly, reasonable expenses attendant to such calculations may be paid by the plan. Thus, the $50,000 expense for calculating the benefits of those opting for the retirement window may be a reasonable expense of the plan. In addition, the $90,000 paid to compute the potential benefits for all eligible employees may be a reasonable expense of the plan, if the fiduciary determines that such an expenditure is a prudent use of plan assets. Even though providing such information to all eligible employees might be viewed as furthering the objectives of the company, this benefit to the employer would not prevent the plan from incurring the expense.[3]

As suggested above, communicating plan information to participants and beneficiaries is an important plan activity and, therefore, expenses attendant to such communications will usually constitute permissible plan expenses, if the expenses are otherwise reasonable. In this regard, administrators and plan fiduciaries generally should be afforded substantial latitude in the method, form and style of their plan communications. Applying the foregoing, the $30,000 to communicate selected components of the window to all eligible participants and the $20,000 to communicate plan benefits to participants that opted for early retirement under the window may constitute reasonable expenses of the plan, even though, like the above benefit calculations, the communication to all eligible participants might be viewed as furthering the objective of the company to induce employees to opt for early retirement.

---

3. The Supreme Court has recognized that plan sponsors receive a number of incidental benefits by virtue of offering an employee benefit plan, such as attracting and retaining employees, providing increased compensation without increasing wages, and reducing the likelihood of lawsuits by encouraging employees who would otherwise be laid off to depart voluntarily. The mere receipt of such benefits by plan sponsors does not convert a settlor activity into a fiduciary activity or convert an otherwise permissible plan expense into a settlor expense. See Lockheed Corp. v. Spink, 517 U.S. 882 (1996), Hughes Aircraft Company v. Jacobson, 525 U.S. 432 (1999).

Fact Pattern Number Three

HIJ, Inc. is a major retailer in Boston, Chicago and San Francisco. During the last two years, it was determined that HIJ's defined benefit plan (plan) was amended to offer a participant loan program and an early retirement window for management employees. The plan is intended to be maintained as a tax-qualified plan. HIJ normally maximizes its tax-deductible contribution to the plan. Upon review of the Plan's financial records, it was determined that the following expenses were paid by the plan:

$100,000 to amend the plan to establish an early retirement window for management employees and to obtain an IRS determination letter;

$50,000 to amend the plan to comply with tax law changes;

$25,000 to amend the plan to establish a participant loan program; and

$20,000 for routine nondiscrimination testing to ensure compliance with the tax qualification requirements

Which of the above expenses, if otherwise reasonable, may be paid by the plan?

Answer

In Advisory Opinion 97-03A, the department expressed the view that the tax-qualified status of a plan confers benefits upon both the plan sponsor and the plan and, therefore, in the case of a plan that is intended to be tax-qualified and that otherwise permits expenses to be paid from plan assets, a portion of the expenses attendant to tax qualification activities may be reasonable plan expenses. The department further clarified its views on tax-qualification expenses in Advisory Opinion No. 01-01. In that opinion, the department expressed the view that a plan fiduciary is not required to take into account the benefits a plan's tax-qualified status confers on an employer in determining whether the expenses attendant to maintaining a plan's tax-qualified status constitute reasonable expenses of the plan. The department further noted that any such benefit should be viewed as an integral component of the incidental benefits that flow to plan sponsors generally by virtue of offering a plan.[4]

In the context of tax qualification activities, it is the view of the department that the design of a plan as a tax-qualified plan clearly involves settlor activities for which a plan may not pay. On the other hand, implementation of the settlor decision to maintain a tax-qualified plan would require plan fiduciaries to undertake activities relating to maintaining the plan's tax-qualified status for which a plan may pay reasonable expenses (*i.e.*, reasonable in light of the services rendered). Implementation activities might include drafting plan amendments required to maintain tax-qualified status, nondiscrimination testing, requesting IRS determination letters.

Applying the above principles, the $50,000 to amend the plan to comply with tax law changes and the $20,000 for routine nondiscrimination testing may constitute reasonable expenses of the plan. The $25,000 to amend the plan to establish a participant loan program would be a plan design/settlor expense inasmuch as the plan fiduciaries have no implementation obligations under the plan until such time as the plan is amended. Subsequent to the plan amendment, however,

---

4. See footnote 3.

expenses attendant to operating the established loan program would be implementation expenses with respect to which the plan may pay reasonable expenses.

The single charge of $100,000 includes expenses for plan design/settlor activities (*i.e.*, amending the plan to establish an early retirement window) and implementation activities (*i.e.*, obtaining an IRS determination letter). Inasmuch as fiduciaries may pay only reasonable expenses of administering the plan, the fiduciaries of the plan would be required to obtain from the service provider a determination of the specific expense(s) attributable to the fiduciaries' implementation responsibilities (*i.e.*, obtaining an IRS determination letter) prior to payment by the plan.

Fact Pattern Number Four

The QRS Corp. is a world-wide shoe manufacturer with plants in the Cincinnati and Detroit areas. A review of the financial records of the QRS Corp. defined benefit plan (the plan) reflected the following expenses:

> $60,000 for consulting fees to analyze the company's options for compliance with Uniformed Services Employment and Reemployment Rights Act of 1994 (USERRA) and Small Business Jobs Protection Act of 1996 (SBJPA);

> $5,000 to amend the plan to comply with USERRA and SBJPA and $5,000 to obtain an IRS determination letter;

> $50,000 in actuary fees to perform nondiscrimination testing due to a plan amendment increasing benefits as a result of union negotiations;

> $5,000 to amend the plan to comply with the requirements of Title I of ERISA

Which of the above expenses, if any, may be paid by the plan?

Answer

The expenses presented in this hypothetical raise some of the same issues as those raised in hypothetical question 3—the extent to which expenses relating to maintenance of tax-qualification may constitute reasonable plan expenses. Applying the principles set forth in the answers to hypothetical question 3, the $5,000 expense to amend the plan, the $5,000 expense for a determination letter and the $50,000 for nondiscrimination testing may be necessary to maintain the plan's tax-qualified status and, therefore, may constitute reasonable plan expenses. The fact that the $50,000 discrimination testing was necessary because of a union-negotiated plan amendment does not affect the expense being treated as a permissible plan expense. On the other hand, if the $50,000 was incurred as part of the plan sponsor's negotiating with the union—in advance of adoption of the plan amendment giving rise to the testing—the expense, as discussed in the Answer to hypothetical question 1, would be viewed as a settlor, rather than plan, expense. The $60,000 for consulting fees to analyze the Company's options for compliance with USERRA and SBJPA would constitute plan design/settlor expenses that may not be paid by the plan.

Similar to a fiduciary's implementation responsibility with regard to maintaining the tax-qualified status of a plan, fiduciaries have an obligation to ensure that administration of their plan comports with the requirements of ERISA, as well as other applicable Federal laws. Accordingly, the $5,000 expense to amend the plan to comply with the requirements of Title I of ERISA would be a permissible plan expense, assuming that the amount is reasonable in light of the services rendered.

Fact Pattern Number Five

The public relations firm, TUV (the Firm), has offices in Philadelphia, Dallas, Los Angeles and New York. The Firm operates a defined benefit plan (plan). From 1993 to 1996, the plan, in addition to distributing a Summary Annual Report (SAR), distributed an individual benefit statement to each participant. The total preparation and distribution costs for the benefit statements were approximately $50,000 annually.

In 1996, the Firm decided it would be a good idea to make sure its employees were aware of all of the benefits provided by the Firm. Accordingly, for 1996 and subsequent years, the individual benefit information was incorporated in a twelve page booklet that included summary information about all the Firm's benefit plans (health, dental, vision), as well as one full page devoted to other Firm benefits (e.g., the physical fitness center, limousine services) and activities (e.g., annual picnic, Holiday party, etc). The booklets are prepared by the plan's actuarial consultant. The booklet costs approximately $125,000 to prepare and distribute annually.

What, if any, of these expenses may be paid by the plan?

Answer

The issues presented by this hypothetical involve the extent to which a plan can pay expenses related to the disclosure of plan information. Clearly, plans may pay those expenses attendant to compliance with ERISA's disclosure requirements (e.g., furnishing and distributing summary plan descriptions, summary annual reports and individual benefit statements provided in response to individual requests). As indicated in the Answer to hypothetical question 2, communicating plan information to participants and beneficiaries is an important plan activity. The department notes that there is nothing in Title I of ERISA that precludes a plan fiduciary from providing more information than that specifically required by statute. Whether or not a particular communication related expense should be incurred by a plan is a fiduciary decision governed by the fiduciary responsibility provisions of Title I of ERISA.

Accordingly, the $50,000 to produce and distribute individual benefit statements would be a permissible plan expense to the extent that the actual costs of preparation and distribution are reasonable. Similarly, a portion of the $125,000 for preparation and distribution of the benefit booklets may also be a permissible plan expense. Clearly, the plan sponsor should pay that portion (1/12) of the costs of the booklet that relates to non-plan matters (*i.e.*, physical fitness center, limousine services, picnic, etc.). In addition, a plan may pay only those reasonable expenses relating to that plan, and therefore, each of the plans should pay their proportionate share of the expenses of the booklet. While plan administrators and fiduciaries should be given considerable deference with regard to their disclosure decisions, plan administrators should be able to explain their disclosure decisions and justify the costs attendant thereto.

Fact Pattern Number Six

The QT, P. C. (QT) is a law firm with satellite offices in most major U. S. cities. QT operates a defined benefit plan (plan). Until 1997, the plan was administered by a ten lawyer benefits committee. In 1997, the plan fiduciaries decided to out-source the administration. Following an in-depth search, the plan's fiduciaries selected Firm, Inc. and agreed to pay $1 million in start-up fees. The start-up fees were paid from the plan and were used to set up data bases and transfer data to Firm that was necessary to administer the plan. The new system operated by Firm provides plan participants with a significantly enhanced level of service than was previously provided by the staff of ten lawyers. Once the plan's administration was transferred to Firm, the plan paid all of Firm's administration fees.

To what extent may the expenses associated with outsourcing the plan's administration be paid by the plan?

Answer

Section 404(a)(1)(A) specifically contemplates the payment of reasonable expenses by an employee benefit plan. Where a plan sponsor has assumed responsibility for the payment of plan expenses and later prospectively shifts that responsibility to the plan, the plan may pay those expenses to the extent reasonable and not otherwise precluded by the terms of the plan.[5]

To the extent that the services provided by Firm are necessary for the administration of the plan, the $1 million start-up fee and ongoing administrative fees may constitute reasonable expenses of the plan if they are reasonable with respect to the services provided, and not otherwise precluded by the plan.

Based on my personal observations, I believe the following expenses can be paid from qualified plan assets:

Defined Benefit Plans: Certain recurring fees, such as the Enrolled Actuary's professional fees for calculating the minimum required contribution and PBGC premiums, clearly are proper expenses that can be paid from the plan assets. Consider that as the Enrolled Actuary compares expected liabilities to plan assets on an annual basis, every dollar paid out for expenses is a dollar that is not available to pay liabilities and will need to be funded. However, a dollar paid today for current expenses might be calculated as an amount less than a dollar as a present value funding component. In a defined benefit plan, expenses for an individual, such as processing a loan or verifying the qualified status of a domestic relations order upon divorce, cannot reduce that individual's accrued benefits.

Defined Contribution Plans: Since ERISA contains no provisions on how plan expenses from a defined contribution plan should be allocated among the accounts, the Department of Labor has indicated that if the governing plan document is silent, then the fiduciary is free to choose a method of allocation for plan expenses (such as pro rata, where general plan expenses are allocated based on an individual account balance as it bears to the total plan accounts, or per capita, where general plan expenses are allocated equally

---

5. The department has taken the position that where a plan document is silent as to the payment of reasonable administrative expenses, the plan may pay reasonable administrative expenses. Where a plan document provides that the employer will pay any such expenses, and if the employer has reserved the right to amend the plan document, ERISA would not prevent the employer from amending the plan to require, prospectively, that the relevant expenses be paid by the plan. The department believes that the prohibition against self-dealing in section 406(b)(1) precludes an employer from exercising fiduciary authority to use plan assets to pay for an amendment that would (retroactively) relieve the employer of an obligation to pay plan expenses. See Advisory Opinion 97-03A.

to each participant).[27] However, the selection of a method must be prudent, based on a rational basis, and solely in the interest of participants. While the fiduciary has discretion on the allocation methods, only limited types of expenses should be wholly borne by the affected participants (such as expenses to calculate and distribute benefits, hardship distributions, loans, or qualified domestic relations orders). The methods must be communicated to the participants through the Summary Plan Description and if they change from time to time, the reason for changing the method cannot be directed at any individual participant. The IRS responded by indicating that allocating the expenses in a defined contribution plan with a reasonable method does not automatically violate the qualification rules, but that the IRS reserves the right to make determinations on a facts and circumstances basis.[28]

2. Special Tax Credits for Small Employers

Statutory Rules at IRC § 45E

Plan expenses paid from general employer assets will usually be deductible on the employer's tax return as a normal and necessary business expense. Furthermore, a small employer pension plan startup cost credit is available to any employer that had no more than 100 employees who received at least $5,000 of compensation from the employer for the preceding year. The credit equals 50% of the qualified startup costs, up to a maximum of $500 per year for each of the first three years that a retirement plan exists. A "qualified startup cost" is any ordinary and necessary expense incurred by an eligible employer in connection with the establishment or administration, or a related employee retirement-education of an eligible employer plan. This nonrefundable income tax credit is available to any small business that adopts a new qualified defined benefit or defined contribution plan (including a 401(k) plan), SIMPLE § 401(k), SIMPLE IRA, or SEP. The credit is a general business credit and it cannot be carried back to years before the effective date of this statutory provision. The 50% of qualifying expenses that are effectively offset by the tax credit are not deductible.

The credit is not available if, during the three-year period preceding the first year that the credit is taken, the employer or any member of the controlled group of the employer established or maintained an eligible employer plan to which contributions were made, or under which benefits accrued for substantially the same employees as are in the eligible employer plan for which the credit is taken.

In order for an employer to be eligible for the credit, the plan must cover at least one NHCE.

For purposes of determining eligibility for the startup cost credit, all employers within the same controlled group of corporations or in trades or businesses under common control or aggregated under leasing or other arrangements will be treated as one employer and all eligible employer plans sponsored by the employer (and other aggregated employers) will be treated as one eligible employer plan.

---

27. DOL Field Assistance Bulletin 2003-3.
28. Rev. Rul. 2004-10.

Chapter 14

ERISA Causes of Action

Overview

What is ERISA preemption?

- ERISA pre-empts any state law that purports to govern employee benefit plans, not employee benefits
- the ERISA "Preemption clause" has three parts to it:
  - the general preemption clause states that, generally, the provisions of Titles I and IV of ERISA shall supersede any and all State laws insofar as they relate to any employee benefits plan,
  - the savings clause excludes (or saves) insurance, banking and securities entities from ERISA preemption since the states heavily regulate these industries, and
  - the deemer clause prohibits anything which fits the definition of an employee benefit plan to be deemed an insurance, banking or securities organization just so it can escape ERISA preemption
- Federal courts, including the U.S. Supreme Court, have not always been consistent in determining ERISA preemption (as a very over-simplified observation, during the first 20 years or so of ERISA, courts were continually expanding ERISA preemption to any state law that even minimally related to employee benefit plans; however, the pendulum seems to be swinging back the other way during the past few years and it appears that courts are now looking as to whether the state law at issue substantially relates to employee benefits plans or whether it is so tangential that it does not realistically relate to employee benefits plans)

What are the criminal remedies under ERISA?

- any person who willfully violates any provision of Part 1 of Title I of ERISA (*i.e.*, reporting and disclosure) is criminally liable:
  - if the convicted person is an individual, then the maximum fine is $100,000 and the maximum prison sentence is ten years
  - If the convicted person is not an individual (*i.e.*, a sponsoring corporation), then the maximum fine is $500,000
  - if a prohibited individual (*i.e.*, a convicted felon) intentionally serves as a plan fiduciary, then such individual can be fined up to $10,000 or imprisoned for up to 5 years, or both

Who has standing to bring an ERISA cause of action?
- There are four classes of parties who can bring an ERISA action:
  - participants (includes anyone that has a "colorable claim" for benefits, such as alternate payees pursuant to a Qualified Domestic Relations Order),
  - beneficiaries,
  - fiduciaries; and
  - the Secretary of Labor (which means the Department of Labor)

What are the common civil causes of actions under ERISA?
- Reporting and disclosure failure:
  - Action: An ERISA § 502(c) action (as cross-referenced under ERISA § 501(a)(1)(A)) is where a participant or beneficiary in an employee benefit plan fails to receive certain mandatory notices or other information required to be disclosed by the Plan Administrator
  - Remedy: Personal liability to the plaintiffs of up to $100 per day of failure plus any other relief the court deems proper.
- Benefits or other rights:
  - Action: An ERISA § 502(a)(1)(B) action is where a participant or beneficiary in an employee benefit plan wishes to recover benefits or to clarify future benefits due, or to enforce his or her rights under the plan
  - Remedy: Recovery or clarification of such alleged benefits, or availing such alleged rights.
- Breach of fiduciary duty:
  - Action: An ERISA § 502(a)(2) action is where a the Secretary of Labor, a participant, or a beneficiary seeks appropriate relief
  - Remedy: Individuals who have breached their fiduciary duty shall be personally liable to: (1) make good to such plan any losses to the plan resulting from each breach; (2) restore to the plan any profits made through the use of plan assets; and (3) shall be subject to other equitable or remedial relief as the court may deem appropriate, including the removal of such fiduciary.
- Equitable relief for actions or inactions (not alleged by the Department of Labor):
  - Action: An ERISA § 502(a)(3) action is where a participant, a beneficiary, or a fiduciary seeks to either enjoin any act or practice which violates any provision of ERISA or the terms of the plan or to obtain other appropriate equitable relief to redress such violations or to enforce any provision of ERISA or this plan.
  - Remedy: A temporary or permanent restraining order, a court order compelling certain actions, or any other appropriate equitable relief.

What are the required claims procedures?
- every ERISA plan must have a claims procedure which provides adequate notice to a participant or beneficiary that a benefit claim has been denied and which provides a reasonable opportunity, through a formal procedure, for the individual to have a full and fair review by a named fiduciary
- there are timing rules (much quicker turn around for claims denied in the group health plan than for claims denied in the retirement plan) and procedural rules imposed on the plan sponsor

What is the relevance of a claims procedure in ERISA civil litigation?

- the plaintiff must show that he or she exhausted all administrative remedies before he or she can sue in court
- once a participant gets a final denial, then he or she may proceed to sue in court (but not until then)
- there are two goals of the benefit claims procedure
  - to ferret out legitimate mistakes or
  - to produce "substantive evidence" for fiduciary decisions
- if a participant or beneficiary is unhappy after completing the plan's claims procedure, then
  - if there is magic language based on Firestone Tire and Rubber Company decision in the plan document (which allows the plan administrator to interpret the plan document and make all benefit decisions, all in its sole discretion), then the district court's standard of review of the second benefit denial is abuse of discretion
  - if no Firestone language is present, then the district court's standard of review is *de novo*

What are ERISA statute of limitations?

- a cause of action for a breach of fiduciary action must be brought by the earlier of:
  - 6 years after the date of the last affirmative act or act of omission on which the fiduciary could have cured the breach, or
  - 3 years after the earliest date on which the plaintiff had actual knowledge of the breach
- in all cases of a fiduciary breach where fraud or concealment is reasonably alleged, then the cause of action can be brought up to 6 years after the discovery of such breach or violation

What attorney fees can be awarded in ERISA litigation?

- certain attorney fees and costs of action may be awarded to either party (other than for the collection of delinquent contributions)
- Courts have developed a five factor test to determine when attorneys fees will be awarded:
  - the degree of offending party's culpability or bad faith,
  - the offending party's ability to personally pay the award,
  - whether or not the awarding of attorneys' fees would deter others under similar circumstances, and
  - the amount of benefit conferred on participants, and the relative merits of the party's position

A. Federal Preemption of State Laws

Statutory Rules at ERISA § 514

All rules discussed in this chapter are the general statutory rules. A form of ERISA federal common law has been developing over the life of ERISA and such rules must be viewed in conjunction with how courts of relevant jurisdiction are actually interpreting and applying the statutory rules.

ERISA provides for the broad preemption of state laws that "relate to" employee benefit plans. The purpose of this provision is to afford employers sponsoring employee benefit plans some comfort that requirements regarding employee benefits will be enforced on a consistent basis, regardless of the state in which the employer, the participant, and/or the plan trust is located. The preemption excludes state regulation of banks, insurance companies, and securities dealers, as long as they are truly regulated under state laws.

The ERISA "Preemption clause" actually has three components:

1. The "general preemption clause" states that, generally, the provisions of Title I (Protection of Employee Benefits Rights) and Title IV (Plan Termination Insurance) of ERISA shall supercede any and all State laws insofar as they relate to any employee benefit plan—but this specifically does not extend to a state criminal law;

2. The "savings clause" excludes (or saves) insurance, banking and securities entities from ERISA preemption since the states heavily regulate these industries; and

3. The "deemer clause" prohibits anything which fits the definition of an employee benefit plan to be deemed an insurance, banking or securities organization just so it can escape ERISA preemption.

Federal courts, including the U.S. Supreme Court, have not always been consistent in determining ERISA preemption. As a very over-simplified observation, during the first 20 years or so of ERISA, courts were continually expanding ERISA preemption to any state law that even minimally related to employee benefit plans. However, the pendulum seems to be swinging back the other way during the past decade and it appears that courts are now looking as to whether the state law at issue substantially relates to employee benefit plans or whether it is so tangential that it does not realistically relate to employee benefit plans. Since the exact state laws that are superceded by ERISA are still not clearly answered, only an attorney can assist the plan administrator in knowing when to follow the single federal law and when to follow one of the respective state laws. Please note that ERISA preemption could be a whole textbook unto itself, and therefore, no attempt to provide a summary of the Supreme Court decisions has been included in this textbook.

Remember, ERISA pre-empts any state law that purports to govern employee benefit plans, not employee benefits. Some of the more recent challenges in regards to retirement plans is whether a state law that automatically eliminates a spouse as a beneficiary on any legal document controls beneficiary designation forms (which, under ERISA, continue to take effect unless and until the plan participant affirmatively changes the beneficiary designation form). This is really the prevue of the plan attorney, so while accountants and other consultants should understand the general rules of preemption, there is no need to go into excruciating detail in this reference book.

In plain English, if a federal law, like ERISA, preempts state law, then a disgruntled employee can only seek redress against the plan or sponsoring employer in federal courts, as opposed to state courts. While the rules and procedures for federal civil actions might make it easier for the employee to have his or her day in court, the federal causes of action under ERISA seem to be skewed in favor of the sponsoring employer, and if the employee is right, is only entitled to limited remedies under ERISA (whereas, under state law, he or she might have been able to receive a larger remedy, including punitive damages).

B. Criminal Causes of Action

Statutory Rules at ERISA § 501

Any person who willfully violates ERISA shall, upon conviction, be fined not more than $100,000 or imprisoned not more than 10 years, or both; except that in the case of such violation by a person not an individual, the fine imposed upon such person shall be a fine not exceeding $500,000.

If a prohibited individual (*i.e.*, a convicted felon) intentionally serves as a plan fiduciary, then such individual can be fined up to $10,000 or imprisoned for up to 5 years, or both.[1]

In the following excerpt from a decision, I willfully have omitted the facts (all I want you to see is the court's analysis).

═══

U.S. v. Phillips
363 F.3d 1167 (11th Cir. 1994)

TJOFLAT, Chief Judge:

This case involves a steel producer's payment of kickbacks, in the form of illegal pension payments, to union officials, in violation of the Labor Management Relations ("Taft-Hartley") Act § 302, 29 U.S.C. § 186 (1988), and its failure to notify the employee pension plan's participants that the plan had been amended to provide for such payments, as required by the Employee Retirement Income Security Act ("ERISA") §§ 101, 102, 104, 29 U.S.C. §§ 1021, 1022, 1024 (1988). A jury found that the steel producer and the union officials, by arranging for the pension payments, violated the Taft-Hartley Act, and it convicted them under the Act's criminal enforcement provisions, 29 U.S.C. § 186(d). In addition, the jury found the steel producer guilty under ERISA's criminal enforcement provision, 29 U.S.C. § 1131 (1988), for failing to notify the pension plan's participants of the change in their pension plan. Finally, the jury found that the steel producer, by making the kickbacks, had engaged in a scheme to defraud the pension plan's beneficiaries*1567 in violation of the mail fraud statute, 18 U.S.C. § 1341 (1988).

The steel producer and the union officials, contending on several grounds that the trial court denied them a fair trial, and, in the case of the union officials, appropriate sentences, ask us to set aside the district court's judgment and order a new trial. We find their contentions meritless, and accordingly affirm their convictions and the union officials' sentences.

* * *

III.

We next address appellants' claim that the district court misinterpreted the term "willfully" as used both in 29 U.S.C. § 186(d)(2) and in 29 U.S.C. § 1131, the applicable criminal enforcement provisions of the Taft-Hartley Act and ERISA, respectively. Appellants argue that the district court's misinterpretations resulted

---

1. ERISA § 411(b).

in jury instructions that set forth a prejudicially low standard of criminal intent for the charges under the Taft-Hartley Act and ERISA.[19]

As the Supreme Court has observed, the term "willfully" has " 'many meanings,' and 'its construction [is] often ... influenced by its context.' " Ratzlaf v. United States, 510 U.S. 135,— —, 114 S.Ct. 655, 659, 126 L.Ed.2d 615 (1994) (quoting Spies v. United States, 317 U.S. 492, 497, 63 S.Ct. 364, 367, 87 L.Ed. 418 (1943)). See also United States v. Murdock, 290 U.S. 389, 395, 54 S.Ct. 223, 225, 78 L.Ed. 381 (1933) ("Aid in arriving at the meaning of the word 'willfully' may be afforded by the context in which it is used."). The interpretation of willfully "turns on [each statute's] own peculiar facts." Screws v. United States, 325 U.S. 91, 101, 65 S.Ct. 1031, 1035, 89 L.Ed. 1495 (1945).

[5] [6] For instance, in some contexts, courts have interpreted "willfully" as requiring a finding of general intent, meaning the intent to engage in the prohibited conduct; that is, acting voluntarily, knowingly, and intentionally, and not accidently or mistakenly. See, e.g., Browder v. United States, 312 U.S. 335, 341, 61 S.Ct. 599, 603, 85 L.Ed. 862 (1941) (interpreting 22 U.S.C. § 220, which provides punishment for a person who knowingly and willfully uses any passport secured by the making of a false statement). Thus, a defendant need not intend to violate the law to commit a general intent crime, but he *1577 must actually intend to do the act that the law proscribes.[20] In other circumstances, courts have construed the term "willfully" to require a finding of specific intent, meaning the intent to violate the law; that is, acting with a "bad purpose" to disobey or disregard the law. See, e.g., Cheek v. United States, 498 U.S. 192, 200, 111 S.Ct. 604, 609, 112 L.Ed.2d 617 (1991) (interpreting the Internal Revenue Code and noting that the specific intent interpretation of "willfully" in the federal tax statutes is an "exception to the traditional rule" that "willfully" requires a finding of only general intent, applied "largely due to the complexity of the tax laws").

This appeal therefore requires us to make the same determination concerning each of the criminal enforcement provisions under which the appellants were convicted: whether the use of the term "willfully" in each statute requires a finding of general or specific intent as we have defined those terms. While our inquiry is the same for the criminal enforcement provisions of both the Taft-Hartley Act, 29 U.S.C. § 186(d)(2), and ERISA, 29 U.S.C. § 1131, we must remain "mindful of the complex of provisions in which they are embedded." Ratzlaf, 510 U.S. at— —, 114 S.Ct. at 659.

* * *

B.

[8] We next consider USX's claim that the district court's charge to the jury with respect to the ERISA violation alleged in Count 16 set forth a prejudicially low standard of criminal intent. Again, the solution to the problem focuses on the proper interpretation of the term "willfully," and on whether the ERISA criminal enforcement provision requires a finding of general or spe-

---

19. Because these contentions present solely a question of law, our review is de novo. See Chandler, 996 F.2d at 1085.

20. The term "law" in this context means the law as a whole, not any specific statute.

cific intent. At issue is section 1131 of ERISA,[28] which makes it a criminal mis-
demeanor willfully to violate Part 1 of ERISA, which contains the reporting
and disclosure requirements governing those who control and administer employee benefit plans. Part 1 of ERISA requires the administrator[29] of a pension plan to notify the Department of Labor and the plan's participants and
beneficiaries of any material modifications in the terms of the pension plan,
such as the creation of a new class of pension beneficiaries. 29 U.S.C. § 1021
(1988).[30]

*1583 The district court charged the jury that a defendant who "knowingly
and intentionally committed acts which [violated Part 1 of ERISA] and ... were
not committed accidentally or by some mistake" was guilty of violating Part 1 of
ERISA. USX argues that section 1131 prohibits violations of Part 1 of ERISA
caused by "act[s] committed voluntarily and purposely, with the specific intent
to do something the law forbids; that is with bad purpose to disobey or disregard the law." In support of this position, USX argues simply that ERISA is a
complex statute; therefore, Congress intended "willfully" to require a finding of
specific intent. USX, however, does not point to anything within the statute itself to support its argument. After examining the language and structure of
ERISA, we cannot agree with USX's interpretation.

As explained by Congress, Part 1 of ERISA is designed: (1) to require the disclosure
of significant information about employee benefit plans and all transactions engaged in by those who control the plans; (2) to provide specific data to plan participants and beneficiaries about the rights and benefits to which they are entitled
and the circumstances that may result in a loss of those rights and benefits; and (3)
to set forth the responsibilities and proscriptions applicable to persons occupying
a fiduciary relationship to employee benefit plans. See House Education and Labor
Committee, Employee Retirement Income Security Act of 1974, H.Rep. No. 533,
93rd Cong., 2d Sess. (1974), reprinted in 1974 U.S.C.C.A.N. 4639, 4648–49. To
achieve the third goal, Congress codified a " 'prudent man' standard for evaluating
the conduct of all fiduciaries." Id. at 4649. In doing so, Congress placed a twofold
duty on every fiduciary: to act in his relationship to the plan's fund as a prudent man
in a similar situation and under like conditions would act, and to act consistently
with the principles of administering the trust for the exclusive purposes previously
enumerated, and in accordance with the documents and instruments governing
the fund unless they are inconsistent with the fiduciary principles of the section.

---

28. The pertinent part of 29 U.S.C. § 1131 (1988) provides as follows:
    Any person who willfully violates any provision of part 1 of [ERISA], ... shall upon convic-
tion be fined not more than $5,000 or imprisoned not more than one year, or both; except that in the
case of such violation by a person not an individual, the fine imposed upon such person shall be a
fine not exceeding $100,000.
29. USX, by a contract with the Administrator of the USX pension fund, had assumed the duty
ERISA imposes to report and disclose material modifications of the pension plan; consequently, USX
was the "administrator" for the purpose of ERISA's reporting and disclosure requirements.
30. The relevant provision in 29 U.S.C. § 1021 (1988), which provides in pertinent part:
    The administrator of each employee benefit plan shall cause to be furnished in accordance
with section 1024(b) of this title to each participant covered under the plan and to each beneficiary
who is receiving benefits under the plan—
    (1) a summary plan description described in section 1022(a)(1) of this title; and
    (2) the information described in sections 1024(b)(3) and 1025(a) and (c) of this title.

Id. at 4651.

Consistent with the codification of a prudent man standard, Congress, in 29 U.S.C. § 1028 (1988), provided a detailed set of exemptions from prohibited transactions and included a good faith defense for reliance on administrative interpretations. Section 1028 provides in pertinent part that

[i]n any criminal proceeding under section 1131 of this title, based on any act or omission in alleged violation of [ERISA Part 1]..., no person shall be subject to any liability or punishment for or on account of the failure of such person to (1) comply with [ERISA Part 1] if he pleads and proves that the act or omission complained of was in good faith, in conformity with, and in reliance on any regulation or written ruling of the Secretary, or (2) publish and file any information required by any provision of this part if he pleads and proves that he published and filed such information in good faith, and in conformity with any regulation or written ruling of the Secretary issued under this part regarding the filing of such reports....

Thus, section 1028 serves to outline clearly the responsibilities of those in a fiduciary relationship to employee benefit plans and to ensure that the statutory codification of the prudent man standard is not undermined by later interpretations of ERISA. In short, Congress, in section 1108, specifically outlined what would serve as a valid defense to a violation of the reporting and disclosure requirements.

This statutory good faith defense is necessary, however, only if a violation of the ERISA criminal enforcement provision in section 1131 is based only upon a finding of general intent. Under USX's construction, section 1108 would be superfluous because the government would have to prove specific intent for violations of Part 1 of ERISA; good faith is a complete defense to specific intent crimes. Although section 1108 could serve to limit the defenses that would be available if section 1131 required a finding of specific intent, this interpretation would, in effect, render "willfully" mere surplusage.

*1584 The only logical interpretation of Part 1 of ERISA is that the term "willfully" in section 1131 requires a finding of only general intent and that section 1108 provides additional statutory defenses not otherwise present for general intent crimes. Under this interpretation, sections 1131 and 1108 serve distinct purposes; the term "willfully" as used in section 1131 ensures that the act was done voluntarily and not by accident or mistake; and section 1131 provides the proper scope of defenses in accordance with the codified "prudent man" standard as determined by Congress. To interpret otherwise would render either the defenses in section 1108 or the term "willfully" in 1131 meaningless surplusage. Consequently, we conclude that the district court's charge to the jury sufficiently and accurately described the mens rea required for violations of ERISA Part 1.

IV.

For the reasons discussed above, we find no merit in any of appellants' claims of error. Accordingly, the judgments of the district court are affirmed.

IT IS SO ORDERED.

C. Civil Causes of Action

Statutory Rules at ERISA § 502

There are four classes of parties who can bring an ERISA action:

1. Participants (includes anyone that has a "colorable claim" for benefits, such as Alternate Payees pursuant to a Qualified Domestic Relations Order)[2]

2. Beneficiaries;

3. Fiduciaries; and

4. The Secretary of Labor (which means any designated agent of the Department of Labor).

Please note that because ERISA preempts other state laws, a disgruntled employee or beneficiary can only receive the remedies detailed below if he or she wins, which, unlike many state civil causes of action, do not allow for punitive damages or damages from pain and suffering.

Below are the only causes of action allowed under ERISA, and the most relevant causes of action seen in qualified retirement plan cases are indicated with an asterisk (*). Again, the plan's attorney, or any ERISA attorney that you know professionally, should be able to explain the pros and cons of each cause of action (from both the plaintiff's and defendant's point of view), and how the federal courts are currently deciding those cases.

*Reporting and Disclosure Failure

Action: An ERISA § 502(c) action (as cross-referenced under ERISA § 501(a)(1)(A)) is where a participant or beneficiary in an employee benefit plan fails to receive certain mandatory notices or other information required to be disclosed by the Plan Administrator.

Remedy: Personal liability to the plaintiffs of up to $100 per day of failure plus any other relief the court deems proper.

*Benefits or Other Rights

Action: An ERISA § 502(a)(1)(B) action is where a participant or beneficiary in an employee benefit plan wishes to recover benefits or to clarify future benefits due, or to enforce his or her rights under the plan.

Remedy: Recovery or clarification of such alleged benefits, or availing such alleged rights.

*Breach of Fiduciary Duty

Action: An ERISA § 502(a)(2) action is where the Secretary of Labor, a participant, or a beneficiary seeks appropriate relief under ERISA § 409 (*i.e.*, liability for the breach of a fiduciary duty).

Remedy: Individuals who have breached their fiduciary duty shall be personally liable to: (1) make good to such plan any losses to the plan resulting from each breach; (2) re-

---

2. Firestone Tire and Rubber Co. v. Bruch, 489 U.S. 101 (1989).

store to the plan any profits made through the use of plan assets; and (3) shall be subject to other equitable or remedial relief as the court may deem appropriate, including the removal of such fiduciary.

*Equitable Relief for Actions or Inactions (Not Alleged by the Department of Labor)

Action: An ERISA § 502(a)(3) action is where a participant, a beneficiary, or a fiduciary seeks to either enjoin any act or practice which violates any provision of ERISA or the terms of the plan or to obtain other appropriate equitable relief to redress such violations or to enforce any provision of ERISA or the plan.

Remedy: A temporary or permanent restraining order, a court order compelling certain actions, or any other appropriate equitable relief.

Please note that the U.S. Supreme Court has held that other equitable relief does not include purely monetary damages, as sought by a plan to recover benefits paid to a participant in a health plan after the participant received money in a tort action.[3]

Reporting and Disclosure Failure (for Plan Registration Statements)

Action: An ERISA § 502(a)(4) action is where the Secretary of Labor, a participant, or a beneficiary seeks appropriate relief under ERISA § 105(c) (*i.e.*, certain plan registration statements).

Remedy: The furnishing of such statement.

Equitable Relief for Actions or Inactions (Alleged by the Department of Labor)

Action: An ERISA § 502(a)(5) action is where the Secretary of Labor seeks to either enjoin any act or practice which violates any provision of ERISA or the terms of the plan or to obtain other appropriate equitable relief to redress such violations or to enforce any provision of ERISA or the plan.

Remedy: A temporary or permanent restraining order, a court order compelling certain actions, or any other appropriate equitable relief.

Enforcement of Civil Penalties Owed to the Department of Labor

Action: An ERISA § 502(a)(6) action is where the Secretary of Labor seeks to enforce the payment of any civil penalties statutorily assessed by the Secretary of Labor for reporting and disclosure failures, prohibited transactions under ERISA § 406, or any breach of fiduciary duty or knowing participation in such breach by another person.

Remedy: Collection of such civil penalties due.

---

3. Great-West Life & Annuity Ins. Co. v. Knudson, 534 U.S. 204 (2002).

Enforcement of QMCSOs

Action: An ERISA § 502(a)(7) action is where a State seeks to enforce compliance with a qualified medical child support order.

Remedy: Compliance with such order.

Certain Medicare and Medicaid Reports

Action: An ERISA § 502(a)(8) action is where the Secretary of Labor or employer seeks equitable relief for a violation of ERISA § 101(f) (which was repealed in 1997).

Remedy: (Since ERISA § 101(f) has been repealed, there is seemingly no longer such cause of action, and thus, no remedy).

Purchase of an Annuity for a Participant or Beneficiary

Action: An ERISA § 502(a)(9) action is where Secretary of Labor, a participant, a beneficiary, or a fiduciary alleges a violation of the fiduciary duties in connection with the purchase of an insured annuity upon the participant's termination of service.

Remedy: To obtain appropriate relief, including the posting of necessary security, to assure receipt by the participant or beneficiary of the appropriate amounts, plus reasonable pre-judgment interest.

Violations of Minimum Coverage or Vesting Rules by a Qualified Plan

Action: An ERISA § 502(b) action is where the Secretary of Labor, if requested by the Secretary of Treasury or by plan participants or beneficiaries, seeks equitable relief for actions or inactions (but not for delinquent contributions to qualified plans or for violations of a group health plan).

Remedy: To obtain appropriate relief.

Equitable Relief for Actions or Inactions of the Secretary of Labor

Action: An ERISA § 502(k) action is where a Plan Administrator, fiduciary, participant or beneficiary seeks to enjoin any act or practice by the Secretary of Labor.

Remedy: A temporary or permanent restraining order, a court order compelling certain actions, or any other appropriate equitable relief.

**Civil Penalties for Certain Prohibited Distributions*

Action: An ERISA § 502(m) action is where the Secretary of Labor seeks to assess a civil penalty for violation of ERISA § 206(e) (*i.e.*, prohibition of certain payments from a DB plan during periods of liquidity shortfall).

Remedy: Assessment of such civil penalties.

Please note: If ERISA preemption exists, then the plaintiff must bring a specific ERISA cause of action and is barred from bringing a state cause of action. All general rules of federal civil procedure apply to ERISA causes of action. The general rule is that no punitive damages are allowed in an ERISA cause of action. However, a few courts have become recently more interested in awarding damages in appropriate circumstances under the phrase "or other appropriate equitable relief" or under the attorney fees or court costs.

D. Importance of Plan Benefit Claims Procedures

Statutory Rules at ERISA § 503

Although ERISA is the single law for employee welfare benefit plans and for employee pension benefit plans, there is a big difference between the two types of benefits. One of the major areas where a single set of rules is viewed as inadequate is in the benefit claims procedures. An improper denial of a medical benefit has an immediate and possibly life threatening implication, whereas an improper denial of a retirement benefit can usually be cured. Through Department of Labor regulations, different time periods and procedures have been established for welfare plans and for pension benefit plans. Every plan must have a claims procedure which provides adequate notice to a participant or beneficiary that a benefit claim has been denied and which provides a reasonable opportunity, through a formal procedure, for the individual to have a full and fair review by a named fiduciary. The plaintiff must usually show that he or she exhausted all administrative remedies before he or she can sue in court.[4] Once a participant gets a final denial, then he or she may proceed to sue in court.

There are two main goals of the claims procedure: to correct mistakes, or to establish the facts and record should the case go to court. The benefit claim is generally first processed by a lower-level employee (either in the sponsoring employer's human resource department or at a third party administrator). The claims review procedure, described below, has two levels. At the first level, a colleague or higher-level employee will review the original benefit denial, and if that person agrees with the first, then the participant or beneficiary can appeal to a second-level review, where a more senior employee will review the benefit determination. Any mistakes made in the earlier determinations will likely be discovered and corrected by the time the appeal is finished. However, if a participant or beneficiary is unhappy after completing the plan's full claims procedure, then he or she can file a law suit against the plan for benefits due. The written appeals determination report will become the record that will be reviewed by the court. If the plan document contains the Firestone Tire and Rubber Company language, allowing the plan administrator to interpret any ambiguities in the plan document, then the district court's standard of review is abuse of discretion; whereas, if the plan document does not include the Firestone language, then the district court's standard of review is de novo.

---

4. Variety Children's Hospital v. Century Medical Health Plan, 57 F3d 1040 (11th Cir. 1995). However, under Labor Regs. § 2560.503-1(l), if the plan administrator fails to establish or follow claims procedures that comply with the Labor Regulations, then the participant or beneficiary is deemed to have exhausted all administrative remedies and can immediately file suit against the plan.

Every ERISA employee benefit plan shall establish and maintain reasonable procedures governing the filing of benefit claims, notification of benefit determinations, and appeal of adverse benefit determinations.[5]

First Level Review

The following requirements must be met by all ERISA plans:

- the claims procedure must comply with any Regulations;
- the Summary Plan Description must adequately describe the plan's claims procedures;
- the claims procedure itself cannot inhibit or hamper a participants rights to protest the denial of a benefit claim;
- the participant or beneficiary must be allowed to authorize a representative to act on his behalf; and
- the procedure itself must ensure that all determinations are made in accordance with the plan documents and that the plan provisions are applied consistently.

In addition, the claims procedures for group health plans must also provide that:

- the claims administrator must notify the participant or beneficiary making a pre-service claim that they failed to follow the claims procedures as soon as possible, but no later than 5 days for a normal claim and no later than 24 hours for an urgent care claim;
- no participant or beneficiary is ever required to file more than two appeals of an adverse benefit determination prior to bringing a civil action;
- arbitration or other forms of dispute resolution can be voluntarily accepted by the claimant, but, if mandatory, then it must be one of the two normal levels of review and can be challenged in a civil action.

The latter two bullet points also apply to the claims procedure for any ERISA plan that provides disability benefits.

As to the timing of denials, the plan administrator must notify the participant or beneficiary of a benefit denial as soon as possible, but no later than:

- for group health plans:
  - 72 hours for an urgent care claim in a group health plan (and if the appeal is incomplete, the plan administrator must notify the claimant as to what additional information is required within 24 hours);
  - a reasonable period of time before ongoing treatment or a number of treatments will be cut-off or denied;
  - 15 days for pre-service claims; and
  - 30 days for post-service claims;
- for disability claims, 45 days; and
- for all other ERISA employee benefit claims, 90 days for all other types of claims.

The time frames start when the participant or beneficiary files the claim, and are not tolled for days or hours that the plan sponsor is not open for business. Therefore, especially due to the time sensitivity of urgent care claims, if a small employer does not have

---

5. Labor Regs. § 2560.503-1(b).

appropriate personnel on call at all times, then the claims review should be done by the insurer or a third party.

The notification of an adverse benefit determination must:

- provide the plan administrator's specific reason(s) for the determination;
- reference the specific provisions of the plan document that support the determination;
- provide a detailed list of additional information that could be submitted for accepting the benefit claim;
- provide a description of the plan's review procedures and a statement of the claimant's right to bring a civil action under ERISA;
- in a group health plan or a plan providing disability benefits, a detailed description of the plan's internal rule, guideline, protocol or other similar criteria that justified the benefit determination or a detailed explanation of the medical necessity, experimental treatment, or similar exclusion limit that justified the determination.

The notification of an adverse benefit determination shall be delivered electronically or in writing, and communicated in a "manner calculated to be understood by the claimant;" however, if the determination is for an urgent care claim in a group health plan, then the plan administrator can provide an immediate oral communication, which would then be followed up with a proper written or electronic notification.

Second Level Review (Appeals)

In addition to the first round of notification of an adverse benefit determination, every plan shall also have a procedure in place where the participant or beneficiary can appeal the adverse determination. The appeals procedure must ensure a full and fair review where the claimant has up to 60 days to receive copies of relevant plan documents, records or other information and then to submit written comments, documents, or other information that supports his or her claim.

The appeals procedure for a group health plan also must:

- extend the period from 60 days to 180 days;
- allow the appeal to be reviewed without any deference to the original benefit determination, and ensure that an individual with at least as much seniority as the original reviewer makes a determination on the appeal;
- ensure that the individual making the determination upon appeal has the knowledge and training to make a reasonable medical decision, or is required to consult with a health care professional that has the appropriate knowledge and training;
- identify the names of all health care professionals consulted during the appeal, regardless of whether their individual advice was actually relied upon by the plan administrator;
- ensure that the health care professionals consulted during the appeal were not the individuals consulted during the original benefit determination, and that the health care professionals consulted during the appeal have at least as much seniority as those individuals consulted during the original review (if they are employed by a common employer);
- if the appeals claim involves a claim involving urgent care, there must be an expedited review process which can involve oral communications in person or via telephone.

The timing for notification of the appeals determination is similar to the timing for the original benefit determination notification, and the content is similar as well.

E. Other Issues in ERISA Litigation

An ERISA cause of action for a breach of fiduciary action must be brought by the earlier of:

- 6 years after the date of the last affirmative act or act of omission on which the fiduciary could have cured the breach; or
- 3 years after the earliest date on which the plaintiff had actual knowledge of the breach.

However, in all cases of a fiduciary breach where fraud or concealment is reasonably alleged, then the cause of action can be brought up to 6 years after the discovery of such breach or violation.[6] For civil actions other than a breach of fiduciary duty, there is no express statute of limitations. "Even though federal courts look to most closely analogous state statute of limitations for ERISA actions, federal law determines when cause of action under ERISA accrues."

An employee benefit plan may sue or be sued.[7]

The U.S. district courts have exclusive jurisdiction for ERISA causes of action (with minor exceptions). Appropriate venue is defined.[8]

Certain attorney fees and costs of action may be awarded to either party (other than for the collection of delinquent contributions).[9] Courts have developed a five factor test to determine when attorneys fees will be awarded:

1. The degree of offending party's culpability or bad faith;
2. The offending party's ability to personally pay the award;
3. Whether or not the awarding of attorneys' fees would deter others under similar circumstances;
4. The amount of benefit conferred on participants; and
5. The relative merits of the party's position.

---

6. ERISA § 413.
7. ERISA § 502(d).
8. ERISA § 502(e),
9. ERISA § 502(g).

Chapter 15

Reporting and Disclosure

Overview

What must be reported annually to the government?

- a plan must provide:
  - an annual report (*i.e.*, form 5500 and attachments); and
  - reports upon plan termination, and any other supplementary reports required by the Secretary of Labor
- there are certain "reportable events" that a qualified defined benefit plan sponsor must communicate with the PBGC to inform them that there is a greater likelihood that they might need to insure unfunded benefits

What must be disclosed to participants of any ERISA covered plan?

- All ERISA plans must provide:
  - a Summary Plan Description (SPD),
  - a Summary of Material Modifications (SMM) to the SPD when plan amendments materially modify it, and
  - a Summary Annual Report (SAR) showing a financial statement and balance sheet for the plan assets
- a plan must also provide the plan document upon request (but can charge reasonable photocopying expenses)

What are the most common communications that must be disclosed to participants of qualified retirement plans?

- benefit statements:
  - at least quarterly in a defined contribution plan with self-directed investments,
  - at least annually in other defined contribution plans, and
  - at least every three years in a defined benefit plan
- in a 401(k) plan:
  - notice of the advantages of asset portfolio diversification,
  - notice of automatic enrollment (if applicable) and notice of default investments (if applicable),
  - notice of impending black out periods,
  - notice that the plan intends to comply with a safe harbor design (if applicable), and
  - notice indicating fees that will be charged to the participant's account

A. Reporting to the Government

1. Annual Filing of Form 5500

Technical Rules Are at IRC § 6058 and ERISA §§ 104 and 4065

Each year, a Form 5500 (Annual Return/Report for Employee Benefit Plan) must be filed for most ERISA pension benefit plan and welfare benefit plan.[1] The employer or plan administrator of an ERISA plan is responsible for filing the Form 5500 return. If no administrator is named specifically in the plan, the plan sponsor (*i.e.,* the employer) is treated as the plan administrator. To reduce the potential for personal liability, individuals signing the Form 5500 should use their name and title (*e.g.,* Joe Smith, Trustee).

The plan administrator for a nonqualified Top-Hat plan does not need to file annual returns, and can instead simply file a statement with the Department of Labor that includes the name and address of the employer, the employer identification number (EIN) assigned by the Internal Revenue Service, a declaration that the employer maintains a plan or plans primarily for the purpose of providing deferred compensation for a select group of management or highly compensated employees, and a statement of the number of SERPs and the number of participants in each plan. This statement must be filed within 120 days after the plan becomes effective. The plan administrator must then provide plan documents as requested by the Department of Labor.

The complete Form 5500 annual report must be filed by the last day of the seventh calendar month after the end of the plan year. For a short plan year, the Form 5500 annual report must be filed by the last day of the seventh calendar month after the end of the short plan year. An automatic extension of time to file the Form 5500 until the due date of the federal income tax return of the employer will be granted if all of the following conditions are met:

- the plan year and the employer's tax year are the same;
- the employer has been granted an extension of time to file its federal income tax return to a date later than the normal due date for filing the Form 5500; and
- a copy of the application for extension of time to file the federal income tax return is attached to the Form 5500.

A chart in the form 5500 instructions assists the plan sponsor in understanding which schedules need to be completed and submitted with the form 5500 (which is always required for all plans that need to file a form 5500):

- Schedule A, Insurance Information—all pension plans and welfare plans that invest in insurance contracts;
- Schedule SB, Actuarial Information—all single-employer defined benefit plans or a Schedule MB, Actuarial Information—all multiemployer defined benefit plans;

---

1. The best place for guidance in completing the forms would be on the instructions for the Form 5500 for that particular year. The instructions for the current year Form 5500 are available at http://www.irs.gov/pub/irs-pdf/i5500.pdf.

- Schedule C, Service Provider Information—large pension plans and large welfare plans if a service provider was paid more than $5000 and/or an accountant or actuary was terminated;
- Schedule D, DFE/Participating Plan Information—only Direct Filing Entities, such as common trusts;
- Schedule E, ESOP Annual Information—all ESOPs
- Schedule G, Financial Transaction Schedules—certain large pension plans and large welfare plans;
- Schedule H, Financial Information—all large pension plans and large welfare plans;
- Schedule I, Financial Information for Small Plans—all small pension plans and certain small welfare plans;
- Schedule R, Retirement Plan Information—all pension plans;
- Schedule SSA, Annual Registration Statement Identifying Separated Participants With Deferred Vested Benefits—all pension plans with separated participants with deferred vested benefits; and
- Accountant's Report—all large pension plans and large welfare plans.

For plan years beginning on or after January 1, 2008, the Form 5500 is required to be filed electronically. The system is called EFAST, and information about all aspects of filing electronically are on the Department of Labor's website.

The Code and Title I of ERISA provide separate penalties for failing to file a Form 5500. The instructions to the Form 5500 series return set forth these penalties in detail. The primary sanction under the Code is $25 per day, up to $15,000 maximum, for failure to file the Form 5500. In addition, ERISA provides for a civil penalty of $1,100 per day for failing or refusing to file a complete Form 5500.

To encourage delinquent filers to come into compliance with their annual reporting obligations under ERISA, the DOL maintains the Delinquent Filer Voluntary Compliance Program (DFVC). The program allows delinquent plans to file a complete report(s), pay a reduced penalty, and bring the plan into compliance. Generally, a plan administrator that elects to participate in the DFVC program must file a complete Form 5500 for each plan year for which the administrator is seeking relief. An administrator may use either the Form 5500 issued for each plan year (or use the most current Form 5500 issued and indicate the year for which it is being filed). The form(s) must be filed with the Employee Benefits Security Administration (EBSA) at the appropriate address listed in the instructions for the most current Form 5500, or electronically in accordance with the applicable electronic filing requirements. A separate submission is required to pay the penalty. DFVC penalties may not be paid from plan assets, as plan administrators are liable personally for civil penalties. It is unclear how plan sponsors will correct once the mandatory electronic filing under EFAST is effective.

The IRS provides administrative relief from late filing penalties imposed under the Code for filers who meet the requirements of the DFVC program. Relief is granted once the plan administrator has satisfied all requirements of the program, including payment of the ERISA penalties. The IRS coordinates with the DOL in determining which filers are eligible for relief. No separate IRS application for relief is required. Relief under the notice is available only to the extent that a Form 5500 is required under Title 1 of ERISA. Thus, Form 5500-EZ filers are not subject to Title I and, thus, are not eligible to participate in the DFVC program.

2. PBGC Reportable Events for Certain Defined Benefit Plans

Statutory Rules at ERISA § 4043

Since the PBGC acts as an insurer of defined benefit plans, a defined benefit plan sponsor is required to report certain events to the PBGC that indicates any increased possibility that the PBGC will need to actually assume the liabilities. The events which must be reported at least 30 days before they actually happen are:

- Change in contributing sponsor or controlled group;
- Liquidation of contributing sponsor or controlled group member;
- Extraordinary dividend or stock redemption;
- Transfer of at least 3% of benefit liabilities;
- Application for minimum funding waiver;
- Loan default;
- Bankruptcy or similar settlement.

Other events that are reportable within 30 days after the plan administrator knows or has reason to know are:

- Disqualification of the plan by the IRS or a determination of noncompliance by the DOL;
- The plan adopts an amendment decreasing benefits payable;
- The number of active participants under a plan is reduced to less than 80 percent of the number of active participants at the beginning of the plan year, or to less than 75 percent of the number of active participants at the beginning of the previous plan year. There is a very important exception for small plans with fewer than 100 participants at the beginning of either the current or the previous plan year;
- The plan terminates or the IRS determines that there is a partial termination;
- The plan fails to make a required minimum funding payment;
- A plan is currently unable or projected to be unable to pay benefits;
- There is a distribution of more than $10,000 to a substantial owner and after the distribution the plan has vested benefits that are unfunded;
- Finally, the plan must report each time the total of unpaid balances of required payments (including interest) exceeds $1 million.[2]

The events are reported on a PBGC Form 10-Advance.

B. Disclosures to Participants and Beneficiaries

In addition to the Summary Plan Description (SPD) and Summary of Material Modifications (SMM) (as discussed in Chapter 12), the plan must also provide the following information.

---

2. ERISA § 302(f)(1).

1. Benefit Statements in a Qualified Retirement Plan

Statutory Rules at ERISA § 105

All qualified retirement plans must provide periodic pension benefit statements to participants and beneficiaries.

- In a defined contribution plan with self-directed accounts, the statements must be delivered at least once every calendar quarter;
- In a defined contribution plan without self-directed accounts, the statements must be delivered at least once every calendar year;
- In a defined benefit plan, the statements must be delivered at least once every 3 years.

Penalties of up to $100 per day apply for failure to furnish the pension benefit statement to a participant or beneficiary. The DOL has indicated that delivery within 45 days of the end of a required period will be deemed timely,[3] and that notices could be delivered electronically.

All statements must include the total benefits accrued, and the portion that are fully vested (or the earliest date on which benefits will become nonforfeitable). For defined contribution plans with self-directed accounts, the statements must also detail the value of each account balance by investment, an explanation of any restrictions on participant direction, and a statement of the importance of diversification. All statements must be written in a manner calculated to be understood by the average plan participant.

The Department of Labor has provided interim guidance allowing multiple documents to, in the aggregate, satisfy the requirements for a defined contribution plan statement. This allows a cover letter from the employer with all of the vesting information, restrictions, and any other plan-wide information, and allows all of the separate banks and financial institutions to then simply send account balances to the respective participants. Additionally, the guidance clarifies that a plan loan does not make the plan self-directed.

For defined contribution plans with self-directed accounts, the plan administrator must also provide a notice indicating the importance of diversification.

2. Summary Annual Reports

Statutory Rules at ERISA § 104

Specific information about the financial position of the pension plan, such as the plan's total assets and liabilities and annual aggregate contributions, must be provided to participants on summary annual reports and properly filed with the Department of Labor as an attachment to the Form 5500.

The SAR must contain specific information:

- for qualified defined contribution plans: financial statement for employee pension benefit plans; and the number of employees, name and address of each fiduciary, the name of and reason any person received compensation to perform services for the plan, and a reason for the change on any material plan advisor.

---

3. DOL Field Assistance Bulletin 2006-03, Q&A-3.

- for qualified defined benefit plans not subject to PBGC coverage: financial statement for employee pension benefit plans; the number of employees, name and address of each fiduciary, the name of and reason any person received compensation to perform services for the plan, and a reason for the change on any material plan advisor; an actuarial statement that summarizes the funded status of the plan; the funded percentage of each plan if there are participants or beneficiaries that have liabilities under 2 or more defined benefit plans sponsored by the employer; and additional information if the employer contributes to a multiemployer plan.

- for qualified defined benefit plans subject to PBGC coverage: information that identifies the plan and plan administrator; for a single-employer plan, a statement as to whether the plan's funding target attainment percentage for the plan year and for the 2 preceding plan years is at least 100 percent (and, if not, the actual percentages), and similar information for a multiemployer plan; for a single-employer plan, a statement of the plan assets, liabilities, prefunding balance, and funding standard carryover balance for the current year and for the 2 preceding plan years and the determination of the PBGC variable premium for the current year; and similar information for a multiemployer plan;

- for welfare plans: financial statement for employee welfare benefit plans; and the number of employees, name and address of each fiduciary, the name of and reason any person received compensation to perform services for the plan, and a reason for the change on any material plan advisor.

The SAR is due:

- for qualified defined contribution plans: not later than 210 days after the end of the plan year.

- for defined benefit plans not subject to PBGC coverage: not later than 210 days after the end of the plan year.

- for defined benefit plans subject to PBGC coverage: for large plans, not later than 120 days after the end of the plan year; and   for small plans that, on each day during the preceding plan year, had 100 or fewer participants, upon the filing of the Form 5500.

- for large welfare plans: for large plans, not later than 210 days after the end of the plan year.

No filing of the SAR is required for:

- a totally unfunded welfare plan;

- a small welfare plan which has less than 100 participants on the first day of the plan year (whether funded or not);

- an apprenticeship or other training plan;

- a Top Hat nonqualified deferred compensation plan;

- a welfare plan for a select group of management or highly compensated employees;

- a day care center;

- a dues financed welfare plan; and

- a dues financed pension plan.

As an alternative to a separate summary annual report, a copy of the annual information return for the plan, *i.e.,* Form 5500, may be provided to participants. This Form

5500 must be accompanied by a cover page indicating that this Form 5500 information is provided as a summary annual report.

3. Other Communications

There are other notices and disclosure requirements that the plan administrator must furnish to plan participants, beneficiaries or other interested parties, either when a certain event occurs at the plan level or when an interested person requests it. One of the most important communications in addition to the Summary Plan Description is providing the legal plan documents to participants and beneficiaries upon request. Upon making a written request to the administrator of an employee benefit plan, any participant in the plan or any beneficiary receiving plan benefits is entitled to receive, after paying reasonable fees, a copy of the latest updated Summary Plan Description and summaries of material modification for amendments not included in the SPD, the latest annual report, any bargaining agreement referencing the plan, and the trust agreement, contract, or other instruments under which the plan is established or operated. A plan administrator also must provide participants and beneficiaries with a copy of the plan, if so requested. The plan administrator also has a duty to disclose information and documents relating to the initial establishment or status of a plan's provisions at a time when those provisions affect a participant's rights. An employer or plan administrator that fails or refuses to comply with the request for information from a participant or beneficiary may be fined an amount up to $110 a day, payable to the participant or beneficiary.[4]

4. Acceptable Methods of Communications

Labor Regs. § 2520.104b-1. Disclosure

(a) **General disclosure requirements.** The administrator of an employee benefit plan covered by Title I of the Act must disclose certain material, including reports, statements, notices, and other documents, to participants, beneficiaries and other specified individuals. Disclosure under Title I of the Act generally takes three forms. First, the plan administrator must, by direct operation of law, furnish certain material to all participants covered under the plan and beneficiaries receiving benefits under the plan (other than beneficiaries under a welfare plan) at stated times or if certain events occur. Second, the plan administrator must furnish certain material to individual participants and beneficiaries upon their request. Third, the plan administrator must make certain material available to participants and beneficiaries for inspection at reasonable times and places.

(b) **Fulfilling the disclosure obligation.**

* * *

(c) **Disclosure through electronic media.**

(1) Except as otherwise provided by applicable law, rule or regulation, the administrator of an employee benefit plan furnishing documents

---

4. ERISA § 502(c)(1); Labor Regs. § 2575.502c-1.

through electronic media is deemed to satisfy the requirements of paragraph (b)(1) of this section with respect to an individual described in paragraph (c)(2) if:

(i) The administrator takes appropriate and necessary measures reasonably calculated to ensure that the system for furnishing documents—

(A) Results in actual receipt of transmitted information (e.g., using return-receipt or notice of undelivered electronic mail features, conducting periodic reviews or surveys to confirm receipt of the transmitted information); and

(B) Protects the confidentiality of personal information relating to the individual's accounts and benefits (e.g., incorporating into the system measures designed to preclude unauthorized receipt of or access to such information by individuals other than the individual for whom the information is intended);

(ii) The electronically delivered documents are prepared and furnished in a manner that is consistent with the style, format and content requirements applicable to the particular document;

(iii) Notice is provided to each participant, beneficiary or other individual, in electronic or non-electronic form, at the time a document is furnished electronically, that apprises the individual of the significance of the document when it is not otherwise reasonably evident as transmitted (e.g., the attached document describes changes in the benefits provided by your plan) and of the right to request and obtain a paper version of such document; and

(iv) Upon request, the participant, beneficiary or other individual is furnished a paper version of the electronically furnished documents.

* * *

Chapter 16

Plan Terminations

Overview

What is the PBGC?

- the Pension Benefit Guaranty Corporation is a "private" corporation established by ERISA and under the federal government's direct control
- basically, the PBGC collects insurance premiums from all defined benefit plans, invests the assets in a trust fund, and will pay certain guaranteed benefits to those terminated defined benefit plans which cannot meet its liabilities
- in cases where the plan itself is so poorly handled, or where the sponsoring employer is defunct or in bankruptcy, the PBGC will become trustee of the plan assets

How can a single employer defined benefit plan be terminated?

- although no employer is required to sponsor a qualified defined benefit plan, those that voluntarily do so need to meet certain requirements before the plan can be terminated
- under a standard termination, the plan has enough assets to pay out all accrued benefit liabilities—here, the plan just communicates certain information to the PBGC about the assets and liabilities, and the plan's Enrolled Actuary certifies certain aspects of the calculated liabilities (in this case, the defined benefit plan paid into the mandatory PBGC insurance system, but received absolutely nothing from it)
- under a distress termination, the plan does not have ample assets to cover its liabilities, and it is apparent that the plan never will because the sponsor is defunct or in bankruptcy (in this case, the plan sponsor asks the PBGC to become plan trustee, to distribute any remaining plan assets, and then pay the balance of guaranteed benefits to the plan participants from the general PBGC trust fund)
- under a PBGC initiated termination, the PBGC determines that the plan must terminate and the PBGC immediately becomes the trustee of all plan assets (here, the PBGC has monitored the plan and noted either negligence or willful fiduciary breaches and the PBGC will try to protect remaining the remaining assets from being mishandled further)

What is withdrawal liability?

- a multi-employer plan is a single plan to which different employers or employee organizations contribute for the benefit of their respective employees
- multi-employer plans are usually a direct result of collectively bargained employees (*i.e.*, union employees) where an individual might have several different em-

ployers throughout his or her career, but where each employer is required, through a collectively bargained agreement, to contribute a certain amount to a certain fund

- employers are not required to negotiate collectively bargained agreements, but if they do so for business reasons, then they can't just withdraw from the fund at any time

- the withdrawal liability represents the cost to a sponsoring employer if it wishes to withdraw from the fund (this helps to ensure that promised benefits will actually be funded, and also serves to prevent a domino effect of several employers withdrawing at once and leaving all liability responsibilities to the remaining employers)

- a withdrawal liability is usually paid over a period of years after the employer withdraws

- a partial withdrawal generally occurs if there is a 70% decline in contributions made by one employer, calculated over a 5 year period—here, such employer is only liable for a portion of the withdrawal liability

A. PBGC Rules for Plan Terminations

1. Single-Employer Defined Benefit Plans

Statutory Rules at ERISA § 4041

This is an extremely short chapter, but I do not want the importance of plan terminations to get lost. Yes, an employer does not otherwise need to offer retirement benefits through a qualified plan, and if it does, it voluntarily agrees to comply with all of the complicated rules in the Code and ERISA. While the plan does not necessarily need to remain in operation in perpetuity, the intention at establishment must be that it is a permanent program, and if business goals demand that it be terminated, there are special rules that must be complied with.

Title IV of ERISA only applies to the termination of single-employer defined benefit plans and the termination or withdrawal liability for multi-employer qualified plans. Title IV of ERISA is organized:

Subtitle A—Pension Benefit Guaranty Corporation (establishment, administrative rules, management of funds, collection of premiums, authority, reporting requirements to the President and to Congress, duties to plans and participants, single-employer guaranteed benefits);

Subtitle B—Coverage (*i.e.*, plans covered by PBGC)

Subtitle C—Termination of single-employer plans

Subtitle D—Liability (*i.e.*, who is responsible for payments)

Subtitle E—Special provisions for Multi employer plans

    Part 1—Employer withdrawals

    Part 2—Merger or transfer of plan assets

    Part 3—Reorganization; Minimum contribution requirement for

    multi-employer plans

Part 4—Financial assistance

Part 5—Benefits after termination

Part 6—enforcement (including civil actions)

Subtitle F—Transition rules and effective dates

Single-employer defined benefit plans can only be terminated if there are enough current assets to pay current accrued benefits, or if the sponsoring employer files for bankruptcy under one of the following three methods:

standard termination: the plan has enough assets to pay out the present value of accrued benefit liabilities. Here, the plan just communicates certain information to the PBGC about the assets and liabilities, and the plan's Enrolled Actuary certifies certain aspects of the calculated liabilities. In this case, the defined benefit plan paid into the mandatory PBGC insurance system, but received absolutely nothing from it. There are special mandatory interest and mortality assumptions that the Enrolled Actuary must use to calculate the present value of plan liabilities upon actual plan termination. The current accrued benefits can be paid out as immediate single lump sums, or the plan can purchase annuities from an insurer on the participants' behalf.

distress termination: the plan does not have ample assets to cover its liabilities, and it is apparent that the plan never will because the sponsor is defunct or in bankruptcy. In this case, the plan sponsor negotiates with the PBGC to become plan trustee, and then distributes all plan assets to the PBGC trust fund so that the PBGC can pay the guaranteed benefits (in annuity form) to the plan participants when they respectively attain the plan's normal retirement age.

PBGC initiated termination: the PBGC determines that the plan must terminate and the PBGC immediately becomes the trustee of all plan assets. Here, the PBGC has monitored the plan and noted either negligence or willful fiduciary breaches and the PBGC will try to protect the remaining assets from being mishandled further.

The Pension Benefit Guaranty Corporation is a "private" corporation established by ERISA and under the federal government's direct control. Basically, the PBGC collects insurance premiums from all defined benefit plans, invests the assets in a trust fund, and will pay certain guaranteed benefits to all participants of terminated defined benefit plans which cannot meet its liabilities. In cases where the plan itself is so poorly handled, or where the sponsoring employer is defunct or in bankruptcy, the PBGC will become trustee of the plan assets.

In the case of the termination of a single-employer plan, the plan administrator shall allocate the assets of the plan (available to provide benefits) among the participants and beneficiaries of the plan in the following order:[1]

First, to that portion of each individual's accrued benefit which is derived from the participant's contributions to the plan which were not mandatory contributions.

Second, to that portion of each individual's accrued benefit which is derived from the participant's mandatory contributions.

Third, in the case of benefits payable as an annuity—

(A) in the case of the benefit of a participant or beneficiary which was in pay status as of the beginning of the 3-year period ending on the termination date

---

1. ERISA § 4044(a).

of the plan, to each such benefit, based on the provisions of the plan (as in effect during the 5-year period ending on such date) under which such benefit would be the least,

(B) in the case of a participant's or beneficiary's benefit (other than a benefit described in subparagraph (A)) which would have been in pay status as of the beginning of such 3-year period if the participant had retired prior to the beginning of the 3-year period and if his benefits had commenced (in the normal form of annuity under the plan) as of the beginning of such period, to each such benefit based on the provisions of the plan (as in effect during the 5-year period ending on such date) under which such benefit would be the least.

For purposes of subparagraph (A), the lowest benefit in pay status during a 3-year period shall be considered the benefit in any status for such period.

Fourth—

(A) to all other benefits (if any) of individuals under the plan guaranteed under this subchapter (determined without regard to section 1322b(a) of this title), and

(B) to the additional benefits (if any) which would be determined under subparagraph (A) if section 1322(b)(5) of this title did not apply.

For purposes of this paragraph, section 1321 of this title shall be applied without regard to subsection (c) thereof.

Fifth, to all other nonforfeitable benefits under the plan.

Sixth, to all other benefits under the plan.

The plan administrator needs to file appropriate notices to the plan participants and with the PBGC and voluntarily to the IRS. If there are missing participants that cannot be located after reasonable efforts, then the plan must notify the PBGC. After a 60-day review period by the PBGC (which begins upon receipt of the completed standard termination notice), and if the termination is filed with the IRS, then after a favorable determination letter is received, the plan administrator must distribute all plan assets as lump sums or purchase annuities by the later of 180 days after the end of the PBGC's 60-day review period or 120 days after receipt of a favorable determination letter from the IRS.

2. PBGC Rules for Single-Employer Defined Contribution Plans

Defined contribution plans are not governed by the PBGC, so all that the plan administrator needs to do is file appropriate notices to the plan participants and voluntarily with the IRS.

If the defined contribution plan is abandoned or orphaned (*i.e.*, no contributions to, or distributions from, the plan have been made for a period of at least 12 consecutive months immediately preceding the date on which the determination is being made or other facts and circumstances (such as a filing by or against the plan sponsor for liquidation under title 11 of the United States Code, or communications from participants and beneficiaries regarding distributions), then a qualified termination administrator may find an individual account plan to be abandoned when, following reasonable efforts to locate or communicate with the plan sponsor, the qualified termination administrator determines that the plan sponsor no longer exists; cannot be located; or is unable to maintain the plan. The qualified termination administrator holds assets of the plan that is considered abandoned and must be eligible to serve as a trustee or issuer of an IRA.

3. PBGC Rules for Multi-Employer Defined Benefit Plans

Statutory Rules at ERISA § 4201

A multi-employer plan is a single plan to which different employers or employee organizations contribute for the benefit of their "employees." Multi-employer plans are usually a direct result of collectively bargained employees (*i.e.*, union employees) where an individual might have several different "employers" throughout his or her career, but where each employer is required, through a collectively bargained agreement, to contribute a certain amount to a certain fund.

Employers are not required to negotiate collectively bargained agreements, but if they do so for business reasons, then they can't just withdraw from the fund at any time. The withdrawal liability represents the "cost" to a sponsoring employer if it wishes to withdraw from the fund. This helps to ensure that promised benefits will actually be funded, and also serves to prevent a domino effect of several employers withdrawing at once and leaving all liability responsibilities to the remaining employers. A withdrawal liability is usually paid over a period of years after the employer withdraws.

A partial withdrawal generally occurs if there is a 70% decline in contributions made by one employer, calculated over a 5 year period. Here, such employer is only liable for a portion of the withdrawal liability.

If a plan is adequately funded, the employer which actually leaves or is deemed to partially leave may not be assessed any withdrawal liability, at the sole discretion of the plan trustees. It is the responsibility of the plan trustees to monitor all contributing employers, and determine whether a withdrawal liability or a partial withdrawal liability is due. The trustees of a multi-employer plan generally consist of several individuals elected from the union, several elected from among the contributing employers, and many full time employees of the fund.

B. IRS Rules for Termination of All Qualified Plans

There are no mandatory rules under the Code for plan terminations, but penalties can be imposed if the plan was not fully compliant. The IRS can go after the individual business owners to collect penalties, especially after the plan distributes all assets as current benefits (whether the individual has retired or not).

1. Procedures to Terminate

Just like a determination letter for the initial qualification of a plan document, a determination request for a plan termination is voluntary. However, it is highly recommended. To do so, the plan files a form 5310 to the IRS to request a final determination letter, and must provide the necessary notices to plan participants in advance of the filing of the request.

Once the plan has been terminated, then all accounts in a defined contribution plan or all accrued benefits in a defined benefit plan are immediately 100% vested. In a defined contribution plan, all of the assets will necessarily be distributed to plan participants. In a defined benefit plan, if there are extra assets after the present value of all fully vested accrued benefits have been paid, then either the balance can be allocated in a nondiscriminatory manner to increase everyone's benefits, or the excess can revert back to the employer, even though a 50% penalty tax will be assessed, or a 20% penalty tax if the reversion is used to fund a replacement plan.[2]

To remain terminated, all plan assets must be distributed as soon as administratively feasible.

Revenue Ruling 89-87

Wasting trusts: terminating plan.

A qualified plan under which benefit accruals have ceased is not terminated if assets of the plan remain in the plan's related trust rather than being distributed as soon as administratively feasible. Rev. Rul. 69-157 clarified and Rev. Rul. 79-237 modified.

ISSUE

Is a pension, profit-sharing, or stock bonus plan terminated if, after an amendment is adopted to terminate the plan, the assets are not distributed as soon as administratively feasible, but are held in the plan's trust which remains in effect in order to make distributions when employees become entitled to payments under the terms of the plan as they exist when the amendment is adopted?

FACTS

For several years before 1988, Plan A was maintained as a qualified plan. In 1987, actions were taken to terminate the plan as of December 31, 1987. All benefit accruals ceased and participants were fully vested in their accrued benefits. However, the plan's trust remained in existence in order to pay benefits when due under the terms of Plan A, on and after plan participants attained the ages necessary for early or normal retirement benefits. The assets of Plan A were not distributed as soon as administratively feasible following the date of plan termination as specified for the plan.

LAW

Section 401(a) of the Internal Revenue Code provides that a trust created or organized in the United States and forming part of a qualified stock bonus, pension, or profit-sharing plan of an employer shall constitute a qualified trust only if the various requirements set out in section 401(a) are met.

Section 501(a) of the Code provides that an organization described in section 401(a) (that is, a trust which is part of a qualified pension, profit-sharing or stock bonus plan) is exempt from taxation.

---

2. IRC § 4980.

Section 1.411(d)-2(c) of the Income Tax Regulations provides that, for purposes of section 411, a plan to which Title IV of the Employee Retirement Income Security Act of 1974 (ERISA) applies is considered terminated as of a particular date if as of that date it was terminated under section 4041 or 4042 of ERISA. Section 1.411(d)-2(c) also provides that a plan that is not subject to Title IV is considered terminated on a particular date if, as of that date, it is voluntarily terminated by the employer or employers maintaining the plan.

Rev. Rul. 69-157, 1969-1 C.B. 115, provides that a trust that is part of a qualified plan will not retain its qualified status after the plan has been terminated. Rev. Rul. 69-157 also provides that a plan is not considered terminated in fact where the plan continues in effect until all the assets have been distributed to participants in accordance with the terms of the plan.

Section 1.416-1, T-4, of the regulations defines a terminated plan as one which has been formally terminated, under which crediting service has ceased for vesting and benefit accruals and under which plan assets have been, or are being, distributed as soon as is administratively feasible. Section 1.416-1, T-5, provides that under a plan for which the assets are not distributed as soon as administratively feasible, minimum contributions or benefit accruals are required under section 416 of the Code.

Section 1.401(a)-20, Q, of the regulations provides that a terminated or frozen plan is subject to the survivor annuity requirements of sections 401(a)(11) and 417 of the Code, unless such plan was terminated prior to September 17, 1985 and all assets were distributed as soon as administratively feasible after the termination date.

Rev. Rul. 79-237, 1979-2 C.B. 190, holds that, once applicable, the minimum funding standards described in section 412 of the Code apply to a pension plan through the date of its termination. Rev. Rul. 79-237 defines the date of termination for plans subject to Title IV as the date described in section 4048 of ERISA.

ANALYSIS

In order to terminate a qualified plan, the date of termination must be established, the benefits of plan participants and other liabilities under the plan must be determined with respect to the date of plan termination, and all plan assets must be distributed to satisfy those liabilities in accordance with the terms of the plan as soon as administratively feasible after the date of termination. Generally, the date of plan termination for a single-employer plan under Title IV of ERISA, will be the date of plan termination for purposes of the Code. In addition, a single-employer plan to which Title IV applies that has not been terminated under Title IV, even though its assets have been distributed, will not have terminated for purposes of the Code. A plan that is amended to terminate and to cease benefit accruals has not, in fact, been terminated under the Code if the assets are not distributed as soon as <Page 82> administratively feasible after the stated date of plan termination, regardless of whether the plan is treated as terminated under other federal law, including Title IV of ERISA. Termination of a multi-employer plan under Title IV of ERISA generally does not result in plan assets being distributed as soon as administratively feasible after the date of plan termination under Title IV. Accordingly, such a plan will not be treated as terminated under section 401(a) of the Code and will have to continue to meet the requirements of section 401(a) to retain its qualified status. In the case of a single-employer plan that is terminated for purposes of Title IV, if plan assets are not distributed as soon as administratively feasible after the date of plan termination under Title IV, the plan will not be treated as terminated for purposes of the Code, except that the plan will be considered as terminated for purposes of section 1.411(d)-2(c) of the regulations. Thus, for example, a plan which is terminated for purposes of Title IV, but under which plan assets are not distributed as soon as administratively feasible, will not be terminated for purposes of Rev. Rul. 79-237 for determining the applicability of the minimum funding standard to such plans.

Whether a distribution is made as soon as administratively feasible is to be determined under all the facts and circumstances of the given case but, generally, a distribution which is not completed within one year following the date of plan termination specified by the employer will be presumed not to have been made as soon as administratively feasible. A plan under which all assets are not distributed as soon as administratively feasible is an ongoing plan and must meet the requirements of section 401(a) of the Code, in order to continue its qualified status. Such a plan remains subject to the minimum funding requirements of section 412, where applicable. Also, in any year in which the trust assets have not been distributed, the plan is subject to the information reporting requirements of sections 6057 and 6058 and, in the case of a defined benefit plan, the actuarial reporting requirements of section 6059.

In this case, Plan A was not in fact terminated when benefit accruals ceased because distributions were not made as soon as administratively feasible thereafter but were delayed until the participants became entitled to receive distributions under the terms of the plan as they existed when the benefit accruals ceased.

HOLDING

A pension, profit-sharing or stock bonus plan, under which benefit accruals have ceased, is not terminated if, after an amendment is adopted to terminate the plan, the plan assets are not distributed as soon as administratively feasible but are held in the trust which remains in existence in order to make distributions when employees become entitled to receive payments as provided under the terms of the plan as they exist when the amendment is adopted. This revenue ruling does not consider whether the cessation of benefit accruals results in a partial termination within the meaning of section 1.411(d)-2 of the regulations.

EFFECT ON OTHER REVENUE RULINGS

Rev. Rul. 69-157 is clarified.

Rev. Rul. 79-237 is modified to provide that for purposes of that revenue ruling, a termination will not occur if plan assets are not distributed as soon as administratively feasible, even if the plan is terminated under Title IV of ERISA.

* * *

2. Frozen Plans and Partial Plan Terminations

A plan can be amended to freeze any further accruals, but not to actually terminate (thus anticipating that sometime in the future an amendment will undo the freeze). However a frozen plan is considered an ongoing plan, and must continually be amended and updated for changes in the law, must continually be operated in accordance with the qualification rules and plan document, and must annually file a form 5500.

There is also a concept of a partial plan termination, where those employees who are involuntarily terminated are fully vested. There is no hard and fast rule for the exact percentage of the workforce, but regulations provide some of the factors or situations:

- The termination of a group of employees formerly covered under the plan;
- A plan amendment excluding a group of employees who have previously been covered;
- A plan amendment that adversely affects the rights of employees to vest in benefits under the plan; or
- In a defined benefit plan, the reduction or cessation of future benefit accruals resulting in a potential reversion to the employer.

Revenue Ruling 2007-43

Minimum vesting standards—partial termination—constructive termination.

In situation where 23% of employees severed employment with employer due to closure of one of employer's locations and were no longer active participants in employer's defined contribution plan, IRS found that partial plan termination had occurred. IRS noted that 20% employee turnover rate creates presumption of partial termination, but that facts and circumstances test might indicate that turnover of 20% or more is routine for employer and wouldn't lead to conclusion that plan was partially terminated. In this scenario, 23% turnover wasn't routine but was caused by shutdown at one location, so partial termination had occurred.

ISSUE

Is there a partial termination of a plan under § 411(d)(3) of the Internal Revenue Code under the facts described in this revenue ruling?

FACTS

Employer X maintains Plan A, a defined contribution plan qualified under § 401(a). The plan year for Plan A is the calendar year. The plan participants include both current and former employees. Plan A provides that an employee of Employer X has a fully vested and nonforfeitable interest in his or her account balance upon either completion of 3 years of service or attainment of age 65. The plan also provides for each participant to have a fully vested and nonforfeitable right to his or her account balance upon the plan's termination or upon a partial termination of the plan that affects the participant.

Employer X ceases operations at one of its four business locations. As a result, 23 percent of the Plan A participants who are employees of Employer X cease active participation in Plan A due to a severance from employment (excluding any severance from employment that is either on account of death or disability, or retirement on or after normal retirement age) during the plan year. Some of these participants are fully vested due to having completed 3 years of service or having attained age 65. Plan A is not terminated.

LAW

Section 411(d)(3) provides in relevant part that a plan will not be qualified unless the plan provides that, upon its partial termination, the rights of all affected employees to benefits accrued to the date of such partial termination, to the extent funded on that date, or the amounts credited to their accounts, are nonforfeitable.

Section 1.411(d)-2(b)(1) of the Income Tax Regulations provides that whether or not a partial termination of a qualified plan occurs (and the time of such event) is determined by the Commissioner with regard to all the facts and circumstances in a particular case. The facts and circumstances include the exclusion, by reason of a plan amendment or severance by the employer, of a group of employees who have previously been covered by the plan, as well as plan amendments that adversely affect the rights of employees to vest in benefits under the plan.

Section 1.411(d)-2(b)(2) provides a special rule with respect to a defined benefit plan that ceases or decreases future benefit accruals under the plan. A partial termination is deemed to occur if a potential reversion to the employer maintaining the plan is created or increased as a result of such cessation or decrease. This special rule does not apply to defined contribution plans.

Section 1.411(d)-2(b)(3) provides that, if a termination occurs, § 411(d)(3) only applies to the part of the plan that is terminated.

In Rev. Rul. 73-284, 1973-2 C.B. 139, an employer established a qualified pension plan that covered all of its 15 employees. The employer later acquired a new business location 100 miles away and closed the original one. All employees were given the opportunity to transfer to the new location and continue to participate in the plan, but only 3 chose to do so. The other 12 employees were discharged and their participation under the plan ended. The employer hired replacements for them at the new location. The revenue ruling concludes that there was a partial termination due to the termination of these employees in connection with the change in business location.

In Rev. Rul. 81-27, 1981-1 C.B. 228, the employer established a qualified defined benefit pension plan that covered employees in the two divisions of its businesses. The plan covered 165 employees. The employer closed down one division and terminated 95 participants. The revenue ruling concludes that the discharge by the employer of 95 of 165 participants constituted a partial termination.

Weil v. Terson Co. Retirement Plan Administrative Committee, 933 F.2d 106 [67 AFTR 2d 91-1131] (2d Cir. 1991), holds that the turnover rate in both vested and nonvested participants is taken into account in determining whether there has been a reduction in the workforce that constitutes a partial termination for purposes of § 411(d)(3). See 933 F.2d at 110.

Matz v. Household International Tax Reduction Investment Plan, 388 F.3d 570 [94 AFTR 2d 2004-6781] (7 Cir. 2004), holds that there is a rebuttable presumption that a 20 percent or greater reduction in plan participants is a partial termination for purposes of § 411(d)(3). The court holds that this presumption is rebuttable depending on other facts and circumstances. See 388 F.3d at 578. The court, relying on Weil, bases the 20 percent calculation on the ratio of those participants who lose coverage, whether or not vested, to all participants, whether or not vested.

ANALYSIS

Based on the foregoing, whether a partial termination of a plan under §411(d)(3) has occurred depends on the facts and circumstances, including the extent to which participating employees have had a severance from employment. If the turnover rate is at least 20 percent, there is a presumption that a partial termination of the plan has occurred. The turnover rate is determined by dividing the number of participating employees who had an employer-initiated severance from employment during the applicable period by the sum of all of the participating employees at the start of the applicable period and the employees who became participants during the applicable period. The applicable period depends on the circumstances: the applicable period is a plan year (or, in the case of a plan year that is less than 12 months, the plan year plus the immediately preceding plan year) or a longer period if there are a series of related severances from employment.

All participating employees are taken into account in calculating the turnover rate, including vested as well as nonvested participating employees. Employer-initiated severance from employment generally includes any severance from employment other than a severance that is on account of death, disability, or retirement on or after normal retirement age. An employee's severance from employment is employer-initiated even if caused by an event outside of the employer's control, such as severance due to depressed economic conditions. In certain situations, the employer may be able to verify that an employee's severance was not employer-initiated. A claim that a severance from employment was purely voluntary can be supported through items such as information from personnel files, employee statements, and other corporate records.

Employees who have had a severance from employment with the employer maintaining the plan on account of a transfer to a different controlled group are not considered as having a severance from employment for purposes of calculating the turnover rate if those employees continue to be covered by a plan that is a continuation of the plan under which they were previously covered (i.e., if a portion of the plan covering those employees was spun off from the plan in accordance with the rules of §414(l) and will continue to be maintained by the new employer).

Whether or not a partial termination of a qualified plan occurs on account of participant turnover (and the time of such event) depends on all the facts and circumstances in a particular case. Facts and circumstances indicating that the turnover rate for an applicable period is routine for the employer favor a finding that there is no partial termination for that applicable period. For this purpose, information as to the turnover rate in other periods and the extent to which terminated employees were actually replaced, whether the new employees performed the same functions, had the same job classification or title, and received comparable compensation are relevant to determining whether the turnover is routine for the employer. Thus, there are a number of factors that are relevant to determining whether a partial termination has occurred as a result of turnover, both in the case where a partial termination is presumed to have occurred due to the turnover rate being at least 20 percent and in the case where the turnover rate is less than 20 percent.

In the present case, there is a presumption that a partial termination has occurred because the turnover rate is 20 percent or more. The facts and circumstances support the finding of a partial termination because the severances from employment occurred as a result of the shutdown of one of the employer's business locations (and not as a result of routine turnover). Therefore, a partial termination of Plan A has occurred.

If a partial termination occurs on account of turnover during an applicable period, all participating employees who had a severance from employment during the period must be fully vested in their accrued benefits, to the extent funded on that date, or in the amounts credited to their accounts.

A partial termination of a qualified plan can also occur for reasons other than turnover. For example, a partial termination can occur due to plan amendments that adversely affect the rights of employees to vest in benefits under the plan, plan amendments that exclude a group of employees who have previously been covered by the plan, or the reduction or cessation of future benefit accruals resulting in a potential reversion to the employer.

HOLDING

Under the facts described in this revenue ruling, a partial termination has occurred.

Chapter 17

Role of the Department of Labor

Overview

Which group within the DOL has jurisdiction over ERISA retirement and health and welfare benefit plans?
- the Employee Benefits Security Administration

What does the EBSA group do?
- they audit ERISA plans for both criminal and civil violations of reporting and disclosure and fiduciary issues (as well as the continuation and the portability and accountability in group health plans)
- they receive calls from plan participants and assist them in understanding their rights under ERISA
- they try to educate plan sponsors and fiduciaries of their obligations under ERISA

What forms of guidance does EBSA provide?
- as an executive agency, they interpret statutory provisions, through regulations, field advisory opinions, and other promulgated guidance
- they have jurisdiction to grant individual transactions between an ERISA plan and a party in interest to proceed with the transaction even though it is statutorily prohibited (and they can extend that PT Exemption to a whole class of parties in)

How does EBSA protect the rights provided to employees under ERISA?
- in some litigation, the Secretary of Labor has the authority to stand in the shoes of a disgruntled participant and actually use its full resources to be a party in civil litigation
- more often than not, however, the EBSA can offer to file an *amicus curie* brief in litigation to show its interpretation of the participant's legal arguments

How does EBSA ensure proper reporting and disclosure?
- EBSA has been designated as the single agency to receive the annual form 5500 reporting form (and attachments), and once processed, shares the information with the IRS and PBGC

A. Organization of the DOL

According to the mission statement on its website:[1] The Department of Labor fosters and promotes the welfare of the job seekers, wage earners, and retirees of the United States by improving their working conditions, advancing their opportunities for profitable employment, protecting their retirement and health care benefits, helping employers find workers, strengthening free collective bargaining, and tracking changes in employment, prices, and other national economic measurements. In carrying out this mission, the Department administers a variety of Federal labor laws including those that guarantee workers' rights to safe and healthful working conditions; a minimum hourly wage and overtime pay; freedom from employment discrimination; unemployment insurance; and other income support.

The Department of Labor (DOL) administers and enforces more than 180 federal laws. These mandates and the regulations that implement them cover many workplace activities for about 10 million employers and 125 million workers.

As pension professionals, we are primarily interested in the Employee Benefit Security Administration (EBSA). The Employee Retirement Income Security Act (ERISA) regulates employers who offer pension or welfare benefit plans for their employees. Title I of ERISA is administered by the Employee Benefits Security Administration (EBSA) (formerly the Pension and Welfare Benefits Administration) and imposes a wide range of fiduciary, disclosure and reporting requirements on fiduciaries of pension and welfare benefit plans and on others having dealings with these plans. These provisions preempt many similar state laws. Under Title IV, certain employers and plan administrators must fund an insurance system to protect certain kinds of retirement benefits, with premiums paid to the federal government's Pension Benefit Guaranty Corporation (PBGC). EBSA also administers reporting requirements for continuation of health-care provisions, required under the Comprehensive Omnibus Budget Reconciliation Act of 1986 (COBRA) and the health care portability requirements on group plans under the Health Insurance Portability and Accountability Act (HIPAA).

Other important divisions of the Department of Labor include:

Wages and Hours

The Fair Labor Standards Act (FLSA) prescribes standards for wages and overtime pay, which affect most private and public employment. The act is administered by the Wage and Hour Division of the Employment Standards Administration (ESA). It requires employers to pay covered employees who are not otherwise exempt from at least the federal minimum wage and overtime pay of one-and-one-half-times the regular rate of pay. For nonagricultural operations, it restricts the hours that children under age 16 can work and forbids the employment of children under age 18 in certain jobs deemed too dangerous. For agricultural operations, it prohibits the employment of children under age 16 during school hours and in certain jobs deemed too dangerous. The Wage and Hour Division also enforces the labor standards provisions of the Immigration and Nationality Act

---

1. www.dol.gov.

(INA) that apply to aliens authorized to work in the U.S. under certain nonimmigrant visa programs (H-1B, H-1B1, H-1C, H2A).

Workplace Safety and Health

The Occupational Safety and Health (OSH) Act is administered by the Occupational Safety and Health Administration (OSHA). Safety and health conditions in most private industries are regulated by OSHA or OSHA-approved state programs, which also cover public sector employers. Employers covered by the OSH Act must comply with the regulations and the safety and health standards promulgated by OSHA. Employers also have a general duty under the OSH Act to provide their employees with work and a workplace free from recognized, serious hazards. OSHA enforces the Act through workplace inspections and investigations. Compliance assistance and other cooperative programs are also available.

Workers' Compensation: The Longshore and Harbor Workers' Compensation Act (LHWCA), administered by ESA's Office of Workers Compensation Programs (OWCP), provides for compensation and medical care to certain maritime employees (including a longshore worker or other person in longshore operations, and any harbor worker, including a ship repairer, shipbuilder, and shipbreaker) and to qualified dependent survivors of such employees who are disabled or die due to injuries that occur on the navigable waters of the United States, or in adjoining areas customarily used in loading, unloading, repairing or building a vessel.

The Energy Employees Occupational Illness Compensation Program Act (EEOICPA) is a compensation program that provides a lump-sum payment of $150,000 and prospective medical benefits to employees (or certain of their survivors) of the Department of Energy and its contractors and subcontractors as a result of cancer caused by exposure to radiation, or certain illnesses caused by exposure to beryllium or silica incurred in the performance of duty, as well as for payment of a lump-sum of $50,000 and prospective medical benefits to individuals (or certain of their survivors) determined by the Department of Justice to be eligible for compensation as uranium workers under section 5 of the Radiation Exposure Compensation Act (RECA).

The Federal Employees' Compensation Act (FECA), 5 U.S.C. 8101 et seq., establishes a comprehensive and exclusive workers' compensation program which pays compensation for the disability or death of a federal employee resulting from personal injury sustained while in the performance of duty. The FECA, administered by ESA's OWCP, provides benefits for wage loss compensation for total or partial disability, schedule awards for permanent loss or loss of use of specified members of the body, related medical costs, and vocational rehabilitation.

The Black Lung Benefits Act (BLBA) provides monthly cash payments and medical benefits to coal miners totally disabled from pneumoconiosis ("black lung disease") arising from their employment in the nation's coal mines. The statute also provides monthly benefits to a deceased miner's survivors if the miner's death was due to black lung disease.

Unions and Their Members

The Labor-Management Reporting and Disclosure Act (LMRDA) of 1959 (also known as the Landrum-Griffin Act) deals with the relationship between a union and its members. It protects union funds and promotes union democracy by requiring labor organizations to file annual financial reports, by requiring union officials, employers, and labor consultants to file reports regarding certain labor relations practices, and by establishing standards for the election of union officers. The act is administered by the Office of Labor-Management Standards (OLMS), which is part of ESA.

Employee Protection

Most labor and public safety laws and many environmental laws mandate whistle-blower protections for employees who complain about violations of the law by their employers. Remedies can include job reinstatement and payment of back wages. OSHA enforces the whistleblower protections in most laws.

Uniformed Services Employment and Reemployment Rights Act

Certain persons who serve in the armed forces have a right to reemployment with the employer they were with when they entered service. This includes those called up from the reserves or National Guard. These rights are administered by the Veterans' Employment and Training Service (VETS).

Employee Polygraph Protection Act

This law bars most employers from using lie detectors on employees, but permits polygraph tests only in limited circumstances. It is administered by the Wage and Hour Division.

Garnishment of Wages

Garnishment of employee wages by employers is regulated under the Consumer Credit Protection Act (CPCA) which is administered by the Wage and Hour Division.

The Family and Medical Leave Act

Administered by the Wage and Hour Division, the Family and Medical Leave Act (FMLA) requires employers of 50 or more employees to give up to 12 weeks of unpaid, job-protected leave to eligible employees for the birth or adoption of a child or for the serious illness of the employee or a spouse, child or parent.

Veterans' Preference

Veterans and other eligible persons have special employment rights with the federal government. They are provided preference in initial hiring and protection in reductions in force. Claims of violation of these rights are investigated by the Veterans' Employment and Training Service (VETS).

Government Contracts, Grants, or Financial Aid

Recipients of government contracts, grants or financial aid are subject to wage, hour, benefits, and safety and health standards under:

> The Davis-Bacon Act, which requires payment of prevailing wages and benefits to employees of contractors engaged in federal government construction projects;

The McNamara-O'Hara Service Contract Act, which sets wage rates and other labor standards for employees of contractors furnishing services to the federal government;

The Walsh-Healey Public Contracts Act, which requires payment of minimum wages and other labor standards by contractors providing materials and supplies to the federal government.

Administration and enforcement of these laws are by ESA's Wage and Hour Division. ESA's Office of Federal Contract Compliance Programs (OFCCP) administers and enforces three federal contract-based civil rights laws that require most federal contractors and subcontractors, as well as federally assisted construction contractors, to provide equal employment opportunity. The Office of the Assistant Secretary for Administration and Management's (OASAM) Civil Rights Center administers and enforces several federal assistance based civil rights laws requiring recipients of federal financial assistance from Department of Labor to provide equal opportunity.

Migrant and Seasonal Agricultural Workers

The Migrant and Seasonal Agricultural Worker Protection Act (MSPA) regulates the hiring and employment activities of agricultural employers, farm labor contractors, and associations using migrant and seasonal agricultural workers. The Act prescribes wage protections, housing and transportation safety standards, farm labor contractor registration requirements, and disclosure requirements. ESA's Wage and Hour Division administers this law.

The Fair Labor Standards Act (FLSA) exempts agricultural workers from overtime premium pay, but requires the payment of the minimum wage to workers employed on larger farms (farms employing more than approximately seven full-time workers). The Act has special child-labor regulations that apply to agricultural employment; children under 16 are forbidden to work during school hours and in certain jobs deemed too dangerous. Children employed on their families' farms are exempt from these regulations. ESA's Wage and Hour Division administers this law. OSHA also has special safety and health standards that may apply to agricultural operations.

The Immigration and Nationality Act (INA) requires employers who want to use foreign temporary workers on H-2A visas to get a labor certificate from the Employment and Training Administration certifying that there are not sufficient, able, willing and qualified U.S. workers available to do the work. The labor standards protections of the H-2A program are enforced by ESA's Wage and Hour Division.

Mine Safety and Health

The Federal Mine Safety and Health Act of 1977 (Mine Act) covers all people who work on mine property. The Mine Safety and Health Administration (MSHA) administers this Act. The Mine Act holds mine operators responsible for the safety and health of miners; provides for the setting of mandatory safety and health standards, mandates miners' training requirements; prescribes penalties for violations; and enables inspectors to close dangerous mines. The safety and health standards address numerous hazards including roof falls, flammable and explosive gases, fire, electricity, equipment rollovers and maintenance, airborne contaminants, noise, and respirable dust. MSHA enforces safety and health requirements at more than 13,000 mines, investigates mine accidents, and offers mine operators training, technical and compliance assistance.

Construction

Several agencies administer programs related solely to the construction industry. OSHA has special occupational safety and health standards for construction; ESA's Wage and Hour Division, under Davis-Bacon and related acts, requires payment of prevailing wages and benefits; ESA's Office of Federal Contract Compliance Programs enforces Executive Order 11246, which requires federal construction contractors and subcontractors, as well as federally assisted construction contractors, to provide equal employment opportunity; the anti-kickback section of the Copeland Act precludes a federal contractor from inducing any employee to sacrifice any part of the compensation required.

Transportation

Most laws with labor provisions regulating the transportation industry are administered by agencies outside the Department of Labor. However, longshoring and maritime industry safety and health standards are issued and enforced by OSHA. The Longshoring and Harbor Workers' Compensation Act (LHWCA), administered by ESA, requires employers to assure that workers' compensation is funded and available to eligible employees. In addition, the rights of employees in the mass transit industry are protected when federal funds are used to acquire, improve, or operate a transit system. Under the Federal Transit law, the Department of Labor is responsible for approving employee protection arrangements before the department of Transportation can release funds to grantees.

Plant Closings and Layoffs

Such occurrences may be subject to the Worker Adjustment and Retraining Notification Act (WARN). WARN offers employees early warning of impending layoffs or plant closings. The Employment and Training Administration (ETA) provides information to the public on WARN, though neither ETA nor the Department of Labor has administrative responsibility for the statute, which is enforced through private action in the federal courts.

B. Employee Benefits Security Administration

1. Organization of EBSA

EBSA oversees nearly 700,000 private-sector retirement plans, approximately 2.5 million health plans, and other welfare benefit plans that provide benefits to approximately 150 million Americans. These plans include assets of approximately $6 trillion (as of June 30, 2008). Basically, EBSA oversees the administration, regulation and enforcement of Title I of the Employee Retirement Income Security Act of 1974 (ERISA). According to their mission statement, EBSA is there to:

- Deter and correct violations of the relevant statutes through strong administrative, civil and criminal enforcement efforts to ensure workers receive promised benefits;
- Develop policies and regulations that encourage the growth of employment-based benefits;

- Assist workers in getting the information they need to exercise their benefit rights; and
- Assist plan officials to understand the requirements of the relevant statutes in order to meet their legal responsibilities.

2. Enforcement

If an investigation reveals a violation of the civil provisions of ERISA, EBSA takes action to obtain correction of the violation. It is EBSA's policy to promote voluntary compliance with ERISA whenever possible. Making corrections to plans includes paying amounts to restore losses, disgorging profits, and paying penalty amounts (when applicable). Labor Department attorneys work with field offices to provide every opportunity for fiduciaries to comply with ERISA. If the persons involved take the proper corrective action, the department will not bring a civil lawsuit with regard to the issues involved. When voluntary compliance is not achieved, EBSA may refer a case to Labor Department attorneys for litigation. Plan assets recovered by EBSA go directly back to the plans and participants involved. See the agency's results fact sheet for the enforcement accomplishments for the last fiscal year.

An important aspect (and metric of success) of EBSA governance is the monetary results, which, for FY 2008, were $1.2 billion ($730.5 million from Prohibited Transactions corrected and plan assets protected; $481.6 million from plan assets restored and participant benefits recovered; and $8.7 million from the voluntary fiduciary correction program). Overall, EBSA's results (below) demonstrate a strong, fair, and effective program that protects the benefits of America's workers and retirees.

Civil Investigations

In FY 2008, EBSA closed 3,570 civil investigations, with 2,696 (75.52%) resulting in monetary results for plans or other corrective action. EBSA often pursues voluntary compliance as a means to correct violations and restore losses to employee benefit plans. However, in cases where voluntary compliance efforts have failed, or which involve issues for which voluntary compliance is not appropriate, EBSA forwards a recommendation to the Solicitor of Labor that litigation be initiated. In FY 2008, 205 cases were referred for litigation. Together, EBSA and the Solicitor of Labor determine which cases are appropriate for litigation, considering the ability to obtain meaningful relief through litigation, cost of litigation, viability of other enforcement options, and agency enforcement priorities. EBSA cases referred to the Solicitor's office for litigation are often resolved, with monetary payments, short of litigation. Nationwide in FY 2008, litigation was filed in 91 civil cases.

Examples of civil wrongdoing include:
- Failing to operate the plan prudently and for the exclusive benefit of participants;
- Using plan assets to benefit certain related parties to the plan, including the plan administrator, the plan sponsor, and parties related to these individuals;
- Failing to properly value plan assets at their current fair market value, or to hold plan assets in trust;
- Failing to follow the terms of the plan (unless inconsistent with ERISA);
- Failing to properly select and monitor service providers; and

- Taking any adverse action against an individual for exercising his or her rights under the plan (*e.g.*, being fired, fined, or otherwise being discriminated against).

Criminal Investigations

EBSA has responsibility to investigate potential violations of the criminal provisions of ERISA and those provisions of Title 18 of the United States Code that relate to employee benefit plans. EBSA conducts most of its criminal investigations under the direction of the United States Attorney for the jurisdiction. Other investigations are conducted in consultation with the appropriate state or local law enforcement authority. Criminal investigations are often conducted jointly with other federal and state law enforcement agencies. In FY 2008, EBSA closed 212 criminal investigations. EBSA's criminal investigations, as well as its participation in criminal investigations with other law enforcement agencies, led to the indictment of 101 individuals—including plan officials, corporate officers, and service providers—for offenses related to employee benefit plans.

Title 18 of the U.S. Code contains three statutes which directly address violations involving employee benefit plans:

- Theft or Embezzlement from Employee Benefit Plan (18 U.S.C. Section 664);
- False Statements or Concealment of Facts in Relation to Documents Required by the Employee Retirement Income Security Act of 1974 (18 U.S.C. Section 1027); and
- Offer, Acceptance, or Solicitation to Influence Operations of Employee Benefit Plan (18 U.S.C. Section 1954).

ERISA also contains the following criminal provisions:

- Section 411, Prohibition Against Certain Persons Holding Certain Positions;
- Section 501, Willful Violation of Title I, Part 1; and
- Section 511, Coercive Interference. Persons convicted of violations enumerated in section 411 are subject to a bar from holding plan positions or providing services to plans for up to 13 years.

Decisions made by EBSA to seek criminal action turn on a number of factors including:

- The egregiousness and magnitude of the violation;
- The desirability and likelihood of incarceration both as a deterrent and as a punishment; and
- Whether the case involves a prior ERISA violator.

Voluntary Compliance

EBSA's Voluntary Fiduciary Correction Program (VFCP) and Delinquent Filer Voluntary Compliance Program (DFVCP) encourage the correction of violations of ERISA by providing significant incentives for fiduciaries and others to self-correct. The VFCP allows plan officials who have identified certain violations of ERISA to take corrective action to remedy the breaches and voluntarily report the violations to EBSA, without becoming the subject of an enforcement action. In FY 2008, EBSA received 1,658 applications for the VFCP. The DFVCP encourages plan administrators to bring their plans into compliance with ERISA's filing requirements. More than 2,200 annual reports were received each month in FY 2008. An online filing and payment option added during FY 2008 has made the program even easier to use.

Informal Complaint Resolution

When workers experience a problem with an employee benefit plan, EBSA has proven effective in resolving their requests for assistance. In FY 2008, EBSA's Benefits Advisors handled nearly 175,000 inquiries and recovered $139.2 million in benefits on behalf of workers and their families through informal resolution of individual complaints. Many of the inquiries were received via EBSA's toll-free number: 1.866.444.EBSA (3272) and Web site: www.askebsa.dol.gov. These inquiries are also a major source of enforcement leads. When EBSA becomes aware of repeated complaints with respect to a particular plan, employer, or service provider, or when there is information indicating a suspected fiduciary breach, the matter is referred for investigation. In FY 2008, 871 new investigations were opened as a result of referrals from Benefits Advisors.

Outreach and Education

EBSA also conducts education and outreach events for workers, employers, plan officials and members of Congress. These nationwide activities include assisting dislocated workers who are facing job loss, educating employers of their obligations under ERISA, using a train-the-trainer format to inform Congressional staff of EBSA programs for their use in constituent services, and providing employees with information concerning their rights under the law. More than 2,000 Education And Outreach Events were held in FY 2008.[2]

EBSA seeks to focus its enforcement resources on areas that have the greatest impact on the protection of plan assets and participants' benefits. To accomplish this goal, EBSA has identified certain national enforcement projects in which field offices are to place particular investigative emphasis.

Health Fraud/Multiple Employer Welfare Arrangements (MEWAs)

A Multiple Employer Welfare Arrangement (MEWA) is a welfare benefit plan or other arrangement which is set up to benefit the employees of two or more employers. When small employers are either unable to find or can't afford the cost of health care coverage for their employees, they may look to MEWAs for coverage. EBSA continues to find instances where MEWAs have been unable to pay claims as a result of insufficient funding and inadequate reserves, or in the worst situations, where they were operated by individuals who drained the MEWA's assets through excessive administrative fees or by outright theft. EBSA's emphasis is on abusive and fraudulent MEWAs created by unscrupulous promoters which sell the promise of inexpensive health benefit insurance, but default on their obligations. The goals of this project are to shut down these abusive MEWAs and to proactively identify known fraudulent MEWA operators to ensure they do not terminate one MEWA just to open another in a different state. EBSA also investigates related criminal activities involving welfare benefit plans. Numerous schemes investigated by EBSA in the last few years have involved mail fraud, wire fraud, bankruptcy fraud, and other ERISA crimes. These criminal MEWA cases, which are prosecuted for the department by U.S. Attorneys' offices, have resulted in jail sentences and court ordered restitution against fraudulent MEWA operators.

---

2. National Enforcement Projects (as of 2009)

Employee Contributions Project

Since 1995, EBSA has pursued an aggressive enforcement project intended to safe-guard employee contributions to 401(k) plans and health care plans by investigating situations in which employers delay forwarding employee contributions into these plans. In some cases, employers do not promptly forward the contributions to the appropriate funding vehicle. In other cases, the employer simply converts the contributions to other uses, such as business expenses. Both scenarios may occur when the employer is having fiscal problems and turns to the plan for unlawful financing. The department's revised participant contribution regulation, effective February 3, 1997, states that such contributions for a pension plan become plan assets as soon as they can reasonably be segregated from the employer's general assets, but in no event later than fifteen business days after the end of the month the contributions are withheld from employees' pay. The national Employee Contributions Project has generated considerable attention from Congress, participants, service providers, and the media. By raising public awareness, the project increased further the volume of participant complaints, which can be valuable leads. An intended impact of the publicity was to put employers on notice that the department would vigorously pursue recoveries of diverted contributions and earnings. The aggressive pursuit of correction and publicity helps EBSA fulfill its mission of correcting and preventing violations of ERISA.

Rapid ERISA Action Team (REACT)

In carrying out its responsibility to protect participants' and beneficiaries' benefits, EBSA has targeted populations of plan participants who are potentially exposed to the greatest risk of loss. One such group of individuals is participants and beneficiaries of plans whose sponsor has filed for bankruptcy. The REACT project, which was begun in FY 2001, enables EBSA to respond in an expedited manner to protect the rights and benefits of plan participants when the plan sponsor faces severe financial hardship or bankruptcy and the assets of the employee benefit plan are in jeopardy. Under REACT, EBSA responds to employer bankruptcies by ensuring that all available legal actions have been taken to preserve pension plan assets. In such situations, it is common to find employers holding assets which belong to or are owed to plans, occasionally intermingling those assets with the employers' own assets. When a plan sponsor faces severe financial hardship, the assets of any plans and the benefits of participants are placed at great risk. Due to the tight time frames and the intricacies of the bankruptcy laws, plan assets and employee benefits are often lost because of the plan fiduciaries' failure to timely identify pension plan contributions that have not been paid to the plan's trust. Under REACT, when a company has declared bankruptcy, EBSA takes immediate action to ascertain whether there are plan contributions which have not been paid to the plans' trust, to advise all affected plans of the bankruptcy filing, and to provide assistance in filing proofs of claim to protect the plans, the participants, and the beneficiaries. EBSA also attempts to identify the assets of the responsible fiduciaries and evaluate whether a lawsuit should be filed against those fiduciaries to ensure that the plans are made whole and the benefits secured.

Employee Stock Ownership Plans

The Employee Stock Ownership Plan (ESOP) project is designed to identify and correct violations of ERISA in connection with ESOPs. ESOPs are designed to invest primarily in employer securities. Due to their unique nature, ESOPs can have distinct violations, as well as violations that might occur in any employee benefit plan. One of the most common violations found is the incorrect valuation of employer securities. This can occur when purchasing, selling, distributing, or otherwise valuing stock. Other issues involve the failure to provide participants with the specific benefits required or allowed under ESOPs, such as voting rights, ability to diversify their account balances at certain times, and the right to sell their shares of stock when received. EBSA will also review the refinancing of ESOP loans following EBSA's issuance of FAB 2002-1.

Consultant/Adviser Project

EBSA's newest National Project focuses on the receipt of improper, undisclosed compensation by pension consultants and other investment advisers. EBSA's investigations will seek to determine whether the receipt of such compensation violates ERISA because the adviser/consultant used its position with a benefit plan to generate additional fees for itself or its affiliates. When ERISA violations are uncovered, EBSA will seek corrective active for past violations as well as prospective relief to deter future violations. EBSA may also need to investigate individual plans to address such potential violations as failure to adhere to investment guidelines and improper selection or monitoring of the consultant or adviser. The CAP will also seek to identify potential criminal violations, such as kickbacks or fraud.

3. Technical Guidance and Prohibited Transaction Exemptions

In addition to regulations that interpret the statutory provisions of ERISA, EBSA promulgates other technical guidance for pension benefit plans and health and welfare benefit plans, such as Advisory Opinions; Field Bulletins; Information Letters; and Interpretive Bulletins. Additionally, they issue class exemptions and individual exemptions from Prohibited Transactions.

The Office of Regulations and Interpretations is primarily responsible for carrying out the Agency's regulatory agenda and interpretive activities. The Office also plays a major role in the development, analysis and implementation of pension and health care policy issues by providing technical assistance and support to the Assistant Secretary, external groups and other offices within EBSA. In addition, the Office coordinates regulatory and interpretive activities with other Federal agencies such as the Department of Treasury, the Internal Revenue Service and the Pension Benefit Guaranty Corporation. The Office is comprised of three divisions, the Division of Regulations, the Division of Fiduciary Interpretations and the Division of Coverage, Reporting and Disclosure. The Division of Regulations is responsible for managing and implementing the Agency's regulatory priorities under Title I of ERISA and coordinating regulatory activities with other Federal agencies. The general interpretive responsibilities of the Office are allocated on a subject matter basis between the Division of Fiduciary Interpretations and the Division of Coverage, Reporting and Disclosure. The Division of Fiduciary Interpretations is responsible for interpretive matters including the fiduciary responsibility, prohibited transaction, qualified domestic relations order and qualified medical child support order provisions of Parts 2, 4, and 6 of Title I of ERISA, as well as related provisions of the Internal Revenue Code and FERSA. The Division of Coverage, Reporting and Disclosure is generally responsible for interpretive matters relating to the coverage, reporting, disclosure, suspension of benefits, preemption, claims procedure, multiple employer welfare arrangements (MEWA), COBRA and other provisions of Parts 1, 2, 5 and 6 of Title I of ERISA.

Technical guidance: EBSA's goal in responding to requests for interpretations and other rulings is to facilitate compliance with ERISA, and the department's regulations through useful and timely interpretive guidance to plan participants, plan sponsors and other members of the employee benefits community. Such requests under Title I of ERISA are handled by EBSA's Office of Regulations and Interpretations (ORI) under the provisions established by ERISA Procedure 76-1 (41 Federal Register 36281, August 27, 1976). The office generally answers inquiries from individuals and organizations in the form of advisory opinions, which apply the law to a specific set of facts, or information letters, which merely call attention to well established principles or interpretations.

PT Exemptions: Applications for exemptions under Title I of ERISA are handled by EBSA's Office of Exemption Determinations (OED). OED staff will advance the protections of ERISA by timely processing of exemption requests under Title I of ERISA, ensuring establishment of effective conditions and safeguards to protect plans, participants and beneficiaries, and facilitating meritorious transactions that would otherwise be prohibited. In processing exemptions, the Department of Labor will minimize regulatory and administrative burdens to the extent feasible, while protecting the rights of plan participants and beneficiaries.

4. *Amicus Curie* Briefs

As discussed in Chapter 14, the Secretary of Labor (through the Assistant Secretary of Labor of the Employee Benefits Security Administration, which is currently Phyllis Borzi) has the authority to act as plaintiff in several ERISA causes of action. While they sometimes take on that role, more often they will simply author an *amicus curie* brief, and will advocate the plaintiff's position (from the Department of Labor's point of view and interpretation) to assist the court. These "friends of the court" briefs are either specifically requested by the judge, or the attorneys from EBSA file a motion with the judge to allow their brief to be submitted because the decision for that individual plaintiff will have ripple effects on many more ERISA plan participants.

5. Form 5500, Annual Reporting Forms

As discussed in Chapter 15, the annual form 5500 is the key component of meeting the reporting requirements for most plans. Several years ago, the federal agencies agreed that the DOL would be responsible for collecting the forms, and then sharing information with the IRS and the PBGC.

Electronic Filing Required Starting in 2009

The ERISA Filing Acceptance System (EFAST) is a system designed to simplify and expedite the receipt and processing of the Forms 5500/5500-EZ. These forms are filed each year by more than one million pension and other employee benefit plans to satisfy annual reporting requirements under ERISA and the Internal Revenue Code. The Department of Labor, Internal Revenue Service and the Pension Benefit Guaranty Corporation created the EFAST system to streamline the forms and the methods by which they are filed and processed. EBSA launched this dedicated web site to provide filers with up-to-date information about filing requirements, electronic filing options, software availability, FAQs, publications, and forms. The Form 5500s do not contain confidential information, and are therefore available to the general public. Before EFAST, a private company posted 5500s on a website called freerisa.com.

EFAST is designed to accept only approved machine print and hand print forms. The system may not properly process forms such as photocopies or non-standard forms that do not meet the Government's specifications. Use of these forms could result in filings being rejected. Under EFAST, filers choose between machine print and hand print computer scannable forms to file the Forms 5500 and 5500-EZ. Machine print forms are completed using computer software from EFAST approved vendors and can be filed electronically or by mail (including certain private delivery services). Hand print forms may be completed by hand, typewriter or by using computer software from EFAST approved vendors.

Desk Reviews of Form 5500 Annual Report Filings

ERISA contains several provisions which were enacted in recognition of the need to establish an effective mechanism to protect the interests of plan participants and beneficiaries, as well as to establish an effective mechanism to detect and deter abusive practices. These provisions include the annual reporting of financial information and activities of employee benefit plans. This is accomplished through the filing of a Form 5500 Series Annual Report. The Secretary of Labor is principally responsible for enforcing ERISA's fiduciary provisions and the annual reporting and disclosure provisions of ERISA. The Office of the Chief Accountant reviews Form 5500 Annual Reports to ensure that the information contained therein is complete and accurate. Where deficient, the Form 5500 Annual Report may be rejected, potentially subjecting the plan administrator to civil penalties not to exceed $1000 per day.

Non-Filer Enforcement Program

The Non-Filer Enforcement Program began in late 1993 as an effort to proactively target employee benefit plans who are required to file annual reports, but have not. Non-Filers are generally companies and corporations, large and small, that have illegally elected not to file annual reports for various reasons. The failure to file annual reports could be a signal that participants' benefits are jeopardy. The program seeks both retroactive (back to 1988) and prospective compliance. Employee benefit plans targeted through the Non-Filer Enforcement Program or referred to the program either through a department investigation or through a referral from the Internal Revenue Service or Pension Benefit Guaranty Corporation are not eligible to participate in other Department of Labor voluntary or reduced penalty programs.

Late-Filer Enforcement Program

For those plan administrators who do not take advantage of the reduced civil penalties offered by the Delinquent Filer Voluntary Compliance Program (DFVC), the department notifies plan administrators of its intent to assess the full penalty for failure to file timely annual reports for the plan years after 1987. Pursuant to ERISA Section 502(c)(2), these plan administrators may be assessed $50 per day for each day an annual report is filed after its required due date, without regard to any extensions to filing. These plan administrators, identified as the result of the department's ongoing investigative efforts are required to submit a Statement of Reasonable Cause to explain the facts for failure to file a timely annual report. Upon review of the Statement of Reasonable Cause, the department determines whether to assess the plan administrator the full late-filer penalty or to provide them a partial or full abatement. This program only targets those plan administrators with delinquent filings who fail to avail themselves of the DFVC Program.

On-Site Reviews of Audit Workpapers

An integral component of the annual reporting and disclosure provisions under Title I of ERISA is the requirement for plans with more than 100 participants, which hold assets in trust, to obtain an annual financial audit by an independent qualified public accountant (IQPA). Audited financial statements and the IQPA's report on the fairness and consistency of their presentation must be filed with the Form 5500. The audit requirement is intended to ensure the integrity of the financial information incorporated in the annual reports. Section 103 of ERISA specifically requires that these audits be conducted pursuant to the standards established by the accounting and auditing profession in the pronouncements which define generally accepted accounting principles (GAAP) and generally accepted auditing standards (GAAS). While ERISA's auditing provisions have worked to provide the DOL and the plan participants and beneficiaries with information about plan operations, experience has shown that IQPA audits do not consistently meet professional standards. In addressing this concern, the Office of the Chief Accountant has established an on-going quality review program for employee benefit plan audits. This program involves a random selection of plan audits that are reviewed to ensure that the level and quality of audit work performed supports the opinion rendered by the IQPA on the plan's financial statements and that such work is adequately documented in the IQPA's work papers as required by established professional standards.

Section IV

Other Employee Benefits Plans

Remember, this textbook focuses on retirement plans, especially qualified retirement plans. Students interested in learning about the rules for other employee benefits plans should look to other textbooks for summaries, or better yet, to the actual statues and regulations. That being said, this section of the textbook just highlights some of the other issues.

Chapter 18 presents the basics of executive compensation. First is a discussion of current compensation issues, such as the employer's deduction, then is a summary of the income tax issues with nonqualified deferred compensation plans for executives, followed by a summary of the types of equity benefit programs that can be offered to executives, and finally, a discussion of securities law issues and financial accounting are highlighted.

Chapter 19 presents the basics of health and welfare benefit plans. First is a discussion of the income tax aspects of different types of health, welfare and fringe benefit plans, then is a discussion of how employers and employees can pay for the benefits, and finally is a discussion of the rights ERISA provides to participants under a group health plan (such as COBRA continuation coverage and HIPAA portability and accountability requirements).

Chapter 20 presents a summary of Social Security Benefits and Individual Retirement Accounts. First is a summary of individual savings (through traditional IRAs and through Roth IRAs), and then is a summary of Social Security benefits.

Chapter 18

Basics of Executive Compensation

Overview

What are some ways to pay executives and other employees with current cash or cash-like compensation?

- there is generally no dollar limit cap on compensation; however, in order for the employer to deduct salary paid as a business expense, the salary must be "reasonable"—over the years, a five factor test has been developed to determine reasonableness

- in a publicly-traded company, the Chief Executive Officer and next top 4 most highly paid employees whose compensation is disclosed under SEC proxy statement rules, the employer's deduction general compensation that is not "performance based" is limited to $1 million

- Golden Parachutes:

    - some key executives will receive certain compensation in the future if there is a change in control of ownership in the employer

    - if this compensation is deemed a "parachute" payment, then, in addition to normal income taxes, the individual will need to pay a 20% excise tax on the "excess amount" (*i.e.*, anything in excess of base salary), and the employer will lose its salary deduction on this amount

    - compensation will be deemed "parachute" payments if they are in excess of three times base salary

    - if a severance agreement is executed within one year prior to the change of control, then the severance payments could lose their protected status and be deemed a "parachute" payment (they are presumed to be parachute, and the employer would need to prove that it was a bona fide severance agreement with no advance knowledge of the eventual change of control)

    - similarly, payments made due to termination of employment within one year following the change in control, then they will be assumed to be "parachute" payments as well

    - a change in control means a change in the actual ownership or effective control, or a change in control of a substantial portion of the corporate assets

- Corporate Owned Life Insurance:

    - the employer can "loan" the employee enough money to pay the premiums for whole life insurance

- to gain the best tax advantages, the employer will be repaid the loan from the cash surrender value of the policy upon the payment of death benefits to the employee's estate (or upon cancellation of the policy)
- the policies can just be general life insurance coverage or can be part of business succession planning
- the IRS has recently changed its position on the proper taxation of split dollar life insurance, and the regulations need to be reviewed before a split dollar policy is drafted
- Phantom Stock Plans:
  - unlike equity based plans where actual ownership rights are transferred to employees, these plans will track certain predetermined stocks or indices and will pay the employee in cash the calculated gain which would have been realized if the employee were actually given such stocks or invested in such indices
- employers can also promise income tax gross-ups, club membership, housing, and other perks

What are some ways to pay executives in their retirement with deferred compensation?

- the employer generally maximizes the use of qualified plans for the broad cross-section of employees.
- then, in order to attract, retain or reward certain favored employees, other plans are set up
- if structured properly, deferred compensation plans for executives will only be subject to minimal reporting and disclosure rules of ERISA
- since these plans are not subject to the minimum vesting and coverage requirements of ERISA, they can be offered to any executive, can offer discriminatory benefits in favor of any one executive or groups of executives, and the benefits can vest and accrue in any manner
- these plans are not subject to the advanced funding requirements of ERISA (in fact, in most instances, they must remain unfunded)
- since these generally represent one-on-one negotiations between the executive and the employer, they are generally enforceable under appropriate state contract laws rather than the federal ERISA law; however, care must be taken because, if enough executives are offered the same non-qualified plan, then a court might determine that, collectively, it looks like a single ERISA plan, subject to all of the rules of ERISA (the whole purpose these plans are excluded from some of the ERISA provisions in the first place is that Congress feels that executives and other favored employees have the ability to negotiate one-on-one with the employer)

How can retirement plans be structured?

- Deferred Compensation Salary Deferral Plans:
  - plans set up where an employee can make an election before service are rendered (generally by the preceding December 1) to defer a portion of currently-taxable compensation to be paid in a future year
  - generally, these plans are set up to complement a qualified 401(k) plan, thus allowing an avenue for employees to save who want to defer more than the annual deferral limit of $15,000 (as adjusted for inflation) — for example, if

a high paid employee wishes to defer $100,000 of compensation she would have otherwise earned, then the maximum amount (*i.e.*, $15,000, as adjusted for inflation) will be deposited into the qualified 401(k) plan and the remainder will be credited under a non-qualified plan

- however, since the excess deferrals are part of the employer's general assets (and not invested in a tax-exempt qualified trust), there is no guarantee that the employees will ever receive their non-qualified deferral promises and associated fund earnings

- there are things that can be done to segregate these deferrals in special employer accounts or trusts, but once the employee no longer has a "substantial risk of forfeiture," then the benefits are immediately taxable to the employee, even if the benefits will not be paid until a future date under the terms of the plan or employment contract

- Supplemental Executive Retirement Plans (SERPs)
  - this will take the form of either a defined benefit plan or a defined contribution plan, where the employer will promise benefits either exclusively through a nonqualified deferred compensation plan or as a supplement to the qualified plan
  - Excess Only Plans:
    - plans set up only to offer benefits lost in a qualified plan due to the benefit limitations imposed by the Code (*i.e.*, IRC §415 maximum benefits)— so employer can provide allocations in excess of $40,000 (as indexed for inflation) per year in a defined contribution model or can pay distributions in excess of $160,000 (as indexed for inflation) per year in a defined benefit model
    - however, other limitations (like the $200,000 salary cap) were added to the Code after ERISA was enacted; therefore, few plans meet the very specific definition of an excess only plan
  - Top Hat Plans:
    - to be excluded from Parts 2, 3 and 4 of Title I of ERISA (Participation and Vesting, Funding, and Fiduciary Responsibility, respectively), a plan, which is commonly referred to as a "Top Hat plan" must be "a plan which is unfunded and is maintained by an employer primarily for the purpose of providing deferred compensation for a select group of management or highly compensated employees."
    - these are unfunded plans (*i.e.*, the assets accumulated to pay liabilities always remain part of the employer's general assets which can be attacked by their creditors).
  - many plans have been designed to be a Top-Hat Plan to avoid the onerous rules of ERISA and qualified plans, but due to poor design or communication, some plans have been deemed by courts to fail the specific definition
  - a "Rabbi Trust" is a very common type of funding vehicle where benefits are "funded" through a trust which can only pay benefits to such favored em-

ployees but which can also pay assets to the employer's creditors pursuant to a court order (thus, keeping the plan unfunded).

How are benefits from nonqualified deferred compensation plans taxed to the executives?

- the deferred compensation benefits have some tax advantages:
  - deferral of income taxation to the employee until there is no longer a substantial risk of forfeiture;
  - deduction by the employer at the same time the employee includes the amount in gross income; and
  - employer pays taxes on fund earnings because the plans are unfunded (*i.e.*, the assets remain part of the general assets of the employer—they are not part of an tax-exempt trust like qualified retirement plan assets)
- in addition to the existing income tax regime, under IRC § 409A, the plan must be drafted to require the executive employee to make an irrevocable election before services are performed in connection with the deferred compensation to only receive the deferred compensation at a certain point in time or upon an event like death, disability, or change in control
  - the employee executive can make elections to further postpone benefits, but cannot accelerate benefits
  - if the plan is not drafted properly, then the employee will pay income taxes as of the year of deferral, plus interest, plus a 20% penalty tax
  - the wording of IRC § 409A causes many unexpected benefits paid to executives to be covered by the statute, but there are some exceptions for short term deferrals and properly structured severance pay

What are some ways to transfer ownership of the business to employees?

- Actual Ownership:
  - ownership generally means stock shares in an incorporated business, interest shares in a partnership, and membership units in a limited liability partnership or corporation; however, publicly-traded businesses are generally corporations, with shares of stock traded on the open market
- Stock Options:
  - in order to encourage employees to perform as well as they are able to, the employer might want to give options to purchase shares of the unrestricted employer stock at a discount
  - the theory is to offer to the employees the right to purchase stock in the future at a reduced rate; thus, if all employees collectively perform well, then market price will rise over the next few years if and when the option is exercised and the employees will purchase the stock at a discount
  - generally, the exercise price is the current market price—for example, if ABC, Inc. is trading today at $23 per share, then a ten year option may be granted today to an individual that allows her to purchase one share of ABC, Inc. stock anytime in the next ten years for $23 per share—if the stock is trading above $23 in the future, the employee will likely purchase the stock by using her own money; if it is trading below $23, then the option will likely not be

exercised until it hopefully rebounds; and if the ten year term expires, then the stock option is valueless

- there are special securities law rules which require certain information for publicly-traded employers to communicate stock option plans with the SEC, and which exempt private companies from any registration
- there are special tax rules on when and how the employee is taxed, and when the employer can take a corresponding deduction as a reasonable business expense
- additionally, there are special accounting rules on how a publicly-traded employer needs to show the stock option on its financial statements
- Incentive Stock Options:
  - ISOs are plans, described at IRC § 422, which are offered to a broad cross-section of employees and which are approved by the shareholders
  - there are limits on the types, amounts, transferability, exercise period, and holding periods of options which can be offered, but the employees will only pay capital gains rates on the gain upon the exercise of the options (the employer gets no deduction)
  - these options are only available to employees
- Nonqualified Stock Options:
  - any option which does not comply with the ISO rules
  - the employer is not limited in how to structure the options or in who they can be offered to (*i.e.,* a select group of employees, members of the board of directors, independent contractors, attorneys, accountants and other business advisors)
  - the individual will pay regular income taxes on the gain upon exercise and the employer will get a corresponding deduction at that time
- Stock Appreciation Rights:
  - ownership generally means stock shares in an incorporated business, interest shares in a partnership, and membership units in a limited liability partnership or corporation
  - however, publicly-traded businesses are generally corporations, with shares of stock traded on the open market

How are benefits from nonqualified deferred compensation plans disclosed to the public in publicly traded companies?

- in the proxy statement of publicly traded companies:
  - all components of the compensation package (including the value of stock options granted) must be disclosed for the CEO, the CFO, and the three next highest paid executives
- in the corporate financial statements:
  - the value of all stock options granted during the year must be shown as an actual cost on the financial statements

A. Issues with Current Compensation for Executives

1. Deductibility of Current Compensation

The difference between current compensation and deferred compensation is basically determined by the tax year that the individual employee includes the compensation in his or her Gross Income.[1] An individual will need to include in his or her Gross Income all "compensation for services, including fees, commissions, fringe benefits, and similar items"[2] when it is actually or constructively received. Basically, the individual has not yet constructively received the compensation "if the taxpayer's control of its receipt is subject to substantial limitations or restrictions."[3] Any portion of compensation that is subject to substantial limitations is considered deferred compensation, and will be taxable in a future tax year when the limitations are removed.

There is generally no dollar limit cap on current compensation. However, in order for the employer to deduct salary paid as a business expense, the salary must be "reasonable."[4] Over the years, a five factor test has been developed to determine reasonableness:[5]

- the employee's role in the company: including the employee's position, hours worked, and duties performed, plus any special duties or role (such as personally guaranteeing corporate loans);

- an external comparison with other companies: salaries paid to comparable employees in similar companies;

- the character and condition of the company: including the sales, net income, capital value, and general economic fitness of the company;

- potential conflicts of interest: ability to "disguise" dividends as salary, particularly when the employee is the sole or majority shareholder, and/or where a large percentage of the compensation is paid as a "bonus"; and

- the internal consistency in compensation: consistency of the compensation system throughout the ranks of the company.

In a publicly-traded company, the Chief Executive Officer and next top 4 most highly paid employees whose compensation is disclosed under SEC proxy statement rules, the deduction allowed for general compensation that is not "performance based" is limited to $1 million.[6] To classify a compensation package as "performance based," which allows a higher deduction for salary than $1 million, it must meet the following criteria:

- the compensation must be paid solely upon account of the attainment of one or more pre-established objective performance goals;

- the performance goals must be established by a compensation committee comprised exclusively of two or more "outside directors";

---

1. Determined in accordance with IRC §§ 83 and 451.
2. IRC § 61(a)(1).
3. Treas. Regs. § 1.451-2.
4. IRC § 162(a)(1).
5. Elliotts, Inc. v. Commissioner, 716 F.2d 1241 (9th Cir.1983).
6. IRC § 162(m). Under IRC § 612(m)(5), the deduction for compensation for "covered executives" is limited to $500,000 in companies that received bail-out money from the federal government through the Troubled Asset Relief Program of the Emergency Economic Stabilization Act of 2008.

- the material terms of the performance goals must be disclosed to and approved by the shareholders; and
- the compensation committee consisting of "outside directors" must certify that indeed the performance goals have been met prior to the payment.

Because of these easy-to-meet exceptions, most CEOs and the next four highest paid executives in a publicly-traded company now have a base salary of $1 million, and then performance goals (such as increasing shareholder equity by 6% over the next 5 years, overseeing the design, patenting and implementation of a new product, or establishing an office and market share in Kenya within the next 3 years) for the remaining tens of millions of dollars most executives receive as compensation.

From the employer's point of view, the proper classification of compensation as either being paid currently or deferred into a future tax year (with the exception of compensation for services rendered this year being paid within the first two and a half months of the following tax year) is crucial for purposes of complying with federal and state tax laws.[7] Therefore, the employer should affirmatively decide when compensation should be taxable to the employee. If it is meant to be currently taxable, then the employer should provide it without substantial limitations or restrictions. However, if it is meant to be deferred compensation, then the employer should be mindful of all of the issues as described below, and determine ahead of time if it will be promised and delivered through a qualified retirement plan, a nonqualified deferred compensation plan, or neither if it is a one-time negotiation that is not part of a plan, fund or program. In addition to the classification of compensation for income tax purposes, the employer must be aware of the rules for deferred compensation if it is delivered through an ERISA plan.

Remember that the term "qualified retirement plan" generally refers to an employer-sponsored pension, profit-sharing, or stock bonus deferred compensation plan that satisfies the specific statutory requirements set forth in §401(a) (or an annuity plan that meets the requirements of §403). If all of the rules of a qualified plan are followed by the sponsoring employer, then both the employer and the employees promised benefits in retirement will receive favorable income tax treatment: the individual employee will generally not be taxed on retirement benefits until actually received; the employer will generally get an immediate tax deduction for contributions to the plan; and the plan assets will generally accumulate tax-free. Non-profit employers that sponsor either a §401(a), 403(b), or 457(b) or (f) plan are not interested in the deduction, but if all of those specific rules are followed by the employer, then the individual employee will generally not be taxed on retirement benefits until actually received.

In nonqualified retirement plans for executives of the employer (or for other non-employees, such as independent contractors or consultants, family members, outside members of the board of directors, or outside consultants), if structured properly, the individual plan participants are only subject to minimal, or perhaps even no, reporting and disclosure rules of ERISA. Since nonqualified deferred compensation plans are not subject to the minimum vesting and coverage requirements of ERISA, they can be offered to any executive, can offer discriminatory benefits in favor of any one executive or groups of executives, and the benefits can vest and accrue in any manner. These plans are not subject to the advanced funding requirements of ERISA (in fact, in most instances, they must

---

7. See IRC §§ 3401 for federal income tax withholding rules; 3121 for federal FICA tax remittance rules; and 3301 for federal FUCA tax remittance rules. The Federation of Tax Administrator's website has links to various state requirements at http://www.taxadmin.org/fta/link/forms.html.

remain unfunded). Since the excess deferrals are part of the employer's general assets (and not invested in a tax-exempt qualified trust), there is no guarantee that the employees will ever receive their non-qualified deferrals and associated fund earnings. There are methods that can be taken to segregate these deferrals into special employer accounts or trusts (such as Rabbi Trusts), but once the employee no longer has a "substantial risk of forfeiture," then the benefits are immediately taxable to the employee, even if the benefits will not be paid until a future date under the terms of the plan or employment contract[8] and the employer will generally get a corresponding tax deduction for the benefits in the same year that they are included in the individual's gross income.[9]

Sometimes deferred compensation benefits represent a one-on-one negotiation between the executive and the employer, and are therefore wholly exempt from ERISA and enforceable under appropriate state contract laws. However, care must be taken because, if enough executives are offered the same non-qualified retirement promises, then a court might determine that, in the aggregate, the separate promises start to look like a single ERISA plan, subject to all of the rules of ERISA.

2. Other Cash-Like Benefits

Golden Parachutes:[10] Some key executives will receive pre-determined compensation in the future if there is a change in control of ownership in the employer. If this compensation is deemed a "parachute" payment, then, in addition to normal income taxes, the individual will need to pay a 20% excise tax on the "excess amount" (*i.e.*, anything in excess of one times base salary if the parachute payment is in excess of three times base salary), and the employer will lose its salary deduction on this amount. A change in control means a change in the actual ownership or effective control, or a change in control of a substantial portion of the corporate assets.[11] Payments paid to key executives in a small business corporation (*i.e.*, S Corporations with fewer than 100 shareholders) due to a change in control are not subject to the penalty.[12] If a severance agreement is executed within one year prior to the change of control, then the severance payments could lose their protected status and be deemed a "parachute" payment (they are presumed to be parachute, and the employer would need to prove that it was a bona fide severance agreement with no advance knowledge of the eventual change of control). Similarly, payments made due to termination of employment within one year following the change in control, then they will be assumed to be "parachute" payments as well. A change in control means a change in the actual ownership or effective control, or a change in control of a substantial portion of the corporate assets.

Corporate Owned Life Insurance: The employer can "loan" a favored employee enough money to pay the premiums for whole life insurance, or just pay the premiums directly. These favored employees can include, at the time the contract is issued, directors[13], highly

---

8. IRC §§ 83 and 451.

9. IRC § 404(a)(5).

10. IRC § 280G. For a complete discussion, see "Golden Parachute Audit Techniques (02-2005)" for a nine step approach that IRS agents will use at an audit, available at http://www.irs.gov/businesses/corporations/article/0,,id=134890,00.html.

11. Treas. Regs. § 1.280G-1, Q&A-27.

12. IRC § 280G(b)(5).

13. IRC § 101(j)(2)(A)(ii)(I).

compensated employees,[14] and highly compensated individuals that are among the top 35% paid employees.[15] If the favored employee dies while still employed, then the death benefits are tax-free to the employer, whether received directly, paid directly to the survivors, or used to purchase the decedent's equity interest in the business. There are certain mandatory notice and consent requirements that must be met before the employer and employee can enjoy the tax attributes.[16] These insurance products will likely become more popular as the income tax rules were cleared up through the Pension Protection Act of 2006.

Phantom Stock Plans: Unlike equity based plans where actual ownership rights are transferred to employees, these plans will track certain predetermined stocks or indices and will pay the employee in cash the calculated gain which would have been realized if the employee were actually given such stocks or invested in such indices.

B. Retirement Plans for Executives

1. Nonqualified Deferred Compensation (NQDC) Plans, Generally

The employer might wish to promise retirement benefits to executives, officers, and other favored employees in addition to the limited benefits allowed in a qualified plan or to workers that are not classified as common-law employees. Excess benefit plans, if drafted properly, are wholly exempt from ERISA, while top-hat plans, if drafted properly, are only subject to limited ERISA governance. However, both types of plans are subject to the taxability provisions under the Code. One important difference with promises of nonqualified deferred compensation is that the promises remain as part of the employer's general assets (thus, subject to the employer's creditors), although certain trusts can be set up to at least separate the desired funding of the promised benefits.

The employer generally maximizes the use of qualified plans for the broad cross-section of employees. Then, in order to attract, retain or reward certain favored employees, other plans are set up. The generic name given to any non-qualified deferred compensation plan for executives is a Supplemental Executive Retirement Plan ("SERP"). They take the forms we have already explored under the rubric of qualified retirement plans:

Deferred Compensation Salary Deferral Plans: Plans set up where an employee can make an election before services are rendered (generally by the preceding December 1) to defer a portion of currently-taxable compensation to be paid in a future year. Generally, these plans are set up to complement a qualified 401(k) plan, thus allowing an avenue for employees to save who want to defer more than the annual limit of $15,000 (as adjusted for inflation), or $20,000 (as adjusted for inflation) if aged 55 or older. For example, if a high paid employee wishes to defer $100,000 of compensation she would have otherwise earned as salary and included in Gross Income this year, and if the executive is eligible to par-

---

14. IRC § 101(j)(2)(A)(ii)(II). Here, highly compensated employees has the same meaning as in § 414(q), but without allowing the employer to make a top-paid group election.

15. IRC § 101(j)(2)(A)(ii)(III), Here, highly compensated individual has the same meaning as in § 105(h)(5)(C), but where 35% is substituted for 25%.

16. IRC § 101(j)(4).

ticipate in the employer's 401(k) plan, then $15,000 will be deposited into the qualified 401(k) plan and the remainder will be credited under a non-qualified deferred compensation plan.

Deferred Compensation Individual Account Plans: This type of plan will take the form of a defined contribution plan. For example, if written as a defined contribution plan and the employer wants to provide an executive with an allocation of $100,000 this year, then if the executive also participates in a qualified plan sponsored by the employer, up to $40,000 (as adjusted for inflation) can be allocated in the qualified defined contribution plan, and the balance can be allocated in a non-qualified deferred compensation plan.

Deferred Compensation Pension Plans: This type of plan will take the form of a defined benefit plan. For example, if the employer wants to provide an annual benefit of $300,000 per year starting at age 65 and continuing for the remainder of the executive's life, then if the executive also participates in a qualified plan sponsored by the employer, $160,000 (as adjusted for inflation and other adjustments) can be funded for and paid through the qualified defined benefit plan, and the balance can be paid each year from a non-qualified deferred compensation plan.

However, since the excess deferrals made to a NQDC salary deferral plan, excess annual additions made to a NQDC individual account plan, and excess annuity promises made from a NQDC pension plan are all part of the employer's general assets (and not invested in a tax-exempt qualified trust), there is no guarantee that the employees will ever receive their non-qualified deferral promises and associated fund earnings. Therefore, the NQDC promises are "unfunded" and subject to the employer's creditors at all times (unfortunately, neither ERISA, its legislative history, nor the associated regulations provide much guidance as to what arrangements qualify as "unfunded," and there was not even guidance from the courts regarding funding with respect to deferred compensation agreements until several years after the enactment of ERISA). As described below, there are a few things that can be done to segregate these deferrals in special employer accounts or trusts, such as funding promises through a "Rabbi trust," but if too much protection is provided by the employer, and once the employee no longer has a "substantial risk of forfeiture," then the benefits are immediately taxable to the employee, even if the benefits will not be paid until a future date under the terms of the plan or employment contract.

2. Excess Benefit Plans and Top-Hat Plans

Excess Only Plans

Plans set up only to offer benefits lost in a qualified plan due to the benefit limitations imposed by the Code (*i.e.*, IRC § 415 maximum benefits).

However, other limitations (like the $200,000 salary cap) were added to the Code after ERISA was enacted; therefore, few plans meet the very specific definition of an excess only plan.[17]

---

17. However, in Kozak, "Sections 415 and 401(a)(17) Harmonized: Bad News for Qualified Retirement Plans, But Potentially Good News for Nonqualified Excess Benefit Plans," *BNA Tax Planning and Compensation Journal, December 2007,* I make the argument that recent regulations for qualified plans seems to eliminate this distinction, but so far, no one at the IRS has either agreed or disagreed with my conclusions.

Top Hat Plans

To be excluded from Parts 2, 3 and 4 of Title I of ERISA (Participation and Vesting, Funding, and Fiduciary Responsibility, respectively), a plan, which is commonly referred to as a "Top Hat plan" must be "a plan which is unfunded and is maintained by an employer primarily for the purpose of providing deferred compensation for a select group of management or highly compensated employees."

These are unfunded plans (*i.e.*, the assets accumulated to pay liabilities always remain part of the employer's general assets which can be attacked by their creditors).

Therefore, designing and establishing NQDC plans requires experience and competence by the employee benefits professional. If a plan is designed to be an excess only plan or a Top Hat plan but upon audit or through litigation, it misses the mark, then it is still a employee benefit pension plan under ERISA, but is subject to all of the onerous rules, and to massive penalties for prior periods of noncompliance. There is a lot of litigation attacking top hat plans (*i.e.*, they are not *primarily* for the purpose of providing deferred compensation or that the group of employees receiving promises of deferred compensation is not *select* enough).[18]

3. Income Taxation of Retirement Plans for Executives

Statutory Rules at IRC §§ 83, 409A, 451, 457A

Until § 409A was added to the Code in 2004, deferred compensation was governed under long-standing Code provisions, some IRS and Treasury guidance published over several decades, and judicially developed tax doctrines. An employee will generally include in Gross Income (and pay taxes on) any compensation in the tax year he or she receives it. Over the years, Treasury and the courts developed three basic tax doctrines:

The economic benefit doctrine: What is taxable as compensation?

The constructive receipt doctrine: When is an amount deemed compensation?

The transfer of property doctrine: Who is taxed on the compensation?

In summary, these three doctrines, in the aggregate, suggested that the employee would include deferred compensation into Gross Income in the tax year that the benefits are no longer subject to a "substantial risk of forfeiture," regardless of whether he or she actually received it or not. This loose and vague definition arguably allowed employers and favored employees to stretch the limits of what a true risk of forfeiture was. There is, however, a provision that allows individuals to voluntarily pay income taxes before receipt of actual benefits, thus gambling that the taxes paid early will be less than taxes paid later, but without the ability to recap the income taxes paid early if the gamble proves wrong.

Largely in response to the collapse of Enron and other corporate implosions, Congress added IRC § 409A to the Code to place tighter restrictions on the timing of when executives deferring income can choose to receive the benefits (specifically, Congress sought to prevent an insider, with non-public knowledge of the employer's immediate financial hardships, from receiving the deferred compensation promises before they ac-

---

18. See, *e.g.,* Chad DeGroot, "Welcome to the Jungle: Plan Sponsors Must Slash Through the Thicket of Top-Hat Plan Litigation," *BNA Tax Management Compensation Planning Journal, June 2008.*

tually become subject to the employer's creditors). Basically, deferred compensation plans under the new rules can only allow distributions under the following circumstances:

- separation from service,
- the date the participant becomes disabled,
- death,
- a specified time (or pursuant to a fixed schedule) specified under the plan at the date of the deferral of such compensation,
- a change in the ownership or effective control of the corporation, or in the ownership of a substantial portion of the assets of the corporation, or
- the occurrence of an unforeseeable emergency.

So, when an individual makes an election to defer compensation not later than the close of the preceding taxable year, the plan must satisfy one of these distribution dates in order for the individual to continue deferring taxes. The participant can elect to further defer distributions for at least an additional 5 years, but if he or she has the ability to receive benefits earlier (regardless of whether or not he or she actually makes the elections), or if there are any other violations of the statute, then all compensation deferred under the plan for the taxable year and all preceding taxable years shall be includible in Gross Income in that year, plus interest calculated at a very unfavorable rate, plus an additional 20% penalty tax, are assessed.

In 2008, adding yet another layer of the tax-compliance onion for NQDC plans, Congress added IRC §457A to the Code to close up some loop holes in the plans maintained by foreign employers.

In response to the economic crisis of 2008, the Obama Administration has set forth proposals to further limit actual or perceived abuses in excessive executive compensation, and any legislative fixes actually implemented will likely come through the Internal Revenue Code.

4. Funding Retirement Promises with Rabbi Trusts

A "Rabbi Trust" is a very common type of funding vehicle where benefits are segregated into a trust to attempt to fund the promised benefits, but the trust is deemed to be unfunded, since any assets held in the trust always remains part of the employer's general assets.[19] With a Rabbi Trust, the individual has at least some security that the assets expected to be used to pay his or her benefits when due. A Rabbi trust can be used for either an excess benefit plan or a Top-Hat plan—if used with an excess benefit plan, then if benefits are not paid the individual can bring a state law breach of contract action against the employer; whereas, if used with a Top-Hat plan, then if benefits are not paid the individual must bring a federal ERISA action against the employer. The assets of the Rabbi trust must generally be located in the United States (and thus, subject to seizure pursuant to proper U.S. court orders).[20]

---

19. PLR 8113107 (12/31/1980) allowed a Rabbi, promised deferred compensation by a Congregation, to defer including the benefits in his Gross Income since the trust was always subject to the Congregation's creditors if they were to declare bankruptcy.
20. IRC §409A(b)(1).

5. Limitations Based on Funding Targets in the Employer's Qualified Defined Benefit Plan

The Pension Protection Act of 2006 added new funding target rules for single-employer qualified defined benefit plans. Under those rules, which arguably have nothing to do with promises made to executives through NQDC plans, If the employer sponsors both a qualified defined benefit plan and a nonqualified deferred compensation plan, and if the funded status of the qualified defined benefit plan is "at-risk," (as discussed in Chapter 6) then assets cannot be set aside or reserved (directly or indirectly) in a trust or other arrangement for purposes of paying deferred compensation to any employee without the individual executive including that amount in Gross Income in the current year.[21]

C. Equity Benefits

The final part of the compensation package can be the transfer of the business from the current owners to employees. If the business is incorporated, then equity compensation usually takes the form of actual stock or stock options. Equity can also be transferred through an Employee Stock Ownership Plan (ESOP), which is a form of qualified retirement plan. Other than the basic discussion herein, equity compensation is beyond the scope of this textbook.

1. Stocks

Stock of a company is deemed a security, and is thus must be registered with the Securities Exchange Commission,[22] and if traded in a secondary market, will be subject to that market's trading rules.[23] When a disinterested investor purchases shares of stock of the issuing employer through a secondary market, they obtain the ownership and voting rights afforded them, and can sell or trade their shares without restrictions. Thus, the investor can sell the stock at a profit if its market value on the day of trade is higher than the value at date of purchase. Similarly, the investor can sell the stock as the market price is falling in order to minimize the losses. Stock is usually classified by the issuing employer as either common stock or preferred stock (where the owners generally have first right to dividend distributions).

When stock certificates are provided to employees as part of the compensation package, they are often restricted. Usually, there will be a vesting period (such as 4 years after receipt) or a performance metric (such as completing a project or increasing the firm's earnings per share ratio by a set percentage) There will also generally be restrictions on how and when the stock can be sold, and how and when the voting rights can be exercised.[24] Unlike stock options, as discussed below, the actual stock certificates, even if restricted,

---

21. IRC § 409A(b)(3)(A).
22. In accordance with the Securities Act of 1933, 48 Stat. 74.
23. In accordance with the Securities Exchange Act of 1934, 48 Stat. 881.
24. There is no current statutory definition of restricted stock, as original IRC § 424 was repealed by the Omnibus Budget Reconciliation Act of 1990.

provide tangible ownership in the employer immediately upon vesting. The employee does not need to take any affirmative actions or expend any money. If the value of the stock increases as a result of his or her employment, the employee will share in the profitability of the business immediately upon vesting. Restricted stock is usually common stock.

2. Stock Options

Stock options give the investor the right to purchase a certain number of shares of stock at a certain strike price, regardless of what they are actually trading for on a secondary market. For a disinterested investor, he or she pays a price for this option, and gambles: he or she wins if the option facilitates the purchase of the actual stock at a price less than true market value, but loses if the stock is actually worth less than the strike price (in which case, the price paid to purchase the option is wasted).

Employers oftentimes use stock options as a form of compensation. The theory is to offer to the employees the right to purchase stock in the future at a reduced rate; thus, if all employees collectively perform well, then market price will rise over the next few years if and when the option is exercised and the employees will purchase the stock at a discount. Employees also gamble with stock options, although they don't pay any money for the option as the regular disinterested investors do: if the market value exceeds the strike price during a set period of time then the employee can dig into his or her pocket and purchase the stock from the employer for the stock price, assuming he or she has access to that amount of cash, and does nothing if the value of the stock falls below the strike price or the period of time to convert an option for a certificate expires (thus neither loses or gains anything from being granted the stock option).

There are special securities law rules which require certain information for publicly-traded employers to communicate stock option plans with the SEC, and which exempt private companies from any registration. Additionally, there are special accounting rules on how a publicly-traded employer needs to show the stock option on its financial statements. Finally, there are special tax rules on when and how the employee is taxed, and when the employer can take a corresponding deduction as a reasonable business expense, and if the stock option is granted at a discount, additional restrictions.[25] Similar to the reasoning of qualified and nonqualified retirement plans, an employer will often offer statutory stock options (Incentive Stock Option Plans and Employee Stock Purchase Plans) to a large cross-section of executives and favored employees, because they are burdened with rules, and then a Nonqualified Stock Option Plan to the more selective group of truly favored executives, officers, and non-employees like directors.

Incentive Stock Option Plans:[26] ISOs are plans that grant stock options to employees. There are limits on the types, amounts, transferability, exercise period, and holding periods of options which can be offered. These options are only available to employees. The strike price must be the market value of the underlying stock on the date the option is granted. Since an employee stock purchase plan is deemed a statutory plan, the exercise of the stock option for actual stock is not a taxable event, the employee will only be taxed at the ultimate sale of the stock, and the employer receives no deduction.[27]

---

25. Under IRC § 409A.
26. IRC § 422(a).
27. IRC § 421(a).

Employee Stock Purchase Plans:[28] An employee stock purchase plan requires an initial investment by the employee to first purchase the stock option, which can then be used to purchase actual shares of stock if the employee wishes to exercise the option. The employee generally funds the plan with payroll deductions. Unlike an ISO, the strike price can be as low as 85% of the market value of the underlying stock on the date the option is granted. Since an employee stock purchase plan is deemed a statutory plan, the exercise of the stock option for actual stock is not a taxable event, the employee will only be taxed at the ultimate sale of the stock, and the employer receives no deduction.[29]

Nonqualified Stock Options Plans: Any plan providing options which does not comply with the ISO or the ESPP rules is, by default, a NSO plan. The employer is not limited in how to structure the options or in who they can be offered to (*i.e.,* NSOs can be offered to a select group of employees, members of the board of directors, independent contractors, attorneys, accountants and other business advisors). The individual will pay regular income taxes on the gain upon exercise and the employer will get a corresponding deduction at that time.

3. Other

There are other ways to use equity to pay compensation, without actually transferring ownership. The most common ways are:[30]

- *Stock Appreciation Rights*: A stock appreciation right provides the right to the monetary equivalent of the increase in the value of a specified number of shares over a specified period of time. It is normally paid out in cash, but it could be paid in shares. SARs often can be exercised any time after they vest. SARs are often granted in tandem with stock options (either ISOs or NSOs) to help finance the purchase of the options and/or pay tax if any is due upon exercise of the options; these SARs sometimes are called "tandem SARs." One of the great advantages of these plans is their flexibility. But that flexibility is also their greatest challenge. Because they can be designed in so many ways, many decisions need to be made about issues such as who gets how much, vesting rules, liquidity concerns, restrictions on selling shares (when awards are settled in shares), eligibility, rights to interim distributions of earnings, and rights to participate in corporate governance (if any).

- *Phantom Stock Plans*: Phantom stock is simply a promise to pay a bonus in the form of the equivalent of either the value of company shares or the increase in that value over a period of time. The taxation of the bonus would be much like any other cash bonus—it is taxed as ordinary income at the time it is received. Phantom stock plans are not tax-qualified, so they are not subject to the same rules as ESOPs and 401(k) plans, provided they do not cover a broad group of employees. If they do, they could be subject to ERISA rules (see below). Unlike SARs, phantom stock may reflect dividends and stock splits. Phantom stock payments are usually made at a fixed, predetermined date.

---

28. IRC § 423(b).
29. IRC § 421(a).
30. definitions found at http://www.nceo.org/library/phantom_stock.html.

D. Securities Law Issues

1. SEC Disclosures

While most employee benefits professionals do not need to be experts in securities law issues, those that consult employers on executive compensation issues, especially in publicly traded companies, do need to understand the complex regulatory scheme.

In response to the Enron, Worldcom, and other major corporate failures, in 2002 Congress passed the Sarbanes-Oxley Act ("SOX").[31] The major theme of the legislation is transparency and proper corporate governance. Some of the issues directly affecting executive compensation are:

- New SEC reporting obligations: SOX requires reporting of a grant, exercise or cancellation of a stock option within 2 business days for directors, officers and 10% shareholders[32] {it was 10 days under the old rules}.

- Loans to directors and officers: SOX prohibits public companies from extending credit in the form of a personal loan, either directly or indirectly, to a director or executive officer (such as the president; any vice president in charge of a principal unit, division or function; or any officer or other individual that performs a policy making function). The issues here include: loan forgiveness; pre-SOX promises for future loans; 401(k) plan loans; split dollar life insurance; cashless exercises of stock options; travel advances; and indemnification and advancement of litigation expenses.[33]

- Insider trading restrictions during blackout periods: During any 401(k) blackout period (a period of more than 3 consecutive business days during which plan participants cannot purchase or sell employer stock), no executive director or officer can trade employer stock, and any realized profits are recoverable from such individuals.[34]

- Disgorgement of executive compensation: If in any year there is material noncompliance with the SEC rules as a result of misconduct, then the CEO and CFO must reimburse the company for any bonus or other incentive or equity based compensation received during the year.[35]

Additionally, the executive compensation packages for the publicly traded company's CEO, CFO, and next three highest paid executives must be disclosed on the annual proxy statements (SEC Form 8-K), which is public information. The following excerpt from the preamble to SEC regulations provides a good summary.

SEC Final Rules, Release 33-8732A (August 2006); Summary

* * *

the new Compensation Discussion and Analysis calls for a discussion and analysis of the material factors underlying compensation policies and decisions reflected in the data

---

31. P.L. 107-204, actually titled the Corporate and Auditing Accountability, Responsibility, and Transparency Act of 2002.
32. SOX §403(a).
33. SOX §402.
34. SOX §306(a).
35. SOX §304.

presented in the tables. This overview addresses in one place these factors with respect to both the separate elements of executive compensation and executive compensation as a whole. We are adopting the overview substantially as proposed, but, in response to comments, we are requiring a separate report of the compensation committee similar to the report required of the audit committee,[1] which will be considered furnished and not filed.[2]

Following the Compensation Discussion and Analysis, we have organized detailed disclosure of executive compensation into three broad categories:

- compensation with respect to the last fiscal year (and the two preceding fiscal years), as reflected in an amended Summary Compensation Table that presents compensation paid currently or deferred (including options, restricted stock and similar grants) and compensation consisting of current earnings or awards that are part of a plan, and as supplemented by a table providing back-up information for certain data in the Summary Compensation Table;

- holdings of equity-related interests that relate to compensation or are potential sources of future gains, with a focus on compensation-related equity interests that were awarded in prior years and are "at risk," whether or not these interests are in-the-money, as well as recent realization on these interests, such as through vesting of restricted stock or the exercise of options and similar instruments; and

- retirement and other post-employment compensation, including retirement and deferred compensation plans, other retirement benefits and other post-employment benefits, such as those payable in the event of a change in control. We are requiring improved tabular disclosure for each of the above three categories and appropriate narrative disclosure that provides material information necessary to an understanding of the information presented in the individual tables.[3]

* * *

2. Financial Statements

Although this text book does not go into detail regarding financial statements for publicly traded companies, a brief discussion of the valuing and accounting for stock options is appropriate here. Publicly traded companies must prepare their financial statements in accordance with generally accepted accounting practices (gaap), as determined by the Financial Accounting Standards Board (FASB). Before FASB required the accounting of

---

1. The Audit Committee Report, required by Item 306 of Regulations S-B [17 CFR 228.306] and S-K [17 CFR 229.306] prior to these amendments, will now be required by Item 407(d) of Regulations S-B and S-K.

2. The Compensation Committee Report that we adopt today is not deemed to be "soliciting material" or to be "filed" with the Commission or subject to Regulation 14A or 14C [17 CFR 240.14a-1 et seq. or 240.14c-1 et seq.], other than as specified, or to the liabilities of Section 18 of the Exchange Act [15 U.S.C. 78r], except to the extent a company specifically requests that the report be treated as filed or as soliciting material or specifically incorporates it by reference into a filing under the Securities Act or the Exchange Act, other than by incorporating by reference the report from a proxy or information statement into the Form 10-K. Instructions 1 and 2 to Item 407(e)(5).

3. This narrative disclosure, together with the Compensation Discussion and Analysis noted above, will replace the narrative discussion that was required in the Board Compensation Report on Executive Compensation prior to these amendments. The narrative disclosure, along with the rest of the amended executive officer and director compensation disclosure, other than the new Compensation Committee Report, will be company disclosure filed with the Commission.

stock options, they were basically granted for free. Remember, a stock option provided to an employee as part of the compensation package simply means that the employee has a right to purchase actual stock certificates in the future at the strike price (*i.e.*, the stock trading price on the date of the stock option grant). There is a possibility that the option will never be exercised—either because the value of the stock does not exceed the strike price any time after the options vest, or because the value of the stock does exceed the strike price but the employee does not have personal cash on hand to purchase the stock certificates he or she is entitled to. Because of this likelihood, the "cost" to the employer of stock options only became a reality if and when an executive or other employee actually exercised the options and purchased the discounted stock certificates.

All that has changed since FASB Statement no. 123(R), Share-Based Payment, became effective for fiscal years beginning after June 15, 2005. Under the new rules, every stock option must be valued at the grant date and shown as a current year cost on the financial statement (mathematical logo-rhythms, such as the Black-Scholes method or more complicated stochastic analyses use probabilities to determine an actual present value of expected stock option exercises).

As stock options now are not free, as many executives feel screwed with all of the underwater options in the late 1990s during the dot com bubble burst, as issues with illegal back-dating of stock options (whether willfully or not), and as public outrage over the perceived excesses of executive compensation, compensation consultants are in a period of re-evaluating the proper mix of stock options, restricted stock certificates, restricted stock units, phantom stock, and all other methods of providing equity compensation in a company's desire to provide long-term incentives to favored employees.

Chapter 19

Health and Welfare Benefit Plans

Overview

How can an employer provide health benefits to employees (and possibly to their families)?

- medical care is the "diagnosis, cure, mitigation, treatment, or prevention of disease, or for the purpose of affecting any structure or function of the body"

- the employer can set aside reserves to reimburse medical expenses (self-funded) or can pay premiums to an insurer or medical services provider

- delivery of health benefits can generally be

  - fee-for-services plan—each expense is reimbursed in full or in part

  - Health Maintenance Organization—a group of doctors and medical staff (usually in a common building) provide all basic medical services

  - preferred provider organizations—a lower out-of-pocket expense is charged to the individual if he or she visits a doctor in the network than if he or she visits a doctor outside of the network

  - point of service plans—as long as the individual's primary physician recommends a specialized medical doctor or procedure, then each expense is reimbursed in full or part

What are some of the types of welfare benefit plans an employer can sponsor?

- Here, the appropriate provision of the Internal Revenue Code dictates what needs to be included in the plan document (and how the plan must be administered) in order for the employer to take a deduction on the cost of the benefits and allow the employees to totally exclude the benefits received from Gross Income

- the most common are:

  - group term life insurance for employees with face amounts up to $50,000

  - group legal services

  - educational assistance programs

  - dependent care assistance programs

  - adoption assistance programs

  - cafeteria plans

    - one of the choices must be cash, and then the employer is free to allow the employee to choose from other benefits like medical expense reimbursement (including dental and vision), disability, life insurance premiums for death benefits in excess of $50,000, day care expenses, prepaid legal services and other qualified benefits

- the employee chooses in December how much pre-tax money, if any, will be withheld from the following year's paychecks and deposited into the cafeteria plan
- Regulations dictate the few reasons an employee can change the election during the year
- contributions are subject to the "use it or lose it" doctrine
- qualified transportation fringe benefits
- other fringe benefits
  - a no-additional cost service,
  - a qualified employee discount,
  - a working condition fringe,
  - a de minimis fringe, or
  - a qualified moving expense reimbursement

How can an employee pay any required out-of-pocket health benefit expenses on a tax-free basis?

- as the cost of providing health care continues to grow, employers are passing all, or a portion, of the cost to employees
- in addition to the actual group health plan, the employer can provide the following plans to help the employee pay for his or her share, and any family members share, on a pre-tax basis (but the cost will be included in the employee's Gross Income if the family member is a same-sex spouse or domestic partner, or a child that is not considered a dependent):
  - Archer Medical Savings Accounts (MSAs)
    - Archer MSAs are only allowed for small employers (defined here as an employer that employed an average of 50 or fewer employees on business days during either of the 2 preceding calendar years)
    - because of the small employer limitations and the temporary basis, Archer MSAs are not too common
  - Cafeteria Plans and Flexible Spending Arrangements (FSAs)
    - the employer can allow employees to elect salary deferrals, or can fund, accounts to pay medical expenses
    - at the end of the year, any unused account balance will be forfeited (which is why many individuals who have lower medical expenses during the year than anticipated will purchase eye glasses or get their teeth cleaned in the waning weeks of December)
  - Health Reimbursement Arrangements
    - The Department of Treasury approved products being marketed, and locked in their tax advantages (so there is no statutory authority, and any variation from the pure vanilla models shown in the Revenue Rulings and IRS Notices can lead to unanticipated tax results)

- the employer sets up notional accounts as part of its general assets, and credits the amount in any employee's account
- unlike cafeteria plans, unused balances at the end of the year can be carried forward
- however, once the individual's service is terminated, the employer can decide to retain all unused account balances

- Health Savings Accounts
  - Congress added a statutory provision to allow employees to open an HSA at the bank or financial institution of their choice
  - HSAs can be funded by employee deferrals or employer contributions
  - The employee owns the account, so unused balances at the end of the year can be carried forward, and the employee keeps the account even if employment is terminated
  - however, in order for the employee to be allowed to fund his or her HSA, the HSA must be tethered to a High Deductible Health Plan, meaning there is a substantial amount of out of pocket expenses the individual must pay (either through the HSA or through other personal assets) before the health plan will cover the cost of additional benefits

- wellness programs
  - the employer can have programs to encourage weight loss or smoking cessation, with the reward being a reduced share of the premium cost

What are the COBRA rules that apply to group health plans?

- COBRA was enacted in 1985 so that terminated employees and their covered family members, who may lose coverage under a group health plan because of termination of employment, death, divorce, or other life events, may be able to continue the coverage under the group health plans for themselves and their covered dependents for limited periods of time for essentially the cost of the full premiums (plus 2%)
- COBRA generally applies to an employer with 20 or more employees on a normal business day in the prior year
- COBRA notices are one of the most important aspects of COBRA, and one of the aspects that is most litigated
  - basically an initial notice informing the employee of his or her COBRA rights must be communicated upon employment, and then another notice must be given timely (within either 30 days or 60 days, depending on the reason) after a "qualifying event"
- generally, if the individual or any qualified beneficiary elects COBRA coverage within 60 days of a qualified event, then as long as premiums are properly paid to the employer, the COBRA coverage will continue for 18 months (or 36 months for some reasons)
- "Qualifying events" are defined, for the employee, as a voluntary or involuntary termination of employment for reasons other than gross misconduct or a reduction in the number of hours of employment

- for the qualified beneficiaries, "qualifying events" are defined to include death of the employee, divorce or legal separation, or, for children and dependents, the loss of such status under the tax laws
- employers that fail to comply with COBRA may be assessed a penalty

What are the HIPAA rules that apply to group health plans?

- HIPAA was enacted in 1996 so that employees, and members of their families, that have a pre-existing medical condition, will not suffer discrimination in future health coverage based on a factor that relates to the individual's health
- in addition, HIPAA imposes uniform standards for the electronic transfer of medical, billing and other information used in the administrative and financial transactions between health care providers, group health plans, and health care clearinghouses; and also imposes new privacy safeguards on certain individually identifiable health information and medical records
- HIPAA generally applies to all group health plans with more than 2 employees, which includes group health plans offered by partnerships, self-employed entities, and churches
- HIPAA generally applies to all types of benefits offered, except for those specifically excluded under the statute (such as accidental death and dismemberment coverage)
- in regards to portability,
  - a preexisting condition refers to any physical or mental conditions for which medical advice, diagnosis, care or treatment was recommended or received before the enrollment date
  - basically, under HIPAA, group health plans can deny coverage for such medical conditions that were problematic to the individual within 6 months of joining the new plan (*i.e.* being hired as an employee for the new employer that sponsors this group health plan)
  - the period that the group health plan can deny coverage for the preexisting condition is limited to 12 months, but must be reduced by the period of time that the individual was covered under a HIPAA plan before enrolling in this plan
- in regards to nondiscrimination and coverage,
  - group health plans can offer whatever benefits it wants and can apply across-the-board limitations on the levels and types of benefits; however, group health plans cannot discriminate in eligibility or enrollment based on health related factors (such as health status, mental or physical medical condition, claims experience, receipt of health care, medical history, genetic information, evidence of insurability, or disability status) and cannot charge an individual a higher premium than is charged to similarly situated individuals
  - therefore, group health plans can (1) exclude coverage for certain diseases or conditions, or certain treatments or drugs, and can (2) limit coverage for annual or lifetime limits, and can set deductibles, co-payments and co-insurance—as long as they are applied uniformly and are not directed to any individual's health related factors

- additionally, plans can deny coverage for sources-of-injury (such as recreational activities), but cannot deny coverage for an individual simply because he or she participates in such activity while not working (for example, bungee jumping)
- however, the plan is allowed to reduce premiums for individuals who comply with a bona fide wellness program (for example, a weight loss or a quit-smoking program that reduces the premiums charged to such individuals who complete the program)
- in regards to privacy,
  - only certain people can see and use "protected health information" (individually identifiable health information related to the past, present, or future physical or mental health or condition of an individual, including demographic information held by the health plan administrator) for specific purposes
  - in all cases, only the minimum amount of PHI necessary can be used
  - all covered entities (other group health plans, insurers and HMOs), as well as any business associate (an agent that conducts business transaction on behalf of the plan or any person who provides legal, actuarial, accounting, consulting, data aggregation, management, administration, accreditation, or financial services involving disclosure of an individual's PHI) need to comply with the privacy regulations
  - under the rules, the employer cannot use PHI from the group health plan to administer any other type of employee benefit program and is prohibited from using it for employment-related purposes (such as performance reviews, promotions, raises, and terminations)
- employers that fail to comply with HIPAA may be assessed a penalty

What other rules apply to group health plans?

- Mental Health Parity Act (MHPA) was enacted in 1996 so that group health plans are prohibited from setting lower lifetime or annual dollar limits for mental health coverage than is set for the medical and surgical benefits for physical health (thus, although a group health plan is not required to offer mental health coverage, if it does, then the dollar limits for the mental health benefits provided cannot be lower than other limits—employers that fail to comply with MHPA may be assessed a penalty)
- Newborn and Mother's Health Protection Act (NMHPA) was enacted in 1996 so that group health plans must allow mothers and newborns to remain in the hospital for at least 48 hours after birth (or 96 hours in the case of a cesarean delivery), and cannot apply pressure for an earlier release (employers that fail to comply with NMHPA may be assessed a penalty)
- Women's Health and Cancer Rights Act (WHCRA) was enacted in 1996 so that group health plans that offer medical and surgical benefits for mastectomies must also offer benefits for reconstructive surgery of the removed breast, for symmetrical appearance of the other breast, and all prostheses and coverage of physical complications at all stages of the mastectomy (employers that fail to comply with MHPA may be assessed a penalty)

A. Taxation of Health and Welfare Benefits

Any part of the compensation package that is not paid in cash is generally deemed to be a health or welfare benefit (or equity compensation, as described in Chapter 18). Health benefits generally include premium payments for accident or health insurance for personal injuries or sickness[1] or amounts received from the insurer.[2] Welfare benefits generally include other non-cash components of compensation that are not health benefits, but that do add to the welfare and well-being of the employee, and sometimes to the employee's family. Many employee benefits experts bifurcate welfare benefits into those that have specific rules under the Code that provide the employer with an immediate deduction and the employee with exclusion from Gross Income and those that do not. In this chapter, the latter type of welfare benefit is simply described as "other," which include fringe benefits, perks, tangible benefits like wellness programs and disease management assistance, and intangible benefits like first choice of job assignments or being allowed to work from home. Like other forms of compensation and employee benefits, regardless of compliance with the requirements under the Code, if the benefits are delivered through an ERISA plan, then they must also comply with those requirements and prohibitions.

1. Health Benefits

Health benefits offered by an employer to an employee come in many different varieties: for example, the employer can purchase insurance, can reimburse out of pocket expenses directly to the employees, or can hire a medical professional to treat employees during working hours. The Code has rules for the various types of health benefits, that, if followed, allow the employer a deduction for their expenses[3] and allow the employee to receive the value of the benefits provided tax-free. If the delivery of health benefits constitutes an ERISA welfare plan, then additional burdens are placed on the employer and additional rights are provided to the participants; and if the welfare plan specifically constitutes a group health plan, then there are even more issues and requirements for compliance.

The starting point for health benefits is in the context of providing access to medical care, or at least a subsidy on an employee's out-of-pocket medical expenses. Medical care, in general, is "the diagnosis, cure, mitigation, treatment, or prevention of disease, or for the purpose of affecting any structure or function of the body."[4] While this definition is the metric normally used for an individual to take a personal deduction for medical expenses on his or her income tax return, the definition is cross-referenced frequently in the Code where tax advantages pass to the employer and employee under a health plan. The definition is a moving target, and the IRS publishes an annual alphabetical listing of costs that are and are not considered medical expenses, and an individual taxpayer can submit a private letter ruling request if he or she has an expense that is not on the list.[5]

---

1. IRC § 105(a).
2. IRC § 104(a)(3).
3. IRC § 162(a)(1) , " … a reasonable allowance for salaries and other compensation for personal services actually rendered." (emphasis added).
4. IRC § 213(d)(1).
5. IRS Pub. 502 (which is updated annually).

In addition, the employer might want to coordinate benefits with the federal Medicare program. Medicare is a broad public program that provides health care benefits for virtually all American citizens who have attained age 65, and for those citizens who become disabled before reaching age 65. The federal Health Care Financing Administration (which is part of the Department of Health and Human Services) administers Medicare.[6]

Medicare Part A: provides inpatient hospital benefits, hospital skilled nursing facility benefits, and related home health services. FICA payroll taxes serve as the premiums (*i.e.*, 1.45% of compensation).

Medicare Part B: provides supplementary medical insurance above and beyond the Part A coverage, but only for those individuals who elect the extra coverage and pay a premium.

Medicare Part C: Medicare Advantage plans, which is an alternative to coverage under Parts A and B.

Medicare Part D: provides prescription drug coverage, but only for those that purchase a proper plan.

Coordinating the group health plan with Medicare is important since employers cannot discriminate against older individuals who are still employees (although plans are allowed to reduce retiree health benefits once the individual qualified for Medicare).[7]

Disability benefits, whether short-term or long-term, are also analyzed as health benefits under the Tax Code,[8] and COBRA continuation protection does not extend to group health plans that provide only disability benefits.[9]

There are several decisions the employer must make. After deciding the array of benefits to offer (such as medical, dental, vision, prescription drugs, and mental health), the employer needs to select how those benefits will be provided (*i.e.,* the choices the covered individuals have in doctors, medical facilities and procedures, and direct out-of-pocket costs). The delivery of health insurance is basically broken down into four main categories:[10]

Fee-for-Service Plans (Indemnity): A Fee-for-Service plan reimburses medical providers for each service a covered individual receives on a case by case basis. For example, if an individual needs an emergency-room x-ray, the hospital will submit a claim to the insurance carrier, who then pays the hospital's fee. There is generally a required annual deductible before it begins to reimburse for covered services. FOS plans provide the covered individuals total freedom to seek whichever doctors, hospitals and clinics are preferable.

Health Maintenance Organizations: The health coverage is paid in advance, rather than paying for each health related service separately. The HMO will offer a range of benefits from preventative care to dental or vision coverage. The doctors and medical staff are generally employees of the health plan. The covered in-

---

6. See http://www.os.dhhs.gov/about/opdivs/hcfa.html.

7. Equal Employment Opportunity Commission Regs. at 29 CFR Parts 1625 and 1627, 72 CFR 72938 (12/26/2007).

8. Rev. Rul. 2004-55 (the applicable statutes and regulations [§§ 104 and 105] do not distinguish between short-term and long-term disability plans).

9. An Employee's Guide to Health Benefits Under COBRA (reprinted September 2006) prepared by the U.S. Department of Labor Employee Benefits Security Administration, available at http://www.dol.gov/ebsa/pdf/cobraemployee.pdf.

10. From http://www.insurelane.com/health/health-insurance-explained.html.

dividual will choose a primary care giver, who will be responsible for coordinating his or her overall health care. The majority of HMO plans require a co-payment for an office visit, a hospital stay, or specialist health service.

Preferred Provider Organizations: A PPO Plan negotiates lower overall fee arrangements with an assortment of doctors, hospitals, clinics, and other health providers. The individual's cost-sharing rate will be lower in-network than out, but the individual still has the freedom to step out of the network for treatment if it is preferred. For example, a PPO may cover 90% of costs when care is received from an in-network provider, but only 70% of costs when received from an out-of-network care provider.

Point of Service Plans: POS plans are HMOs that allow individuals to manage their own health care, rather than insisting on referrals from their primary care physician. Whenever a medical need arises, the individual will generally have the following choices: go through the primary care physician, and receive coverage under HMO guidelines; receive care through a PPO provider and receive coverage under the PPO's in-network rules; or choose the services of a health-care professional outside of the HMO or PPO networks, and receive coverage under out-of-network rules.

The employer then needs to decide:

- whether to self-fund the plan;
- whether to pass some of the costs along to employees;
- whether to allow spouses, children, dependents, and other family members of the employee to participate in the plan;
- whether the health benefits will coordinate with Medicare[11]; and
- once implemented, whether to outsource the administration and operation of the plan.

The decisions should coordinate what the particular group of covered individuals (meaning the employees and family members) desire with the costs that the employer can afford.

2. Welfare Benefits

In general, welfare benefits are benefits that add to the general welfare of an employee, and possibly his or her family members. The benefits that Congress specifically encourages through favorable taxation are:

Group Term Life Insurance:[12] If the employer purchases a group-term life insurance policy for its non-key employees,[13] then the premiums for death benefits up to $50,000

11. According to the Medicare website, some employer-provided health insurance policies can continue or switch over to provide coverage for individuals when they are 65 and retired. In addition, Medicare has special rules that apply to beneficiaries who have group health plan coverage through their own or their spouse's current employment—if the sponsoring employer has 20 or more employees, then the plan must offer these people the same health insurance benefits under the same conditions that younger workers and spouses receive. Visit http://www.medicare.gov/Choices/Employer.asp.

12. IRC § 79.

13. IRC § 79(d)(1)(A). Key employee has the same meaning as under § 416(i).

for each individual are excluded from that individual's Gross Income. Premiums must be determined uniformly, but may be computed on the basis of 5-year age brackets.[14] The plan must be nondiscriminatory,[15] and may exclude certain employees.[16] Generally, there must be at least 10 employees to constitute a group.[17]

Group Legal Services:[18] If the employer establishes a qualified group legal services plan[19] for its employees, then the contributions into the plan, or the benefits from the plan, are excluded from that individual's Gross Income. The contributions or benefits can be for the employee, his or her spouse, and his or her dependents. The plan must be nondiscriminatory.[20]

Educational Assistance Programs:[21] If the employer establishes a qualified educational assistance program[22] for its employees, then the contributions into the program, or the benefits from the program, are excluded from that individual's Gross Income. The contributions or benefits can be for the employee, his or her spouse, and his or her dependents. In any calendar year, the maximum exclusion from gross income for any individual is $5,250.[23] Educational assistance includes the expenses incurred by the employee, spouse or dependent (such as tuition and supplies) or by the employer in providing courses of instruction (such as books, supplies and equipment), but does not include property that will be retained by the employee after the education (such as tools or supplies), does not include meals, lodging or transportation, and does not include education involving sports, games or hobbies.[24] No more that 5% of the amounts paid or incurred by the employer in any year can be for principal shareholders or owners.[25]

Dependent Care Assistance Programs:[26] If the employer establishes a qualified dependent care assistance program[27] for its employees, then the contributions into the program, or the benefits from the program, are excluded from that individual's Gross Income. In any calendar year, the maximum exclusion from gross income for any individual is $5,000.[28] Dependent care assistance means the payment or provision of employment-related expenses for household and dependent care services necessary for gainful employment.[29] No more that 25% of the amounts paid or incurred by the employer in any year can be for prin-

---

14. IRC §79(c); Treas, Regs. §1.79-3.

15. IRC §79(d)(3)(A); Treas. Regs. §1.79-4T (note that Temporary Regulations are only supposed to be effective for 3 years after publication, and these Temporary Regulations were published on 1/29/86).

16. IRC §79(d)(3)(B).

17. Treas. Regs. §1.79-1(c).

18. IRC §120.

19. IRC §§120(b) and 120(d)(7), and Treas. Regs. §1.120-3 (the employer must provide notice to the IRS to apply for recognition status).

20. IRC §120(c)(3). No more than 25% of the contributions can be for Highly Compensated Employees, as defined at §414(q).

21. IRC §127.

22. Treas. Regs. §1.127-2.

23. IRC §127(a)(2).

24. IRC §127(c)(1).

25. IRC §127(c)(3), which includes any individual that owns more than 5% of the stock or capital assets of the employer.

26. IRC §129.

27. Treas. Regs. §1.127-2.

28. IRC §129(a)(2) ($2,500 in the case of a separate return filed by a married individual). Under IRC §129(b), the individuals might be limited in their exclusion based on their earned income.

29. IRC §129(e)(1) (referencing the definition in IRC §21(d)(2) for the earned income tax credit available to certain individuals).

cipal shareholders or owners.[30] The plan must be nondiscriminatory.[31] The employer might also be able to provide an on-site facility.[32]

Adoption Assistance Programs:[33] If the employer establishes a qualified adoption assistance program[34] for its employees, then the contributions into the program, or the benefits from the program, are excluded from that individual's Gross Income. In all aggregated calendar years, the maximum exclusion from gross income for any individual for the adoption of any single child is $10,000.[35] Adoption assistance means the payment or provision of employment-related expenses for the legal adoption of an eligible child who is not a child of the taxpayer's spouse.[36]

Cafeteria Plans:[37] If the employer establishes a qualified cafeteria plan[38] for its employees, then the voluntary employee salary reductions into the plan to purchase the desired benefits are excluded from that individual's Gross Income. A cafeteria plan must be a premium-only-plan, or must offer participants the opportunity to elect between at least one permitted taxable benefit and at least one qualified benefit.[39] A premium-only-plan is a cafeteria plan that offers as its sole benefit an election between cash (for example, salary) and payment of the employee share of the employer-provided accident and health insurance premium.[40] The only qualified benefits[41] allowed to be offered under a cafeteria plan are:

- premiums for group-term life insurance (for face amounts up to $50,000);
- premiums for accident and health plans;
- certain premiums for COBRA continuation coverage;
- premiums for accidental death and dismemberment insurance policy;
- premiums for long-term or short-term disability coverage;
- premiums for dependent care assistance program;
- premiums for adoption assistance programs;
- elective deferrals into a qualified 401(k) plan;
- certain plans maintained by educational organizations; and
- contributions to Health Savings Accounts.

---

30. IRC § 129(d)(4), which includes any individual that owns more than 5% of the stock or capital assets of the employer.

31. IRC § 129(d)(2). Under IRC § 129(d)(8)(A), no more than 55% of the contributions can be for Highly Compensated Employees, as defined at § 414(q).

32. IRC § 129(e)(8).

33. IRC § 137.

34. IRC § 137(c).

35. IRC § 137(b), but an additional amount is allowed for the adoption of a special needs child (the individuals might be limited in their exclusion based on their earned income). Under § 137(f), this aggregate lifetime threshold will be adjusted for inflation.

36. IRC § 129(e)(1) (referencing the definition in § 23(d)(1) for the adoption tax credit available to certain individuals).

37. IRC § 125.

38. IRC § 125(d).

39. Proposed Treas. Regs. § 1.125-1(b)(4) (The Proposed Regulations were issued on 8/6/2007, and according to § 1.125-1(s), should be effective as of January 1, 2009; however, according to the preamble, employers may rely on the Proposed Regulations pending publication of the final regulations).

40. Proposed Treas. Regs. § 1.125-1(a)(5).

41. Proposed Treas. Regs. § 1.125-1(a)(4).

Additionally, cafeteria plans must be written,[42] and cannot discriminate in favor of highly compensated individuals[43] or Key Employees.[44]

Flexible Spending Arrangements:[45] A special type of cafeteria plan is a Flexible Spending Arrangement, which reimburses the employee for certain out-of-pocket expenses specified in the FSA. In addition to actual salary reductions, the employer is allowed to provide non-elective employer contributions, called flex-credits.[46] Under the use-or-lose rule, in order to avoid any deferral of income, any amounts contributed by employees not reimbursed by the end of the calendar year are forfeited;[47] however, the employer can choose to recapture the forfeitures to defray administrative expenses[48] or allocate the forfeitures among employees on a reasonable and uniform basis.[49] An employer is generally allowed to limit participation in a health FSA to those employees who actually participate in the employer's accident and health plan,[50] and can specify salary reduction intervals.[51]

Qualified Transportation Fringe Benefit Arrangement:[52] If the employer establishes a qualified transportation fringe benefit arrangement for its employees, then the voluntary employee salary reductions into the arrangement to purchase the desired benefits are excluded from that individual's gross income.[53] The qualified transportation fringe benefits are: transportation in a commuter highway vehicle if such transportation is in connection with travel between the employee's residence and place of employment;[54] any transit pass;[55] qualified parking;[56] or qualified bicycle commuting reimbursements.[57] The maximum amount that can be excluded from income for travel reimbursement and transit passes is $100 per month,[58] and for qualified parking is $175 per month.[59]

3. Other Fringe Benefits

In general, all other welfare benefits are those that are considered fringe benefits under the Code, but which are not viewed as employee benefit plans by Employee Benefits practitioners. However, they are still benefits that employees may value, and will only provide a deduction for the employer and exclusion from Gross Income by individuals if the rules of the respective Code section are followed. Under the general tax rules, anything of value that an individual receives in exchange for services rendered should be included in his or her gross income, unless there is a specific provision in the Code that excludes

---

42. IRC § 125(d)(1).
43. IRC § 125(b)(1), not the same definition as a Highly Compensated Employee under § 414(q).
44. IRC § 125(b)(2), the same definition as Key Employee under § 416(i)(1).
45. Proposed Treas. Regs. § 125-5.
46. Proposed Treas. Regs. § 1.125-5(b)(1).
47. Proposed Treas. Regs. § 1.125-5(c)(1).
48. Proposed Treas. Regs. § 1.125-5(o)(1)(ii)(C).
49. Proposed Treas. Regs. § 1.125-5(o)(1)(ii)(A).
50. Proposed Treas. Regs. § 1.125-5(g)(1).
51. Proposed Treas. Regs. § 1.125-5(g)(2).
52. IRC § 132(f).
53. Treas. Regs. § 1.132-9, Q&A-11.
54. IRC § 132(f)(1)(A).
55. IRC § 132(f)(1)(B).
56. IRC § 132(f)(1)(C).
57. IRC § 132(f)(1)(G).
58. IRC § 132(f)(2)(A).
59. IRC § 132(f)(2)(B).

it.[60] The IRS provides an explanation of the following fringe benefits that confer tax advantages, as well as a summary of their employment tax treatment:[61]

Achievement Awards: the value of any tangible personal property given to an employee as an award for either length of service or safety achievement (however, 2% shareholders in an S Corporation can not be treated as an employee);

Athletic Facilities: the value of an employee's use of an on-premises gym or other athletic facility operated by the employer (can be on any property owned or leased by the employer, as long as it is not for residential use);

De minimis (minimal) benefits: any property or service provided to an employee that has "so little value" that accounting for it would be unreasonable or administratively impracticable. Examples include: occasional use of a company copying machine; holiday gifts of property with a low fair market value; group-term life insurance with a death benefit of up to $2000, occasional parties or picnics for employees or their guests; or occasional tickets for entertainment or sporting events;

Employee discounts: price reductions given to employees on property or services offered to customers in the ordinary course of business (but not on real property or discounts of investment property). Under the Publication, the IRS allows the employer to provide de minimus fringe benefits to current, retired and disables employees, their widow(er)s, certain leased employees, and partners of the partnership that provide services. There are limits to the amount that can be excluded from the individual's gross income, and the benefits need to be available to all employees on a nondiscriminatory manner;

Lodging on business premises: the value of lodging furnished to an employee if: it is on the business premises, it is for the employer's convenience, and the employee accepts it as a condition of employment;

De Minimus Meals: the value of de minimus meals provided to an employee that has "so little value" that accounting for it would be unreasonable or administratively impracticable. Examples include: coffee, doughnuts, and soft drinks; occasional meals or money provided to allow an employee to work overtime; or occasional parties or picnics for employees and their invited guests. Additionally, the value of meals provided to employees at an employer-operated eating facility can be excluded if revenue from the facility equals or exceeds its direct costs and if it does not discriminatory in favor of Highly Compensated Employees.

Moving expense reimbursements: any direct or indirect payments of moving expenses that the employee would have been able to deduct on his or her individual income tax return if not for the reimbursement;

No-additional-cost services: services usually provided in the ordinary course of business that are provided to an employee that does not cause any substantial additional costs (such as airline travel, bus or train tickets, hotel rooms, and telephone services provided for free). Additionally, the value of no-additional cost services cannot be discriminatory in favor of Highly Compensated Employees;

Retirement Planning Services: the value of retirement planning advice or information provided to an employee or his or her spouse, which can include general advice and information on retirement, but which cannot include services for tax preparation, accounting, legal, or brokerage advice or operations;

---

60. IRC § 61(a).

61. IRS Publication 15-B (2010), "Employer's Tax Guide to Fringe Benefits, (for use in 2010)", available at http://www.irs.gov/pub/irs-pdf/p15b.pdf.

Tuition reduction: the value of undergraduate education expenses paid from the employee's wages, and the value of graduate education expenses if the graduate student performs certain teaching or research activities; and

Working condition benefits: the value of property and services provided to an employee so he or she can perform his or her job (such use of a company car for business or work-related education).

In addition to the delineated fringe benefits, employers can provide tangible benefits, like sick leave, paid family and medical leave, wellness programs and disease management, as well as intangible perks, like first choice in job assignments or vacation schedules, casual Fridays, the ability to work at home, or covered parking spaces. The employer can be as creative as it wants, but from an income tax point of view the value of the benefit will be taxable to the employee if it does not meet the definition of a specific section of the Code, and from an ERISA point of view the benefit cannot be randomly reduced or taken away if it is delivered through an ERISA plan.

B. Paying for Health and Welfare Benefits

Like many other aspects of employee benefit plans, the interaction of tax attributes under the Code and mandates placed on the employer under ERISA is quite fuzzy. Technically, there is no definition of a group health plan under the Code, and the only definition is found in ERISA; however, the ERISA definition contains cross-references to Code sections. A group health plan is an employee welfare benefit plan providing medical care[62] to participants or beneficiaries directly or through insurance, reimbursement, or otherwise.[63] However, a group health plan does not include any plan substantially all of the coverage under which is for qualified long-term care services.[64]

1. Fully Insured or Self-Funded

Health care benefit plans and disability plans can be classified as: fully insured, fully self-funded, or partially insured and partially self-funded. Under a fully insured plan, benefits are provided solely through an insurance company or similar organization (such as a health maintenance organization), and premiums are paid directly by the employer from its general assets or partly from the employer's general assets and partly from contributions made by employees or members. Under a fully self-funded plan, benefits are paid, as needed, solely from the general funds of the employer maintaining the plan. Under a partially insured and partially self-funded plan, benefits are provided by using a combination of insurance and benefits paid from the general funds of the employer.

Because there is no specific exclusion under ERISA, by default, group health plans are subject to ERISA, regardless of whether fully insured or not (thus, subject to Reporting and Disclosure, Fiduciary Duties, Civil Action and Enforcement, and the special rules for group health plans pursuant to COBRA and HIPAA). However, under the preemp-

---

62. As defined in IRC § 213(d).

63. ERISA § 607(1).

64. As defined in IRC § 7702B(c).

tion clause of ERISA, if an insurance company providing benefits in a fully-insured plan (or stop-loss insurance for a combination plan) is regulated by a state insurance agency, then the State laws are not preempted.[65] Employers should determine whether ERISA is preemptive or not before entering into any insurance contracts.

2. Cost-Sharing with Employees

In order to reduce the overall outlay by employers, the trend is for employers to require the covered employees to pay a portion of the premiums. Employers generally charge more when employees also elect to cover their non-employee spouses, children, dependents, or other members of their families. Congress has provided some funding vehicles for employees to use pre-tax money to pay their share.

In addition to paying a portion of the premiums, the other more recent trend is what is called consumer driven health care. Here, covered individuals will be required to pay a certain limited amount out of their pockets, commonly referred to as a deductible (such as a $15 co-pay for any doctor's visit, regardless of how much the doctor actually charges, a $12 fee for any prescription drug, regardless of the true cost of providing such medication, or even a limited $1000 for any type of necessary surgery, irrespective of the final cost charged to and covered by the health insurer). The idea behind consumer driven health care is to gradually raise the amount of out-of-pocket expenses bourn by the individual. This shift, in theory, would assist each individual in taking more control of what health treatment is necessary and worthwhile in his or her own situation. One of the advantages of Health Savings Accounts (as described below) is that financial gain will inure to those individuals that exercise thriftiness in their personal health care decisions. However, opponents fear that individuals will not seek out preventive health care due to the cost, and will only go to the doctors after conditions rise to the crucial or emergency level.

a. Subsidy for Employees

The employer does not need to provide health benefits in the first place, and does so on a voluntary basis. When the employer wants to pass some of the costs over to the employees, it sometimes tries to put a positive spin on the communications. Many employers indicate that because they are part of a group, they are able to negotiate better premiums than the individuals can usually do on their own outside of the group health plan. Then, the employer proclaims that instead of requiring the employees to pay the full premium, the employer will subsidize a portion. A typical subsidy is 70%, so that the employee that chooses medical benefits will only pay 30% of the total premium. A positive communications spin like this might mitigate any low morale by employees that are asked to pay for a portion of their health care benefits.

b. Subsidy for Employees' Spouses, Children, Dependents and Domestic Partners

Once an employer negotiates a group health plan contract with an insurer (or decides to self-insure), then it can allow the employees who choose to be covered to also enroll members of their family. For income tax purposes, the value of medical coverage for the

---

65. ERISA § 514(b)(2)(A).

employee's spouse, children and statutory dependents will not be included in the employee's Gross Income. While employers are allowed to let employees enroll other individuals, the value of the benefits for these non-traditional family members will be imputed into the employee's gross income as compensation. The term domestic partner can be viewed in a broad sense as not only same-sex individuals in a committed relationship[66] but also opposite-sex couples that could marry but choose not to (and even other members of a mixed family that do not meet the children or dependents definitions). A recent study looking at taxes lost to all same-sex and opposite-sex couples classified as "unmarried" concluded that "employees with partners now pay on average $1,069 per year more in taxes than would a married employee with the same coverage. Collectively, unmarried couples lose $178 million per year to additional taxes. U.S. employers also pay a total of $57 million per year in additional payroll taxes because of this unequal tax treatment."[67] In this period where some states are expanding spousal rights while others are contracting them, employers (and their benefits professional advisors) are cautioned to determine if there are any requirements or prohibitions on offering domestic partner benefits to their employees, especially if they contract or do business with state or local municipalities, or if they do business in multiple states.

If the family members are employed and can participate in their employer's health plan, then the family must decide which plan provides more valued benefits and which is more cost effective. Similarly, the employees eligible for their plan should see if they would be better off by being considered a family member in another plan.

c. Pre-Tax Funding Vehicles for Employees

In order to allow employees to pay the premiums or deductibles for medical expenses incurred by them, or their spouses, children or dependents, employers can establish additional employee benefit plans. Flexible Spending Accounts ("FSAs") are accounts that can be offered to employees through employer provided cafeteria plans that provide employees with coverage which reimburse specified, incurred expenses (subject to reimbursement maximums and any other reasonable conditions).[68] FSAs allow employees to elect to defer a portion of their salary, on a pre-tax basis,[69] into accounts that can be used to reimburse their "qualified medical expenses"[70] incurred during the period of coverage. The major problem with these accounts is the "use it or lose it" rule.[71] In order to be reimbursed, participants must substantiate expenses through an independent third party.[72] Therefore, although these

---

66. According to "State By State: the Legal Battle over Gay Marriage (updated Sept. 1, 2009)," available at www.npr.org, New Hampshire, Vermont, Massachusetts, Connecticut and Maine had legalized same-sex marriage. California has about 11,000 same-sex married couples, but voters overturned it in 2009, and Washington and New Jersey have forms of recognized same-sex civil unions.

67. Center for American Progress and the Williams Institute report by M. V. Lee Badgett, "Unequal Taxes of Equal Benefits: The Taxation of Domestic Partner Benefits (December 2007)," available at http://www.americanprogress.org/issues/2007/12/pdf/domestic_partners.pdf.

68. Proposed Treas. Regs. § 1.125-5(a) (72 F.R. 43937, 8/6/2007). According to the Preamble, this provision will be effective on 1/1/2009, but can be relied on pending the issuance of final regulations.

69. IRC § 125(a), unless the individual is a highly compensated employee or key employee and the plan is discriminatory under IRC § 125(b).

70. As defined in IRC § 213(d).

71. Since Cafeteria Plans cannot allow for the deferral of income, under Proposed Treas. Regs. § 1.125-5(c) (72 F.R. 43937, 8/6/2007) any unused balance at the end of the calendar year is forfeited. However, under Proposed Regs. § 1.125-1(e), a grace period of up to 2½ months after the plan year end may be adopted to allow for the reimbursement of qualified expenses incurred during that grace period.

72. Proposed Treas. Regs. § 1.125-6(b)(3) (72 F.R. 43937, 8/6/2007).

accounts provide a tax-favored way for employees to fund their anticipated medical expenses on a year-by-year basis, there is no incentive for frugality. In fact, most individuals are forced to go on a scavenger hunt at the end of each year to spend the remaining balance of their account on non-essential medical expenses, such as new eyeglasses or teeth whitening.

Archer Medical Savings Accounts

Medical Savings Accounts ("MSA"s) were introduced on a pilot basis in 1996,[73] and were renamed as Archer Medical Savings Accounts ("Archer MSAs") when the program was renewed in 2000.[74] Archer MSAs are only allowed for small employers (defined here as an employer that employed an average of 50 or fewer employees on business days during either of the 2 preceding calendar years).[75] One catch is that the medical benefits must be pursuant to a high deductible health plan, where the annual deductible is between $1500 and $2250 for the employee if only the employee participates, or between $3000 and $4500 in the case of family coverage.[76] High Deductible Health Plans may be offered by a variety of entities, including insurance companies and health maintenance organizations.[77] Employees can elect to contribute, on a pre-tax basis, salary deferrals into an Archer MSA to be used to cover their individual qualified medical expenses,[78] but, on a monthly basis, only up to 1/12 of 65% of the deductible amount if only the employee participates and 75% of the deductible amount if the employee chooses family coverage.[79]

Since these Archer MSAs do not follow the use-it-or-lose-it doctrine of their FSAs brethren,[80] they can actually further the goal of consumer driven health care since they allow accumulations from year to year and over time, and thus encourage frugality. The downside of this Archer MSA experiment, however, is that only a limited number of taxpayers may establish them,[81] and their status is temporary, originally set to become obsolete in 2000, and through recent legislation, extended several times, most recently until 2007.[82]

Health Reimbursement Arrangements

The next step in furtherance of consumer driven health care came in 2002, not by legislative mandate, but through approval and acquiescence by the U.S. Department of Treasury of certain products being promoted by insurers and financial institutions. Basically, Treasury recognized that certain accounts were being set up by employers to provide individuals with a source of income to cover their personal health expenses. These

---

73. The Health Insurance Portability and Accountability Act of 1996 § 301, P. L. 104-191.

74. The Community Renewal Tax Relief Act of 2000 § 1(a)(7), P.L. 106-554.

75. IRC § 220(c)(4).

76. IRC § 220(c)(2).

77. IR Notice 96-53, Q&A-5.

78. IRC § 220(d)(2).

79. IRC § 220(b)(2).

80. Under IRC § 220(e), while the account continues to qualify as an Archer MSA, it is not subject to tax. Under § 220(f) qualified distributions are excluded from Gross Income and excess contributions can be returned without tainting the Archer MSA. Therefore, amounts can be taken out at any time, even in future tax years.

81. IRC § 220(j). Employers can allow employees to choose their own MSA trustee or custodian (in the same way they can choose an IRA trustee or custodian), or the employer can select the trustee or custodian. However, because of this cap on allowed participants, IR Notice 96-53, Q&A-9, 10, and 11, the trustees need clearance from the IRS before establishing any new accounts.

82. IRC § 220(i)(2).

Health Reimbursement Arrangements ("HRAs") were generally provided in conjunction with a high deductible health insurance plan that caused employees to be personally responsible for higher out-of-pocket expenses. Treasury blessed these products and practices, and locked in the tax advantages and consequences for the plain vanilla products that were then being marketed.[83] Like the Archer MSAs, these accounts do not follow the use-it-or-lose-it doctrine, and allow the accumulation and compounding of remaining account balances at the end of each year.[84] Any amount distributed for an individual that is not the employee's spouse, child or dependent will be included in the employee's Gross Income.[85]

The two main disadvantages of HRAs, however, seems to be that (1) unlike Archer MSAs, or even FSAs, these HRAs are just a marketing idea approved by the Department of Treasury through their regulatory authority, but are not actually statutory provisions of the Code that are debated and legislated by Congress; and (2) unlike Archer MSAs or FSAs, there is no actual money segregated and invested for individuals, but is rather a notional account where a bookkeeper merely maintains HRA account balances within the employer's general assets (which is always subject to the employer's other creditors).

Health Savings Accounts

Regardless of employer involvement, individuals that are covered under a High Deductible Health Plan can establish Health Savings Accounts (HSAs) to accumulate personal assets for the intended purpose of helping them pay qualified medical expenses.[86] The trustee must be a bank, insurance company or other financial institution.[87] The individual owns his or her account, and any balance is portable when he or she moves from one employer to another. The amounts invested in a HSA are not subject to income tax,[88] and as long as distributions are for qualified medical expenses[89] for the account holder or for his or her spouse or dependents, then the distributions are not included in Gross Income.[90] Upon death, if the HSA is rolled over to a spouse,[91] or if transferred to a former spouse upon divorce,[92] then the spouse is deemed to be the proper account beneficiary and there is no taxable event. If amounts are used for anything other than qualified medical expenses, then the distribution is subject to income tax[93] and an additional 10% penalty tax.[94]

The medical benefits must be pursuant to a High Deductible Health Plan.[95] The HDHP must be the only plan that provides medical benefits for the individual. However, an alternate plan can provide benefits for accidents, disability, dental care, vision care, and

---

83. IR Notice 2002-45 and Rev. Rul. 2002-41.
84. In fact, under Rev. Rul. 2005-24, any distribution of the unused portion will generally be included in Gross Income.
85. Rev. Rul. 2006-36.
86. IRC § 223(d)(1).
87. IRC § 223(d)(1)(B).
88. IRC § 223(e)(1).
89. IRC § 223(d)(2).
90. IRC § 223(f)(1).
91. IRC § 223(f)(8).
92. IRC § 223(f)(7).
93. IRC § 223(f)(2).
94. IRC § 223(f)(4).
95. IRC § 223(c)(2)(A).

other permitted insurance.[96] Additionally, a plan that allows for preventative care without being subject to a deductible is still a good HDHP.[97] There are special coordination rules for married individuals, each having access to family coverage from their respective employers.[98]

Contributions each month are limited to $2250 for the employee if only the employee participates, or $4500 in the case of family coverage.[99] In addition if the individual is 55 or older, then he or she can contribute an additional annual contribution of up to $1000.[100] If an employer makes a contribution, within permissible limits, to the HSA on behalf of an employee who is an eligible individual, the contribution is deductible by the employer[101] and is excluded from the employee's Gross Income and wages.[102] A partnership may also contribute to a partner's HSA and an S corporation may contribute to the HSA of a 2-percent shareholder-employee.[103] Additionally, balances from the employee's MSA or HRA can be rolled into an HSA.[104]

With the introduction of HSAs in 2003, Congress seemed to have solved the two disadvantages of the HRAs; namely, (1) HSAs have legal effect as they are codified in the statute, and (2) HSAs represent actual individual accounts rather than notional crediting accounts. The Bureau of Labor Statistics (BLS) recently reported that 8 percent of private industry workers have access to a health savings account,[105] and the number of enrollees and dependents covered by an HSA-eligible plan increased from about 438,000 in September 2004 to about 1 million in March 2005 and to about 3 million in January 2006.[106]

d. Wellness Programs

In addition to actually subsidizing the cost of medical benefits, employers have the ability to establish a wellness program. A wellness program is any program designed to promote health or prevent disease where healthy individuals, or individuals who improve their health, can receive a higher subsidy from the employer for health benefit premiums charged. If none of the conditions for obtaining a reward under a wellness program is based on an individual satisfying a standard that is related to a health factor, then the wellness program is compliant if participation in the program is made available to all similarly situated individuals.[107] However, there are some things the employer can do if any of the conditions for obtaining a reward under a wellness program is based on an individual satisfying a standard that is related to a health factor.[108] Wellness programs have been around since 1996, but will likely become more popular due to the recent regulations published by the Department of Labor

---

96. IRC § 223(c)(1)(B).

97. IRC § 223(c)(2(C).

98. IRC § 223(b)(5).

99. IRC § 223(b)(2). The limits are adjusted annually, and are $3000 and $5950, respectively, in 2009 pursuant to Rev. Proc. 2008-29.

100. IRC § 223(b)(3).

101. IRC § 223(a).

102. IRC § 106(d).

103. IR Notice 2005-8, 2005-4 IRB 368.

104. IRC § 223(f)(5).

105. U.S. Bureau of Labor Statistics "Program Perspectives on Health Benefits (October 2008)," available at www.hls.gov/opub/perspectives/issue1.pdf.

106. The United States Government Accountability Office report, "Consumer-Directed Health Plans: Early Enrollee Experiences with Health Savings Accounts and Eligible Health Plans" (August 2006), available at http://www.gao.gov/new.items/d06798.pdf.

107. Labor Regs. § 2590.702(f)(1).

108. Labor Regs. § 2590.702(f)(2).

and an employer checklist.[109] In addition, a recent study shows that employers can save $1.65 in health care expenses for every dollar spent on a comprehensive employee wellness program.[110]

C. ERISA Rules for Health and Welfare Benefits

Employers that sponsor group health plans must comply with continuation requirements under COBRA and portability and accountability requirements under HIPAA. The compliance rules are set forth in ERISA, and penalties for noncompliance are set forth in the Code.

1. COBRA

The Consolidated Omnibus Budget and Reconciliation Act of 1985 (COBRA)[111] was enacted so that terminated employees and their covered family members, who may lose coverage under a group health plan because of termination of employment, death, divorce, or other life events, may be able to continue the coverage under the group health plans for themselves and their covered dependents for limited periods of time for essentially the cost of the full premiums. COBRA requires that each qualified beneficiary who would lose coverage under the plan as a result of a qualifying event is entitled, under the plan, to elect, within the election period, continuation coverage under the plan.[112]

While the technical COBRA-related rules for group health plans are defined in ERISA, and regulations promulgated by the Department of Labor,[113] the penalties for noncompliance are defined in the Code, and regulations promulgated by the Department of Treasury.[114] The Code imposes on the employer excise taxes of up to $100 per day for any period during which the employer fails to comply with respect to a qualified beneficiary.[115] In addition, ERISA authorizes a person entitled to a notice of COBRA rights under ERISA to recover $110 per day for each day after the notice is due and not provided.[116]

COBRA applies to employers that normally employed fewer than 20 employees on a typical business day during the preceding calendar year.[117] Even if COBRA does not apply, the plan may be subject to state law that regulates insurance and requires continuation of coverage.[118]

Continuation Requirements: After a qualifying event, a qualified beneficiary must be offered identical coverage as provided to similarly situated current employees[119] for at least

---

109. DOL Field Assistance Bulletin 2008-02.

110. Press Release on BenefitsLink issued by Highland Blue Cross Blue Shield, "Newly Published Study Demonstrates Return on Investment for Employee Wellness Program (2/11/2008), available at http://benefitslink.com/pr/detail.php?id=41609.

111. P.L. 99-272; IRC § 4980B; ERISA §§ 601–609.

112. ERISA § 601(a).

113. ERISA, Title I, Subtitle B, Part 6, §§ 601 to 609.

114. IRC § 4980B.

115. IRC § 4980B(a), (b), (c), and (e).

116. ERISA § 502(c)(1).

117. ERISA § 601(b).

118. See ERISA § 514(b)(2)(A).

119. ERISA § 602(1).

18 months.[120] However, they can be charged up to 102% of the premium (not just the portion that they were responsible for while employed).[121] The most common qualifying event for an employee include termination of employment or a reduction in hours;[122] whereas, other important qualifying events for the employee's family members are the death of the covered employee,[123] the divorce or legal separation of a spouse who is covered under the plan,[124] or a dependent child covered under the plan ceasing to be a dependent child.[125] A qualifying beneficiary is limited to the employee's spouse and dependents,[126] and thus does not include domestic partners or other family members that the employer specifically allows to b covered under the group health plan.

Notices: Fortunately for the qualified beneficiaries, but unfortunately for the employer that sponsors a group health plan, there are very strict and crucial communication issues. In order for the qualifying beneficiary to properly make an election for continuation coverage,[127] the employer must comply with the notice requirements.[128] Employers and plan administrators are cautioned that personnel in payroll departments or human resources departments need to be acutely aware of these notice requirements, and that the COBRA administration should be delegated to a third party administrator if there is any doubt of the attention that internal personnel can pay to the COBRA continuation requirements.

2. HIPAA

The Health Insurance Portability and Accountability Act of 1996 (HIPAA)[129] was enacted so that employees, and members of their families, that have a pre-existing medical condition, will not suffer discrimination in future health coverage based on a factor that relates to the individual's health. In addition, HIPAA imposes uniform standards for the electronic transfer of medical, billing and other information used in the administrative and financial transactions between health care providers, group health plans, and health care clearinghouses; and also imposes new privacy safeguards on certain individually identifiable health information and medical records.

The special group health plan requirements do not apply to any group health plan has less than 2 participants who are current employees on the first day of the plan year.[130] However, these small plans must comply with the requirements for minimum hospital stays for mothers and newborns (as described below).[131]

---

120. ERISA § 602(2).
121. ERISA § 602(3). The American Recovery and Reinvestment Act of 2009 allows eligible individuals a subsidy of up to 65% of their COBRA charge if the individual became eligible for COBRA between Sept. 1, 2008, and Dec. 31, 2009.
122. ERISA § 603(2).
123. ERISA § 603(1).
124. ERISA § 603(3).
125. ERISA § 603(5).
126. ERISA § 607(3)(a).
127. ERISA § 605(a).
128. ERISA § 606(a).
129. P.L. 104-191; IRC § 9801, *et seq*; ERISA §§ 701, *et seq.*
130. ERISA § 732(a).
131. *Id.* (cross-referencing ERISA § 711).

While the technical HIPAA-related rules for group health plans are defined in ERISA, and regulations promulgated by the Department of Labor,[132] the penalties for noncompliance are defined in the Code, and regulations promulgated by the Department of Treasury.[133] The basic penalty tax is $100 per day per effected individual.[134] If the violation is discovered upon audit, then a minimum penalty per individual of $2500 is imposed if the violations are de minimis, otherwise minimum penalty of $15,000 (church plans excluded).[135] However, there is no tax if the violation is discovered when exercising reasonable diligence[136] or if it is timely corrected (*i.e.*, within 30 days) and was not due to willful neglect.[137] There is an overall limitation on the tax[138] and the IRS has the authority to waive all or a portion of the penalty taxes under appropriate circumstances.[139] An important exception to penalty taxes altogether applies to a group health plan of a small employer which provides health insurance coverage solely through a contract with a health insurance issuer,[140] where a small employer is defined as an employer who employed an average of at least 2 but not more than 50 employees on business days during the preceding calendar year and who employs at least 2 employees on the first day of the plan year.[141]

Portability

In regards to portability, a preexisting condition refers to any physical or mental conditions for which medical advice, diagnosis, care or treatment was recommended or received before the enrollment date.[142] Basically, a group health plan can deny coverage for those medical conditions that were problematic to the individual within 6 months of joining the new plan (*i.e.* being hired as an employee for the new employer that sponsors this group health plan). The period that the group health plan can deny coverage for the preexisting condition is limited to 12 months,[143] but must be reduced by the period of time that the individual was covered under a HIPAA plan before enrolling in this plan.[144]

Accountability

In regards to accountability (or more precisely, nondiscrimination and coverage), group health plans can offer any mix of benefits and can apply across-the-board limitations on the levels and types of benefits.[145] However, group health plans cannot discriminate in eligibility or enrollment based on health related factors (such as health

---

132. ERISA, Title I, Subtitle B, Part 7, §§701 to 734. Basically identical definitions are found in the Code, Subtitle K, Chapter 100, §§9801–9833 (although there is no corresponding Code provision that mirrors ERISA §713, which requires reconstructive surgery following a mastectomy).

133. IRC §4980D.

134. IRC §4980D(b)(1).

135. IRC §4980D(b)(3).

136. IRC §4980D(c)(1).

137. IRC §4980D(c)(2).

138. IRC §4980D(c)(3).

139. IRC §4980D(c)(3).

140. IRC §4980D(d)(1).

141. IRC §4980D(d)(2).

142. ERISA §701(a)(1).

143. ERISA §701(a)(2).

144. ERISA §701(a)(3).

145. ERISA §702(a)(2).

status, mental or physical medical condition, claims experience, receipt of health care, medical history, genetic information, evidence of insurability, or disability status)[146] and cannot charge an individual a higher premium than is charged to similarly situated individuals.[147]

Therefore, group health plans can (1) exclude coverage for certain diseases or conditions, or certain treatments or drugs, and can (2) limit coverage for annual or lifetime limits, and can set deductibles, co-payments and co-insurance—as long as they are applied uniformly and are not directed to any individual's health related factors. Additionally, plans can deny coverage for sources-of-injury (such as recreational activities), but cannot deny coverage for an individual simply because he or she participates in such activity while not working (such as bungee jumping).

Privacy

In regards to privacy, only certain people can have access to and use "protected health information" (individually identifiable health information related to the past, present, or future physical or mental health or condition of an individual, including demographic information held by the health plan administrator) for specific purposes. In all cases, only the minimum amount of PHI necessary can be used. The health privacy rules are pursuant to Regulations promulgated by the Department for Health and Human Services since Congress did legislate rules in the time period set forth in HIPAA.[148] Basically, all covered entities (group health plans, insurers and HMOs), as well as any Business Associate (an agent that conducts business transaction on behalf of the plan or any person who provides legal, actuarial, accounting, consulting, data aggregation, management, administration, accreditation, or financial services involving disclosure of an individual's PHI) need to comply with the privacy regulations,[149] and must protect the individually identifiable health information of the plan participants.[150] There are permitted uses and disclosure requirements in the Regulations, but the bottom line is that the employer should limit the number of personnel in the payroll or human resources department that have access to protected health information, ensure that medical records are at the very least in a separate locked file cabinet or in different password-protected electronic files than other personnel records, and that health information is not in any way used to make employment decisions. Common sense should be used as well, such as making sure the officer of the company that the assigned privacy officer's computer monitor cannot be seen by any non-authorized personnel.[151]

Other Provisions of HIPAA

In addition to the most publicized components of HIPAA (portability, accountability, and privacy), the law affects group health plans by:

---

146. ERISA § 702(a)(1). Labor Regs. § 2590.702(a)(2) defines evidence of insurability as conditions arising out of acts of domestic violence and participation in activities such as motorcycling, snowmobiling, all-terrain vehicle riding, horseback riding, skiing, and other similar activities.

147. ERISA § 702(b)(1). Labor Regs. § 2590.702(d) define similarly situated individuals, and Labor Regs. § 2590.702(e) clarifies the nonconfinement and actively at work provisions.

148. 45 CFR Parts 160, 162, and 164, as amended through February 16, 2006.

149. 45 C.F.R. §§ 160.102, 160.103. Although small group health plans had a delayed effective date until 2004, there are no other special provisions or relief granted to small group health plans.

150. 45 C.F.R. § 160.103.

151. The complete privacy rules and obligations, as well as general advice, can be found at http://www.hhs.gov/ocr/hipaa/.

- requiring that if an employer participates in a multi-employer group health plan or a multiple employer welfare arrangement (MEWA), renewability in the plan is guaranteed as long as contributions are timely paid; there is no fraud or other intentional misrepresentation of material fact by the employer; the employer complies with material plan provisions; the plan continues to offer coverage in that particular geographic area; in the case of a plan that offers benefits through a network plan, there is still at least one individual enrolled through the employer who lives, resides, or works in the service area of the network plan; and if applicable, the collectively bargained agreement requires or authorizes contributions to the plan;

- allowing a group health plan to reduce premiums for individuals who comply with a bona fide wellness program, (for example: a weight loss or a quit-smoking program that reduces the premiums charged to such individuals who complete the program);[152]

- requiring group health plans to issue certificates of creditable coverage when an individual no longer is covered under the plan (due to termination of employment, voluntary withdrawal from the plan, or plan termination).[153]

3. Mental Health Parity Act

The Mental Health Parity Act of 1996[154] required that a group health plan (or health insurance that funds a group health plan provided by an employer) that provided both medical and surgical benefits and mental health benefits may not impose an annual or lifetime limit on mental health benefits unless it imposes an annual or lifetime limit on medical and surgical benefits.[155] Although this provision has been extended several times, in 2008, Congress made the provisions permanent, and renamed the section by adding "substance abuse."[156]

4. The Newborns' and Mothers' Health Protection Act

The Newborns' and Mothers' Health Protection Act of 1996[157] applies to group health plans sponsored by employers of all sizes and group health insurance. The statute prohibits group health plans and group health insurance from restricting hospital stays in connection with childbirth for mother and child following normal vaginal delivery to less than 48 hours or, following cesarean section, to less than 96 hours. The hospital stay may be less than the minimum if approved by the attending physician in consultation with the mother.[158] Restrictions on eligibility, monetary payments, and rebates, penalties on providers, incentives to providers, and limitation of benefits during this portion of a hos-

---

152. Labor Regs. § 2590.702(f).
153. ERISA § 701(e).
154. P.L. 104-204; IRC § 9812; ERISA § 712.
155. ERISA § 712(a).
156. Congress passed the "Technical Correction in Mental Health Parity Effective Date Act," P.L. 110-460, which deleted paragraph (f), which had the original sunset date.
157. P.L. 104-204; IRC § 9811; ERISA § 711.
158. ERISA § 711(a)(2).

pital stay are also prohibited.[159] This rule must be included in the summary description for the plan within 60 days after the first day of the first plan year in which it is required.[160]

5. Women's Health and Cancer Rights Act

The Women's Health and Cancer Rights Act of 1998[161] applies to all group health plans, insurance companies, and health maintenance organizations (HMOs) that provide coverage for medical and surgical benefits. Thus, group health plans sponsored by small employers of all sizes must comply with the requirements contained in the Act. All group health plans, insurance companies, and health maintenance organizations that provide coverage for medical and surgical benefits with respect to a mastectomy must provide coverage for reconstructive surgery in a manner determined in consultation with the attending physician and the patient.[162] Coverage includes reconstruction of the breast on which the mastectomy was performed, surgery and reconstruction of the other breast to produce a symmetrical appearance, and prostheses and treatment of physical complications at all stages of the mastectomy, including lymphedemas.[163] The health plan may impose deductibles or coinsurance requirements for reconstructive surgery in connection with a mastectomy only if the deductibles and coinsurance requirements are consistent with those established for other benefits under the plan.

Group health plans may not deny to a participant eligibility (or continued eligibility) to enroll in or renew coverage under the plan solely to avoid this new requirement.[164] Health plans also may not provide financial incentives or disincentives to medical providers in order to avoid this requirement.[165] In addition, group health plans, insurance companies, and HMOs must satisfy notice requirements associated with the enactment of this law.[166]

---

159. ERISA § 711(b).
160. ERISA § 711(d).
161. P.L. 105-277, IRC § 9802; ERISA § 713.
162. ERISA § 713(a).
163. ERISA § 713(a)(1)–(3).
164. ERISA § 713(c)(1).
165. ERISA § 713(c)(2).
166. ERISA § 713(b).

Chapter 20

Social Security Benefits and Individual Retirement Accounts

Overview

What is a traditional IRA?
- IRAs can only have a bank, investment company, or other qualifying financial institution serve as custodian
- the contribution is a deduction from the individual's tax return (*i.e.,* it's a pre-tax contribution) or is a non-taxable rollover from a qualified plan
- individual tax payers may deposit up to $5,000 (as adjusted for inflation) each year; however, the limit is phased out depending on the taxpayers Adjusted Gross Income or if an individual is a participant in a qualified retirement plan
- individuals older than 50 can make additional "catch up" contributions of $1,000 (as adjusted for inflation) each year
- the money accumulates tax-free until withdrawn
- the individual pays taxes in the year distributed on contributions plus investment earnings actually received
- there will generally be a 10% penalty for withdrawals taken before attaining age 59½ (unless used for certain expenses like education or the purchase of a home— however, there are very specific rules for these qualified expenses)
- individuals must start taking out money at age 70½ and therefore cannot use it as a wealth transfer device

What is a Roth IRA?
- Roth IRAs can only have a bank, investment company, or other qualifying financial institution serve as custodian
- the contribution is made after it is included in the individual's Gross Income (*i.e.,* it's an after-tax contribution) or is a non-taxable rollover from a Roth account in a qualified plan
- individual tax payers may deposit up to $5,000 (as adjusted for inflation) each year into a Roth IRA; however, the limit is phased out depending on the taxpayers Adjusted Gross Income or if an individual is a participant in a qualified retirement
- individuals older than 50 can make additional "catch up" contributions of $1,000 (as adjusted for inflation) each year
- the money accumulates tax free until withdrawn

- the individual pays no taxes on any amounts received as long as he is older than 59½ and the money has been deposited for at least 5 years
- individuals do not need to start taking out money at age 70½ and therefore can use it as a wealth transfer device

How does the U.S. Social Security system generally work?

- in 1935, the United States created the Social Security system as part of the New Deal to help combat the Great Depression
- the Old Age, Survivors and Disability Insurance part of the system (OASDI) provides retirement benefits to Americans who have worked 40 quarter-years over their careers (equal to an annuity starting at Social Security Retirement Age of 65, 66 or 67, and continuing for the life of the individual annuitant), survivor benefits to the surviving spouse and dependent children of the covered worker upon his or her death, and disability benefits to the worker who becomes disabled before retirement
- the Health Insurance part of the system (HI) provides Medicare benefits to individuals who have attained age 65 and Medicaid for indigent individuals who have not attained age 65
- FICA requires that
  - 6.2% of each employee's paycheck, up to the Social Security Taxable Wage Base ($106,800 for 2010) is paid into the system to cover the OASDI portion of the premium and
  - 1.45% of the entire paycheck to cover the HI portion of the premium
  - the employer must deposit an equal amount
  - a self-employed individual pays both portions of the premium (*i.e.,* 12.4% of self-employed earned income up to the SSTWB plus 2.9% of total self-employed earned income)
- the system is a "pay as you go system" in that there is neither any pre-funding by the government nor are any true reserves established
  - current workers pay into the system and benefits are paid out in the same year

A. Individual Savings

1. Traditional IRAs

Statutory Rules at IRC §§ 219 and 408

Traditional Individual Retirement Accounts (IRAs) can only have a bank, investment company, or other qualifying financial institution serve as custodian, through a written contract, but no part of the account can be invested in insurance contracts. When an individual makes a contribution to his or her IRA, then the individual is entitled to a deduction on the tax return (*i.e.,* it's a pre-tax contribution). The individual has until the filing of the return to make a contribution, so for the 2010 tax year, can make the contribution by April 15, 2011 (or later, if extensions are properly applied for).

Alternatively, an individual retirement annuity, which seems a bit less popular, is a contract issued by an insurance company where certain aspects of the annual premium charged to the individual comply with statutory limits and requirements.

Individual tax payers may deposit up to $5,000 (as adjusted for inflation) each year into a traditional IRA. Individuals older than 50 can make additional "catch up" contributions of up to $1,000 (as adjusted for inflation) each year. However, in no year can an individual contribute more to the traditional IRA than he or she received as earned income included in Gross Income for that year (there is a special rule for determining earned income with a married couple). This deduction limit might be phased out depending on the taxpayers Adjusted Gross Income for the year.

Additionally, if an individual is a participant in a qualified retirement plan, then, depending on his or her AGI, the deduction may be limited through a mathematical formula (first, determine the fraction of [(AGI for the year—$80,000) / $20,000], and second, multiply that fraction by the contribution; note that $50,000 replaces $80,000 in the numerator, and $10,000 replaces $20,000 in the denominator, if the filing status of the taxpayer is anything other than married filing jointly). This provision in the Code is due to sunset on January 1, 2011, where it will revert back to the provisions in effect on January 1, 2001.[1] There are specific rules on determining whether an individual is a participant in a qualified retirement plan, with special rules for married participants, volunteer firefighters, and reservists in the Armed Forces.

In addition to the normal deduction, low income individuals might also be entitled to a credit against taxes for either 10%, 20% or 50% of the first $2,000 contributed for the year.[2]

The distribution rules from an IRA are similar to the distribution rules from a qualified retirement plan, as discussed in Chapter 9. The money in a traditional IRA accumulates tax-free until withdrawn. The individual pays taxes in the year distributed on contributions plus investment earnings actually received. There will generally be a 10% penalty for withdrawals taken before attaining age 59½ (unless used for certain expenses like education or the purchase of a home—however, there are very specific rules for these qualified expenses). Individuals must start taking out money at age 70½ and therefore can not use it as a wealth transfer device.

If a participant in a qualified retirement plan terminated employment and decides to rollover his or her plan distribution, then the rollover can be deposited into an individual's already existing IRA; similarly, an individual can make annual contributions into an IRA which includes a rollover. For simplicity, and to protect the individual from any

---

1. This is the only place in the text where I need to discuss the 10 year sunset provisions of the Economic Growth and Tax Relief Reconciliation Act of 2001 (EGTRRA). Due to U.S. Senate rules, if a tax law that is not revenue neutral does not pass with at least 60 Senators, then the provisions automatically sunset in 10 years. If you remember, in each State of the Union Speech from 2002 through 2008, President Bush asked Congress to make his tax cuts permanent, but they basically did not (therefore, tax rates and estate taxes are due to sunset on January 1, 2011 and revert to the provisions as they were on January 1, 2001). Luckily for pension plan purposes, all of the pension changes in EGTRAA were specifically made permanent through the Pension Protection Act of 2006, so we mostly do not need to be concerned with the sunset of the other EGTRAA rules. For sunset provisions, see Sec. 901, EGTRRA, P.L. 107-16.

2. IRC § 25B.

errors, most banks or other IRA custodians will create sub-accounts in the same IRA to segregate rolled-over contributions from individual contributions.

IRAs can be used as part of an employer plan, such as SIMPLEs. Part of President Obama's stated initiative is to establish automatic enrollment IRAs for employers that don't otherwise sponsor a qualified retirement plan.

2. Roth IRAs

Statutory Rules at IRC § 408A

"Except as provided in this section, [§ 408A] a Roth IRA shall be treated for purposes of this title in the same manner as an individual retirement plan."[3] Therefore, other than the income tax issues, everything is the same (such as Roth IRAs can only have a bank, investment company, or other qualifying financial institution serve as custodian).

The contribution is made after it is included in the individual's Gross Income (*i.e.,* it's an after-tax contribution). The contribution limit is the same as for traditional IRAs (*i.e.,* $5,000 (as adjusted for inflation) plus a catch-up of $1,000 (as adjusted for inflation)). Therefore, an individual has up to $5,000 (or $6,000 if aged 50 or older) each year to allocate between all of his or her traditional IRAs and Roth IRAs. However, similar to the traditional IRA rules, the contribution allowed is phased out depending on his or her AGI, where $15,000 is the amount in the denominator of the fraction (or $10,000 for a married person filing as an individual). Please note that the rules used to be more complicated, such as requirements that no contribution was allowed in a year when the AGI exceeded $100,000, but those restrictive provisions have been repealed.

Any "qualified distribution" from a Roth IRA shall not be includible in Gross Income, where a "qualified distribution" means any payment or distribution:

- made on or after the date on which the individual attains age 59½,
- made to a beneficiary (or to the estate of the individual) on or after the death of the individual,
- attributable to the individual's being disabled (within the meaning of section 72(m)(7)), or
- which is a qualified special purchase distribution (*i.e.,* used to purchase a first home or for qualified higher education expenses).

A payment or distribution from a Roth IRA shall not be treated as a qualified distribution if the payment or distribution is made within the 5-taxable year period beginning with the first taxable year for which the individual made a contribution to a Roth IRA (or such individual's spouse made a contribution to a Roth IRA) established for such individual.

Unlike traditional IRAs, individuals do not need to start taking out money at age 70½ and therefore can use it as a wealth transfer device. They can also continue making contributions to a Roth IRA after attaining age 70½.

---

3. IRC § 408A(a).

B. Social Security Benefits

Statutory Rules at IRC § 3121 and the Social Security Act,
Codified at Title 42 of the U.S. Code, §§ 301 to 710

The paternalistic concept developed after the world economy changed from local agrarian to global industrialization in the 19th Century (first for railroad and factory workers, then for others). Many credit the first law as the Oppression Code of 1910 (Germany), where the masters were required to take care of their servants so that they did not become wards of society. The first international treaty on social security seems to be the Franco-Italian treaty, where residents of one country would be entitled, under certain circumstances, to benefits from the other country while they were employed in that country. Currently, European Union member nations are required to harmonize their respective social security programs so that they do not represent barriers to the free movement of labor between member nations.

In 1935, the United States created the Social Security system as part of the New Deal to help combat the Great Depression.

The Old Age, Survivors and Disability Insurance part of the system (OASDI) provides retirement benefits to Americans who have worked 40 quarter-years over their careers (equal to an annuity starting at Social Security Retirement Age of 65, 66 or 67, and continuing for the life of the individual annuitant), survivor benefits to the surviving spouse and dependent children of the covered worker upon his or her death, and disability benefits to the worker who becomes disabled before retirement. The monthly benefits are based on a mathematical formula that takes into account the individual's average salary over his or her career, subject to a maximum monthly benefit, (which is $3140 for 2010).[4] Although this looks like a qualified defined benefit plan, promising a guaranteed monthly annuity based on a predefined formula, it is not funded in advance like a qualified defined benefit plan is required to be—the system is a "pay as you go system" in that there is neither any pre-funding by the government nor are any true reserves established. Current workers pay into the system and benefits are paid out in the same year.

The Health Insurance part of the system (HI) provides Medicare benefits to individuals who have attained age 65 and for disabled individuals who have not attained age 65.

The Federal Income Contributions Act (FICA) requires that 6.2% of each employee's paycheck, up to the Social Security Taxable Wage Base ($106,800 for 2010) is paid into the system to cover the OASDI portion of the premium and 1.45% of the entire paycheck to cover the HI portion of the premium. The employer must deposit an equal amount. A self-employed individual pays both portions of the premium (*i.e.,* 12.4% of self-employed earned income up to the SSTWB plus 2.9% of total self-employed earned income).

By all actuarial estimates, as the "baby boomers" retire over the next quarter of a century, there will be more retirees than current workers. Additionally, people have greater current life expectancies than they did in 1935, and current health care and prescription costs are greater than they were in 1935. Therefore, the "health" of the American Social Security System and possible solutions are currently being debated.

---

4. According to http://www.ssa.gov/pressoffice/colafacts.htm.

Social Security benefits can be "taxable"—when the individual completes an individual income tax return, the full Social Security benefits received are shown in Gross Income,[5] but only the taxable portion is actually added into Gross Income.[6] For the 2008 Form 1040, the worksheet to determine whether the SS benefits are received tax-free, or if 50% or 85% of the benefits will be included in Gross Income, is at page 27 of the instructions.

The following is taken from ElderLawAnswers.com[7] Please note that Social Security itself, and any possible fixes to the system, are political issues. I am personally a proponent of the idea of Social Security benefits, so I find that this group provides information I am comfortable with. There are other viewpoints, and I am sure that if you do a quick Google search, you will find other organizations that might dispute any or all of the following statements.

Myths about Social Security

If you are wondering about your future Social Security benefits, you are not alone. Social Security is a strange political animal. On the one hand, it is politically sacrosanct—both Democrats and Republicans have kept it off-limits in their efforts to balance the federal budget. At the same time, when polled, most younger Americans say that they do not expect Social Security to be around for them when they retire.

Both attitudes towards Social Security reflect misunderstandings about the program's funding. Those without faith in the program should be assured that it will be around to contribute to the retirements of today's workers, even if no one should depend on it as his or her sole retirement income.

Myth 1: The Social Security "Trust Fund"

Although the Social Security Administration measures its surplus or deficit in terms of a "trust fund," in fact no such entity exists. As a result of this terminology, most Americans believe that their payroll taxes go into an account to be drawn on when they retire. In fact, their taxes simply go to pay benefits to current retirees, with the surplus going to pay other costs of government.

Currently, the payroll tax is bringing in more than is necessary to pay current retirees and those on disability: In 1999, there were revenues of $527 billion and distributions of $393 billion, resulting in a $134 billion surplus. The federal government keeps track of the surplus and in effect signs an IOU to repay the Social Security system with interest when needed.

Myth 2: Workers get less out of the system than they paid in

While the current Social Security payroll tax is 15.3 percent on income up to $106,800 a year (2009 figure), the tax rates and the wage base were much lower when most current retirees were working and contributing to the system. As recently as 1972, the maximum payroll tax paid (by the employee) was only $419 a year. Even including interest earned since the contributions were made, most retirees receive back significantly more than they contributed.

This may not be true for current workers, since both the tax and the wage base upon which the tax is determined have increased dramatically since the

---

5. line 20a
6. line 20b.
7. http://www.elderlawanswers.com/Elder_Info/Elder_Article.asp?id=700.

1970s. Whether current workers will recover their entire investment will depend in part on how long they live, whether they are married and whether they earned a high or low wage.

Myth 3: The Social Security system is bankrupt

Due to anticipated demographic developments, at some time in the future Social Security benefits will exceed revenues from the payroll tax. This means that benefits will have to be cut or postponed, or that the difference will have to be made up from federal tax revenues, or both. The federal government can't go bankrupt like an individual or company. It must meet its obligations, and it will do so. Additionally, dire predictions abut the insolvency of the system fail to consider the possibility of immigration or another "baby boom" increasing the number of wage earners in future years, or the effect of an increasingly productive economy.

Myth 4: Proportionality

While most people expect to receive retirement benefits proportional to their lifetime earnings, this is not exactly how Social Security benefits are determined. In calculating a retired worker's monthly benefit check, the SSA determines a "primary insurance amount" (PIA) based on the worker's earnings over 35 years. But it weights the first few hundred dollars of average monthly income highest, and income over $4,483 a month (in 2009) lowest. The result is that low-wage earners receive a higher benefit relative to their lifetime earnings than do higher wage earners. (This is somewhat offset by the fact that the payroll tax is based on only a portion of the higher wage earners' taxable income.)

Myth 5: The system favors two-income couples

While the system of determining the PIA may seem to favor two-income married couples, in fact single-income married couples do better in most cases. This is because spouses of retirees are entitled at a minimum to one-half of the benefits of the retired worker. So, in effect, the married worker with a non-working spouse receives 150 percent of the benefits received by a non-married retiree with the same work history. A working spouse must have an earnings history nearly comparable to that of the main wage earner to receive benefits substantially exceeding what he or she would be entitled to without having worked.

Myth 6: "I can invest better"

Many people feel that they could do better if they took their payroll tax (including the employer's contribution) and invested it on their own. That's possible, but by no means assured. As is discussed above, if you are married and the sole or primary wage earner, it would be almost impossible to beat the extra 50 percent of benefits that come to your spouse. In addition, any calculation must take into account the disability benefits and programs for disabled children and other dependents in measuring the return on the Social Security investment. Due to the redistributive nature of Social Security, it would be very difficult for lower-wage earners to do as well investing on their own.

Social Security also has the advantage of forcing workers to save. You and your employer have to make the contributions each month. It's portable, meaning you lose nothing by changing jobs. It's guaranteed against bankruptcy or an employer misusing the funds. There's no risk that you'll dip into the funds prior to retirement for other pressing needs. Finally, for most Social Security beneficiaries, the monthly checks come tax free. Finally, Social Security is not an investment program. It's a system under which current taxpayers support current retirees. If it is to be replaced with a forced investment program, as some suggest, provisions need to be made for today's retirees.

Conclusion

In short, the Social Security system provides a secure base income for most retirees, and it will continue to do so in the future. Its redistributive nature benefits lower-wage earners at the expense of higher-wage earners, but they and their employers contribute a higher proportion of their earnings as well. Under any measure, most current retirees receive back significantly more than they contributed. Due to significant increases in the payroll tax and the wage base, this result cannot be assured for future retirees. But that does not mean that the system is at risk of going bankrupt, as many Americans fear.

Section V

Final Issues

This section is short, and I truly hope you read through it (which should not take that much time). Put down your pens (unless your professor indicates that you might be tested on the material)—just relax, read, enjoy, and think.

Chapter 21 is a simple overview of some of the ethical issues that attorneys and other benefits professionals should consider.

Chapter 22 is simply a compendium of career advice essays written specifically for this text book by nine colleagues who I consider friends. The essays, when read collectively, should really demonstrate what talents and drive you need to bring to the table if you're interested in a career as a benefits professional, and that those who are good at their jobs go far and are provided interesting career options along the way.

Chapter 23 simply contains some of my personal final thoughts on America's public policy of an aging population.

Chapter 21

Ethics Issues

Overview

Who does the benefits professional represent?
- the client is owed the professional's loyalty, confidentiality and zealous representation, and can be:
  - the employer sponsoring an ERISA plan;
  - the union providing employee benefits;
  - individual officers in their individual capacities;
  - the Board of Directors or Board of Trustees;
  - the Plan Administrator;
  - the Plan;
  - an individual participant or beneficiary; or
  - the class of participants and beneficiaries of the Plan
- it is important to know who the client is:
  - so that proper waivers can be secured if the professional is representing multiple parties;
  - so that confidentiality and client privileges can be properly established;
  - so that attorney work product, prepared in anticipation of litigation, can be properly established; and
  - so that the retainer agreement will comply with local bar rules and other professional codes of ethics

What are some of the issues any benefits professional who practices in front of the IRS be concerned with?
- all attorneys, CPAs, Enrolled Actuaries, Enrolled Agents, and now Enrolled Retirement Plan Agents who represent a plan in front of the IRS (generally communications to and from the IRS and representing the plan during an audit) must comply with Circular 230
- under Circular 230, they need to:
  - follow general best practices;
  - comply with certain requirements with respect to tax returns, documents, affidavits and other papers;
  - advise clients as to potential penalties if they take certain tax positions; and

> • carefully and artfully include many specific provisions in any written opinion.

1. Other Laws That Impact Employee Benefits Plans

While ERISA preempts other state laws that regulated employee benefits, it does not preempt other federal laws or state laws that don't regulate employee benefits. Whether an attorney or other benefits professional, you should at least become familiar with some of these other laws—not necessarily to provide advice, but to spot issues and know when you need to find an expert on that subject.

- Federal securities laws
- Age Discrimination in Employment Act (ADEA)
- Federal Social Security laws
- Americans with Disabilities Act (ADA)
- Fair Labor Standard Acts (FLSA)
- Family and Medical Leave Act (FMLA)
- Federal bankruptcy laws
- Title IV of the Civil Rights Act
- State insurance laws
- State banking laws

2. Whom Does the ERISA Attorney or Other Professional Represent?

There are many individuals you will deal with as a benefits professional (the owner of a small business, the director of human resources in a large corporation, an already-hired outside consultant, …). The individuals who walk in to your office or deal with you over the phone or email are most likely in one of the following roles:

- The Employer sponsoring an ERISA plan
- The union providing employee benefits
- Individual officers in their individual capacities
- The Board of Directors or Board of Trustees
- The Plan Administrator
- The Plan
- An individual participant or beneficiary

It is important to know who the client is:

- so that proper waivers can be secured if the attorney or other professional is representing multiple parties;
- so that confidentiality and any privilege (such as attorney-client privilege) can be properly established;
- so that work product (such as attorney work product), prepared in anticipation of litigation, can be properly established; and

- so that the retainer agreement will comply with local bar rules for attorneys or other codes of professional conduct.

With attorneys, the core ethical duty generally is to zealously advocate the client's legal position. With accountants, the core ethical duty is generally to protect the public. Other benefits professionals have as their core ethical duty shades of either of those two opposite ends of the spectrum. Therefore, in a textbook like this that will hopefully appeal to a variety of benefits professionals, I just want you at the starting point to understand who your client is, regardless of who actually pays your fees, and then use your applicable code of professional conduct to figure out who your loyalty is owed to.

3. Practice in Front of the IRS (Circular 230)

As discussed in Chapter 3, Attorneys, Enrolled Actuaries, CPAs, Enrolled Agents, and now Enrolled Retirement Plan Agents, are granted authority to practice in front of the IRS pursuant to the rules of Circular 230. They are actually provided power of attorney through a form 2848 (as discussed in Chapter 10).

Circular 230 (Revised April, 2008), "Regulations Governing the Practice of Attorneys, Certified Public Accountants, Enrolled Agents, Enrolled Actuaries, Enrolled Retirement Plan Agents, and Appraisers before the Internal Revenue Service" is actually located at Title 31 of the U.S. Code of Federal Regulations, Subtitle A, Part 10.[1] It is important for all benefits professionals who want to represent their clients on audits, self correction discussions, determination letter requests, or any other official capacity to familiarize themselves with Circular 230. One of the most important aspects of Circular 230 are written opinions. Back in the 1980s and 1990s, "tax shelters" were all based on legal opinions written by attorneys, or other written opinions drafted by other tax professionals. The general recourse was to go after the taxpayer trying to inappropriately defer or exclude taxable income from Gross Income, but not the professionals writing opinions that the particular series of transactions would yield favorable tax treatment allowed under the Internal Revenue Code. In the 2000s, the new term of art used by the IRS is "Abusive Tax Avoidance Transactions" (ATATs), and the current thinking, as reflected in the current iteration of Circular 230, is to go after the professionals writing the advice (usually for an incredibly hefty fee). Thus, in order to maintain a favorable professional status in regards to the IRS, the professional (CPA, attorney, EA, Enrolled Agent, and ERPA) must comply with some general best practices and must take certain considerations into account before issuing a written opinion. One of the most abused provisions so far is that by making it clear that something written down is absolutely not legal advice, then that communication with a client or potential client is not a written opinion subject to all of the requirements under Circular 230 (that's why many firms, where a professional might inadvertently send an email to a client that can possibly rise to the level of legal tax advice, automatically include a tag line at the bottom of the email that the content does not in any way constitute legal advice). Below are relevant provisions from Circular 230—please note the different thresholds (highlighted in bold) that must be considered for different purposes—regardless of your professions, these terms of art rise to the level of legal terms, and if you are a benefits professional of any sort, you might want to personally seek advice from an attorney as to how each metric is measured (is it a 40% probability, a 51% probability, a 60% probability, ...).

---

1. but can be found at http://www.irs.gov/taxpros/index.html?navmenu=menu1.

As to general best practices for tax advisors, the regulations suggest[2]

- Communicating **clearly** with the client regarding the terms of the engagement. For example, the advisor should determine the client's expected purpose for and use of the advice and should have a **clear understanding** with the client regarding the form and scope of the advice or assistance to be rendered.

- Establishing the facts, determining which facts are relevant, evaluating the **reasonableness** of any assumptions or representations, relating the applicable law (including potentially applicable judicial doctrines) to the relevant facts, and arriving at a **conclusion supported by the law and the facts.**

- Advising the client regarding the importance of the conclusions reached, including, for example, whether a taxpayer may avoid accuracy-related penalties under the Internal Revenue Code if a taxpayer acts in reliance on the advice.

- Acting **fairly** and with **integrity** in practice before the Internal Revenue Service.

As to standards with respect to tax returns and documents, affidavits and other papers, the regulations suggest[3]

- A practitioner may not advise a client to take a position on a document, affidavit or other paper submitted to the Internal Revenue Service unless the **position is not frivolous.**

- A practitioner may not advise a client to submit a document, affidavit or other paper to the Internal Revenue Service—

  - The purpose of which is to delay or impede the administration of the Federal tax laws;

  - That is **frivolous**; or

  - That contains or omits information in a manner that demonstrates an intentional disregard of a rule or regulation unless the practitioner also advises the client to submit a document that evidences a good faith challenge to the rule or regulation.

As to advising clients on potential penalties, affidavits and other papers, the regulations suggest[4]

- A practitioner must inform a client of any penalties that are **reasonably likely** to apply to the client with respect to—

  - A position taken on a tax return if—(A) The practitioner advised the client with respect to the position; or (B) The practitioner prepared or signed the tax return; and Any document, affidavit or other paper submitted to the Internal Revenue Service.

- The practitioner also must inform the client of any opportunity to avoid any such penalties by disclosure, if relevant, and of the requirements for adequate disclosure. This paragraph applies even if the practitioner is not subject to a penalty under the Internal Revenue Code with respect to the position or with respect to the document, affidavit or other paper submitted.

---

2. Circular 230, § 10.33.
3. Circular 230, § 10.34(b).
4. Circular 230, § 10.34(c).

A practitioner advising a client to take a position on a tax return, document, affidavit or other paper submitted to the Internal Revenue Service, or preparing or signing a tax return as a preparer, generally may rely in good faith without verification upon information furnished by the client. The practitioner may not, however, ignore the implications of information furnished to, or actually known by, the practitioner, and must make reasonable inquiries if the information as furnished appears to be incorrect, inconsistent with an important fact or another factual assumption, or incomplete.[5]

A covered opinion is written advice (including electronic communications) by a practitioner concerning one or more Federal tax issues arising from—[6]

- A transaction that is the same as **or substantially similar** to a transaction that, at the time the advice is rendered, the Internal Revenue Service has determined to be a tax avoidance transaction and identified by published guidance as a listed transaction under 26 CFR 1.6011-4(b)(2);

- Any partnership or other entity, any investment plan or arrangement, or any other plan or arrangement, **the principal purpose** of which is the avoidance or evasion of any tax imposed by the Internal Revenue Code; or

- Any partnership or other entity, any investment plan or arrangement, or any other plan or arrangement, **a significant purpose** of which is the avoidance or evasion of any tax imposed by the Internal Revenue Code if the written advice—

  - Is a reliance opinion (if the advice concludes at a confidence level of at least **more likely than not a greater than 50 percent likelihood** that one or more significant Federal tax issues would be resolved in the taxpayer's favor);

  - Is a marketed opinion (if the practitioner knows or has reason to know that the written advice will be used or referred to by a person other than the practitioner (or a person who is a member of, associated with, or employed by the practitioner's firm) in promoting, marketing or recommending a partnership or other entity, investment plan or arrangement to one or more taxpayer(s));

  - Is subject to conditions of confidentiality (if the practitioner imposes on one or more recipients of the written advice a limitation on disclosure of the tax treatment or tax structure of the transaction and the limitation on disclosure protects the confidentiality of that practitioner's tax strategies, regardless of whether the limitation on disclosure is legally binding. A claim that a transaction is proprietary or exclusive is not a limitation on disclosure if the practitioner confirms to all recipients of the written advice that there is no limitation on disclosure of the tax treatment or tax structure of the transaction that is the subject of the written advice.); or

  - Is subject to contractual protection (if the taxpayer has the right to a full or partial refund of fees paid to the practitioner (or a person who is a member of, associated with, or employed by the practitioner's firm) if all or a part of the intended tax consequences from the matters addressed in the written advice are not sustained, or if the fees paid to the practitioner (or son other than the practitioner (or a person who is a person who is a member of, as-

---

5. Circular 230, § 10.34(d).
6. Circular 230, § 10.35(c).

sociated with, or employed by the practitioner's firm) are contingent on the taxpayer's realization of tax benefits from the transaction. All the facts and circumstances relating to the matters addressed in the written advice will be considered when determining whether a fee is refundable or contingent, including the right to reimbursements of amounts that the parties to a transaction have not designated as fees or any agreement to provide services without reasonable compensation).

As to the requirements for a covered opinion, the regulations state—[7]

Factual Matters

(i) The practitioner must use reasonable efforts to identify and ascertain the facts, which may relate to future events if a transaction is prospective or proposed, and to determine which facts are relevant. The opinion must identify and consider all facts that the practitioner determines to be relevant.

(ii) The practitioner must not base the opinion on any unreasonable factual assumptions (including assumptions as to future events). An unreasonable factual assumption includes a factual assumption that the practitioner knows or should know is incorrect or incomplete. For example, it is unreasonable to assume that a transaction has a business purpose or that a transaction is potentially profitable apart from tax benefits. A factual assumption includes reliance on a projection, financial forecast or appraisal. It is unreasonable for a practitioner to rely on a projection, financial forecast or appraisal if the practitioner knows or should know that the projection, financial forecast or appraisal is incorrect or incomplete or was prepared by a person lacking the skills or qualifications necessary to prepare such projection, financial forecast or appraisal. The opinion must identify in a separate section all factual assumptions relied upon by the practitioner.

(iii) The practitioner must not base the opinion on any unreasonable factual representations, statements or findings or of the taxpayer or any other person. An unreasonable factual representation includes a factual representation that the practitioner knows or should know is incorrect or incomplete. For example, a practitioner may not rely on a factual representation that a transaction has a business purpose if the representation does not include a specific description of the business purpose or the practitioner knows or should know that the representation is incorrect or incomplete. The opinion must identify in a separate section all factual representations, statements or finds of the taxpayer relied upon by the practitioner.

Relate Law to Facts

(i) The opinion must relate the applicable law (including potentially applicable judicial doctrines) to the relevant facts.

(ii) The practitioner must not assume the favorable resolution of any significant Federal tax issue except as provided in paragraphs (c)(3)(v) and (d) of this section, or otherwise base an opinion on any unreasonable legal assumptions, representations, or conclusions.

---

7. Circular 230, § 10.35(d).

(iii) The opinion must not contain internally inconsistent legal analyses or conclusions.

Evaluation of Significant Federal Tax Issues

(i) *In general.* The opinion must consider all significant Federal tax issues except as provided in paragraphs (c)(3)(v) and (d) of this section.

(ii) *Conclusion as to each significant Federal tax issues.* The opinion must provide the practitioner's conclusion as to the **likelihood** that the taxpayer will prevail on the merits with respect to each significant Federal tax issue considered in the opinion. If the practitioner is unable to reach a conclusion with respect to one or more of those issues, the opinion must state that the practitioner is unable to reach a conclusion with respect to those issues. The opinion must describe the reasons for the conclusions, including the facts and analysis supporting the conclusions, or describe the reasons that the practitioner is unable to reach a conclusion as to one or more issues. If the practitioner fails to reach a conclusion at the confidence level of **at least more likely than not** with respect to one or more significant Federal tax issues considered, the opinion must include the appropriate disclosure(s) required under paragraph (e) of this section.

(iii) *Evaluation based on chances of success on the merits.* In evaluating the significant Federal tax issues addressed in the opinion, the practitioner must not take into account the possibility that a tax return will not be audited, that an issue will not be raised on audit, or that an issue will be resolved through settlement if raised.

(iv) *Marketed opinions.* In the case of a marketed opinion, the opinion must provide the practitioner's conclusion that the taxpayer will prevail on the merits at a confidence level of **at least more likely than not** with respect to each significant Federal tax issue. If the practitioner is unable to reach a more likely than not conclusion with respect to each significant Federal tax issue, the practitioner must not provide the marketed opinion, but may provide written advice that satisfies the requirements in paragraph (b)(5)(ii) of this section.

(v) *Limited scope opinions.*

(A) The practitioner may provide an opinion that considers less than all of the significant Federal tax issues if—

(1) The practitioner and the taxpayer agree that the scope of the opinion and the taxpayer's potential reliance on the opinion for purposes of avoiding penalties that may be imposed on the taxpayer are limited to the Federal tax issue(s) addressed in the opinion;

(2) The opinion is not advice described in paragraph (b)(2)(i)(A) of this section (concerning listed transactions), paragraph (b)(2)(i)(B) of this section (concerning the principal purpose of avoidance or evasion) or paragraph (b)(5) of this section (a marketed opinion); and

(3) The opinion includes the appropriate disclosure(s) required under paragraph (e) of this section.

(B) A practitioner may make reasonable assumptions regarding the favorable resolution of a Federal tax issue (as assumed issue) for purposes of providing an opinion on less than all of the significant Federal tax issues as provided in this paragraph (c)(3)(v). The opinion must identify in a separate section all issues for which the practitioner assumed a favorable resolution.

Overall Conclusion

(i) The opinion must provide the practitioner's overall conclusion as to the **likelihood** that the Federal tax treatment of the transaction or matter that is the subject of the opinion is the proper treatment and the reasons for that conclusion. If the practitioner is unable to reach an overall conclusion, the opinion must state that the practitioner is unable to reach and overall conclusion and describe the reasons for the practitioner's inability to reach a conclusion.

(ii) In the case of a marketed opinion, the opinion must provide the practitioner's overall conclusion that the Federal tax treatment of the transaction or matter that is the subject of the opinion is the proper treatment at a **confidence level of at least more likely than not.**

Excluded Advice

Luckily for many tax professionals (especially benefits professionals), there is certain advice excluded from the requirements for a covered opinion, which are:[8]

(A) Written advice provided to a client during the course of an engagement if a practitioner is reasonably expected to provide subsequent written advice to the client that satisfies the requirements of this section;

(B) Written advice, other than advice described in paragraph (b)(2)(i)(A) of this section (concerning listed transactions) or paragraph (b)(2)(i)(B) of this section (concerning the principal purpose of avoidance or evasion) that—

> (1) Concerns the qualification of a qualified plan;

> (2) Is a State or local bond opinion; or

> (3) Is included in documents required to be filed with the Securities and Exchange Commission.

(C) Written advice prepared for and provided to a taxpayer, solely for use by that taxpayer, after the taxpayer has filed a tax return with the Internal Revenue Service reflecting the tax benefits of the transaction. The preceding sentence does not apply if the practitioner knows or has reason to know that the written advice will be relied upon by the taxpayer to take a position on a tax return (including for these purposes an amended return that claims tax benefits not reported on a previously filed return) filed after the date on which the advice is provided to the taxpayer;

(D) Written advice provided to an employer by a practitioner in that practitioner's capacity as an employee of that employer solely for purposes of determining the tax liability of the employer; or

(E) Written advice that does not resolve a Federal tax issue in the taxpayer's favor, unless the advice reaches a conclusion favorable to the taxpayer at any confidence level (e.g., not frivolous, realistic possibility of success, reasonable basis or substantial authority) with respect to that issue. If written advice concerns more than one Federal tax issue, the advice must comply with the requirements of paragraph (c) of this section with respect to any Federal tax issue not described in the preceding sentence.

---

8. Circular 230, § 10.35(d).

Final Thoughts

Okay, that's enough discussion about Circular 230 for purposes of this textbook. The reason I am spending so much time is because in addition to our own professional-specific codes of conduct based on the professional associations we join, we need to make sure we additionally comply with the written advice rules and general best practices included in Circular 230 if we want to represent our clients in the front of the IRS. In the regulations, in addition to the OPR's ultimate decision to disbar, suspend or censure a tax professional, they will also send referrals and information to any professional association that the professional belongs to.

4. Other Ethical Concerns

Although ERISA is a federal law and attorneys can practice anywhere, they need to make sure that they do not violate the Multi-Jurisdictional Practice Issues (some professionals, such as attorneys, are licensed by the state, so an attorney who takes the Illinois bar exam and is licensed to practice in Illinois may have problems if he or she physically goes to California and provides legal advice there, even if the client's business is incorporated in Illinois, or even if he or she remains physically in Illinois, there may be problems if he or she provides legal advice to a business incorporated in California). This is not meant to scare or dissuade any professional, because there are many ways to do this properly, but at least think about it before putting your professional license in jeopardy.

If the benefits professional has any control over plan assets, then he or she might be deemed a fiduciary of the plan (thus subject to personal liability for any fiduciary breaches). Similarly, if the client (often times a small business) has a pattern of blindly following any suggestions made by the benefits professional, and doesn't generally weigh the options to make an affirmative decisions, then the benefits professional should realize the client's reliance, and should try to make clear that unless the client makes certain decisions about the investment of employee benefit plan assets that the benefits professional might be deemed a plan fiduciary (and therefore should charge a higher fee to protect against any inadvertent personal liability for a breach of fiduciary duty).

There are also special rules for attorneys appearing and practicing before the SEC (which are rapidly developing after enactment by the Sarbanes-Oxley Act of 2002).

Chapter 22

Career Advice Essays

Now we get to one of the roles I enjoy the most and take most seriously, that of being a mentor. And from the essays you are about to read, I am not the only one who values his or her role as a mentor to up and coming benefits professionals.

When I teach this class, in the waning hours of the final class, after we've explored the regulatory framework of employee benefit plans, I like to talk about careers so that anyone who actually enjoys the subject matter will think about pursuing it as a career. I generally discuss my career path—from math major to pension consultant to Enrolled Actuary to attorney in private practice to attorney in academia. I discuss how there are many employers looking for talented benefits professionals—ranging from traditional law firms, actuarial firms and accounting firms, to in-house human resources departments, to financial institutions, to governmental agencies, and to think tanks. I highlight how understanding a federal law, like the Code or ERISA, allows the individual to move to any geographic area to accept a job offer or to be near one's family and friends—even if an attorney or CPA might need to take another professional exam to be licensed to practice there. I also like to discuss, especially to law students, that there are many different aspects of the profession that they can specialize in—not just whether to focus in on health and welfare benefit plans or retirement plans or executive compensation plans, but also whether they want to be a business consultant on the front end (to draft documents and train their clients to only promise benefits that they can actually deliver and then to deliver them) or a litigator at the back end (to seek justice when something goes awry). As you can see, I love my chosen field of focus, and after getting to know students as individuals and teaching them how to think about and understand the regulation of employee benefits plans, I whole-heartedly encourage anyone else who has the patience to learn all of the rules and the desire to be a valuable member of the client's business planning team to go for it.

In the classroom setting, I usually try to invite a guest in to help me discuss careers as an employee benefits professional, since by now, my students are probably excited to hear a new voice. For this textbook, I have done the next best thing—I have asked nine colleagues I call friends (some of whom have mentored me and some of whom I have mentored) to just write an essay on careers. They are nine very diverse individuals in their backgrounds, employers, specialties, professional designations, and optimism. Collectively, their essays all say the same thing—that considering a career as a benefits professional is probably at least a worthwhile exercise. At the end of the day, even if you decide to pursue a different career path, at the very least, the essays will provide a small sample of the wonderful, intelligent, compassionate and motivated people who have chosen (or stumbled) upon this area of specialty.

Out of respect for each of the nine essayists, they appear simply in alphabetical order, because there was no other way I could possibly order them.

Nevin E. Adams, JD

Nevin is Editor-in-Chief of PLANSPONSOR magazine and its web counterpart PLANSPONSOR.com.

"(My) Career Path"

Ultimately, the thing that has kept me in this business—and happily engaged in this business—for more than a quarter century is that it is always changing. There have been major legislative changes on the order of every 18 months or so ever since I started, and technology continues to play a major role, even as demographic trends (everybody gets older) continue to make it more relevant. It is a business in which "history" matters, but in which the old rules become just that in no time at all. Consequently, it's relatively easy for someone with intelligence, dedication, and passion to succeed and prosper.

The best career advice I ever got—and I hand it out whenever I'm given half a chance— keep your eyes open for opportunity. It is highly unlikely that the path that I took—or that anyone else has taken—will be able to provide a workable roadmap for your career in employee benefits. However, along the way you learn things—and while some lessons are more easily learned than others, perhaps those experiences can shed light on the road you're on, or stepping off on.

I've been in this business of employee benefit plans ever since I was a senior in college—a senior with an affinity for numbers, and a passion for helping people understand complex things. I would have been a teacher, but—having come from a long line of teachers—I probably had a better sense for what I'd be getting into than some. In any event, I decided early in my college career that I loved business; was fascinated by the way a finance curriculum took the theories of economics, the art of marketing, the precision of mathematics, and the clarity of accounting and turned them into something meaningful and practical.

That didn't help me when it came to making a career choice, unfortunately. But it did position me, as a member of a business fraternity at DePaul University, to take advantage of a part-time intern position at Northern Trust Bank in Chicago. I didn't yet know what I wanted to do, but as a Finance major with no real idea as to what I wanted to "do" with my life, a bank looked like a logical place to accumulate some relevant experience on my largely empty resume.

As fate would have it, I landed there just as a major trend in accounting consolidation for pension trusts was taking root—a trend that, as it turned out, converged with a period in time where automation had not yet caught up with the needs of the industry. Which brings me to another point of advice: The demands of the business, the regimen of the law, and the needs of the community frequently outpace the ability of technology to provide a ready solution. Take advantage of those opportunities to learn how to do what needs doing manually—and you'll be able to build a better solution in the long term. Too many people wait for someone else to find the right answer—and then too frequently blindly accept suboptimal approaches simply because that is how the resulting "package" was built.

After a couple of years doing pension accountings, I had an opportunity to move to another group within the firm—lower profile within the company (to put it mildly), but it was a group that had its own computer. Now, I realize that in today's environment, that sounds pretty archaic—but the point is that they had the ability to shape their own priorities at a time when everyone else had to wait for their chance in the mainframe queue—and that ability gave them the ability to influence their own destiny. Now, that also meant that I had to learn how to load paper in a printer, that on more than one late evening I had to watch the printer spit out the paper I had put in. But the important thing is to put yourself in a position where you have some control over your destiny/direction. I've been able to do that in two very large firms now, basically by being willing to work in "black boxes" nobody else seems to know—or, frankly, want to know—anything about. By the way, that group that had its own computer was doing participant accountings for defined contribution plans—years before the 401(k) was a reality—and being part of it then put me in a position to grow with that business.

There was a brief interlude in this time—about 30 days' worth—where I learned another valuable lesson. Never say you'll never work for someone. Because you just might have to.

It was also during this period that I began to feel a need to get more education. I debated pursuing an MBA, but since I already had a business undergrad, finally decided that a law degree would allow me to learn things that were truly different, as opposed to just more about things I already knew about. Moreover, by this time, I was routinely being asked to read, interpret, and apply the contents of legal plan documents.

Now, I'd love to tell you that law school allowed me to do that job of reading and interpreting legal documents better—but the truth is, it didn't, at least not in any noticeable way. Don't get me wrong—I learned a lot of interesting and valuable things in law school, and I wouldn't trade the experience for the world, but, having accumulated a number of years of experience in the field, I was already operating at a level beyond the law school basics. However, my law school education provided two extraordinarily valuable things: a confidence in my ability to accurately interpret and apply the law and—more importantly—the confidence of my superiors, co-workers, and clients in my ability to do so. Credentials matter in this business—and it's worth pursuing the right ones.

One shouldn't conclude from all this that this has been a smooth, upward, and forward career path. For example, more than one person told me when I joined the participant accounting unit that I was nuts for doing so (including my boss's boss)—and, honestly, things could have worked out very differently. There also came a time several years back when a change in management totally derailed the career path that I had in mind. The subsequent changes basically took half my staff and gave them to another department. It was a very demoralizing time for me—I had not done anything wrong or anything different, but all of a sudden a door was slammed in my face (at the time it felt like it had also been slammed on my foot).

For most of my career, I have been in very demanding jobs—the kind that don't afford much idle time for introspection or contemplation. I've counseled others on the wisdom of an annual assessment of where you are, and what you are doing—but, as in many things in life, I've also found it easier to hand out good advice than to take my own. Nonetheless, one of the good things about having lots of your job responsibilities ripped out of your control is that you do have more time to think—and, once I got over the hurt and the anger (I'm not sure there are 12 steps, but there are definite phases of job-change acceptance), I began to try and figure out a plan of action. You can't always control what is done "to" you, after all—but you can control how you respond/react to it.

The reality is, even when you can't do anything to change things in the short-term, taking action—reconnecting with old associates and mentors, talking to recruiters, and even making a special effort to get to know the new management—is the best way to avoid feeling like a victim. As it turned out, my new responsibilities gave me a chance to focus on something that I'm sure would have received very little of my time or attention under other circumstances: communication. I "discovered" a talent for writing, heretofore largely obscured by the strictures of corporate memorandums (and professional decorum). That talent, coupled with my experience and an ability to help make complex subjects approachable, found an outlet in a series of internal and external publications, including a newsletter that, thanks to the advent of e-mail, began to find its way not only outside my department ... but eventually outside the company.

By then, that job "focus" had begun to get lost among other responsibilities. In my experience, the more you can do well, the more you are asked to do, and that has always been the case in my career. Still, I continued to do the newsletter, and as I began to be asked to add people to it, a friend of mine from years back suggested that I share it with an associate of hers. An associate who, it turned out, founded PLANSPONSOR magazine. Now, at the time, I couldn't imagine that someone who did that kind of thing for a living would find any merit in my little daily e-mail. Indeed, I found the notion of sharing that with a professional writer more than a little embarrassing. Still, my friend was persistent, and one Christmas week, as much to cross at least one thing off my "to do" list as anything else, I sent a copy to him.

A couple of weeks later, I heard back from him. Much to my amazement he liked it—and wanted to talk to me about producing it for them! Well, that discussion expanded, and within a few months we were talking about a permanent position; not only producing the newsletter I had been doing as a "hobby" as a career, but also building a Web site, and taking on responsibility for what has become the nation's leading information resource for retirement plan sponsors. Once again, keeping an eye open for opportunity—and being willing to take a chance—paid off. And in ways I could not even have imagined.

Nearly a decade later, I've had the opportunity and the privilege not only to help plan sponsors—the folks that keep our private retirement system running every day—but to speak out on their behalf. Over 50,000 individuals across our planet now read that daily e-mail (NewsDash) that I started doing as a "hobby" nearly 15 years ago. However, the thing I treasure most is the 20–50 e-mails a week I get back from readers—either to highlight a point of clarification, to ask a question, to request more information or—more often than you might think—to give us a pat on the back.

When all is said and done, success in this business—as well as success in life—comes down to a few basic considerations: listen at least as much as you talk, be willing to share timely information that is useful (and entertaining), and do so at a time—and in a setting—that is convenient for those whom you want to reach.

These are good people, doing great things—making a difference in real people's lives every day. Welcome to the "club!"

Mark A. Davis, QPFC, AIF®

Mark is Vice President and Financial Advisor at Captrust Financial Advisors.

I am an independent investment advisor that provides fiduciary services to sponsors of qualified retirement plans. Working with qualified plans requires a very specialized focus that is quite different from what most traditional investment advisors do. I help organizations to form and operate Investment Committees that take on the responsibility of selecting and monitoring the investments that are made available for participant directed retirement plan menus. I create customized Investment Policy Statements that drive the selection and monitoring process. I report to my clients on a quarterly basis as to the status of the investments they have chosen. I help them to understand the way their participants are actually using the investments that they are being offered and I recommend both policy and strategic changes as appropriate. I need to understand the ins and outs of various plan designs from both and IRS and a DOL perspective. I need to stay current on legal, regulatory and investment best practices in order to help my clients to provide the best possible employee benefit within a given organization's unique constraints. I am best at my job when I work in concert with the other retirement plan professionals, lawyers, auditors, record-keepers, Trustees and custodians etc. that provide services to a given plan client.

I am pleased and thankful to be able to make my living in the world of qualified retirement plans. There is a very real "mission" to what I do that gives me a strong sense of meaning and purpose. Most Americans will never see a professional investment consultant, fewer will have the opportunity to work with an investment advisor who functions as a fiduciary and truly looks out for their interest in a manner that is free from potential product bias. By serving as a fiduciary at the Plan level I can play a critical role in helping to define the universe of investments that participants in my clients' plans can use. If I can influence my clients to offer investments that are less expensive or better diversified, or both, I believe I can make a difference, if indirectly, in participants' retirement outcomes which can have an effect on families for generations to come.

Providing investment advisory services to plans allows me to combine multiple skill sets and interests that are quite different from those needed when providing services to individuals. I need to have expertise in plan design issues, the politics of ERISA and other legislation and regulations in addition to an understanding of the capital markets and other principles of investing. Through my career I have been fortunate to have had the opportunity to serve as an advisor to politicians and regulators and to help influence policy making on a national scale. I have also had the opportunity to testify before the House Education and Labor Committee and also to the House Ways and Means Committee to express my thoughts on defined contribution plan issues. I have been grateful for the chance to input into the national dialogue.

The employee benefit plan field has been very rewarding personally and a great means of providing a living for me and my family.

Chad R. DeGroot, JD

Chad is an Associate at Bryan Cave LLP in their Employee Benefits and Executive Compensation group.

It seems appropriate to begin by explaining how I came to be interested in employee benefits because that interest is still quite fresh. When I entered law school, I had never even known employee benefits to be its own discipline, or even questioned the concept for that matter. It seemed like something that would just get lumped together with employment law or tax law (this was the case in law firms for a long time). In fact, it was not until I took a course on income taxation, that I even looked at the Internal Revenue Code, but it was at that point that I began to gain an appreciation for it. It may have been attributable to an undergraduate study of philosophy, but I started to see the Code not as a compilation of a number of different sections, but rather as a self-referential whole. As a definition in the dictionary can only define a word by using other words within that same collection, so too does the tax code seem to explain its rules. For example, among the laundry list of requirements for a qualified plan under section 401(a), there are roughly 60 cross references to other sections and subsections of the Code. Many, if not most of those cross-referenced sections contain references to other sections to help explain or clarify. It is because of this that one can seemingly get lost in the Code when simply trying to clarify just a single provision. Because of this, many consider the Code to be too complex, and again, maybe it's just my background, but to me employee benefits and, similarly, tax law, are areas of concentration that exemplify the notion that law will always be a practice—never just a job.

The first thing I noticed as an associate in the employee benefits and executive compensation group at a large law firm was the sheer depth and never-ending nature of employee benefits. Although I began my career after having received an LL.M. in employee benefits law, which did provide a great base of knowledge with which to enter the field, it was not until I began practicing that the breadth of the area became apparent, and how necessary experience would be to gain a true understanding. Of course, one can basically break the field down into its three main categories: retirement, health and welfare, and executive compensation. But, what makes this field so expansive, is the depth of each of those categories and the endless and impossible issues that develop within a human resources department due to employees, boards of directors and executives, and their ability to always come up with, or create a scenario that has never been contemplated by lawmakers or commentators.

Although you will not be expected to master all things employee benefits in your first few years, you will notice that partners seemingly have. I recall sitting in on lunch meetings where senior associates or partners would be discussing an issue that had recently come up, and I would realize I am absolutely incapable of even discussing the topic intelligently, let alone able to provide an answer. Because of this, as a new associate, I began spending much of my time feeling overwhelmed and frustrated. However, always keep in mind that as intimidating as partners or principles, and experienced attorneys and senior consultants may seem when you are in school training to one day fill those roles, they really are just people who want to help. One senior associate in my group (who has since made partner) explained to me that she spent her entire first year feeling like she could barely keep her head above water and as though she was unable to make any sense of the area. This was comforting because I feel that way everyday, as well. In addition, a former adjunct professor corroborated this account of the overwhelming nature of the first two years of practice. After sending her a late night email asking whether I would ever truly get a grip on my so-called "expertise," she responded describing a "two-year click" that seems to occur with most, if not all, associates. That is supposedly the time at which everything begins to come together and at which point young associates begin to develop the confidence that is generally lacking as they begin their careers. I had mistakenly thought everything "clicked" at about 6 months in, and that I was an exception. However, as soon as I started developing that confidence, I was brought back down to earth following an avoidable error on my part. I am still awaiting the "click."

To further exacerbate the complex nature of employee benefits, you will often be asked questions that seem to be outside of your practice area. For example, you might be asked about the specifics of a present value calculation or what payroll practice to employ to solve a given problem—issues that are generally better suited for actuaries or accountants, respectively. Although you will find yourself often working with other professionals such as these, it will be very helpful to familiarize yourself, generally, with these other disciplines to not only make yourself a more well-rounded associate, but to also assist when discussing these issues with other professionals. The best way to do this is to pick up a brief overview of an applicable area of expertise. For example, a basic accounting book for lawyers that simply teaches you about the concept of a balance sheet, revenues and expenses, and not necessarily the intricacies of cost accounting can go a long way to increase your knowledge of not only general accountancy, but make you a better employee benefits associate. Of course, the same holds true for actuaries or accountants who often interact with employee benefits attorneys — it certainly helps to have a general idea of what an employee benefits attorney does so that you are best able to utilize that expertise.

I have found that the best way to learn employee benefits, in addition to, of course, doing the research necessary for assigned projects, is to not only stay on top of current events in the area, but also to do as much as possible with respect to the benefits community outside of your office. Attending meetings and seminars of not only the American Bar Association, but also local bar associations and other trade groups, not only allows you to network with other benefits professionals and experts in the field, but it provides members and attendees with further review of current trends and changes. Before you know it, you'll be asked to present on a relevant topic to that group, or publish a brief article on something of current interest. This is a great way to essentially force yourself to become an expert in as many areas of the practice as possible.

Employee benefits is always changing, and that is a great thing for a young associate. In my first employee benefits class in law school, an influential professor (who later came to author this textbook) made a point about how Congress has been advancing major new benefits legislation at least every two years, and that pattern has held true. This ever-changing nature of employee benefits, should guarantee an abundance of work in the area for years to come. This is certainly welcome as this essay is being written during a time in which many young associates are losing their jobs and having difficulty finding work. In addition to general ERISA and Code compliance work, and the drafting of plans and amendments, much of my work as a young associate is attributable to this seemingly constant production of new legislation. Generally, it is young associates who are charged with reading and understanding the new laws and ensuring that our clients do as well — just ask some senior partners who began practicing law around the time when ERISA was signed into law how they came to find themselves practicing employee benefits.

Kathryn J. Kennedy, JD, FSA

Kathryn ("Katie") is a professor at The John Marshall Law School, and currently serves as Director of its Center for Tax Law and Employee Benefits and as Associate Dean for Advanced Studies and Research.

One of the most common questions posed by well-educated young adults is the selection of a chosen profession. While my parents' generation may have answered this question with a single recommendation, the current generation of young adults realizes that they may have multiple professions during their lifetime. Thus, the ability to keep current and abreast of changes that are occurring in the world — especially technological and legal changes — is essential. If an individual is interested in the legal profession, it's imperative to select an area of law that is expected to continue to be in demand and to provide on-going challenges. I believe employee benefits law has been and will continue to provide such challenges for the next generation of practitioners.

When I was a college student back in the early 1970s, I solicited advice from professionals including my father, a labor union attorney, and a family friend, a pension actuary, as to fruitful areas of law to pursue. They all directed me to employee benefits law—an area that was just becoming subject to federal regulation through ERISA, which was passed in 1974. Since my undergraduate interest focused on mathematics, I continued to pursue a degree in actuarial science at Drake University. This later led to the passage of the requisite exams for my Fellowship from the Society of Actuaries in 1976. While my interest in pensions from actuarial perspective was fulfilled, I realized that a true understanding of employee benefits law would require legal training. Thus, I enrolled in Northwestern University's School of Law in 1977 and attained my J.D. degree in 1980. The combination of actuarial and legal training has been extremely fruitful in my understanding and practice of employee benefits law. I would recommend such training to any individual who has the stamina and interest in seeing employee benefits law from a variety of perspectives.

As the director for The John Marshall Law School's Center for Tax Law & Employee Benefits and a professor of law, I am constantly encouraging existing students and current practitioners to embark on an advanced degree in employee benefits law (either a Master of Science degree or an Master of Legal Letters (LL.M.) degree) in order to successfully practice in this area of law. The reason why employee benefits practitioners are in such demand is that the area of law changes so rapidly, both legislatively and regulatory. It is also exceedingly complex and inter-disciplinary, affording employee benefits attorneys the opportunity to interact with accountants, actuaries, and human resource personnel.

Many students are willing to jump onboard until they realize the commitment requires the following:

- diligent readings of regulations, guidance, advice;

- dialogue with other HR professionals (including actuaries, accountants, HR professionals); and

- perpetual educational training to remain current with the changes in the law.

I, of course, counsel such students that these are the very reasons employee benefits practitioners are in such demand. And it's certainly the reason that drew me to the field. For some students, this can serve as a challenge, while others may be overwhelmed at the prospect to constantly learning new legislation and regulatory guidance.

As we begin a new century with an increasingly proportion of the population concentrated in the age 65 plus category, the issue of employee benefits becomes increasingly important—as individuals hope to retire in dignity, both with sufficient retirement income and sufficient health insurance. These challenges will be exceedingly difficult as the past and current generations have not sufficiently saved for retirement and employers are shifting to defined contribution plans and away from defined benefit plans. Also retiree health care coverage, as provided by the employer, proved to be a legacy cost that employers could not afford, and thus are a benefit of the past. President Obama in his inaugural address pledged that government would assist in assuring Americans "a retirement that is dignified." Hopefully this means that the federal government will promote and encourage the private employer-provided retirement system. Given the challenges that faced all Americans with the credit crisis and the declines in the stock market during 2008, it will take forward thinkers to develop a retirement system that can withstand the perils of the stock market and afford Americans a dignified retirement. I believe there is no greater time to be an employee benefits attorney or practitioner than now. Good luck and God speed!

Gary S. Lesser, JD

Gary is the principal of GSL Galactic Consulting

"What a Long, Strange Trip It's Been": From Career Planning to Retirement Planning

So you're thinking about a career involving retirement plans. There are only three things you need to know:

(1) Where will your career begin?

(2) Where do you want your career to end?

(3) What is the best type of retirement plan?

You're starting out with your shiny new law degree, full of plans. Things may seem confusing or chaotic at first—just like retirement planning itself—and they may seem that way for a while. Sometimes, if you're lucky and you do your research, a pattern will reveal itself quickly, and you'll be able to follow it. But more often, the pattern doesn't begin to emerge for some time—and it's only in retrospect that it all begins to make sense. Either way, you need to balance your goals with a healthy dose of reality and flexibility.

Take my story. I never would have predicted my end-point based on my beginnings. I entered the job market in 1973 with an accounting degree and a law degree, with plans to become an estate and gift tax attorney in the private sector after working for a few years in the Estate & Gift Tax Division (E&G) of the Internal Revenue Service. I applied. Needing a job, I also applied to the CIA and FBI. The economy, like now, was suffering from a blooming recession.

I also wrote cover letters and forwarded my resume to law firms, accounting firms, and insurance companies. Getting a job, other than as a life insurance salesman, was going to be more difficult than I thought. Granted, I was offered several positions that would provide me with "experience," but little or no real compensation to speak of. Young and blustery, with a young person's typically overinflated sense of my own worth, I was insulted. But why should these firms have hired me, when rookies and veterans were being offered the same salary? I may have been green, but I was capable and ready to work—if only I could get a job.

Strange things happen. Several months later, after thanking me profusely for applying, the IRS informed me that there was a federal job freeze and they would keep my application on file for six more months. (I can't talk about the FBI and the CIA.) But it was 1974, and, lucky for me, a proposed new law called the Employee Retirement Income Security Act of 1974 (ERISA) was being debated in Congress. Its passage was imminent and government agencies were beginning to prepare.

Notwithstanding a federal job freeze, the IRS was going to hire agents to staff the new Employee Plans and Exempt Organization Division (EP/EO) in 1975. The Department of Labor and the Pension Benefit Guaranty Corporation would also be hiring.

I interviewed on a Friday and was hired that afternoon. ERISA training started on Monday, and I was told not to be late. Six weeks later, I was a Tax Law Specialist/Attorney with the IRS in Brooklyn, New York—one of the original eleven hired by the IRS to administer and enforce ERISA law across the country. The position had nothing to do with estate and gift taxes, but I could always transfer to that division. My position paid $13,800 to start. I was really close to my career goal—the Estate & Gift Tax Division was next to the EP/EO Division. I could see it from my desk. I actually spoke to people who worked there!

I was being molded by the IRS, but it looked good—like my official identification packet containing my picture along with the very finely engraved etching of the Treasury Department building in Washington, DC. It was very useful for cashing checks (just kidding). My division chief and immediate supervisor at the IRS were both attorneys. Whenever they wanted something done, they assigned it to me. Whenever a volunteer was needed to coordinate special projects (for example, blood drives, charitable donations drives, U.S. Savings bond drives, and so forth), they encouraged me to apply. It would "look good" on my record.

I would stay with the IRS for nearly five years. In addition to my position ruling on the qualified status of employer plans—we read each one in those days—I managed a special taxpayer services hotline for retirement plan questions, and was the division disclosure officer for Privacy and Freedom of Information Act purposes. The IRS was grooming me. Keeping up with the new laws and regulations was interesting and challenging. They also trained us often.

I learned much and it was good experience. But I was itchy to start my "real" career and to reap greater fame, higher glory, and more money in the private sector. I said goodbye to my friends, a $20,000 paycheck, my last 8 to 5 job, and my government pension.

My next position was managing the day-to-day operations of a small pension consulting and actuarial organization in New York City whose owner had moved to California. The owners also sold life insurance. There was an opportunity to become a partner in this organization, and I was earning considerably more. But the small-firm atmosphere turned out to be too confining. The firm was located in a building high above Times Square. It had a walk-out balcony that made me think I was on the set of Rosemary's Baby. We met with clients Monday through Thursday, and Friday was dress-down day. One summer morning, I opened the office door wearing my clogs, shorts, and beach tie-dye shirt and was startled to see a man standing there in a suit. He said that he was the new owner and that my services were no longer needed. The year was 1980, and the recession was ending, not yet over. I wanted to jump.

After working for another and much larger pension consulting and administration firm for a while—during which time I continued to hone my knowledge of defined benefit and defined contribution plan design and administration—I was eventually hired as the Director of Retirement Plans by a small mutual fund manager and distributor on Wall Street. After designing the retirement plan documents and marketing packages, it was my responsibility to help the wholesalers promote our fund's sales throughout the broker-dealer community. I didn't know what a wholesaler was, had no idea what they did, how they did it, or how I was possibly going to help them do it. One day I was called into the managing partner's office. The firm, he told me, needed someone who understood how financial products were distributed—and my replacement had been hired. But, in addition to giving me six months severance pay, he had arranged for me to have an interview with a major brokerage firm that was looking for an attorney with knowledge of the new pension laws.

The brokerage firm wanted to build a retirement plan department to support its registered representatives. It was a specialized marketing department, but we did our own legal work. I began to understand how financial products are created, distributed, administered, and marketed. After five years and four bosses, I also began to understand how Wall Street worked—and didn't work. I bought some Maalox and began to look for a new position. Industry-wise, I was branded with arcane and hard-to-understand terms like ERISA, IRA, SEP, and, worst of all, prohibited transaction. SEPs were good plans for registered representatives to start with, especially new representatives with small business owner clients. I supported the firm effort: generating commissions on recurring annual contributions irrespective of market conditions. Our marketing department also worked with all of the individual product departments. Small elephants that hide in the grass may become big elephants. It was thought that such animals eat financial products.

The ensuing years found me working for the marketing department in another mutual fund complex and several insurance companies, and suddenly, it was 1993—nearly twenty years since I'd first set foot inside the offices of the IRS. My estate-and-gift-tax dreams long abandoned, I had learned the hard way that the financial services industry is a dangerous and volatile place, especially in a recession. Marketing department positions are not very secure, to put it mildly. But I did enjoy the work. So, armed with years of experience as well as some pretty solid knowledge in an esoteric field, I decided to strike out on my own. Looking for suitable projects, I approached a publisher about writing a book on SEPs in the Q&A format. That book, the Simple, SEP and SARSEP Answer Book, is now in its 15th edition. At the same time, realizing I'd cultivated a sophisticated understanding of a little-comprehended—but financially viable—area, I began to offer consulting services and even tried my hand at developing number crunching software that could help financial planners better serve their clients. In other words, I identified a need and then proceeded to fill it—or, maybe more accurately, the need identified itself to me, because by then I had the requisite tools. It turned out I had picked up a few things along the way that not many people understood—things that they needed to understand if they wanted to design and market retirement plans.

Happily, the software and consulting took off, and people in the industry began to connect my name with a specialized knowledge of retirement plans and services, which were becoming more and more profitable. Soon I was being asked to speak on retirement planning at professional meetings around the country, to help the people who were selling these services actually understand what they were selling—and how to sell it. Over the years, in addition to that first book, I've authored several other books for my publisher, Aspen Publishers, and a few for the American Institute of Certified Public Accountants (AICPA). Today, each new law opens the possibility of a new book, a course, or a lecture.

Why do I mention all this, you may ask? Well, choosing a career is not unlike designing the best retirement plan. The more you know, the easier it is to design the best plan or to follow the right path.

Simply stated, the best retirement plan is the one that comes closest to satisfying the needs and objectives of the client, the adopting employer. Matching those needs to the various types of available plans and the myriad possible plan designs is often more difficult than defining the employer's needs and objectives. The benefits and costs associated with establishing, maintaining, and terminating the plan, and the life of the plan, must all be considered. The motivation of the employees and the demographics of an employer may also be relevant factors in choosing the right plan.

For example, a tax-sanctioned simplified employee pension plan (SEP) program can compare favorably with a qualified plan pension or profit-sharing plan even though fully vested SEP contributions would generally be made for employees with three or more years of service. Because a qualified plan has a shorter eligibility requirement (generally, a service requirement of one year and the performance of 1,000 hours of service), contributions may have to be made or allocated to more employees. Although the qualified plan would most likely have a vesting schedule applied to employer-derived accrued benefits or account balances, it is applied to an additional two years of contributions made by the employer. Under a SEP, fully vested contributions would be allocated to fewer participating employees. The plan that offers the least employee cost at all points along an employee's employment time line can be determined only after:

- Considering many factors, such as potential growth of business, employee turnover, age, whether employed on the last day of the plan year, worked at least 500 or 1,000 hours, work patterns, and so on.

- Analyzing a group's eligibility to participate initially and then to receive contributions, and the extent to which those contributions will be vested upon an employee's termination of service.

The right plan can be selected by design, but the decision often involves the elimination of unsuitable plan types followed by the selection and design of the best plan from those that remain. For example, an employer that is unable to commit to a contribution level would not ordinarily adopt a pension plan. A traditional 401(k) plan may not be suitable for a smaller business owner whose lower-paid workers—known as "non-highly compensated employees"—choose not to make elective contributions. A SEP may be more suitable for a smaller business owner if there is high employee turnover. In some cases, not having a qualified or tax-sanctioned plan is a better business decision than adopting a plan that will cost too much and/or may not benefit owners and other key-employees. Nonqualified executive compensation planning must also be considered, especially in situations when a qualified or tax-sanctioned plan is not effective—tax-wise or otherwise.

The design of the best—or most suitable plan—is both an art and a science. The enormous complexity of the IRS, DOL, and PBGC regulations in this area provides both opportunities and pitfalls for the practitioner. The need to have competent assistance on an initial and ongoing basis cannot be overemphasized. This is not an area in which the intelligent practitioner can afford to go it alone.

The funding of plan benefits is generally accomplished by investing in securities, as opposed to or in addition to life insurance, guaranteed investment contracts, annuities, and real estate. If an individual provides advice on such matters, he or she may have to be registered as an investment adviser. If life insurance is purchased in a qualified plan, numerous tax and nontax issues also need to be considered.

Strange things happen. Sometime you choose your path, sometimes a path chooses you. I sometimes wish I had stayed with the IRS. I would have been earning in the low six figures and would be retiring in four years with a 55 percent of compensation pension from the Treasury Department. A check you can count on. Do your research and choose your path and your plans carefully. Good luck.

Stuart M. Lewis, JD

Stuart is a shareholder at Buchanan Ingersoll & Rooney PC, and is co-chair of its ERISA Litigation Group and Executive Compensation Group.

"Careers in Employee Benefits — Come on in"

In my role as an adjunct professor at Georgetown University Law School and in my role as head of the Employee Benefits Practice Group in my law firm, my students and associates often ask me whether they should pursue a career in employee benefits. As with almost all my answers to legal questions, I tell them, "It depends."

A career in employee benefits has its pluses and minuses, like any specialty area of the law. Among the factors that would recommend a career in this field would be the three EVERs:

- Everlasting (remember death and taxes employee benefits are largely part of taxes). Issues in this field will never go away, meaning that there will always be a need for legal help involving these issues.

- Ever-changing. This is a subject area that never rests. Employee benefits is both a favorite revenue-raiser by Congress (which means they are continually tinkering with the rules) and at the same time, a favorite whipping boy of Congress (which has the same result as being a favorite revenue-raiser except that it affects non-tax areas as well). This requires continual, and sometimes exhausting, due diligence to keep up with developments.

- Ever-in-need. Most companies, even very large companies, are woefully under-staffed with necessary technical help in this area. Often tax counsel or other members of the legal department will handle employee benefits issues but will usually admit that they do not have the necessary expertise to deal with many of the issues involved. This means that at both the corporate and private-practice level there will be a need for expertise in this area.

My students also tell me that this field is hard to break into. Those doing the hiring are typically looking for experience. Those wanting to be hired typically want to get the experience but that leaves a gap that can be difficult for a student to bridge. The solution to bridging this gap is not easy and may require a bit of luck.

Probably the key component that an aspiring employee benefits student should focus on is developing a strong technical knowledge of this field. The rules are intricate, complex and often difficult to understand. It may, in fact, take years to develop sufficient breadth of knowledge to feel entirely comfortable giving advice.

As students, it is essential that you take any courses in the field that are available to you. If you are considering getting an LLM, you should consider a law school that has a strong course offering in the field and should take all of the courses you can related to employee benefits.

Practical experience is highly valued. If you can work as a volunteer, get involved with bar association committees or simply do any type of self-study that will give you experience, that will definitely provide an important component that can help you break into the field.

In approaching this area, it should be kept in mind that while many students consider employee benefits to be a specialty area, people who specialize in the area consider it a general practice area with numerous specialties (or sub-specialties, if you will). Areas such as executive compensation, retirement planning, health plans, welfare plans, ERISA litigation, ERISA lobbying, SEC and labor law are areas that ERISA practitioners consider to be specialty areas. Anyone trying to develop expertise in the employee benefits field who has an opportunity to delve into any of these areas should take full advantage of that opportunity. From there, it will be easier to evolve into other areas in the employee benefits field that may be of interest.

As a final thought, I would stress flexibility. It is often difficult to follow a pre-selected path of career development. I know that I backed into an employee benefits specialty by chance more than by design and I believe many people in the field did as well. Anyone seeking to go this route should take advantage of whatever is available, but stay flexible, stay focused, and stay interested.

J.J. McKinney, CPC, QPA, QKA

J.J. is Chief Operations Officer at Retirement Strategies, Inc.

I do not know that any child wakes up and one day immediately revolves a dream from professional ball player to employee benefits specialist or in my case Popeye to employee benefits. As someone who has neither sailed a ship nor taken much of a liking to spinach I am not sure where that dream came from. Nonetheless, guided by the waves of life I found myself amid the clouds of the IRS and DOL on the ever changing seas of ERISA, Internal Revenue Code (IRC) and Treasury Regulations.

Pension is an industry for everyone and no one at the same time; in other words, one loves it, hates it or loves to hate it. If you enjoy research, numbers, change, problem solving, variables, statistics, presenting, writing or reading you can find a comfortable place to nestle yourself for the next 30 to 40 years.

By the time I entered college the Popeye pipe dreams had gone and I felt a call to teaching. After 5 years and a successful BA in English and Spanish I landed a job teaching middle school Spanish. Aside from the obnoxious children, bad administration and low pay it was not a bad gig. I had the summer off and found employment through a temporary leasing organization that sent me to a third party administrator to compile enrollment packets. I share this anecdote to demonstrate how becoming a benefits professional is no accident. The Spanish degree paid off—the company hired me to answer phones on their bi-lingual line.

We find challenges at every corner every day in this industry primarily easily forewarned by the name "Employee Benefits." Currently legislators and practitioners wrestle with fee disclosure and investment advice. The industry grapples with a dramatic shift in pension philosophy—the pension plan as a means to provide benefits for employees who have given their lives to the company has revolved into savings plans to provide investment opportunity and portability for employees whose loyalty remains until the next best opportunity calls. Like the internet to the personal computer, the 401(k) feature to a profit sharing plan exploded into the lives of millions of Americans without a real understanding of both its rewards and risks. Lawmakers scramble to reevaluate pension laws and regulations because the philosophical shift has turned the 200 year history of retirement plans in America on its head in the last 20 years.

Understanding the moving parts to a qualified retirement plan plays a vital role for every plan sponsor. However, most plan sponsors do not place the qualified plan in a list of their top 10, 50 or even 100 priorities. Generally, the plan sponsor runs a business that does involve plan administration. As you have read in previous chapters complex rules and regulations frame the qualified plan landscape. The government works prolifically to amend the IRC and regulations as administrations and economies change. Plan sponsors must rely on outside experience to meet plan administration responsibilities.

Qualified plan rules affect tax laws, business practices, individual finance planning and many other areas. Attorneys and CPAs who understand specific areas of the law or Code may not realize how the qualified plan works with other areas of the plan sponsor's business or personal needs. The wise plan sponsor hires a third party administrator to keep the plan in compliance with regulatory mandates, a recordkeeper to book keep the assets and a consultant to constantly review and fit the plan to the tax payer's situation.

Our firm services plan sponsors at three levels: we are a third party administrator, recordkeeper and consultant for our clients. Each proficiency serves to check and balance the other two.

Third party administrator (TPA)

The complex nature of plan operation lends itself to unintended oversights and mistakes. The TPA performs many of the control functions on the plan sponsor's behalf to ensure that the retirement plan operates in accordance with the written plan document and maintains compliance within the guidelines of the IRC. A TPA directs the plan sponsor to make decisions to fulfill the provisions of the document in plan operation.

Plans with 401(k) features may be in compliance in written form; however, the TPA performs necessary tests to ensure that the plan operates in compliance with the document. Preliminary and continuous testing throughout the year help the plan sponsor prepare for either the budgetary constraints of an additional contribution or communication to Highly Compensated Employees (HCE) about corrective distributions. Retirement Strategies, Inc. (RSI) converted a case where a group of HCEs sued the plan sponsor over corrective distributions and forfeited matching contributions. The plan sponsor's employment contract read that the employee could defer up to the statutory limit and explained the plan's match formula. The employer ultimately settled and paid the lost contributions and match as a bonus to each of the HCEs. The plan sponsor could have avoided the lawsuit and myriad fees and expenses by allowing the TPA to review the employment contract containing the plan related details.

The TPA is an invaluable resource even in a "safe harbor" plan by helping fulfill the necessary notice and allocation requirements to satisfy the rules and regulations. The safe harbor plan is often sold as a "free-ride" which leads the plan sponsor to believe that once it is up and running the plan is self sufficient. The plan may easily drop safe harbor protection, incur testing failures and possibly penalties by neglecting a simple annual notice. TPAs monitor the timing of these requirements and calculate the contributions as prescribed in the document to help maintain the safe harbor.

Recordkeeper

A recordkeeper plays two basic and important functions; maintaining records for participants and monitoring deposits coming into the plan. The complexity of the detail relies on technology to accomplish proper book keeping to the level required by the IRC. The plan separately maintains records for each participant, source of money, investment and often the basis level for contributions as well as tax basis for post-tax monies. Additionally, the IRC has been changed at various intervals in history to affect new rules on certain types of contributions. Depending on how long the plan has been in existence the record keeper might maintain 401(k) deferrals made before 1987 separately from those contributed after 1986. The plan might also have matching contributions subject to a vesting schedule separately accounted from safe harbor matching contributions. A recordkeeper can handle this level of detail at a reasonable cost by using software to handle multiple plans and plan sponsors while a plan sponsor trying to maintain the same level of records for one plan could easily spend over a hundred-thousand dollars a year in-house.

Each source of money is subject to different rules especially as they relate to distributions from a qualified plan. The recordkeeper provides information so the third party administrator can determine how much a participant may withdraw by reviewing vesting on each source and calculating basis. The TPA reviews the plan document to determine whether the participant may take the disbursement. Improper distributions will not likely return to the plan and could cause plan qualification issues. RSI corrected a case where the plan sponsor insisted on calculating vesting and reporting it directly to the recordkeeper. The participant received $25,000 more than allowed. When the recordkeeper took the discovery to a higher level the plan sponsor spent time and money retrieving the overdrawn amount from the receiving institution. This is a success story. Often the plan sponsor pays the overdrawn amount to the plan of pocket. The plan sponsor is the ultimate authority, but the plan sponsor can save time, effort and expense by trusting the recordkeeper to exercise expertise in maintaining proper vesting records.

Recordkeepers expertise extends beyond simple book keeping. The well advised plan sponsor uses the recordkeeper as an assets to operate the plan properly.

Consultant

Consultants have the fun job in the pension industry. Always the opportunist who brightens poor compliance results through enhanced plan design or plan amendment. Consultants can work with a CPA to help an overwhelmed tax payer and teach him how to save and shelter more through a qualified plan. The same consultant eases the transition for new participants during a merger or acquisition. The pension consultant sustains a variety of skills and knowledge and solves problems by applying them to fact patterns. Consultants recognize the abilities of the plan sponsor and match them with the appropriate service model solution. Consultants review plan sponsor cash flow, goals, objectives, demographics, retention and spending patterns to best fit plan design. The consultant continually monitors all facets of the company as it transforms. The consultant understands how the recordkeeper works, how to read and write a plan document, how to correct failed, compliance testing or foresee when a failure is imminent and make preemptive improvements. Experienced consultants have likely worked as a TPA and recordkeeper and understand their roles and challenges.

Consultants typically review their clients' situations throughout the year so that changes may be made during the year. Plan sponsors generally prepare too late to optimize a tax situation with a qualified plan when a banner year arises. RSI reviews several small business cases each year in this exact scenario. Midway through the year a plan sponsor notices that his projected numbers are double what he factored at the beginning of the year; however, the 401(k) profit sharing plan in place will only allow a moderate level of shelter for the extra income (appropriate for most years). We analyze information and discuss forecasting with the plan sponsor and research trends in the sponsor's industry and geographic region. We correspond with the sponsor's CPA to get another expert's view of the situation. We may explore adding a defined benefit plan to the practice as an appropriate option. If this one year is an anomaly we might suggest waiting to see if the business will sustain this level of revenue and profit.

Consultants' fees for a specific project might be as much as the plan sponsor pays for either their recordkeeping or third party administration for a full year, but the outcome is worth it. The above scenario could go two ways. The consultant who acts in haste may help the sponsor establish a defined benefit plan immediately that may be difficult to afford in future years. The consultant who takes the cautious approach and appropriately researches the information will make a sound recommendation while providing the sponsor with all of the pros and cons that accompany the decision. The sponsor pays the consultant's fee whether the decision is to add a new plan or do nothing and wait. The consultant's recommendation adds value at both ends—the sponsor knows about new options and realizes best when to exercise them.

The TPA, recordkeeper and consultant each play vital roles as organs in the body of the pension industry. These services can be bundled into one service provider like RSI or the sponsor may engage each separately. In any case, understanding their roles and why the roles are important allows plan sponsors to hire for the appropriate need and keep themselves out of unnecessary trouble.

Tom Reeder, JD

Tom is Senior Benefits Counsel on the Democratic U.S. Senate Finance Committee staff (at the time he wrote this essay, he was the Benefits Tax Counsel in the Office of Tax Policy at the Department of the Treasury).

"Tax and the City"

I am delighted that Professor Kozak has given me this invitation to share my thoughts to those entering the employee benefits tax practice and am flattered that he contemplates that some of my observations may be of use. With that in mind, I offer the following thoughts based on my own experiences inside and outside of the practice of law.

1. It's all happening in the Internal Revenue Code. On a hot day in the summer of 2008, I found myself doing a little extra sweating indoors. I was being cross-examined by a Member of the Ways and Means Committee at a hearing at which I had just testified. The subject was getting people to save more. I found myself in the awkward position of having to argue that the Internal Revenue Code might not be the best mechanism for influencing behavior. But then, realizing where I was, I caught myself. In the hearing room of the House Ways and Means Committee, you NEVER admit that the Internal Revenue Code is not the best way to influence behavior. So I used some lighthearted quip to bail myself out.

The exchange got me thinking, though, about what drew me so much to tax law, and particularly, employee benefits. Most serious students of public policy believe that the tax code works best as a revenue raiser and not as a fundamental organ of social policy. The history of the Internal Revenue Code, however, is a series of massive tax laws the purpose of which has been largely to stimulate (or regulate) behavior, and much less to raise revenue. This is most obvious in the area of employee benefits, with retirement savings and health coverage being the two largest tax expenditure items in the Code.

Most people who go into the legal profession are looking to have a positive influence on other people. Some of us, of course, end up working in areas that might be very remunerative, but don't really have that much effect on our human environment, but most of us go home at night feeling good about what we do. What better area of practice is there than the area where the real action is taking place?

2. Never underestimate the value of a first career. Virtually everyone I know who practices law in the employee benefits arena got into their specialty by what seems to be a series of chance events. In my case, one of the biggest employers in Austin when I graduated from the University of Texas in the early seventies was the Internal Revenue Service regional service center. I went to work there for two years as a tax examiner and got a good grounding in the general tax rules and a healthy dose of how things do or don't work in a bureaucracy. Plowing through tax returns was not my idea of fun, however, and I went back to school to become a teacher and had a tremendously rewarding and fun career as a high school teacher, including two years in the Peace Corps in West Africa. However fun that was, I began to realize that wasn't going to keep me interested over the long haul, so I decided to try my hand in the law.

When I began to practice law, I sometimes felt disadvantaged compared to others in my age group, because many of them had so much more legal experience. But I would not do it any differently, even if given the opportunity for a re-do. I believe the richness of the experiences gained with another career is more valuable to me than had I been practicing law during that time. Also, it gave my views on retirement savings an unexpected twist. Many of us in the retirement policy area pay much attention to leakage from the retirement system. We commonly have a holier-than-thou attitude towards the sanctity of the 401(k) account or the IRA and profess that participants should do without whatever they think they need before raiding their retirement savings. However, I have the experience of having spent my entire 403(b) account on my law school education. Since I graduated from law school with no debt, I have no regrets.

3. Build on what you already know. I was fortunate to be able to remain in Austin to attend the University of Texas School of Law. I did well in my studies, but I found that I really excelled in tax classes. I assume it was the background from the IRS, because what seemed convoluted to my classmates made (and still makes) perfect sense to me. I benefited greatly from a tax professor who emphasized why tax rules were written the way they were, not just the study of the rules themselves. Ever since, I have often been able to get to the meaning of a mysterious tax rule by thinking of what the policy makers was trying to do with the statute instead of focusing on the otherwise meaningless words on the page. So when I graduated from law school, I considered myself a tax lawyer. Little did I know — really. I thought (and still think) the opportunities for a sophisticated tax practice were greater in a big city, and, if I had any ambitions in tax policy, that city should be Washington. My spouse reluctantly agreed and we packed up the U-Haul headed to the big city.

4. Specialize. If you asked most Americans about whether they thought tax lawyers were specialized, they would respond that tax law was a very narrow area of the law. However, in a big firm, such as the one where I practiced, one soon learns that tax law is a relatively broad area of the law, and it is increasingly rare for someone to call themselves a general tax lawyer. I realized this as I struggled to grasp various areas of tax law. My early years of practice were spent learning areas of the tax law that I didn't even know existed when I was in law school.

Right after the enactment of the Tax Reform Act of 1986, when the tax world was boning up on all of the new rules, one of the new rules was section 89. It generally prohibited discrimination in employer-provided health benefits. Because the rule was so new, I was on a relatively equal footing with everyone else, so I decided that, with the help of a capable and willing mentor, I would become the firm's expert on that new area of the law that promised to be the next big thing. I worked many non-billable hours with the statute, committee reports, articles, and proposed regulations and slogged through long meetings devoted to the fine points of the statutory requirements. I did become one of the firm's experts on the subject, but Congress, in a rare recognition of the fact that the law really was too complex, repealed the statute.

5. But not too much. Large firms will commonly suck up junior associates in areas outside of their area of "expertise" whenever the firm needs a grunt in another department. Those experiences added breadth to my background from which I continue to draw benefits, including the rare opportunity to argue motions in court (I'm 2–0 in that category).

6. Seek out pro bono. As a complement to that broadening experience, MY firm was a strong proponent of pro bono work. As a result, I was able to work on issues that made a real and immediate difference in an individual's life. One of the most memorable cases involved a pension claim of a widow in West Virginia. When I was first considering the case, one of the partners in the employee benefits practice objected saying that the case might involve a subject matter conflict with our paying clientele, *i.e.*, plan sponsors. A senior partner overruled that objection, however, and I was off to the races. I won the case and a warm "God bless you, Mr. Reeder" from the client. There are plenty of opportunities in the area of pro bono tax work (e.g., working with Volunteers in Tax Assistance and obtaining tax exempt status for charitable organizations) and employee benefits work (e.g., taking case referrals from the Pension Rights Center and the Legal Counsel for the Elderly).

7. Don't be afraid to move. After a few years of getting my feet wet, I joined the ranks of the extremely sought-after; that is, the experienced employee benefits associate. Although I was doing fine and did not want to move, I received dozens of calls from headhunters. Then one day I got the offer that I absolutely had to think about. The senior partner of the employee benefits practice was moving to another firm, and most of the rest of the practice appeared to be following him. I could stay where I was and be the only fish in a very big pond or I could move with most of my practice group. I chose the latter and I learned something that would have been virtually impossible to find out if I had stayed. Many of the clients for which I was working and thought were someone else's clients had actually become my clients. To my pleasant surprise, as soon as I indicated I was moving, many of my clients asked where they should tell my old firm to send their files. I had actually gained a book of business I did not know I had. My practice really took off in my new firm and I benefitted from a tremendous working relationship with the attorneys in the new firm and all of the associates reaped some of the rewards of what one of the partners called the "fiscal fecundity" of the firm.

8. Don't fight the call to government service. The number of calls from headhunters increased with my experience level and I began to get a new type of call—from government officials asking if I would like to come to work in the government. Washington has a wealth of practice opportunities for employee benefits professionals interested in government service. The tax-writing committees and the labor committees of both houses of Congress have employee benefits lawyers and of course there are lots of opportunities at the Departments of Labor and Treasury and the IRS and PBGC. Some of these agencies hire freshly minted lawyers and actuaries and some require several years of specialized practice before taking someone on.

In my case, after several years in a large law firm, there was a desire to earn the status of equity partner. There is a tremendous attraction of working with other great lawyers who view you as a partner. So I resisted the urge to go into government service and continued to work the ungodly hours taking on as much as I possibly could in return for an ungodly amount of money.

A short time after making partner, however, I began to wonder whether I would ever find the ideal time to move. Also, my social conscience began to nag me about whether I was part of the problem or part of the solution. About once a day something happened to remind me that my value to clients was not just to help them follow the law, but to also help them to achieve a result that the law was intended to prevent. For example, I actually had a client ask me, "How do I get rid of my older workers?" What bothered me more than the question was the fact that I actually had some advice for the client, which included the notion of not asking questions quite like that. It was soon after that experience that the Benefits Tax Counsel at Treasury repeated his request that I come to work at Treasury. I happily accepted.

The Treasury Department offers a healthy mix of legislative and regulatory work. You must keep your technical skills honed as you work through regulatory projects (with the IRS Office of Chief Counsel and the Employee Plans Division of the IRS). You also work on the development of the tax provisions in the President's annual budget and are called upon by the tax writing committees of Congress to assist in drafting legislation. In short, you are placed in a position in which you can promote good social policy and stop bad ideas.

9. Always have and be a mentor. I have been extremely fortunate in both my teaching career and in the law to be able to work with someone from whom I have learned something every day I am at work. Those times when I did not have such a person who took an interest in my well being and success and whom I could look to for advice, support, and a good example coincided with those times when I was thinking about going to work somewhere else. The success of any organization depends largely on the availability of mentors in the workplace. In any discussion comparing places to work, especially the very frank ones that are commonly found online, the topic of the availability of mentors ranks close to money and interesting work as reasons lawyers like or dislike a firm.

10. Put your own mask on first. Every time I travel, I look forward to the spiel at the beginning of a flight when the flight attendant or television monitor shows the passengers how to use the emergency oxygen mask system. The line of particular interest to me goes something like, "If you're traveling with persons who need assistance, make sure you have arranged your own mask before helping them." That advice is very useful in other contexts. You are not going to be of very much use to others if you don't take care of yourself. This is an area where I perhaps need the most work. To me, most important in self-care is the maintenance of a life outside of the office. Though at times a challenge, the rewards are far reaching for both your personal and professional well being.

Tom Terry, FSA, EA

Tom is a Managing Director of JPMorgan and CEO of that firm's Compensation and Benefits Strategies consulting unit.

I've been a consulting actuary in the employee benefits field for nearly 35 years. One afternoon last year, the phone rang. On the other end was a long-standing client. Bob is a corporate head of HR whose firm was then in the midst of an acquisition. As Bob poured over the corporate charter of the company his firm was preparing to buy, he found that he was struggling with the compensation significance of a particularly complex section. Could I help?

He emailed me the section of the charter that had him stumped and I looked it over quickly. Four things hit me immediately: I was completely unfamiliar with corporate charters; I didn't understand what I was reading; I failed to see any connection in this information to compensation or employee benefits; and I was clueless as to why he thought to call me!

Unsure how I was going to help Bob, we nevertheless started to dig in. Forty-five minutes later, our call ended—with Bob thanking me profusely. It was a very satisfying moment, career-wise—and it was indicative of why I've so much enjoyed working in employee benefits.

As an actuary fresh out of school years ago, I saw employee benefits as a series of laws, regulations and formulas. From that perspective, I believed the essential exchange between employers and their employees was financial. I also thought the chief value I could bring clients was my technical knowledge, my mastery of detail and my comfort with complex formulas that left most people in the dark.

Today, my perspective is vastly different. Instead of a series of contractual arrangements, I now see employee benefits as the key ingredients to defining a company's culture. And I now see my contribution differently as well. Yes, I'm proud of what I've learned and the technical detail I've mastered. Yet the greater value I can bring to any dialogue today is what I've learned about relationships and collaboration. I don't have to know all the answers. My impact can come from influencing how people look at a problem and how they work with others to solve it. Done right, I think employee benefits is about teamwork and collaboration across disciplines toward a good answer—not the one correct or compliant answer. That's the contribution I was able to make to Bob.

When I talk to students and others considering a career in employee benefits, I like to emphasize that the field offers infinite possibilities. Many are attracted to the field because of its rich technical content. But—laws come and go, while people and organizations will always be there. And so the infinite possibilities derive from the richness of the relationships with those people and organizations. For me, the learning never ends.

Chapter 23

Public Policy of an Aging Population

Overview

What are some problems with ERISA?
- the rules are extremely complex, from all aspects (a participant's appreciation of the benefits promised; the plan sponsor's understanding in advance of a transaction or decision as to its legality; and the plan's professional counsel, like attorney or accountant, in their ability to properly advise the plan)
- the business practices from 1974 are not the same as they are today (*i.e.,* in 1974 most employers had a defined benefit plan as the primary plan and then supplemented it with a defined contribution plan, whereas a 401(k) plan is the primary plan for most current employers; also, there are far more mergers, acquisitions, joint ventures, temporary employees, leased employees, and phased retirement issues in today's business environment than there were back then)
- the whole state of health benefits has changed dramatically due to longer life expectancies, greater health care costs, and the Health Maintenance Organization (HMO) becoming a predominant health plan arrangement
- Communication is far better these days, so some of the original protections for "uninformed" participants and beneficiaries might not still be a concern
- few, if any, congressmen, senators, or federal judges truly understand ERISA
- new federal laws are enacted almost annually which effect employee benefit plans

What are some retirement issues with an aging population?
- in this author's opinion:
  - the main problem with the current employer-provided retirement plan regime is the reliance on defined contribution plans that mostly pay out single lump sums, or defined benefit plans that offer the option of converting a life annuity into a single lump sum
  - the longevity risk (*i.e.,* living longer than expected and depleting the entire retirement account while still alive) is wholly borne by the individual
  - unless health reform is actually accomplished, the health care costs during retirement eat up most of the individual's retirement income

1. Problems with ERISA in Its Current Form

Here are some of my personal concerns with the current state of the the the regulatory framework of employee benefits plans. I don't mean to discourage any student, because I truly believe in the original goals of ERISA—protecting the rights of employees promised benefits through an employer plan. This textbook has hopefully provided you with a basic knowledge of how the rules work, and this final chapter will hopefully arm you with issues that you can help to address as you become a benefits professional.

The rules are extremely complex, from all aspects (a participant's appreciation of the benefits promised; the plan sponsor's understanding in advance of a transaction or decision as to its legality; and the plan's professional counsel, like attorney or accountant, in their ability to properly advise the plan).

The business practices from 1974 are not the same as they are today (*i.e.*, in 1974 most employers had a defined benefit plan as the primary plan and then supplemented it with a defined contribution plan, whereas a 401(k) plan is the primary plan for most current employers; also, there are far more mergers, acquisitions, joint ventures, temporary employees, leased employees, and phased retirement issues in today's business environment than there were back then).

The whole state of health benefits has changed dramatically due to longer life expectancies, greater health care costs, and the Health Maintenance Organization (HMO) becoming a predominant health plan arrangement.

Communication is far better these days, so some of the original protections for "uninformed" participants and beneficiaries might not still be a concern.

Few, if any, congressmen, senators, or federal judges truly understand ERISA, even after 35 years of its existence.

New federal laws are enacted almost annually which effect employee benefit plans.

More federal agencies have regulatory authority and concerns regarding employee benefits plans than the original DOL, IRS and PBGC.

2. Aging Population

Aside from the economic and corporate controversies and tragedies of the last decade, a major concern is adequate retirement benefits for the aging population—not just here in the United States, but globally.

According to a new report, "[t]he average age of the world's population is increasing at an unprecedented rate. The number of people worldwide 65 and older is estimated at 506 million as of midyear 2008; by 2040, that number will hit 1.3 billion. Thus, in just over 30 years, the proportion of older people will double from 7 percent to 14 percent of the total world population."[1]

The report starts out with a 20 question quiz (I did not get an A on the quiz even though I have been thinking about these issues for many years), which I encourage you to find online and consider.

---

1. Kinsella, Kevin and Wan He, U.S. Census Bureau, International Population Reports, P95/09-1, An Aging World: 2008, U.S. Government Printing Office, Washington, DC, 2009.

The report identified nine trends that offer a snapshot of global challenges:[2]

- The world's population is aging: People aged 65 and over will soon outnumber children under age 5 for the first time in history.

- Life expectancy is increasing: Most countries show a steady increase in longevity over time, which raises questions about the potential for the human lifespan.

- The number of the oldest old is rising: The world's population aged 80 and over is projected to increase 233 percent between 2008 and 2040, compared with 160 percent for the population aged 65 and over and 33 percent for the total population of all ages.

- Some populations are aging while their size declines: While the world's population is aging, total population size is simultaneously declining in some countries, and the list of these countries is projected to expand.

- Noncommunicable diseases are becoming a growing burden: Chronic noncommunicable diseases are now the major cause of death among older people in both developed and developing countries.

- Family structures are changing: As people live longer and have fewer children, family structure are transformed and care options in older age may change.

- Patterns of work and retirement are shifting: Shrinking ratios of workers to pensioners and people spending a larger portion of their lives in retirement increasingly tax existing health and pension systems.

- Social insurance systems are evolving: As social insurance expenditures escalate, an increasing number of countries are evaluating the sustainability of these systems and revamping old-age security provisions.

- New economic challenges are emerging: Population aging has and will have large effects on social entitlement programs, labor supply, and total savings around the globe."

I encourage students to read the full report at some point, not necessarily for this course on employee benefits plans rules in America, but more to get an understanding of the similarity of issues of an aging population that affect many countries and their respective retirement pension and social programs.

Some final quotes, this time from a different report on global aging. "We are aging—not just as individuals or communities but as a world. In 2006, almost 500 million people worldwide were 65 and older. By 2030, that total is projected to increase to 1 billion—1 in every 8 of the earth's inhabitants. Significantly, the most rapid increases in the 65-and-older population are occurring in developing countries, which will see a jump of 140 percent by 2030."[3] And then, in regards to shifting patterns of work and retirement, the report concludes "[n]o set of issues has stimulated public discourse about population aging more than work, retirement, and economic security in old age. In Western democracies, in Eastern Europe's transitional economies, and in much of the less developed world, policymakers struggle with the balance between public and private income security systems." The report continues with two additional points: "In response to escalating pension expenditures, an increasing number of countries across the development spectrum are evaluating the sustainability of old-age social insurance systems" and "Popula-

---

2. Id.
3. Dobriansky, Paula J., Richard M. Suzman and Richard J. Hodes, "Why Population Aging Matters: A Global Perspective," National Institute on Aging (2007).

tion aging will have dramatic effects on local, regional, and global economies. Most significantly, financial expenditures, labor supply, and total savings will be affected."

3. Collection of Short Articles

Over my career as a benefits professional, I have been concerned with the aging population and the adequacy of retirement income. I am closing this textbook with just a few of those articles. I am not asking you to agree with my concerns and conclusions, all I am asking is that you think about how you, as a professional, outside of your billable hours helping specific clients with their employee benefits issues, can write articles, give speeches, perform pro bono services, participate in professional organizations that write white papers or comments to proposed regulations, or find other ways to help to highlight problems with the systems and possibly to advocate solutions. The first article expresses my views on defined contribution plans (especially 401(k) plans), the second expresses my views on defined benefit plans, and the third gets off the subject of public policy with an aging population, and goes back to the first part of this chapter, and reflects the views on simplifying the regulation of qualified plans (where I was recording secretary for a tax force).

"How To Make Your 401(k) Plan Retirement Account Balance Last Through Retirement"
By Barry Kozak, 2009
Not yet published

Your retirement account is only really valuable to you if it is sufficient to pay for your retirement expenses. This article proposes a two-part approach to properly funding your 401(k) account. First, you need to reasonably determine how much money you need in your 401(k) account upon retirement. Second, you need to determine how much money needs to be contributed during your working years that will accumulate to the required amount. Along the way, you will need to monitor your investment choices, and might need to re-evaluate your needs during retirement or at what age you will retire. Congress gave us a great way of saving for our retirement through employer-sponsored 401(k) plans. However, we need to take the responsibility for making sure that the 401(k) plan will properly fund our desired retirement goals. This article suggests how you can manage such responsibility.

How Much Do You Need At Retirement?

This is probably the more important question to ask, rather than how much do you contribute and how do you invest the money along the way. If you participate in a 401(k) plan, then at retirement, you will have a pot of money to spend during your retirement, without many restrictions. The best planning you can do is to determine how much money you will need to spend each year, determine how long you expect to live, and then determine the account balance you will need when you "retire." With this determination, you can then plan on making the appropriate contributions and investment choices along the way; understanding, of course, that there might be some years that you can contribute more and some years you need to contribute less.

While you do not need to be a high-level mathematician for this, I will try to show the main mathematical concepts through the following case study. Mary is a single woman. She is 50 years old and is earning $40,000 per year at her job. Her employer just established a 401(k) plan, and Mary must determine how much money she wants to defer from her paycheck for the next 15 years. As suggested, Mary should first determine how much she needs accumulated at age 65, and then figure out how much should be contributed annually over the next 15 years. Mary would like to retire at age 65, and although she will spend less on work clothes and commuting, she still thinks that she will need about $30,000 per year to enjoy her years in retirement in a similar lifestyle as she is currently accustomed to. Mary expects to receive $12,000 per year from Social Security. Assuming Mary has no other income sources, her 401(k) account balance, whatever it is, will therefore need to provide $18,000 per year for the rest of her life.

How long will Mary live beyond age 65. Perhaps she can go to a good psychic to find out. Joking aside, no one knows how long they will live, but we can make educated guesses based on published life expectancies. According to a U.S. Department of Health and Human Services special project, at www.4woman.gov, the female life expectancy at birth is 79 years. In statistical terms, that means that 50% of women will die before age 79, and 50% will live longer. How does this help Mary? If Mary is in fairly good health, and if her family history indicates longevity, then Mary should probably assume that she will live longer than age 79.

Let's assume that Mary decides that she expects to live until age 85. If she assumes age 85, and dies at some other age, then the issue is whether her estimate is too conservative or too liberal. If she was too conservative, and she dies sometime before age 85, then she will have had enough retirement income while she was alive, and will additionally have some remaining assets to pass through her estate upon her death. However, if she is too liberal, and she actually lives beyond age 85, then her 401(k) account will probably be depleted at age 85. Therefore, other than the Social Security payments, after age 85, she will have no other retirement income. In such a case, Mary, as an older woman, might need to move in order to reduce her rent and other living expenses, might need to sell off some of her assets, or might have to become a ward of the state and collect some sort of welfare. This latter case is very scary for most people, and is the main reason that everyone, including Mary, should assume a long life instead of a short life. In light of advancing medical breakthroughs, it might even be reasonable to conservatively assume living until age 100.

Okay, so Mary determines that she will live until age 85, and will need to withdraw $18,000 each year. If she can guarantee that the 401(k) account balance will earn 5% each year, then in order to fund an annuity of $18,000 per year for each of the next 20 years, Mary would need an account balance of about $236,000 accumulated at her age 65 (any financial calculator or software program would show a Present Value of about $236,000 is needed for a 20 year annuity of $18,000 at an assumed rate of return of 5%). This means that Mary withdraws $18,000 in the first year, and the remaining balance earns 5% interest, then she withdraws $18,000 in the second year, with that remaining balance earning 5%, and so on, so in the twentieth year, the account balance will be about $18,000, and once Mary withdraws it, the account is wholly depleted. Again, if Mary is still alive at age 86, she has no further money to withdraw from her 401(k) account balance. Please note that assuming an interest rate is as unpredictable as assuming the age at which we will die. However, it is as important, so a conservative assumption is always preferable.

Just to show a few different scenarios, if Mary could find an investment that would be expected to earn 6% interest from age 65 to age 85, then in order to withdraw the same $18,000 per year, she would only need to accumulate about $219,000. On the other hand, if she invested the money that produced a 3% earnings yield per year, then she would need to accumulate about $276,000. Therefore, the earnings that are expected on the account once Mary begins retirement is just a guess. In a similar analysis, if she assumes a conservative rate like 3%, and accumulates $276,000, but she actually earns 6%, then she can withdraw $18,000 for 35 years, until age 90. However, if she assumes 6%, accumulates $219,000, but she actually earns 3%, then she will only have 15 years of an $18,000 distribution, meaning her account would be depleted at age 80, and would not last until her assumed life expectancy of age 85. Again, it is always better to assume a conservative rate of interest, and if Mary's investment choices produce a better-than-expected rate of return, then her money can last longer, or she can splurge on a vacation or two and withdraw an extra $3000 here and there.

How Do You Determine How Much to Contribute and How to Invest It?

After estimating a conservative life expectancy based on your health and family history, and after figuring out how much money you will need per year and a conservative rate of return, you have determined the pot of money needed at retirement. Now, you have to make a plan on how to get there. This includes an election each year on how much money should be withheld from your paycheck and deposited into the 401(k) plan, a diversified investment portfolio strategy that has the best chance of providing your account with a favorable rate of return, and monitoring the accumulation along the way.

First, you need to realize that the optimum contribution may be too expensive for you. If that's the case, then you can possibly contribute more money in some years and less in other. However, at the end of the day, if you cannot afford the targeted contributions while you are working, then you can expect a lesser total account balance upon retirement.

In Mary's case, if she assumes that she will earn 5% interest on her accounts, then to accumulate $236,000 at age 65, she will need to contribute about $10,400 each year. This contribution can partially consist of an employer's match. Assuming the employer's match would equal $2000 (a very generous match for most employers), under Mary's determination above, she would need to defer $8,400 each year out of her $40,000 salary to accumulate the targeted account balance of $236,000 (which is 21% of her entire pay check). Unfortunately, Mary probably cannot afford such a cut in current salary just to fund her required retirement income.

In this case, and Mary is certainly not alone, Mary might need to plan to retire later than age 65. If she now changed her plans to retire at age 70, but still expected to live until age 85 and still expected her account to earn 5% interest both before retirement and after retirement, then Mary would only need to defer a total contribution of $5,645 per year for the next 20 years until age 70, in order to accumulate $196,000, which should fund a distribution of $18,000 per year from age 70 until age 85 (again, a portion of the $5,645 could consist of an employer match). Many people do not like to hear news like this, but if Mary can only rely on Social Security benefits and her accumulated 401(k) account during retirement, and she can't conceivably afford what is required as contributions along the way, then she either needs to postpone retirement beyond age 65 or figure out how to live on a distribution from the 401(k) plan of less than $18,000 per year.

This is the reason that all advisors suggest that people start contributing to their 401(k) plans as early as possible. The effect of compounding of interest over a longer number of years produces higher account balances with less funding. Also, if there is a longer period of time, then there is a better chance of the average rates of returns coming close to the assumed rate (if there are some down years, there is more of a chance for some up years to bring the average up).

How to Determine the Proper Investment Strategy

In a 401(k) plan, if your employer allows you to direct the investments, then there are certain things that the employer must do. However, once those obligations are met, you are basically on your own to make the proper investment choices. Your employer has a fiduciary duty, under a federal law called the Employee Retirement Income Security Act (ERISA), to prudently select the investment options that you can choose from. This means that your employer must exercise due diligence and select the mutual fund families or other investment choices that basically have a good performance record, don't charge excessive fees to your individual accounts, provide general investment education, offer at least three choices that provide a diversified risk, and that provide you with all of the information and rights that you would get if you invested in that product outside of the 401(k) plan.

Therefore, a typical employer might offer you, as a participant in the 401(k) plan, a mutual fund family that has 12 options that vary in risk (such as a risky international fund, a less risky small cap growth or value fund, a moderately risky large cap growth or value fund, a conservative balanced or fixed income fund, and a very conservative stable value fund). You have no control over the selection of the mutual fund family, and all you can do is choose from among the options you are provided with through the plan. Legally, if the employer made a prudent and reasonable choice in selecting this family of funds, then you probably cannot sue the employer or the plan if you make improper investment decisions and your account loses money or does not earn your expected rate of return. While this rule is beneficial for the employers, and actually encourages them to sponsor 401(k) plans in the first place, it places the full risk of improper investment decisions on the shoulders of each individual participant.

Similar to the discussion of expected age at death, since you never know the actual rate of return on any asset until after it has been earned (or lost), you can either err by being too conservative, or err by being too liberal. If you are conservative, then you have a better chance of earning what is expected, and even a chance of earning more than expected. On the other hand, if your assumption is too liberal, then there is a chance your account will do as well as expected, but there is a greater chance that it will under-perform. If your account under-performs, then you will either accumulate less than is needed at retirement, or you might need to increase your contribution level in later years to make up for the lost investment earnings. Therefore, you should diversify your 401(k) account so that in the aggregate, if some funds do better-than-expected while others do less-than-expected, your account should still see an overall rate of return that matches your realistic conservative expectations.

This requires monitoring the individual investment options, and setting strict strategies for when your portfolio diversification will be changed. Although many of us have access to computers, and many 401(k) plans allow daily trading, unless you are a licensed investment advisor privy to all of the public information, it is highly suggested that you refrain from changing your portfolio every minute you see a performance indicator that you do not like. On the other hand, if you are too scared to re-evaluate your earlier decisions, and wait several years before making changes, you might equally hinder the chance for your account to earn the expected returns. Most advisors suggest that an evaluation every three months, or at least every year, assures the best chance of making proper on-going investment decisions. You should set personal goals, such as "I expect my small cap value fund to earn 5% per year, and once there is a 6 month period where the return is less than 4.5%, I will sell." Please note, however, that the goals you set for yourself should directly relate to your toleration for investment risk, and another person might change the above criteria to something like "I expect the small cap fund to earn 5% per year, and once there is a 2 month period where the return is less than 5.9%, I will sell." All that I am suggesting is that you set realistic trigger points for each of your investment choices, and only sell if they fall below your target point, and not on a whim (other than learning relevant news, such as an investigation of the fund manager or something severe like that).

In this age of bear markets and corporate scandals, many 401(k) accounts have lost value. Part of the explanation is that many accounts were too heavily skewed towards highly-risky investments (including the sponsoring employer's own stock). However, an account that is too heavily skewed towards highly-conservative investments (such as government bonds) will probably never yield a high enough accumulation at retirement. Therefore, a properly diversified account (with some risky investments offset by some conservative investments) is the best way to invest your 401(k) account, especially if the 401(k) account represents a substantial part of your expected retirement income.

Unfortunately, this means that you, the individual participant, need to understand investments and how to properly diversify your account. Most employers will provide their 401(k) plan participants with general investment education (such as "a typical 40 year old should have X% in a risky international fund, Y% in a large cap growth fund, and Z% in a conservative US Treasury bond fund; whereas, a typical 60 year old should have A%, B%, and C%, respectively"). This is at least a good start, assuming you are a typical 40 year old or a typical 60 year old. Although Congress changed the law in 2006 to allow employers to provide more directed individual investment advice to the 401(k) plan participants (through either the plan's investment advisor or through a neutral third-party investment advisor). Surveys are indicating that many employers are being slow to adopt this strategy. Therefore, many employees who participate in a 401(k) plan should expect to find, on their own, and pay for, out of their pocket, investment advice specifically tailored to his or her personal situation and level of risk that can be tolerated. If such individual advice is too costly, then he or she should, at the very least, follow the general advice provided for their age group.

Conclusion

Therefore, my suggestion is to determine a realistic targeted 401(k) account balance needed at retirement, and then determine how much is needed to be deferred from salary along the way. The investment portfolio should be as diversified as possible so that the chance of actually earning or exceeding your assumed rate of return is optimized. However, the accumulations must be monitored along the way, and if the account earns less than expected in any year, or if other personal expenses prevent you from contributing the proper amount for any given year, then: larger contributions will be required in future years; you will need to take less distributions during retirement; or, you will need to postpone retirement. On the other hand, a better-than-expected investment return, or the ability to put in larger contributions (such as deferring your holiday bonus instead of spending it on gifts) could allow: lower contributions in later years; or, the ability to either takes distributions for a longer period of time during retirement or allow you to take more than budgeted in any given year.

Please note that many calculators and spread-sheet computer programs have the basic financial mathematics functions needed to determine present values, future values, and payments. You should always seek professional help in determining how to best diversify you investments so that the risk of a devastating loss is minimal.

Discussions on "Averting the Retirement Income Crisis" by Carol R. Sears, FSPA, MAAA, FCA, CPC, EA and Scott D. Miller, FSPA, MAAA, FCA, CPC, EA — Comments on the Paper by Barry Kozak, MAAA, MSPA, EA

The Society of Actuaries, "The Pension Forum,"
Volume 17, Number 1 (October 2008)

I enjoyed reading the article, and appreciate how Carol Sears and Scott Miller propose to change the current thinking about retirement, in general, and how employers should consider and adopt retirement benefit plans that take into account longer life expectancies and the risk of outliving retirement assets. They are advocating a "RISP" as an additional benefit for employees. Under their proposal, a RISP would provide an annuity-only benefit, starting at age 65, regardless of employment status, and increasing at strategic ages (25% of benefit from 65 to 67, 50% of benefit from ages 68 to 71, 75% from 72 to 74, and then 100% of benefit thereafter, terminating at death) If the participant is married at commencement date, then annuity would need to satisfy the Qualified Joint and Survivor rules under current law. The article suggests legislative changes to encourage these benefit promises (such as amendments to IRC Sections 415 and 411, and specific exclusions from IRC Sections 416, 401(a)(26), 410(b), and 401(a)(9), and changes in FASB reporting). The design and purpose of a RISP benefit is laudable, and I believe that it can be structured into a defined benefit plan under the current rules, although such suggested statutory amendments would better support the RISP.

However, my concern is that their RISP idea, while potentially useful, might be better framed as an insurance program rather than a retirement program. As described below, retirement benefits generally represent a tangible portion of wages that are owed to employees who forfeit current salary for deferred compensation, and insurance represents a peace of mind (or safety net) that compensates them if (and only if) a catastrophic event happens. RISPs would be attractive to employees "fearful" of outliving the account balance accrued at retirement from the employer's existing defined contribution plan or defined benefit plan that allows lump sum distributions.

Compensation:

In order to attract, retain and reward employees, the employer needs to offer a total compensation package comparable to its competitors in the labor market. Retirement plans represent pecuniary pay as part of the complete compensation package—instead of paying an employee $1 today for her services today, the employer will determine the present value of $1 and pay her that present value today in the form of a contribution into a qualified retirement plan. It will mature and will be paid when she has retired. If the employer uses a defined benefit annuity-only plan to deliver the retirement benefits, and if its calculation of the true present value is understated, then the employer will have underfunded the plan; whereas, if the employer delivers the benefits through a defined contribution plan or through a lump sum distribution from a defined benefit plan, and if the calculated present value is understated, then the employee will have a lower account balance than expected.

Understanding retirement benefits in the context of a component of the total compensation package is crucial to my criticism. This view was expressed by Sears and Miller, and was around long before there was an ERISA or even a formalized Internal Revenue Code. For example, Albert DeRoode starts his article titled "Pensions as Wages"[1] with:

> The growing demand on the part of employees for pensions is really a demand for higher wages, using the expression wages in its broad sense, as the return for which the employee gets from his labor. A pension is as much a part of an employee's real wages as are conditions of labor, guarantee of steady employment, board and lodging (where they are included), medical attention, half pay in the case of sickness, and other features not included in the actual money wages received. Theoretically, the simplest way of dealing with labor would be the payment of a money wage, requiring the employee to provide for the hazards of employment and his old age. While here and there an employee does this, by and large the mass of employees do not.

Given that retirement income represents an appropriate and tangible portion of the employee's total compensation package, then the first level of risk, which the participant's generally have no control over, is how the employer chooses to fund and deliver the retirement benefits (*i.e.*, through a defined benefit plan or a defined contribution plan). As the retirement plan is just a formalized method of converting deferred compensation into an expected present value, the employer should be maximizing each employee's actual and perceived compensation in retirement (obviously within its current and projected budgetary constraints). Just like underestimating the value of current salary, where disgruntled "capable" employees will migrate elsewhere where their skills can earn a higher wage and where disgruntled "incapable" employees remain but shirk in their duties, the risk is on the employer if it underestimates the present value of retirement benefits.

---

1. The American Economic Review, Vol. 3, No. 2, 287–295. Jun., 1913.

Longevity Risk:

Their article properly defines and discusses longevity risk, but longevity risk is, in my opinion, not a separate issue since it is already incorporated into the methods of allowable distributions from qualified defined benefit or defined contribution plans (*i.e.*, as an annuity or a single lump sum distribution).

If retirement benefits are paid as an annuity (the normal form under a traditional defined benefit plan), then there is no longevity risk on the part of the employee, and proper funding is wholly borne by the employer and the plan's actuary. Those retirees that are "lucky" will live longer than their life expectancy and, because they will receive benefits until the day they die, the extra benefit payments will cause an actuarial loss in the plan. On the other hand, those retirees that are "unlucky" will die earlier than expected and, because they will receive fewer benefits than expected, the balance of unpaid benefit distributions will cause an actuarial gain in the plan. Thus, the employer, through the plan's actuary, bears the risk of underestimating substantial benefit levels based on compensation and service, and the associated present values (either through life expectancies, rates of return, ages and elections made at retirement, or any other assumptions).

If retirement benefits are paid as a single lump sum (the traditional form under a defined contribution plan, although offered as an option in far too many defined benefit plans and statutory hybrid plans), then there is no longevity risk on the part of the employer, and it is wholly borne by the employee (assuming that the appropriate parties made rational and prudent investment decisions over the retirement assets). Those retirees that are "unlucky" will live longer than their life expectancy and, because they will most likely outlive their accumulated accounts as of retirement, they will personally bear the risk of not having other sources of income during the remainder of their lives. On the other hand, those retirees that are "lucky" will die earlier than expected and, if there is any unused portion of the accumulated account as of retirement, then the balance can be passed through a bequest upon their deaths. Thus, the employer has no longevity risk for the retirees, either individually or collectively.

I am purposely being dramatic with the use of the terms "lucky" and "unlucky" — but it supports my argument. In their article, Sears and Miller are proposing that a RISP is an additional benefit paid to the retirees, funded by the employer, and delivered through an additional retirement plan (or through the same defined benefit plan, potentially with a bifurcated formula). However, if the primary retirement benefits are promised through a traditional defined benefit plan as an annuity for life, and are promised at a level that provides adequate retirement income for the whole of retirement, whether 4 short months or 40 long years, then no participant of the plan will in any way need to worry about longevity risk. As the benefits are being funded, the plan's actuarial assumptions should be adjusted from time to time to reflect true expectancies and contingencies. If the defined benefit plan cannot pay substantial benefits, then the employer should reassess how salary is divided between current pay and deferred compensation, and how deferred compensation is being discounted.

Insurance:

The RISP idea, in my opinion, therefore represents a form of insurance that protects the employee against longevity risk if they participate in a defined contribution plan or a defined benefit plan that allows a lump sum distribution. The premiums should either come from the employees themselves, or can be paid by the employer as an additional employee benefit (like other forms of insurance, but not as a form of retirement benefit). The RISP will then be available to the "unlucky" cashed-out retirees who are still alive after their life expectancy expires but who have spent down their account balances.

Going back to the total compensation package for a moment, although premiums for such things as health, life, disability, and workers compensation are dollars that if not used to purchase premiums would be available to compensate employees with higher salaries or more robust retirement benefits, most employees view insurance premiums differently than retirement benefits. Inherently, situations that are insured represent events that are generally undesirable, and most employees generally don't count the dollars spent on insurance premiums as part of their compensation; rather, they look at the benefits contingent on the event happening as a valuable buffer from catastrophe. Retirement benefits, on the other hand, represent a promise of being paid in the future for services performed today.

Therefore, a RISP as described in the article could be better expressed as an insurance product that, in the event that the employer's retirement benefits, when aggregated with Social Security and personal savings, are not adequate for a retiree that lives beyond his or her life expectancy, then the insurance benefit can kick in. However, to keep it in terms of insurance rather than an additional retirement benefit, it should be tied in to the poverty level, or some other objective metric, rather than an individual's compensation or years of service as an employee. As with all insurance, however, the moral hazard arises as individuals with such insurance coverage can affirmatively or carelessly overspend other assets knowing that if they live a long and healthy life, they will have another source of income.

Conclusion:

If the employer sponsors a traditional defined benefit plan that pays annuities, then there is no longevity risk borne by the employees, and any excessive actuarial losses from too many people outliving their life expectancies is purely error on the part of the actuary. I am an Enrolled Actuary (as are the authors) and defend our profession, but the article even starts with the warning that "[a]n actuarial train wreck is fast approaching." I take this to mean that the actuaries of defined benefit plans are being too liberal in their assumptions (albeit because of penalty taxes associated with assets that revert to the employer) and are erring on the side of under funding the plans rather than over funding them (and I am not sure if the new funding mandates introduced by PPA will result in any true difference in funding levels when it comes to actuarial losses by retirees living longer than their life expectancies, since plan mortality assumptions are not affected by the funding mandates).

If an employer sponsors a defined contribution plan, then it is most likely doing so to control annual contribution costs. If an employer sponsors a defined benefit plan that allows lump sums, then it is most likely doing so because the employees place a value on the option of receiving a single lump sum. The employer costs for funding RISPs, either through contributions to a trust separate from the qualified plan or as premiums to an insurer, would likely be less expensive than converting a defined contribution plan into a defined benefit plan providing a RISP or in eliminating the lump sum option in the existing defined benefit plan. This solution would need legislative changes to allow the economic benefit of the RISP to be excluded from the participants' Gross Income and to be deductible by the employer if it is not considered a normal and reasonable business deduction.

The RISPs as outlined in the article would likely be better appreciated by employees based on a pure insurance concept rather than a retirement concept. They will receive whatever retirement benefits are promised and delivered through the qualified plan, which will usually be based on their compensation and service, and if they are lucky and live beyond their life expectancy, then they will additionally receive an annuity stream tied into the poverty level, without any reference to actual wages or service.

MEMO

TO: Members of the American Bar Association Section of Taxation, Employee Benefits Taskforce on Pension Simplification, Kurt L.P. Lawson, Chair

FROM: Barry Kozak, member

DATE: January 22, 2001

RE: Preliminary discussion on the meaning of "simplification."

At Kurt's request, I am starting one of the most important dialogues of our task force: What is simplification? The answer is not so simple! Black's Law Dictionary doesn't even provide a definition of "simplification."

As you are each aware, the Joint Committee on Taxation has requested comments from the American Bar Association Section of Taxation regarding simplification of the Tax Code. Our Task Force will be responsible for pension simplification. As discussed below, there are different ways of defining simplification. Kurt and I believe that we must all agree on our definition of simplification before we start thinking about the actual suggestions.

First and foremost, I am assuming that we will work within the current framework of federal taxation (*i.e.*, a graduated income tax scheme where everything is included in the taxpayer's Gross Income unless specifically excluded by a statutory provision) as opposed to alternative tax structures, like a flat tax, a value added tax, or a sales tax. The remainder of this memo will therefore assume that retirement plans will remain qualified under IRC § 401 and that trusts holding pension assets will remain qualified under IRC § 501. Our job, then, is to make legislative suggestions to the U.S. congress about simplification of IRC § 401 (and references to all other Code provisions governing qualified retirement plans).

The way I see it, there are several broad categories where the definition of "simplification" is quite ambiguous. Our primary task is forming the parameters of our proposal paper. Then, we must decide whether our suggestions relate to simplification in the Tax Code itself, or whether congress should defer simplification to the proper regulatory agencies. Finally, we need to determine whether our paper will be limited to tax simplification, or whether it should extend to other federal laws which impact pension plans.

First, does simplification mean less or more? The answer isn't so obvious. Some pension plan sponsors want "less" rules because they enjoy the flexibility in plan design, even if there are more hoops to jump through (*i.e.*, annual testing). Others want "more" rules because they enjoy an array of choices which diminish flexibility but ensure compliance. Less, although meeting the definition of simplification in the truest sense of the word, might eliminate the flexibility necessary in plan design for complex business organizations. More, on the other hand, seems to contradict the concept of simplification, but might really simplify the annual administration of plans. At the LA meeting of our task force, a Treasury attorney seemed to indicate that in his personal view, adding more safe harbors to the nondiscrimination regulations would simplify those regulations. I had a short debate with him expressing my view that lessening the difficulty of the general test would simplify things more than adding more safe harbors. I understand that our job here is to make proposals to congress about simplification of the actual statutes, but the debate of less vs. more in regulations will have the same arguments in tax laws.

Second, does simplification make the Tax Code easier for the plan sponsor or for the benefits professional? Although we might not like to admit it, some can view simplification as a plan sponsor being able to read and interpret the Code provisions with less help from benefits professionals (attorneys, actuaries, accountants, …). Others will say that if we benefits professionals can better understand the Code, then, although the plan sponsors will still depend on us, we can provide better and less expensive advice with more confidence and assurance that our advice and services will not be challenged. Most individual taxpayers view tax simplification as allowing them to prepare their tax returns without help from their accountants. Are these same individuals, some who are the administrators and fiduciaries of qualified plans, going to have the same view of pension simplification? For example, does expanding the availability of SIMPLE plans to more plan sponsors simplify the system (with more homogenous plans) or add more complexity to it (less control and monitoring by attorneys which might lead to more operational failures and more litigation)?

Third, does pension simplification mean updating the Code for current business practices or leaving it as business practices existed in 1974? When ERISA was drafted, defined benefit plans were the dominant plans in any organizations' retirement program and profit sharing plans merely supplemented them; there were no cash or deferred arrangements nor were there any hybrid plans; mergers, acquisitions, spinoffs, and joint ventures only nominally occurred; there was a clear distinction between employees, independent contractors and leased employees; and most individuals actually stopped working when they "retired." As we all know, none of this is true in our current environment. We have to determine whether simplification means short term simplification (*i.e.*, tweaking the rules as they currently exist so we can get immediate simplification) or a long term process (*i.e.*, changing the whole structure, which might take years to perfect and understand fully).

Fourth, does simplification mean more comprehensive statutes (resulting in the need for less regulations) or less comprehensive statutes (resulting in the need for more regulations)? In the almost-passed pension legislation of 2000, congress mandated that the Secretary of Treasury must review the original minimum distribution proposed regulations of 1987 (which were never finalized), simplify them, and finalize them. The proposed regulations which were issued last week seem to comply with the mandate (even though this bill never became law). Do we want to suggest that congress make similar mandates for all other complexities of the law (nondiscrimination testing, determination of controlled groups, …) or do we want to suggest that congress take a more active role in codifying statutes that don't need agency interpretations?

Finally, although not specifically requested by the Joint Committee on Taxation, should our simplification suggestions include omnibus amendments to other federal laws which have an impact on pension administration (*i.e.*, ERISA, ADEA, bankruptcy, securities, …)? If congress looks at tax simplification in a vacuum without simplification for the interdependent labor and other rules, then their actions might actually complicate pension administration (even as the tax aspects are simplified). On the other hand, if the scope of our paper starts expanding indefinitely, an actual paper may never be completed, which negates the whole purpose of our task force in the first place.

We have a new 107th congress, and there are new chairs of both the House Ways and Means and the Senate Finance Committees. In addition, we have a completely new executive agenda and policy concerns. Therefore, it is unknown how the current congress will define simplification. However, if we look at how recent congresses have viewed pension simplification, we might have a better understanding of what the current congress wants from us.

106th Congress: In July, 2000, Senator Bingaman introduced S. 2922 entitled "Pension Reform and Simplification Commission Act," where a bipartisan commission of non-government individuals would be formed to study the existing pension scheme, review and assess regulatory statutes, and recommend changes in the law. Section 4(b) of the bill regards issues to be studied by the commission, and paragraph (13) states:

"any proposals for major simplification of Federal legislation and regulation regarding qualified pension plans, in order to mitigate problem areas identified under this subsection, with the goal of—

(A) strengthening the private pension system;

(B) expanding the availability, adoption, and retention of tax-favored savings plans by all Americans;

(C) eliminating rules that burden the pension system beyond the benefits they provide, for low and moderate income workers, including minorities and women, with specific emphasis on—

(i) eligibility and coverage;

(ii) contributions and benefits;

(iii) minimum distributions, withdrawals, and loans:

(iv) spousal and beneficiary benefits;

(v) portability between plans;

(vi) asset recapture;

(vii) plan compliance and terminations;

(viii) income and excise taxation; and

(ix) reporting, disclosure, and penalties; and

(D) identification of the trade-offs involved in simplification under sub-paragraph (C)."

While the furthest this bill got was introduction to the Senate Finance Committee, it might give insight into what our current congress might want from us regarding proposals of pension simplification. Even if congress fails to create such a commission, our ABA paper might have a good chance of having an impact on pension simplification if our proposals follow these instructions from the Senate bill. By the way, the bill further states, at section 4(c)(2), that the Commission should make simultaneous findings or recommendations concerning ERISA as well as with the Internal Revenue Code. Therefore, we would likely be justified in expanding our Task Force comments to include simplification of other federal laws, in addition to taxation, even if our report is going to the Joint Committee on Taxation.

105th Congress: On the other hand, if we go back to the Taxpayer Relief Act of 1997, title XV, subtitle A uses the term "Pensions and Employee Benefits—Simplification." There, simplification is seemingly accomplished by a variety of methods: elimination of certain statutory provisions, clarification or modification of others, and the addition of new statutory provisions. This brings us back to the purpose of this memo: what is pension simplification? This tax law shows that in 1997, congress lacked a uniform agreement on the definition of simplification. Hopefully, however, we can form a unified consensus among our Task Force.

Anyway, I hope that this memo will be the genesis of productive discussions between our Task Force members.

* * *

Appendix A

Law 101 Concepts for Non-Law Students

As this textbook will hopefully be used by non-attorney benefits professionals (or soon to be professionals), this appendix will explain some basic legal issues.

The U.S. Constitution

Under Article I, Congress enacts federal laws, such as the Internal Revenue Code, ERISA, Securities laws, generally under the rubric of raising revenue or regulating interstate commerce. For employee benefits plans, the most important committees are generally the Senate Finance Committee and the Senate Health, Education, Labor & Pensions Committee, the House Ways & Means Committee and the House Education & Labor committee, and the professional non-partisan staff of the Joint Committee on Taxation. Additionally, the cost to revenues (*i.e.* scoring) for any legislation is performed by the Congressional Budget Office. In enacting laws, the legislative history (hearings, floor speeches, reports, ...) can be instructive in understanding the spirit of a particular law or statutory provision.

Under Article II, the President enforces federal laws. In addition, the President is in charge of the executive agencies, such as the IRS (through the Department of Treasury), the Employee Benefits Security Administration (through the Department of Labor) and the PBGC (loosely through the Departments of Labor and Commerce).

Under Article III, the federal courts interpret federal laws when ambiguous, or when several federal laws are at odds with each other. Certain federal laws preempt state laws (such as ERISA preemption of all state laws that relate to any employee benefit plan, with certain enumerated exceptions).

Congress

You can keep up with activities of Congress through their respective websites. A very good site to track specific legislation at every stage, from introduction to the assignment of a Public Law number is at the official Library of Congress website http://thomas.loc.gov (notice there is no "www" in the site's URL). Public Law numbers are XXX-YY, where XXX is the session (the 111th session of Congress reflects January 2009 to December

2010), and YY is simply the numerical ordering of laws either signed by the President or where the President's veto was overwritten. The Public Law is then physically placed somewhere in the United States Code (for example, Title 26 of the USC contains all of the federal income tax provisions, and Title 29 of the U.S. Code contains all of the labor provisions, including ERISA, but also including others like the National Labor Relations Act and the Family Medical Leave Act). That explains why benefits practitioners generally cite to the section of ERISA whereas other attorneys, especially in official court documents, cite that same provision in title 29 of the U.S. Code. Therefore, in Appendix E is a quick conversion chart for ERISA provisions.

There are many resources on the thomas.loc site, such as committee reports and Congressional records (to find legislative history), as well as useful information, such as treaties with other countries, how the U.S. Supreme Court operates, and links to the U.S. Constitution and Declaration of Independence.

Executive Agencies

While each agency has its own internal procedures, there are some similarities between them. In this book, the important aspects of IRS regulation of qualified retirement plans are in Chapter 10, and the important aspects of EBSA regulation of ERISA employee benefit plans are in Chapter 17. Basically, each agency performs audits and examinations, issues regulations and other guidance, and provides education and outreach services.

As to the audits and examinations, each agency has information on their respective websites on what the target can expect, what documents they need to provide, and how the agency is supposed to act. If there is a dispute that cannot be resolved at the agency level (even by going to more senior officers), then the dispute can ultimately be resolved through the federal court system. As to the education and outreach, just look at their respective websites.

Regulations

The most important aspect of agencies for benefits professionals, however, is the guidance they publish. The most important guidance they can promulgate is in the form of a final regulation, which will be published in the Code of Federal Regulations (CFR). All regulations are published in proposed form in the Federal Register, with a public comment period. The proposed regulations might be published in final form, published in temporary form (which are only supposed to be effective for 3 years), remain proposed (if the agency's business priorities shift away from that project), or repealed. If Congress specifically instructed the agency to issue regulations, then they are considered "Legislative" Regulations, and when published in final form, have the effect of law (as per the U.S. Supreme Court's holding in Chevron U.S.A. Inc. v. Natural Resources Defense Council, 467 U.S. 837 (1984)). Otherwise, if Congress didn't specifically require the agency to issue regulations, but it just does so under its general authority, then those regulations, when published in final form, will be "Interpretive" Regulations, which do not have the effect of law, but courts will presume them to be authoritative. Proposed regulations have no legal effect, but provide signals on how the agency wishes to issue final regulations—subject to public comments. The regulations are usually published with a preamble, which explains the background, why regulations needed to be issued, and how and why the final regulations differ from the proposed regulations. While the preamble has no binding effect, they are still useful when trying to understand regulations.

Treasury regulations are arranged by corresponding Internal Revenue Code sections. They are in the form of either Treasury Regulations §X.Y-Z, or 26 CFR §X.Y-Z, where X is "1" if they relate to a Code section that is in Subtitle A, Income Taxes (sections 1 through 1563), a "54" if they relate to a Code section that is in Subtitle D, Miscellaneous Excise Taxes (sections 4001 through 5000), and other numbers corresponding to other Subtitles; where Y is the actual Code section; and where Z is the part (if there is a table of contents due to multiple parts, then the TOC will be at -0, otherwise, if there is only one part to the regulations, it will be at -1). All Treasury regulations are first published as Treasury Decisions (T.D.), in sequential order, so if the service you are using does not directly link to preambles, then if you see reference to a T.D., that will be where you can find the preamble.

Department of Labor Regulations are organized a bit differently. They are in the form of either Labor Regulations §X.Y-Z, or 29 CFR §X.Y-Z, where X is a portion of ERISA, such as "2520" are the rules and regulations for reporting and disclosure and "2530" are the rules and regulations for minimum standards; where Y is the actual ERISA section; and where Z is the part (there are no tables of contents like there are in Treasury Regulations).

Other Guidance

If guidance is not issued in the form of regulations, then it is either hard guidance (such as Revenue Rulings, Revenue Procedures, Notices, and Announcements from the IRS or Advisory Opinions, Exemptions or Field Assistance Bulletins from the EBSA), which lock in the agency's legal position, but the Taxpayer/target can prove to the court that there is a different, yet reasonable and consistent interpretation of the statutory provision; or the guidance is soft guidance (such as Private Letter Rulings and Field guidance from the IRS or Information Letters or Interpretive Bulletins from the EBSA), which are only made public by Freedom of Information Act and have no legally binding effect (although they are instructive, when used properly, to see the agency's position taken on similar issues).

Federal Courts

There are three tiers to the federal judiciary system: district courts, courts of appeal, and the U.S. Supreme Court.

Federal District Courts

Controversies originate in a district court, where the facts are "developed" (based on rules of evidence which allow certain documents, statements or testimonies to be introduced and others to be excluded). ERISA litigation, as discussed in Chapter 14 of this textbook, has special rules for evidence and discovery, juries as opposed to simply judges, which geographic location of a district court is the proper venue for the controversy, and which district courts have jurisdiction over both the plaintiff and the respondent (the terms "prosecutor" and "defendant" are generally only used in criminal actions, where someone can go to jail or lose his life; whereas, in civil actions, generally the losing party can only be ordered to pay some money, or in order to provide equity, to either do something or refrain from doing something). In income tax litigation, it is a little more complex—when the IRS and taxpayer disagree, the taxpayer can pay the amount of taxes supposedly owed to the IRS and then sue the IRS for a refund in either the local district court or at the U.S. Court of Claims in Washington DC, or the taxpayer can refuse to pay the amount of taxes arguably owed and the IRS can sue the taxpayer in U.S. Tax Court. The litigation strategies are quite complex and outside of the scope of this book.

Federal Circuit Courts of Appeal

The losing party from the district court (or U.S. Court of Claims or U.S. Tax Court) can appeal the decision to the appropriate Court of Appeals, which are arranged by geographic location:

- Federal Circuit (Washington)
- D.C. Circuit (Washington)covers District of Columbia
- 1st Circuit (Boston)covers Maine, Massachusetts, New Hampshire, Puerto Rico, and Rhode Island
- 2nd Circuit (New York)covers Connecticut, New York, and Vermont
- 3rd Circuit (Philadelphia) covers Delaware, New Jersey, Pennsylvania, and U.S. Virgin Islands
- 4th Circuit (Richmond) covers Maryland, North Carolina, South Carolina, Virginia, and West Virginia
- 5th Circuit (New Orleans) covers Louisiana, Mississippi, and Texas
- 6th Circuit (Cincinnati) covers Kentucky, Michigan, Ohio, and Tennessee
- 7th Circuit (Chicago) covers Illinois, Indiana, and Wisconsin
- 8th Circuit (St. Louis) covers Arkansas, Iowa, Minnesota, Missouri, Nebraska, North Dakota, South Dakota
- 9th Circuit (San Francisco) covers Alaska, Arizona, California, Guam, Hawaii, Idaho, Montana, Nevada, Northern Mariana Islands, Oregon, and Washington
- 10th Circuit (Denver) covers Colorado, Kansas, New Mexico, Oklahoma, Utah, and Wyoming
- 11th Circuit (Atlanta) covers Alabama, Florida, and Georgia

The appellate court is generally reviewing the judge's actions from the district court. The losing party might argue that the facts are incorrect because the district court erred in applying the rules of evidence, or the losing party might argue that the judge accepted a wrong rule of law or misapplied a correct rule of law. The appellate court will generally only overrule the lower court's ruling if the judge acted arbitrarily and capriciously; however, if the controversy is over the correct rule of law to apply, then the appellate court might review the case *de novo* (from the beginning). However, in most appeals, if the lower court did in fact misapply the law, the appellate court will remand the case back to the lower court, with instructions on what the correct rule of law is (*i.e.*, which test must be used or what factors should be considered). An appellate court decision is binding on all district courts within its geographical jurisdiction for all future litigation over the same controversy—although losing parties from other district courts who petition the other court of appeals to review their case, can argue that the logic of one circuit should be adopted in the current circuit. The court of appeals decision can either be written by a small panel of judges (usually 3), or by the entire roster of appellate court judges in that Circuit (*per curium*).

The U.S. Supreme Court

The Supreme Court is a second level of appeals. The losing party at the Circuit level can petition the U.S. Supreme Court to hear the case by filing a *writ of certiorari*. The Supreme Court will generally only accept the case for review if there is a split in the lower Circuits over the prevailing federal law. The Supreme Court's decision (either to affirm or reverse the Circuit's opinion, or to remand back to the district court) is binding on all federal courts for all future litigation over the same controversy (unless and until a future U.S. Supreme Court case comes to a different conclusion or Congress amends the underlying statutory provision in controversy). U.S. Supreme Court opinions (and some Circuit Court of Appeals opinions) are complicated to read, since the "majority" decision may in fact simply be a "plurality"—one of the 9 Supreme Court justices writes the official opinion explaining which party prevails and the legal roadmap that gets to that result, and some justices might concur (meaning that they agree with the end result, but do not agree with the writing justice's legal roadmap) while others might dissent (meaning that they either agree with the legal roadmap but come to a different result, or disagree with the legal roadmap and the end result).

Court Opinions

Court opinions are recorded in different reporter "books"—which was a lot more important before the age of computer research. Therefore, a U.S. Supreme Court case can have a cite that looks like P v R, X U.S. Y (Z); where P is the name of the Petitioner, R is the name of the Respondent, X is the volume number, U.S. is the official reporter, Y is the page number, and Z is the year the decision was published. So, when I cited the Chevron case above as Chevron U.S.A. Inc. v. Natural Resources Defense Council, 467 U.S. 837 (1984)—Chevron U.S.A. Inc. is the party that petitioned the U.S. Supreme Court, Natural Resources Defense Council had to respond, 467 is the numerical volume of the U.S. reporter, 837 is the first page of the opinion, and 1984 is the year it was decided. There are other reporters, so the same exact case is also found at 104 S.Ct. 2778 (*i.e.*, page 2778 of the 104th volume in the Supreme Court reporter) and in other reporters—but for purposes of this textbook. U.S. Supreme Court cases simply have the single cite to the U.S. reporter. For Court of Appeals opinions, in this book they will be cited as P v R, X F.3d Y (Gth Cir. (S) Z); where P is the name of the petitioner and R is the name of the respondent, X is the volume of the Federal Reporter, 3rd Series (earlier cases might be in the F.2d or F.1t series), Y is the page number, G is the circuit's number, S is the state within the circuit, and Z is the year of the decision. For district court opinions, in this book they will be cited as P v R, X F.Supp.3d Y (D S, Z); where P is the name of the petitioner and R is the name of the respondent, X is the volume of the Federal Supplement Reporter, 3rd Series (earlier cases might be in the F.Supp.2d or F.Supp.1t series), Y is the page number, D is the geographic district within the state, S is the name of the state, and Z is the year of the decision.

It's really not difficult, once you understand the convention for citing a case. You can find cases at libraries, especially law libraries, and online (some services charge a fee). The paid service I used to research this book is Westlaw, and they include editorial coordination between cases, so if you see a number in square brackets, like [1] or [4], they are editorial conveniences that have nothing to do with the official opinion. Likewise, there might be numbers following an asterisk or two, which just show in electronic research the official page number (for example, in the Chevron case, the opinion starts at 837 of the U.S. reporter and at page 2778 of the Supreme Court reporter, so the electronic version of the case will show *838 where page 838 of U.S. would start and *839 where page 839 of U.S. would start, and at different points would show **2779 where page 2779 of S.Ct. would start and **2880 where page 2880 of S.Ct. would start.

Conclusion

Of course, this Appendix A is not a substitute for 3 years of law school and the Juris Doctorate (JD) degree. It will, hopefully, provide the non-law student or non-attorney professional at least a comfort zone in reading this book. There are many official governmental sites that provide more information on any of the three branches of government.

The hierarchy of guidance can be summarized as:

Document	Legal Effect
Statute in the U.S. Code	Absolutely binding
U.S. Supreme Court holding	Absolutely binding
Final Regulations—if instructed by Congress and if reasonable	Absolutely binding
Final Regulations—if not instructed by Congress	Presumed binding (but plaintiff can prove his/her interpretation of the law is better)
U.S. Court of Appeals holding	Binding only in that circuit
U.S. District Court holding	Binding only in that district
Documents intended to be publicly released (Revenue Rulings, Procedures, Notices and Announcements)	Official agency position for all individuals and plans
Documents intended to remain private, but which are made public per the Freedom of Information Act (Private Letter Rulings, Internal IRS Technical Memorandum, Audit Procedures and Alerts)	Indication of how the agency might treat similarly situated individual or plans
Proposed regulations (or Temporary regulations that, if not published in final form within 3 years, are supposed to be withdrawn)	The position the agency plans to take when published in final form, but it can be changed pursuant to public comments
All other written documents (like the Grey books from the Enrolled Actuaries meetings) and other communications (like an IRS officer sitting on a panel and answering Q&As)	Unofficial indication of how the agency might act
Circular 230, Actuarial Standards of Practice (ASOPs) and Codes of Professional Responsibility	What you need to follow in order to keep your professional license and to avoid a disgruntled client effectively suing you for malpractice.

Appendix B

Adjustments to Statutory Limitations and Thresholds Due to Inflation

Description	Provision	Statutory Amount	Adjustment	2008 Limit	2009/2010 Limit
Compensation limit for qualified plan benefits	IRC § 401 (a)(17)	$200,000 (as of 2001)	As per § 415(d), rounded to next lowest $5,000	$230,000	$245,000
Highly Compensated Employee— compensation test	IRC § 414 (q)(B)(i)	$80,000 (as of 2001)	As per § 415(d)	$105,000	$110,000
Key Employee— officer test	IRC § 416 (i)(1)(A)(i)	$130,000 (as of 2001)	As per § 415(d), rounded to next lowest $5,000	$150,000	$160,000
Defined Contribution Plan—annual additions limit	IRC § 415 (c)(1)(A)	$40,000 (as of 2001)	Exact method described at IRC § 415(d)	$46,000	$49,000
Defined Benefit Plan— annual benefit limit	IRC § 415 (b)(1)(A)	$160,000 (as of 2001)	Exact method described at IRC § 415(d)	$185,000	$195,000
Elective Deferral limit (for 401(k), 403(b) and 457 plans); and designated Roth contribution limit	IRC § 402 (g)(1)(B)	$15,000 (as of 2006)	As per § 415(d), rounded to next lowest $500	$15,500	$16,500

Note: due to poor growth in the Consumer Price Index in 2009, there are no cost of living adjustments for 2010 (under the stated procedures).

Description	Provision	Statutory Amount	Adjustment	2008 Limit	2009/2010 Limit
Catch-up Deferral limit (for 401(k), 403(b) and 457 plans); and designated Roth contribution limit	IRC §414 (v)(2)(B)(i)	$5,000 (as of 2006)	As per §415(d), rounded to next lowest $500	$5,000	$5,500
Elective Deferral limit (for SIMPLE plans)	IRC §408 (p)(2)(E)(i)	$10,000 (as of 2005)	As per §415(d), rounded to next lowest $500	$10,500	$11,500
Catch-up Deferral limit (for SIMPLE plans)	IRC §414 (v)(2)(B)(ii)	$2,500 (as of 2006)	As per §415(d), rounded to next lowest $500	$2,500	$2,500
IRA and Roth IRA deduction limitation	IRC §219 (b)(5)(A)	$5,000 (as of 2008)	Exact method described at IRC §219 (b)(5)(D)	$5,000	$5,000
IRA and Roth IRA catch-up deduction limitation	IRC §219 (b)(5)(B)	$1,000 (as of 2006)	Exact method described at IRC §219 (b)(5)(D)	$1,000	$1,000
Social Security Taxable Wage Base	IRC §401 (l)(5)(E)	N/A	Exact method described at section 230 of the Social Security Act (for 2009, see Rev. Rul. 2009-2)	$102,000	$106,800

Appendix C

ERISA and Code Organizational Charts

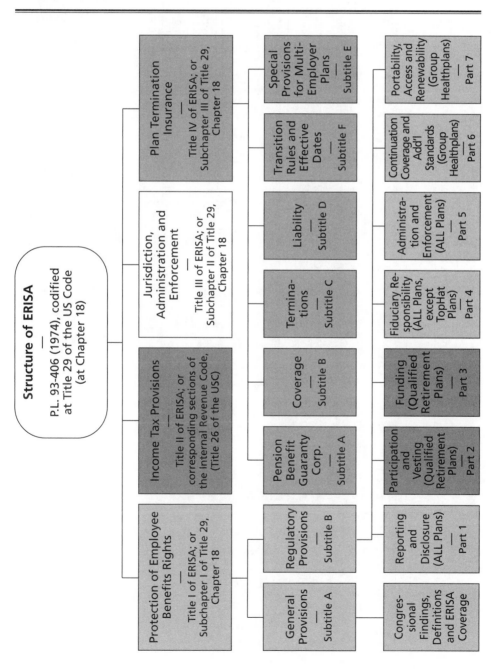

Structure of ERISA
—
P.L. 93-406 (1974), codified at Title 29 of the US Code (at Chapter 18)

Protection of Employee Benefits Rights
—
Title I of ERISA; or Subchapter I of Title 29, Chapter 18

Income Tax Provisions
—
Title II of ERISA; or corresponding sections of the Internal Revenue Code, (Title 26 of the USC)

Jurisdiction, Administration and Enforcement
—
Title III of ERISA; or Subchapter II of Title 29, Chapter 18

Plan Termination Insurance
—
Title IV of ERISA; or Subchapter III of Title 29, Chapter 18

General Provisions
—
Subtitle A

Regulatory Provisions
—
Subtitle B

Pension Benefit Guaranty Corp.
—
Subtitle A

Coverage
—
Subtitle B

Termina-tions
—
Subtitle C

Liability
—
Subtitle D

Special Provisions for Multi-Employer Plans
—
Subtitle E

Transition Rules and Effective Dates
—
Subtitle F

Congres-sional Findings, Definitions and ERISA Coverage

Reporting and Disclosure (ALL Plans)
—
Part 1

Participation and Vesting (Qualified Retirement Plans)
—
Part 2

Funding (Qualified Retirement Plans)
—
Part 3

Fiduciary Re-sponsibility (ALL Plans, except TopHat Plans)
—
Part 4

Administra-tion and Enforcement (ALL Plans)
—
Part 5

Continuation Coverage and Add'l Standards (Group Healthplans)
—
Part 6

Portability, Access and Renewability (Group Healthplans)
—
Part 7

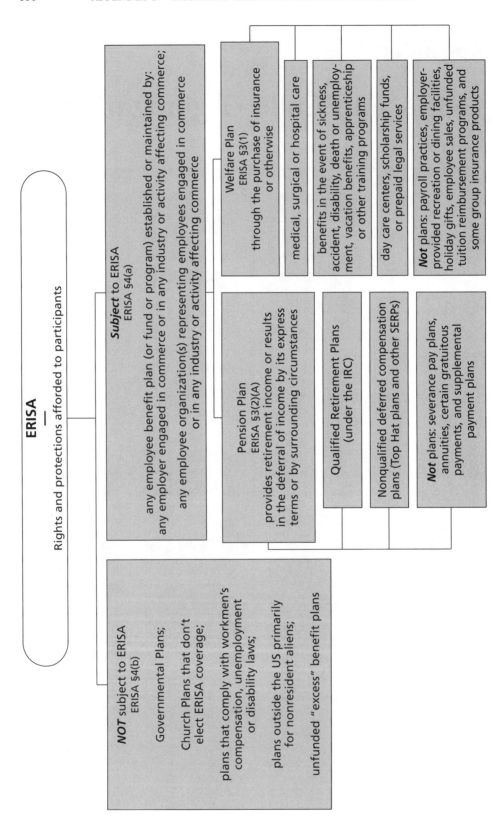

ERISA

Rights and protections afforded to participants

Subject to ERISA
ERISA §4(a)

any employee benefit plan (or fund or program) established or maintained by: any employer engaged in commerce or in any industry or activity affecting commerce;

any employee organization(s) representing employees engaged in commerce or in any industry or activity affecting commerce

Welfare Plan
ERISA §3(1)
through the purchase of insurance or otherwise

medical, surgical or hospital care

benefits in the event of sickness, accident, disability, death or unemployment, vacation benefits, apprenticeship or other training programs

day care centers, scholarship funds, or prepaid legal services

Not plans: payroll practices, employer-provided recreation or dining facilities, holiday gifts, employee sales, unfunded tuition reimbursement programs, and some group insurance products

Pension Plan
ERISA §3(2)(A)
provides retirement income or results in the deferral of income by its express terms or by surrounding circumstances

Qualified Retirement Plans (under the IRC)

Nonqualified deferred compensation plans (Top Hat plans and other SERPs)

Not plans: severance pay plans, annuities, certain gratuitous payments, and supplemental payment plans

NOT subject to ERISA
ERISA §4(b)

Governmental Plans;

Church Plans that don't elect ERISA coverage;

plans that comply with workmen's compensation, unemployment or disability laws;

plans outside the US primarily for nonresident aliens;

unfunded "excess" benefit plans

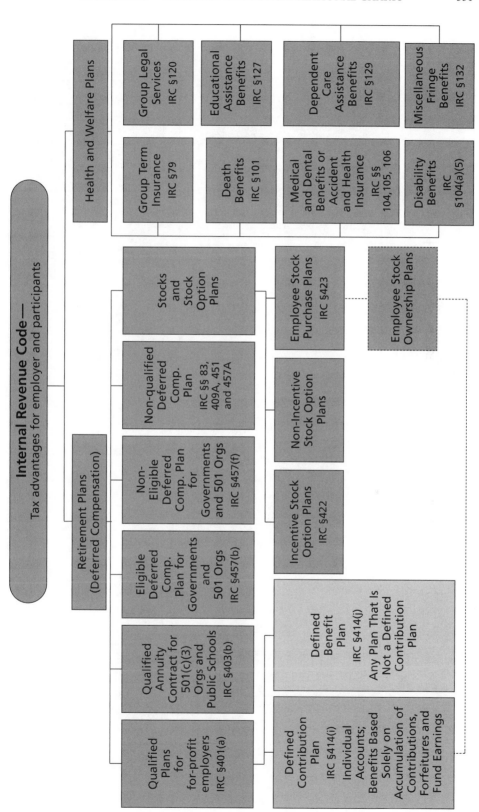

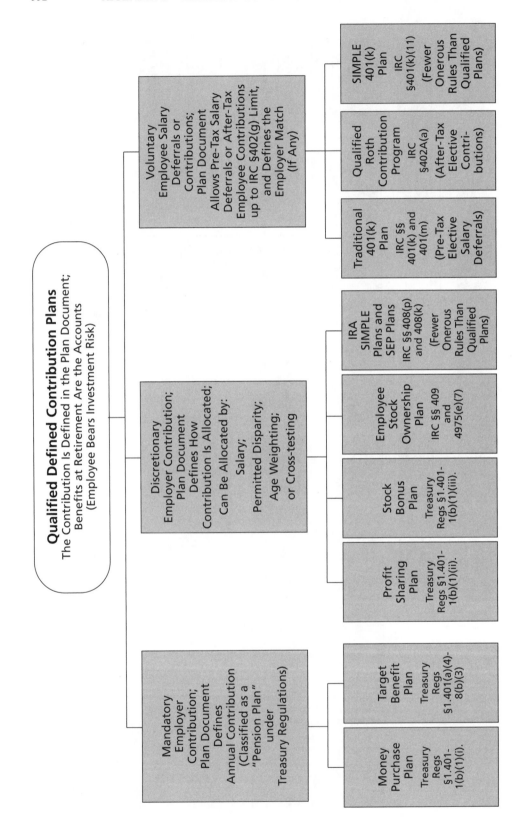

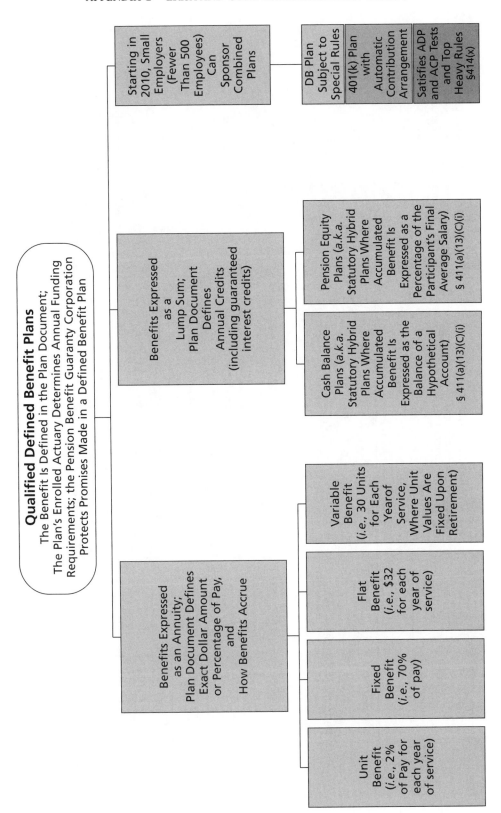

	Defined Benefit Plan	Defined Contribution Plan
Benefit	whatever is promised	accumulation of account
Guarantees	PBGC (up to a statutory limit)	none
Funding	whatever Actuary demands (plus a cushion amount, if desired)	discretionary or at least budgeted (up to 25% of payroll)
Investment Risk	on Employer	on Employee
Better for	older (than 42)	younger (than 42)
Early Retirement "Sweeteners"	allowed	not allowed (other than catch-up contributions)
Focus	output ("benefits")— accrued benefits defined in plan; statutory limitations ($160,000 or 100% of avg. comp.)	input ("contributions")— allocation methods defined in plan; statutory limitations ($40,000 or 100% of comp.)
Communication	portion of normal retirement benefit accrued	account balance to date
General Costs	high (actuary's fee, PBGC premiums)	controllable (passed to accounts)
Accruals	must avoid excessive backloading	account at any point in time
In-Service Distributions	allowed after 62; new rules for definition of Normal Retirement Age	allowed after 5 years; but salary deferrals ONLY through hardship distributions

Appendix D

ERPA Learning Objectives and Mapping

The exams for the Enrolled Retirement Plan Agent (ERPA) designation are administered by the American Institute of Retirement Education, and all information about the exams is at https://erpaexam.org/. Ultimately, the IRS is responsible for certifying those candidates who successfully complete the ERPA exams, and all information about the actual credentials is at http://www.irs.gov/retirement/article/0,,id=185433,00.html.

Below are all of the learning objectives for the two ERPA exams, and a key to the chapter of this book where the topic is discussed. However, I would strongly suggest first reading the entire book, and then reviewing the material per these learning objectives.

Internal Revenue Service

Enrolled Retirement Plan Agent — Special Enrollment Examination (ERPA-SEE)

2009 Syllabus

Part I Syllabus

Part I: Compliance and Operations Issues

Topic A — Participation, Coverage and Vesting

#	ERPA Learning Objective	Chapter
1	Identify allowable minimum age and service requirements for eligibility	8.C.1
2	Define the eligibility computation period	8.C.1
3	Determine breaks-in-service and identify how they impact eligibility and vesting	7.A.1
4	Identify permissible plan entry dates	8.C.1
5	Determine which plans must meet minimum coverage requirements	8.C
6	Identify excludable employees for coverage testing	8.C.2
7	Calculate the ratio percentage test to determine whether coverage is satisfied	8.C.3
8	Define the minimum participation rules applicable to a defined benefit plan	8.D
9	Identify permissible vesting schedules, vesting service and vesting changes under PPA	7.A.1, 2, 3
10	Identify impact of a change of vesting schedule	7.A.1
11	Determine when forfeitures may occur and their permitted uses	7.A.1

Topic B—Contributions, Allocation and Benefit Formulas and Accrual Rules

#	ERPA Learning Objective	Chapter
1	Distinguish among the types of contributions made to a qualified plan	6.A.1, 2 6.B.1
2	Differentiate between a plan contribution and a participant allocation	7.B.2.b
3	Identify conditions that may be imposed on a participant to receive an allocation	7.B.2.b
4	Identify whether the defined benefit plan benefit formula satisfies permitted disparity rules	5.C.4
5	Explain the difference between safe harbor allocation and non-safe harbor allocation	8.E.2, 3
6	Calculate an accrued benefit for a participant in a defined benefit plan	7.B.3.c
7	Calculate career average and final average pay benefit formulas	5.C.5
8	Identify characteristics of a cash balance/hybrid plan and describe the impact of PPA on cash balance conversions	5.D.2

Topic C—Limitations on Benefits, Contributions and Compensation

#	ERPA Learning Objective	Chapter
1	Identify annual limitations on elective deferrals	6.B.1.c
2	Calculate permissible catch-up contributions for catch-up eligible participants	6.B.1.d
3	Determine the taxation of excess deferrals and identify effects of the timing of correction	8.F.4
4	Explain the annual additions limit for defined contribution plans	7.C.1
5	Calculate maximum annual additions limit under a defined contribution plan	7.C.1
6	Identify the basic limitation on benefits from a defined benefit plan	7.C.2
7	Calculate the maximum benefit limit under a defined benefit plan	7.C.2
8	Explain the effects of a short plan year	7.C
9	Calculate the maximum compensation used for determining contributions or benefits	7.C.1
10	Describe the definition of IRC 414(s) compensation and contrast with IRC §415 compensation, including what compensation can be excluded	8.E.5
	Calculate the compensation ratios in an IRC 414(s) test	8.E.5

Topic D—General Nondiscrimination Rules

#	ERPA Learning Objective	Chapter
1	Define a highly compensated employee	8.B.1
2	Describe the top-paid group rule, including which employees can be excluded	8.B.1
3	Identify plans that use general test for nondiscrimination in amount of benefits and contributions	8.E.3
4	Describe a safe harbor design for defined contribution and defined benefit plans to satisfy the nondiscrimination rules	8.E.2

5	Describe the uniformity requirements for benefits under a design-based safe harbor defined benefit plan	8.E.2
6	Identify the determination and grouping of allocation rates and benefit accrual rates	8.E.3
7	Identify the use of aggregation, disaggregation and restructuring on nondiscrimination testing	8.E.4
8	Explain the concept of defined contribution cross-testing and how the general test works on a cross-tested basis	8.E.4
9	Calculate the gateway test to determine whether the test is satisfied in a cross-tested defined contribution plan	8.E.4
10	Describe the benefits, rights and features provided under a plan, and understand the current and effective availability test	8.E.6

Topic E — ADP/ACP Testing

#	ERPA Learning Objective	Chapter
1	Explain the special nondiscrimination tests (ADP/ACP) applicable to 401(k) plan contributions	8.F.1, 2
2	Calculate an average deferral ratio and the ADP or an average contribution ratio and the ACP	8.F.1, 2
3	Identify contributions that are included in the ADP or ACP test	8.F.1, 2
4	Distinguish between the prior-year and current-year testing methods	8.F.1
5	Define qualified nonelective contributions and when they can be used to correct a testing failure	8.F.4
6	Identify correction methods that can be used to cure failed ADP/ACP tests	8.F.4
7	Calculate the corrective distribution amounts in a failed ADP/ACP test	8.F.4
8	Describe the tax treatment of different correction methods	8.F.4
9	Compute the excise tax on excess contributions and excess aggregate contributions	8.F.4

Topic F — Top-Heavy Testing

#	ERPA Learning Objective	Chapter
1	Define a key employee and former key employee	8.G
2	Determine whether a plan is top-heavy	8.H
3	Describe the permissive and required aggregation of plans for purposes of the top-heavy determination	8.H
4	Identify the consequences of being a top-heavy defined contribution plan	8.H
5	Identify the consequences of being a top-heavy defined benefit plan	8.H

Topic G — Related Employers

#	ERPA Learning Objective	Chapter
1	Identify factors that are relevant in determining whether an employer is part of a controlled group or an affiliated service group	8.A.1, 2
2	Explain the consequences of a controlled group or affiliated service group relationship	8.A.1, 2
3	Explain the application of the qualification rules to multiple employer plans	4.A.3, 4

Topic H—Elective Deferral Arrangements

#	ERPA Learning Objective	Chapter
1	Explain traditional 401(k) safe harbor plans and how the testing exemptions work	8.F.3
2	Identify the requirements of a qualified automatic contribution arrangement safe harbor 401(k) plans	5.B.4.c
3	Describe the 401(m) safe harbor arrangement	8.F.3
4	Describe the safe harbor notice requirements	8.F.3
5	Identify the requirements of a SIMPLE 401(k) plan	5.B.5
6	Explain the advantages of adopting an automatic enrollment plan	5.B.4.c
7	Define Roth 401(k) contribution requirements	5.B.4.b

Topic I—Deduction and Funding Rules

#	ERPA Learning Objective	Chapter
1	Explain the application of the deduction rules to both defined benefit and defined contribution plans	6.C.1, 2
2	Calculate the maximum deduction limit applicable to a defined contribution plan	6.C.2
3	Calculate the maximum deductible contribution when a plan sponsor maintains both a defined contribution and defined benefit plan	6.C.1, 2
4	Define the contribution and compensation components used in determining the deduction limit	6.C.1, 2
5	Calculate the earned income for a self-employed individual or partner in a partnership	8.E.5
6	Identify the excise tax on nondeductible contributions to qualified plans and on failure to meet minimum funding requirements	6.C.1, 2
7	Explain general concepts of minimum funding	6.A.2.b

Topic J—Miscellaneous Plans

#	ERPA Learning Objective	Chapter
1	Describe the characteristics of an IRC § 403(b) arrangement	4.A.1.c
2	Describe the operational requirements of a 403(b) arrangement	4.A.1.c
3	Identify the characteristics of a fully insured plan under IRC § 412(i)	6.A.2.d
4	Identify the characteristics of IRA funded employer sponsored arrangements	5.B.5

Topic K—Legal Framework

#	ERPA Learning Objective	Chapter
1	Compare and contrast the jurisdiction of DOL/IRS/PGBC	3.C.1, 3
2	Identify which plans are covered under ERISA Titles I and IV	11.A.1, 2
3	Explain the reliance permitted on different levels of government guidance (*i.e.*, regulations, revenue procedures, private letter rulings, etc.)	3.C.2 Appx A

Part II: Plan Documents, Reporting and Distribution Issues

Topic L—Plan Documents and Amendments

#	ERPA Learning Objective	Chapter
1	Identify who can sponsor and adopt a qualified plan	4.A.2
2	Distinguish between the trust agreement, the plan document and an adoption agreement	4.C.1, 3
3	Identify the different types of plan documents	4.C.1, 3
4	Identify the limitations on changes that would be allowed to be made to pre-approved plans	4.C.1.a, b
5	Describe the reliance rules on advisory, opinion and determination letters	4.C.1 10.B.3
6	Describe the role of a sponsoring prototype organization	4.C.1.a, b
7	Distinguish between the role of the plan trustee and plan administrator	3.E.1
8	Differentiate between required and discretionary amendments and their timing, including remedial amendment periods	4.C.2
9	Distinguish when plan amendments can and cannot be made retroactively	4.C.2
10	Identify protected benefits that cannot be eliminated/changed by means of plan amendment	7.B.3.h
11	Describe the remedial amendment cycle	4.C.2 10B.3

Topic M—Government Filings and Submissions

#	ERPA Learning Objective	Chapter
1	Describe Form 2848 and who may represent the client before the IRS in retirement plan matters	10.B.6 21.3
2	Explain the procedure to submit a plan to the IRS for qualification review	10.B.3
3	Explain the use of Forms 5300, 5307 and 5310	16.B.1 10.B.3
4	Identify who is required to file Form 5500 series and the due dates	15.A.1
5	Based on a set of facts identify which schedules are required to be submitted in the Form 5500 series	15.A.1
6	Explain Form 5500 series filing requirements for final plan year, amended returns and short plan years	16.B.1, 2
7	Determine penalties for failure to report or late filing for Form 5500 series and understand the DOL Delinquent Filers Voluntary Compliance program (DFVC)	17.B.5
8	Identify the audit report requirements for Form 5500 series	15.A.1 3.E.2

Topic N—Participant Communications

#	ERPA Learning Objective	Chapter
1	Define Summary Plan Description requirements and timing	12.B
2	Identify required notices to employees on plan submission and plan termination	N/A
3	Define Summary of Material Modifications requirements and timing	12.B
4	Define annual notices to participant, including the Summary Annual Report and PPA-required funding notice for defined benefit plans	15.B.2
5	Determine how often benefit statements must be given to participants and the content of such statements, including the changes required under PPA	15.B.1
6	Understand the requirements for distribution and rollover notices, including the IRC § 402(f) Special Tax Notice and the timing of payouts	9.C.2
7	Identify and contrast acceptable methods of delivering employee communications	15.B.4

Topic O—Rollovers

#	ERPA Learning Objective	Chapter
1	Explain the general rules governing eligible rollovers to and from qualified plans, including the PPA-allowed Roth IRA rollovers	14.C.2
2	Identify the criteria used to determine eligibility for rollover	14.C.3
3	Explain the distinction between direct rollovers and plan-to-plan transfers, including the PPA changes to the non spouse beneficiary rollover rules	14.C.3
4	Describe the 60-day rule as it applies to distributions and rollovers	14.C.3
5	Explain the options relating to automatic IRA rollover	14.C.3

Topic P—Distributions

#	ERPA Learning Objective	Chapter
1	Determine the general tax consequences of qualified plan distributions	14.C.1
2	Identify the rules on distributions subject to withholding	14.C.2
3	Summarize the rules, penalties and exceptions that apply to premature distributions	14.C.4
4	List the categories of nontaxable distribution amounts	14.C.1
5	Describe the tax treatment of employer securities distributed in kind	14.C.1
6	Outline the tax treatment of installment payments/annuities from a qualified plan	14.C.1
7	Describe an involuntary cash-out and any notification requirements to plan participants	14.A.4 14.C.2
8	Calculate a required minimum distribution amount	14.C.5
9	Describe the reporting requirements for plan distributions	14.C.2

Topic Q—Annuity Requirements and Spousal Consent

#	ERPA Learning Objective	Chapter
1	Identify plans subject to the survivor annuity requirements	14.A.4
2	Explain the QPSA and QJSA requirements including the changes under PPA and how these benefits can be waived	14.A.4
3	Describe the impact of the spousal consent rules on participant loans	14.A.4

Topic R—Death Benefits and Beneficiaries

#	ERPA Learning Objective	Chapter
1	Explain the incidental death benefit rules for life insurance under a defined contribution or defined benefit plan	7.B.4.a
2	Identify the options under the distribution rules for beneficiaries	N/A
3	Describe the rules for nonspousal beneficiaries	N/A

Topic S—Participant Loans

#	ERPA Learning Objective	Chapter
1	Define the requirements for a participant loan to satisfy IRC § 72(p)	9.B.5
2	Explain how a loan can be a prohibited transaction under IRC § 4975	9.B.5
3	Calculate the maximum available loan amount based on a participant's vested account balance	9.B.5
4	Identify situations that can result in a loan default	9.B.5
5	Distinguish between deemed distributions under IRC § 72(p) and loan offset	9.B.5

Topic T—QDROs

#	ERPA Learning Objective	Chapter
1	List the requirements for a domestic relations order to be considered a QDRO, including the administrative procedures for a QDRO	9.B.3
2	Describe taxation of QDRO distributions	9.B.3

Topic U—Plan Audit and Correction Programs

#	ERPA Learning Objective	Chapter
1	Describe the process of an IRS audit, including where an audit can be conducted	4.A.2.d 10.B.4
2	Describe the EPCRS program, including what failures qualify, fees and typical EPCRS corrections	4.A.2.d 10.B.4
3	Describe the general requirements for SCP	4.A.2.d 10.B.4
4	Describe the general requirements for VCP	4.A.2.d 10.B.4
5	Describe the general requirements for Audit CAP	4.A.2.d 10.B.4
6	Outline the differences between significant and insignificant operational failures, plan document failures and demographic failures	4.A.2.d 10.B.4
7	Describe the purpose and requirements of the DOL VFC program	4.A.2.d 10.B.4

Topic V — Prohibited Transactions under IRC § 4975

#	ERPA Learning Objective	Chapter
1	Identify the types of transactions which are prohibited	13.B.1, 2
2	Understand prohibited transaction exemptions, corrections and excise taxes	13.B.3

Topic W — Plan Terminations

#	ERPA Learning Objective	Chapter
1	Outline the process to terminate a plan: IRS, DOL, PBGC required forms, documents and deadlines	16.A.1 16.B.1, 2
2	Identify the rules specific to a defined benefit plan termination: standard vs distress, PBGC vs non-PBGC, ERISA § 4044 asset priority	16.A.1 16.B.1, 2
3	Distinguish among a frozen plan, a partial plan termination and a full termination	16.B.2

Topic X — Ethics and Professional Responsibility

#	ERPA Learning Objective	Chapter
1	Describe the rules governing an ERPA's authority to practice before the IRS	21.3
2	Describe the duties and restrictions applicable to an ERPA practicing before the IRS	21.3
3	Describe the sanctions for violating regulations outlined in Circular 230	21.3

Appendix E

Conversion of ERISA Section Cites and US Code Section Cites

ERISA was enacted as a self-contained law, with 4 Titles (Title II being the corresponding changes to the Internal Revenue Code, codified at Title 26 of the US Code). Then, ERISA section was placed at Chapter 18 of Title 29 of the US Code, with only 3 Subchapters (*i.e.*, no need to place Title II of ERISA section into a subchapter of Chapter 18 of Title 29 of the US Code). The chart below shows the conversions:

Title 29 — Labor
Chapter 18 — Employee Retirement Income Security Program
Subchapter I — Protection of Employee Benefit Rights
Subtitle A — General Provisions

ERISA § 2	29 USC § 1001	Congressional findings and declaration of policy.
ERISA § 3	29 USC § 1001a	Additional Congressional findings and declaration of policy.
[not part of ERISA]	29 USC § 1001b	Findings and declaration of policy.
ERISA § 3	29 USC § 1002	Definitions.
ERISA § 4	29 USC § 1003	Coverage.

Subtitle B — Regulatory Provisions
Part 1 — Reporting and Disclosure

ERISA § 101	29 USC § 1021	Duty of disclosure and reporting.
ERISA § 102	29 USC § 1022	Summary plan description.
ERISA § 103	29 USC § 1023	Annual reports.
ERISA § 104	29 USC § 1024	Filing and furnishing of information.
ERISA § 105	29 USC § 1025	Reporting of participant's benefit
ERISA § 106	29 USC § 1026	Reports made public information.
ERISA § 107	29 USC § 1027	Retention of records.
ERISA § 108	29 USC § 1028	Reliance on administrative interpretations.
ERISA § 109	29 USC § 1029	Forms.
ERISA § 110	29 USC § 1030	Alternative methods of compliance.
ERISA § 111	29 USC § 1031	Repeal and effective date.

Part 2 — Participation and Vesting

ERISA § 201	29 USC § 1051	Coverage.
ERISA § 202	29 USC § 1052	Minimum participation standards.
ERISA § 203	29 USC § 1053	Minimum vesting standards.
ERISA § 204	29 USC § 1054	Benefit accrual requirements.
ERISA § 205	29 USC § 1055	Requirement of joint and survivor annuity and preretirement survivor annuity.
ERISA § 206	29 USC § 1056	Form and payment of benefits.
ERISA § 207	29 USC § 1057	Repealed.
ERISA § 208	29 USC § 1058	Mergers and consolidations of plans or transfers of plan assets.
ERISA § 209	29 USC § 1059	Recordkeeping and reporting requirements.
ERISA § 210	29 USC § 1060	Multiple employer plans and other special rules.
ERISA § 211	29 USC § 1061	Effective dates.

Part 3 — Funding

ERISA § 301	29 USC § 1081	Coverage.
ERISA § 302	29 USC § 1082	Minimum funding standards.
ERISA § 303	29 USC § 1083	Minimum funding standards for single-employer defined benefit pension plans.
ERISA § 304	29 USC § 1084	Minimum funding standards for multiemployer plans.
ERISA § 305	29 USC § 1085	Additional funding rules for multi-employer plans in endangered status or critical status.
ERISA § 306	29 USC § 1085a	Repealed.
ERISA § 307	29 USC § 1085b	Repealed.
ERISA § 308	29 USC § 1086	Repealed.

Part 4 — Fiduciary Responsibility

ERISA § 401	29 USC § 1101	Coverage.
ERISA § 402	29 USC § 1102	Establishment of plan.
ERISA § 403	29 USC § 1103	Establishment of trust.
ERISA § 404	29 USC § 1104	Fiduciary duties.
ERISA § 405	29 USC § 1105	Liability for breach of co-fiduciary.
ERISA § 406	29 USC § 1106	Prohibited transactions.
ERISA § 407	29 USC § 1107	Limitation with respect to acquisition and holding of employer securities and employer real property by certain plans.
ERISA § 408	29 USC § 1108	Exemptions from prohibited transactions.
ERISA § 409	29 USC § 1109	Liability for breach of fiduciary duty.
ERISA § 410	29 USC § 1110	Exculpatory provisions; insurance.
ERISA § 411	29 USC § 1111	Persons prohibited from holding certain positions.
ERISA § 412	29 USC § 1112	Bonding.
ERISA § 413	29 USC § 1113	Limitation of actions.
ERISA § 414	29 USC § 1114	Effective date.

Part 5 — Administration and Enforcement

ERISA § 501	29 USC § 1131	Criminal penalties.
ERISA § 502	29 USC § 1132	Civil enforcement.
ERISA § 503	29 USC § 1133	Claims procedure.
ERISA § 504	29 USC § 1134	Investigative authority.
ERISA § 505	29 USC § 1135	Regulations.
ERISA § 506	29 USC § 1136	Coordination and responsibility of agencies enforcing this subchapter and related Federal laws.
ERISA § 507	29 USC § 1137	Administration.
ERISA § 508	29 USC § 1138	Appropriations.
ERISA § 509	29 USC § 1139	Separability.
ERISA § 510	29 USC § 1140	Interference with protected rights.
ERISA § 511	29 USC § 1141	Coercive interference.
ERISA § 512	29 USC § 1142	Advisory Council on Employee Welfare and Pension Benefit Plans.
ERISA § 513	29 USC § 1143	Research, studies, and reports
ERISA § 514	29 USC § 1144	Other laws.
ERISA § 515	29 USC § 1145	Delinquent contributions.
ERISA § 516	29 USC § 1146	Outreach to promote retirement income savings.
ERISA § 517	29 USC § 1147	National Summit on Retirement Savings.

Part 6—Continuation Coverage and Additional Standards for Group Health Plans

ERISA § 601	29 USC § 1161	Plans must provide continuation coverage to certain individuals.
ERISA § 602	29 USC § 1162	Continuation coverage.
ERISA § 603	29 USC § 1163	Qualifying event.
ERISA § 604	29 USC § 1164	Applicable premium.
ERISA § 605	29 USC § 1165	Election
ERISA § 606	29 USC § 1166	Notice requirements.
ERISA § 607	29 USC § 1167	Definitions and special rules.
ERISA § 608	29 USC § 1168	Regulations.
ERISA § 609	29 USC § 1169	Additional standards for group health plans.

Part 7—Group Health Plan Requirements
Subpart A—Requirements Relating to Portability, Access, and Renewability

ERISA § 701	29 USC § 1181	Increased portability through limitation on preexisting condition exclusions.
ERISA § 702	29 USC § 1182	Prohibiting discrimination against individual participants and beneficiaries based on health status.
ERISA § 703	29 USC § 1183	Guaranteed renewability in multi-employer plans and multiple employer welfare arrangements.

Subpart B—Other Requirements

ERISA § 711	29 USC § 1185	Standards relating to benefits for mothers and newborns.
ERISA § 712	29 USC § 1185a	Parity in application of certain limits to mental health benefits.
ERISA § 713	29 USC § 1185b	Required coverage for reconstructive surgery following mastectomies.

Subpart C—General Provisions

ERISA § 731	29 USC § 1191	Preemption; State flexibility; construction.
ERISA § 732	29 USC § 1191a	Special rules relating to group health plans.
ERISA § 733	29 USC § 1191b	Definitions.
ERISA § 734	29 USC § 1191c	Regulations.

Subchapter II—Jurisdiction, Administration, Enforcement; Joint Pension Task Force, etc.
Subtitle A—Jurisdiction, Administration, and Enforcement

ERISA § 3001	29 USC § 1201	Procedures in connection with the issuance of certain determination letters by the Secretary of the Treasury covering qualifications under Internal Revenue Code.
ERISA § 3002	29 USC § 1202	Procedures with respect to continued compliance with Internal Revenue requirements relating to participation, vesting, and funding standards.
ERISA § 3003	29 USC § 1203	Procedures in connection with prohibited transactions.

Subtitle B—Joint Pension, Profit-sharing, and Employee Stock Ownership Plan Task Force; Studies
Part 1—Joint Pension, Profit-sharing, and Employee Stock Ownership Plan Task Force

ERISA § 3021	29 USC § 1221	Establishment.
ERISA § 3022	29 USC § 1222	Duties.

Part 2—Other Studies

ERISA § 3031	29 USC § 1231	Congressional study.
ERISA § 3032	29 USC § 1232	Protection for employees under Federal procurement, construction, and research contracts and grants.

Subtitle C—Enrollment of Actuaries

ERISA § 3041	29 USC § 1241	Joint Board for the Enrollment of Actuaries.
ERISA § 3042	29 USC § 1242	Enrollment by Board; standards and qualifications; suspension or termination of enrollment.

Subchapter III—Plan Termination Insurance
Subtitle A—Pension Benefit Guaranty Corporation

ERISA § 4001	29 USC § 1301	Definitions.
ERISA § 4002	29 USC § 1302	Pension Benefit Guaranty Corporation.
ERISA § 4003	29 USC § 1303	Operation of corporation.
ERISA § 4004	29 USC § 1304	Repealed.
ERISA § 4005	29 USC § 1305	Pension benefit guaranty funds.
ERISA § 4006	29 USC § 1306	Premium rates.
ERISA § 4007	29 USC § 1307	Payment of premiums.
ERISA § 4008	29 USC § 1308	Annual report by the corporation.
ERISA § 4009	29 USC § 1309	Portability assistance.
ERISA § 4010	29 USC § 1310	Authority to require certain information.
ERISA § 4011	29 USC § 1311	Repealed.

Subtitle B—Coverage

ERISA §4021	29 USC §1321	Coverage.
ERISA §4022	29 USC §1322	Single-employer plan benefits guaranteed.
ERISA §4022A	29 USC §1322a	Multiemployer plan benefits guaranteed.
ERISA §4022B	29 USC §1322b	Aggregate limit on benefits guaranteed; criteria applicable.
ERISA §4023	29 USC §1323	Plan fiduciaries.

Subtitle C—Terminations

ERISA §4041	29 USC §1341	Termination of single-employer plans.
ERISA §4041A	29 USC §1341a	Termination of multiemployer plans.
ERISA §4042	29 USC §1342	Institution of termination proceedings by the corporation.
ERISA §4043	29 USC §1343	Reportable events.
ERISA §4044	29 USC §1344	Allocation of assets.
ERISA §4045	29 USC §1345	Recapture of payments.
ERISA §4046	29 USC §1346	Reports to trustee.
ERISA §4047	29 USC §1347	Restoration of plans.
ERISA §4048	29 USC §1348	Termination date.
ERISA §4049	29 USC §1349	Repealed.
ERISA §4050	29 USC §1350	Missing participants.

Subtitle D—Liability

ERISA §4061	29 USC §1361	Amounts payable by corporation.
ERISA §4062	29 USC §1362	Liability for termination of single-employer plans under a distress termination or a termination by corporation.
ERISA §4063	29 USC §1363	Liability of substantial employer for withdrawal from single-employer plans under multiple controlled groups.
ERISA §4064	29 USC §1364	Liability on termination of single-employer plans under multiple controlled groups.
ERISA §4065	29 USC §1365	Annual report of plan administrator.
ERISA §4066	29 USC §1366	Annual notification to substantial employers.
ERISA §4067	29 USC §1367	Recovery of liability for plan termination.
ERISA §4068	29 USC §1368	Lien for liability.
ERISA §4069	29 USC §1369	Treatment of transactions to evade liability; effect of corporate reorganization.
ERISA §4070	29 USC §1370	Enforcement authority relating to terminations of single-employer plans.
ERISA §4071	29 USC §1371	Penalty for failure to timely provide required information.

Subtitle E — Special Provisions for Multiemployer Plans
Part 1 — Employer Withdrawals

ERISA § 4201	29 USC § 1381	Withdrawal liability established; criteria and definitions.
ERISA § 4202	29 USC § 1382	Determination and collection of liability; notification of employer.
ERISA § 4203	29 USC § 1383	Complete withdrawal.
ERISA § 4204	29 USC § 1384	Sale of assets.
ERISA § 4205	29 USC § 1385	Partial withdrawals.
ERISA § 4206	29 USC § 1386	Adjustment for partial withdrawal; determination of amount; reduction for partial withdrawal liability; procedures applicable.
ERISA § 4207	29 USC § 1387	Reduction or waiver of complete withdrawal liability; procedures and standards applicable.
ERISA § 4208	29 USC § 1388	Reduction of partial withdrawal liability.
ERISA § 4209	29 USC § 1389	De minimis rule.
ERISA § 4210	29 USC § 1390	Nonapplicability of withdrawal liability for certain temporary contribution obligation periods; exception.
ERISA § 4211	29 USC § 1391	Methods for computing withdrawal liability.
ERISA § 4212	29 USC § 1392	Obligation to contribute.
ERISA § 4213	29 USC § 1393	Actuarial assumptions.
ERISA § 4214	29 USC § 1394	Application of plan amendments; exception.
ERISA § 4215	29 USC § 1395	Plan notification to corporation of potentially significant withdrawals.
ERISA § 4216	29 USC § 1396	Special rules for plans under section 404(c) of title 26.
ERISA § 4217	29 USC § 1397	Application of part in case of certain pre-1980 withdrawals; adjustment of covered plan.
ERISA § 4218	29 USC § 1398	Withdrawal not to occur because of change in business form or suspension of contributions during labor dispute.
ERISA § 4219	29 USC § 1399	Notice, collection, etc,. of withdrawal liability
ERISA § 4220	29 USC § 1400	Approval of amendments.
ERISA § 4221	29 USC § 1401	Resolution of disputes.
ERISA § 4222	29 USC § 1402	Reimbursements for uncollectible withdrawal liability.
ERISA § 4223	29 USC § 1403	Withdrawal liability payment fund.
ERISA § 4224	29 USC § 1404	Alternative method of withdrawal liability payments.
ERISA § 4225	29 USC § 1405	Limitation on withdrawal liability.

Part 2 — Merger or Transfer of Plan Assets or Liabilities

ERISA § 4231	29 USC § 1411	Mergers and transfers between multiemployer plans.
ERISA § 4232	29 USC § 1412	Transfers between a multiemployer plan and a single-employer plan.
ERISA § 4233	29 USC § 1413	Partition.
ERISA § 4234	29 USC § 1414	Asset transfer rules.
ERISA § 4235	29 USC § 1415	Transfers pursuant to change in bargaining representative.

Part 3 — Reorganization; Minimum Contribution Requirement for Multiemployer Plans

ERISA § 4241	29 USC § 1421	Reorganization status.
ERISA § 4242	29 USC § 1422	Notice of reorganization and funding requirements.
ERISA § 4243	29 USC § 1423	Minimum contribution requirement.
ERISA § 4244	29 USC § 1424	Overburden credit against minimum contribution requirement.
ERISA § 4244A	29 USC § 1425	Adjustments in accrued benefits.
ERISA § 4245	29 USC § 1426	Insolvent plans.

Part 4 — Financial Assistance

ERISA § 4261	29 USC § 1431	Assistance by corporation.

Part 5 — Benefits after Termination

ERISA § 4281	29 USC § 1441	Benefits under certain terminated plans.

Part 6 — Enforcement

ERISA § 4301	29 USC § 1451	Civil actions.
ERISA § 4302	29 USC § 1452	Penalty for failure to provide notice.
ERISA § 4303	29 USC § 1453	Election of plan status.

Subtitle F — Transition Rules and Effective Dates

ERISA § 4402	29 USC § 1461	Effective date; special rules.

Table of Statutes and Regulations

United States Constitution, 28, 31
Article I, Section 7, of the Constitution of the United States, 36
The 16th Amendment to the United States Constitution, 31
IRC §25B, 121, 485
IRC §45E, 388
IRC §61(a), 11, 446, 470
IRC §61(a)(1), 446
IRC §72(c), 271
IRC §72(d), 271
IRC §72(p), 269–270, 561
IRC §72(t), 274
IRC §79, 466–467, 551
IRC §79(c), 467
IRC §79(d)(1)(A), 466
IRC §79(d)(3)(A), 467
IRC §79(d)(3)(B), 467
IRC §83, 15–16, 446, 448, 451, 551
IRC §101(j)(2)(A), 448–449
IRC §101(j)(4), 449
IRC §104, 18, 464, 551
IRC §104(a)(3), 464
IRC §105, 464
IRC §105(a), 464
IRC §106, 138, 476
IRC §106(d), 476
IRC §120, 467, 551
IRC §120(b), 467
IRC §120(c)(3), 467
IRC §120(d)(7), 467
IRC §125, 175, 468–469, 473
IRC §125(a), 473
IRC §125(b), 469, 473
IRC §125(b)(1), 469
IRC §125(b)(2), 469
IRC §125(d), 468–469
IRC §125(d)(1), 469
IRC §127, 467, 551
IRC §127(a)(2), 467

IRC §127(c)(1), 467
IRC §127(c)(3), 467
IRC §129, 467–468, 551
IRC §129(a)(2), 467
IRC §129(d)(2), 468
IRC §129(d)(4), 468
IRC §129(d)(8)(A), 468
IRC §129(e)(1), 467–468
IRC §129(e)(8), 468
IRC §132(f), 469
IRC §132(f)(1), 469
IRC §132(f)(1)(A), 469
IRC §132(f)(1)(B), 469
IRC §132(f)(1)(C), 469
IRC §132(f)(1)(G), 469
IRC §132(f)(2)(A), 469
IRC §132(f)(2)(B), 469
IRC §137, 468
IRC §137(b), 468
IRC §137(c), 468
IRC §137(f), 468
IRC §152, 18
IRC §162(a)(1), 18, 446, 464
IRC §162(m), 446
IRC §162(m)(5), 446
IRC §170(b)(1)(A)(ii), 60
IRC §213(d), 464, 471, 473
IRC §213(d)(1), 464
IRC §219, 484, 548
IRC §220(b)(2), 474
IRC §220(c)(2), 474
IRC §220(c)(4), 474
IRC §220(d)(2), 474
IRC §220(e), 474
IRC §220(f), 474
IRC §220(i)(2), 474
IRC §220(j), 474
IRC §223(a), 476
IRC §223(b)(2), 476
IRC §223(b)(3), 476

IRC §223(b)(5), 476
IRC §223(c)(1)(B), 476
IRC §223(c)(2)(A), 475
IRC §223(c)(2)(C), 476
IRC §223(d)(1), 475
IRC §223(d)(1)(B), 475
IRC §223(d)(2), 475
IRC §223(e)(1), 475
IRC §223(f)(1), 475
IRC §223(f)(2), 475
IRC §223(f)(4), 475
IRC §223(f)(5), 476
IRC §223(f)(7), 475
IRC §223(f)(8), 475
IRC §280G, 175, 448
IRC §280G(b)(5), 448
IRC §401(a), 17, 47–48, 51, 62, 77, 84,
    89, 91, 95, 113–114, 116–117,
    119–121, 128, 131, 133–134, 137–140,
    143, 156, 163, 173–174, 176, 179, 184,
    186–187, 243, 247, 250–253, 260,
    262–264, 275, 284–285, 340, 551
IRC §401(a)(2)(B)(i)(I), 138
IRC §401(a)(4), 131, 187, 260, 285
IRC §401(a)(9), 137, 243, 275
IRC §401(a)(9)(G), 137
IRC §401(a)(11), 252–253, 340
IRC §401(a)(11)(D), 253
IRC §401(a)(13), 264
IRC §401(a)(14), 251, 262
IRC §401(a)(23), 95
IRC §401(a)(25), 134, 247
IRC §401(a)(26), 186
IRC §401(a)(27), 91
IRC §401(a)(31), 273
IRC §401(a)(36), 263
IRC §401(b), 70, 284
IRC §401(c)(1), 201
IRC §401(c)(3), 8
IRC §401(h), 139
IRC §401(k), 96–97, 204, 219, 263, 265,
    552
IRC §401(k)(2)(B)(i), 263
IRC §401(k)(3), 204
IRC §401(k)(8), 263
IRC §401(k)(12), 219
IRC §401(k)(13), 97
IRC §401(l), 102
IRC §401(m), 96, 219
IRC §401(m)(2), 219

IRC §402(a), 70, 270–271
IRC §402(c)(4), 273
IRC §402(e)(4), 272
IRC §402(f), 272, 560
IRC §402(g), 119, 140, 552
IRC §402A, 96, 263, 552
IRC §402A(d)(2), 263
IRC §403(b), 47, 551, 558
IRC §404, 17, 70, 121–122, 201, 448
IRC §404(a)(5), 448
IRC §404(a)(8)(c), 201
IRC §408, 98, 552
IRC §408(a), 98
IRC §408(k), 98, 552
IRC §408(p), 552
IRC §408A, 486
IRC §408A(a), 486
IRC §409(h), 95
IRC §409(o), 95
IRC §409A, 15–16, 175, 444, 451–454
IRC §409A(b)(1), 452
IRC §409A(b)(3)(A), 453
IRC §410(a), 176
IRC §410(b), 176, 179, 184, 285
IRC §411(a), 106, 128, 134, 138, 249, 262
IRC §411(a)(7), 134, 249
IRC §411(a)(7)(A)(i), 134
IRC §411(a)(8), 262
IRC §411(a)(9), 138, 249
IRC §411(a)(13), 106
IRC §411(b)(1), 134–135
IRC §§ 411(b)(1)(G), 135
IRC §411(b)(1)(H), 135
IRC §411(b)(2), 133
IRC §411(b)(5), 106–107
IRC §411(b)(8), 135
IRC §411(d)(6), 137, 185, 260
IRC §412, 77, 112–113, 117, 252, 291,
    558
IRC §412(d)(2), 77
IRC §412(e)(3), 112, 117, 291
IRC §414(b), 156
IRC §414(c), 156
IRC §414(d), 51
IRC §414(e), 54
IRC §414(f), 117
IRC §414(i), 84, 551
IRC §414(j), 85, 551
IRC §414(k), 85, 108
IRC §414(m), 163–164

IRC §414(n), 8
IRC §414(p), 264
IRC §414(q), 174–175
IRC §414(r), 173
IRC §414(s), 556
IRC §414(u), 120
IRC §414(v), 120
IRC §414(w), 263
IRC §414(w)(2), 263
IRC §414(x), 107
IRC §415(b), 140, 143
IRC §415(c), 139, 195, 201
IRC §416(i), 235
IRC §417(a)(3), 340
IRC §417(e), 253, 270
IRC §417(e)(4), 270
IRC §420, 139
IRC §421(a), 454–455
IRC §422(a), 454
IRC §423(b), 455
IRC §430, 114
IRC §431, 117
IRC §432, 117
IRC §436, 116
IRC §451, 15
IRC §457(a), 70
IRC §457(b), 47–48, 51, 53, 551
IRC §457(f), 47–48, 54, 551
IRC §457A, 16, 452
IRC §501(a), 17, 314
IRC §501(c)(3), 48, 61
IRC §512, 17
IRC §§3121, 16, 487
IRC §3301, 16, 447
IRC §3405(c), 273
IRC §3401, 447
IRC §4963(e)(1), 362
IRC §4971, 111, 113
IRC §4972, 123
IRC §4974(a), 275
IRC §4975(d)(1), 270
IRC §4975(d)(17), 364
IRC §4975(e), 362
IRC §4975(f), 270, 363
IRC §4975(f)(6), 270, 363
IRC §4980, 112, 418
IRC §4980B, 477
IRC §4980D, 479
IRC §4980D(b)(1), 479
IRC §4980D(b)(3), 479

IRC §4980D(c)(1), 479
IRC §4980D(c)(2), 479
IRC §4980D(c)(3), 479
IRC §4980D(d)(1), 479
IRC §4980D(d)(2), 479
IRC §4980F, 137
IRC §6058, 406
IRC §7702B(c), 471
IRC §9801, 478
IRC §9811, 481
IRC §9802, 482
Treas. Regs. §1.79-1(c), 467
Treas, Regs. §1.79-3, 467
Treas. Regs. §1.79-4T, 467
Treas. Regs. §1.120-3, 467
Proposed Treas. Regs. §1.125-1(a)(4), 468
Proposed Treas. Regs. §1.125-1(a)(5), 468
Proposed Treas. Regs. § 1.125-1(b)(4),
   468
Proposed Treas. Regs. §125-5, 469
Proposed Treas. Regs. §1.125-5(a), 473
Proposed Treas. Regs. §1.125-5(b)(1), 469
Proposed Treas. Regs. §1.125-5(c)(1), 469
Proposed Treas. Regs. §1.125-5(g)(1), 469
Proposed Treas. Regs. §1.125-5(g)(2), 469
Proposed Treas. Regs. §1.125-
   5(o)(1)(ii)(C), 469
Proposed Treas. Regs. §1.125-
   5(o)(1)(ii)(A), 469
Proposed Treas. Regs. §1.125-6(b)(3), 473
Treas. Regs. §1.127-2, 467
Treas. Regs. §1.132-9, Q&A-11, 469
Treas. Regs. §1.280G-1, Q&A-27, 448
Treas. Regs. §1.401-1, 87, 90, 95, 132
Treas. Regs. §1.401(a)-1(b), 251
Treas. Regs. § 1.401-1(b)(1)(i), 90, 132
Treas. Regs. § 1.401-1(b)(1)(ii), 132
Treas. Regs. § 1.401-1(b)(1)(iii), 95
Treas. Regs. §1.401-14, 139
Treas. Regs. §1.401(a)(4)-1 through -13,
   188
Treas. Regs. §1.401(a)(4)-1(c), 202
Treas. Regs. §1.401(a)(4)-2, 189
Treas. Regs. §1.401(a)(4)-4, 202
Treas. Regs. §1.401(a)(4)-4(b)(1), 202
Treas. Regs. §1.401(a)(4)-4(c)(1), 202
Treas. Regs. §1.401(a)(4)-5, 202
Treas. Regs. §1.401(a)(4)-8, 105, 194
Treas. Regs. §1.401(a)(4)-10, 203

Treas. Regs. §1.401(a)(4)-11, 184, 227, 234

Treas. Regs. §1.401(a)(5)-1(c), 194

Treas. Regs. §1.401(b)-1(e)(3), 284

Treas. Regs. §1.401(k)-1(d)(3), 222

Treas. Regs. §1.401(k)-2, 210, 226

Treas. Regs. §1.401(k)-3, 220

Treas. Regs. §1.401(l)-1(c)(16)(i), 102

Treas. Regs. §1.401(l)-1(c)(25), 102

Treas. Regs. §1.401(l)-3, 102

Proposed Treas. Regs. §1.402(e)-2(f), 273

Treas. Regs. §1.402A-1, Q&A-8, 269

Treas. Regs. §1.410(b)-2, 180

Treas. Regs. §1.410(b)-3, 177

Treas. Regs. §1.410(b)-4, 181

Treas. Regs. §1.410(b)-5, 183

Treas. Regs. §1.410(b)-8, 184

Treas. Regs. §1.411(c)-1(e), 248

Treas. Regs. §1.411(c)-1(f)(1), 250

Treas. Regs. §1.411(c)-1(f)(2), 250

Treas. Regs. §1.411(d)-3(g)(2)(ii), 138

Treas. Regs. §1.414(b)-1, 156

Treas. Regs §1.414(c)-2, 157

Proposed Treas. Regs. § 1.414(m)-2, 164

Treas. Regs. §1.414(s)-1, 195

Treas. Regs. §1.417(a)-3(a)(4), 340

Treas. Regs. §1.451-2, 446

Treas. Regs. §53.4963-1(e), 362

Treas. Regs. §54.4974-2, Q&A-7, 275

Treas. Regs. §54-4980F-1, Q&A-11, 340

29 USC, 308, 563–570

§1001; ERISA §2, 308

§1001a; (no corresponding provision in ERISA), 309, 563

§1001b; (no corresponding provision in ERISA), 310, 563

§1002(1); ERISA §3(1), 321, 322, 325, 326

§1002(2); ERISA §3(2), 316, 321

§1002(3); ERISA §3(3), 321

§1002(5); ERISA § 3(5), 69

§1002(14); ERISA §3(14), 204, 383

§1002(21)(A); ERISA §3(21)(A), 349, 352

§1002(34); ERISA §3(34), 85, 365, 373, 374

§1002(35); ERISA §3(35), 85

§1002(40); ERISA §3(40), 69

§1003(b); ERISA §4(b), 297, 550, 563

§1021(i); ERISA §101(i), 375

§1024; ERISA §104, 406, 409, 551, 563

§1024(b)(1); ERISA §104(b)(1), 329

§1025; ERISA §105, 339, 398, 409, 551, 563

§1054(h); ERISA §204(h), 137, 339, 340

§1056(a)(3); ERISA §206(a)(3), 250

§1082(f)(1); ERISA §302(f)(1), 408

§1101; ERISA §401, 349, 565

§1102(a)(1); ERISA § 402(a)(1), 314

§1102(b)(3); ERISA §402(b)(3), 328

§1104; ERISA §404, 355, 565

§1104(c); ERISA §404(c), 364

§1105; ERISA §405, 377, 565

§1106; ERISA §406, 361, 398, 565

§1106(b); ERISA §406(b), 357

§1107(d)(4); ERISA §407(d)(4), 358

§1107(d)(5); ERISA §407(d)(5), 358

§1108; ERISA §408, 363, 565

§1109; ERISA §409, 376, 397,565

§1110; ERISA §410, 376, 565

§1111; ERISA §411, 349, 565

§1111(b); ERISA §411(b), 393

§1112; ERISA §412.,377, 565

§1113; ERISA § 413, 377, 403, 565

§1131; ERISA §501, 393, 397, 565

§1132(a)(1)(B); ERISA §502(a)(1)(B), 340, 390, 397

§1132(a)(2); ERISA §502(a)(2), 377, 390, 397

§1132(b); ERISA §502(b), 399

§1132(c); ERISA §502(c), 390, 397

§1132(c)(1); ERISA §502(c)(1), 411, 477

§1132(d); ERISA §502(d), 403

§1132(e); ERISA §502(e),, 403

§1132(g); ERISA §502(g), 351, 403

§1133; ERISA §503, 340, 400, 565

§1134(a); ERISA §504(a), 376

§1144; ERISA §514, 391, 565

§1144(b)(2)(A); ERISA §514(b)(2)(A), 472, 477

§1161(a); ERISA §601(a), 477

§1161(b); ERISA §601(b), 477

§1162(1); ERISA §602(1), 477

§1162(2); ERISA §602(2), 478

§1162(3); ERISA §602(3), 478

§1163(1); ERISA §603(1), 478

§1163(2); ERISA §603(2), 478

§1163(3); ERISA §603(3), 478

§1163(5); ERISA §603(5), 478

§1165(a); ERISA §605(a), 478

§1166; ERISA §606, 341, 565

§1166(a); ERISA §606(a), 478
§1167(1); ERISA §607(1), 471
§1167(3)(a); ERISA §607(3)(a), 478
§1181(a)(1); ERISA §701(a)(1), 479
§1181(a)(2); ERISA §701(a)(2), 479
§1181(a)(3); ERISA §701(a)(3), 479
§1181(a)(1); ERISA §701(e), 481
§1182(a)(1); ERISA §702(a)(1), 480
§1182(a)(2); ERISA §702(a)(2), 479
§1182(b)(1); ERISA §702(b)(1), 480
§1185; ERISA §711, 478, 481, 565
§1185(a)(2); ERISA §711(a)(2), 481
§1185(b); ERISA §711(b), 482
§1185(d); ERISA §711(d), 482
§1185a; ERISA §712, 481, 565
§1185a(a); ERISA §712(a), 481
§1185b; ERISA §713, 479, 482
§1185b(a); ERISA §713(a), 482
§1185b(a)(1)-(3); ERISA §713(a)(1)-(3), 482
§1185b(b); ERISA §713(b), 482
§1185b(c)(1); ERISA §713(c)(1), 482
§1185b(c)(2); ERISA §713(c)(2), 482
§1191a(a); ERISA §732(a), 478
§1302; ERISA §4002, 124, 567
§1305; ERISA §4005, 124, 567
§1306; ERISA §4006, 124, 567
§1307; ERISA §4007, 124, 567
§1341; ERISA §4041, 414, 419, 568
§1343; ERISA §4043, 408, 568
§1344(a); ERISA §4044(a), 415

§1365; ERISA §4065, 406, 568
§1381; ERISA §4201, 417, 569
Labor Regs. §2509.75-8, FR-11, 358
Labor Regs. §2509.94-1, 358
Labor Regs. §2509.94-3, 358
Labor Regs. §2509.95-1(c)(6), 355
Labor Regs. §2510.3-1, 305
Labor Regs. §2510.3-2, 301
Labor Regs. §2510.3-3, 298
Labor Regs. §2510.3-102, 359–360
Proposed Labor Regs. §2510.3-102, 360
Labor Regs. §2520.102-2 through -4, 329
Labor Regs. §2520.102-2, 329–330
Labor Regs. §2520.102-3, 331
Labor Regs. §2520.104b-1, 411
Labor Regs. §2530.200b-1, 128
Labor Regs. §2530.200b-2.,128
Labor Regs. §2550.404c-1, 364
Labor Regs. §2550.404c-1(c)(4), 364
Labor Regs. §2550.404c-5(c), 375
Labor Regs. §2560.503-1(b), 401
Labor Regs. §2560.503-1(l), 400
Labor Regs. §2575.502c-1, 411
Labor Regs. §2590.606-1(c), 341
Labor Regs. §2590.606-4(b)(4), 341
Labor Regs. §2590.702(d), 480
Labor Regs. §2590.702(e), 480
Labor Regs. §2590.702(f), 476, 481
Labor Regs. §2590.702(f)(1), 476
Labor Regs. §2590.702(f)(2), 476

Table of Cases

Achiro v. Commisioner, 77 TC 881 (1981), 161

Aiken v. Policy Management Sys. Corp, 13 F.3d 138 (4th Cir. 1993).,328, 338

Boggs v. Boggs, 520 U.S. 833 (1997), 254

Branch v. G. Bernd Co, 955 F.2d 1574 (11th Cir. 1992), 328

Burke v. Kodak Ret. Income Plan, 336 F.3d 103 (2nd Cir. 2003), 328

Burstein v. Ret. Account Plan for Employees of Allegheny Health Edu. and Research Found, 334 F.3d 365 (3rd Cir. 2003), 328

Cerasoli v Xomed, Inc, 47 F.Supp2d 401 (WD NY 1999), 327

Chiles v. Ceridian Corp, 95 F.3d 1505 (10th Cir. 1996), 328

Commissioner v. Glenshaw Glass, 348 U.S. 426 (1955), 11

Commissioner of Internal Revenue Service v. Keystone Consolidated Industries, Inc, 508 US 152 (1993), 358

Custer v. Sweeney, 89 F.3d 1156 (4th Cir. 1996), 350

Diak v. Dwyer, Costello & Knox, P.C, 33 F.3d 809 (7th Cir. 1994), 315

Edwards v. State Farm Mut. Auto. Ins. Co, 851 F.2d 134 (6th Cir.1988), 328

Elliotts, Inc. v. Commissioner, 716 F.2d 1241 (9th Cir.1983), 446

Firestone Tire & Rubber Co. v. Bruch, 489 US 101 (1989), 328, 329, 391, 397, 400

Great-West Life & Annuity Ins. Co. v. Knudson, 534 U.S. 204 (2002), 398

Govoni v. Bricklayers, Masons & Plasterers International Union, Local No. 5 Pension Fund, 732 F.2d 250 (1st Cir. 1984), 328

Health Cost Controls, Inc, v. Washington, 187 F.3d 703, 712 (7th Cir. 1999), 327

Hickman v. GEM Ins. Co, 299 F.3d 1208, 1212 (10th Cir. 2002), 341

Horn v. Berdon, Inc. Defined Benefit Pension Plan, 938 F.2d 125 (9th Cir. 1991), 328

Landry v. Airline Pilots Ass'n, 892 F.2d 1238 (5th Cir. 1990), 327

LaRue v. DeWolff, Boberg & Assoc, 128 S.Ct. 1020 (2008), 364, 377

Marolt v. Alliant Techsystems, 146 F.3d 617 (8th Cir.1998), 328

Nationwide Mut. Ins. Co. v. Darden, 503 U.S. 318, 323 (1992), 8

O'Leary v. Provident Life & Accident Ins. Co, 456 F.Supp2d 285 (DC Mass, 2006), 317

Palmisano v. Allina Health Sys, 190 F.3d 881 (8th Cir. 1999), 328

Riley v. Murdock, 890 F.Supp. 444, 458 (E.D.N.C. 1995), 357

Sigman v. Rudolph Wurlitzer Co, 11 N.E.2d 878 (Ohio App, 1937), 24

U.S. v. Phillips, 363 F.3d 1167 (11th Cir. 1994), 393

Variety Children's Hospital v. Century Medical Health Plan, 57 F3d 1040 (11th Cir. 1995), 400

Washington v. Murphy Oil USA, Inc, 497 F.3d 453 (5th Cir. 2007), 328

Wilson v. Southwestern Bell, 55 F.3d 399, 407 (8th Cir. 1995), 341

Index

benefits professionals, 1, 23, 32, 155, 204, 280, 284, 289–290, 456, 491, 495, 500, 503, 509, 521, 538, 541–542

accountant, 39–40, 42, 50, 73, 123, 201, 315, 355, 407, 437–438, 525–526

actuary, 39–40, 50, 72, 80, 83, 86, 93–94, 105–106, 109–110, 112–117, 123, 127, 134, 151, 153, 180, 240, 245, 248, 385, 387, 407, 413, 415, 503, 510, 522–523, 535–536, 553–554

attorney, 24, 39–40, 43, 50, 53, 60, 71–75, 94, 165, 168, 226, 265, 281, 289, 293–295, 327, 350–352, 355, 357, 391–392, 397, 400, 403, 432, 493–495, 501, 503, 509–512, 525–526, 538

Enrolled Retirement Plan Agents (ERPAs), 24, 43

insurance advisor, 41

investment advisor, 39, 41–42, 355, 506–507, 532

record keepers, 23, 42

third party administrators, 23, 42

compensation, 1, 3–6, 10–12, 14–16, 18, 24–25, 29, 36, 40, 45, 47–49, 51, 53–54, 58, 63, 70, 74, 84–86, 90–93, 96–106, 108, 110, 118–119, 122, 127–128, 132–133, 135–136, 139–143, 150, 154–155, 171–172, 174–175, 179, 181, 187, 189–191, 193–201, 206–211, 213–217, 219–222, 224–225, 231, 235–236, 259–260, 268, 270–271, 285, 297, 300–301, 303, 306–308, 316, 318–320, 326, 347–348, 350, 352, 354, 363, 380, 383, 388, 406, 409–410, 423, 427, 430, 435, 439, 441–458, 464–465, 473, 498, 503, 507–508, 511, 514–516,
522–523, 533–537, 547, 550–551, 556, 558

earned income, 11, 13, 40, 48, 100, 119, 122, 140–141, 164, 177, 201, 236, 467–468, 484–485, 487, 558

in general, 1, 4, 37, 42, 89, 103, 107, 157–158, 177–178, 180–181, 184, 195, 198, 221, 226, 251–252, 260, 266, 269, 279, 281–282, 287, 295, 349, 364–365, 371, 464, 466, 469, 499, 533

death benefits, 3, 6, 48, 117, 131, 137, 261, 276, 442, 449, 460, 466, 551, 561

Department of Labor, 1, 22, 24, 29, 31, 34, 38, 43, 69, 75, 124, 281, 291, 293, 296–297, 300, 306, 323, 325, 334, 336–339, 349, 352, 355–359, 363, 376–379, 381, 387, 390, 395, 397–398, 400, 406–407, 409, 425–438, 465, 476–477, 479, 511, 541, 543

amicus curie briefs, 296, 436

enforcement, 30, 32, 34, 50, 65, 119, 289, 292–293, 296, 320, 364, 381, 393–394, 396, 398–399, 415, 429–434, 437, 471, 549, 565, 567–568, 570

civil investigations, 431

consultant/adviser project, 435

criminal investigations, 432

employee contributions project, 434

health fraud/Multiple Employer Welfare Arrangements (MEWAs), 433

informal complaint resolution, 433

outreach and education, 76, 433

voluntary compliance program, 407, 432, 437, 559

form 5500, 43, 69, 108, 114, 286, 293–294, 334–335, 405–407, 409–411, 421, 425, 436–438, 559
   desk reviews, 437
   electronic filing, 407, 436–437
technical guidance, 282, 296, 435–436
Employee Benefits Security Adminis-tration, 22, 31–32, 296, 336–337, 407, 425–426, 430, 436, 465, 541
   PT exemptions, 347, 436

employees, 1, 3–11, 14–15, 17–19, 21–31, 35, 37, 45–46, 48–49, 51–64, 66, 68–70, 73–75, 79–82, 87–100, 102, 106–107, 110–114, 117–121, 125–126, 128, 131–133, 135–136, 138–142, 149–156, 161–168, 170–186, 188–193, 196–205, 208–209, 214–219, 221–225, 227, 234–237, 245, 247, 252, 255, 257, 260–263, 268, 270, 274, 283, 285–286, 289–291, 294–295, 297–303, 305–309, 313–320, 322–323, 325–326, 328–329, 331, 333, 336–337, 347, 360–363, 376, 380–381, 383–384, 386, 388, 406, 409–410, 413, 417–418, 420–430, 433–434, 439, 441–451, 453–455, 458–462, 464–475, 477–479, 508, 513–514, 516–517, 523, 525–526, 532–534, 536–538, 550, 553, 555–556, 560, 567
common-law, 1, 4, 7–8, 11, 13, 151, 196, 255, 449
independent contractors, 1, 4, 8, 11, 89, 175, 445, 447, 455, 538
leased employees, 8, 89, 470, 525–526, 538
partners in a partnership, 8, 11, 89, 270
self-employed, 4, 8, 11, 13, 48, 69, 71, 88, 118–119, 122, 140–141, 196, 198–199, 201, 211, 236, 280, 298, 462, 484, 487, 558
sole proprietors, 4, 8, 11, 89, 99, 201, 270, 363
owners, 4, 40, 48, 73–74, 118, 124, 166–168, 170, 172, 201, 218, 363, 417, 453, 467–468, 512, 514

employers, 1, 3–8, 15–16, 21–22, 24, 28–30, 34–35, 42–43, 45, 47, 49, 51, 54–55, 60–61, 63–73, 75–76, 82–83, 86, 90, 92, 96, 98–100, 107, 110, 112, 117, 119–120, 122, 126, 128–129, 132, 136, 138–140, 149, 155, 173–174, 185–186, 188, 203, 210, 235–236, 247, 262, 282–283, 285, 288, 301, 307–310, 316, 318, 324, 331–332, 337–339, 350, 359, 363, 388, 392, 413–414, 417, 419, 426–430, 433–434, 439, 442, 445, 447, 451–452, 454, 456, 460, 462–463, 465, 468, 471–474, 476–478, 481–482, 486, 490, 503, 510, 520, 523, 525–526, 530–533, 551, 553, 557, 568
church, 45, 47–48, 51, 54–60, 64, 70, 119, 131, 140, 179, 297, 338, 479, 550
for-profit, 6, 45, 51–52, 61, 70, 123, 338, 551
governmental, 3, 22, 29–30, 47, 51–55, 119, 121, 197, 273, 292, 295, 297, 503, 546, 550
non-profit, 6, 45, 47–48, 51, 61, 64, 119, 281, 447
public school, 48, 60–61, 70
various roles in an employee benefit plan
   plan administrator, 38, 75, 77, 82, 94, 96, 129, 150, 152, 174, 180, 232–233, 235, 240, 242, 245, 248, 251, 253–254, 256, 264–265, 269, 271–275, 284, 289, 293, 313–314, 329–336, 338, 350, 356, 373, 378, 390–392, 397, 399–402, 406–411, 415–416, 431, 437–438, 463, 480, 493–494, 559, 568
   fiduciary over plan assets, 38, 349

equity ownership, 3, 6

executive compensation, 4, 6, 45, 139, 439, 441–458, 503, 507–508, 514–516
deductibility of current compensation, 446
   equity benefits, 453
   stock certificates, 453, 458
   stock options, 444–445, 453–458

employee stock purchase plans, 454–455, 551

incentive stock option plans, 454, 551

golden parachutes, 6, 441, 448

nonqualified deferred compensation plans, 16, 439, 444–445, 447, 550

excess benefit plans, 297, 300, 449–450, 550

income taxation, 263, 269–270, 444, 451, 507

individual account plans, 258, 355, 450

limitations based on funding targets, 453

pension plans, 33, 60–61, 87, 90, 132, 241, 247, 249, 251, 255, 257–258, 263, 300, 304, 309–311, 315–316, 333, 383, 406–407, 450, 537, 539, 564

Rabbi trusts, 16, 448, 452

phantom stock plans, 442, 449, 455

stock appreciation rights, 445, 455

Top-Hat plans, 300, 449–450

Employee Retirement Income Security Act, 1, 5, 21–43, 60, 204, 254, 315, 318, 334, 350, 364, 366, 379, 393, 395, 419, 426, 430, 432, 511, 531

advanced funding, 21, 29, 442, 447

civil enforcement, 30, 565

communication of promised benefits, 29

federal agencies that regulate employee benefit plans, 31

Department of Labor, Employee Benefits Security Administration, 337, 465

Pension Benefit Guaranty Corporation, 1, 22, 30–31, 43, 64, 80, 86, 106, 124, 291, 413–415, 426, 435, 437, 511, 553, 567

fiduciary duties, 21, 23, 30, 38–39, 42, 100, 314–316, 345–346, 348, 350, 355–358, 376–377, 399, 471, 565

group health plans, 21–22, 30, 333, 341, 401, 425, 461–463, 465, 471, 477–482, 566

continuation coverage, 30, 335, 439, 468, 477–478, 549, 566

portability, 22, 30, 37, 425–426, 439, 462, 474, 477–480, 516, 539, 549, 566–567

income tax provisions, 1, 22–23, 31, 54, 542, 549

minimum vesting, 21, 29, 48, 60, 62, 126, 128, 131, 421, 442, 447, 564

need for Congress to act, 28

preemption, 28, 30, 98, 389, 391–392, 399, 436, 472, 541, 566

termination of retirement plans, 30

ERISA Plans, 40, 295–311, 327, 338, 352, 401, 405, 425

causes of action, 21–22, 28, 30, 33, 295, 320, 389–403, 436

attorney fees, 391, 400, 403

benefit claims procedures, 400

civil actions, 392, 403, 415, 544, 570

benefits or other rights, 390, 397

breach of fiduciary duty, 111, 348, 351, 357, 364, 375, 390, 397–398, 403, 501, 565

reporting and disclosure failures, 398

criminal actions, 544

federal preemption of state laws, 391

statute of limitations, 65, 286, 391, 403

employee benefit pension plans, 300

governed, 15, 22, 31, 51, 54–55, 60–61, 281, 297–298, 300, 304, 318, 320, 324, 326, 379, 386, 416, 451

not governed, 51, 54, 298, 300, 304, 416

employee benefit plans, 1, 4, 7–8, 10–11, 14–15, 22, 29–34, 40–43, 168, 257–258, 282, 291, 297–298, 305, 307–309, 321, 323, 325, 337–338, 341, 349, 378, 389, 392, 395–396, 431–432, 436–437, 469, 471, 473, 503–504, 525–526, 542

governed, 15, 22, 31, 51, 54–55, 60–61, 281, 297–298, 300, 304, 318, 320, 324, 326, 379, 386, 416, 451

employee benefit plans, *continued*
  not governed, 51, 54, 298, 300, 304,
    416
employee welfare benefit plans, 301,
    305, 321, 331, 333, 400, 410
  governed, 15, 22, 31, 51, 54–55,
    60–61, 281, 297–298, 300, 304,
    318, 320, 324, 326, 379, 386,
    416, 451
  not governed, 51, 54, 298, 300, 304,
    416
fiduciary over plan assets, 38, 349
  bonding requirements, 354, 377
  co-fiduciaries, 348, 377
  delegation, 324, 345, 358, 377
  duties for each decision, 295, 355
  personal liability, 38, 40, 295,
    354–355, 376–377, 390, 397,
    406, 501
  solely in the interest of plan partici-
    pants, 355
  with the care, skill prudence and
    diligence of a prudent man, 355
investment policy statement, 75, 359
investments allowed, 357, 359
paying plan expenses, 378
  as administrator, 318
  tax credits, 13, 388
prohibited transactions, 34, 38, 292,
    295, 347, 357, 361–363, 396, 398,
    431, 435, 562, 565, 567
  exemptions, 9, 12, 34, 66, 296, 347,
    363, 396, 435–436, 543, 558,
    562, 565
    class, 75, 123, 159–160, 274,
      298, 302, 321, 379, 381, 395,
      425, 435, 493, 503, 509
    individual, 3–17, 21–24, 29–30,
      33, 35, 38, 43, 46, 48–49,
      51–52, 58, 61–62, 64, 73–75,
      79–88, 90, 98–100, 106, 110,
      112, 118–120, 125, 127–128,
      134–138, 140, 154–155, 160,
      167–168, 170, 173, 175–176,
      180, 187–188, 196, 200–202,
      209, 211, 228, 235–237,
      239–241, 243–246, 250–252,
      254–255, 258–260, 262–264,
      270–271, 273, 275–276, 280,
      294–295, 297–302, 304, 316,

      322–323, 325–326, 336,
      339–341, 345–350, 352,
      354–355, 357, 362, 364–365,
      368, 370–374, 376–377,
      386–390, 393, 395, 400, 402,
      411–413, 415–417, 425,
      432–433, 435–436, 439, 441,
      444–450, 452–453, 455–457,
      459, 461–470, 472–476,
      478–481, 483–490, 493–494,
      503, 509–510, 513–514, 517,
      521, 525, 531–532, 536, 538,
      546, 551, 558, 566
  statutory, 14–16, 34, 36–37, 40,
    45, 63, 65, 71–73, 79–84,
    96–97, 102, 105–109,
    112–114, 116–117, 119–121,
    124, 128, 132–135, 137,
    139–143, 155–156, 163–164,
    170–174, 176–177, 179, 184,
    186–187, 204, 211, 219, 225,
    235–237, 242, 245, 247, 250,
    252, 254, 257–258, 264–265,
    269–270, 272–276, 279, 282,
    284, 293, 297–298, 300, 304,
    325, 329, 336, 338, 341,
    346–347, 349, 355, 361–364,
    375–377, 388, 391–393,
    396–397, 400, 408–409, 414,
    417, 425, 435, 447, 451,
    453–455, 460–461, 473, 475,
    484–487, 517, 521, 533, 535,
    537, 540–541, 543, 545,
    547–548, 553–554
  under ERISA, 7, 21–22, 29–30, 32,
    36, 38, 42, 55, 69, 137, 252,
    295–296, 314, 316, 321,
    323–327, 335–338, 347,
    351–352, 354, 361–362,
    379–380, 389–390, 392–393,
    397–398, 402–403, 407, 425,
    433, 436, 451, 471, 477, 558
  civil penalties, 38, 362, 398–399,
    407, 437
  parties in interest, 204, 361
  under the Code, 14, 69, 98, 139,
    254, 274, 347, 407, 417, 419,
    449, 464, 469, 471
  disqualified persons, 362

penalty tax, 13, 16, 109, 111, 113, 119, 121, 123, 137, 242–244, 252, 270–271, 274–275, 340, 347, 362, 418, 444, 452, 475, 479

remittance of employee salary deferrals, 359

reporting and disclosure, 29, 38, 76, 100, 119, 289, 295, 325, 328, 330, 337–338, 378, 389–390, 395–398, 405–412, 425, 427, 435, 437–438, 442, 447, 471, 543, 549, 563

to the government, 100, 338, 405–406

form 5500, 43, 69, 108, 114, 286, 293–294, 334–335, 405–407, 409–411, 421, 425, 436–438, 559

PBGC reportable events, 408

to the participants, 29, 100, 109, 171, 263, 338, 364, 383, 388, 464

benefit statements, 339, 342, 386, 405, 409, 560

self-directed 401(k) plans, 295, 364

black out periods, 375, 405

termination of defined benefit plans

multi-employer plans, 118, 379, 413–414, 417

withdrawal liability, 22, 30, 66, 413–414, 417, 569

single employer plans, 49, 113

distress termination, 413, 415, 568

procedures, 29–30, 32, 38, 43, 66, 74–75, 186, 227–228, 243, 251, 254, 265, 270, 274, 279–280, 286–288, 290, 313–314, 317, 321, 324, 327–328, 331, 333–334, 340, 349, 352, 354–356, 366–368, 378, 390, 392, 400–402, 417, 465, 542–543, 546–547, 558, 561, 567, 569

for IRS, 74, 76

frozen plans, 420

full termination, 562

partial termination, 131, 408, 420–424

standard termination, 413, 415–416

written plan document, 39, 49, 75, 99, 270, 295, 313–314, 338, 517

ability to amend or terminate, 328

controlling plan document, 71, 295, 314, 336, 340, 357

Summary Plan Description (SPD), 226, 313–314, 338, 405, 408

ethical issues, 491

client, 8, 42, 50, 54, 64, 112, 123, 156, 163, 175, 202, 226, 244, 276, 343, 352, 493–497, 500–501, 503, 507, 513, 521–522, 546, 559

other federal laws, 494, 537, 539–540

health and welfare benefits plans, 21, 304

health benefit delivery plans

fee-for-service plans, 465

Health Maintenance Organizations (HMOs), 482

Medicare, 399, 465–466, 484, 487

group health plans, 21–22, 30, 333, 341, 401, 425, 461–463, 465, 471, 477–482, 566

Consolidated Omnibus Budget Reconciliation Act (COBRA)

continuation requirements, 22, 477–478

notices, 22, 32, 64, 82–83, 100, 154, 223, 232, 254, 271–272, 337–343, 348, 390, 397, 409, 411, 416, 418, 460–461, 478, 518, 543, 546, 560

Health Insurance Portability and Accountability Act (HIPAA), 426

accountability requirements, 439, 477

portability requirements, 426

Mental Health Parity Act, 463, 481

tax-free funding vehicles

Archer Medical Savings Accounts, 460, 474

Health Reimbursement Arrangements, 460, 474–475

Health Savings Accounts, 19, 461, 468, 472, 475–476

high deductible health plan, 461, 474–475

wellness programs, 461, 464, 471, 476

group health plans, *continued*
  Women's Health and Cancer Rights
    Act, 463, 482
welfare benefits, 3, 6, 10, 12, 17, 19,
    21, 28–31, 52, 58, 69, 197, 297,
    304, 314, 327, 381, 426, 464, 466,
    469, 471, 477
  adoption assistance programs, 459,
    468
  cafeteria plans, 19, 140, 175, 236,
    459–461, 468–469, 473
  dependent care assistance programs,
    174, 459, 467
  educational assistance programs,
    459, 467
  flexible spending arrangements, 19,
    460, 469
  fringe benefits, 3, 11, 18, 197, 446,
    460, 464, 469–471, 551
    achievement awards, 470
    athletic facilities, 470
    employee discounts, 470
    lodging on business premises,
      470
    moving expense reimburse-
      ments, 470
    no-additional cost services, 470
    qualified transportation fringe
      benefits, 460, 469
    retirement planning services, 18,
      470
    tuition reduction, 471
    working condition benefits, 471
  group legal services, 174, 459, 467,
    551
  group term life insurance, 459, 466

income tax, 1, 3–7, 9–17, 22–24, 31,
    35–36, 45–46, 48–49, 51, 54, 56, 58,
    62, 65, 70–71, 83, 85, 87, 95–99, 121,
    140, 162–163, 171, 236, 243–244, 247,
    270–272, 274–276, 281–282, 286, 295,
    315–316, 337, 388, 406, 419, 422, 439,
    442, 444, 447, 449, 464, 467, 470–472,
    475, 486, 488, 537, 542, 544, 549
  Adjusted Gross Income, 12–14, 99,
    121, 267, 483, 485
  Alternative Minimum Tax, 9, 12, 121
  corporate income tax, 14, 49, 316

  credits, 9, 13–14, 62, 83, 106,
    117–118, 125, 129, 139, 187, 270,
    354, 388, 461, 553
  deductions, 9, 11–14, 16–17, 23, 37,
    40, 68, 86, 121, 123, 201–202, 270,
    280, 291, 305, 308, 316, 323, 353,
    360–361, 455
  exemptions, 9, 12, 34, 66, 296, 347,
    363, 396, 435–436, 543, 558, 562,
    565
  Gross Income, 1, 9–19, 31, 37, 49, 54,
    65, 70, 81–82, 96–99, 119, 121,
    163, 197, 202, 230, 232–233, 242,
    244, 267, 270–273, 275, 280, 286,
    444, 446, 448–449, 451–453,
    459–460, 464, 467–470, 473–476,
    483, 485–486, 488, 495, 537
  income tax liability, 9–11, 13–14

income tax advantages, 1, 3, 5, 10–11,
    15, 17, 22, 24, 35, 45, 48–49, 51, 70,
    87, 95, 244, 276, 337
  of non-qualified deferred compensa-
    tion, 10, 15
  of qualified retirement plans, 8, 17, 49,
    156, 280, 405, 449, 506–507, 542
  of health and welfare benefit plans, 17,
    30, 439

Individual Retirement Accounts, 3, 7,
    98–99, 301–302, 439, 483–490
  Roth, 17, 81–83, 96–99, 109–111,
    118–119, 121, 126–127, 130, 138,
    140, 154, 204, 227, 230, 242–243,
    263, 269, 271, 273, 275, 291, 346,
    364, 439, 483, 486, 547–548, 552,
    558, 560
    deduction limits, 123
      normal, 12–13, 39, 63, 67, 70,
        80, 84–87, 95, 100–107,
        113–117, 123, 125–127,
        130–131, 134–136, 138,
        142–147, 151, 153, 172, 180,
        188, 193–194, 204, 239–242,
        245, 247–254, 259–262,
        270–271, 273, 276, 301, 306,
        332, 335, 353, 379, 388, 401,
        406, 415–416, 418, 421, 423,
        441, 448, 461, 481, 485, 535,
        537, 554

distributions, 9, 11, 13, 15–17,
    38–39, 46, 54, 62–64, 67, 70, 77,
    82, 86, 90, 96, 98–99, 110, 115,
    119, 121, 135–136, 220, 227,
    229–231, 234, 239–277, 289,
    299, 347, 350, 388, 399, 416,
    418, 420, 443, 452–453, 455,
    474–475, 488, 517–518,
    533–535, 539, 554, 560–561
rollovers, 202, 271, 273–274, 291,
    429, 560
traditional, 7, 10, 81, 87, 96–98,
    106–107, 110, 119, 121, 131, 135,
    243, 256, 263, 269, 273, 292, 356,
    358, 394, 439, 483–486, 503, 506,
    514, 535–536, 552, 558
    deduction limits, 123
    normal, 12–13, 39, 63, 67, 70,
        80, 84–87, 95, 100–107,
        113–117, 123, 125–127,
        130–131, 134–136, 138,
        142–147, 151, 153, 172, 180,
        188, 193–194, 204, 239–242,
        245, 247–254, 259–262,
        270–271, 273, 276, 301, 306,
        332, 335, 353, 379, 388, 401,
        406, 415–416, 418, 421, 423,
        441, 448, 461, 481, 485, 535,
        537, 554
    distributions, 9, 11, 13, 15–17,
        38–39, 46, 54, 62–64, 67, 70, 77,
        82, 86, 90, 96, 98–99, 110, 115,
        119, 121, 135–136, 220, 227,
        229–231, 234, 239–277, 289,
        299, 347, 350, 388, 399, 416,
        418, 420, 443, 452–453, 455,
        474–475, 488, 517–518,
        533–535, 539, 554, 560–561
    rollovers, 202, 271, 273–274, 291,
        429, 560

Internal Revenue Service, 22, 31, 52, 60,
    72, 75, 99, 232, 279–294, 358, 376,
    406, 435, 437, 495–497, 500, 511, 520,
    555
    Circular 230, 43, 281, 293, 493,
        495–498, 500–501, 546, 562
        general best practices, 493,
            495–496, 501

professionals that can practice in
    front of the IRS
    Attorneys, 1, 7, 13, 23–24,
        38–40, 43, 50, 74–76, 280,
        293–294, 327, 329, 337–339,
        345, 350–352, 354, 391, 403,
        431, 433, 436, 445, 455, 491,
        493, 495, 501, 508–510, 512,
        517, 521, 538, 542
    Certified Public Accountants, 43,
        293, 495, 513
    Enrolled Actuaries, 40–41, 43,
        112–113, 281, 293, 493, 495,
        546
    Enrolled Agents, 24, 43, 281,
        293, 493, 495
    Enrolled Retirement Plan Agents,
        24, 43, 281, 293, 493, 495
    written opinions, 495
Employee Plans group, 22, 31–32, 46,
    279, 281
    Customer Education & Outreach,
        282
    Examinations, 22, 40–41, 43, 66,
        279–280, 282, 289–290,
        292–293, 542
        Employee Plans Compliance
            Unit (EPCU), 289
        focused examinations, 289–290
        international issues, 292
    Rulings & Agreements, 279, 282
        favorable determination letters,
            56, 106
    Employee Plans Correction Resolu-
        tion System, 66, 286
        voluntary correction program
            (VCP), 280
Tax Exempt / Government Entities op-
    erating division, 32

paid time off, 3, 5

qualified retirement plans, 1, 4, 6, 8,
    16–18, 21–23, 45–49, 51, 54, 62, 70,
    73, 128, 132, 156, 176, 186, 237, 243,
    247, 271, 275, 279–280, 295, 300, 314,
    327, 349, 405, 409, 439, 449–450,
    506–507, 537, 542, 549–550

qualified retirement plans, *continued*

accruals, 48, 62, 67, 110, 114, 116,
125–147, 152, 176, 185, 188, 237,
250, 339, 418–422, 424, 554
annual additions in defined contribution plans, 141
definitely determinable benefits,
90, 127, 132–134, 247
maximum, 27, 45, 63, 79, 86,
100, 103–105, 110, 112,
119–123, 127, 139–140,
142–147, 158, 176, 193, 195,
233, 256, 266, 359, 377,
388–389, 407, 443, 450,
467–469, 487–488, 556, 558,
561
benefit accruals in a defined benefit
plan, 137age discrimination, 32,
83, 135, 262, 494
alternate forms of distribution, 136
joint life annuity, 127, 137
single life annuity, 127,
136–137, 247
single lump sum distribution,
535
definitely determinable benefits,
90, 127, 132–134, 247
early retirement benefits, 114,
135–136, 241, 259–260, 262
maximum, 27, 45, 63, 79, 86,
100, 103–105, 110, 112,
119–123, 127, 139–140,
142–147, 158, 176, 193, 195,
233, 256, 266, 359, 377,
388–389, 407, 443, 450,
467–469, 487–488, 556, 558,
561
normal form of benefit, 134,
240–241, 249, 251, 253, 260
normal retirement benefits, 135,
418
non-retirement type benefits, 137
disability benefits, 138, 318,
320–321, 324, 326–327,
401–402, 465, 484, 487, 489,
551
life insurance, 6, 137–139, 249,
291, 347, 441–442, 448, 456,
459, 466, 468, 470, 511–512,
514, 561

retiree health benefits, 139, 465
amendments, 33, 35–36, 71–72,
76–77, 105, 110, 117, 124, 135,
137, 152–153, 173, 184, 187,
202–203, 249, 279, 284, 313, 327,
329–330, 353, 357, 363, 380, 384,
405, 411, 422, 424, 457, 509, 533,
539, 559, 569
prospective, 42, 76, 106, 355, 427,
435, 437, 498
retroactive, 50, 76, 227, 437
annual testing, 40, 45, 91, 149–237,
289, 378, 538
aggregation of employers, 155
affiliated service groups, 149,
152, 185, 235
controlled group of corporations, 74, 149, 156, 161–163,
177, 388
Highly Compensated Employees
(HCEs)
calendar year data election, 150,
174
identification, 72, 77, 174, 279,
285, 291, 293, 366, 406, 512,
540
top-paid group election, 150,
174, 449
minimum coverage testing, 120,
152, 176–177, 179, 184–185, 188
mathematical tests, 62, 151–152,
176, 179, 186
Average Benefits Percentage
Test
Average Benefits Test,
179–180
Allocation Rates, 153,
189–191, 193–194, 557
Nondiscriminatory Classification test, 171–172, 179,
181, 190–192
Reasonable Classification,
179–181, 190
Nondiscriminatory Classi-
fication, 171–172,
179–181, 190–192
NHCE concentration,
180